CCNA and Beyond

By Stuart Fordham
CCIE #49337

Copyright

Notice of Rights

Superhero flying up copyright Maxutov | Dreamstime.com
Ethernet cable from www.pd4pic.com

Notice of Liability

Trademarks

To those who have given me both the opportunity to learn, and the inspiration to do so.

Thanks to Morgan for keeping me company during the long hours spent making this book.
Miss you little buddy.

Thanks

I would like to thank my family, especially my wife Nicky and Jake and Caleb, my children.

Thanks to everyone else who supported and encouraged me.

Table of Contents

About xii
    About the Author.. xii
    Following this book... xii

About the CCNA exam xiii

Topology.. xv

1. The Operation of IP Data Networks 1
    1.1 Recognize the purpose and functions of various network devices such as routers, switches, bridges and hubs 2
        Hubs 2
        Bridges... 3
        Switches 4
        Routers 5
    1.2 Select the components required to meet a given network specification 5
    1.3 Identify common applications and their impact on the network 5
        Email... 6
        DNS... 7
        HTTP 7
        FTP 7
        TELNET... 7
    1.4 Describe the purpose and basic operation of the protocols in the OSI and TCP/IP models............... 8
        The TCP/IP model 9
        The OSI model 11
    1.5 Predict the data flow between two hosts across a network 16
    1.6 Identify the appropriate media, cables, ports, and connectors to connect Cisco network devices to other network devices and hosts in a LAN 24

2. LAN Switching Technologies 29
    2.1 Determine the technology and media access control method for Ethernet networks 29
    2.2 Identify basic switching concepts and the operation of Cisco switches 30
        2.2.a Collision Domains 31
        2.2.b Broadcast Domains.. 31
    2.3 Configure and verify initial switch configuration including remote access management 36
        2.3.a hostname... 36
        2.3.e enable secret password 47
        2.3.f console and VTY logins 48
        2.3.g exec-timeout 51
        2.3.h service password encryption.. 53
        2.3.i copy run start 54
    2.4 Verify network status and switch operation using basic utilities such as.......................... 55
        2.4.a Ping... 55
        2.4.b Telnet 57
        2.4.c SSH 57
    2.5 Describe how VLANs create logically separate networks and the need for routing between them .. 59

2.5.a Explain network segmentation and basic traffic management concepts 60
2.6 Configure and verify VLANs..60
2.7 Configure and verify trunking on Cisco switches...65
2.7a DTP 66
2.7b Auto-Negotiation 70
VTP 72
2.8 Identify enhanced switching technologies 87
2.9 Spanning Tree..88
2.9.a Describe root bridge election 88
2.9.b Spanning tree mode 96
2.8.a RSTP...96
2.8.b PVSTP 96
2.9 Configure and verify PVSTP operation 98
2.8.c Etherchannels 105

3. IP Addressing (IPv4/IPv6) 116
Binary conversion 117
Calculating subnet addresses (the hard way)..122
Calculating subnet addresses (the easy way)..124
3.1 Describe the operation and necessity of using private and public IP addresses for IPv4 addressing
....126
3.2 Identify the appropriate IPv6 addressing scheme to satisfy addressing requirements in a LAN/WAN
environment..126
3.3 Identify the appropriate IPv4 addressing scheme using VLSM and summarization to satisfy
addressing requirements in a LAN/WAN environment..129
3.4 Describe the technological requirements for running IPv6 in conjunction with IPv4 136
3.4.a dual stack 136
3.5 Describe IPv6 addresses 137
3.5.a global unicast 137
3.5.b multicast 137
3.5.c link local...137
3.5.d unique local...138
3.5.e EUI-64 138
3.5.f auto-configuration 139
Unspecified address ::/128 139
Default route ::/0 140
Documentation 2001:db8::/32 140
Site-local fec0::/10 140
Anycast addresses 140
Configuring IPv6 140

4. IP Routing Technologies 151
4.1 Describe basic routing concepts...151
4.1.a packet forwarding 151
4.1.b router lookup process 152
4.1.c Process Switching/Fast Switching/CEF 154
4.2 Configure and verify utilizing the CLI to set basic Router configuration 155

4.2.a hostname...155
4.2.b local user and password 156
4.2.c enable secret password...157
4.2.d console & VTY logins 158
4.2.e exec-timeout 158
4.2.f service password encryption 158
4.2.g interface IP Address 158
4.2.g (i) loopback 161
4.2.h banner 163
4.2.i motd 165
4.2.j copy run start 167
4.3 Configure and verify operation status of a device interface 167
4.3.a Serial 167
4.3.b Ethernet 171
4.4 Verify router configuration and network connectivity using................................171
4.4.a ping 171
4.4.a (i) extended 172
4.4.b traceroute 174
4.4.c telnet 176
4.4.d SSH 176
4.4.e sh cdp neighbors 177
4.5 Configure and verify routing configuration for a static or default route given specific routing requirements 181
4.6 Differentiate methods of routing and routing protocols.....................................184
4.6.a Static vs. dynamic 184
4.6.b Link state vs. distance vector 187
4.6.c next hop 190
4.6.d ip routing table 192
4.6.e Passive Interfaces (how they work) 196
4.7 Configure and verify OSPF 200
4.7.a Benefit of single area 201
4.7.b Configure OSPFv2 202
4.7.c Configure OSPFv3 219
4.7.d Router ID 224
4.7.e Passive Interface 225
4.7.f Discuss multi-area OSPF 225
4.7.g Understand LSA types and purpose 237
4.8 Configure and verify interVLAN routing (Router on a stick) 241
4.8.a sub interfaces 242
4.8.b upstream routing 243
4.8.c encapsulation 243
4.9 Configure SVI interfaces 248
4.10 Manage Cisco IOS Files 253
4.10.a Boot Preferences 255
4.10.b Cisco IOS Images (15) 259
4.11 Configure and verify EIGRP (single AS) 261
4.11.a Feasible Distance/Feasible Successors/Administrative distance.........................264

4.11.b Feasibility condition 265
4.11.c Metric composition 265
4.11.d Router ID 277
4.11.e Auto summary...279
4.11.f Path Selection 283
4.11.g Load Balancing 287
4.11.g (i) Unequal 287
EIGRP for IPv6 (EIGRPv6)..290

5. IP Services.. 297
5.1 Configure and verify DHCP (IOS Router) 297
5.1.a Configuring router interfaces to use DHCP 299
5.1.b DHCP options (Basic overview and functionality) 306
5.1.c Excluded addresses 307
5.1.d Lease time 307
5.2 Describe the types, features, and applications of ACLs.........................308
5.2.a standard (editing and sequence numbers) 310
5.2.b extended 312
5.2.c named...315
5.2.d numbered...316
5.2.e Log option 317
5.3 Configure and verify ACLs in a network environment...........................318
5.3.a named 319
5.3.b numbered..321
5.3.c Log option..322
5.4 Identify the basic operation of NAT 324
5.4.a purpose 325
5.4.b pool 325
5.4.c static 325
5.4.d 1to1 325
5.4.e overloading 325
5.4.f source addressing 325
5.4.g one way NAT 326
5.5 Configure and verify NAT for given network requirements 326
5.6 Configure and verify NTP as a client 333
5.7 Recognize High availability (FHRP) 334
5.7.a VRRP 335
5.7.b HSRP 339
5.7.c GLBP 342
5.8 Configure and verify syslog 348
5.8.a Utilize syslog output..351
5.9 Describe SNMP v2 and v3...353

6. Network Device Security 359
6.1 Configure and verify network device security features.........................359
6.1.a Device password security 359
6.1.b Enable secret vs. enable 359

6.1.c Transport 360

6.1.c.1 disable telnet 361

6.1.c.2 SSH 361

6.1.d VTYs 362

6.1.e physical security 362

6.1.f service password 363

6.1.g Describe external authentication methods 364

6.2 Configure and verify Switch Port Security 365

6.2.a Sticky MAC 365

6.2.b MAC address limitation 366

6.2.c static/dynamic 369

6.2.d violation modes... 370

6.2.d (i) err disable 371

6.2.d (ii) shutdown 371

6.2.d(iii) protect restrict 373

6.2.e Shutdown unused ports 374

6.2.f err disable recovery 374

6.2.g Assign unused ports in unused VLANs 374

6.2.h Putting Native VLAN to other than VLAN 1 374

6.3 Configure and verify ACLs to filter network traffic 375

6.4 Configure and verify ACLs to limit telnet and SSH access to the router 378

7. Troubleshooting... 380

7.1 Troubleshoot and correct common problems associated with IP addressing and host configurations

.... 383

7.2 Troubleshoot and resolve VLAN problems 386

7.2.a Identify that VLANs are configured 388

7.2.b Verify port membership correct... 388

7.2.c Correct IP address configured 389

7.3 Troubleshoot and resolve trunking problems on Cisco switches 389

7.3.a Verify correct trunk states.. 389

7.3.b Verify correct encapsulation configured 390

7.3.c Correct VLANs allowed 391

7.4 Troubleshoot and resolve ACL issues 392

7.4.a Verify statistics 394

7.4.b Verify permitted networks 394

7.4.c Verify direction 395

7.4.c (i) Interface 398

7.5 Troubleshoot and resolve Layer 1 problems 400

7.5.a Framing.. 400

7.5.b CRC 401

7.5.c Runts 401

7.5.d Giants 401

7.5.e Dropped packets 401

7.5.f Late collisions 401

7.5.g Input/output errors 402

7.6 Identify and correct common network problems... 403

7.7 Troubleshoot and resolve spanning tree operation issues 403
    7.7.a Verify root switch 403
    7.7.b Verify priority 404
    7.7.c Verify mode is correct 404
    7.7.d Verify port states 406
7.8 Troubleshoot and resolve routing issues 407
    7.8.a Verify routing is enabled (sh ip protocols) 408
    7.8.b Verify routing table is correct 410
    7.8.c Verify correct path selection 411
7.9 Troubleshoot and resolve OSPF problems 411
    7.9.a Verify neighbor adjacencies 411
    7.9.b Verify hello and dead timers 413
    7.9.c Verify OSPF area 414
    7.9.d Verify interface MTU 414
    7.9.e Verify network types 417
    7.9.f Verify neighbor states 419
    7.9.g Review OSPF topology table 420
7.10 Troubleshoot and resolve EIGRP problems 421
    7.10.a Verify neighbor adjacencies 421
    7.10.b Verify AS number 425
    7.10.c Verify load balancing 426
    7.10.d Split horizon 427
7.11 Troubleshoot and resolve interVLAN routing problems 430
    7.11.a Verify connectivity 430
    7.11.b Verify encapsulation 431
    7.11.c Verify subnet 433
    7.11.d Verify native VLAN 433
    7.11.e Port mode trunk status 434
7.12 Troubleshoot and resolve WAN implementation issues 436
    7.12.a Serial interfaces 437
    7.12.b Frame Relay 438
    7.12.c PPP 440
7.13 Monitor NetFlow statistics 443
7.14 TS EtherChannel problems 445

8. WAN Technologies 449
8.1 Identify different WAN Technologies 449
    8.1.a Metro Ethernet 449
    8.1.b VSAT 449
    8.1.c Cellular 3g/4g 449
    8.1.d MPLS 450
    8.1.e T1/E1 450
    8.1.f ISDN 450
    8.1.g DSL 451
    8.1.h Frame Relay 451
    8.1.i Cable 452
    8.1.j VPN 452

8.2 Configure and verify a basic WAN serial connection 452
8.3 Configure and verify a PPP connection between Cisco routers 456
8.4 Configure and verify Frame Relay on Cisco routers.. 468
8.5 Implement and troubleshoot PPPoE 475

9. Beyond the CCNA: Redistribution... 486

10. Exam time.. 499

Appendix A: CIDR Notation 500

Appendix B: Powers of 2... 501

Appendix C: Binary to Hex conversion 502

Appendix D: Wireshark Captures 503

About

About the Author

I have been working in IT for around 15 years - starting off in desktop support, moving up the chain to third line and more recently and specifically finding my "home" within networking. I have worked for a number of companies, including local health authorities, Hedge Funds, and software houses.

I studied Psychology at university; however, at the end of the degree, I really didn't fancy spending years and years studying in order to progress up the ladder. So, I moved into IT, and have spent years and years studying in order to progress up the ladder. I have a number of qualifications including; CCIE Routing and Switching, CCDP, CCNP, CCSA, CCDA, CCNA, JNCIP, CEH, RHCSA, MCITP, MCSE, MCSA: Security, Network+, Security+, A+ and I think that's about it. I tend to collect certifications; some I have purposefully let lapse in order to concentrate more on the Cisco side of things. Others are still current.

I released my first book, BGP for Cisco Networks, in March 2014. I enjoyed the process of creating it so much that I continued with Volume II; MPLS for Cisco Networks, right away, and after that came VPNs and NAT for Cisco Networks.

I am married with twin sons, and I live in Bedfordshire in the UK.

I can be contacted at stu@802101.com. I am always happy to hear feedback and suggestions. My website address is http://www.802101.com.

Following this book

When entering configuration mode, IOS always adds "Enter configuration commands, one per line. End with CNTL/Z" I have removed these lines from all output. Occasionally, due to space requirements, I will truncate interfaces (Eth instead of Ethernet). This is purely for formatting reasons, and only where necessary. Generally, I will remove interface up notifications as well.

The narrative of this book is written in Calibri font.

    Console output is written in Menlo font, and this is what you should see
    and type into your routers and switches.

The bits written in Chalkduster font are the bits you will need a pen and paper for.

About the CCNA exam

Congratulations on making a wise decision to study for the CCNA certification! It will be a rewarding experience, but it won't be an easy one. Hopefully, this book will help shorten the time it takes for you to pass, and your career as the next networking superhero can begin.

There are two ways you can become a CCNA; you can take two exams, or one exam. Pearson VUE proctors all the exams, and this is where you register to book the exam. The website address is: **http://www.pearsonvue.com/cisco/**.

No matter whether you take the two-exam route or one exam route, you get the same certification.

The two-exam route entails taking the Interconnecting Cisco Networking Devices part 1 (ICND1, exam code 100-101). It is a 90-minute exam, with between 50 to 60 questions. You do get the CCENT (Cisco Certified Entry Network Technician) certification though. Following a successful pass of this, you then take Part 2 (ICND2, 200-101), which is slightly shorter at 75 minutes, but has the same number of questions.

Alternatively, you can take one exam. The CCNAX, or Interconnecting Cisco Networking Devices (exam code 200-120): Accelerated. This is a 90-minute exam, again with between 50 and 60 questions.

Which should you take? Should you sit two exams or just one? Well, it's kind of up to you. The CCENT was not around when I studied for this, but my personal preference would be to take one exam instead of two. The questions won't be any harder or easier; there will just be less of them!

My own CCNA journey

I started my CCNA studies on the 20th September 2006 after enrolling in an evening class at my local college. I had to drop out due to changing jobs, but picked my studies up again after being made redundant and studied during a new job, finally passing on the 15th June 2009. I passed on my second attempt.

That's nearly three years from start to finish, and I found it tough.

By comparison, I started studying for the CCNP in January 2012 (due to the fact that the CCNA validation would expire in September 2012), completing it on 9th July 2013. This took about a year and a half. I started my CCIE studies straight after, and became CCIE certified on the 11th July 2015, nearly two years to the day.

Why did the CCNA take me so long?

Because the learning curve from very basic networking skills to becoming a CCNA is a very big one.

It was all new to me, and topics such as subnetting got me completely flummoxed. It was not an easy certification by any means. So, don't expect this to be an easy ride. However, I hope that I can make it easier.

Apart from the wealth of material you need to digest and be able to regurgitate on the day of the exam, there were other reasons why I found it hard, and this book will address some of those. Most importantly, we will start as we mean to go on; with UNetLab. You can find a post of how to set up UNetLab on the CCNA and Beyond website (**http://www.ccnaandbeyond.com**). So please do read that first. If you don't have the resources to run your own set up, then you can sign up with **http://www.unlcloud.com**. UNL Cloud is a virtual SaaS hosted platform that you can access from anywhere. It's run by my mate Vic, and he's a great guy.

I started by using Cisco's Packet-Tracer program, and while it has come a long way since I used it, it's only good for the CCNA level exams. You can only perform limited tasks with it and it will not carry you forward. For my CCNP I switched to using GNS3, which is a great product and I will not knock it, but when you reach the time when you want to start studying for your CCIE (and I hope that time does come for you), then you need a platform that will carry you on. UNetLab is superb for this. I only wish it had been around when I started my journey, so you are far luckier than me in that respect. It is much easier than buying a rack full of equipment, that will only serve you for a year or two, and then get left in the garage gathering dust.

Why should you choose this book?

There were four books for my CCNA, they were big weighty tomes and were hard to pick up some days. I don't want this book to be like that. Networking should be fun; you should want to study because the material is interesting and, like a good novel, keeps you hooked. That's the plan for this book.

I will follow the syllabus very closely, starting each chapter with a recap of what the weight (the percentage scoring) of the section is, and the topics we should cover. Occasionally we will head beyond the CCNA and tread on the toes of the CCNP, but don't be scared. It'll be fun! We will build a network, from the ground up. After all, this is why you are learning networking, right?

Most networking books use explanations and configurations with just a couple of routers, or switches. We have a full network, as this is the kind of thing you will be dealing with in real-life.

The next page shows the network we will be building.

Topology

This is going to be our main network:

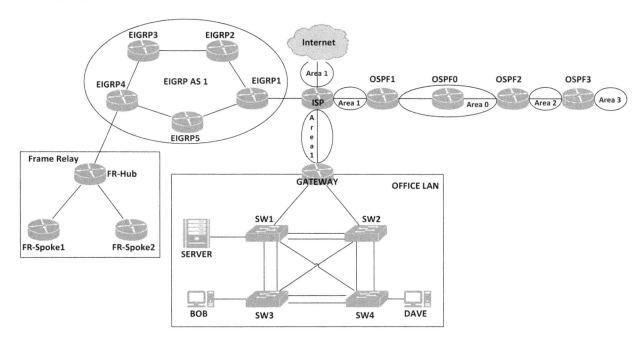

We have a (small) local area network with four switches, a server and our users; Bob and Dave. This network uses a gateway router to connect to the rest of the world, and we will use these routers to see how information routes around the Internet.

Hopefully you are already eager to get started. If you are feeling overwhelmed already then don't worry, we'll be breaking each section down and tackling them bit by bit.

We will use a separate topology for the troubleshooting section.

We will start to get our hands dirty in chapter 2 when we look at switching, from that point on it will be very hands-on. We do have to go through some theory first though, so let's start by looking at how a network operates.

1. The Operation of IP Data Networks

Chapter one, and the biggest question; how do networks operate? To answer this would actually take the length of the entire book, so we will start with a what, a how, another what, a why, and two more how's. If you are thinking "What?", then you are off to a good start.

Although this chapter only accounts for 5% of the CCNA exam weighting, it does provide the basic knowledge of how to connect the varying devices that make up a network, and to see how data moves across it.

Let's start by defining what a network is, as that would be a good place to start. This will also help us define the topology (the way the network is laid out) that we will be using as we go through the book.

Dictionary.com defines a "network" as:

"a system containing any combination of computers, computer terminals, printers, audio or visual display devices, or telephones interconnected by telecommunication equipment or cables: used to transmit of receive information".

While a network therefore, could comprise of a couple of routers, I like to take a different approach to my books. Most networking books will have little examples of a network, so say you are connecting a router to a switch, there will be just the two components, they will not connect to anything else, and this example may bear no relevance or, more importantly, bear no significance to another section in the same book. What do I mean by significance? Well, when you make a change on one router, you are either going to have happy customers, or angry customers - this book will prepare you for the consequences and impacts of network changes. This is vital in your career in networking.

Many moons ago, before my CCNA days, I was at a client site and I was asked to give one user an external IP address on a Cisco PIX firewall. I only had limited experience with these and, to cut a long story short, that business had no Internet for a number of hours. I did not know what consequence my changes would have on the rest of the network. I did not research, no one else knew the answer and I was under pressure. My actions caused a detrimental effect.

Hence the fact that we are using a large topology to simulate a decent sized network, with a number of devices. I have never come across a network made of just two devices; networks have many components, such as routers, firewalls, switches, bridges and hubs. But what are these devices and what do they do? Let's have a look at these now.

1.1 Recognize the purpose and functions of various network devices such as routers, switches, bridges and hubs

If we start in reverse order, we can cover the devices that are now considered to be old technology (hubs and bridges) and get to the important ones (switches and routers).

Hubs

When I first started doing home networking, hubs were the only cost-effective purchase. Switches were excessively expensive, and a hub was relatively cheap. Hubs are now seldom used as switches have dropped dramatically in price and are far more accessible. The chances of encountering a hub in an enterprise are getting slimmer every year.

A hub is device that connects multiple Ethernet devices, such as PCs, together. They all go to form a single network segment (a group). Hubs are, however, pretty simple. Imagine we have a four-port hub, with four PCs (PC-A, PC-B, PC-C, PC-D) connected. If PC-A wants to send some data to PC-D, then it sends it out of its Ethernet port to the hub and then the hub sends it to PC-D. The hub also sends the same data to PC-B and PC-C, a very inefficient method. The only recipient that the hub does not send the data to is the source, PC-A.

So, a hub is really down at the lower end of the scale of intelligent devices. This is because a hub operates at the very first layer of the OSI model, which we shall look at shortly. It just repeats the signal that it receives; it does not understand the data it is being sent at the frame or IP address levels. This is why is can also be referred to as a multiport repeater. There are a couple of slightly more intelligent aspects to a hub, one of which is collision detection. A collision occurs when two devices try to send data at the same time. Devices will wait until they see that the line is clear, but two (or more) devices can see that that line is clear and will attempt to send data at the same time, therefore the packets collide. When the hub detects a collision it sends a jam signal, and no device can send any more data until a random interval time completes (which they independently choose, so that one device's interval will be different to the other's). This is known as Carrier Sense Multiple Access with Collision Detection (CSMA/CD). In a busy network, with many devices, a hub can quickly cause issues, but this is predominantly in older networks. Modern networks operate at full-duplex; they can send and receive data at the same time. Hubs operate at half-duplex. Either they can send, or they can receive at any given time. CSMA/CD is now referred to as "obsolete", along with the physical connections that used it such as 10BASE5 and 10BASE2, though it is still supported (referred to as "legacy" support).

There is also CSMA/CA, which stands for Carrier Sense Multiple Access with Collision Avoidance, where nodes in a shared environment (such as Ethernet is), listen for the channel to be 'idle' before they try to transmit. CSMA/CA is common in Wireless networking.

The issue of using hubs and collision detection does actually dictate how the network must be designed, and when taking network speeds into account (either 10Mbit/s (Megabits per second), or 100Mbit/s) we actually find that our network can be much smaller than is actually required. If we are running a slow network, of 10Mbit/s, then we hit a rule, called the 5-4-3 rule. The 5-4-3 rule specifies that in a collision domain, there can be at most 5 segments, a maximum of 4 hubs or repeaters, and a maximum of three user segments in a line.

Think of a segment as the actual network cable connecting a pc to a hub, or a hub to another hub. A more succinct definition would be an electrical connection between networked devices using a shared medium.

If our network is faster, running at 100Mbit/s then we can only have 3 segments between end stations.

Let's get a visual of this:

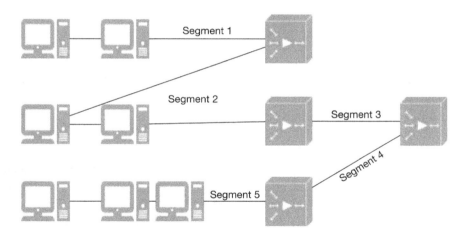

As you can see, hubs have an effect on how we design our network, right down to the cables we use. In the picture above, there are a number of hubs joined together. The capabilities of the hub we have determine what cable we will use to connect them together. If the hubs have an uplink port then you can use any standard straight-through cable in this port to connect the two together. If they do not have an uplink port, then you will need a crossover cable to connect them together, we will look at cables later in the chapter, but the point is that networking is all about control; we should control the routing, the switching, access-lists should determine a persons access. We should never let a hardware choice control how our network is designed.

Bridges

As the name would suggest, a bridge connects two network segments, creating an aggregate network. Bridging technology is predominantly used in relation to Wi-Fi networks, bridging the wireless client to the wired network. Bridging is different to routing as although routers can join two or more networks together, the networks remain completely separate, and this operates at a higher layer of the OSI model. Bridging operates at the first two layers of the OSI model, and can operate in different modes, transparent bridging, simple bridging, multiport bridging and source route bridging.

Bridges also separate devices into different collision domains, allowing for a more efficient network, as the number of devices affected by collisions will decrease, and the bandwidth available to each of the collision domains increases.

One of the biggest issues with a hub is that it does not retain any knowledge about what is connected where. On the other hand, when performing transparent bridging, bridges use a forwarding table to send frames. As they receive data, they check the address with the table, which is initially empty. If there is no address match found in the database, then the bridge (like a hub) floods this data out of all ports (apart from the one that the data was received on). The destination network will then respond, and an entry in the forwarding database will be created. Typically, bridges have fewer ports than hubs.

Switches

A switch combines the port density of hubs, with the intelligence of bridges, only forwarding data to one host, instead of sending it to all hosts (apart from the original sender). As the switch learns of connected hosts it build up an address table of the hardware address that belongs to the host (the MAC address), so that it can perform this one-to-one communication between hosts.

Switches perform three main functions. They make forwarding or filtering decisions, based on the destination MAC address, they learn MAC addresses based on the source MAC address, and they create a loop-free layer-2 topology, using the Spanning-Tree protocol. Spanning-Tree prevents frames bouncing around the network indefinitely. Switches also have the added bonus of creating separate collision domains, and we will look at how a switch benefits the network more than a hub in the next chapter.

There are different types of switches. They can be unmanaged, simply plugging them into your network and letting them do as they should, or managed. Managed switches are controlled through a number of methods, such as through a web interface, or through a CLI (Command Line Interface) using SSH or Telnet. We can also use protocols such as SNMP (Simple Network Management Protocol) to monitor the device, and react to issues or potential issues (based on threshold values). Such reactions can include a simple email alert sent to the network administrators, through to logging into the device and making changes, such as turning ports off, changing access-lists, or making routing changes.

Switches can also operate at one or more layers of the ISO model. Often they operate at layer-2, simply forwarding traffic between hosts, but they can also function at layer-3, offering routing functionality, layer-4, where they can provide Network Address translation, or even layer-7, taking part in content delivery, or acting as a web cache (storing web pages).

Routers

A router will pass data between different networks, such as from you to the Internet and back again. Routers live at a layer up from switches (well, a layer-2 switch at least), and use routing tables to learn where to pass data. A routing table can be as simple as one or two lines, such as pass everything this way, or pass all internal traffic one way and anything else another way, right through to having thousands of entries.

I am keeping the explanation of switches and routers brief, as we will cover their functions in much greater detail in chapters two and four.

1.2 Select the components required to meet a given network specification

So, in what scenario would you use a hub instead of a switch? Never, given the option. Seriously. If you ever have to choose then wrong question is being asked. The answer will always be switch, unless of course the question is "Can I connect two computers together using a hub, or a bit of string and some sticky tape?" Nine times out of ten, a switch will always be the right answer. A switch would also be used to connect multiple hosts to the same subnet (who we can talk to without needing a router).

So when would you use a router? Any time you need to connect to the Internet, you would use a router. Whilst some switches can provide routing capabilities, you certainly would not use one as your connection to the Internet. Typically, they do not offer any form of security for devices. A router would be used to connect different subnets. Routers also separate broadcast domains, which we will look at in the next chapter.

1.3 Identify common applications and their impact on the network

Let's look at a typical day in the office.

You grab a coffee, sit at your desk and turn on your computer. Once you are logged into the network, then you'll probably go and check your email, do some web browsing and catch up on the news, maybe you will work on some documents, some more web browsing, more email and so on and so forth. Each of these actions uses a different application, many will use different protocols, and each has an effect on the network traffic.

Here we will have a look at some of the protocols and how they communicate. We will leave DHCP out for the moment, as there is a big section on that later.

Email

The first email was sent in 1971 by the late Ray Tomlinson, on the ARPANET system; the precursor to the modern Internet. Before this messages could only be sent and received by people on the same computer, but Ray came up with a system that used the @ sign to allow messages to be sent between hosts, separating the user from the machine. Ray forgot what his first email was, a bit sad really, but he wasn't aware of how important email would be to us years down the line. He could have gone down in history as the man who said "One little send for man, giant amounts of spam for mankind", or something. Now there is something in the region of 4.5 billion email accounts, and email traffic is in the region of 204 billion emails per day, though about three quarters of this is spam.

We read our email using a client, this can be web-based such as Gmail and delivered using HTTP, or HTTPS, or through a dedicated application such as Outlook, and can use different protocols such as POP3 (Post Office Protocol 3), IMAP (Internet Message Access Protocol), or MAPI (Messaging Application Programming Interface), used by Microsoft Exchange. Each of these protocols will connect to the email server using a specific port.

If you were to send an email from user@domain.org, to me (stu@802101.com) then the email would be sent to the local mail submission agent (MSA). The MSA would be something like smtp.domain.org. This server would then work out whether the email was to be delivered locally or remotely, using the domain name (802101.com). In this case it is remote, so the server smtp.domain.org does a DNS (Domain Name System) lookup to find the mail server for 802101.com.

The DNS server for 802101.com would reply with an MX record for the domain, and this is a list of Mail eXchange servers, which would be my mail server (smtp.802101.com).

The server smtp.domain.org would then send the email to smtp.802101.com using the SMTP protocol (Simple Mail Transfer Protocol), on TCP port 25. My mail server would accept the message and store it in my mailbox, ready for me to collect with my mail client.

When we sent the email, we did so because of DNS (and the MX servers). When we visit a website, or send an email, it goes to an IP address. DNS is the protocol that converts names like www.google.com or www.802101.com to IP addresses.

DNS

DNS maps IP addresses to hostnames. It is used heavily both in the Local Area Network (downloading a spreadsheet from a local server by browsing to it using the path \\server1\fileshare), and the Internet (opening a browser and typing in http://www.google.com for example).

When we request a resource, such as a domain name (also referred to as a Fully Qualified Domain Name or FQDN), we will first query a DNS server using UDP on port 53.

If the DNS server has an entry then it will return it straight away. If it does not, it will query one of the root nameservers on the Internet. This will tell us where to go, starting with the top-level domain (TLD), which in the above two cases will be COM. The .COM nameserver will then have an entry for google.com, or 802101.com, and will point us to the nameservers for those domains. These servers will then return the IP address for the web server (www.google.com), or the SMTP server (smtp.802101.com).

HTTP

HTTP traffic is our web traffic. It uses the HyperText Transfer Protocol, or HTTP, to display web pages. We have the inventor of the Internet, Tim Berners-Lee, to thank for this. By default an HTTP server listens on TCP port 80 to incoming requests such as www.802101.com or www.google.com. Again this makes heavy usage of DNS to convert the name to an IP address. We will look at this in greater detail when we set up our DNS server in chapter 9.

FTP

FTP is the File Transfer Protocol, and we use it to transfer files between a server and a client. FTP uses two ports, as the control of FTP (TCP port 21) is separate to the data connection (TCP port 20).

TELNET

The last application we will discuss is Telnet. Telnet is used for remotely managing devices, including Windows and Linux based servers and, as we will see soon, our Cisco devices. Telnet is a client-server protocol, meaning one side (the client) will call in to the other (the server).

Telnet is not the preferred method, however. Telnet is insecure as all the usernames and passwords used to connect to the devices are sent in clear text (over TCP port 23). SSH (Secure Shell) is preferred to Telnet, as it is (as the name suggests) secure.

The second half of this section is to identify the impact of these applications on the network. How do you evaluate the impact an application has on the network? It can be done from two angles; capacity and security. The more users you have, the more traffic they will generate. Different applications will use different amounts of bandwidth (how much Internet capacity we have). Video streaming uses far more bandwidth than the average email, for example. As your user base increases your bandwidth needs may also increase. Then we have security. As mentioned, there are secure protocols, such as SSH and insecure ones such as Telnet. This has a security implication on the network; wherever possible you should turn off access (both internal and external) to insecure protocols. Though, this is not a network design, nor is it a security exam. So, let's get back to Routing and Switching.

In this chapter so far we have discussed some protocols, ports, layers and the basic operation of some of them. Now we will look at how these protocols and ports interact with the network from the user's application right down to how they are sent as electrical signals across the wire.

1.4 Describe the purpose and basic operation of the protocols in the OSI and TCP/IP models

The applications we use, no matter whether it is email, FTP, or watching an online video, all use the same process to get from point A to point B. The data will go through several layers from how it is transmitted across the wires that connect us to the rest of the network, to how we see the data on our screen. The number of layers differs depending on what model we choose to follow.

There are a couple of "models", and these state how many layers data will go through. We have the OSI model, which is a standardized version and has seven layers, or we have the TCP/IP model, which has five layers, but used to have four before they modified it.

We will start with a quick overview of the OSI model and the TCP/IP model before we discuss these in more depth.

Examples	OSI model	TCP/IP (new)	TCP/IP (old)	Examples
HTTP, FTP, SMTP, TELNET	Application			DNS, DHCP, FTP, HTTP, SMTP, TELNET
HTML, CSS	Presentation	Application	Application	
SSL, SQL	Session			
TCP, UDP	Transport	Transport	Transport	TCP, UDP
IP, ICMP	Network	Network	Internet	IP, ICMP
PPP, MAC	Data Link	Data Link	Link	ARP, OSPF, PPP, MAC
DSL, USB, ISDN	Physical	Physical		

My preference for trying to remember the OSI model is through the pneumonic "**P**lease **D**o **N**ot **T**hrow **S**ausage **P**izza **A**way". We also have the earlier TCP/IP model, which is a LITA version (pronounced "lighter") of the OSI model, and the later version, which took the PS out of the OSI model (PS referring to Presentation and Session, naturally). We will start our comparison with the TCP/IP model.

The TCP/IP model

TCP/IP stands for Transmission Control Protocol / Internet Protocol. The Transmission Control Protocol (TCP) is a core protocol within the Internet Protocol (IP) suite. I have already spoken about TCP, when we looked at the different applications, and how each of these had its own port number. We also spoke about UDP, in the case of DNS. UDP is the fire-and-forget protocol; it's built for speed, not reliability. TCP is reliable, it ensures packets are received in the right order, and are checked for errors. TCP is built for accuracy.

UDP is a connectionless protocol, meaning that we do not wait to see if the end device is ready to listen (known as handshaking). There is also no guarantee of delivery, duplication, or of packets arriving in the correct order. Depending on the application that is using this UDP data, there may be logic built in to handle the delivery and receipt of data. Despite this, it is useful for data that is required to arrive in sequence, such as voice, audio and video data, where retransmission of data would cause the stream to become garbled.

IP looks after how the TCP (or UDP) segment is delivered after being encapsulated in an IP datagram. Encapsulated is a fancy term for "sandwiched"; where the important filling is placed between a header and a trailer.

The TCP/IP model came about through DARPA, the old US military network. DARPA was the precursor to the Internet, and because of this, the TCP/IP model is known as the DoD (Department of Defense) or Internet model. Starting from the top, we have the Application layer, then the Transport layer, the Internet layer and lastly the Link layer. We will look at these layers in more detail as we see how an application that uses UDP creates a packet.

TCP/IP - Application layer

At the application layer we use protocols such as HTTP, FTP, SMTP and DHCP. The data at this level is then encapsulated into TCP or UDP ready for the transport layer. Encapsulation is where each layer adds a header and maybe a trailer or footer to the packet. Through these headers we can see where one layer ends and another starts. It is at this layer that we are concerned with the port numbers of particular services, such as port 80 for HTTP traffic. The TCP/IP model application layer comprises the OSI models Session, Presentation and Application layers.

Our data at this level looks very simple:

Data

The data is then passed to the Transport layer.

TCP/IP – Transport layer

A UDP header encapsulates the data we received from the Application layer; the data becomes "UDP data". Whereas the application layer is concerned with process-to-process connectivity, the transport layer is all about host-to-host connectivity. The transport layer looks after a lot of the more protective aspects of data transfer, such as error control, segmentation, flow control, congestion control, as well as the application port numbers used.

UDP header	UDP data

TCP/IP – Internet layer

The Internet layer is where routing occurs; the process of sending data from one network to another (also known as Internetworking). This layer is concerned with host addressing and identification, which we will look at in chapter three, and packet routing, which is the sending of packets to a router closer to the destination than we are.

Our UDP header and UDP data become the IP data part of the packet, and we now have an IP header at the beginning (again we have been encapsulated).

IP header	IP data

We are then passed down to the final layer.

TCP/IP - Link layer

The final layer is the link layer. Here the IP packet (the header and the data) becomes the frame data and are encapsulated in a frame header and footer. This is the layer where software meets hardware, and here the frame is transmitted over the physical medium (such as the Ethernet cable).

Our packet now looks like this:

Frame header	Frame Data	Frame footer

The complete process looks a little like this:

Application				Data	
Transport			UDP header	UDP data	
Internet		IP header	IP Data		
Link	Frame header	Frame Data			Frame footer

The actual mechanics of how a packet travels does not differ between the TCP/IP model and the OSI model, apart from the fact that the OSI model adds more levels of abstraction. An abstraction level is a way of separating roles and duties. Think of it in the way a restaurant operates, we have the greeter, who shows you your seat, the people who serve you your food and drink, and the people who actually cook the food. These are all separate roles (abstraction layers) that lead to the overall success of the functioning of the restaurant. Both models achieve the same outcome, but the OSI model (to keep with the restaurant analogy), has different people to bring you the bread, drink and food.

The OSI model

The OSI (Open Systems Interconnection) model has seven layers, and in most likelihood, is the one you will come across the most. It is the "standard", vendor neutral model, coming from the International Organization for Standardization (who are also known as ISO). Whilst the focus on the exam does seem to be the OSI model, by the end of the 1990s the TCP/IP model was the most predominantly used, and still is today.

We will use a TCP packet for this example, so we can see the differences and similarities between that and a UDP packet, starting at the user interface.

OSI - Application layer

We start with the layer closest to the user. Here we will have applications such as Outlook or Thunderbird for email, Filezilla for FTP, or PuTTY for SSH. This layer will create a data PDU (Protocol Data Unit). These PDUs contain a payload, which is the data we create and this is known as the Service Data Unit (SDU). We also have the header (and sometimes) footer related to the protocol.

The start of our packet, at this layer, looks like this:

	AH	Data

We have our data, and an application layer header (AH).

Our PDU is then passed down to the presentation layer.

OSI – Presentation layer

The presentation layer creates context between the application layer and the session layer. Here we start to build translations between the data in the PDU sent to us from the application layer, to something that the session layer will understand (and vice-versa if the data is coming into the application layer), such as strings being converted into XML data and HTML character encoding.

Encryption and decryption also occurs at this layer, when you log into to your bank's secure website the web page displayed by the application layer was decrypted by the presentation layer.

The data at the Presentation layer is then passed to the Session layer.

OSI – Session Layer

The session layer looks after the connections between our local application and the remote one. It establishes the connection, maintains it, and closes it. The session layer is where full-duplex or half-duplex come into play to ensure the correct establishment of the connections between the two ends.

OSI – Transport layer

The transport layer is where our data and application layer header become one, and we have ours encapsulated in a TCP header:

	TCP Header	Application Data

Our protocols at this layer will be TCP and UDP. The PDU is now known as a segment. The transport layer handles reliability. It can keep track of flows and will retransmit segments that have failed or, if no failures have been detected, the next segment. It keeps track of the segments using sequence numbers. In the event that sequences 1,2,4 and 5 are received, but not 3, it will request sequence 3 to be resent.

The transport layer also handles flow control, congestion avoidance, multiplexing, and connection-oriented communication.

When two computers talk, it is no different to when people talk, both sides need to talk at a rate (speed) that the other can understand. In networks, this is performed through flow control. Flow control prevents buffer overruns, where one side sends data at a faster rate than the other can receive it, and improves efficiency by reducing buffer under-run (the other side waiting for more data).

Congestion avoidance is about making sure that the link(s) we use are not overwhelmed by the amount of data being pushed down them, otherwise we could experience packet loss. There are a number of ways that congestion avoidance (and by extension of this, congestion control) is implemented. One of these is Carrier Sense Multiple Access with Collision Avoidance (CSMA/CA), which uses a "Request to Send" and a "Clear to Send" (RTS/CTS) communication between the sender, who sends the RST, and the recipient, who replies with a CTS, thus allowing the sender to send the data. Another method of congestion avoidance is window reduction.

As we are sent information, we send an acknowledgement in return, to say that we have received a segment. Sliding windows allow us to accept multiple segments with a single acknowledgement. The size of the available window depends on the amount of data in the memory buffer that sits between the application layer and the data link layer. This capacity is stated in a 16-bit field in the TCP header. This places a limit on the size of the window; this limit is 64 kilobytes (2^{16}). Sliding windows go hand-in-hand with another of these congestion avoidance methods; slow-start. In slow-start we set a one-to-one relationship between the data we are sent and the acknowledgements we send back in return. They send us a segment, we "ACK" it. We then increase the window, sending one ACK for every two segments, then moving to three packets for one ACK, then four, and so on up to the window limit, at which stage we go back to a one-to-one relation, and start building up again.

The final method we will discuss is the implementation of quality of service (QoS) measures, which are concerned with (and are classed as) queue management. Whilst these are not part of the CCNA, we should briefly discuss a couple. These are Explicit Congestion Notification (ECN) and Backwards Explicit Congestion Notification (BECN). ECN allows for end-to-end (i.e. all the routers along the way) notification of network congestion. The benefit of using ECN is that the packets are not dropped, which is usually the way that the network shows that there is congestion. However, there is a caveat here. This does depend on the age of the hardware that you are using. Older hardware would drop packets marked with the ECN bit, but now the number of devices that will drop packets marked with the ECN bit stands at around 1%. Even Apple has adopted the use of ECN. BECN uses ICMP source quench messages to achieve a similar effect as ECN, but without the need for the end-points to signal that they want to use this, unlike ECN where both sides have to agree to use it.

The ports we spoke about earlier (port 25 for SMTP traffic, 80 for HTTP web traffic, 23 for Telnet and so on), allow us to perform multiplexing. Multiplexing is where we can have multiple applications on one device, all listening on their own ports, allowing the device to do multiple functions at the same time, such as serving email, HTTP pages and file sharing.

Finally we have connection-oriented communication, where we establish a session and then pass data over it so that it might be received in the order that it was sent. This differs to connectionless communication, where the data can be delivered out of order. This puts greater burden on the receiver, as either it has to reorder them, or the packets are dropped. Frame Relay, MPLS and TCP are all connection-oriented.

OSI – Network layer

Our segments from the transport layer now become datagrams, or packets, as they pass into this layer; we also gain an IP header, which contains our source and destination IP addresses:

	IP Header	TCP Header	Application Data

This layer maps the IP (network) address to the physical (MAC) address, and is where data will be fragmented in order to pass over the physical medium. The network layer handles packet forwarding and routing.

Protocols at this level include IPv4 and IPv6, ICMP, IPSec (as used in the encryption of VPN traffic), the routing protocol RIP, and the multicast protocols; DVMRP (Distance Vector Multicast Routing Protocol), PIM-SM (Protocol Independent Multicast Sparse Mode) and PIM-DM (Dense Mode).

We have connectionless communication at this layer, where the recipient is not required to send an acknowledgement in return.

OSI – Data link layer

The data link layer defines the protocol for connection creation between nodes (such as us and an upstream router), including the flow control protocol and looks after error corrections for the physical layer.

Within the data link layer, we have two sub layers, the Media Access Control or MAC layer and the Logical Link Control, or LLC layer.

The LLC layer sits between the network layer and the MAC layer. Its main function is to allow the networks protocols to be transported (multiplexing) and to provide node-to-node flow and error control.

The MAC layer takes care of addressing, using the physical address on the network interface. It generates and checks Frame Check Sequences (FCS), and controls access to the physical layer. The MAC layer adds on the Ethernet header, which contains the source and destination MAC addresses and a trailer, containing the FCS.

Ethernet Header	IP Header	TCP Header	Application Data	Ethernet trailer

Frame Check Sequences (FCS) are calculated by the sender, using a cyclic redundancy check, and are based on the data in the layer-2 frame. They are then stored as a number within the FCS field. The destination node can then create their own FCS and compare it against the one that they have been sent. If an error is found then the packet can be discarded, or retransmission can be requested.

OSI – Physical layer

The final layer is the physical layer. It is this layer in which our zeros and ones, our bits and bytes, get sent as electrical signals across the transport medium (i.e. copper wire). The physical layer is an interface between the binary data and the electrical signal, translating the data link layer requests into hardware-specific operations for the sending and receiving of the electrical signals. This is done at blisteringly fast speed, where the voltage increases and decreases to encode the 0s and 1s takes place at $1/10,000,000^{th}$ of a second.

This layer performs auto-negotiation between nodes (so that both agree on the duplex and speed of a link).

We can see how the packets actually look using a packet capture utility such as tcpdump (on linux), or Wireshark. Wireshark is much easier to use (though you can use tcpdump to generate the capture and Wireshark to look at it). We will look at some Wireshark captures in the next section, which will also solidify some of the differences in how the data looks as it passes through the layers of the OSI model.

Before we move on, we will return to look at our end packet. From the TCP/IP model we saw that the end result looked a little like this:

Frame header	Frame Data	Frame footer

We should break this down a little more though, as it will help us going forward.

Header						Trailer
Preamble	SFD	Destination MAC	Source MAC	Type	Data and Pad	FCS
7 bytes	1 bytes	6 bytes	6 bytes	2 bytes	46 – 1500 bytes	4 bytes

The preamble is used for clock synchronization. The SFD (Start of Frame Delimiter) is used to mark a new incoming frame, and then we have our destination and source MAC addresses. The EtherType (Type) identifies the protocol that will be used in the data, and then we have our data and padding and lastly the FCS, which is our means of testing whether the frame is good or bad. The preamble, SFD, destination and source MAC addresses, type and FCS all have a fixed size. The data can vary in size between 46 and 1500 bytes. The 802.3 specification means that there is a limit on how much we can pack into a frame, and this is called the MTU; the Maximum Transmission Unit. We can use "jumbo frames" to increase the MTU, but only in certain scenarios, so for the majority of time, we are bound by this 1500-byte limit.

> 802.3 is the name given to the Ethernet standard. The Institute of Electrical and Electronics Engineers (IEEE) are the people who hand out these designations.
>
> 802 itself refers to the standards for local area networks and metropolitan area networks.

The complete sequence looks like this:

Application					AH	Data
Presentation					AH	Data
Session					AH	Data
Transport				TCP header	Application data	
Network			IP Header	TCP header	Application data	
Data Link		Ethernet header	IP header	TCP header	Application data	Ethernet trailer
Physical	Frame header	Frame data				Frame footer

1.5 Predict the data flow between two hosts across a network

How does data get from host A to host B across a network? As we saw from the previous section, we use different data at different layers. We use IP addresses for the majority of the layers, but once we get to the data link and physical layers, we rely on the MAC address. We will look at MAC addresses in greater detail in section 2.1. One of the critical factors here is that the IP address never changes (unless we are behind a NAT device, which will switch one IP address for another; usually a private address for a public one), but the MAC address will change as the frame goes from device to device.

Let's look at an example of how this works and, more importantly, why. If you want to follow along on your topology, then either jump ahead to chapter 4 (just for a moment) and set up the IP addressing for the EIGRP1, ISP and OSPF1 routers, along with the routing as specified, or come back to this part later, at least once you have got up to that part of chapter 4.

We have three routers. EIGRP1 needs to communicate with OSPF1. They are on separate networks and are connected by a router (ISP).

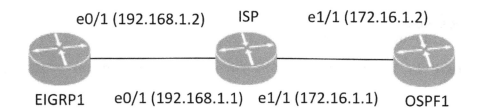

e0/1 (192.168.1.2)   ISP   e1/1 (172.16.1.2)

EIGRP1   e0/1 (192.168.1.1) e1/1 (172.16.1.1)   OSPF1

Device	Interface	IP Address	MAC address
EIGRP1	E0/1	192.168.1.2	aabb.cc00.1110
ISP	E0/1	192.168.1.1	aabb.cc00.0c10
ISP	E1/1	172.16.1.1	aabb.cc00.0c11
OSPF1	E1/1	172.16.1.2	aabb.cc00.0b11

The EIGRP1 router does not have an explicit routing entry for OSPF1. All it knows is to send everything to ISP. This is through a default gateway. We will go into this in more detail in chapter 4, but our routing table is shown below:

```
EIGRP1#show ip route | b Gate
Gateway of last resort is 192.168.1.1 to network 0.0.0.0

S*     0.0.0.0/0 [1/0] via 192.168.1.1
       192.168.1.0/24 is variably subnetted, 2 subnets, 2 masks
C         192.168.1.0/24 is directly connected, Ethernet0/1
L         192.168.1.2/32 is directly connected, Ethernet0/1
EIGRP1#
```

The same is true for OSPF1, and its routing table is show below:

```
OSPF1#show ip route |  b Gate
Gateway of last resort is 172.16.1.1 to network 0.0.0.0

S*     0.0.0.0/0 [1/0] via 172.16.1.1
       172.16.0.0/16 is variably subnetted, 2 subnets, 2 masks
C         172.16.1.0/24 is directly connected, Ethernet1/2
L         172.16.1.2/32 is directly connected, Ethernet1/2
OSPF1#
```

The line(s) we need to concern ourselves with are the ones with S*, these are static routes, and both EIGRP1 and OSPF1 point to the ISP router.

Our upper level layers create the packet, which passes down through the layers to the network layer. We will use (for our first example) a simple ping from one side to the other:

```
EIGRP1#ping 172.16.1.2
Type escape sequence to abort.
Sending 5, 100-byte ICMP Echos to 172.16.1.2, timeout is 2 seconds:
!!!!!
Success rate is 100 percent (5/5), round-trip min/avg/max = 20/29/60 ms
EIGRP1#
```

From this we can see the source and destination IP addresses, as shown in the Wireshark screenshot below.

```
  7 192.168.1.2        172.16.1.2        ICMP  Echo (ping) request  id=0x0000, seq=0/0, ttl=255 (reply in 10)
  8 aa:bb:cc:00:0c:10  Broadcast         ARP   Who has 192.168.1.2? Tell 192.168.1.1
  9 aa:bb:cc:00:11:10  aa:bb:cc:00:0c:10 ARP   192.168.1.2 is at aa:bb:cc:00:11:10
 10 172.16.1.2         192.168.1.2       ICMP  Echo (ping) reply    id=0x0000, seq=0/0, ttl=254 (request in 7)
▶ Frame 10: 114 bytes on wire (912 bits), 114 bytes captured (912 bits) on interface 0
▶ Ethernet II, Src: aa:bb:cc:00:0c:10 (aa:bb:cc:00:0c:10), Dst: aa:bb:cc:00:11:10 (aa:bb:cc:00:11:10)
▶ Internet Protocol Version 4, Src: 172.16.1.2, Dst: 192.168.1.2
▶ Internet Control Message Protocol
```

Wireshark capture: 1

The packet from EIGRP1 to OSPF1 is forwarded to the ISP router, according to our routing table (line 7). We do not need to know OSPF1's MAC address, as MAC addresses are only significant between two points (EIGRP1 to ISP and from ISP to OSPF1), but the ISP router does need to know the MAC address of EIGRP1. It performs an ARP query to get this information in line 8, and receives a reply in line 9. As MAC addresses are only relevant between one host and its neighbor, although the ping reply packet is addressed to EIGRP1 (192.168.1.2), the layer-2 frame is sourced from the ISP router (aabb.cc00.0c10), even though the layer-3 IP address is that of OSPF1.

The exclamation marks in the output above show that our ping was successful. We will cover ping in chapter 4, but this indicates that we have a successful end-to-end connectivity at the network layer (and therefore the layers beneath it as well), even though we are still unaware on OSPF1's MAC address. We can confirm this from the contents of our ARP cache:

```
EIGRP1#show arp
Protocol  Address        Age (min)  Hardware Addr   Type   Interface
Internet  192.168.1.1           15  aabb.cc00.0c10  ARPA   Ethernet0/1
Internet  192.168.1.2            -  aabb.cc00.1110  ARPA   Ethernet0/1
EIGRP1#
```

We have our own MAC address in the second entry (aabb.cc00.1110), and don't worry that I have written the MAC addresses differently to how they are shown in Wireshark, as both are valid representations of the same thing; aabb.cc00.1110 is the same as aa:bb:cc:00:11:10.

The ISP router has a larger ARP cache, as it knows about the router OSPF1 as well as EIGRP1:

```
ISP#sh arp
Protocol  Address       Age (min)  Hardware Addr   Type   Interface
Internet  172.16.1.1        -       aabb.cc00.0c11  ARPA   Ethernet1/1
Internet  172.16.1.2        32      aabb.cc00.0b11  ARPA   Ethernet1/1
Internet  192.168.1.1       -       aabb.cc00.0c10  ARPA   Ethernet0/1
Internet  192.168.1.2       29      aabb.cc00.1110  ARPA   Ethernet0/1
ISP#
```

OSPF1 has a smaller ARP cache; it just knows about itself and the ISP router:

```
OSPF1#sh arp
Protocol  Address       Age (min)  Hardware Addr   Type   Interface
Internet  172.16.1.1        29      aabb.cc00.0c11  ARPA   Ethernet1/1
Internet  172.16.1.2        -       aabb.cc00.0b11  ARPA   Ethernet1/1
OSPF1#
```

As you can see, EIGRP1 only needs to know about the MAC addresses for the direct connection to the ISP router, similarly OSPF1 only needs to know about the MAC address of itself, and the one that it connects to on the ISP router.

If we do not already know the MAC addresses, then the routers will perform an ARP request (lines 8 and 9 of the capture above) to gain this vital information.

We start by broadcasting our own MAC address (a gratuitous ARP). This is sent to the broadcast MAC address ff:ff:ff:ff:ff:ff:

```
    8 aa:bb:cc:00:0c:10  Broadcast        ARP    Who has 192.168.1.2? Tell 192.168.1.1
▶ Frame 8: 60 bytes on wire (480 bits), 60 bytes captured (480 bits) on interface 0
▼ Ethernet II, Src: aa:bb:cc:00:0c:10 (aa:bb:cc:00:0c:10), Dst: Broadcast (ff:ff:ff:ff:ff:ff)
  ▶ Destination: Broadcast (ff:ff:ff:ff:ff:ff)  ◀
  ▶ Source: aa:bb:cc:00:0c:10 (aa:bb:cc:00:0c:10)
    Type: ARP (0x0806)
    Padding: 000000000000000000000000000000000000
▼ Address Resolution Protocol (request)
    Hardware type: Ethernet (1)
    Protocol type: IPv4 (0x0800)
    Hardware size: 6
    Protocol size: 4
    Opcode: request (1)
    Sender MAC address: aa:bb:cc:00:0c:10 (aa:bb:cc:00:0c:10)
    Sender IP address: 192.168.1.1
    Target MAC address: 00:00:00_00:00:00 (00:00:00:00:00:00)
    Target IP address: 192.168.1.2
```

EIGRP1 then sends a reply, with its own MAC address:

```
     9 aa:bb:cc:00:11:10  aa:bb:cc:00:0c:10  ARP    192.168.1.2 is at aa:bb:cc:00:11:10
▶ Frame 9: 60 bytes on wire (480 bits), 60 bytes captured (480 bits) on interface 0
▶ Ethernet II, Src: aa:bb:cc:00:11:10 (aa:bb:cc:00:11:10), Dst: aa:bb:cc:00:0c:10 (aa:bb:cc:00:0c:10)
▼ Address Resolution Protocol (reply)
     Hardware type: Ethernet (1)
     Protocol type: IPv4 (0x0800)
     Hardware size: 6
     Protocol size: 4
     Opcode: reply (2)
     Sender MAC address: aa:bb:cc:00:11:10 (aa:bb:cc:00:11:10)
     Sender IP address: 192.168.1.2
     Target MAC address: aa:bb:cc:00:0c:10 (aa:bb:cc:00:0c:10)
     Target IP address: 192.168.1.1
```

Now the MAC address of EIGRP1 is known by ISP, and is in our ARP cache. The same is true for the other side of the connection, ISP uses the same process to learn the MAC address of OSPF1, and the ping succeeds.

As you can see from the Wireshark capture, the source and destination MAC addresses are only known as far as the neighboring router. We visualize this in a better way:

Now, what would happen if the connection from the ISP router to OSPF1 were unavailable? What would happen to the packet?

Actually, this depends where the problem lies.

If we shut down the e1/1 interface on OSPF1, and try pinging from EIGRP1 to OSPF1 then the packets are just lost:

```
OSPF1(config)#interface e1/1
OSPF1(config-if)#shutdown
OSPF1(config-if)#
```

```
EIGRP1#ping 172.16.1.2
Type escape sequence to abort.
Sending 5, 100-byte ICMP Echos to 172.16.1.2, timeout is 2 seconds:
.....
Success rate is 0 percent (0/5)
EIGRP1#
```

We can see this in Wireshark:

```
 15 192.168.1.2  172.16.1.2  ICMP  Echo (ping) request  id=0x0002, seq=0/0, ttl=255 (no response found!)
▶ Frame 15: 114 bytes on wire (912 bits), 114 bytes captured (912 bits) on interface 0
▶ Ethernet II, Src: aa:bb:cc:00:11:10 (aa:bb:cc:00:11:10), Dst: aa:bb:cc:00:0c:10 (aa:bb:cc:00:0c:10)
▶ Internet Protocol Version 4, Src: 192.168.1.2, Dst: 172.16.1.2
▼ Internet Control Message Protocol
    Type: 8 (Echo (ping) request)
    Code: 0
    Checksum: 0x178b [correct]
    Identifier (BE): 2 (0x0002)
    Identifier (LE): 512 (0x0200)
    Sequence number (BE): 0 (0x0000)
    Sequence number (LE): 0 (0x0000)
  ▶ [No response seen]
  ▶ Data (72 bytes)
```

Wireshark capture: 2

If we shut down the e1/1 interface on the ISP router, we get a different response:

```
ISP(config)#int e1/1
ISP(config-if)#shutdown
ISP(config-if)#

EIGRP1#ping 172.16.1.2
Type escape sequence to abort.
Sending 5, 100-byte ICMP Echos to 172.16.1.2, timeout is 2 seconds:
U.U.U
Success rate is 0 percent (0/5)
EIGRP1#
```

The ISP router will respond with a Destination Unreachable ICMP message:

```
 39 192.168.1.1  192.168.1...  ICMP  Destination unreachable (Host unreachable)
▶ Frame 39: 70 bytes on wire (560 bits), 70 bytes captured (560 bits) on interface 0
▶ Ethernet II, Src: aa:bb:cc:00:0c:10 (aa:bb:cc:00:0c:10), Dst: aa:bb:cc:00:11:10 (aa:bb:cc:00:11:10)
▶ Internet Protocol Version 4, Src: 192.168.1.1, Dst: 192.168.1.2
▼ Internet Control Message Protocol
    Type: 3 (Destination unreachable)
    Code: 1 (Host unreachable)
    Checksum: 0xe539 [correct]
    Unused: 00000000
  ▶ Internet Protocol Version 4, Src: 192.168.1.2, Dst: 172.16.1.2
  ▶ Internet Control Message Protocol
```

This does give us a degree of problem isolation to help us troubleshoot, if we get a "Destination Unreachable" ICMP message then the problem is on the next router (ISP in this case), if the problem is on a remote router then the request packet will receive no reply.

Because we have started to look into the contents of a packet, it makes sense to return to the previous section and look at a capture that shows all the layers.

We will turn the ports on ISP and OSPF1 back on again, and then telnet from EIGRP1 to OSPF1 (we will set up telnet in subsequent chapters, as well as the below commands):

```
OSPF1(config)#int e1/1
OSPF1(config-if)#no shutdown
OSPF1(config-if)#

ISP(config)#int e1/1
ISP(config-if)#no shut
ISP(config-if)#

OSPF1(config-if)#line vty 0 4
OSPF1(config-line)#login
% Login disabled on line 2, until 'password' is set
% Login disabled on line 3, until 'password' is set
% Login disabled on line 4, until 'password' is set
% Login disabled on line 5, until 'password' is set
% Login disabled on line 6, until 'password' is set
OSPF1(config-line)#password cisco
OSPF1(config-line)#transport input telnet
OSPF1(config-line)#

EIGRP1#telnet 172.16.1.2
Trying 172.16.1.2 ... Open


User Access Verification

Password:cisco
OSPF1>exit

[Connection to 172.16.1.2 closed by foreign host]
EIGRP1#
```

We type in the password "cisco", and now we can examine the Wireshark capture:

```
   17 192.168.1.2   172.16.1.2   TCP      55717 → 23 [SYN] Seq=0 Win=4128 Len=0 MSS=536
► Frame 17: 60 bytes on wire (480 bits), 60 bytes captured (480 bits) on interface 0
► Ethernet II, Src: aa:bb:cc:00:11:10 (aa:bb:cc:00:11:10), Dst: aa:bb:cc:00:0c:10 (aa:bb:cc:00:0c:10)
► Internet Protocol Version 4, Src: 192.168.1.2, Dst: 172.16.1.2
► Transmission Control Protocol, Src Port: 55717 (55717), Dst Port: 23 (23), Seq: 0, Len: 0
```

Wireshark capture: 3

As we can see, we have the source IP address of EIGRP1, the destination IP address of OSPF1, the source MAC address of EIGRP1 and the destination MAC address of the ISP router. The destination port number is set to 23, and our source port (55717) is one of the higher ports (outside of the range reserved for specific applications, which is 0-1023).

We then have the data stream:

```
   20 192.168.1.2   172.16.1.2   TELN… Telnet Data ...
► Frame 20: 66 bytes on wire (528 bits), 66 bytes captured (528 bits) on interface 0
► Ethernet II, Src: aa:bb:cc:00:11:10 (aa:bb:cc:00:11:10), Dst: aa:bb:cc:00:0c:10 (aa:bb:cc:00:0c:10)
► Internet Protocol Version 4, Src: 192.168.1.2, Dst: 172.16.1.2
► Transmission Control Protocol, Src Port: 55717 (55717), Dst Port: 23 (23), Seq: 1, Ack: 1, Len: 12
▼ Telnet
   ► Do Suppress Go Ahead
   ► Will Terminal Speed
   ► Will Negotiate About Window Size
   ► Will Remote Flow Control
```

In the above capture we can see the layer-7, 6 and 5 data (Telnet), the layer-4 transport layer segment (our Transmission Control Protocol), the layer-3 network layer IP packet, the layer-2 Data link frame with our MAC addresses, and our layer-1 physical Bit layer.

You can see that Wireshark has included [SYN] in Frame 3. This is part of the TCP three-way handshake that is used when two devices communicate. The full sequence can be seen in the capture:

```
   17 192.168.1.2   172.16.1.2    TCP    55717 → 23 [SYN] Seq=0 Win=4128 Len=0 MSS=536
   18 172.16.1.2   192.168.1…    TCP    23 → 55717 [SYN, ACK] Seq=0 Ack=1 Win=4128 Len=0 MSS=536
   19 192.168.1.2   172.16.1.2    TCP    55717 → 23 [ACK] Seq=1 Ack=1 Win=4128 Len=0
```

This handshake must complete before the two devices can send data to each other. A diagram of what this looks like is below:

We start with a Synchronize message (SYN), which is acknowledged by the other router (SYN, ACK), and then we acknowledge the acknowledgement in the last message.

Similarly, a connection should also be closed, which we can also see in the Wireshark capture:

```
65  172.16.1.2   192.168.1…   TCP    23 → 55717  [FIN, PSH, ACK] Seq=90 Ack=44 Win=4085 Len=0
66  192.168.1.2  172.16.1.2   TCP    55717 → 23  [ACK] Seq=44 Ack=91 Win=4039 Len=0
67  192.168.1.2  172.16.1.2   TCP    55717 → 23  [FIN, PSH, ACK] Seq=44 Ack=91 Win=4039 Len=0
68  172.16.1.2   192.168.1…   TCP    23 → 55717  [ACK] Seq=91 Ack=45 Win=4085 Len=0
```

The TCP connection termination consists of a FIN (FIN meaning "finished"), an acknowledgment, another FIN, followed by a final acknowledgement.

Let's finish this chapter by looking at the physical connections we will use.

1.6 Identify the appropriate media, cables, ports, and connectors to connect Cisco network devices to other network devices and hosts in a LAN

When I did my CCNA I needed to learn every cable that has been used in networking since networking began, I felt that I could go into any server room and correctly identify and use the myriad of cables they would have in a real environment. I have used two types. The everyday reality is that you will only ever use a handful of different cables, unless you happen to step into a network that has not changed since the early 1990s.

Most of the traffic we transfer locally will be through copper cables, but these have a finite limit on cable length. We can also use fibre, which enables a much longer cable length. The Ethernet standard is known as 802.3, the early 10Mbps cable uses the standard IEEE name of 802.3, and each variation and subsequent improvement on this gains a new suffix. Each also has an informal standard name, which uses the speed, "base" meaning baseband and either -T or -X, which denotes either UTP cable (T), or fibre (X).

The following table shows the maximum cable speed, along with the naming standards:

Category (UTP)	Speed	Name	Informal name	Formal name	Type, maximum length
Cat.3	10 Mbps	Ethernet	10BASE-T	802.3	Copper, 100 metres
Cat.5	100 Mbps	Fast Ethernet	100BASE-T	802.3u	Copper, 100 metres
Cat.5/5e	1000 Mbps	Gigabit Ethernet	1000BASE-T	802.3ab	Copper, 100 metres
Cat.6	10 Gbps	10 Gig Ethernet	10GBASE-T	802.3an	Copper, 100 metres
	1000 Mbps	Gigabit Ethernet	1000BASE-X	802.3z	Fibre (see below)

In the second column, we have the speeds, which are measured in Bits per second (bps). A bit is the smallest unit of storage and can be either a zero (0) or a one (1). These can then be used in the physical layer to generate the voltages on/off sequence required for the physical layer.

We need to understand the difference between bits and bytes, mainly as when people complain that their Internet is slow and never matches up to the bytes they should be getting, you can point out that it is measured in bits, not bytes.

Speeds of links are usually measured in bits, whereas the size of something (such as a file) is generally measured in bytes. 8 bits (b) make up a byte (B), the letter "a" in a text file would account for one byte. An IP address is 32 bits, or 4 bytes.

A kilo*byte* (kB) is 1,024 bytes, and a mega*byte* (MB) is 1,048,576 bytes, but it is easier to remember this as 1,024 kilobytes.

A kilo*bit* (kb) however is 1000 bits, a mega*bit* (Mb) is 1,000,000 bits and a Giga*bit* (Gb) is 1,000,000,000 bits. A gigabyte (GB) would therefore be 1,073,741,824 bytes, or 8,000,000,000 bits. You can see why many people are easily confused between a megabit and a megabyte confused.

The last column specifies whether we are using UTP copper, or fibre. UTP stands for Unshielded Twisted-pair. It comprises eight separate copper cables that are twisted together. They are twisted together to cancel out electromagnetic interference (EMI) and crosstalk. We can thank the guy who invented the telephone, Alexander Graham Bell, for this. The eight wires go to form four pairs.

The physical connector used with UTP is an RJ-45 connector. Depending on the purpose of the cable, (and on the age of the equipment) the cables either will be connected in pairs, or will be crossed over. An image of an RJ-45 connector is shown below:

The standard cable is known as a patch cable (Cisco calls this a straight-through cable), and this is used to connect a PC to a switch, or a switch to a router. To connect two switches we may need a different type of cable. If we are using older equipment then we need to use a crossover cable, newer switches will automatically detect what device they are connected to and will look after the pin assignment automatically, which is called auto-mdix. As a general rule of thumb (and I mean in the exam), when connecting two switches together, you would use a crossover cable.

A straight-through cable is exactly as the name suggests:

Pin	Color		Pin	Color
1	White/Orange		1	White/Orange
2	Orange		2	Orange
3	White/Green		3	White/Green
4	Blue		4	Blue
5	White/Blue		5	White/Blue
6	Green		6	Green
7	White/Brown		7	White/Brown
8	Brown		8	Brown

The important pins are 1, 2, 3 and 6. On one side we transmit using pins one and two and receive on pins three and six, the other side will then receive on pins one and two, and transmit on three and six.

A crossover cable has the order of the pins changed (but only on one side):

Pin	Color		Pin	Color
1	White/Orange		1	Blue
2	Orange		2	White/Blue
3	White/Green		3	White/Green
4	Blue		4	White/Orange
5	White/Blue		5	Orange
6	Green		6	Green
7	White/Brown		7	White/Brown
8	Brown		8	Brown

Again the important pins are 1, 2, 3 and 6, but both receive on pins one and two, and transmit on pins three and six.

1000BASE-T is a bit different, it uses all four pairs of wires; it can also send and receive at the same time on each wire pair.

There is a third type of cable, known as a rollover cable. This is used to connect the COM port (serial port) of a computer to the console port of a Cisco router or switch. This is usually flat and light blue in color.

Below is a small table with the right cables for the right purpose.

Device	Device	Cable
PC	Switch	Straight-through (patch cable)
Switch	Router	Straight-through
Switch	Switch	Crossover
PC (Serial port)	Switch or router console port	Rollover

1000BASE-X covers a wide range of mediums. Whilst most of these are fiber based, there are a couple of copper based variants, so we should not assume that all 1000BASE-X implementations are fiber.

1000BASE-TX uses Cat.6 or Cat.7 UTP, 1000BASE-CX uses shielded balanced cable, and 1000BASE-KX uses copper backplane. The others do use fiber. Fiber allows networks to span several kilometers using a single cable. Whereas an electrical signal over copper suffers attenuation (loss of signal strength the further along the line it goes), a fiber optic cable uses light transmitted across a strand of glass or plastic to achieve the longer distances, without a loss of signal strength. It is also immune to electromagnetic interference.

Fiber comes in two modes, multi-mode and single-mode. Multi-mode fiber has a larger core diameter than single mode fiber, and allows for cheaper light sources, such as LEDs to be used. Generally, both forms are more expensive than copper cabling. However, they do span much further distances:

Name	Mode	Distance
1000BASE-SX	Multi	220 - 550 meters
1000BASE-LX	Multi	550 meters
1000BASE-LX	Single	5 Kilometers
1000BASE-LX10	Single (pair)	10 km
1000BASE-EX	Single	40 km
1000BASE-ZX	Single	70 Kilometers
1000BASE-BX10	Single	10 Kilometers

Finally, we should discuss serial cables, before we look at an example of how the local area network (LAN) connects to the Wide Area Network (WAN).

Serial cables

Serial cables are generally big chunky things and are used to connect modems and routers together. One end must send clocking information; this is so that both sides send data at the same speed. The end that supplies the clocking information is referred to as the DCE, the Data Communications Equipment. The other end is known as the DTE or Data Terminal Equipment. You can get one cable with DCE embossed on one end and DTE embossed on the other, alternatively you can get a DTE cable and a DCE cable and join them together. Serial interfaces often have a function called a Channel Service Unit/Data Service Unit (CSU/DSU) built into them, which provides the clocking function. If the serial interface does not support this then a separate CSU/DSU is required. The CSU/DSU is required to connect the DTE (router) to the ISP's digital circuit (such as a T1 line, which we will discuss in chapter eight). Modems are CSU/DSUs. We will discuss this in greater depth in chapter eight when we look at WAN technologies. Below is a diagram of a "basic" network, including cabling, and where the LAN meets the WAN.

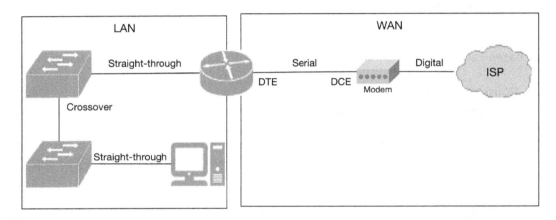

We have already seen a few port configurations, using the e0/1 and e1/1 interfaces on EIGRP1, ISP and OSPF1. The "e" refers to the type of interface, meaning it is an Ethernet interface. Serial interfaces would use "s". Routers can host a number of different cards. These cards can supply Ethernet or serial interfaces. The first digit (bolded) of e0/1, or e1/1, refers to the slot that the card is in, and the final digit refers to the interface on that card. Therefore, the connection between ISP and EIGRP1 is using the card in the first slot (which are numbered from 0), and port number 1 (e0/1). The e1/1 connection is using the port 1 on the card in slot number one.

So now we know what we can connect up, how we can connect it, and how traffic passes and changes as it travels along it, let's start creating our own network, starting with a Local Area Network (LAN).

2. LAN Switching Technologies

This section makes up a huge 20% of the scoring, so expect Cisco to ask a larger number of questions from this section!

In this section, we will look at how our data moves around our local area network (LAN). This is known as a switched network, because the packets will be switched, rather than routed. Devices in a network use different information, depending on whether it is a switched environment, or a routed environment. Switched networks use the Media Access Control method.

2.1 Determine the technology and media access control method for Ethernet networks

Switches use MAC addresses to deliver packets, these are Media Access Control addresses, and these are unique and are formed of two parts.

The MAC addresses we refer to are called MAC-48 addresses, but are also referred to as EUI-48, which is now the preferred term. MAC-48 addresses are only used for hardware, whereas EUI-48 addresses can be used for hardware and software, which we will look at in more detail when we cover IPv6 addressing.

The MAC address is 48-bits long, so there can be 281,474,976,710,656 unique addresses. They are formed of six groups, and in each group are two hexadecimal digits, 0-9 and a-f. A MAC address can take the format of 01:02:03:ab:cd:ef, or can be written as 01-02-03-ab-cd-ef, or even 0102.03ab.cdef.

The first half of the MAC address (24-bits) is assigned to the manufacturer of the interface card. Cisco has a large number of these. To see a complete list you can look at the following URL: http://www.coffer.com/mac_find/?string=cisco. These are "universally administered addresses", and are referred to as the Organizationally Unique Identifier (OUI). The IEEE (Institute of Electrical and Electronics Engineers) manages the OUI assignment.

The second half of the MAC address can be assigned however the organization sees fit. MAC addresses can be duplicated, either in error, or on purpose. The IEEE mitigates the latter though, by setting a target lifetime of 100 years, so the chances of this happening will be slim.

We can also change our MAC address, at which point it becomes known as a "locally administered address".

The MAC address is very important for the switch, as this tells the switch what kind of data it is handling.

Let's start with a MAC address (a fictional one) of 01:02:03:ab:cd:ef, this is the BIA or Burned-In Address, that is hardcoded into the network interface card's (NIC) read-only memory (ROM). We have an OUI of 01:02:03, this would be assigned by the IEEE to 802101.com. We would then use this to make up the first half of the MAC address, and append ab:cd:ef as the identifier assigned to the NIC. This address will then be broken down into a range, starting with the most significant, to the least significant.

01 would be the most significant byte. This is then broken down into binary. We will look at how we convert to binary in Chapter 3, so don't worry too much about how this works at the moment. This in binary will be 00000001. We can tell from this which is a universally administered address, and which is a locally administered address. In our example, this would be a universally administered address, as the second-least-significant bit is a zero, shown in bold: 0000000**1**. The least significant bit would be one: 0000000**1**. This second-least significant bit is known as the Universal/Local bit (U/L bit), regardless of whether it is a zero or a one. If our fictional MAC address started with 02, then this would be 00000010 in binary. As the second-least-significant bit is 1 (000000**1**0) this would be a locally administered address.

All OUIs will have this bit as 0. A zero means that the frame is only intended to reach one other host, and is therefore a unicast frame. If the switch already knows about the intended recipient, meaning that it has an entry in its CAM table for it (which we will discuss shortly), then the switch will forward it to that port. If the switch does not have an entry in its CAM table, then the frame is forwarded on all of its ports, apart from the one it was received on, to all the nodes in the broadcast domain.

As well as the unicast MAC addresses, we also have the group addresses, which are broadcast addresses and multicast addresses. If the U/L bit is a 1 then the frame will still only be sent once, but more information from the MAC address is then used to forward the frame. If the MAC address is all F's (ff:ff:ff:ff:ff:ff) then this will be a broadcast address. A MAC address starting with FF will have the binary value of 11111111. Therefore, the U/L bit will be 1.

A multicast MAC address will start with 01, its U/L bit will therefore be a zero, but it uses a reserved range (from 01:00:5E:00:00:00 to 01:00:5E:7F:FF:FF), specifically for multicast. It is the rest of the address which determines to which nodes on the network the frame is sent.

2.2 Identify basic switching concepts and the operation of Cisco switches

Previously we saw that if the switch, through the use of the U/L bit, has a unicast frame then it will check its CAM table for a matching entry. If it does not have an entry in its CAM table then it will send the frame to all of the nodes in its collision domain. So what, exactly, is a "collision" domain, and how does it differ from a "broadcast" domain?

2.2.a Collision Domains

In a wired network, well, modern wired networks, the concept of collision domains is fading away fast, though they are still very prevalent in wireless networks. A collision domain is where multiple hosts are connected to a shared medium, such an environment would be computers connected to a hub. When two devices try sending data at the same time, these packets can collide.

In these early networks, only one host could "talk" at one time. Having too many hosts in one collision domain would make the lights on the hubs go crazy, usually bathing the server room in a red glow (many collision lights were red). These collisions were (obviously) a bad thing, and the devices would have to abort and try to transmit the same packets again.

Collisions are resolved using Carrier Sense Multiple Access with Collision Detection (CSMA/CD). CSMA/CD allows the packets to be discarded and re-sent one at a time. This is still inefficient, which is why switches became so popular.

Switches break down each connected device into its own separate collision domain, if it is running at half-duplex. If the connected device is running at full duplex, then there will be no chance of collisions.

> In half-duplex a node can either receive data, or send data. It cannot do both at the same time. In full-duplex a device can send and receive at the same time. Imagine half-duplex like a walkie-talkie and full-duplex like a telephone conversation.

2.2.b Broadcast Domains

A broadcast domain is one where the nodes within it can all reach each other (broadcast) at the data link layer. When a hub is used, nodes connected to the hub are part of one collision domain and are part of one broadcast domain.

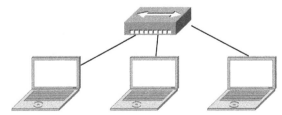

One collision domain
One broadcast domain

If there are multiple hubs connected together, then they are still part of the same broadcast domain and the same collision domain.

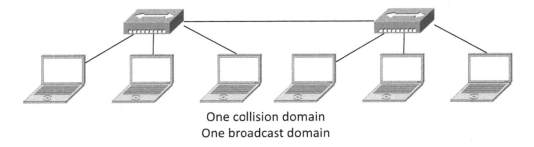

One collision domain
One broadcast domain

If we break the two hubs apart by placing a layer-2 switch in-between them (assuming all hosts are on the same VLAN), then we would have two collision domains and one broadcast domain.

All devices in VLAN 1

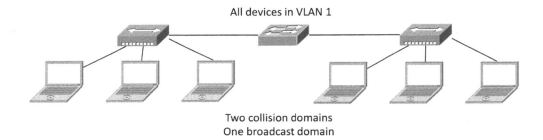

Two collision domains
One broadcast domain

We can break up broadcast domains by introducing layer-3 devices, such as a router, into the network. We could also achieve the same thing through the creation of additional VLANs. Below we have a router connecting two hubs. We now have two collision domains and two broadcast domains (one of each per-side of the router). Only layer-3 devices, such as a router, or a VLAN can do this, though additional VLANs by themselves would have no means of communicating; a layer-3 device would still be required, we shall look at Inter-VLAN routing in Chapter 4.

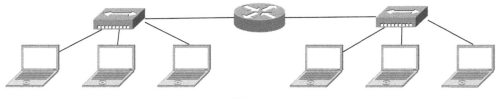

Two collision domains
Two broadcast domains

We can also use VLANs (which we will discuss shortly) to increase the number of broadcast domains. Next we can see that we have eight collision domains (one per link connection), and three broadcast domains:

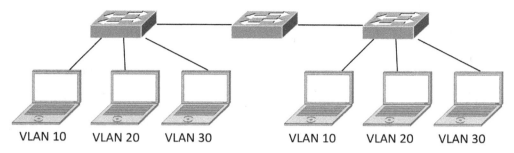

Eight collision domains
Three broadcast domains (one per-VLAN)

These are switches, so can operate at full-duplex, therefore each switch port is a separate collision domain and the three VLANs create three separate broadcast domains.

Now that we have seen how a switch learns what traffic is what, and how it plays a role in the network, let's get under the hood, and see how it manages the traffic that passes through it.

2.2.c Ways to switch

When a sender (in this case Dave) sends a packet to Bob, he will send the data, which will be sent as a single frame, or if the data is larger than 1500-bytes, it will be separated into multiple frames, according to the MTU size we discussed earlier. The switch that Dave connects to will receive the frame and will forward it to Bob. This switching process can take one of two methods. The switch can wait till it has the complete frame, and then send it, which is known as store-and-forward, or wait till it has just enough information to know where the packet should be sent and start sending it, which is known as cut-through.

2.2.c (i) Store

2.2.c (ii) Forward

Really, store and forward are parts of the same process. I don't know why the blueprint lists them separately when even Cisco use the term "store-and-forward" in their documentation, so we will discuss it as one process; store-and-forward.

Store-and-forward does as the name suggests, it will store the entire frame and once it has performed error (integrity) checking on the received data, will then forward it to the destination. The switch will check the destination and source addresses and will compare the CRC (Cyclic Redundancy Check), which is stored in the FCS field and is used to check the length of the packet to make sure that it has not been tampered with, or is corrupt, as we saw in the previous chapter. If these three are all fine, it will send the frame out to Bob.

The benefit of store-and-forward is that Bob does not need to perform error checking on the frame.

Because these frames are stored in a buffer, an area of memory used to hold traffic passing through the switch, a busy switched environment can start to experience severe latency with this method due to the amount of traffic and the switch needing to perform the CRC check on each frame. For this reason cut-through switching was created.

2.2.c (iii) Cut through

In cut-through switching the switch will start to forward the frame before the entire frame has been received, usually as soon as it has processed the destination address (the DMAC or Destination MAC address). The benefit of this is that it reduces latency (the period of which the frame is sent between devices), but the flip side to this is that all the error checking must take place on the destination device. This means that if a frame is corrupt, or truncated, then network performance could be degraded because the switch does not look at the FCS field at the end of the frame. Such an example would be frames truncated due to collisions.

There is some dispute as to how much of the frame is stored in cut-through forwarding. Many sources cite is as being the first 6 bytes (after the preamble), which is enough for the switch to read the destination MAC address, though in practice this is slightly larger. The EtherType (a two-octet field indicating the protocol that is encapsulated within the payload), which is either 0800 for IPv4, or 86DD for IPv6, can be considered before the frame is forwarded and if there are any filtering mechanisms (such as filtering HTTP traffic) on the port, then this will also need to be read before the frame is forwarded. In this instance the amount of data that the switch will process before it starts forwarding can be as much as 54 bytes.

Fragment-free, a variation on cut-through switching, offers a solution to this issue. Collision fragments are not forwarded as the switch holds the frame until the first 64 bytes are read in order to detect a collision before forwarding the frame. A frame smaller than 64 bytes is called a runt, and will be discarded by the switch.

With cut-through the speeds of the outgoing and incoming interfaces should be the same, ideally; otherwise the benefits of reduced latency will be lost.

Whilst cut-through, or fragment-free sound ideal, there are scenarios where store-and-forward are more appropriate, such as when the devices are a long way from each other, or where the network experiences high error rates.

So this explains how a switch manages the traffic volume that passes through it, but how does it know where to send it?

2.2.d CAM Table

When a switch is newly set up, it does not automatically know whom its connected users are. It needs to learn them and to store what it learns. It does this by adding (and removing) entries from a portion of memory known as the Content Addressable Memory (CAM) table.

The CAM table keeps a list of MAC addresses, the switch port that the MAC address has been seen on, a timestamp and its VLAN assignment.

The timestamp is so that entries can be deleted, or aged out, the default time for this is 300 seconds (five minutes). This ensures that the CAM table is constantly up-to-date.

Let's take a newly powered up switch, with a number of connected hosts attached to it as an example.

We have two hosts, AA and DD. Their MAC address are 01:02:03:aa:bb:cc and 01:02:03:dd:ee:ff. At the moment the switch does not know who these two machines are, but when host AA starts to send data to host DD, the switch performs a number of steps.

When the switch receives the frame, it stores the MAC address of host AA in its CAM table, along with the port that the frame was received on, the VLAN and a timestamp. It knows which VLAN to use, as this is configured on the interface.

Because the switch does not yet know where host DD is located, it floods the unicast frame out of all ports that are in the same VLAN, except the port that it now knows is connected to host AA (the source port).

Host DD will respond to the frame and the switch will add this into the CAM table, again keeping the MAC address of host DD, the port ID, VLAN ID and the timestamp.

For future traffic between host AA and host DD the switch will perform a lookup in the CAM table and send the frames directly between the hosts, without needing to flood it to other hosts. The process is very similar to the ARP request that we saw in the previous chapter.

I think it's about time we did some actual configuration!

2.3 Configure and verify initial switch configuration including remote access management

2.3.a hostname

Now the fun actually starts, and we can start configuring the network.

First, let's start by making our switches easily identifiable. By default they will all be named "switch", which is fine if you just have one, but any more than that and management of the switches will become much harder. The switches don't care what they are called, for the most part; this is more for our benefit. You can call switches anything you like, you can name them after cartoon characters if you want, or name them so that that are easily identifiable in a rack, such as SW1R1 for Switch 1 in Rack 1, SW2R1 for Switch 2 Rack 1, and so on, though this becomes an issue if switches are moved. Using printed labels on the switches is certainly beneficial.

Let's kick off our first task by renaming our switches. Within the lab, right click each switch, and then click on Start. The black square should turn into a black triangle, and then you can click on the switch to launch the telnet session.

When we first start our telnet sessions, the switch will prompt us as to whether we want to enter the initial configuration dialog?

```
        --- System Configuration Dialog ---

Would you like to enter the initial configuration dialog? [yes/no]:
no


Press RETURN to get started!
```

We need to type in *"no"*, or just *"n"* here and then press return. This is standard for devices that do not have a configuration file, and this will be covered in more detail in section 4.10. We should now see this:

```
Switch>
```

The bracket (>) means we are in the "User EXEC" mode. Our abilities here are very limited. To see what commands we can run, just type a question mark (?) and you will see a long list of commands we can use. In User EXEC mode we can connect to other devices using the *"connect"* command, switch between users using the *"login"* command and perform some basic troubleshooting; using the *"ping"* and *"traceroute"* commands for example. There are a few other commands, some we will need, and some we will not. For the moment though, the command we want is *"enable"*. The enable command will take us into the Privileged EXEC mode, so lets do that now. Type *"enable"* and press enter:

```
Switch>enable
Switch#
```

You can see that the prompt has now changed and this is how we can differentiate between the two modes. If you use the question mark again, you'll see that the list of available commands is much larger now. For the moment though, type *"exit"* and press enter. You will get back to the User EXEC mode; press enter again to get the prompt back.

Why have I tempted you with the privileged mode, only to drag you back? Well, right off the bat, we should learn those little time savers that will become second nature to you.

> This book is called CCNA and Beyond. It is designed to teach you what you need for the CCNA exam and what you need to be a network engineer. It is not just for the exam, hence the commands I use will most often be truncated, allowing you to get to the information you need quickly. Some truncated commands may not be available during the CCNA exam though, so understand what I am truncating. Please do practice using the context sensitive help, and the question mark.

If you enter a question mark, you'll see the available commands again. How many start with the letter "e"? Three; "enable", "ethernet" and "exit". How many start with "h"? One; help. Type "*h*" and press enter:

```
Switch>h
Help may be requested at any point in a command by entering
a question mark '?'.  If nothing matches, the help list will
be empty and you must backup until entering a '?' shows the
available options.
Two styles of help are provided:
1. Full help is available when you are ready to enter a
   command argument (e.g. 'show ?') and describes each possible
   argument.
2. Partial help is provided when an abbreviated argument is entered
   and you want to know what arguments match the input
   (e.g. 'show pr?'.)

Switch>
```

Because the help command was the only command that started with "h", we can type in "*h*" and get to the right command. The IOS is clever this way, if we start to type a command and up to that point, there are no alternatives, it will use that command. Type "*e*" and press return.

```
Switch>e
% Ambiguous command:  "e"
Switch>
```

Because there are three results, the IOS does not know which one to choose. What can we do then, if we know the first letter of a command, but not the rest of it? In this case, we can use the letter and the question mark:

```
Switch>e?
enable  ethernet  exit

Switch>e
```

The switch will now list the available options. Notice, also, that it is quite helpful and puts the letter or letters we have typed in on the new line. Enable is a unique command at the second letter (**en**), so anything from "en" onwards will be a 100% match to "enable", so type "*en*" and press enter:

```
Switch>en
Switch#
```

Great, we are back at the privileged mode. OK, so how do we change the hostname? Use the question mark to display our command options. There is nothing even close to what we might need. This is because we need to move into another mode. So far we have been in exec modes (either User EXEC, or Privileged EXEC). These are for executing commands (exec meaning executing), what we need to do is configure the switch, so we need to be in configuration mode. To do this we can type in *"configure"* and press enter, or we can find the shorter method, by typing in *"co?"*:

```
Switch#co?
configure   connect   copy

Switch#co
```

The shortest command we can use here will be *"conf"*:

```
Switch#conf
Configuring from terminal, memory, or network [terminal]?
```

We have three options. We can configure from the terminal, from memory, or from the network. The option we want is already selected. Here the word "terminal" is in square brackets, indicating that this is the default choice, we can just press enter here, or press *"t"* and then press enter, so that your prompt shows:

```
Switch#conf
Configuring from terminal, memory, or network [terminal]? t
Switch(config)#
```

Now type exit and press enter to go back to privileged mode. Don't worry; it's the last time I'll get you to do this. The quickest way into global configuration mode, from where we are now, is to type *"conf t"* and press enter:

```
Switch(config)#exit
Switch#conf t
Enter configuration commands, one per line.  End with CNTL/Z.
Switch(config)#
```

Now this is where we can start to have some fun, but also where it is most dangerous. Changes you make here have an immediate effect. Other platforms, such as the IOS-XR switches, need to have their changes committed before they are "live" (the same is true if you use Juniper networking equipment). IOS is not the same; if you make a change here it will take effect straight away. It's like Yoda says, "Do, or do not. There is no try". My dad always said, "measure twice, cut once", I think the two are applicable here. Either way, you get the idea. Something like changing the hostname will not have much of an impact, but when we look at routing, or access-rules later on, then you'll see the effect such changes can have on a network, for good and for bad.

Anyway, let's actually configure something. First off, we should change our hostnames to something more distinctive. To change the hostname we type in "*hostname*" followed by the name we want to call our switch. We will call them "SW1", "SW2", "SW3", and "SW4":

```
Switch(config)#hostname SW1
SW1(config)#
```

OK, that's the first one done. Now you do the rest of them. See what the shortest length you can make the command. In the end, we should have the following prompts:

```
SW1(config)#

SW2(config)#

SW3(config)#

SW4(config)#
```

The shortest command would be "*ho*" followed by the name of the switch ("*ho SW1*" etc).

Just to do a quick recap of the commands for SW2, the process (in both long and short format) would be:

```
Switch>
Switch>enable
Switch#configure terminal
Switch(config)#hostname SW2
SW2(config)#

Switch>
Switch>en
Switch#conf t
Switch(config)#ho SW2
SW2(config)#
```

Now that our switches are properly named, we will know what switch we are on when we manage them remotely. But how are we going to manage them remotely?

2.3.b mgmt ip address

There are three ways that we can set our switches up for remote management and by remote management I mean so that we can log in to them from Dave's PC. These different ways will have different repercussions on how our network is designed.

The first way is to create a loopback interface. A loopback interface is a virtual interface, meaning we cannot plug anything into it, but we can use it for a number of purposes, as we will see when we look at routing in chapter 4. The loopback interface method would require a routing protocol to pass the IP addresses around, but we are not going to do that (at least not just yet).

The second method is to assign an IP address to one of our physical interfaces (or all of them if we wanted complete switch-to-switch management connectivity). Taking SW1 as the example, we would need five IP addresses in order for it to talk to the other switches on all of its switch-to-switch links. For all our switches to talk to each other we would need twenty IP addresses, and we would need ten different subnets as well. That would be both time consuming, make for a very complicated network and as we will find out in the next chapter, a massive waste of IP addresses.

The third way is the easiest method and the one that we will be using. That is to assign an IP address to a VLAN. We spoke about VLANs earlier in this chapter and how they are beneficial in creating additional, but smaller broadcast domains and enhance security. We are now going to create a VLAN interface.

VLAN 1 already exists on all of our switches. It is one of the default set of VLANs that every switch comes with, either to get you up and running, i.e. for remote management like VLAN 1 is, or for backwards compatibility, such as VLANs 1002 to 1005, which are the default VLANs for FDDI and Token Ring, these cannot be deleted or used for Ethernet.

What we will do now is create an interface for VLAN 1, which is known as a VIF (Virtual Interface). To do this we use the command *"interface vlan 1"*:

```
SW1(config)#interface vlan 1
SW1(config-if)#
%LINEPROTO-5-UPDOWN: Line protocol on Interface Vlan1, changed state to
down
SW1(config-if)#
```

We could also use *"int vlan 1"* to get to the same place. Note that again the prompt has changed and that the interface state changes to "down". We are now in the interface configuration mode. Now, let's give the interface an IP address:

```
SW1(config-if)#ip address 10.1.1.1 255.255.255.0
SW1(config-if)#
SW1(config-if)#no shut
SW1(config-if)#
%LINK-3-UPDOWN: Interface Vlan1, changed state to up
%LINEPROTO-5-UPDOWN: Line protocol on Interface Vlan1, changed state to
up
SW1(config-if)#
```

I have assigned the IP address 10.1.1.1, with a subnet mask of 255.255.255.0 (a class C, or /24 subnet). The command *"no shut"*, which is a shortened form of *"no shutdown"*, is also used in order to bring up the interface.

We'll now set the other switches up with IP addresses as well:

```
SW2(config)#int vlan 1
SW2(config-if)#
%LINEPROTO-5-UPDOWN: Line protocol on Interface Vlan1, changed state to
down
SW2(config-if)#ip address 10.1.1.2 255.255.255.0
SW2(config-if)#no shut
SW2(config-if)#
%LINK-3-UPDOWN: Interface Vlan1, changed state to up
%LINEPROTO-5-UPDOWN: Line protocol on Interface Vlan1, changed state to
up
SW2(config-if)#

SW3(config)#int vlan 1
SW3(config-if)#
%LINEPROTO-5-UPDOWN: Line protocol on Interface Vlan1, changed state to
down
SW3(config-if)#ip add 10.1.1.3 255.255.255.0
SW3(config-if)#no shut
SW3(config-if)#
%LINK-3-UPDOWN: Interface Vlan1, changed state to up
%LINEPROTO-5-UPDOWN: Line protocol on Interface Vlan1, changed state to
up
SW3(config-if)#

SW4(config)#int vlan 1
SW4(config-if)#
%LINEPROTO-5-UPDOWN: Line protocol on Interface Vlan1, changed state to
down
SW4(config-if)#ip add 10.1.1.4 255.255.255.0
SW4(config-if)#no shut
SW4(config-if)#
%LINK-3-UPDOWN: Interface Vlan1, changed state to up
%LINEPROTO-5-UPDOWN: Line protocol on Interface Vlan1, changed state to
up
SW4(config-if)#
```

We can't test this out just yet, as we need to do a little bit more work before we can see the fruits of our labours. Nonetheless, we are off to a good start. Our switches are nearly ready to talk to each other, but how will they talk to other devices, such as the gateway router, or to devices that they do not have an entry for in their routing table?

2.3.c ip default-gateway

For a device to communicate with devices outside of their own network, we need to define a default-gateway. Usually this is a router, firewall, or a VLAN interface. In this section, we will configure SW1, which will have a default gateway pointing to the Gateway router.

We are still in interface configuration mode on SW1, so we should go back a level, to global configuration mode. I say, "should", we could still type in the command, if we know it, but we lose the context-sensitive help and tab completion. Below I try using tab completion to finish the command off (line 1), and underneath that I try using the context-sensitive help (line 2), both fail. If I typed the full command, however, it would accept the command, and drop me back into global configuration mode.

```
1.  SW1(config-if)#ip defaul
2.  SW1(config-if)#ip defaul?
3.  % Unrecognized command
4.  SW1(config-if)#ip defaul
```

For the moment though, let's type exit and then set our default gateway, using the command "*ip default-gateway*" followed by the IP address of the Gateway router:

```
SW1(config-if)#exit
SW1(config)#ip def
SW1(config)#ip default-?
default-gateway  default-network

SW1(config)#ip default-gat
SW1(config)#ip default-gateway 10.1.1.254
```

Above, you can see that I have used tab completion a couple of times. Now that we have done this on SW1, it will know where to look to for any device that is outside of its own network (10.1.1.0/24), we will explain the command in chapter 4.

Although we have not yet configured the routers that will make up the "outside world", we should make sure that when we do, we are safe and secure. If we were to go ahead and connect ourselves to the rest of the devices then, as we do not need to enter a username or password to gain access to our switches, neither would anyone else.

2.3.d local user and password

Although local usernames and passwords are not exactly the best method to secure devices (in both terms of defence or manageability), they are still recommended. It makes sense as the number of devices in the network increases, to centrally manage your usernames and passwords. This can then be linked, through a protocol such as LDAP, RADIUS, or TACACS, into AD (Active Directory), and is essential if you are working for a company that is bound by regulations, such as PCI (the Payment

Card Industry). There is no need for us to go this deep, the CCNA syllabus does not list any of the above as a requirement, and so we will just create some local users instead.

We have two users; Bob and Dave. They need to be able to log onto each of the devices as themselves, using a password of either Bob123, or Dave123, depending on who is logging in. To create a user we use the command (in configuration mode) *"username"* followed by the username, then we also need to specify a password. We can achieve this in a couple of ways, we could use the command *"username Bob"*, which would create the user Bob and then we could set the password, by using the command *"username Bob password Bob123"*. The second way will create the user, if is not already created, as well as setting the password, so this way is much easier for us:

```
SW1(config)#username Bob password Bob123
SW1(config)#username Dave password Dave123
SW1(config)#
```

There are a couple of other things we should look at when creating users. If we had a user that, for one reason or another, did not need to have a password, then we could use the command *"username Bob nopassword"*. This however, is not recommended for the majority of environments. Another useful command is *"username Bob privilege"* followed by the privilege level assigned to that user. This can range from 0 to 15, and can be used to allow some users to execute some commands, and other users the ability to execute more commands:

```
SW1(config)#username Bob privilege ?
  <0-15>  User privilege level

SW1(config)#username Bob privilege
```

We can then set restrictions on the commands that Bob can or cannot use. It's useful, but we are not required to configure any such restrictions. We also have the command *"username Bob secret"*, followed by a secret password, we will look at this shortly. For the moment though, please create the same users, with the same passwords, on the other three switches. There is a way to save you doing the typing here, and it's a neat little trick that will save you time, over and over again.

On SW1 type in *"end"*, so that we return to the Privileged EXEC mode:

```
SW1(config)#end
SW1#
```

Now type in *"sh run | i usern"* like I have below:

```
SW1#sh run | i usern
username Bob password 0 Bob123
username Dave password 0 Dave123
SW1#
```

We will cover part of this in more detail in a few moments, but I'll explain the command now. The *"sh"* is the short(est) form of the command *"show"*. If you type in show along with the questions mark (*"show ?"*) then you'll see the long list of items we can look at, along with their descriptions. Some will be more useful to you than others. The next word *"run"* is short for *"running-config"*, so we have told the router to show us the running-config. Remember I said that the changes we do here are effective immediately? Well, any changes we make are made to a file called the running-config. When we boot up our router or switch, it will load the configuration from the startup-config file, which is copied into memory as the running-config. If changes in the running-config have not been copied to the startup-config, then when we reboot our router or switch, these changes will be lost. We will look at how the running-config and the startup-config files can by made to be the same later on.

So far, we have said, "show me the running configuration", then we have the pipe character ("|"). This is an output modifier. Meaning that we can be more selective with what we actually want to see. The options are:

```
SW1#show run | ?
  append     Append redirected output to URL
  begin      Begin with the line that matches
  count      Count number of lines which match regexp
  exclude    Exclude lines that match
  format     Format the output using the specified spec file
  include    Include lines that match
  redirect   Redirect output to URL
  section    Filter a section of output
  tee        Copy output to URL
SW1#show run |
```

The useful ones are begin, exclude, include and section. We can jump to a particular part of the configuration using the begin keyword, show a section (such as a routing configuration), we can exclude certain items, or just show the ones we want. In the command above I have used "i" for include, along with a shorter form of "username". The command is now "show me the running configuration, but only include anything that starts with, or includes the keyword usern". So now, we will only get back the lines that start with "usern". If we had, say, an access-list called "my_usernumbers", then this would have also been included in the results.

Returning to the purpose of the command, we now have a very succinct set of results returned, we can then copy them from SW1 by highlighting the two lines, and then within configuration mode on the other switches, paste them onto the console.

Try highlighting the two username commands and pasting them onto the other switches. Depending on what program you are using, then this can be as simple as highlighting them on SW1, and (in configuration mode) on the other switches, pressing the right mouse button. I am using SecureCRT from VanDyke software, and for the price of $99, it does make life much easier!

Once this is done, we should be able to check each of the switches and confirm that the users are all present and correct:

```
SW2#sh run | i usern
username Bob password 0 Bob123
username Dave password 0 Dave123
SW2#

SW3#sh run | i usern
username Bob password 0 Bob123
username Dave password 0 Dave123
SW3#

SW4#sh run | i usern
username Bob password 0 Bob123
username Dave password 0 Dave123
SW4#
```

It would be good to be able to test this now, right? Let's configure Dave's machine with an IP address and test out our access.

If it's not already started, then turn on Dave's computer, and connect to it. It should get to the message about entering the "initial configuration dialog", type "no" and press enter.

When we get to the prompt that says "Router>", go into the privileged exec mode by typing "enable" (or "en"), and then into configuration mode, by typing "conf t". Notice that although this is a router, there is no difference (so far) between this and the switches we are used to:

```
Router#conf t
Enter configuration commands, one per line.  End with CNTL/Z.
Router(config)#
```

First of all, we should change the hostname to something a little more interesting. Let's call this one "Dave-PC":

```
Router(config)#hostname Dave-PC
Dave-PC(config)#
```

Notice how the prompt changes immediately? This easily shows how a command can have an instant effect.

Now let's configure an IP address on the interface connecting us to SW4:

```
Dave-PC(config)#int e0/0
Dave-PC(config-if)#ip add 10.1.1.21 255.255.255.0
```

```
Dave-PC(config-if)#no shut
Dave-PC(config-if)#
%LINK-3-UPDOWN: Interface Ethernet0/0, changed state to up
%LINEPROTO-5-UPDOWN: Line protocol on Interface Ethernet0/0, changed
state to up
Dave-PC(config-if)#
```

At this stage if we try and remotely manage SW4, we will find that it fails. Below you can see that I am trying to connect to SW4's 10.1.1.4 IP address:

```
Dave-PC(config)#end
Dave-PC#
Dave-PC#telnet 10.1.1.4
Trying 10.1.1.4 ... Open


Password required, but none set

[Connection to 10.1.1.4 closed by foreign host]
Dave-PC#
```

It does however make the initial connection, so at least we are headed in the right direction.

Before we go ahead and fix this, let's look at the next section; "enable secret password".

2.3.e enable secret password

The enable secret password offers another level of security, forcing the user to type in another password when moving from the user mode to the exec mode. Let's try this out, with a password of cisco:

```
SW4(config)#enable secret 0 cisco
SW4(config)#
```

Now let's go back to the user mode and see what happens when we try to move to the privileged exec mode:

```
SW4(config)#end
SW4#exit

SW4 con0 is now available

Press RETURN to get started.

SW4>en
Password:
```

We are now prompted for a password, so type in "cisco" and press enter:

```
Password:
SW4#
```

Now we are back in the privileged exec mode.

How is this a better form of security? We have already seen that our user passwords for Bob and Dave are stored in clear text, in that they are easily readable, so how is adding another password any better if that too is readable? Well, with the enable secret the password is encrypted using an MD5 hash, so that it is not humanly readable. We can check this by returning to the exec prompt and using the command "*sh run | i enable*":

```
SW4#sh run | i enable
enable secret 5 $1$hQM5$nDVRu8j9nMwWTQL1v5Ax1.
SW4#
```

There is a less secure format of this, and that is "*enable password*" command, but this is not encrypted. Let's try this out on SW3:

```
SW3(config)#enable password cisco
SW3(config)#end
SW3#sh run | i enable
enable password cisco
SW3#
```

Not the most ideal form of security in the world, but there are ways to fix this, which we will cover shortly. Before we do that, let's see how we can allow Dave to connect to SW4.

2.3.f console and VTY logins

We saw earlier that when we tried to telnet from Dave's PC to SW4 we almost got there, but we were turned away with the message "Password required, but none set". At the moment SW4 does not have any way of checking how someone trying to log in to the switch should be authenticated. We can authenticate users through a number of methods, such as checking against a local list of users, or using a remote service, such as RADIUS to authenticate users.

We need to set up local authentication on SW4. But where do we set this? The switches (and routers) have different "lines". There are lines for the physical connections to the console and AUX ports, and on the virtual interfaces that are used for Telnet and SSH connections. The way in which we tell the switch to authenticate the users is identical for each of these lines, so we will look at the virtual interfaces, but the process would be the same if we wanted to secure our console line (the method UNetLab uses to connect us to the device).

We can find the current configuration of these lines by running the command *"show running-config"*, or if we wanted to just show just this part of the configuration, then we can use the command *"sh run | s line"*, where "s" is short for "section". Remember earlier we used a similar command with the "include" directive, well, the include will show us the lines that include the keyword we need, whereas "section" will include all of the section we need, and this includes the configuration within.

Let's compare the two for this example, starting with the include:

```
SW4#sh run | i line
line con 0
line aux 0
line vty 0 4
SW4#
```

Now let's have a look at the output if we use "section" (or "s") instead of "include":

```
SW4#sh run | s line
line con 0
 logging synchronous
line aux 0
line vty 0 4
SW4#
```

The result is pretty similar, but notice that the console has the *"logging synchronous"* command within it. That particular line is indented, meaning that it is a command that applies to "line con 0", which is our console interface. Let's sort out the login from Dave's PC and see how this affects our output.

Because we created users; Bob and Dave, on each of our switches, we have created a database of local users. We can instruct our switches to use this database to authenticate connections to the device. As we want to authenticate our telnet session, we do this under the VTY lines, which are also used for SSH connections. We have five VTY lines by default; VTY 0, VTY 1 and so on, up to VTY 4. To configure them we type in, from the configuration mode, *"line vty 0 4"*.

> We can create more VTY lines if we wanted to, using the command *"line vty 5 15"*, for example, which would create an additional 11 VTY lines.
>
> From a security standpoint it is useful to limit the number of VTY lines that are usable.

In order to tell the switch to authenticate users against its local database of users for the first five VTY lines we use the command *"login local"*:

```
SW4(config)#line vty 0 4
SW4(config-line)#login local
SW4(config-line)#
```

Now, when we try connecting to SW4 from Dave's PC, we need to enter our username (Dave) and password (Dave123).

```
Dave-PC#telnet 10.1.1.4
Trying 10.1.1.4 ... Open

User Access Verification

Username:Dave
Password:Dave123
SW4>exit

[Connection to 10.1.1.4 closed by foreign host]
Dave-PC#
```

Now we have full access to SW4 from our PC, which is very handy for remote management.

If security is not so much of a requirement, we can set it so that anyone can connect with the same password. To do this we need to change our setting from *"login local"* to *"login"*. When we do this though, we are informed that we will need to set a password:

```
SW4(config-line)#login
% Login disabled on line 2, until 'password' is set
% Login disabled on line 3, until 'password' is set
% Login disabled on line 4, until 'password' is set
% Login disabled on line 5, until 'password' is set
% Login disabled on line 6, until 'password' is set
SW4(config-line)#
```

Let's set a password:

```
SW4(config-line)#password cisco
SW4(config-line)#
```

Now let's try logging in from Dave's PC, and see what happens. If you are still connected to SW4 then type *"exit"* to return to the prompt on Dave-PC:

```
Dave-PC#telnet 10.1.1.4
Trying 10.1.1.4 ... Open

User Access Verification
```

```
Password:
SW4>en
Password:
SW4#exit
```

For both the password prompts, I entered a password of "cisco".

Clearly, being prompted for a username and password is a little bit more secure than just entering a password, yet both are only very basic forms of security. If we look at the switch configuration, as it currently stands, then no matter what authentication method we use, someone could easily find out what the passwords are:

```
SW4(config-line)#end
SW4#sh run | i password
no service password-encryption
username Bob password 0 Bob123
username Dave password 0 Dave123
 password cisco
SW4#
```

If these passwords are used on other devices, then, because the passwords are stored in clear text, those devices could also be compromised. It doesn't take much skill to realise a password used on one switch might be used on another. There is an answer to this (apart from using a third-party authentication solution, such as RADIUS), and we will look at this in a moment. Until then, let's fix something.

2.3.g exec-timeout

I don't know about you, but having to log back into the device after we leave it for a while, gets a little bit annoying. You have probably seen it yourself, either from coming back to the console after reading, grabbing a cup of coffee or something, only to be faced with this:

```
SW4 con0 is now available



Press RETURN to get started.
```

This process, of returning us to the user mode is annoying, but does increase security (somewhat), after all, how many times have you stepped away from the keyboard without locking your system so that it returns to a login page?

For our purposes though, we can disable this behaviour. From the console line we can set a timeout, the default for which is ten minutes. We can set this to be shorter, longer, or off completely. The command we will use is *"exec-timeout <time in minutes> <time in seconds (optional)>"*. So, we could set the timeout for five and a half minutes using the command *"exec-timeout 5 30"*.

Time for a little quiz!

1: What would be the command that you enter to set the timeout back to 10 minutes?
2: How would the command be shown in the IOS if you were to look at the configuration?

OK, so hands up who put the first answer as *"exec-timeout 10 0"*? Excellent. I would also accept *"exec-timeout 10"* as well, as the seconds is optional.

Now the tricky question; how would this be shown in the IOS? Would the answer be *"exec-timeout 10 0"*, *"exec-timeout 10"*, something else, or nothing? The answer is actually nothing. It wouldn't be shown in the configuration, because ten minutes is the default. Our command will be accepted, but not shown in the configuration. This is important to learn early on. If you enter a command that is the same as the default, then the command will not be shown. This applies to all parts of the IOS, not just the console lines.

Let's see this in action, then set the console timeout to zero, and disable it completely:

```
1.  SW4(config)#line con 0
2.  SW4(config-line)#exec-t 10
3.  SW4(config-line)#do sh run | s line
4.  line con 0
5.   logging synchronous
6.  line aux 0
7.  line vty 0 4
8.   password cisco
9.   login
10. SW4(config-line)#exec-t 0
11. SW4(config-line)#do sh run | s line
12. line con 0
13.  exec-timeout 0 0
14.  logging synchronous
15. line aux 0
16. line vty 0 4
17.  password cisco
18.  login
19. SW4(config-line)#end
```

As you can see, if I set the timeout to be ten minutes (line 2), it doesn't appear in the configuration. If I set it to 0 (do not timeout) in line 10, using the short version of the command (*"exec-t 0"*), then the command does show up in the configuration, and it shows the long version; *"exec-timeout 0 0"* (line 13).

You'll see above that I didn't need to go out of configuration mode in order to run commands that I would usually run from the privileged exec mode (the *"show"* commands). Instead I used the command that I usually would (*sh run | s line*), but I put *"do"* in front of it. Using *"do <exec command>"* allows us to run such commands without moving between modes. It can save a bit of time, but we still need to pay attention to where we are in the IOS (i.e. which mode we are in). We cannot use *"do"* in privileged exec mode, only in configuration mode.

You may want to disable the exec-timeout on the other switches and on Dave-PC as well.

Now that that little "issue" is fixed, let's fix our insecure password problem.

2.3.h service password encryption

As we have seen so far, most of our passwords have been stored in clear text. If anyone were to get access to our devices, or the backups we store of our configurations, then they would be able to read these easily. The exception to this has been the enable secret password in 2.3.e, which was stored in its encrypted form.

Thankfully, for us, there is a way that the IOS can encrypt all our current and future passwords. This is the command *"service password-encryption"*.

Let's see the before and after effects of this command:

```
SW4#sh run | i password
no service password-encryption
username Bob password 0 Bob123
username Dave password 0 Dave123
 password cisco
SW4#conf t
SW4(config)#service password-encryption
SW4(config)#end
SW4#
SW4#sh run | i password
service password-encryption
username Bob password 7 047904045E731F
username Dave password 7 072B205A4B584B56
 password 7 13061E010803557878
SW4#
```

So, is that all we need to do? Well, no, not really. This is far from a secure method. It is actually extremely easy to decrypt these passwords using a little bit of JavaScript. I have posted such a page on my website: http://www.802101.com/p/cisco-type-7-password-decoder.html.

The preferred method is to use the secret keyword, as we did earlier. So instead of using the command "*username Bob password Bob123*", we would actually use "*username Bob secret 0 Bob123*". Let's see how this looks when we try it out. We cannot keep our existing user password though, so we have to remove it, using the "*no*" form of the command we used to enter it in:

```
SW4(config)#username Bob secret 0 Bob123
ERROR: Can not have both a user password and a user secret.
Please choose one or the other.
SW4(config)#
SW4(config)#no username Bob password Bob123
SW4(config)#
```

We can paste in a SHA256 or MD5 encrypted password, or specify that the password is unencrypted, which is also the default:

```
SW4(config)#username Bob secret ?
  0     Specifies an UNENCRYPTED secret will follow
  4     Specifies a SHA256 ENCRYPTED secret will follow
  5     Specifies a MD5 ENCRYPTED secret will follow
  LINE  The UNENCRYPTED (cleartext) user secret

SW4(config)#username Bob secret 0 Bob123
```

The default behaviour will be to store this password using SHA256 encryption. How does this show in the configuration now?

```
SW4(config)#do sh run | i username
username Dave password 7 072B205A4B584B56
username Bob secret 4 qYDuFS4vL4CX308mk1SbUVm1X14kiq/mo2.lhnMqq3g
SW4(config)#
```

As you can see, it looks much more secure. It will take more than a few lines of JavaScript to decrypt that! We are nearly done with this section and are ready to move on to some basic verification methods, but before we move on, we really should save the work we have done so far.

2.3.i copy run start

As I mentioned earlier, there are two configuration files. The one we spend 99.9% of our time dealing with is the running-config. The changes we make here have an immediate effect, but are only good for as long as they are in memory, which is where the running-config lives. If we want our modifications to survive a reboot, then we must copy these changes to the startup-config.

To do this we use the privileged exec command *"copy running-config startup-config"*. The short form of this is *"copy run start"*. You can also use the command *"write memory"*, but this is deprecated, which means that it's the older format that Cisco supports for legacy purposes but may take it away at some stage.

On SW4 in privileged exec mode, save the configuration:

```
SW4#copy run start
Destination filename [startup-config]?
Building configuration...
Compressed configuration from 1274 bytes to 895 bytes[OK]
SW4#
```

Note that I needed to confirm the destination filename. The choice is in square brackets, so I just press enter, and it "builds" the configuration and compresses it, saving it over the current startup-config.

Now would be a good time to save the configurations on all the devices, so we can move on to look at some basic troubleshooting techniques.

2.4 Verify network status and switch operation using basic utilities such as

There are a couple of tools we can use to test end-to-end connectivity. We have already seen one, in the form of telnet, which we used to test connectivity between Dave-PC and SW4. We will talk a little more about telnet in a moment and see how it is useful, but less than ideal from the security aspect. We will then look at a more secure method. Before we do this though, we will look at the most popular and simplest method of testing connectivity, Ping.

2.4.a Ping

Ping stands for "Packet Internet Groper". It works in the same manner as active SONAR on a submarine does. The device sends an ECHO request and waits for a response. This response is then used to measure the round-trip time.

PING uses ICMP (Internet Control Message Protocol) to send the request (or response), and this request-response pairing is defined in RFC 1122: "Requirements for Internet Hosts — Communication Layers". ICMP is a network layer protocol; therefore ping works at the network layer and is used to verify network connectivity.

Let's see this in action. From Dave-PC, type in *"ping 10.1.1.4"*:

```
Dave-PC#ping 10.1.1.4
Type escape sequence to abort.
Sending 5, 100-byte ICMP Echos to 10.1.1.4, timeout is 2 seconds:
!!!!!
Success rate is 100 percent (5/5), round-trip min/avg/max = 4/11/20 ms
Dave-PC#
```

Above we have sent five 100-byte requests to SW4, with a timeout of two seconds. All five were successful, in that we received a reply for each of them. There are two ways we know that we received a reply for all five requests. The first is that we have five exclamation marks. This indicates a successful request-reply pairing. The second way we know that these were successful is that we are given the success rate in the last line. We also get the round-trip statistic, telling us the shortest (4 milliseconds), longest (20 milliseconds) and average round-trip times (11 milliseconds) of the five requests. Because ping works at the network layer, it also helps in troubleshooting, as a successful ping means that our network layer, data link layer, and our physical layer are all working.

So, if an exclamation mark means success, what means failure?

Actually there are a number of reasons that a ping can fail and there is a different character for each failure type.

Character	Failure reason
.	Timeout while waiting for a reply
U	Destination unreachable (via a Destination Unreachable PDU)
Q	Destination too busy to reply, and sent a source quench instead
M	Packet could not be fragmented (too big for the MTU of the link)
?	Packet type is unknown
&	Packet lifetime exceeded

We can create failures (to a degree) using the extended ping command, which we will look at in chapter 4. We can create fragmentation issues by creating a large packet and setting the Do Not Fragment bit, others will be harder recreate, such as the packet lifetime exceeded error. We would have to have a pretty big network in order to go past the TTL (Time To Live) limit of 255 that we spoke about in the previous chapter. Actually, if your network does consist of 255 hops then it has not been designed correctly!

Ping is not 100% reliable though. Many hosts on the Internet actually disable ping replies for security reasons. If it's not easily visible then it makes it a harder target to pinpoint, which is known as "security through obscurity".

2.4.b Telnet

Telnet is old. It's one of the oldest protocols we will discuss, and was created in 1969 under RFC 15 (https://tools.ietf.org/html/rfc15). Yes, it is that old, and no, the RFCs that came before this are not very interesting.

If ping worked well to help us troubleshoot the bottom three layers, then telnet, which is an application layer protocol, must be even better. We have used telnet a couple of times already, but not really spoke about it in any depth.

Telnet works at the application layer. Therefore, if we have a successful telnet session then we know that all of our layers are working. Telnet uses TCP port 23, and is a client-server protocol. In our example, SW4 is acting as the server and Dave-PC is the client. As we have seen, we can do a lot with telnet. It has been extremely popular since the start of the Internet and continues to be useful now. However, it is inherently insecure. There is no encryption, so usernames and passwords are sent in clear text. If someone were to be sniffing the packets on the wire, then they could easily capture all they needed to take over a device or two, or maybe even the entire network.

Thankfully, there is a more secure option.

2.4.c SSH

SSH, which stands for Secure Shell, is also an application layer protocol, so it provides the end-to-end connectivity and, as the name would suggest, is secure.

One of the most popular SSH clients is PuTTY, though it does much more than just SSH. You can download it from the following URL: http://www.chiark.greenend.org.uk/~sgtatham/putty/download.html.

For SSH to work, especially on Cisco IOS, we need to run a couple of commands first. Firstly we need to set a domain name, and then generate a key:

```
SW4(config)#ip domain-name 802101.local
SW4(config)#crypto key generate rsa general-keys modulus ?
  <360-4096>  size of the key modulus [360-4096]

SW4(config)#crypto key generate rsa general-keys modulus 2048
The name for the keys will be: SW4.802101.local

% The key modulus size is 2048 bits
% Generating 2048 bit RSA keys, keys will be non-exportable...
[OK] (elapsed time was 1 seconds)
```

```
SW4(config)#
%SSH-5-ENABLED: SSH 1.99 has been enabled
SW4(config)#
```

As you can see above, the crypto key command enables SSH, but requires the hostname and domain name to be set first. We can generate keys of varying sizes, from 360 up to 4096. The length of the key will determine how easy it is to crack. 1024 bit keys have already been cracked, so the logical approach would be to use 2048 as a minimum. A large key, such as 4096 will be harder to crack, but will put greater processing power on the devices when they use it to encrypt or decrypt data.

Let's try connecting from Dave-PC to SW4:

```
Dave-PC#ssh 10.1.1.4
% No user specified nor available for SSH client
Dave-PC#
```

We need to send a username and password when we use SSH. We can do this using -l to specify the user, which needs to be one either local to SW4, or one that SW4 can find through another means, such as RADIUS.

```
Dave-PC#ssh -l Dave 10.1.1.4
Password:Dave123

[Connection to 10.1.1.4 closed by foreign host]
Dave-PC#
```

Still no luck and this is because we haven't quite finished our configuration yet. We still need to add another command and we'll put one in as best practice:

```
SW4(config)#ip ssh version 2
SW4(config)#do sh run | s line vty
line vty 0 4
 password 7 13061E010803557878
 login
SW4(config)#line vty 0 4
SW4(config-line)#login local
SW4(config-line)#end
```

We should enable SSH version 2. Notice that when we enabled SSH before, it showed the version as being 1.99. This version actually came after version 2.1; it is used for backward compatibility to identify a server that supports both version 1 and version 2 (RFC 4253). Version 2 has a number of improvements over version 1, such as better security through Diffie-Hellman key exchange and integrity checking. So, whenever you implement SSH, make sure that it is set to be version 2.
That takes care of the first line, but what about the rest of the output? In the second line I have shortened the command "*do* (meaning I really should do this from the privileged mode but don't want

to switch modes at the moment) *show running-config*" and narrowed it down to the section related to the VTY lines.

Here we can see that we have used the "*login*" command, which we switched to in section 2.3.f. For SSH we need to use the command "*login local*" which is then entered and we now have SSH access (using the password "Dave123"):

```
Dave-PC#ssh -l Dave 10.1.1.4
Password:

SW4>en
Password:
SW4#
SW4#! Hello from Dave
SW4#
SW4#exit

[Connection to 10.1.1.4 closed by foreign host]
Dave-PC#
```

When we switch to enable mode, using the "*en*" command, we need to use the password "cisco", as this is the one defined on SW4, not Dave's own password which we used in the second line. We then get full access to SW4 from the comfort of our own seat at Dave's PC. The Hello from Dave line is just a comment; we can create comments by starting the line with an exclamation mark. These are not saved in our configuration, but are useful from time to time.

There is another very useful troubleshooting command, traceroute, which we will look at in chapter 4. But now we can move on to the next section, and look at VLANs in greater detail.

2.5 Describe how VLANs create logically separate networks and the need for routing between them

At the moment, all of our switches and devices operate in one VLAN (Virtual Local Area Network), which is VLAN 1. This is enabled by default and cannot be removed. From a security stance, the main purpose of VLAN 1 is for remote management, not for carrying user data. We also have a couple of other VLANs, 1002 through to 1005. These are the legacy VLANs (used for compatibility with Token Ring and Fiber Distributed Data Interface, or FDDI), like VLAN 1 these legacy VLANs cannot be deleted, but unlike VLAN 1, these cannot be used for Ethernet based traffic.

This means that we have from VLAN 2 to 1001 to play with and also an extended range, from 1006 to 4094. That's a lot of VLANs that we can use to carve up our network, separate our users and make things look a little more logical.

That's what we *could* do, but why *should* we do it?

2.5.a Explain network segmentation and basic traffic management concepts

Creating more VLANs has a number of benefits for the network. Additional VLANs create additional broadcast domains in switched networks, meaning that whilst the number of broadcasts may not decrease, they are contained and will be received by fewer devices, thus the size of the broadcast domain is reduced.

VLANs increase security, allowing you as the network administrator to separate user access by department; the Marketing department does not need to have visibility of the confidential employee data held by the Human Resources department and the Finance team does not need to have login access to the switches, for example. This also means that people can have more flexibility in where they sit in the office, as it just requires a small change on the switch. So VLANs offer flexibility for users, whilst retaining security.

We can separate network access down to such a level that means we actually have more efficient bandwidth usage. Many logical networks can exist on the same physical network infrastructure, without competing for resources.

The increase in logical networks allows the placement of users to be based on department, rather than physical location. Not all members of the Finance department have to sit together, they can be spread out across the office space, yet this does not need to affect their work, the port they connect into can be configured for their appropriate VLAN easily, and they can continue working.

Let's go and create some VLANs.

2.6 Configure and verify VLANs

We can create VLANs in a couple of different ways. We can create them all locally, though either the VLAN database method or by assigning a port to a VLAN, or we can have them created for us by another switch. We will create a number of VLANs now and see these different methods. First of all, let's start by verifying what VLANs we have at the moment:

```
SW4#show vlan

VLAN Name                 Status    Ports
---- -------------------- --------- ---------------------------
1    default              active    Et0/0, Et0/1, Et0/2, Et0/3
                                    Et1/0, Et1/1, Et1/2, Et1/3
1002 fddi-default         act/unsup
1003 token-ring-default   act/unsup
1004 fddinet-default      act/unsup
1005 trnet-default        act/unsup

VLAN Type  SAID   MTU  Prnt RingNo BrdgNo Stp BrdgMo
---- ----- ------ ---- ---- ------ ------ --- ------
1    enet  100001 1500 -    -      -      -   -
1002 fddi  101002 1500 -    -      -      -   -
1003 tr    101003 1500 -    -      -      -   -
1004 fdnet 101004 1500 -    -      -      ieee -
1005 trnet 101005 1500 -    -      -      ibm  -

SW4#
```

There is quite a lot of information there. I even had to remove a couple of columns that were empty to make it fit properly. We can see that all of our switch ports are in VLAN 1, and we have VLANs 1002 to 1005. We can make it a bit easier on ourselves, and look at the "brief" output:

```
SW4#show vlan brief

VLAN Name                 Status    Ports
---- -------------------- --------- ---------------------------
1    default              active    Et0/0, Et0/1, Et0/2, Et0/3
                                    Et1/0, Et1/1, Et1/2, Et1/3
1002 fddi-default         act/unsup
1003 token-ring-default   act/unsup
1004 fddinet-default      act/unsup
1005 trnet-default        act/unsup

SW4#
```

That's a little better. We can make it even more succinct though:

```
SW4#show vlan brief | e unsup

VLAN Name                 Status    Ports
---- -------------------- --------- ---------------------------
1    default              active    Et0/0, Et0/1, Et0/2, Et0/3
                                    Et1/0, Et1/1, Et1/2, Et1/3
SW4#
```

Alternatively, we can specify a VLAN according to its ID:

```
SW4#sh vlan id 1

VLAN Name                       Status    Ports
---- -------------------------- --------- ------------------------------
1    default                    active    Et0/0, Et0/1, Et0/2, Et0/3
                                          Et1/0, Et1/1, Et1/2, Et1/3

VLAN Type  SAID   MTU  Parent RingNo BridgeNo Stp BrdgMode Trans1 Trans2
---- ----  ----   ---  ------ ------ -------- --- -------- ------ ------
1    enet  100001 1500 -      -      -        -   -        0      0

Primary Secondary Type        Ports
------- --------- ----------- ------------------------------------------

SW4#
```

For the sake of four lines, this is probably overkill, but we can use the exclude command to remove the lines beginning with 1002, 1003, 1004 and 1005 from the output. It's useful to know how to manipulate the exclude and include commands to make searching for the relevant information easier and quicker, the command would be *"show vlan brief | exclude unsup"*.

OK, let's start by creating some VLANs. We will create five VLANs, this is more than we will need, but it will give us a nice output later. These will be our VLANs:

VLAN	Purpose
10	Main users
20	Servers
30	Bob
40	Printers
50	Guests

All our VLANs will be in the "normal" VLAN range (1-1001), we can have up to 4094 vlans and those from 1006 to 4094 live in the "extended VLAN" range. There is actually VLAN 4095 (and a VLAN 0), but these are reserved, and cannot be edited or deleted, so they are hidden from view. VLANs 40 and 50 won't be used, but the rest will. Dave will be in VLAN 10, our Server will live in VLAN 20, and Bob will be on his own in VLAN 30.

On SW4 switch to configuration mode and type in *"vlan 10"*:

```
SW4(config)#vlan 10
SW4(config-vlan)#
```

Notice that we are in a new mode, as indicated by "config-vlan". We have some options here, though not many will ever be used. We can name our VLAN and you should name your VLANs, as it will make your life much easier. There are a couple of other commands, such as shutdown and private-vlan that you may use. Private-VLANs are something you'll come across in greater depth the CCNP (Routing and Switching). For the moment though, let's just give our new VLAN a name:

```
SW4(config-vlan)#name Main
SW4(config-vlan)#
```

Now, let's create our other VLANs:

```
SW4(config-vlan)#vlan 20
SW4(config-vlan)#name Servers
SW4(config-vlan)#vlan 30
SW4(config-vlan)#name Bob
SW4(config-vlan)#vlan 40
SW4(config-vlan)#name Printers
SW4(config-vlan)#
```

Notice that I have not done VLAN 50 yet, we will do that one in a bit. So we have four new VLANs. Or do we? Let's use the "*do show vlan brief*" command to find out:

```
SW4(config-vlan)#do sh vlan bri

VLAN Name                             Status    Ports
---- -------------------------------- --------- -------------------------------
1    default                          active    Et0/0, Et0/1, Et0/2, Et0/3
                                                Et1/0, Et1/1, Et1/2, Et1/3
10   Main                             active
20   Servers                          active
30   Bob                              active
1002 fddi-default                     act/unsup
1003 token-ring-default               act/unsup
1004 fddinet-default                  act/unsup
1005 trnet-default                    act/unsup

SW4(config-vlan)#
```

I only count three new VLANs. So what happened to VLAN 40? We entered the same commands, so it should work, right? Well, this is a bit of a "gotcha" with Cisco IOS, with the last VLAN you add, you need to exit out of VLAN configuration mode for it to be added to the VLAN database:

```
SW4(config-vlan)#exit
% Applying VLAN changes may take few minutes.  Please wait...

SW4(config)#
```

```
SW4(config)#do sh vlan bri | e 00

VLAN Name                Status      Ports
---- -------------------- ---------- ------------------------
1    default              active     Et0/0, Et0/1, Et0/2, Et0/3
                                     Et1/0, Et1/1, Et1/2, Et1/3
10   Main                 active
20   Servers              active
30   Bob                  active
40   Printers             active
SW4(config)#
```

I have used the exclude command to exclude the 1002, 1003, 1004, and 1005 VLANs, because I do not have any VLANs with double zeros, I can do this. If I had created VLAN 100 though, this would also have been excluded form the results.

We have four new VLANs, but what about the last VLAN? There is another way to create VLANs. If we pick a random (unused) port on a switch, and assign it to a (new) VLAN then, depending on the version, the VLAN will be created for us. The problem with this approach is that if a switch is in VTP client mode (which we will see shortly), this method will not create the needed VLAN. For the moment though, let's just go ahead and add it properly, and add an interface to it:

```
SW4(config)#vlan 50
SW4(config-vlan)#name Guests
SW4(config-vlan)#exit
% Applying VLAN changes may take few minutes.  Please wait...

SW4(config)#do sh vlan bri | e 00
VLAN Name                Status      Ports
---- -------------------- ---------- --------------------------------
1    default              active     Et0/0, Et0/1, Et0/2, Et0/3
                                     Et1/0, Et1/1, Et1/2, Et1/3
10   Main                 active
20   Servers              active
30   Bob                  active
40   Printers             active
50   Guests               active
SW4(config)#interface e0/3
SW4(config-if)#switchport mode access
SW4(config-if)#switchport mode trunk
SW4(config-if)#end
```

Now we have our five new VLANs.

Assigning hosts to a VLAN also has an effect on the packets that they send. They now have an extra field, which contains the VLAN ID, the position of which depends on our encapsulation method, which we shall see shortly.

That was two methods of creating VLANs; there is a third (VTP), but we need to skip forward before we can set this up. Before we can use SW4 to send its VLANs to the other switches, it needs to have a medium to do this.

2.7 Configure and verify trunking on Cisco switches

In order for our other switches, SW1, SW2 and SW3, to receive the VLAN list from SW4 and add it to their own database, we need a couple of things. Firstly, we need a medium for the VLANs to pass along and secondly we need a protocol that will handle the adding (as well as subtracting) of VLAN information.

We will look at the first requirement, trunking, now and move on to the second part shortly.

For the moment we will concentrate on the link between SW4 and SW3. We have two links; e0/2 and e1/2. We will just be looking at e0/2 at this stage.

Let's have a look at the interface's configuration:

```
SW4#sh run int e0/2
Building configuration...

Current configuration : 42 bytes
!
interface Ethernet0/2
 duplex auto
end

SW4#
```

There is nothing all that interesting there. Let's dig a little deeper:

```
SW4#sh int e0/2 switchport
Name: Et0/2
Switchport: Enabled
Administrative Mode: dynamic desirable
Operational Mode: trunk
Administrative Trunking Encapsulation: negotiate
Operational Trunking Encapsulation: isl
Operational Dot1q Ethertype:  0x8100
Negotiation of Trunking: On
Access Mode VLAN: 1 (default)
```

```
Trunking Native Mode VLAN: 1 (default)
Administrative Native VLAN tagging: enabled
Operational Native VLAN tagging: disabled
Voice VLAN: none
Administrative private-vlan host-association: none
Administrative private-vlan mapping: none
Operational private-vlan: none
Trunking VLANs Enabled: ALL
Pruning VLANs Enabled: 2-1001
Capture Mode Disabled
Capture VLANs Allowed: ALL

SW4#
```

I have bolded the interesting lines. The first bolded line shows that the administrative mode is "dynamic desirable". Dynamic Desirable means that we can be a trunk if we wanted to, though it does depend on what the other side is set up. Our operational mode is "trunk", we will negotiate the trunking protocol (either dot1q or ISL, more on those in a moment), and our native mode VLAN will be VLAN 1 (no surprise as this is the default VLAN). Lastly, we will tag the native VLAN. These settings are all part of what is known as DTP.

2.7a DTP

DTP, the Dynamic Trunking Protocol, is a proprietary Cisco protocol that will negotiate a trunk on a link between two VLAN-aware switches.

OK, this all sounds good, but what actually is a trunk? To explain what a trunk is we should explain the issues they prevent.

We now have a fairly healthy number of VLANs, but only a few connections between the switches, which is good. The fewer connections between switches, the less chance there is for a loop in the network. Taking two switches from our topology as an example, if SW4 wants to send data to SW1 then it can only do this (directly) over one link. That one link can either carry one VLAN, meaning we would then need to add another four cables for the other VLANs, or we could turn that one connection into a trunk link, which could carry all of our VLANs at the same time.

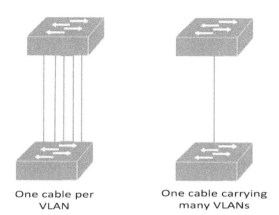

One cable per
VLAN

One cable carrying
many VLANs

Although both are very valid approaches and both achieve the same end-goal; relaying your data from one place to another, clearly we would have an issue in scalability if we were to use the first option. Once you start increasing the number of VLANs and the number of switches, the first method would become an administrative nightmare and a waste of ports.

Let's set up our first trunk between SW4 and SW3. SW3 and SW4 have two links connecting them, for the moment we will just be configuring E0/2 on each switch.

Refer back to the previous output; the administrative mode is set on SW4 to dynamic desirable:

```
SW4#sh int e0/2 switchport | i Administrative Mode
Administrative Mode: dynamic desirable
SW4#
```

This means that SW4 will try and make this port a trunk port if the other side is set to trunk, dynamic desirable, or dynamic auto mode. If we look at SW3's port settings then what would we expect to find? Hopefully the same as SW4's E0/2 port!

```
SW3#sh int e0/2 switchport | i Administrative Mode
Administrative Mode: dynamic desirable
SW3#
```

So, in theory, we should have at least one trunk between SW3 and SW4.

We can check our trunk status using the command "*show interface trunk*" (*sh int trunk*):

```
SW3#sh int trunk

Port            Mode            Encapsulation   Status          Native vlan
Et0/2           desirable       n-isl           trunking        1
Et0/3           desirable       n-isl           trunking        1
Et1/1           desirable       n-isl           trunking        1
Et1/2           desirable       n-isl           trunking        1
Et1/3           desirable       n-isl           trunking        1

Port            Vlans allowed on trunk
Et0/2           1-4094
Et0/3           1-4094
Et1/1           1-4094
Et1/2           1-4094
Et1/3           1-4094

Port            Vlans allowed and active in management domain
Et0/2           1
Et0/3           1
Et1/1           1
Et1/2           1
Et1/3           1

Port            Vlans in spanning tree forwarding state and not pruned

Port            Vlans in spanning tree forwarding state and not pruned
Et0/2           1
Et0/3           1
Et1/1           none
Et1/2           1
Et1/3           none
SW3#
```

As you can see, SW3 has all of its switch-to-switch links set up as trunks, and did this without intervention on our part. From the output we can see that the interfaces have all defaulted to desirable (dynamic desirable) mode and are using ISL as their encapsulation method.

ISL (Inter-Switch Link) is a proprietary trunking protocol developed by Cisco, so it is not surprising that this is set as the default, however the industry standard, 802.1Q (or dot1q), is far more popular and is the preferred protocol to use.

With ISL, the VLAN tag is appended to the Ethernet frame along with a new ISL FCS trailer encapsulating the entire frame, whereas 802.1Q puts the tag within the frame (between the Source MAC and EtherType fields), which allows these tagged frames to be transported across standard Ethernet links. The different frames are shown next:

802.1Q:

Preamble	SFD	D.MAC	Source MAC	**802.1Q**	Type	Data and Pad	FCS
7 bytes	1 bytes	6 bytes	6 bytes	4 bytes	2 bytes	46 – 1500 bytes	4 bytes

ISL:

ISL header	D.MAC	Source MAC	Type	Data and Pad	FCS	**ISL FCS**
26 bytes	6 bytes	6 bytes	2 bytes	46 – 1500 bytes	4 bytes	4 bytes

Returning to the output of *"sh int trunk"* on SW3, we can see that our status is trunking, and that our native VLAN is VLAN 1.

A native VLAN is one where the frames are untagged (the packets do not have the VLAN tag). So if a switch receives an untagged frame, then it will assume that these frames are part of the VLAN that is designated as the native VLAN. These frames will remain untagged, whereas frames that do not belong on the native VLAN will be tagged. The native VLAN should be the same at each end, otherwise the switches will complain about a native VLAN mismatch.

Having a native VLAN is a good idea in some respects, but is open to being abused. Additional headers, tagging the frame as say VLAN 4, can be placed before the existing VLAN tag allowing the packet to pass through one switch as one VLAN (VLAN 1 in this example), this header is then stripped off and the malicious packet passes through the network in a different VLAN, VLAN 4 in this example. This is referred to as "VLAN hopping". Although this is not required knowledge for the CCNA exam, it is best practice to follow a few guidelines.

- Unused ports should be placed in a separate unused VLAN, such as VLAN 999.
- Unused ports should be shut down and set to be in access mode.
- VLAN 1 should not be used for devices (start using VLANs from number two onwards).
- Trunks should have a separate native VLAN as well.
- Trunks should have tagging performed explicitly.

Returning again to the output above, SW3 will trunk for any of the VLANs that it knows about, so by default will trunk VLANs 1 - 4094, though according to the next line, "VLANs allowed and active in the management domain", SW3 is only aware of VLAN 1. We will get on to spanning tree in a short while, but pruning means that if a VLAN is deemed to be "unused" by the switch, then it will stop trunking for it.

As we have seen so far, without any work on our part, a port connected to a host will work as an access port and a port connected to another switch will act as a trunk port. This use useful, but not very secure, so when we are configuring ports for either user access, or to be a trunk, we should specify its role.

For interface e0/0 on SW4, we should set its role to be an access port, as we have just the one host connected to it:

```
SW4(config)#int e0/0
SW4(config-if)#switchport mode access
SW4(config-if)#
```

For interface e0/2 the process is slightly different, slightly being the operative word:

```
SW4(config-if)#int e0/2
SW4(config-if)#switchport mode trunk
Command rejected: An interface whose trunk encapsulation is "Auto" can
not be configured to "trunk" mode.
SW4(config-if)#
```

2.7b Auto-Negotiation

We cannot just move our port to being a trunk port. All the automatic behaviour that Cisco puts in (i.e. all the "Cisco magic" that gets us up and running out of the box) is only good as long as we don't need to make any changes. Once we start making changes, then we start to find ourselves bound to certain ways of doing things. This is one of those times. The Cisco default for trunks is ISL, this will happily form a trunk with the default port mode of dynamic desirable, yet once we force our trunk to be a trunk port, using the command "*switchport mode trunk*", we must explicitly state what our operational trunking encapsulation is. Our options are ISL, dot1q, or negotiated:

```
SW4(config-if)#switchport trunk encapsulation ?
  dot1q      Interface uses only 802.1q trunking encapsulation when trunking
  isl        Interface uses only ISL trunking encapsulation when trunking
  negotiate  Device will negotiate trunking encapsulation with peer on
             interface

SW4(config-if)#switchport trunk encapsulation dot1q
SW4(config-if)#
```

Dot1q will always be preferred over the other two options, and the encapsulation method on both sides should match. How has this change affected our "*show interface e0/2 switchport*" output?

Here is the (truncated) output as it was originally:

```
SW4#sh int e0/2 switchport
Name: Et0/2
Switchport: Enabled
Administrative Mode: dynamic desirable
Operational Mode: static access
Administrative Trunking Encapsulation: negotiate
```

Operational Trunking Encapsulation: native
Negotiation of Trunking: On

Here it is after we set our encapsulation and the mode:

```
SW4(config-if)#do sh int e0/2 swi
Name: Et0/2
Switchport: Enabled
Administrative Mode: dynamic desirable
Operational Mode: trunk
Administrative Trunking Encapsulation: dot1q
Operational Trunking Encapsulation: dot1q
Negotiation of Trunking: On
```

Now we can see the effect our commands had. We definitely have a trunk, and we are definitely using dot1q encapsulation. This is important going forward, where possible values should be fixed, such as port modes and encapsulation methods. Do not leave these things up to chance, as it increases the possibility of error. Now that we have set SW4's e0/2 port as a dot1q trunk, what effect has that had on SW3's e0/2 port?

```
SW3#sh int e0/2 swi
Name: Et0/2
Switchport: Enabled
Administrative Mode: dynamic desirable
Operational Mode: trunk
Administrative Trunking Encapsulation: negotiate
Operational Trunking Encapsulation: dot1q
Negotiation of Trunking: On
```

SW3 has negotiated its mode to be a trunk and the operational trunking encapsulation has, again through negotiation, moved to dot1q instead of ISL. Our administrative trunking encapsulation is still set to negotiate, which is why the two switches are still communicating with each other.

If we look at our trunk status (*show interface trunk*) then we can see here also whether we have hard-coded our trunk status, or whether it has been set through negotiation (note that the output has been truncated):

```
SW3#sh int trunk

Port     Mode        Encapsulation   Status      Native vlan
Et0/2    desirable   n-802.1q        trunking    1
Et0/3    desirable   n-isl           trunking    1
Et1/1    desirable   n-isl           trunking    1
Et1/2    desirable   n-isl           trunking    1
Et1/3    desirable   n-isl           trunking    1
SW3#
```

```
SW4(config-if)#do sh int trunk

Port      Mode        Encapsulation  Status     Native vlan
Et0/1     desirable   n-isl          trunking   1
Et0/2     desirable   802.1q         trunking   1
Et1/0     desirable   n-isl          trunking   1
Et1/1     desirable   n-isl          trunking   1
Et1/2     desirable   n-isl          trunking   1
SW4(config-if)#
```

Here we can see that SW3 has negotiation 802.1q encapsulation, as denoted by "n-802.1q", the "n-" meaning negotiated, whereas SW4 is fixed at 802.1q.

Let's go ahead and set SW3 to have the same fixed trunk status that SW4 has:

```
SW3(config)#int e0/2
SW3(config-if)#
SW3(config-if)#switchport trunk encapsulation dot1q
SW3(config-if)#switchport mode trunk
SW3(config-if)#
SW3(config-if)#end
SW3#
SW3#sh int trunk

Port      Mode        Encapsulation  Status     Native vlan
Et0/2     on          802.1q         trunking   1
Et0/3     desirable   n-isl          trunking   1
Et1/1     desirable   n-isl          trunking   1
Et1/2     desirable   n-isl          trunking   1
Et1/3     desirable   n-isl          trunking   1
<truncated>

SW3#
```

Now that we have our trunks set up, let's use them as they were designed to be and pass our VLANs across them. For this we require another protocol; VTP

VTP

VTP stands for the VLAN Trunking Protocol. Again, this is a proprietary Cisco invention, and it is designed to carry VLAN information from one switch to another. By default, the switches will already have VTP enabled. But if this is the case, then why does SW3 not have the same amount of VLANs that SW4 does?

```
SW4#sh vlan brief

VLAN Name                     Status    Ports
---- ------------------------ --------- --------------------
1    default                  active    Et0/0, Et1/3
10   Main                     active
20   Servers                  active
30   Bob                      active
40   Printers                 active
50   Guests                   active
1002 fddi-default             act/unsup
1003 token-ring-default       act/unsup
1004 fddinet-default          act/unsup
1005 trnet-default            act/unsup

SW4#

SW3#sh vlan bri

VLAN Name                     Status    Ports
---- ------------------------ --------- --------------------
1    default                  active    Et0/0, Et0/1, Et1/0
1002 fddi-default             act/unsup
1003 token-ring-default       act/unsup
1004 fddinet-default          act/unsup
1005 trnet-default            act/unsup

SW3#
```

The answer is that VTP has three different modes; Server, Client and Transparent. The default is for the switch to be in Server mode. We can find out what mode we are in using the command *"show vtp status"*

```
SW4#sh vtp status
VTP Version                     : 3 (capable)
Configuration Revision          : 8
Maximum VLANs supported locally : 1005
Number of existing VLANs        : 10
VTP Operating Mode              : Server
VTP Domain Name                 :
VTP Pruning Mode                : Disabled (Operationally Disabled)
VTP V2 Mode                     : Disabled
VTP Traps Generation            : Disabled
MD5 digest                      : 0xDA 0xA8 0xCB 0xFB 0xD6 0xF3 0xE3 0x14
Configuration last modified by 0.0.0.0 at 12-31-15 13:39:18
Local updater ID is 0.0.0.0 (no valid interface found)
VTP version running             : 1
SW4#
```

```
SW3#sh vtp status
VTP Version                     : 3 (capable)
Configuration Revision          : 0
Maximum VLANs supported locally : 1005
Number of existing VLANs        : 5
VTP Operating Mode              : Server
VTP Domain Name                 :
VTP Pruning Mode                : Disabled (Operationally Disabled)
VTP V2 Mode                     : Disabled
VTP Traps Generation            : Disabled
MD5 digest                      : 0x57 0xCD 0x40 0x65 0x63 0x59 0x47 0xBD
Configuration last modified by 0.0.0.0 at 0-0-00 00:00:00
Local updater ID is 0.0.0.0 (no valid interface found)
VTP version running             : 1
SW3#
```

Both switches are running in Server mode, meaning SW3 will not populate its VLAN database with entries from SW4. Let's spend a few moments going through this output.

There are three versions of VTP. Version 1 supports the normal VLAN range (1-1001), pruning, and clear text and MD5 passwords. Pruning is where a switch will not forward traffic for VLANs that are not required on the other switch, so say SW3 only had access ports in VLAN 10, then SW4 would, after a period, not send information about the other VLANs, including broadcasts and unknown unicast traffic. If ports are added into the pruned VLANs, then they will be added back automatically.

VTP version 2 added support for Token Ring, which was a huge benefit to the three people still using Token Ring. OK, there may have been a few more than three, but more usefully it also added consistency checking, the ability to pass on unrecognized TLVs (Type-length-value) and it can forward VTP messages without checking the version number or domain when running in transparent mode.

Version 3 added support for the extended VLAN range (1006 – 4095), the transfer of private VLAN structure information, support for MST (Multiple Spanning-Tree) and other databases, protection from being overwritten by new switches being added to the network and more password protection.

Returning to the output for SW4 above, we can see that we are capable of running version 3 (top), but we are actually running version 1 (the last line). Our configuration revision is 8 (though yours may show a lower number). The revision number acts as a form of protection in the event that another VTP server is added to the network. The highest revision will always win. We have more VLANs on SW4 (10 instead of the default 5), our operating mode is as a server, but we do not have a VTP domain name set, and pruning is disabled. We have trap generation disabled, this is linked to the consistency checking feature in VTP version 2, our device ID, configuration update data (who and when updted our VLAN database). We then have our MD5 digest, and data for when the VTP database was updated (and by whom).

Let's have a little play around and see this in action. We are going to do a lot of configuration here, but at the end of it, we should have a very healthy switched network.

We will start by setting our interfaces to be trunks, before moving on to creating some VLANs on another switch and seeing the effect that the revision number has on a client.

We will only be using single links between switches for the moment.

```
SW1(config)#int e0/2
SW1(config-if)#switchport trunk encapsulation dot1q
SW1(config-if)#switchport mode trunk
SW1(config-if)#int e0/3
SW1(config-if)#swi trun encap dot
SW1(config-if)#swi mo trunk
SW1(config-if)#int e1/1
SW1(config-if)#swi trun encap dot
SW1(config-if)#swi mo trunk
SW1(config-if)#end
SW1#

SW2(config)#int e0/2
SW2(config-if)#swi trun enc dot
SW2(config-if)#swi mo tru
SW2(config-if)#int e0/1
SW2(config-if)#swi trun enc dot
SW2(config-if)#swi mo tru
SW2(config-if)#int e1/1
SW2(config-if)#swi trun enc dot
SW2(config-if)#swi mo tru
SW2(config-if)#end
SW2#

SW3(config)#int e0/3
SW3(config-if)#swi trun enc dot
SW3(config-if)#swi mo trunk
SW3(config-if)#int e1/1
SW3(config-if)#swi trun enc dot
SW3(config-if)#swi mo trunk
SW3(config-if)#end
SW3#
```

```
SW4(config)#int e0/1
SW4(config-if)#swi trun encap dot
SW4(config-if)#swi mo trunk
SW4(config-if)#int e1/1
SW4(config-if)#swi trun encap dot
SW4(config-if)#swi mo trunk
SW4(config-if)#end
SW4#
```

If you now do a *"show interface trunk | i Status|trunking"* on each of the switches (so we capture the header line and the interfaces), you should see that each looks like this:

```
SW1#show interface trunk | i Status|trunking
Port            Mode            Encapsulation   Status          Native vlan
Et0/2           on              802.1q          trunking        1
Et0/3           on              802.1q          trunking        1
Et1/1           on              802.1q          trunking        1
Et1/2           desirable       n-isl           trunking        1
Et1/3           desirable       n-isl           trunking        1
SW1#

SW2#show interface trunk | i Status|trunking
Port            Mode            Encapsulation   Status          Native vlan
Et0/1           on              802.1q          trunking        1
Et0/2           on              802.1q          trunking        1
Et1/0           desirable       n-isl           trunking        1
Et1/1           on              802.1q          trunking        1
Et1/2           desirable       n-isl           trunking        1
SW2#

SW3#show interface trunk | i Status|trunking
Port            Mode            Encapsulation   Status          Native vlan
Et0/2           on              802.1q          trunking        1
Et0/3           on              802.1q          trunking        1
Et1/1           on              802.1q          trunking        1
Et1/2           desirable       n-isl           trunking        1
Et1/3           desirable       n-isl           trunking        1
SW3#

SW4#sh int trunk | i Status|trunking
Port            Mode            Encapsulation   Status          Native vlan
Et0/1           on              802.1q          trunking        1
Et0/2           desirable       802.1q          trunking        1
Et1/0           desirable       n-isl           trunking        1
Et1/1           on              802.1q          trunking        1
Et1/2           desirable       n-isl           trunking        1
SW4#
```

Notice that SW4 still shows "desirable" on its E0/2 interface. Although this differs to the other switch's port setting, this will still work fine.

A port configured as dynamic desirable will, through DTP, form a trunk link if the other side is set as trunk, dynamic desirable or dynamic auto. Let us quickly step back into DTP to go through the port states and what they mean when setting up a trunk. Below is a quick chart, a "Y" means a trunk will form and an "N" means that no trunk will form.

	Access	Trunk	Dynamic Auto	Dynamic desirable	Nonegotiate
Access	N	N	N	N	N
Trunk	N	Y	Y	Y	
Dynamic auto	N	Y	N	Y	
Dynamic Desirable	N	Y	Y	Y	
Nonegotiate	N				

I have left the nonegotiate column and row empty on purpose. Nonegotiate turns off DTP, so you will lose all the automatic trunk creation benefits, but you do gain an element of security back. If a trunk port is set with nonegotiate it will have to have "*switchport mode trunk*" set manually.

Access mode puts the port into a permanent non-trunking mode and it will not matter what the other side is configured as, a trunk will never form on an access port.

Trunk as the name suggests will form a trunk with another trunk and will actively try to convert the other side into a trunk. If the other side does not agree to become a trunk link, the port will still show as a trunk link (as we have hard-coded the mode).

Dynamic auto will form a trunk on a link where the other side is set to trunk, or dynamic desirable. This is the default mode on newer switches. Dynamic desirable will form a trunk with a trunk port, another dynamic desirable port, or a dynamic auto port.

Let's change the mode on SW4 and crack on:

```
SW4(config)#int e0/2
SW4(config-if)#switchport mode trunk
SW4(config-if)#end
SW4#sh int trunk | i Status|trunking
Port        Mode            Encapsulation  Status       Native vlan
Et0/1       on              802.1q         trunking     1
Et0/2       on              802.1q         trunking     1
Et1/0       desirable       n-isl          trunking     1
Et1/1       on              802.1q         trunking     1
Et1/2       desirable       n-isl          trunking     1
SW4#
```

This is so much neater.

Now we will start to set up our VTP domain. We will eventually have one VTP server, which will be SW4, but really, we should look at what happens when we have more than one server with different revisions and how transparent mode works.

On SW1 we will create three VLANs:

```
SW1(config)#vlan 4000
SW1(config-vlan)#vlan 4001
% Applying VLAN changes may take few minutes.  Please wait...

SW1(config-vlan)#vlan 4002
% Applying VLAN changes may take few minutes.  Please wait...

SW1(config-vlan)#exit
% Applying VLAN changes may take few minutes.  Please wait...

SW1(config)#end
SW1#
```

We then confirm that they are in the VLAN database and in a state of "active":

```
SW1#sh vlan bri

VLAN Name                             Status    Ports
---- -------------------------------- --------- -----------------------
1    default                          active    Et0/0, Et0/1, Et1/0
1002 fddi-default                     act/unsup
1003 token-ring-default               act/unsup
1004 fddinet-default                  act/unsup
1005 trnet-default                    act/unsup
4000 VLAN4000                         active
4001 VLAN4001                         active
4002 VLAN4002                         active
SW1#
```

We can confirm that SW1 is set as a VTP server, but its revision is still zero:

```
SW1#show vtp status
VTP Version                     : 3 (capable)
Configuration Revision          : 0
Maximum VLANs supported locally : 1005
Number of existing VLANs        : 5
VTP Operating Mode              : Server
VTP Domain Name                 :
VTP Pruning Mode                : Disabled (Operationally Disabled)
```

```
VTP V2 Mode                       : Disabled
VTP Traps Generation              : Disabled
MD5 digest                        : 0x57 0xCD 0x40 0x65 0x63 0x59 0x47 0xBD
Configuration last modified by 0.0.0.0 at 0-0-00 00:00:00
Local updater ID is 0.0.0.0 (no valid interface found)
VTP version running               : 1
SW1#
```

Let's try to set the VTP domain name:

```
SW1(config)#vtp domain 802101.com
Changing VTP domain name from NULL to 802101.com
SW1(config)#
```

Now, using the "*do*" command, as we don't want to have to switch backwards and forwards between modes, we can see the domain name:

```
SW1(config)#do sh vtp status | i Domain|Revision
Configuration Revision            : 0
VTP Domain Name                   : 802101.com
SW1(config)#
```

Now, let's add another VLAN:

```
SW1(config)#vlan 4003
SW1(config-vlan)#exit
% Applying VLAN changes may take few minutes.  Please wait...

SW1(config)#
SW1(config)#do sh vtp status | i Revision
Configuration Revision            : 0
SW1(config)#
```

The revision is still at zero. What we need to do is also set the version:

```
SW1(config)#vtp version 2
SW1(config)#
SW1(config)#do sh vtp status | i Revision
Configuration Revision            : 1
SW1(config)#
```

Now we have a new revision number. Let's set SW4 up in the same way:

```
SW4(config)#vtp version 2
VTP version is already in V2.
SW4(config)#
```

```
SW4(config)#do sh vtp status
VTP Version                   : 3 (capable)
Configuration Revision        : 1
Maximum VLANs supported locally : 1005
Number of existing VLANs      : 5
VTP Operating Mode            : Server
VTP Domain Name               : 802101.com
VTP Pruning Mode              : Disabled (Operationally Disabled)
VTP V2 Mode                   : Enabled
VTP Traps Generation          : Disabled
MD5 digest                    : 0xDD 0xBC 0x76 0x9F 0xFB 0xEE 0xF6 0x79
Configuration last modified by 0.0.0.0 at 12-31-15 14:10:31
Local updater ID is 0.0.0.0 (no valid interface found)
VTP version running           : 2
SW4(config)#do sh vtp status | i version
VTP version running           : 2
SW4(config)#
```

Notice that we are told that we are already that the version is already set to version 2. We can see that our configuration was modified by comparing the "Configuration last modified by" line on SW4, note that there will be a difference in the times between the first use of the command and now.

More importantly, the VLANs we created earlier, are now missing from SW4:

```
SW4#sh vlan bri

VLAN Name                     Status    Ports
---- ------------------------ --------- --------------------
1    default                  active    Et0/0, Et1/3
1002 fddi-default             act/unsup
1003 trcrf-default            act/unsup
1004 fddinet-default          act/unsup
1005 trbrf-default            act/unsup
SW4#
```

Our other two switches are also complaining. On the console of SW3 you should see:

```
%SW_VLAN-4-VTP_USER_NOTIFICATION: VTP protocol user notification: MD5
digest checksum mismatch on receipt of equal revision summary on trunk:
Et1/3

%SW_VLAN-4-VTP_USER_NOTIFICATION: VTP protocol user notification: MD5
digest checksum mismatch on receipt of equal revision summary on trunk:
Et0/3
```

Now you have first-hand experience of how dangerous it could be to connect a switch into a network without doing some work to prepare it. A box-fresh switch should not have any VLANs preconfigured on it, but what about a switch someone has brought in from home and connected up to a free network port? Even more reason to explicitly configure the trunk ports you need to be trunk ports and set the rest of them to be access ports (and also shut them down and put them in a separate VLAN). Hopefully you will never come across this in real life!

Before we fix this we will cover the third VTP mode; Transparent. In transparent mode we have our own set of VLANs, that need to be configured locally on the switch, but we will also pass VTP advertisements across. These will not affect our own VLANs, but we can have a switch configured in transparent mode passing VLANs from a server to a client:

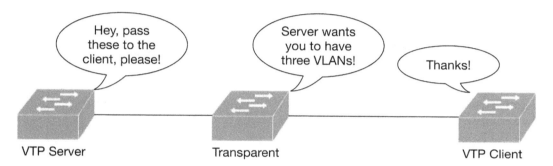

Let's fix our network. We will start by making SW1, SW2 and SW3 VTP clients, so that when we put the VLANs back onto SW4, we do not experience any odd or unexpected behaviour:

```
SW1(config)#vtp mode ?
  client       Set the device to client mode.
  off          Set the device to off mode.
  server       Set the device to server mode.
  transparent  Set the device to transparent mode.

SW1(config)#vtp mode client
Setting device to VTP Client mode for VLANS.
SW1(config)#

SW2(config)#vtp mode client
Setting device to VTP Client mode for VLANS.
SW2(config)#

SW3(config)#vtp mode client
Setting device to VTP Client mode for VLANS.
SW3(config)#
```

We should also set SW4 to be the server.

```
SW4(config)#vtp mode server
Device mode already VTP Server for VLANS.
SW4(config)#
```

We are told that it is already a server, so why do we do this? Well, this is just one of those best practice things. Strictly speaking, you don't need to, but good networking is all about following a process. This will help eliminate chances for error and you are 100% sure that SW4 is set as a server.

Now let's add our VLANs back again:

```
SW4(config)#vlan 10
SW4(config-vlan)#name Main
SW4(config-vlan)#vlan 20
SW4(config-vlan)#name Servers
SW4(config-vlan)#vlan 30
SW4(config-vlan)#name Bob
SW4(config-vlan)#vlan 40
SW4(config-vlan)#name Printers
SW4(config-vlan)#vlan 50
SW4(config-vlan)#name Guests
SW4(config-vlan)#exit
SW4(config)#
```

If we now check the other switches, we should see that these VLANs have been propagated to the other switches:

```
SW1(config)#do sh vlan bri | e unsup

VLAN Name                      Status    Ports
---- ------------------------- --------- --------------------
1    default                   active    Et0/0, Et0/1, Et1/0
10   Main                      active
20   Servers                   active
30   Bob                       active
40   Printers                  active
50   Guests                    active
4000 VLAN4000                  active
4001 VLAN4001                  active
4002 VLAN4002                  active
4003 VLAN4003                  active
SW1(config)#
```

```
SW2(config)#do sh vlan brief | e unsup

VLAN Name                            Status     Ports
---- -------------------------------- ---------- --------------------
1    default                         active     Et0/0, Et0/3, Et1/3
10   Main                            active
20   Servers                         active
30   Bob                             active
40   Printers                        active
50   Guests                          active

SW2(config)#

SW3(config)#do sh vlan bri | e unsup

VLAN Name                            Status     Ports
---- -------------------------------- ---------- --------------------
1    default                         active     Et0/0, Et0/1, Et1/0
10   Main                            active
20   Servers                         active
30   Bob                             active
40   Printers                        active
50   Guests                          active

SW3(config)#
```

That looks much better now! This is so much easier that manually creating VLANs on each individual switch!

If we look at the output from *"show interface trunk"* on SW4 and another switch, such as SW1, we can confirm that our trunks are working as intended (please note that the following output has been truncated for ease of reading):

```
SW4(config)#do sh int trunk

Port       Mode         Encapsulation  Status       Native vlan
Et0/1      on           802.1q         trunking     1
Et0/2      on           802.1q         trunking     1
Et1/0      desirable    n-isl          trunking     1
Et1/1      on           802.1q         trunking     1
Et1/2      desirable    n-isl          trunking     1

Port       Vlans allowed and active in management domain
Et0/1      1,10,20,30,40,50
Et0/2      1,10,20,30,40,50
Et1/0      1,10,20,30,40,50
Et1/1      1,10,20,30,40,50
Et1/2      1,10,20,30,40,50
```

```
Port            Vlans in spanning tree forwarding state and not pruned
Et0/1           none
Et0/2           none
Et1/0           none
Et1/1           1,10,20,30,40,50
Et1/2           none
SW4(config)#

SW1(config)#do sh int trunk

Port            Mode            Encapsulation  Status       Native vlan
Et0/2           on              802.1q         trunking     1
Et0/3           on              802.1q         trunking     1
Et1/1           on              802.1q         trunking     1
Et1/2           desirable       n-isl          trunking     1
Et1/3           desirable       n-isl          trunking     1

Port            Vlans allowed and active in management domain
Et0/2           1,10,20,30,40,50,4000-4003
Et0/3           1,10,20,30,40,50,4000-4003
Et1/1           1,10,20,30,40,50,4000-4003
Et1/2           1,10,20,30,40,50,4000-4003
Et1/3           1,10,20,30,40,50,4000-4003

Port            Vlans in spanning tree forwarding state and not pruned
Et0/2           1,10,20,30,40,50,4000-4003
Et0/3           1,10,20,30,40,50,4000-4003
Et1/1           1,10,20,30,40,50,4000-4003
Et1/2           1,10,20,30,40,50,4000-4003
Et1/3           1,10,20,30,40,50,4000-4003
SW1(config)#
```

We will not need some of the VLANs between 10 and 50 going across the trunks if the other switches do not need them. To avoid this behavior and unnecessary traffic, we can enable pruning. This can only be enabled on a VTP server, as we can see if we try to enable it on a VTP client (SW1):

```
SW1(config)#vtp pruning
Cannot modify pruning unless in VTP server mode
SW1(config)#
```

So, let's enable it on SW4 instead:

```
SW4(config)#vtp pruning
Pruning switched on
SW4(config)#
```

Now we can see that pruning is enabled on the other switches:

```
SW1(config)#
%SW_VLAN-6-VTP_PRUNING_CHANGE: VTP Operational Pruning Enabled.
SW1(config)#

SW2(config)#
%SW_VLAN-6-VTP_PRUNING_CHANGE: VTP Operational Pruning Enabled.
SW2(config)#

SW3(config)#
%SW_VLAN-6-VTP_PRUNING_CHANGE: VTP Operational Pruning Enabled.
SW3(config)#
```

Notice the immediate effect that this has on our trunks:

```
SW1(config)#do sh int trunk | b pruned
Port            Vlans in spanning tree forwarding state and not pruned
Et0/2           1,4000-4003
Et0/3           1,4000-4003
Et1/1           1,50,4000-4003
Et1/2           1,4000-4003
Et1/3           1,4000-4003
SW1(config)#
```

SW1 shows VLANs 10, 20, 30 and 40 (and 50 on one interface) as being pruned, as does SW2:

```
SW2(config)#do sh int trunk | b pruned
Port            Vlans in spanning tree forwarding state and not pruned
Et0/1           1
Et0/2           1,50
Et1/0           1
Et1/1           1
Et1/2           none
SW2(config)#end
```

The same is true for SW3 and SW4. Let's start to open our network back up again, by adding a few machines back into their respective VLANs, starting with the server connected to SW1:

```
SW1(config)#int e1/0
SW1(config-if)#swi mode acc
SW1(config-if)#swi acc vl 20
SW1(config-if)#end
SW1#
```

Now let's add Bob to his personal VLAN on SW3:

```
SW3(config)#int e0/0
SW3(config-if)#swi mode access
SW3(config-if)#swi access vlan 30
SW3(config-if)#end
SW3#
```

Finally, let's put Dave back into the main VLAN:

```
SW4(config)#int e0/0
SW4(config-if)#swi mode acc
SW4(config-if)#swi acc vlan 10
SW4(config-if)#end
SW4#
```

What effect has this had on our trunking? If we look at the output of show interface trunk and limit it down to beginning at the line that says pruned, we can see:

```
SW1#sh int trunk | b pruned
Port          Vlans in spanning tree forwarding state and not pruned
Et0/2         1,4000-4003
Et0/3         1,30,4000-4003
Et1/1         1,10,50,4000-4003
Et1/2         1,4000-4003
Et1/3         1,4000-4003
SW1#

SW2#sh int trunk | b pruned
Port          Vlans in spanning tree forwarding state and not pruned
Et0/1         1
Et0/2         1,10,20,30,50
Et1/0         1
Et1/1         1
Et1/2         none
SW2#

SW3#sh int trunk | b pruned
Port          Vlans in spanning tree forwarding state and not pruned
Et0/2         1
Et0/3         1,10,20,50
Et1/1         none
Et1/2         1
Et1/3         none
SW3#
```

```
SW4#sh int trunk | b pruned
Port          Vlans in spanning tree forwarding state and not pruned
Et0/1         none
Et0/2         none
Et1/0         none
Et1/1         1,20,30
Et1/2         none
SW4#
```

Looks a bit confusing, doesn't it! SW2 is a good example to help us understand the effects of pruning though. SW2 will still forward traffic for the VLANs as SW1 will need VLAN 20, for the server, SW3 will need VLAN 30 for Bob and SW4 will need VLAN 10 for Dave. Yet, because SW2 does not have any active ports in those VLANs, the others will not forward those VLANs to SW2. Therefore, the unnecessary traffic is eliminated, which is the purpose of pruning. So why, then, does SW1 still forward the VLANs 4000 to 4003? Well, firstly this is because extended VLANs (1006 – 4095) are ineligible for pruning, secondly the other switches do not receive these VLANs though as they did not come from our VTP server (SW4).

> If you want to be 100% sure that a VLAN will not be pruned, number it in the extended VLAN range.

So far, this is fine, but what happens when we experience a link failure in our network? We have no form of redundancy in our switched network. If we look at the outputs above, they all say "Vlans in spanning tree forwarding state and not pruned". The one word (well two to be exact) we have not mentioned yet is spanning tree. Let's have a look at that now.

2.8 Identify enhanced switching technologies

Enhanced switching technologies is a bit of a broad statement, and confused by the fact that the syllabus takes our final two different sections (spanning-tree and etherchannels), and then mashes them up, slaps them back together and expects you to make sense of it. Really, we should discuss the spanning-tree modes (2.9.b), which are (amongst others) RSTP (2.8.a) and PVSTP (2.8.b), then look at how we configure and verify PVSTP (2.9), how the root bridge is elected (2.9.a), and then move on to Etherchannels (2.8.c). It must have been beer-o-clock in the Cisco office when they were planning the syllabus layout!

Spanning Tree is a form of loop prevention within a network. Recall from the first chapter we said that one of the three (main) functions of a switch was to create a loop-free layer two topology, well it does this through the Spanning-Tree Protocol (STP).

Consider our topology, we have a number of links between the switches. This is great for redundancy, but can result in a loop. A loop in the network is not a fun thing to fix. One wrong cable can cause your switches to lock up, all the lights turn on full (instead of blinking happily) and the network grinds to a halt. If you can find the correct cable to unplug then the network can recover, but finding the correct cable can take time. I am speaking from experience here, and yes, I did learn my lesson! It was in my early days in networking, I knew that redundant connections would be a good idea, I knew that there was a single point of failure in the network and that having multiple connections between the switches could mitigate this, but I did not know enough to see the possible consequences. Thankfully, I knew which cable I had plugged in and the network recovered quickly. However, it was still a very worrying few minutes.

With properly implemented spanning tree, all those problems could have been avoided.

2.9 Spanning Tree

The Spanning-Tree Protocol was standardized under 802.1D and (excuse the pun) there have been several branches to the original, such as Rapid Spanning Tree (RSTP / 802.1w), Multiple Spanning Tree (MST / 802.1s) and Per-VLAN Spanning Tree (PVST), which is Cisco proprietary, so does not get a swanky "802" name. Each of these has been designed to overcome some of the limitations of its predecessor. It makes sense, therefore, that we start this section by looking at the original Spanning Tree protocol.

Spanning Tree allows us to have multiple links within a network for the purposes of redundancy. These links all build a "tree"; a data path through the network. To avoid loops in the layer-2 network, the spanning tree will disable the links that do not form part of the tree. Should a tree link become unavailable, one of these disabled links will be enabled and become part of the tree. All the links will either be blocking traffic or forwarding traffic, which is when the network is "fully converged".

The "base" of the tree is called the root bridge. Each other switch should have a connection to this, either directly, or indirectly (through another switch). We can have different root bridges for different VLANs if we wanted, so we can exercise great control over how our spanning-tree topology looks, or we can choose to let the switches decide who will be the bridge. But how do they decide who gets the role?

2.9.a Describe root bridge election

When the switches elect a root bridge, the switch with the smallest bridge ID becomes the root bridge. The bridge ID can either be manually configured, or the switch will use a priority number and its MAC address. The default bridge priority is 32768 and when we configure the priority manually, we must do so in blocks of 4096 (0, 4096, 8192, 12288 and so on). If there is a tie in the priority (as there will be unless we have manually specified one), then the switches will compare the MAC addresses (lower being preferred). Once they have compared each other, one switch will be the root. This usually means that without any configuration on your part, the oldest switch will become the root, as it will have a lower MAC address. All the more reason to protect yourself against people attaching their own switches to the network!

Lets go through this with a bit of an example.

We have two switches, SW1 and SW2. SW1 has a MAC address of aabb.cc00.0100 and SW2 has a MAC address of aabb.cc00.0200, neither has had their priority changed. Which one will become the root bridge?

SW1 will be the root bridge. They will have a tie over the default priority, and will use the MAC address to break the tie. Because SW1 has the lower MAC address (0100) it wins the tie and becomes the root bridge.

We can see this in action on our own switches. On SW1 and SW2 type in the command *"show spanning-tree"*. It will show you a separate entry for each VLAN, so for the moment, just press the space bar so that we can see all of the entry for VLAN0001 and then press *"q"* to stop the command. An alternative is to use the command *"show spanning-tree vlan 1"*:

```
SW1#show spanning-tree

VLAN0001
  Spanning tree enabled protocol ieee
  Root ID    Priority    32769
             Address     aabb.cc00.0100
             This bridge is the root
             Hello Time   2 sec  Max Age 20 sec  Forward Delay 15 sec

  Bridge ID  Priority    32769  (priority 32768 sys-id-ext 1)
             Address     aabb.cc00.0100
             Hello Time   2 sec  Max Age 20 sec  Forward Delay 15 sec
             Aging Time  300 sec

Interface           Role Sts Cost      Prio.Nbr Type
------------------- ---- --- --------- -------- --------------------
Et0/0               Desg FWD 100       128.1    Shr
Et0/1               Desg FWD 100       128.2    Shr
Et0/2               Desg FWD 100       128.3    Shr
Et0/3               Desg FWD 100       128.4    Shr
Et1/1               Desg FWD 100       128.34   Shr
Et1/2               Desg FWD 100       128.35   Shr
Et1/3               Desg FWD 100       128.36   Shr
SW1#
```

```
SW2#show spanning-tree vlan 1

VLAN0001
  Spanning tree enabled protocol ieee
  Root ID    Priority    32769
             Address     aabb.cc00.0100
             Cost        100
             Port        3 (Ethernet0/2)
             Hello Time   2 sec  Max Age 20 sec  Forward Delay 15 sec

  Bridge ID  Priority    32769  (priority 32768 sys-id-ext 1)
             Address     aabb.cc00.0200
             Hello Time   2 sec  Max Age 20 sec  Forward Delay 15 sec
             Aging Time  300 sec

Interface           Role Sts Cost      Prio.Nbr Type
------------------- ---- --- --------- -------- --------------------------
Et0/0               Desg FWD 100       128.1    Shr
Et0/1               Desg FWD 100       128.2    Shr
Et0/2               Root FWD 100       128.3    Shr
Et0/3               Desg FWD 100       128.4    Shr
Et1/0               Desg FWD 100       128.33   Shr
Et1/1               Desg FWD 100       128.34   Shr
Et1/2               Altn BLK 100       128.35   Shr
Et1/3               Desg FWD 100       128.36   Shr
SW2#
```

Above we can see the MAC address we are using (Bridge ID Address), our priority (32769), which is the default of 32768 with the extended system ID, which is 1 because it is VLAN 1 (VLAN 10 would mean a priority of 32778, which would be the default of 32768 + 10 for example).

If we are not the root bridge, we will have a port cost and this is based on a fixed list, depending on what version of spanning tree we are running. The original spanning tree did not leave much room for speeds greater than 10GBit/s, so Rapid Spanning Tree (RSTP) gave us a new set of numbers, with room for future growth:

Interface speed	STP cost	RSTP cost
4 Mbit/s	250	5,000,000
10 Mbit/s	100	2,000,000
16 Mbit/s	62	1,250,000
100 Mbit/s	19	200,000
1 Gbit/s	4	20,000
2 Gbit/s	3	10,000
10 Gbit/s	2	2,000

We then, on SW2, have the port, in this case it is e0/2. This is known as the root port (RP), which is the port with the lowest cost to the root bridge. SW2 has two interfaces that could have been the root port, e0/2 and e1/2. Both connect to SW1, but e0/2 will be more likely to be chosen as it is the lower numbered of the two. The root bridge will not have any root ports, as it cannot have a shortest path to itself, all its ports will be "designated" though.

We then have our timers, which we will discuss in a moment, and then a list of our ports, what roles they are performing and the states they are in. We will come back to the roles in a moment, but in traditional STP, the states would be blocking, listening, learning, forwarding, or disabled. All of SW1s ports will be in the forwarding state (FWD), but SW2 will place its E1/2 port in the blocked state, so that a loop does not occur, this is known as a Non-designated port (NDP). The other ports, those that are forwarding that is, will become Designated Ports (DP); these will forward BPDUs (Bridge Protocol Data Units). We will see what BPDUs are used for in the next section.

Let's build up a little diagram of how this affects our network.

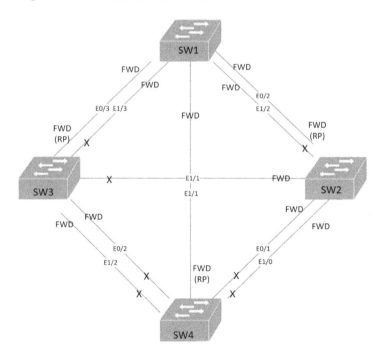

As we can see, each of the non-root switches (SW2, SW3 and SW4) have a Root Port, which will usually be the lowest numbered port, unless there is a direct link to the root switch, as is such in the case of SW4. The other ports, marked with an X, are blocked and therefore there must be a shorter path to the root bridge elsewhere.

So, what would happen if the direct link between SW1 and SW4 were to go down? In a nutshell we would send a bunch of BPDUs and go through a number of different states until all was healthy again. SW4 is a great example to look at to get an idea about BPDUs and the different states that a switch port can go through in STP. SW4 only has one forwarding port, which is its direct connection to SW1, so let's break it and see what happens.

The switches have decided amongst themselves who should be the root bridge, and which of their ports should be either forwarding or blocked. They do this using Bridge Protocol Data Units (BPDUs). BPDUs are used to build the spanning tree and are the switches way of learning about bridge IDs and costs.

BPDUs are sent to the multicast address 01:80:C2:00:00:00 (or 01:00:0C:CC:CC:CD if we are using Per VLAN Spanning Tree) and are sourced from the MAC address of the port that the BPDU comes out of. Traditional STP has three different BPDUs. The first BPDU is the Configuration BPDU (CBPDU) and is used to build up the tree. The second is used to keep the other switches updated with any changes in the network, and is known as the Topology Change Notification (TCN) BPDU. The third one is a TCA, Topology Change Acknowledgement, sent in receipt of a TCN. These TCNs are sent every two seconds, by default and are the "Hello" time shown in the output previously.

Let's try to capture the states that a switch goes through in the event that it has to recompute the spanning tree.

I will be trying to get just the few lines that we need, so the command I will be using, once I shut down the link to SW1, is *"do show spanning-tree | b Role"*. I have already put myself under the interface we are going to shut down, and these are the current port states:

```
SW4(config)#int e1/1
SW4(config-if)#do sh spanning-tree vlan 10 | b Role
Interface        Role Sts Cost      Prio.Nbr Type
---------------- ---- --- --------- -------- --------------------
Et0/0            Desg FWD 100       128.1    Shr
Et0/1            Altn BLK 100       128.2    Shr
Et0/2            Altn BLK 100       128.3    Shr
Et1/0            Altn BLK 100       128.33   Shr
Et1/1            Root FWD 100       128.34   Shr
Et1/2            Altn BLK 100       128.35   Shr

SW4(config-if)#
```

Let's shut it down, and keep pressing the up arrow and enter so, hopefully, we can capture the state changes:

```
SW4(config-if)#shut
SW4(config-if)#do sh spanning-tree vlan 10 | b Role
Interface            Role Sts Cost      Prio.Nbr Type
-------------------  ---- --- --------- -------- --------------------
Et0/0                Desg FWD 100       128.1    Shr
Et0/1                Root LIS 100       128.2    Shr
Et0/2                Altn BLK 100       128.3    Shr
Et1/0                Altn BLK 100       128.33   Shr
Et1/2                Altn BLK 100       128.35   Shr

SW4(config-if)#
```

Immediately, even before we are notified that the port has been shut down, the e0/1 port goes into listening mode (LIS). It stays in this state for 15 seconds, which is the forward delay timer shown in the output of *"show spanning-tree"*. In the listening state we will process (send and receive) BPDUs, but we will not start to learn MAC addresses, nor will we forward or process user data. That data will simply be dropped. It is in this state that the loop-free computation takes place and this is where we would transition to the blocking state if a loop were to be found.

If all is well then from here we go into a learning state (LRN):

```
SW4(config-if)#do sh spanning-tree vlan 10 | b Role
Interface            Role Sts Cost      Prio.Nbr Type
-------------------  ---- --- --------- -------- --------------------
Et0/0                Desg FWD 100       128.1    Shr
Et0/1                Root LRN 100       128.2    Shr
Et0/2                Altn BLK 100       128.3    Shr
Et1/0                Altn BLK 100       128.33   Shr
Et1/2                Altn BLK 100       128.35   Shr

SW4(config-if)#
```

We still won't forward user traffic in this state, but we will start to learn MAC addresses, building up our CAM table. We stay in the learning state for another 15 seconds (again this is the forward delay). Then we move into the forwarding state (FWD):

```
SW4(config-if)#do sh spanning-tree vlan 10 | b Role
Interface            Role Sts Cost      Prio.Nbr Type
-------------------  ---- --- --------- -------- --------------------
Et0/0                Desg FWD 100       128.1    Shr
Et0/1                Root FWD 100       128.2    Shr
Et0/2                Altn BLK 100       128.3    Shr
Et1/0                Altn BLK 100       128.33   Shr
Et1/2                Altn BLK 100       128.35   Shr

SW4(config-if)#
```

Once we are in the forwarding state, we can send and receive data in a normal fashion. The whole process takes roughly 30 seconds. The process is very similar if we were to connect a new switch to one of our existing switches, but (through the BPDUs) if this were to introduce a loop in the network, then the port would go into a blocking state (BLK), instead of forwarding.

A blocking port is not truly blocking. It will block user data from being sent or received, but it will still process BPDUs (otherwise it would not know that the loop has been fixed).

As a recap, the STP port states are Blocking (20 seconds), Listening (15 seconds), Learning (15 seconds) and Forwarding (and disabled, where an administrator has shut down the port).

Let's return SW4 back to full working order:

```
SW4(config-if)#no shut
SW4(config-if)#do sh spanning-tree vlan 10 | b Role
Interface          Role Sts Cost      Prio.Nbr Type
------------------ ---- --- --------- -------- --------------------
Et0/0              Desg FWD 100       128.1    Shr
Et0/1              Root FWD 100       128.2    Shr
Et0/2              Altn BLK 100       128.3    Shr
Et1/0              Altn BLK 100       128.33   Shr
Et1/2              Altn BLK 100       128.35   Shr

SW4(config-if)#
%LINK-3-UPDOWN: Interface Ethernet1/1, changed state to up
%LINEPROTO-5-UPDOWN: Line protocol on Interface Ethernet1/1, changed
state to up
SW4(config-if)#do sh spanning-tree vlan 10 | b Role
Interface          Role Sts Cost      Prio.Nbr Type
------------------ ---- --- --------- -------- --------------------
Et0/0              Desg FWD 100       128.1    Shr
Et0/1              Root FWD 100       128.2    Shr
Et0/2              Altn BLK 100       128.3    Shr
Et1/0              Altn BLK 100       128.33   Shr
Et1/1              Desg LIS 100       128.34   Shr
Et1/2              Altn BLK 100       128.35   Shr

SW4(config-if)#
```

We have to wait a few moments for them to go into the listening state, at this stage the e0/1 port is still forwarding, but a moment later, it moves to the blocked state:

```
SW4(config-if)#do sh spanning-tree vlan 10 | b Role
Interface           Role Sts Cost      Prio.Nbr Type
------------------- ---- --- --------- -------- --------------------
Et0/0               Desg FWD 100       128.1    Shr
Et0/1               Altn BLK 100       128.2    Shr
Et0/2               Altn BLK 100       128.3    Shr
Et1/0               Altn BLK 100       128.33   Shr
Et1/1               Root LIS 100       128.34   Shr
Et1/2               Altn BLK 100       128.35   Shr

SW4(config-if)#
```

At this point, we are not able to process any user data on this port. After the 15 seconds forward delay timer has expired, we move to the learning state:

```
SW4(config-if)#do sh spanning-tree vlan 10 | b Role
Interface           Role Sts Cost      Prio.Nbr Type
------------------- ---- --- --------- -------- --------------------
Et0/0               Desg FWD 100       128.1    Shr
Et0/1               Altn BLK 100       128.2    Shr
Et0/2               Altn BLK 100       128.3    Shr
Et1/0               Altn BLK 100       128.33   Shr
Et1/1               Root LRN 100       128.34   Shr
Et1/2               Altn BLK 100       128.35   Shr

SW4(config-if)#
```

After another 15 seconds we move to the forwarding state:

```
SW4(config-if)#do sh spanning-tree vlan 10 | b Role
Interface           Role Sts Cost      Prio.Nbr Type
------------------- ---- --- --------- -------- --------------------
Et0/0               Desg FWD 100       128.1    Shr
Et0/1               Altn BLK 100       128.2    Shr
Et0/2               Altn BLK 100       128.3    Shr
Et1/0               Altn BLK 100       128.33   Shr
Et1/1               Root FWD 100       128.34   Shr
Et1/2               Altn BLK 100       128.35   Shr

SW4(config-if)#
```

Again, the process takes between 30 to 50 seconds. We can, however, speed this up a bit.

2.9.b Spanning tree mode

There are a number of modes of STP, and these include Rapid-Spanning Tree (RSTP), Per-VLAN Spanning Tree (PVST), and Multiple Spanning Tree (MST). Our focus will be PVST, but we will discuss RSTP first.

2.8.a RSTP

The original version of STP could take 50 seconds to recover after a link failure, which is a long time and longer than most people would find acceptable in todays networked world. Therefore, in 2001, RSTP came out. RSTP has a number of benefits that reduces the time it takes for the topology to reconverge and for the ports to transition to the forwarding state. RSTP is backwards compatible with STP (802.1D), but expanded on STP through the additional port roles of Alternate and Backup. The alternate port is an alternate path to the root bridge and the backup port is another path to a different segment.

RSTP achieves the quicker transition times by only having three states; Discarding, Learning and Forwarding. These roles are similar to STP, in that in the discarding state no user data is sent, in the learning state we can start to populate our CAM table and in the forwarding state we are working normally. So we save 15 seconds by not moving into the listening state.

So, this kind of begs the question, if we have a listening state (which we saw when we watched the spanning-tree reconverge) then we should be running STP, but we have the alternate (Altn) port roles of RSTP, so what are we running here?

2.8.b PVSTP

Actually, we are running neither of the two. We are running Per-VLAN Spanning Tree (Plus), or PVST+, but you would have to do some digging to know that. There are a couple of ways to see what mode of STP you are running. Our port costs are all 100, meaning that we cannot be running RSTP. However, you still need to know the costs to be able to tell from this. Even showing the detailed output of spanning tree does not tell us much:

```
SW4#show spanning-tree vlan 10 detail | section VLAN0010
 VLAN0010 is executing the ieee compatible Spanning Tree protocol
   Bridge Identifier has priority 32768, sysid 10, address aabb.cc00.0400
   Configured hello time 2, max age 20, forward delay 15
   Current root has priority 32778, address aabb.cc00.0100
   Root port is 6 (Ethernet1/1), cost of root path is 100
   Topology change flag not set, detected flag not set
   Number of topology changes 9 last change occurred 00:36:32 ago
         from Ethernet1/1
```

```
        Times:  hold 1, topology change 35, notification 2
                hello 2, max age 20, forward delay 15
        Timers: hello 0, topology change 0, notification 0, aging 300

    SW4#
```

We can see that we are running *"ieee compatible Spanning Tree"*, but there is nothing there to tell us that we are running PVST+. We can tell from the running configuration though:

```
    SW4#sh running-config | i spanning-tree
    spanning-tree mode pvst
    spanning-tree extend system-id
    SW4#
```

Above we can see that our mode is PVST. The line *"spanning-tree extend system-id"* is where we start adding the VLAN number onto our priority. The other telltale sign is that we do have an STP instance for each of our VLANs, as *"show spanning-tree"* shows, and hence the name.

The final way to confirm what version of spanning tree we are running is to use the command *"show spanning-tree vlan <vlan> summary"*

```
    SW1#sh spann vlan 10 summ
    Switch is in pvst mode
    Root bridge for VLAN0010 is this bridge.
    EtherChannel misconfig guard       is enabled
    Extended system ID                 is enabled
    Portfast Default                   is disabled
    Portfast Edge BPDU Guard Default   is disabled
    Portfast Edge BPDU Filter Default  is disabled
    Loopguard Default                  is disabled
    Platform PVST Simulation           is enabled
    PVST Simulation Default            is enabled but inactive in pvst mode
    Bridge Assurance                   is enabled but inactive in pvst mode
    Pathcost method used               is short
    UplinkFast                         is disabled
    BackboneFast                       is disabled

    Name             Blocking Listening Learning Forwarding STP Active
    ---------------- -------- --------- -------- ---------- ----------
    VLAN0010                0         0        0          5          5
    SW1#
```

PVST is the default mode for our switches. To be more precise, it is PVST+. PVST is only compatible with ISL, whereas PVST+ supports 802.1Q as well. In the end, Cisco stopped support for PVST and just used PVST+, but the command to implement PVST+ is the same as PVST (*spanning-tree mode pvst*).

So, we are already running PVST. What can we do now to configure it? Well, because Cisco made it into a separate topic, quite a bit!

2.9 Configure and verify PVSTP operation

One of the major benefits of PVST+ is that it allows the root switch location to be decided on and optimised on a per-VLAN basis. Therefore, we could make each of our switches the root for a particular VLAN, and specify whom the secondary root will be in the event that the primary goes down. We could therefore have a topology configured like this:

VLAN	Primary	Secondary
10	SW1	SW2
20	SW2	SW1
30	SW3	SW4
40	SW4	SW3
50	SW1	SW1

I am deliberately leaving VLAN 50's root bridge as SW1.

Cisco makes the setting of the roles (primary or secondary) very easy for us. We could do it by using the priority values, or we can specify primary or secondary:

```
SW1(config)#spanning-tree vlan 10 root primary
SW1(config)#spanning-tree vlan 20 root secondary
SW1(config)#

SW2(config)#spanning-tree vlan 20 root primary
SW2(config)#spanning-tree vlan 10 root secondary
SW2(config)#
```

We can now confirm that this is working how we would expect, starting with VLAN 10:

```
SW1(config)#do sh spann vlan 10
VLAN0010
  Spanning tree enabled protocol ieee
  Root ID    Priority    24586
             Address     aabb.cc00.0100
             This bridge is the root
             Hello Time   2 sec  Max Age 20 sec  Forward Delay 15 sec

  Bridge ID  Priority    24586  (priority 24576 sys-id-ext 10)
             Address     aabb.cc00.0100
             Hello Time   2 sec  Max Age 20 sec  Forward Delay 15 sec
             Aging Time   300  sec
```

```
Interface           Role Sts Cost       Prio.Nbr Type
------------------- ---- --- ---------- -------- --------------------
Et0/2               Desg FWD 100        128.3    Shr
Et0/3               Desg FWD 100        128.4    Shr
Et1/1               Desg FWD 100        128.34   Shr
Et1/2               Desg FWD 100        128.35   Shr
Et1/3               Desg FWD 100        128.36   Shr
SW1(config)#
```

Let's compare this to SW2:

```
SW2#sh span vlan 10

VLAN0010
  Spanning tree enabled protocol ieee
  Root ID    Priority    24586
             Address     aabb.cc00.0100
             Cost        100
             Port        3 (Ethernet0/2)
             Hello Time   2 sec  Max Age 20 sec  Forward Delay 15 sec

  Bridge ID  Priority    28682  (priority 28672 sys-id-ext 10)
             Address     aabb.cc00.0200
             Hello Time   2 sec  Max Age 20 sec  Forward Delay 15 sec
             Aging Time  300 sec

Interface           Role Sts Cost       Prio.Nbr Type
------------------- ---- --- ---------- -------- --------------------
Et0/1               Desg FWD 100        128.2    Shr
Et0/2               Root FWD 100        128.3    Shr
Et1/0               Desg FWD 100        128.33   Shr
Et1/1               Desg FWD 100        128.34   Shr
Et1/2               Altn BLK 100        128.35   Shr

SW2#
```

Does anything stand out here?

Notice that the priorities have changed. When we use the command *"spanning-tree vlan <vlan> root primary|secondary"*, this is converted into numbers. We can only go in multiples of 4096 as both of these are (with the addition of the VLAN number due to the command *"spanning-tree extend system-id"*), these numbers were chosen to be the numeric equivalent of root primary and root secondary.

We can check VLAN 20 on SW1 and SW2 now and should see the same. For the sake of brevity I will be using the command *"show spanning-tree vlan 20 summary | i Root"*:

```
SW1(config)#do sh spann vlan 20 summ | i Root
Root bridge for VLAN0020 is 24596.aabb.cc00.0200.
SW1(config)#

SW2(config)#do sh spann vlan 20 summ | i Root
Root bridge for VLAN0020 is this bridge.
SW2(config)#
```

SW2 is our root bridge for VLAN 20, and its priority is 24596, which is the priority number (24576) and the VLAN ID (20) added together. We can set SW3 and SW4 up using these values and achieve the same results. The difference here is that we do not have to add the VLAN ID ourselves. In fact, we cannot even if we try to:

```
SW3(config)#spanning-tree vlan 30 priority 24606
% Bridge Priority must be in increments of 4096.
% Allowed values are:
  0     4096  8192  12288 16384 20480 24576 28672
  32768 36864 40960 45056 49152 53248 57344 61440
SW3(config)#
SW3(config)#spanning-tree vlan 30 priority 24576
SW3(config)#spanning-tree vlan 40 priority 28672
SW3(config)#

SW4(config)#spanning-tree vlan 40 priority 24576
SW4(config)#spanning-tree vlan 30 priority 28672
SW4(config)#
```

Now we have specified our root primary and root secondary, we can confirm that they are performing the right roles:

```
SW3(config)#do sh spanning-tree vlan 30 summ | i Root
Root bridge for VLAN0030 is this bridge.
SW3(config)#

SW4(config)#do sh spanning-tree vlan 30 summ | i Root
Root bridge for VLAN0030 is 24606.aabb.cc00.0300.
SW4(config)#
```

As you can see, SW3 has automatically added the VLAN ID of 30 to the priority of 24576 that we set. So, what would happen if we were to go onto SW1 and set a lower priority for VLAN 20?

```
SW1(config)#spanning-tree vlan 20 priority 0
SW1(config)#end
```

Again we use the command "*show spanning-tree vlan 20*" to confirm:

```
SW1#sh spanning-tree vlan 20

VLAN0020
  Spanning tree enabled protocol ieee
  Root ID    Priority    20
             Address     aabb.cc00.0100
             This bridge is the root
             Hello Time   2 sec  Max Age 20 sec  Forward Delay 15 sec

  Bridge ID  Priority    20    (priority 0 sys-id-ext 20)
             Address     aabb.cc00.0100
             Hello Time   2 sec  Max Age 20 sec  Forward Delay 15 sec
             Aging Time  15  sec

Interface          Role Sts Cost      Prio.Nbr Type
----------------   ---- --- --------- -------- --------------------
Et0/2              Desg FWD 100       128.3    Shr
Et0/3              Desg FWD 100       128.4    Shr
Et1/0              Desg FWD 100       128.33   Shr
Et1/1              Desg FWD 100       128.34   Shr
Et1/2              Desg FWD 100       128.35   Shr
Et1/3              Desg FWD 100       128.36   Shr
SW1#
```

As you can see, there is nothing preventing us from configuring a lower (and therefore more preferred) priority and in doing so seizing the root bridge role from another switch. If both switches had the priority set at zero, then the one with the lowest MAC address would win the tie.

So, how do we protect ourselves? Actually, it's not that easy. There is a function called root guard, which as the name suggests, should protect our root port, no matter how or where we configure it. Lets try this out:

```
SW2(config)#int e0/2
SW2(config-if)#
SW2(config-if)#spanning-tree guard root
SW2(config-if)#
%SPANTREE-2-ROOTGUARD_CONFIG_CHANGE: Root guard enabled on port
Ethernet0/2.
SW2(config-if)#
%SPANTREE-2-ROOTGUARD_BLOCK: Root guard blocking port Ethernet0/2 on
VLAN0040.
SW2(config-if)#
%SPANTREE-2-ROOTGUARD_BLOCK: Root guard blocking port Ethernet0/2 on
VLAN0050.
SW2(config-if)#
SW2(config-if)#end
SW2#sh spann vl 20 | b Role
```

```
Interface         Role Sts Cost      Prio.Nbr Type
---------------   ---- --- --------- -------- ----------------------------
Et0/1             Desg FWD 100       128.2    Shr
Et0/2             Desg BKN*100       128.3    Shr *ROOT_Inc
Et1/0             Desg FWD 100       128.33   Shr
Et1/1             Desg FWD 100       128.34   Shr
Et1/2             Root FWD 100       128.35   Shr
SW2#
```

Root guard is now working on e0/2 and has placed the port into a root-inconsistent state. This is pretty much the same are the listening state, but is not enough to reclaim back our root status. What we will do now is set up root guard on our other connection to SW1. Set SW1 back to being root secondary and see what happens when we change SW1's priority to zero again:

```
SW2(config)#int e1/2
SW2(config-if)#spann guard root
SW2(config-if)#
%SPANTREE-2-ROOTGUARD_CONFIG_CHANGE: Root guard enabled on port
Ethernet1/2.
%SPANTREE-2-ROOTGUARD_BLOCK: Root guard blocking port Ethernet1/2 on
VLAN0050.
%SPANTREE-2-ROOTGUARD_BLOCK: Root guard blocking port Ethernet1/2 on
VLAN0040.
SW2(config-if)#

SW1(config)#span vl 20 root sec
SW1(config)#

SW2(config-if)#
%SPANTREE-2-ROOTGUARD_UNBLOCK: Root guard unblocking port Ethernet0/2 on
VLAN0020.
SW2(config-if)#do sh spann vl 20 | section Root
   Root ID    Priority    24596
              Address     aabb.cc00.0200
              This bridge is the root
              Hello Time   2 sec  Max Age 20 sec  Forward Delay 15 sec

SW2(config-if)#
```

SW2 becomes the root again. In a properly placed design, root guard will work well. It is not designed to prevent topology changes caused by purposeful configuration changes, as we did above, but will prevent rogue downstream devices from causing havoc. Clear planning of the priority numbers of the root bridge will certainly help keep things the way you want them to be in your network.

If we wanted to be very strict about how we deal with such events as a rogue switch, we could even go so far as automatically shutting down the port using BPDU guard.

Because SW1 was sending superior (more preferred) BPDUs to SW2, it was allowed to take over the root bridge role. However, we could have been very strict and implemented BPDU guard on SW2, under the interfaces we wanted to protect. The interface-level command for this would be *"spanning-tree bpduguard enable"*. Our topology is not designed to show the effect of this command, but if this were placed on a different port and someone were to connect a switch to it, then upon receipt of a superior BPDU (therefore trying to become the root), the port would actually be shut down, by being placed in an error disabled (err-disable) state.

This is one of those commands that should be entered at the global level, once you have designed where you want your root bridge to be. Once this is done, your spanning tree has converged and you are happy with the results, go into config mode and use the command *"spanning-tree portfast edge bpduguard default"*. This will enable it on all the interfaces, so you don't have to do it one by one.

> On some IOS versions, the command will be *"spanning-tree portfast bpduguard default"*. You can see what version you need to use through the context-sensitive help: *"spanning-tree portfast ?"*

Lets do this on SW1 and see the effects:

```
SW1(config)#spanning-tree portfast edge bpduguard default
SW1(config)#do sh spanning-tree vlan 10 summ
Switch is in pvst mode
Root bridge for VLAN0010 is this bridge.
EtherChannel misconfig guard      is enabled
Extended system ID                is enabled
Portfast Default                  is disabled
Portfast Edge BPDU Guard Default  is enabled
Portfast Edge BPDU Filter Default is disabled
Loopguard Default                 is disabled
Platform PVST Simulation          is enabled
PVST Simulation Default           is enabled but inactive in pvst mode
Bridge Assurance                  is enabled but inactive in pvst mode
Pathcost method used              is short
UplinkFast                        is disabled
BackboneFast                      is disabled

Name               Blocking Listening Learning Forwarding STP Active
------------------ -------- --------- -------- ---------- ----------
VLAN0010                  0         0        0          5          5
SW1(config)#
```

You can now see that that "Portfast Edge BPDU Guard Default" is enabled. We have quite a few disabled items though, such as portfast and portfast BPDU filter.

Portfast is a great way of speeding up the time it takes for a connected host to start sending and receiving data. These portfast-enabled ports will transition from blocked or disabled directly to forwarding.

Portfast is recommended only for ports connected to hosts such as PCs (depending on the IOS version, we will be warned about this when we enable it):

```
SW1(config)#spanning-tree portfast network default
SW1(config)#do sh spanning-tree vlan 10 summ | i Portfast
Portfast Default                        is network
Portfast Edge BPDU Guard Default        is enabled
Portfast Edge BPDU Filter Default       is disabled
SW1(config)#
```

On some IOS versions, the command will be "*spanning-tree portfast default*".

We can disable it on a per-port basis using the interface command "*spanning-tree portfast disable*":

```
SW1(config)#int e0/2
SW1(config-if)#spanning-tree portfast disable
SW1(config-if)#
```

To disable it on the other ports connecting to switches, I will use the range command:

```
SW1(config-if)#interface range e0/0, e0/3, e1/1 - 3
SW1(config-if-range)#spanning-tree portfast disable
SW1(config-if-range)#end
```

Now we can see that portfast is enabled globally, which is good for our users and disabled for our switch-to-switch links and our connection to the gateway router.

We will quickly talk about BPDU filter, loopguard, uplink fast and backbone fast before moving on.

Portfast BPDU filter stops the port from sending BPDU messages or receiving them, this effectively removes it from STP. However, if a BPDU is received on that port, then portfast is disabled, as is bpdufilter, and the port will take part in STP again. This can be enabled globally ("*spanning-tree portfast edge bpdufilter default*", or on earlier IOS versions, just "*spanning-tree portfast bpdufilter default*"), or at an interface level ("*spanning-tree bpdufilter enable*").

Loopguard will prevent alternate or root ports becoming designated ports. BPDUs will not be sent on these ports. This feature is enabled using the global command "*spanning-tree loopguard default*".

UplinkFast is useful where we have redundant links, such as our network. When we shutdown the connection from SW4 to SW1 we saw that we went through the different states, from blocked to listening, to learning and then to forwarding until we were converged again. UplinkFast makes this process quicker, by skipping the listening and learning states. Uplinkfast is a very useful feature, which can be enabled at the global level, using the command "*spanning-tree uplinkfast*".

Next, we have BackboneFast, which goes hand-in-hand with UplinkFast. BackboneFast will detect failures between other switches, so if SwitchA (the root) loses its connection to SwitchB, both SwitchA and SwitchB can go through SwitchC to get to each other.

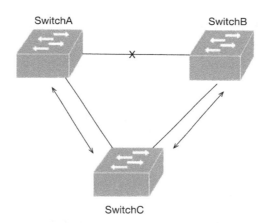

Usually SwitchC would have its link to SwitchB in the blocked state, as it has a direct link to SwitchA, the root. If SwitchA loses the link to SwitchB, SwitchB will start to send BPDUs identifying itself as the root to SwitchC, who is still getting them from SwitchA at the same time. The BPDUs from SwitchB will be inferior BPDUs and because of this, SwitchC will unblock its port to SwitchB, moving from listening to learning and then into the forwarding state.

The final setting we need to talk about is EtherChannel guard. However, before we learn how to guard an EtherChannel, let's find out what one is first.

2.8.c Etherchannels

EtherChannels are a number of links all acting as one, allowing for load-balancing and greater speeds; two 1-Gbps links can become one 2-Gbps inks for example. It became a standard in 2000, referred to as 802.3ad. Before this it was a Cisco proprietary protocol, which is why we have two versions; the industry standard LACP (Link Aggregation Control Protocol), and Cisco's PAgP (Port Aggregation Protocol). If you have trouble remembering which is which, try to remember **P**robably **Ag**ain **P**roprietary.

Lets set up some, shall we? We will have PAgP between SW1 and SW2 and between SW3 and SW4. We will also set up LACP between SW1 and SW3 and use the "on" mode to form an EtherChannel between SW2 and SW4, without the aid of either PAgP or LACP.

Before we start doing this, we should make sure that all our trunk interfaces are using 802.1Q encapsulation. The easiest way will be to use the interface range command again:

```
SW1#conf t
SW1(config)#interface range e0/2 - 3, e1/1 - 3
SW1(config-if-range)#
SW1(config-if-range)#switchport trunk encap dot
SW1(config-if-range)#swi mode trunk
SW1(config-if-range)#

SW2#conf t
SW2(config)#int range e0/1 - 2, e1/0 - 2
SW2(config-if-range)#
SW2(config-if-range)#switchport trunk encap dot
SW2(config-if-range)#switchport mode trunk
SW2(config-if-range)#

SW3#conf t
SW3(config)#int ran e0/2 - 3, e1/1 - 3
SW3(config-if-range)#
SW3(config-if-range)#switchport trunk encap dot
SW3(config-if-range)#switchport mode trunk
SW3(config-if-range)#

SW4#conf t
SW4(config)#int ra e0/1 - 2, e1/0 - 2
SW4(config-if-range)#
SW4(config-if-range)#switchport trunk encap dot
SW4(config-if-range)#switchport mode trunk
SW4(config-if-range)#
```

We can confirm that they are all set up correctly:

```
SW1(config-if-range)#do sh int trunk | i trunking
Et0/2        on              802.1q          trunking        1
Et0/3        on              802.1q          trunking        1
Et1/1        on              802.1q          trunking        1
Et1/2        on              802.1q          trunking        1
Et1/3        on              802.1q          trunking        1
SW1(config-if-range)#
```

```
SW2(config-if-range)#do sh int trunk | i trunking
Et0/1         on                802.1q          trunking       1
Et0/2         on                802.1q          trunking       1
Et1/0         on                802.1q          trunking       1
Et1/1         on                802.1q          trunking       1
Et1/2         on                802.1q          trunking       1
SW2(config-if-range)#

SW3(config-if-range)#do sh int trunk | i trunking
Et0/2         on                802.1q          trunking       1
Et0/3         on                802.1q          trunking       1
Et1/1         on                802.1q          trunking       1
Et1/2         on                802.1q          trunking       1
Et1/3         on                802.1q          trunking       1
SW3(config-if-range)#

SW4(config-if-range)#do sh int trunk | i trunking
Et0/1         on                802.1q          trunking       1
Et0/2         on                802.1q          trunking       1
Et1/0         on                802.1q          trunking       1
Et1/1         on                802.1q          trunking       1
Et1/2         on                802.1q          trunking       1
SW4(config-if-range)#
```

With EtherChannels, it is important that, so we don't have issues, we get the settings the same.

Let's create our first EtherChannel group between SW1 and SW2, which will be PAgP. We do this in interface mode using the channel-group command (which is used for creating all of the Etherchannel modes). We then need to specify a group number, and a mode:

```
SW1(config-if-range)#exit
SW1(config)#interface range e0/2, e1/2
SW1(config-if-range)#channel-group ?
  <1-255>  Channel group number

SW1(config-if-range)#channel-group 1 ?
  mode  Etherchannel Mode of the interface

SW1(config-if-range)#channel-group 1 mode ?
  active     Enable LACP unconditionally
  auto       Enable PAgP only if a PAgP device is detected
  desirable  Enable PAgP unconditionally
  on         Enable Etherchannel only
  passive    Enable LACP only if a LACP device is detected

SW1(config-if-range)#channel-group 1 mode desirable
Creating a port-channel interface Port-channel 1
```

```
SW1(config-if-range)#
%LINEPROTO-5-UPDOWN: Line protocol on Interface Ethernet0/2, changed
state to down
%LINEPROTO-5-UPDOWN: Line protocol on Interface Ethernet1/2, changed
state to down
SW1(config-if-range)#
%LINEPROTO-5-UPDOWN: Line protocol on Interface Ethernet1/2, changed
state to up
%LINEPROTO-5-UPDOWN: Line protocol on Interface Ethernet0/2, changed
state to up
SW1(config-if-range)#
```

We can create up to 255 channel groups (though you may find that the virtual switch we are using here does have an issue with the higher numbers) and we need to specify a mode, to differentiate between the different Etherchannel modes. We can use auto or desirable for PAgP, and I have set both to desirable. Our PAgP Etherchannel is created.

The steps for SW2 are no different:

```
SW2(config-if-range)#int ra e0/2, e1/2
SW2(config-if-range)#
SW2(config-if-range)#channel-group 1 mode desirable
Creating a port-channel interface Port-channel 1

SW2(config-if-range)#
```

We now have a new interface on both switches; Port-channel 1, which seems to be happily trunking our VLANs:

```
SW1(config-if-range)#do sh int trunk | i trunking
Et0/3        on              802.1q          trunking     1
Et1/1        on              802.1q          trunking     1
Et1/3        on              802.1q          trunking     1
Po1          on              802.1q          trunking     1
SW1(config-if-range)#

SW2(config-if-range)#do sh int trunk | i trunking
Et0/1        on              802.1q          trunking     1
Et1/0        on              802.1q          trunking     1
Et1/1        on              802.1q          trunking     1
Po1          on              802.1q          trunking     1
SW2(config-if-range)#
```

We no longer have the individual interfaces in our list of trunks and we did not have to set any trunking properties on the new interface. It is very happy taking part in STP:

```
SW1(config-if-range)#do sh spanning vlan 10 | b Interface
Interface          Role Sts Cost      Prio.Nbr Type
------------------ ---- --- --------- -------- --------------------
Et0/3              Desg FWD 100        128.4    Shr
Et1/1              Desg FWD 100        128.6    Shr
Et1/3              Desg FWD 100        128.8    Shr
Po1                Desg FWD 56         128.65   Shr

SW1(config-if-range)#

SW2(config-if-range)#do sh spanning vlan 10 | b Interface
Interface          Role Sts Cost      Prio.Nbr Type
------------------ ---- --- --------- -------- --------------------
Et0/1              Desg FWD 100        128.2    Shr
Et1/0              Desg FWD 100        128.33   Shr
Et1/1              Desg FWD 100        128.34   Shr
Po1                Root FWD 56         128.514  Shr

SW2(config-if-range)#
```

Notice the lower cost in the interface, 56 instead of 100 (making it more preferred). We now know from the perspective of VTP and STP that our Etherchannel is working well, but how do we find out that it is working if we are not using these technologies? We can use the command *"show etherchannel"* and *"show etherchannel summary"*:

```
SW1(config-if-range)#show etherchannel
                Channel-group listing:
                ----------------------

Group: 1
----------
Group state = L2
Ports: 2   Maxports = 4
Port-channels: 1 Max Port-channels = 1
Protocol:   PAgP
Minimum Links: 0

SW1(config-if-range)#sh etherchannel summ
Flags:  D - down         P - bundled in port-channel
        I - stand-alone s - suspended
        H - Hot-standby (LACP only)
        R - Layer3      S - Layer2
        U - in use       f - failed to allocate aggregator

        M - not in use, minimum links not met
        u - unsuitable for bundling
        w - waiting to be aggregated
        d - default port
```

```
        w - waiting to be aggregated
Number of channel-groups in use: 1
Number of aggregators:          1

Group  Port-channel  Protocol    Ports
------+-------------+-----------+------------------------------------
1      Po1(SU)       PAgP        Et0/2(P)     Et1/2(P)

SW1(config-if-range)#
```

I am sure that they have those two commands the wrong way round. The summary has much more information than the other command! Nevertheless, both show that our first Etherchannel is working well. As a quick reference, use the summary version of the command and if you can see (SU) and each interface in the group has (P), then you are in good stead.

Let's create our other PAgP Etherchannel. This time both will be set at Auto, which is the other option in PAgP:

```
SW3(config-if-range)#do sh cdp neighbors | i SW4
SW4.802101.local Eth 0/2     168         R S   Linux Uni Eth 0/2
SW4.802101.local Eth 1/2     162         R S   Linux Uni Eth 1/2
SW3(config-if-range)#int ra e0/2, e1/2
SW3(config-if-range)#channel-group 3 mode auto
Creating a port-channel interface Port-channel 3

SW3(config-if-range)#
%LINEPROTO-5-UPDOWN: Line protocol on Interface Ethernet0/2, changed
state to down
%LINEPROTO-5-UPDOWN: Line protocol on Interface Ethernet1/2, changed
state to down
%LINEPROTO-5-UPDOWN: Line protocol on Interface Ethernet0/2, changed
state to up
%LINEPROTO-5-UPDOWN: Line protocol on Interface Ethernet1/2, changed
state to up
SW3(config-if-range)#

SW4(config-if-range)#do sh cdp neighbors | i SW3
SW3              Eth 0/2     146         R S   Linux Uni Eth 0/2
SW3              Eth 1/2     152         R S   Linux Uni Eth 1/2
SW4(config-if-range)#int ra e0/2, e1/2
SW4(config-if-range)#channel-group 3 mode auto
Creating a port-channel interface Port-channel 3

SW4(config-if-range)#
%LINEPROTO-5-UPDOWN: Line protocol on Interface Ethernet1/2, changed
state to down
```

```
%LINEPROTO-5-UPDOWN: Line protocol on Interface Ethernet1/2, changed
state to up
SW4(config-if-range)#
```

Let's do some checking to confirm if our etherchannel is working or not. The etherchannel summary command is a good place to start:

```
SW4(config-if-range)#do sh etherchannel summary | b Group
Group  Port-channel  Protocol    Ports
------+-------------+-----------+-------------------------------
3      Po3(SD)        PAgP        Et0/2(I)    Et1/2(I)

SW4(config-if-range)#

SW3(config-if-range)#do sh etherchannel summ | b Group
Group  Port-channel  Protocol    Ports
------+-------------+-----------+-------------------------------
3      Po3(SD)        PAgP        Et0/2(I)    Et1/2(I)

SW3(config-if-range)#
```

Rats! Not good. This is one of those times that when two sides are set to "auto", no one is actually leading the conversation. Let's change SW3 to desirable and see what happens:

```
SW3(config-if-range)#channel-group 3 mode desirable
SW3(config-if-range)#
%LINEPROTO-5-UPDOWN: Line protocol on Interface Port-channel3, changed
state to up
SW3(config-if-range)#do sh etherchannel summ | b Group
Group  Port-channel  Protocol    Ports
------+-------------+-----------+-------------------------------
3      Po3(SU)        PAgP        Et0/2(P)    Et1/2(P)

SW3(config-if-range)#

SW4(config-if-range)#
%LINEPROTO-5-UPDOWN: Line protocol on Interface Port-channel3, changed
state to up
SW4(config-if-range)#do sh etherchannel summary | b Group
Group  Port-channel  Protocol    Ports
------+-------------+-----------+-------------------------------
3      Po3(SU)        PAgP        Et0/2(P)    Et1/2(P)

SW4(config-if-range)#
```

That's better!

The same is true with LACP; two passive devices will not form an EtherChannel, but two active devices will.

```
SW1(config-if-range)#do sh cdp neigh | i SW3
SW3          Eth 1/3       127              R S    Linux Uni Eth 1/3
SW3          Eth 0/3       131              R S    Linux Uni Eth 0/3
SW1(config-if-range)#int range e0/3, e1/3
SW1(config-if-range)#channel-group 13 mode ?
  active     Enable LACP unconditionally
  auto       Enable PAgP only if a PAgP device is detected
  desirable  Enable PAgP unconditionally
  on         Enable Etherchannel only
  passive    Enable LACP only if a LACP device is detected

SW1(config-if-range)#channel-group 13 mode active
Creating a port-channel interface Port-channel 13

SW1(config-if-range)#

SW3(config-if-range)#do sh cdp neigh | i SW1
SW1            Eth 1/3     142              R S    Linux Uni Eth 1/3
SW1            Eth 0/3     155              R S    Linux Uni Eth 0/3
SW3(config-if-range)#int ran e0/3, e1/3
SW3(config-if-range)#channel-group 13 mode active
Creating a port-channel interface Port-channel 13

SW3(config-if-range)#
%LINK-3-UPDOWN: Interface Port-channel13, changed state to up
SW3(config-if-range)#
%LINEPROTO-5-UPDOWN: Line protocol on Interface Port-channel13, changed
state to up
SW3(config-if-range)#do sh etherchannel 13 summ | b Group
Group  Port-channel  Protocol    Ports
------+-------------+-----------+-----------------------------------
13     Po13(SU)      LACP        Et0/3(P)       Et1/3(P)

Last applied Hash Distribution Algorithm:    -

SW3(config-if-range)#

SW1(config-if-range)#do sh etherchannel 13 summ | b Group
Group  Port-channel  Protocol    Ports
------+-------------+-----------+-----------------------------------
13     Po13(SU)      LACP        Et0/3(P)       Et1/3(P)

Last applied Hash Distribution Algorithm:    -

SW1(config-if-range)#
```

We could also run SW3 in passive mode:

```
SW3(config-if-range)#channel-group 13 mode passive
SW3(config-if-range)#
%LINK-3-UPDOWN: Interface Port-channel13, changed state to down
%LINEPROTO-5-UPDOWN: Line protocol on Interface Port-channel13, changed
state to down
%LINK-3-UPDOWN: Interface Port-channel13, changed state to up
%LINEPROTO-5-UPDOWN: Line protocol on Interface Port-channel13, changed
state to up
SW3(config-if-range)#
SW3(config-if-range)#do sh etherchannel 13 summ | b Group
Group  Port-channel  Protocol    Ports
------+-------------+----------+---------------------------------
13     Po13(SU)      LACP        Et0/3(P)        Et1/3(P)

Last applied Hash Distribution Algorithm:   -

SW3(config-if-range)#
```

Our final etherchannel is much easier:

```
SW2(config-if-range)#do sh cdp neigh | i SW4
SW4.802101.local Eth 0/1      174           R S    Linux Uni Eth 0/1
SW4.802101.local Eth 1/0      141           R S    Linux Uni Eth 1/0
SW2(config-if-range)#int ran e0/1, e1/0
SW2(config-if-range)#channel-group 24 mode on
Creating a port-channel interface Port-channel 24

SW2(config-if-range)#
%LINEPROTO-5-UPDOWN: Line protocol on Interface Port-channel24, changed
state to up
SW2(config-if-range)#

SW4(config-if-range)#do sh cdp neigh | i SW2
SW2          Eth 1/0      149           R S I  Linux Uni Eth 1/0
SW2          Eth 0/1      149           R S I  Linux Uni Eth 0/1
SW4(config-if-range)#int ran e0/1, e1/0
SW4(config-if-range)#channel-group 24 mode on
Creating a port-channel interface Port-channel 24

SW4(config-if-range)#
%LINEPROTO-5-UPDOWN: Line protocol on Interface Port-channel24, changed
state to up
SW4(config-if-range)#
```

And a quick check:

```
SW2(config-if-range)#do sh etherchannel summary | b Group
Group  Port-channel  Protocol    Ports
------+-------------+-----------+------------------------------
1      Po1(SU)       PAgP        Et0/2(P)    Et1/2(P)
24     Po24(SU)      -           Et0/1(P)    Et1/0(P)

SW2(config-if-range)#

SW4(config-if-range)#do sh etherchannel summary | b Group
Group  Port-channel  Protocol    Ports
------+-------------+-----------+------------------------------
3      Po3(SU)       PAgP        Et0/2(P)    Et1/2(P)
24     Po24(SU)      -           Et0/1(P)    Et1/0(P)

SW4(config-if-range)#
```

Nice, we now have a good set of Etherchannels running between our switches!

So how has this affected VTP and STP?

```
SW1(config-if-range)#do sh int trunk | i trunking
Et1/1              on          802.1q              trunking       1
Po1               on          802.1q              trunking       1
Po13              on          802.1q              trunking       1
SW1(config-if-range)#do sh spannin vl 10 | b Interface
Interface          Role Sts Cost      Prio.Nbr Type
------------------ ---- --- --------- -------- --------------------
Et1/1              Desg FWD 100       128.34   Shr
Po1                Desg FWD 56        128.514  Shr Network
Po13               Desg FWD 56        128.515  Shr Network

SW1(config-if-range)#
```

Not much has changed form the point of view of SW1, it is still forwarding on all of its ports and SW4 still prefers the direct link to SW1, even though it has a higher cost:

```
SW4(config-if-range)#do sh spann vl 10 | b Interface
Interface          Role Sts Cost      Prio.Nbr Type
------------------ ---- --- --------- -------- --------------------
Et0/0              Desg FWD 100       128.1    Shr
Et1/1              Root FWD 100       128.34   Shr
Po3                Altn BLK 56        128.514  Shr
Po24               Altn BLK 56        128.515  Shr

SW4(config-if-range)#
```

So far, we have only looked at layer-2 EtherChannels. We can have a layer-3 EtherChannel if we want to. To do this all we need do is assign an IP address to the interface. We do need to change it's mode though, using the command "*no switchport*", which turns it into a layer-3 port:

```
Switch(config)#int ran gi 0/0 - 1
Switch(config-if-range)#no shut
Switch(config-if-range)#channel-group 24 mode on
Creating a port-channel interface Port-channel 24

Switch(config-if-range)#int po 24
Switch(config-if)#
%LINEPROTO-5-UPDOWN: Line protocol on Interface Port-channel24, changed
state to up
Switch(config-if)#ip address 24.24.24.24 255.255.255.0
                     ^
% Invalid input detected at '^' marker.

Switch(config-if)#ip addre?
% Unrecognized command
Switch(config-if)#no switchport
Switch(config-if)#ip add 24.24.24.24 255.255.255.0
Switch(config-if)#
%LINEPROTO-5-UPDOWN: Line protocol on Interface Port-channel24, changed
state to up
Switch(config-if)#
```

Without the "*no switchport*" command, we are unable to configure an IP address on the port.

Are there any benefits of having a layer-3 EtherChannel over a layer-2 one? Well, it depends on the purpose. For trunking between switches, we would not need a layer-3 interface, if we have a IP address that could benefit from this link aggregation, then yes, a layer-3 EtherChannel would be appropriate.

We can finish this chapter by returning to EtherChannel guard. EtherChannel guard will detect EtherChannel misconfiguration, and place the interfaces into the error-disabled state. It is enabled using the global command "*spanning-tree etherchannel guard misconfig*".

Our LAN is off to a good start. Our next step will be to get it communicating with the outside world and also to set up inter-VLAN communication. In order to do this we will need to assign more IP addresses. In the next chapter, we will find out how to choose the IP addresses we will use and see how we can work out IP addresses and their binary equivalents!

3. IP Addressing (IPv4/IPv6)

There are 10 types of people in the world:
Those who understand binary and those that don't.

We have now reached chapter 3, or, as I like to call it, chapter 11. Although this section only accounts for 5% of the exam weight, it is a <u>very</u> important topic to learn. When I was trying to understand IP addressing it would give me nightmares, though not as bad as the dream I had before my CCIE exam, when I dreamt that I was given a couple of bits of Lego, and asked to configure EIGRP on it. I think it was my minds way of telling me not to take it so seriously. However, never try to design a network out of Lego. It'll look awesome and fun, but won't function very well.

IP addressing does not have to be a complicated subject. The conversion from decimal to binary looks difficult, but once you have done it a few times, it is not.

Each IP (version 4) address is a 32-bit address, made up of four octets. An octet is a unit consisting of eight bits, 8+8+8+8=32. It comes from the Latin "octo" meaning eight. These octets are separated by dots, to give us an IP address (called Dotted-Decimal Notation).

Octet 1	Octet 2	Octet 3	Octet 4	IP Address
192	168	1	1	192.168.1.1
10	1	1	4	10.1.1.4

Each of these addresses can then be broken down into the network portion (what network we belong to) and the host portion (who we are on the network), depending on the subnet mask that we use.

There are different types of IP addresses; these are broken down into "classes" and, within these different classes, whether they are public or private addresses.

Public addresses are used on the Internet; they give you a presence on the Internet and connect you to other public addresses. Private addresses (known as RFC 1918 addresses) cannot be used on the Internet, they are not addressable on the public Internet and are reserved for use within a Local Area Network, like the one we have been setting up in the previous chapter.

There are five different classes of IP addresses (A through to E) and each class has a default subnet mask. This subnet mask allows us to work out what is the network ID and what is the host ID. This controls who we can talk to, without additional help in the form of additional routing. In the following table, N refers to the part of the address signifying the network, and H refers to the host portion of the address:

Class	Range	Default Subnet Mask	Network / Host	Example
A	1-126	255.0.0.0	NHHH	10.1.1.1: 10.0.0.0 is the network, .1.1.1 is the host
B	128-191	255.255.0.0	NNHH	172.16.1.1: 172.16 is the network, .1.1 is the host
C	192-223	255.255.255.0	NNNH	192.168.1.1: 192.168.1 is the network, .1 is the host
D	224-239	Reserved for Multicasting		
E	240-254	Reserved for experimental use		

The numbers in the range column are the numbers in the first octet of the IP address. The 127.0.0.0 to 127.255.255.255 range is used for loopback and diagnostic functionality.

Within each of the first three classes are private addresses:

Class	Range
A	10.0.0.0 – 10.255.255.255
B	172.16.0.0 – 172.31.255.255
C	192.168.0.0 0 – 192.168.255.255

In order to communicate with another host across a wire, the IP addresses need to be converted in to the zeros and ones of binary, so that, in turn, it can be converted into electrical pulses. This is what we are going to start looking at now.

Binary conversion

Recall from the previous chapter, we looked at how a switch breaks down a MAC address and looks for the least-significant-bit and from that gains the U/L bit in order to ascertain whether it is a universally administered address, or a locally administered address. In there we saw that if the first octet of the MAC address was 01, then the binary equivalent would be 00000001 and if the first octet was 02, then the binary would be 00000010. Now we are going to see why this is.

Grab a pen and some paper. At the top of the paper write down the following numbers, making sure that you leave some spaces in between the numbers.

128   64   32   16   8   4   2   1

It is important to note that the above numbers add up to 255. Because we start counting at 0 with IP addresses (for the network, or for a host, depending on our subnet mask), this means that in any individual octet, the most we can go up to is 256. Now let's do some counting. We will start with 10. What numbers from the list above will make 10 when added together? Clearly, we can only add 8 and

2. So to make 10, we would put a zero under any number that we cannot use and a one under the number that we can use. Your piece of paper should now look like this:

```
128   64   32   16   8    4    2    1
 o    o    o    o    1    o    1    o   = 10
```

If we apply this to SW4, which has an IP address of 10.1.1.4, then the binary version of the first octet (10) will be 00001010. The second and third octets are all be one, so they would be 0000001. The final octet is four, so that would be 00000100. The binary version of its IP address will therefore be 00001010 00000001 00000001 00000100.

Let's take a slightly more complicated number, 192.168.64.8. How would we convert this into binary?

Let's start with 192. Can we subtract 128 from 192? Of course, we can. Therefore, we can put a one under 128:

```
128   64   32   16   8    4    2    1
 1
```

192 minus 128 leaves us with 64. We have a column for this, so we now have:

```
128   64   32   16   8    4    2    1
 1    1    o    o    o    o    o    o   = 192
```

The second octet is 168. We can take 128 away from this, which leaves 40:

```
128   64   32   16   8    4    2    1
 1    1    o    o    o    o    o    o   = 192
 1
```

We cannot take 64 away from 40, so we would put a zero under the 64 column:

```
128   64   32   16   8    4    2    1
 1    1    o    o    o    o    o    o   = 192
 1    o
```

We can take 32 away from 40, leaving us with 8, so we can fill in the rest of the line:

```
128   64   32   16   8    4    2    1
 1    1    o    o    o    o    o    o   = 192
 1    o    1    o    1    o    o    o   = 168
```

The third octet is easy, 64:

128	64	32	16	8	4	2	1	
1	1	0	0	0	0	0	0	= 192
1	0	1	0	1	0	0	0	= 168
0	1	0	0	0	0	0	0	= 64

The final octet is also easy:

128	64	32	16	8	4	2	1	
1	1	0	0	0	0	0	0	= 192
1	0	1	0	1	0	0	0	= 168
0	1	0	0	0	0	0	0	= 64
0	0	0	0	1	0	0	0	= 8

Therefore, the binary equivalent of 192.168.64.8 is 11000000 10101000 01000000 00001000.

Now, why do we care what the binary equivalent of an IP address is? An IP address on its own is useless to us; it needs a corresponding subnet mask (also known as the bitmask) so that we can know what other machines we can talk to, without the need to leave our own network; the hosts on our network. A "basic" or default subnet mask is made up of one or more 255's and one or more 0's. A common one would be 255.255.255.0 for a class C address, as we saw previously.

Think about the subnet mask as the devices' way of asking "Do I care?". Taking the example IP address above (192.168.64.8), if we apply a class C subnet to it (255.255.255.0), we can work out how many hosts we can talk to, and the device (a router or a switch) can differentiate one subnet from another. It does this by using a bitwise AND operation to compare two values. This takes two values and if they match each other then the answer is true. For example, comparing 1 and 1 would be true, comparing 2 and 2 would be true, comparing 3 and 4 would be false.

Let's compare two IP addresses, our current example (192.168.64.8) and 192.168.64.48. Both are using a subnet mask of 255.255.255.0.

We know that the first three octets of both these IP addresses, when converted to binary, are 11000000 10101000 01000000. Our first IP address's last octet is 00001000, and the second one would be 00110000:

128	64	32	16	8	4	2	1	
0	0	1	1	0	0	0	0	= 48

So now, we can compare the two. Write down the following numbers, leaving a two-line gap between the IP1 and IP2 lines:

```
IP1   1 1 0 0 0 0 0 0   1 0 1 0 1 0 0 0   0 1 0 0 0 0 0 0   0 0 0 0 1 0 0 0


IP2   1 1 0 0 0 0 0 0   1 0 1 0 1 0 0 0   0 1 0 0 0 0 0 0   0 0 1 1 0 0 0 0
```

Our subnet mask is 255.255.255.0. If we add up all our numbers (128+64+32+16+8+4+2+1) we get 255, so we can put 1's under all of our first three sets of numbers:

```
IP1   1 1 0 0 0 0 0 0   1 0 1 0 1 0 0 0   0 1 0 0 0 0 0 0   0 0 0 0 1 0 0 0
SN1   1 1 1 1 1 1 1 1   1 1 1 1 1 1 1 1   1 1 1 1 1 1 1 1

IP2   1 1 0 0 0 0 0 0   1 0 1 0 1 0 0 0   0 1 0 0 0 0 0 0   0 0 1 1 0 0 0 0
SN2   1 1 1 1 1 1 1 1   1 1 1 1 1 1 1 1   1 1 1 1 1 1 1 1
```

The 1's mean that we care about the matches between IP1 and IP2. So far, we match on all of our numbers. The final octet of our subnet mask is zero, so we can add this as well:

```
IP1   1 1 0 0 0 0 0 0   1 0 1 0 1 0 0 0   0 1 0 0 0 0 0 0   0 0 0 0 1 0 0 0
SN1   1 1 1 1 1 1 1 1   1 1 1 1 1 1 1 1   1 1 1 1 1 1 1 1   0 0 0 0 0 0 0 0

IP2   1 1 0 0 0 0 0 0   1 0 1 0 1 0 0 0   0 1 0 0 0 0 0 0   0 0 1 1 0 0 0 0
SN2   1 1 1 1 1 1 1 1   1 1 1 1 1 1 1 1   1 1 1 1 1 1 1 1   0 0 0 0 0 0 0 0
```

So now, we have entered all of our subnet in binary. The device (the router or switch that needs to do the calculation) cares about the numbers matching in the first three octets. The final octet of the subnet mask is a zero, meaning we don't care what comes next. The bitwise AND is then performed on the two subnet masks:

```
IP 1   1 1 0 0 0 0 0 0   1 0 1 0 1 0 0 0   0 1 0 0 0 0 0 0   0 0 0 0 1 0 0 0
SN 1   1 1 1 1 1 1 1 1   1 1 1 1 1 1 1 1   1 1 1 1 1 1 1 1   0 0 0 0 0 0 0 0
AND    1 1 0 0 0 0 0 0   1 0 1 0 1 0 0 0   0 1 0 0 0 0 0 0   0 0 0 0 0 0 0 0
IP 2   1 1 0 0 0 0 0 0   1 0 1 0 1 0 0 0   0 1 0 0 0 0 0 0   0 0 1 1 0 0 0 0
SN 2   1 1 1 1 1 1 1 1   1 1 1 1 1 1 1 1   1 1 1 1 1 1 1 1   0 0 0 0 0 0 0 0
AND    1 1 0 0 0 0 0 0   1 0 1 0 1 0 0 0   0 1 0 0 0 0 0 0   0 0 0 0 0 0 0 0
```

Both the AND values match so we know that these two IP addresses are within the same subnet.

Let's look at another couple of examples.

Is the host 10.16.8.2 in the same network as 10.16.28.3 if both have a subnet mask of 255.255.0.0?

Breaking the IP addresses down into binary, we have the following:

128	64	32	16	8	4	2	1	
0	0	0	0	1	0	1	0	= 10
0	0	0	1	0	0	0	0	= 16
0	0	0	0	1	0	0	0	= 8
0	0	0	0	0	0	1	0	= 2

As the first two octets are the same, we'll start from 28 for the second IP address:

128	64	32	16	8	4	2	1	
0	0	0	1	1	1	0	0	= 28
0	0	0	0	0	0	1	1	= 3

So our binary equivalents would be 00001010 00010000 00001000 00000010 and 00001010 00010000 00011100 00000011.

Now we write in our "do we care" 1's, and our "I don't care" 0's, and perform the AND:

IP 1	0 0 0 0 1 0 1 0	0 0 0 1 0 0 0 0	0 0 0 0 1 0 0 0	0 0 0 0 0 0 1 0
SN 1	1 1 1 1 1 1 1 1	1 1 1 1 1 1 1 1	0 0 0 0 0 0 0 0	0 0 0 0 0 0 0 0
AND	0 0 0 0 1 0 1 0	0 0 0 1 0 0 0 0	0 0 0 0 0 0 0 0	0 0 0 0 0 0 0 0
IP 2	0 0 0 0 1 0 1 0	0 0 0 1 0 0 0 0	0 0 0 0 1 1 0 0	0 0 0 0 0 0 1 1
SN 2	1 1 1 1 1 1 1 1	1 1 1 1 1 1 1 1	0 0 0 0 0 0 0 0	0 0 0 0 0 0 0 0
AND	0 0 0 0 1 0 1 0	0 0 0 1 0 0 0 0	0 0 0 0 0 0 0 0	0 0 0 0 0 0 0 0

Again the AND lines show that we have a match, therefore these two hosts are in the same subnet.

Let's try a different subnet. This time, keeping the same IP addresses, but the subnet mask is 255.255.240.0. 240 in binary is:

128	64	32	16	8	4	2	1	
1	1	1	1	0	0	0	0	= 240

Would we have a match now?

IP 1	0 0 0 0 1 0 1 0	0 0 0 1 0 0 0 0	0 0 0 0 1 0 0 0	0 0 0 0 0 0 1 0
SN 1	1 1 1 1 1 1 1 1	1 1 1 1 1 1 1 1	1 1 1 1 0 0 0 0	0 0 0 0 0 0 0 0
AND	0 0 0 0 1 0 1 0	0 0 0 1 0 0 0 0	0 0 0 0 0 0 0 0	0 0 0 0 0 0 0 0
IP 2	0 0 0 0 1 0 1 0	0 0 0 1 0 0 0 0	0 0 0 1 1 1 0 0	0 0 0 0 0 0 1 1
SN 2	1 1 1 1 1 1 1 1	1 1 1 1 1 1 1 1	1 1 1 1 0 0 0 0	0 0 0 0 0 0 0 0
AND	0 0 0 0 1 0 1 0	0 0 0 1 0 0 0 0	0 0 0 1 0 0 0 0	0 0 0 0 0 0 0 0

No, we do not. The fourth bit in the third octet (bolded) is not a match in the two AND values; therefore these two hosts are not in the same subnet.

There is a lot more that these numbers tell us. They also tell us the network ID we are in, and broadcast address for that network. Keeping with the same IP addresses above, we can work out the network subnet that both belong to.

Calculating subnet addresses (the hard way)

The subnet address tells us which network we belong to and how many other devices there can be in this subnet.

There are a couple of methods we can use to calculate the subnet address. If we already have worked out the binary AND we can use this. We just add up the numbers. For the first IP address the AND is 00001010 00010000 00000000 0000000. The second IP address's AND is 00001010 00010000 00010000 00000000.

Using our table, we can then put this into readable numbers. For the first IP address:

128	64	32	16	8	4	2	1	
0	0	0	0	1	0	1	0	= 10
0	0	0	1	0	0	0	0	= 16
0	0	0	0	0	0	0	0	= 0
0	0	0	0	0	0	0	0	= 0

And now the second IP address:

128	64	32	16	8	4	2	1	
0	0	0	0	1	0	1	0	= 10
0	0	0	1	0	0	0	0	= 16
0	0	0	1	0	0	0	0	= 16
0	0	0	0	0	0	0	0	= 0

This shows that the first IP address is on the 10.16.0.0 subnet, and the second is in the 10.16.16.0 subnet.

The next way is slightly harder, especially without the aid of a scientific calculator.

We take the subnet mask from our previous example (255.255.240.0) in its binary form and start counting the number of 0's from right to left. There are 12 of them.

1 1 1 1 1 1 1 1 1 1 1 1 1 1 1 1 1 1 1 1 0 0 0 0 0 0 0 0 0 0 0 0

We then need to take this 12 and do a power of 2. 2^12 gives us 4096.

$$2^{12} = 4096$$

4096 is the maximum number of hosts per subnet, meaning there is up to 4096 other devices (less two, which we will see in a moment) that we can communicate with, without needing to know about how to get to other networks. We will always do a power of 2 on the number of zeros we have, so for a class C subnet of 255.255.255.0, there would be 8 zeros, and we would do 2^8, which would give us 256, or if we were using a class B network of 255.255.0.0, there would be 16 zeros, so we would do 2^16, which equals 65536. The general formula is 2^h-2, where h is the number of host bits (12 in our case above). We then subtract 2 to get the number of hosts available. There is a table of these in Appendix B.

If we divide 4096 by 256 (the maximum number that an octet can add up to) we get 16.

$$4096 \div 256 = 16$$

We can have 16 subnets, each with 256 addresses contained within it, starting from subnet 0, within our network. Therefore, our subnet ID is 10.16.0.0 for the first IP address, and the range is from 10.16.0.0 to 10.16.15.255. The next range would be from 10.16.16.0 to 10.16.31.255, which is where our second IP is. If we had a third IP address of 10.16.35.2 (with the same 255.255.240.0 subnet mask), then this would live in the 10.16.32.0 subnet, and the range for which would be 10.16.32.0 to 10.16.47.254. This would be another way of confirming that the two IP addresses are not in the same subnet.

We always need to remember to subtract two from the final number of hosts per subnet, the first number will be our subnet ID (10.16.0.0), it identifies the subnet we are in and the last one (10.16.15.255) will be the broadcast address, which is unusable, as a broadcast address will never be the source address of any frame. So really, we get 4094 usable addresses.

From this we can make a number of subnetworks, we could have 16 networks, starting with subnet zero. They would, really, all be part of the same network though, as they use the same subnet mask:

	Subnet	Usable Range	Number of hosts
0	10.16.0.0	10.16.0.1 - 10.16.0.255	255
1	10.16.1.0	10.16.1.0 - 10.16.1.255	256
2	10.16.2.0	10.16.2.0 - 10.16.2.255	256
3	10.16.3.0	10.16.3.0 - 10.16.3.255	256
4	10.16.4.0	10.16.4.0 - 10.16.4.255	256
5	10.16.5.0	10.16.5.0 - 10.16.5.255	256
6	10.16.6.0	10.16.6.0 - 10.16.6.255	256
7	10.16.7.0	10.16.7.0 - 10.16.7.255	256
8	10.16.8.0	10.16.8.0 - 10.16.8.255	256
9	10.16.9.0	10.16.9.0 - 10.16.9.255	256
10	10.16.10.0	10.16.10.0 - 10.16.10.255	256
11	10.16.11.0	10.16.11.0 - 10.16.11.255	256
12	10.16.12.0	10.16.12.0 - 10.16.12.255	256
13	10.16.13.0	10.16.13.0 - 10.16.13.255	256
14	10.16.14.0	10.16.14.0 - 10.16.14.255	256
15	10.16.15.0	10.16.15.0 - 10.16.15.254	255
Total:			**4094**

Notice that only the first subnet starts with a one, as the zero is the network address and only the last one, subnet 15, has one removed for the broadcast address. This is only because the hosts would still be using the 255.255.240.0 subnet mask; in this case, the intermediate subnets can legitimately use .0 or .255 as the last octet in their IP address. We could use these subnets to further subdivide the network, and carve it up as we see fit, and we will get onto Variable Length Subnet Masks later.

Calculating subnet addresses (the easy way)

So, if we were asked to find out the broadcast address for a given subnet, how would we go about that? What if we were to say the IP address is 10.16.8.2/20?

When we refer to subnet masks, we refer to a prefix length. This is often written in the CIDR (Classless Inter-Domain routing) format, /8, /16, /24 or any valid number in between (refer to Appendix A for a list of the CIDR notations). We have already been through how to convert an IP address, or a subnet mask into binary and this is purely follow-on from that. We have used 255.255.240.0 for our previous examples and this can be expressed in CIDR notation just by adding up the number of 1's that we have:

```
1 1 1 1 1 1 1 1   1 1 1 1 1 1 1 1   1 1 1 1 0 0 0 0   0 0 0 0 0 0 0 0
8 + 8 + 4 = 20
```

Therefore in CIDR notation 255.255.240.0 becomes /20. Similarly a class A subnet mask of 255.0.0.0 becomes /8, a class B subnet of 255.255.0.0 becomes /16 and a class C subnet of 255.255.255.0 becomes /24.

Because we have 20 bits set to one in a /20 subnet this means that the third octet will add up to 240 (128+64=32+16) and we can subtract 240 from 256, giving us 16. Now we are back at counting in batches of 16; 0, 16, 32 and so on. Because 16 is our third octet, and as we know that the range of the fourth octet will be from 0 to 256. Starting at 0 we can go so far as 15.255 in the first subnet before we get into the next subnet. Therefore, 15.255 will be our broadcast address.

As you can see, this way seems much faster. Let's have a look at one more example, then we can move on.

What would the subnet ID, broadcast address, and usable range be for 176.34.92.15/26, and how many hosts could we have?

A /26 subnet would mean we have 26 bits out of a maximum of 32 used. Because it is greater than a /24 we immediately know that the first three octets of the subnet mask must all be 255.

$$1\ 1\ 1\ 1\ 1\ 1\ 1\ 1 \quad 1\ 1\ 1\ 1\ 1\ 1\ 1\ 1 \quad 1\ 1\ 1\ 1\ 1\ 1\ 1\ 1 \quad 1\ 1\ 0\ 0\ 0\ 0\ 0\ 0$$
$$8+8+8+2 = 26$$

We then just need to add 128 and 64 together, to get 192. These are the bits we care about in the last octet. Then we subtract them from 256, which gives us 64.

$$256 - 192 = 64$$

We can then work out how many subnets we have, starting at 0:

Subnet	Starts at	IP address range	Usable
0	0	176.34.92.0 - 176.34.92.63	62
1	64	176.34.92.64 - 176.34.92.127	62
2	128	176.34.92.128 - 176.34.92.191	62
3	192	176.34.92.192 - 176.34.92.255	62

Therefore, in our example of 176.34.92.15/26, the subnet ID would be 176.34.92.0. The broadcast address would be 176.34.92.63 and we have 62 addresses that we can assign to hosts.

I hope that you are still following along. Once you have done this a few times, it becomes much easier, and, generally, outside of an exam or interview, you'll probably never need to do this by hand again! There will also be more subnetting worksheets posted on the website. Let's move on.

3.1 Describe the operation and necessity of using private and public IP addresses for IPv4 addressing

As mentioned at the start of the chapter, IP addresses can be broken down into one of two categories, private and public. IP addresses are 32-bits in length, which gives us a maximum of 4,294,967,296 unique addresses (2^32). This may seem like a lot, but as of September 9th 2015, the population of China was at 1,371,980,000 and that of India was at 1,276,860,000. So really, there is not that many in all in comparison to the number of people who might need one. For this reason IPv4 addresses were split into private (RFC 1918) and public addresses. In September 2015, ARIN (The American Registry for Internet Numbers, who hand out IP addresses in the United States) ran out of IPv4 addresses completely (https://www.arin.net/resources/request/ipv4_countdown.html).

Public IPv4 addresses are now in extremely short supply; this has been a concern since the late 1980s. Let's face it, the Internet has been very popular and everyone wants to be on it. Originally, blocks of IP addresses were handed out without worrying about future depletion. Because of this we now have technologies such as Network Address Translation, where one or more private IP addresses are "translated" to one or more public IP addresses, and CIDR notation, which we spoke of earlier, which allows address blocks to be divided up amongst a number of different customers. The biggest change to come from this depletion of IPv4 addresses is IPv6.

3.2 Identify the appropriate IPv6 addressing scheme to satisfy addressing requirements in a LAN/WAN environment

An IPv6 address is 128-bits long. Far longer than an IPv4 address, meaning that we have many more addresses. So many in fact that organizations can have an entire /48 (2^80) address block assigned to them, which is actually greater than the total number of IPv4 addresses (2^32)! In fact there are in the region of 340 trillion trillion IPv6 addresses, which makes comparing the amount of IPv4 addresses to IPv6 addresses quite crazy.

IANA, the Internet Assigned Numbers Authority, hand out large address blocks to the RIRs, the Regional Internet Registries.

The RIRs are:

- AFRINIC (African Network Information Center) for Africa
- ARIN (American Registry for Internet Numbers) for the USA, Canada
- APNIC (Asia-Pacific Network Information Center) for Asia, Australia, New Zealand
- LACNIC (Latin America and Caribbean Network Information Center) for Latin America
- RIPE NCC (Réseaux IP Européens Network Coordination Center) for Europe, Russia, Middle East and Central Asia

Taking a typical /23 block, this can be broken down into 512 separate /32 blocks, which are then handed to the ISPs. The ISPs then divide this /32 block into 65536 /48 blocks, and then hand out these to customers. The customers can then create 65536 /64 blocks of networks and each of these /64 blocks still has more IPv6 addresses than then entire IPv4 address pool.

So, why do we have all these statistics? Well, when you start looking at how IPv6 addresses are designed, it can be a little off-putting, they look confusing, but the stats are designed to put your mind at rest and highlight why IPv6 is required.

Let's start by looking at an IPv6 address.

An IPv6 address consists of eight groups of four hexadecimal digits, separated by a colon (:). Each group represents sixteen bits, such as 2001:db8:AABB:0000:1234:5678:9000:0001. Similarly to IPv4 addresses, IPv6 addresses are classified into different groupings. We have unicast, multicast and anycast. These addresses will be explained in more detail in section 3.5. For the moment, we should concentrate on subnetting within IPv6.

Before we jump into this though, we should help ourselves a little. IPv6 addresses are long. I cannot fit two IPv6 addresses in one line, but thankfully, we can shorten them, albeit within certain constraints.

Let's take a commonly used example; 2001:db8::/32. This range is actually reserved for documentation, such is the luxury of using IPv6 that 79,228,162,514,264,337,593,543,950,336 addresses can be reserved just for us to talk about! Anyway, back to the point. IPv6 addresses are long, it takes time to write these out by hand, but there are ways in which we can shorten them, but only if they have multiple zeros in them.

We can shorten a block of zeros, by replacing them with a single zero. Taking our example above (2001:db8:AABB:<u>0000</u>:1234:5678:9000:0001), we have one continuous block of zeros in the fourth octet, so this can be replaced with a single zero, which gives us 2001:db8:AABB:<u>0</u>:1234:5678:9000:0001.

We can also remove the zeros at the start of an octet, such as the eighth octet, leaving us with just the one: 2001:db8:AABB:0:1234:5678:9000:<u>1</u>. This makes it a little easier for us. We cannot remove the trailing zeros in the seventh octet though, as this would be interpreted as 0009, instead of 9000.

If we have multiple octets that all have zeros, then we can remove these as well, but instead of replacing them with a single zero as we did above, they can be replaced with a double colon (::). If our IPv6 address had been 2001:db8:AABB:<u>0000:0000</u>:5678:9000:0001, then it could be written as 2001:db8:AABB<u>::</u>5678:9000:1. We can only do this once however. If we had the address 2001:db8:<u>0000:0000</u>:AABB:<u>0000:0000</u>:1001, then we could not write it as 2001:db8<u>::</u>AABB<u>::</u>1001, instead we would have to write it as 2001:db8<u>::</u>AABB:<u>0:0</u>:1001. So, wherever possible, use lots of zeros in your IPv6 addresses, as it will make them much easier to read! Now that we can make our addresses smaller and easier to read, let's look at what addresses we can use and where we can use them.

For this we will assume that we have been leased the address space 2001:ABCD::1234:0:0:0/48 (or to use the full address 2001:ABCD:0000:0000:1234:0000:0000:0000/48) by our ISP. With this subnet, we have the capacity to make 65,536 different /64 subnets. Our first would start at 2001:abcd::/64 and would end at 2001:abcd:0:ffff::/64, the next subnet would start at 2001:abcd:0:0001:ffff::/64, and so on right up to final subnet 2001:abcd:0001:ffff::/64. We are not short of addresses here, so we can afford to be less strict with IPv6 addresses than we would be with IPv4 addresses. There are, however, some guidelines.

Loopback interfaces

For loopback interfaces you should use /128 addresses. You could have several loopback interfaces, using IP addresses such as 2001:abcd::0001/128, 2001:abcd::0002/128 and so on. It is good practice to use single IP addresses for loopback addresses (such as 1.2.3.4/32 for IPv4, which is the same as 1.2.3.4 255.255.255.255) and if you ever configure MPLS, then this is actually a requirement for the underlying Label Distribution Protocol (LDP).

Point-to-point

Point-to-point interfaces should use /127 prefixes, which allows for two hosts, such as 2001:abdc::1234:0:0:2/127 and 2001:abdc::1234:0:0:3/127. This would be used between two hosts, such as a WAN link.

End-User LAN

A /64 subnet is generally considered ideal for an local area network, your hosts could have addresses such as 2001:abdc::1234:0:0:1/64, 2001:abdc::1234:0:0:2/64, 2001:abdc::1234:0:0:3/64 and so on (and now you can see why I wanted to shorten these addresses!).

A /64 is also a requirement of Auto-configuration, which we will talk about shortly.

End Sites

According to RFC 6177, a /56 subnet is recommended as the minimal end sites assignments, it used to be /48, but this is now for "larger" sites. From this /56 we can still make 256 /64 networks.

Larger sites

Larger end-sites can get a /48 subnet mask. From this they can make 65536 /64 networks.

The large number of addresses available in IPv6 means that we can be very generous with our address assignments, however the same cannot be done with IPv4 addresses.

3.3 Identify the appropriate IPv4 addressing scheme using VLSM and summarization to satisfy addressing requirements in a LAN/WAN environment

We have just seen that we can be a bit casual with IPv6 addresses, but we have to be a little stricter with IPv4 addresses.

Internally, within our own LAN, we can decide on any IP addressing scheme we desire, but networks are very fluid in their nature, in that they can, and do, change. Whilst they are still bound by the restrictions we place on them, they do still experience growth as business functions change, staffing levels increase and technologies change. This means that without proper planning an IP addressing scheme can either be wasteful (too many addresses being unused) or over-subscribed (not enough addresses for everyone).

So, what is the perfect answer to this? Well, without being able to see into the future, there is none. However, we can make an educated guess by looking at previous staff growth and by asking about future expansion plans. Generally, it is safe to estimate about 10% growth and to pick a subnet size large enough to accommodate this growth. So, what do we do if we need to implement restrictions, such as separation of users through VLANs? Do we add additional subnets; potentially wasting even more addresses, or make better use of the ones we have?

Assume, for the moment that we are looking at the IP addressing scheme for our LAN. In the previous chapter, we started to address our switches and hosts, but we did not go into the rationale of why we are using the addressing scheme that we are.

We gave the switches IP addresses of 10.1.1.1 for SW1, 10.1.1.2 for SW2 and so on. Dave-PC got the IP address 10.1.1.21. This is a class A private address range, but is using a custom /24 subnet mask (255.255.255.0). This gives us 254 addresses to use (remember that the first address, 10.1.1.0, is the network address, and the last address, 10.1.1.255, is the broadcast address). If I had stuck with the default subnet mask (/8, or 255.0.0.0), then we would have 16,777,216 addresses to use (well, less the network and broadcast addresses), which is far, far more than we need. Not only that, but what would happen when we needed to carve up our network to make way for the other VLANs? If we had used the default /8 subnet then we have used up all of the private class A network range, and would have to move to either the class B, or class C, and what then if, again, we use the default subnet masks? We would be facing the same shortage of usable ranges, due to the wasting of IP address space we have already allocated. This is why although we are using a class A range, we have used a class C subnet range. We have given ourselves room for expansion. We have subnetted a subnet and this process is referred to as Variable Length Subnet Masking (VLSM).

VLSM

VLSM allows us to carve up a network as we see fit. We can take a full 10.0.0.0/8 subnet, and divide it to suit our needs. Let's do this now, following a brief:

Hey,
Thanks for doing the network expansion. We need you to carve up our network as follows:

VLAN	Purpose	Users or Devices
1	Management	180
10	Main users	350
20	Servers	50
30	Bob	5
40	Printers	28
50	Guests	30

Thanks and have a good weekend!

How would we tackle this? Firstly, let's start by writing down what we need, with room to make notes:

VLAN	Purpose	Required	Network address	Usable addresses
1	Management	180		
10	Main users	350		
20	Servers	50		
30	Bob	5		
40	Printers	28		
50	Guests	30		

VLAN 1

We already have VLAN 1, which is using the 10.1.1.0/24 subnet, so we can keep using this for VLAN 1.

VLAN	Purpose	Required	Network address	Usable addresses
1	Management	180	10.1.1.0/24	256
10	Main users	350		
20	Servers	50		
30	Bob	5		
40	Printers	28		
50	Guests	30		

We cannot make this smaller, as a /25 subnet would only give us 126 usable addresses.

VLAN 10

The next logical subnet would be 10.1.2.0, but a /24 subnet is not large enough to accommodate VLAN 10, it would only offer 254 usable addresses and we need 350. To do this we are going to borrow a bit from the netmask, and use a /23 subnet (255.255.254.0), which gives us 512 addresses. This is plenty; it fulfils the brief and leaves us room for expansion.

The /23 subnet allows us to use the address range 10.1.2.0 – 10.1.3.255.

VLAN	Purpose	Required	Network address	Usable addresses
1	Management	180	10.1.1.0/24	256
10	Main users	350	10.1.2.0/23	512
20	Servers	50		
30	Bob	5		
40	Printers	28		
50	Guests	30		

VLAN 20

VLAN 20 needs 50 addresses. We need to start at 10.1.4.0, but how do we work out the number of host bits to use? The last one was easy; this one is a little more difficult.

We start with our usual set of numbers:

128 64 32 16 8 4 2 1

All we need to do is work our way from right to left, adding up until we get to the position that will give us enough hosts.

1+2 = 3
1+2+4 = 7
1+2+4+8 = 15
1+2+4+8+16 = 31
1+2+4+8+16+32 = 63

We can therefore use six host bits (1+2+4+8+16+32), which would give us 64 addresses, more than enough for the 50 that we require. This means that the network portion of the address is 26 bits long (8+8+8+2), therefore this is a /26 subnet, and the subnet mask would be 255.255.255.192.

VLAN	Purpose	Required	Network address	Usable addresses
1	Management	180	10.1.1.0/24	256
10	Main users	350	10.1.2.0/23	512
20	Servers	50	10.1.4.0/26	64
30	Bob	5		
40	Printers	28		
50	Guests	30		

VLAN 30

Bob needs five IP addresses, no one knows why, he's somewhat important though, so we'll let him have them. Our next subnet begins at 10.1.4.64, so let's see how many host bits we need:

$$1+2 = 3$$
$$1+2+4 = 7$$

We need three host bits, we have 29 network bits (8+8+8+5), which gives us exactly five usable addresses from our /29 subnet (255.255.255.248).

VLAN	Purpose	Required	Network address	Usable addresses
1	Management	180	10.1.1.0/24	254
10	Main users	350	10.1.2.0/23	510
20	Servers	50	10.1.4.0/26	62
30	Bob	5	10.1.4.64/29	5
40	Printers	28		
50	Guests	30		

VLAN 40

We have 28 printers and spend a fortune on laser toner. Our previous network range ends at 10.1.4.71, but this is not to say that with a different subnet mask our next range would start at 10.1.4.72. First, let's work out the subnet range we will need. Working in the same fashion as above:

$$1+2 = 3$$
$$1+2+4 = 7$$
$$1+2+4+8 = 15$$
$$1+2+4+8+16 = 31$$

We are using five bits for our host address, which leaves us with a netmask of 255.255.255.224, or a /27 (8+8+8+3). This gives us 30 usable addresses. However, if we started at 10.1.4.72, applying a /27 subnet would actually make our subnet assignment overlap with VLAN 30. Let's break out the pen and paper to work this out:

VLAN 30 has a subnet mask of 255.255.255.248. We can subtract 248 from 256, which gives us 8. 8 is therefore our "jump" number. We start at 64 as the first subnet (VLAN 20) ends at 10.1.4.63, and add 8, add 8 repeatedly until we have a nice set of numbers:

    64
    72
    80
    88
    96
    104

Now let's work it out using a /27, firstly finding the "jump" number:

    256-224 = 32

    64
    96
    128
    160

Therefore, we can see that our first /27 subnet would actually overlap with four /29 subnets. The point at which they "agree" is 96. Therefore our first /27 subnet needs to begin at 10.1.4.96:

VLAN	Purpose	Required	Network address	Usable addresses
1	Management	180	10.1.1.0/24	254
10	Main users	350	10.1.2.0/23	510
20	Servers	50	10.1.4.0/26	62
30	Bob	5	10.1.4.64/29	5
40	Printers	28	10.1.4.96/27	30
50	Guests	30		

VLAN 50

VLAN 50 is a bit easier, because we need the same number as VLAN 40. Our last network range (VLAN 40) will end at 10.1.4.127, so our next subnet will start at 10.1.4.128. We can use the same subnet mask as VLAN 40, which will give us exactly the 30 usable addresses that we need.

VLAN	Purpose	Required	Network address	Usable addresses
1	Management	180	10.1.1.0/24	254
10	Main users	350	10.1.2.0/23	510
20	Servers	50	10.1.4.0/26	62
30	Bob	5	10.1.4.64/29	5
40	Printers	28	10.1.4.96/27	30
50	Guests	30	10.1.4.128/27	30

We now have used Variable Length Subnet Masking to make best use of our available range; we also have scope for future growth. Whilst although I said that adding 10% to allow for growth was a good idea, I have worked above as you should do in the CCNA exam. So, just to reiterate, in the exam do what they ask for, if they ask for 30 addresses, give them 30, not 33. 33 would take you out of one subnet mask into a larger one, and you would waste addresses, and (more critically) lose points in the exam. Just give them 30. In real life, give yourself room for future growth; having to re-IP a network is never a fun task. Also, it is much easier to work starting with the largest number you need, and working downwards, so we would start with VLAN 10, then VLAN 1, then VLAN 20 and so on, as the examples in the downloads section of the website will show.

Part of the remit was to make sure that we still use the 10.0.0.0/8 subnet, as this is being advertised "upstream", meaning that the gateway router is (or at least will be once we set it up), advertising that particular network to the rest of the "world". This means that we are summarizing our six different networks into one and just advertising this one network, instead of six.

Summarization

There was a big worry in August 2014 that the Internet would fall over due to the amount of Internet routes (BGP routes) passing the 500,000 mark. 500,000 routes on Internet-carrier grade routers really do not seem like much, but it's all about the amount of memory available to the routers. The routers that run the Internet are big and full of very expensive technology. They are not the kind of equipment that can be swapped out easily, or cheaply. Because of this, many of the older routers had a limit on the number of routes they could store (500,000 strangely enough), which is pretty much the maximum their 4GB of memory can handle. A router with 8GB can handle about a million routes. On the actual day there were "issues", the Internet was a bit sluggish from time to time, but generally, it held up pretty well. For a good write up on the causes have a read of the BGPMon article: http://www.bgpmon.net/what-caused-todays-internet-hiccup/. Currently (October 3rd 2015) there are 564,798 IPv4 prefixes in the global BGP table, just over half of which are /24 (54.52%). By contrast there are 24,486 IPv6 prefixes, 45.24% are /48 prefixes. These stats came from @bgp4_table and @bgp6_table via Twitter, which offers a great way of tracking the growth of the Internet, or alternatively, a distinct lack of summarization.

Passing the 500,000 mark (the first time) caused a few issues, but nothing too major. It was actually caused by a failure to aggregate addresses by one of the major ISPs, an additional 15,000 prefixes were added to the BGP routing table, and disappeared a short while after. Summarization (which is the same as aggregation) keeps routing tables smaller. Smaller tables are quicker to read.

We have just developed a hierarchical addressing scheme for our network. A hierarchical addressing scheme allows us to reduce our routing table entries, and is much easier to manage and troubleshoot.

We can summarize our networks as the major 10.0.0.0/8 network, which is one routing entry instead of six. However, this is not the most efficient way. If we had other offices using addresses in the 10.x.x.x range, we would have issues in routing. Therefore, we should summarize a little more succinctly.

So, how would we do this?

Our used range is 10.1.1.0 to 10.1.4.159. We start by working out the network and host bits for the third octet:

```
128   64   32   16   8   4   2   1

1+2 = 3 (not enough)
1+2+4 = 7 (this works)
```

We need to borrow three bits from the network address to give us enough room for our used range. This means that we can have the following subnets:

10.1.0.0 – 10.1.0.255
10.1.1.0 – 10.1.1.255
10.1.2.0 – 10.1.2.255
10.1.3.0 – 10.1.3.255
10.1.4.0 – 10.1.4.255
10.1.5.0 – 10.1.5.255
10.1.6.0 – 10.1.6.255
10.1.7.0 – 10.1.7.255

Because we have borrowed three host bits, this leaves us with five network bits, giving us a netmask of 21 (8+8+5). The subnet for this would be 255.255.248.0 (128+64+32+16+8). Therefore, it would make sense to advertise this 10.1.0.0/21 subnet to the rest of the world, rather than the 10.0.0.0/8 as specified in the remit from the boss. This would be one of those times that you would go to them and suggest a change, pointing out (politely) that your suggestion would be better in the long run.

So, if you do start to run short on IPv4 addresses and are looking to move towards IPv6, how would you go about this? Thankfully, you can migrate from IPv4 to IPv6 with ease. There are a number of technologies available to accomplish this.

3.4 Describe the technological requirements for running IPv6 in conjunction with IPv4

Whilst the move from IPv4 to IPv6 is not an easy undertaking, there are a number of migration technologies designed to make the process smoother. There are three typical approaches for migration. These are dual-stack, tunnelling, or translations.

We can tunnel using IPv6-over-IPv4 (6to4), where IPv6 packets are encapsulated within IPv4 packets. The sending and receiving router must be configured as dual stack (which we will cover shortly), Teredo tunnelling where the hosts perform the tunnelling, again both must be dual stack, or Intra-Site Automatic Tunnel Addressing Protocol (ISATAP), where virtual links are used to connect two IPv6 islands together using boundary routers, which again need to be dual stack.

We then have the translation methods, such as NAT-PT, which performs translation between IPv4 and IPv6, but the focus for the CCNA is on dual stack technologies.

3.4.a dual stack

Dual stack entails running both IPv4 and IPv6 on the same router. It can therefore communicate with both IP versions. Only the devices that require access to both the IPv4 and IPv6 need to be dual stack, those devices that only need access to the one protocol (IPv4 or IPv6), need only run a single stack. An example of such a network might look like this:

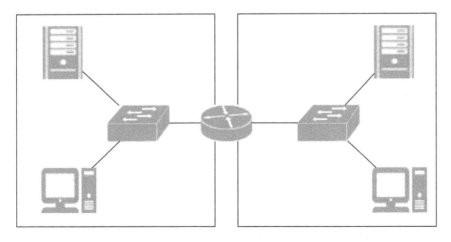

IPv4 Network   IPv6 Network

We will set up a few of our routers to be dual stack shortly, but before we do, we need to look at the type of IPv6 addresses we can actually assign.

3.5 Describe IPv6 addresses

3.5.a global unicast

Global addresses use the 2000::/3 prefix and are the IPv6 version of a public address. Because of the wealth of addresses, this may not always be the case and this range may be expanded, but it's certainly true for now.

Global addresses can be broken down into the 2000, the global routing prefix, the subnet ID and the interface ID.

Each address starts with 2000, this in hex is 0010000000000000 and this takes up 3 bits. Next, we have the global routing prefix (45 bits), which is the part of the address assigned to an organization. The subnet ID follows, which is 16 bits and is where you, as the network administrator, can start to apply some logic to your addressing scheme (such as hierarchical addressing, which we spoke about earlier). This accounts for 64-bits out of the 128-bit address and then we have the interface ID, which must be unique, accounting for the final 64-bits.

128-bits			
64-bits			64-bits
3-bits	45-bits	16-bits	64-bits
2000	Db8	subnet	Interface ID

3.5.b multicast

Multicast is used for a number of reasons, the most common purposes being to request an IP address through DHCP and for sending and receiving messages within an IGP (Internal Gateway Protocol). We haven't covered any of the IGPs yet, so we will look at IPv6 multicast addresses when we do that in the next chapter. IPv6 multicast addresses use the address space ff00::/8

3.5.c link local

We have two types of link-local addresses, ::1/128 and fe80::/10.

::1/128 is our loopback interface, used for testing. It is the IPv6 equivalent of 127.0.0.1/8.

The addresses in the fe80::/10 range are our link-local addresses. A link-local address is required on every IPv6-enabled interface; it allows a node to communicate with another node on the same link. This does not matter whether the interface even has an IPv6 address configured. If I type "ifconfig" in my Mac's terminal window, I can see that it has an IPv6 address of fe80::6aa8:6dff:fe0c:41f0:

```
en0: flags=8863<UP,BROADCAST,SMART,RUNNING,SIMPLEX,MULTICAST> mtu 1500
    ether 68:a8:6d:0c:41:f0
    inet6 fe80::6aa8:6dff:fe0c:41f0%en0 prefixlen 64 scopeid 0x4
```

You can see that the Mac's operating system has shortened the IPv6 address by removing joined blocks of zeros, replacing them with a double colon after the fe80.

The least significant bits (the bits at the end of the address) are taken from the MAC address of the interface (68:a8:6d:0c:41:f0) and is referred to as a "modified EUI-64" address. The 48-bit MAC address is broken in half, has FF:FE inserted into it in the middle of the third and fourth octets and this becomes our EUI-64 address: 6aa8:6dff:fe0c:41f0. We then put fe80: at the beginning, and fill in the missing characters with zeros. Notice, also, that the U/L bit is inverted. The "8" at the second position in my MAC address becomes an "a". This is because with the link-local address the U/L bit gets inverted. This is to make it easier when configuring the local scope identifiers (apparently).

The link-local address is (in the long, full, format) fe80:0000:0000:0000:6aa8:6dff:fe0c:41f0. However, we can shorten it, following the rules we spoke about in section 3.2. The purpose of this address is to make the machine know that it is IPv6 capable, it is closer to the IPv4 auto-configuration addresses (169.254.0.0/16) than to a loopback address, but its purpose is more to say, "Yes, I can do IPv6, you just haven't configured an address, so I'll use this one as a place-holder". This is a necessity, and every IPv6 interface must have a link-local address.

3.5.d unique local

Unique Local Addresses (ULAs) have been assigned the address space fc00::/7 and are broken down into two blocks. The first block fd00::/8 are for local communication and is a 40-bit random address, which generates a /48 address space. The second half, fc00::/8, is unallocated, but is the closest thing in the IPv6 world to the private IP addresses in IPv4.

3.5.e EUI-64

As we saw from the link-local address, the EUI-64 format interface ID is created from a 48-bit MAC address by inserting 0xFFFE between upper three bytes and the lower three bytes of the MAC address. The EUI-64 format is very handy, we can use it ourselves and it is used in IPv6 auto-configuration.

3.5.f auto-configuration

Whilst the thought of rolling out IPv6 strikes a fear of dread into the hearts of a large number of network engineers, there are many factors that can actually make it easier than one would expect. One of these is IPv6 autoconfiguration. IPv6 is actually fairly chatty, probably more so that IPv4 and this is due to the added ease of setting IPv6, such as auto-configuration.

Auto-configuration actually comes in two flavors; stateful and stateless. Stateful autoconfiguration uses DHCPv6 (the IPv6 version of DHCP), whereas stateless (also known as Stateless Address Autoconfiguration, or SLAAC) uses the Neighbor Discovery Protocol (NDP) and employs the EUI-64 address format. NDP performs several functions, including router discovery and duplicate address detection.

There are a number of steps that must be performed for the routers to get the auto-configuration IP address. Firstly, the devices must discover the default router. The host device (or router) sends out an initial Router Solicitation message (RS). This is sent to the all-IPv6-routers multicast address (FF02::2). This solicitation gets the IPv6-speaking routers to identify themselves to the first device. They respond with a Router Advertisement message (RA). The RA includes the link-local IPv6 address, the IPv6 address and prefix, and is sent either to the IPv6 unicast address of the host, or to the all-IPv6-hosts multicast address (FF02::1).

The address prefixes learned through the RS/RA messages are used by SLAAC to generate the first half of the new IPv6 address. The interface portion of the address is then generated using the EUI-64 format.

Before the final address is used, duplicate address detection (DAD) is performed. DAD uses another set of messages; the Neighbor Solicitation and Neighbor Advertisement. These act as ARP does in IPv4, the host uses neighbor solicitation to ask who has a particular address, and the neighbor advertisement answers this. The NS message is sent out and includes the address that the node wants to use in it, if no one responds with an NA message, then the host is safe to use that address.

Unspecified address ::/128

Think of this one as a placeholder. As a computer boots up, it will go through various phases before it's totally usable. One of these phases will be obtaining an IP (v4 or v6) address. This relies on a number of other components within the OS (Operating System) to have already started up. So, what happens while a machine is waiting for an IP address? Does it stop other services from starting up? What if it never gets an IP address, then the computer boot up would stall and the machine would be useless. No, instead a computer will continue to boot and periodically retry to get an IP address. If there are services that reside on that computer that are listening for network connections, they need an address to listen on. This is what the unspecified address is; it is a placeholder address. If we list the processes on the computer that are listening for connections and we see the ::/128 listed, then this is because it is listening on all interfaces for that service.

Default route ::/0

Default routes in IPv6 will be displayed as ::/0, we have seen the IPv4 counterpart way back in chapter one, and we will look at the IPv6 default route later in this chapter.

Documentation 2001:db8::/32

As we have already seen, because the IPv6 address space is so large there is a special block set aside for documentation purposes.

Site-local fec0::/10

This is now deprecated, meaning that it is no longer used. Its original purpose was to specify an address within an organizations site network. However, *site* was excessively ambiguous and instead we now use Unique Local Addresses instead.

Anycast addresses

Anycast addresses blew my mind when I first came across them. They seem to defy all the rules of never duplicating an address. With Anycast, groups are created and multiple devices in the group have the same address. When a request to that particular address is made it is routed to the nearest member of that group. This is known as a one-to-nearest communication model. Anycast can span the globe and a popular implementation of this is for DNS providers, where DNS requests are sent to the nearest server in the group.

Comparing IPv4 to IPv6, has there been a glaring omission? We have unicast, multicast, anycast, but not broadcast. In IPv6, there is no broadcast address equivalent to IPv4. This is supposedly one of the major bonuses for IPv6 (the other being auto-configuration), that Cisco recommends as a reason to adopt IPv6 instead of IPv4. In reality, such as decision on version adoption should not be made based on these two factors. Whilst we may struggle to get new addresses from providers, IPv4 certainly won't disappear for the next few years.

Configuring IPv6

Let's start doing some basic IPv6 address configuration now and see how we can enable some of our routers for IPv6, and how we can test connectivity. Let's start by seeing how far autoconfiguration gets us!

Starting with the router EIGRP1, we need to enable it for IPv6 routing. The command to do this is *"ipv6 unicast-routing"*:

```
EIGRP1(config)#ipv6 unicast-routing
EIGRP1(config)#
```

Then we use the command *"ipv6 address autoconfig"* to enable autoconfiguration:

```
EIGRP1(config)#int e0/1
EIGRP1(config-if)#no shutdown
EIGRP1(config-if)#ipv6 address autoconfig
EIGRP1(config-if)#
```

That's all we need to do! But what address has it given us? Let's find out:

```
EIGRP1(config-if)#do sh run int e0/1
Building configuration...

Current configuration : 69 bytes
!
interface Ethernet0/1
 no ip address
 ipv6 address autoconfig
end
EIGRP1(config-if)#
```

Nothing helpful there. Let's make life a little easier and switch back to privileged exec mode so we can enjoy the benefits of tab completion and the context-sensitive help:

```
EIGRP1(config-if)#end
EIGRP1#sh ipv6 int bri | s Ethernet0/1
Ethernet0/1          [up/up]
    FE80::A8BB:CCFF:FE00:1110
EIGRP1#
```

We have one IPv6 address listed; FE80::A8BB:CCFF:FE00:1110, which is a link-local address (recall that these start FE80).

We can also see the other addresses configured (if there are any) as well as any multicast groups we have joined using the command *"show ipv6 interface <interface>"*:

```
EIGRP1#sh ipv6 interface e0/1
Ethernet0/1 is up, line protocol is up
  IPv6 is enabled, link-local address is FE80::A8BB:CCFF:FE00:1110
  No Virtual link-local address(es):
  Stateless address autoconfig enabled
```

```
     No global unicast address is configured
     Joined group address(es):
       FF02::1
       FF02::2
       FF02::FB
       FF02::1:FF00:1110
     MTU is 1500 bytes
     ICMP error messages limited to one every 100 milliseconds
     ICMP redirects are enabled
     ICMP unreachables are sent
     ND DAD is enabled, number of DAD attempts: 1
     ND reachable time is 30000 milliseconds (using 25657)
     ND advertised reachable time is 0 (unspecified)
     ND advertised retransmit interval is 0 (unspecified)
     ND router advertisements are sent every 200 seconds
     ND router advertisements live for 1800 seconds
     ND advertised default router preference is Medium
     Hosts use stateless autoconfig for addresses.
   EIGRP1#
```

Let's see what happens when we configure the same commands on the ISP router:

```
   ISP(config)#ipv6 unicast-routing
   ISP(config)#int e0/1
   ISP(config-if)#ipv6 address autoconfig
   ISP(config-if)#no shut
   ISP(config-if)#
```

We now have IPv6 addresses on both routers:

```
   ISP(config-if)#do sh ipv6 int bri | s Ethernet0/1
   Ethernet0/1            [up/up]
       FE80::A8BB:CCFF:FE00:C10
   ISP(config-if)#do sh ipv6 int e0/1
   Ethernet0/1 is up, line protocol is up
     IPv6 is enabled, link-local address is FE80::A8BB:CCFF:FE00:C10
     No Virtual link-local address(es):
     Stateless address autoconfig enabled
     No global unicast address is configured
     Joined group address(es):
       FF02::1
       FF02::2
       FF02::FB
       FF02::1:FF00:C10
     MTU is 1500 bytes
     ICMP error messages limited to one every 100 milliseconds
     ICMP redirects are enabled
     ICMP unreachables are sent
```

```
    ND DAD is enabled, number of DAD attempts: 1
    ND reachable time is 30000 milliseconds (using 30000)
    ND advertised reachable time is 0 (unspecified)
    ND advertised retransmit interval is 0 (unspecified)
    ND router advertisements are sent every 200 seconds
    ND router advertisements live for 1800 seconds
    ND advertised default router preference is Medium
    Hosts use stateless autoconfig for addresses.
  ISP(config-if)#
```

Can we communicate between the two devices? We can:

```
  ISP(config-if)#do ping FE80::A8BB:CCFF:FE00:1110
  Output Interface: Ethernet0/1
  Type escape sequence to abort.
  Sending 5, 100-byte ICMP Echos to FE80::A8BB:CCFF:FE00:1110:
  Packet sent with a source address of FE80::A8BB:CCFF:FE00:C10%Ethernet0/1
  !!!!!
  Success rate is 100 percent (5/5)
  ISP(config-if)#
```

Note we need to specify the output interface (bolded) and that I have removed the timeout and the route-trip time statistics, this is just to make the output a little easier to read. Now we have two IPv6 addresses, let's just go back over why they have chosen the addresses that they have:

Router	Interface	MAC Address	IPv6 Address
EIGRP1	E0/1	aabb.cc00.1110	FE80::A8BB:CCFF:FE00:1110
ISP1	E0/1	aabb.cc00.0c10	FE80::A8BB:CCFF:FE00:C10

Firstly, both have FF:FE inserted between the third and fourth octets of the MAC address. Secondly both have the "a" at the second position has been replaced with an "8".

We have confirmed connectivity using the ping command, so far so good. Let's add the link between ISP and OSPF1 and see how things look:

```
  ISP(config-if)#int e1/1
  ISP(config-if)#ipv6 add autoconfig
  ISP(config-if)#no shut
  ISP(config-if)#

  OSPF1(config)#ipv6 unicast-routing
  OSPF1(config)#int e1/1
  OSPF1(config-if)#ipv6 address autoconfig
  OSPF1(config-if)#no shut
  OSPF1(config-if)#
```

Let's test connectivity, first by checking what address we have generated:

```
ISP(config-if)#do sh ipv6 int e1/1 | i :
  IPv6 is enabled, link-local address is FE80::A8BB:CCFF:FE00:C11
  No Virtual link-local address(es):
  Joined group address(es):
    FF02::1
    FF02::2
    FF02::FB
    FF02::1:FF00:C11
  ND DAD is enabled, number of DAD attempts: 1
ISP(config-if)#
```

Then we can test by pinging:

```
OSPF1(config-if)#do ping ipv6 FE80::A8BB:CCFF:FE00:C11
Output Interface: Ethernet1/1
Type escape sequence to abort.
Sending 5, 100-byte ICMP Echos to FE80::A8BB:CCFF:FE00:C11:
Packet sent with a source address of FE80::A8BB:CCFF:FE00:B11%Ethernet1/1
!!!!!
Success rate is 100 percent (5/5)
OSPF1(config-if)#
```

Again, we have success. What we won't be able to do is ping using IPv6 from OSPF1 to EIGRP1, the addresses we have are link-local, and therefore they are only usable between two links. Instead, we will need to use a different address. I am going to use the documentation range for this:

```
EIGRP1(config)#int e0/1
EIGRP1(config-if)#ipv6 address 2001:db8::/64 eui-64
EIGRP1(config-if)#

ISP(config-if)#int e0/1
ISP(config-if)#ipv6 add 2001:db8::/64 eui-64
ISP(config-if)#do sh run int e0/1 | b interface
interface Ethernet0/1
 mac-address aabb.cc00.0c10
 no ip address
 ipv6 address 2001:DB8::/64 eui-64
 ipv6 address autoconfig
end

ISP(config-if)#
%IPV6_ND-6-ADDRESS: 2001:DB8::/64 can not generate auto-configured
address on Ethernet0/1, 2001:DB8::A8BB:CCFF:FE00:C10 already configured
using a different method
ISP(config-if)#
```

Despite this warning, do we have connectivity between EIGRP1 and ISP?

```
ISP(config-if)#do sh ipv6 int bri | s Ethernet0/1
Ethernet0/1            [up/up]
    FE80::A8BB:CCFF:FE00:C10
    2001:DB8::A8BB:CCFF:FE00:C10
ISP(config-if)#
```

```
EIGRP1(config-if)#do ping ipv6 2001:DB8::A8BB:CCFF:FE00:C10
Type escape sequence to abort.
Sending 5, 100-byte ICMP Echos to 2001:DB8::A8BB:CCFF:FE00:C10:
!!!!!
Success rate is 100 percent (5/5)
EIGRP1(config-if)#
```

Yes, we do, and note that we are not asked to specify which interface we want to use. Let's try the other side:

```
OSPF1(config-if)#ipv6 add 2001:db8::/64 eui-64
OSPF1(config-if)#
```

```
ISP(config-if)#ipv6 add 2001:db8::/64 eui-64
%Ethernet1/1: Error: 2001:DB8::/64 is overlapping with 2001:DB8::/64 on
Ethernet0/1
ISP(config-if)#
```

This error does make sense, as the address space overlaps. As you can see, while autoconfiguration works well, its application is limited; it is not a scalable solution. Therefore, it makes sense to plan your IPv6 addresses, and this way you can have a fully functioning network.

Let's set this up properly now. First, we will remove our IPv6 addresses from our routers, and then check that all the addresses have been removed:

```
EIGRP1(config-if)#no ipv6 add
EIGRP1(config-if)#do sh ipv6 int bri | i :
EIGRP1(config-if)#
```

```
ISP(config-if)#no ipv6 add
ISP(config-if)#int e0/1
ISP(config-if)#no ipv6 add
ISP(config-if)#do sh ipv6 int bri | i :
ISP(config-if)#
```

```
OSPF1(config-if)#no ipv6 add
OSPF1(config-if)#do sh ipv6 int bri | i :
OSPF1(config-if)#
```

Let's set up some new addresses, giving ISP's e0/1 interface the IPv6 address 2001:db8:a1::1/64:

```
ISP(config-if)#ipv6 add 2001:db8:a1::1/64
ISP(config-if)#do sh ipv6 int bri | i :
    FE80::A8BB:CCFF:FE00:C10
    2001:DB8:A1::1
ISP(config-if)#
```

There are two ways we can configure an IPv6 address on EIGRP1. We can use autoconfiguration again, or we could use a specific address. We will use the autoconfiguration method for a moment:

```
EIGRP1(config-if)#ipv6 add auto
EIGRP1(config-if)#do sh ipv6 int bri | i :
    FE80::A8BB:CCFF:FE00:1110
    2001:DB8:A1:0:A8BB:CCFF:FE00:1110
EIGRP1(config-if)#
```

We have reachability:

```
EIGRP1(config-if)#do ping 2001:db8:a1::1
Type escape sequence to abort.
Sending 5, 100-byte ICMP Echos to 2001:DB8:A1::1:
!!!!!
Success rate is 100 percent (5/5)
EIGRP1(config-if)#
```

Let's set up the other side, using "planned" addresses (2001:db8:a2::/64):

```
ISP(config-if)#int e1/1
ISP(config-if)#ipv6 add 2001:db8:a2::1/64
ISP(config-if)#

OSPF1(config-if)#ipv6 add 2001:db8:a2::2/64
OSPF1(config-if)#
```

Next, we can test reachability:

```
OSPF1(config-if)#do ping ipv6 2001:db8:a2::1
Type escape sequence to abort.
Sending 5, 100-byte ICMP Echos to 2001:DB8:A2::1:
!!!!!
Success rate is 100 percent (5/5)
OSPF1(config-if)#
```

With our current setup, EIGRP1 and OSPF1 can both reach the ISP router, which is half of our goal (the other half being that they can reach each other). So, why would you use one method over another?

The second way offered us a greater level of control, but on a large-scale rollout, it would be more time consuming. The first option would be far more suited to a large-scale deployment, allowing you to have a template configuration (in a text document) that you can cut and paste into the router. The network could be configured much faster, apart from the odd device or two that require an easy to remember address (DNS servers, gateway routers and so on). Both strategies will though, work very well. Are there any other issues with one method over another? Have a look at the IPv6 routing table. Remember that EIGRP1 is using autoconfiguration:

```
EIGRP1(config-if)#do sh ipv6 route
IPv6 Routing Table - default - 3 entries
Codes: C - Connected, L - Local, S - Static, U - Per-user Static route
       B - BGP, HA - Home Agent, MR - Mobile Router, R - RIP
       H - NHRP, I1 - ISIS L1, I2 - ISIS L2, IA - ISIS interarea
       IS - ISIS summary, D - EIGRP, EX - EIGRP external, NM - NEMO
       ND - ND Default, NDp - ND Prefix, DCE - Destination, NDr - Redirect
       O - OSPF Intra, OI - OSPF Inter, OE1 - OSPF ext 1, OE2 - OSPF ext 2
       ON1 - OSPF NSSA ext 1, ON2 - OSPF NSSA ext 2, la - LISP alt
       lr - LISP site-registrations, ld - LISP dyn-eid, a - Application
NDp 2001:DB8:A1::/64 [2/0]
      via Ethernet0/1, directly connected
L    2001:DB8:A1:0:A8BB:CCFF:FE00:1110/128 [0/0]
      via Ethernet0/1, receive
L    FF00::/8 [0/0]
      via Null0, receive
EIGRP1(config-if)#

OSPF1(config-if)#do sh ipv6 route
IPv6 Routing Table - default - 3 entries
Codes: C - Connected, L - Local, S - Static, U - Per-user Static route
       B - BGP, R - RIP, H - NHRP, I1 - ISIS L1
       I2 - ISIS L2, IA - ISIS interarea, IS - ISIS summary, D - EIGRP
       EX - EIGRP external, ND - ND Default, NDp - ND Prefix, DCE - Destination
       NDr - Redirect, O - OSPF Intra, OI - OSPF Inter, OE1 - OSPF ext 1
       OE2 - OSPF ext 2, ON1 - OSPF NSSA ext 1, ON2 - OSPF NSSA ext 2, l - LISP
C    2001:DB8:A2::/64 [0/0]
      via Ethernet1/1, directly connected
L    2001:DB8:A2::2/128 [0/0]
      via Ethernet1/1, receive
L    FF00::/8 [0/0]
      via Null0, receive
OSPF1(config-if)#
```

The first entry differs. EIGRP1 has NDp, whereas OSPF1 has C. NDp (from the codes above) means ND Prefix, and C stands for connected. Both look similar and are correct for the device, it just means that EIGRP1 has learnt the route via the neighbor discovery protocol.

So, do you want to see something cool? Of course you do. The books say that you must start off by using the command "*ipv6 unicast-routing*" in order to enable the router for IPv6, well, that's not quite correct in real-life. In the exam if you are prompted with either a question saying to outline the steps needed to implement IPv6 on a router, or a question asking why IPv6 isn't working, then yes, you need to include this as step number one, or the answer is to "enable IPv6 globally". Nevertheless, we can actually help ourselves here, and remove this command:.

```
EIGRP1(config-if)#no ipv6 unicast
EIGRP1(config)#do sh run int e0/1 | b interface
interface Ethernet0/1
 no ip address
 ipv6 address autoconfig
end

EIGRP1(config)#
```

We still have our IPv6 address command under the interface and we still have an address:

```
EIGRP1(config)#do sh ipv6 int bri | s Ethernet0/1
Ethernet0/1            [up/up]
    FE80::A8BB:CCFF:FE00:1110
    2001:DB8:A1:0:A8BB:CCFF:FE00:1110
EIGRP1(config)#
```

What have we lost? Nothing. What have we gained? Everything:

```
EIGRP1(config)#do sh ipv6 route | b /
ND  ::/0 [2/0]
     via FE80::A8BB:CCFF:FE00:C10, Ethernet0/1
NDp 2001:DB8:A1::/64 [2/0]
     via Ethernet0/1, directly connected
L   2001:DB8:A1:0:A8BB:CCFF:FE00:1110/128 [0/0]
     via Ethernet0/1, receive
L   FF00::/8 [0/0]
     via Null0, receive
EIGRP1(config)#
```

We have gained a default route (::/0) through the link local address of the ISP router. If we do the same on OSPF1, we gain the same route and get the end-to-end connectivity between OSPF1 and EIGRP1 that we would hope for:

```
OSPF1(config-if)#no ipv6 unicast
OSPF1(config)#
OSPF1(config)#do sh ipv6 route | b /
ND  ::/0 [2/0]
     via FE80::A8BB:CCFF:FE00:C11, Ethernet1/1
C   2001:DB8:A2::/64 [0/0]
     via Ethernet1/1, directly connected
```

```
L   2001:DB8:A2::2/128 [0/0]
      via Ethernet1/1, receive
L   FF00::/8 [0/0]
      via Null0, receive
OSPF1(config)#

EIGRP1#ping 2001:db8:a2::2
Type escape sequence to abort.
Sending 5, 100-byte ICMP Echos to 2001:DB8:A2::2:
!!!!!
Success rate is 100 percent (5/5)
EIGRP1#
```

If we put the command back in on OSPF1 we lose this default route:

```
OSPF1(config)#ipv6 unicast-routing
OSPF1(config)#do sh ipv6 route | b /
C   2001:DB8:A2::/64 [0/0]
      via Ethernet1/1, directly connected
L   2001:DB8:A2::2/128 [0/0]
      via Ethernet1/1, receive
L   FF00::/8 [0/0]
      via Null0, receive
OSPF1(config)#
```

In order to get the end-to-end connectivity working again we need to add a static IPv6 route (we'll cover what a static route is in the next chapter):

```
OSPF1(config)#ipv6 route ::/0 2001:db8:a2::1
OSPF1(config)#do sh ipv6 route | b /
S   ::/0 [1/0]
      via 2001:DB8:A2::1
C   2001:DB8:A2::/64 [0/0]
      via Ethernet1/1, directly connected
L   2001:DB8:A2::2/128 [0/0]
      via Ethernet1/1, receive
L   FF00::/8 [0/0]
      via Null0, receive
OSPF1(config)#

EIGRP1#ping 2001:db8:a2::2
Type escape sequence to abort.
Sending 5, 100-byte ICMP Echos to 2001:DB8:A2::2:
!!!!!
Success rate is 100 percent (5/5)
EIGRP1#
```

We have end-to-end connectivity again.

In the next chapter, we will look at default routes, static routes and the fun bit: dynamic routing.

4. IP Routing Technologies

This is going to be a fun chapter. It will also be a long chapter. We have a lot to cover, but by the end of it, we should have a complete network, encompassing our LAN and our WAN. This chapter accounts for 20% of the exam weighting. The good thing about this chapter is that we have already covered some of the areas in chapter two when we looked at switching.

Our focus for this chapter will be on routing. This is how packets get from one network to another. So far, we have been looking at switching within a LAN, now we want access to the outside world.

4.1 Describe basic routing concepts

Routers are designed to forward packets. They receive a packet on one interface and need to make a decision as to where to forward it.

4.1.a packet forwarding

We are not concerned with MAC addresses now, just IP addresses. We have already seen, from the previous chapter, how an IP address and subnet mask pairing can influence what packets are local and which are destined for remote networks, but now we will look at how these decisions are made by the router.

We looked at (in chapter one) a basic routing table and in a moment, we will actually create this routing table. This table is consulted every time the router needs to make a forwarding decision. We have some IP addresses that are local to the router; the ones configured on the router's interfaces. These can be assigned to physical interfaces, such as our Ethernet or serial interfaces, or they can be assigned to a virtual interface, such as the VLAN virtual interface, we configured in chapter two. There are also loopback interfaces, which are virtual interfaces and these can be used for testing, or providing a fixed point for other routers to connect to, as they offer more stability in a network that has multiple paths. We will cover loopback interfaces later in this chapter.

Packet forwarding is simply the process of sending a packet from A to B, though there can be a number of devices, such as routers along the way. The important aspect of this is the routing table, which is used in the router lookup process.

4.1.b router lookup process

Much like a switch creates an ARP cache of MAC addresses in order to correctly send frames from one node to another; a router also needs to know where to send packets. It does this through a routing table.

Routing is all about selecting the best path to send a packet. We use a routing table to keep a list of available routes and from this we select the best path to a particular destination network.

Routing tables, which are known as the RIB or Routing Information Base, can be anything from a single line (send all traffic to this next-hop router), to a couple of lines, or even thousands of lines. Each of these lines is known as a route.

Each route has a metric and this is used to select the best path if two (or more) routes exist pointing to the same destination. The first of these we will look at is Administrative Distance (AD). Whilst this is not a true "metric", it is the one we will become most familiar with. We will discuss this in greater detail in section 4.6.f, but for the moment the AD and other metrics are designed to prioritize the routing table, ordering the routes in it from most believable (the best option we have for sending traffic and getting it there), to least believable (most likely to disappear somewhere along the route).

We will start with a quick example, which will become clearer as we move forward.

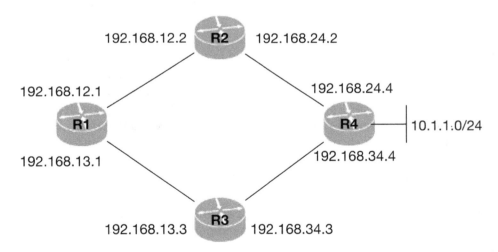

Above we have a host (R1), who wants to send a packet to Server1, which is in the 10.1.1.0/24 network. R1 connects to R2 and R3. R2 and R3 both connect to R4, which is where the 10.1.1.0/24 network is. R1 has two possible routes to send traffic to Server1. It knows about the 10.0.0.0/8 network (learned through RIP) as well as the 10.1.1.0/24 network (learned through EIGRP). One route will go via R2, the other via R3, and these are shown in bold:

```
R1#sh ip route | b Gate
Gateway of last resort is not set

      10.0.0.0/8 is variably subnetted, 2 subnets, 2 masks
R        10.0.0.0/8 [120/2] via 192.168.12.2, 00:00:02, Eth0/0
D        10.1.1.0/24 [90/435200] via 192.168.13.3, 00:00:21, Eth0/1
      192.168.12.0/24 is variably subnetted, 2 subnets, 2 masks
C        192.168.12.0/24 is directly connected, Ethernet0/0
L        192.168.12.1/32 is directly connected, Ethernet0/0
      192.168.13.0/24 is variably subnetted, 2 subnets, 2 masks
C        192.168.13.0/24 is directly connected, Ethernet0/1
L        192.168.13.1/32 is directly connected, Ethernet0/1
R     192.168.24.0/24 [120/1] via 192.168.12.2, 00:00:02, Ethernet0/0
D     192.168.34.0/24 [90/307200] via 192.168.13.3, 00:00:21, Eth0/1
R1#
```

Which route will R1 choose?

When we have multiple routes, the longest match will always win. We read the IP address from left to right and the routing entry chosen will be the one that matches the closest. In the above example, we have two routes and the longest match will be the route taken (via R3).

We can confirm this using traceroute:

```
R1#trace 10.1.1.1 n
Type escape sequence to abort.
Tracing the route to 10.1.1.1
VRF info: (vrf in name/id, vrf out name/id)
  1 192.168.13.3 0 msec 5 msec 0 msec
  2 192.168.34.4 1 msec *  0 msec
R1#
```

If you are ahead of the game and thinking that the administrative distance (AD) is the deciding factor here, not the longest match, then we can change the AD and get the same result:

```
R1#sh ip route | b Gate
Gateway of last resort is not set

      10.0.0.0/8 is variably subnetted, 2 subnets, 2 masks
R        10.0.0.0/8 [120/2] via 192.168.12.2, 00:00:12, Ethernet0/0
D        10.1.1.0/24 [120/435200] via 192.168.13.3, 00:00:01, Eth0/1
      192.168.12.0/24 is variably subnetted, 2 subnets, 2 masks
C        192.168.12.0/24 is directly connected, Ethernet0/0
L        192.168.12.1/32 is directly connected, Ethernet0/0
      192.168.13.0/24 is variably subnetted, 2 subnets, 2 masks
C        192.168.13.0/24 is directly connected, Ethernet0/1
L        192.168.13.1/32 is directly connected, Ethernet0/1
```

```
R       192.168.24.0/24 [120/1] via 192.168.12.2, 00:00:12, Ethernet0/0
D       192.168.34.0/24 [120/307200] via 192.168.13.3, 00:00:01, Eth0/1
R1#
```

If we perform the same traceroute, we see that it takes exactly the same path as before, preferring the longest match in the routing table:

```
R1#trace 10.1.1.1 n
Type escape sequence to abort.
Tracing the route to 10.1.1.1
VRF info: (vrf in name/id, vrf out name/id)
  1 192.168.13.3 4 msec 5 msec 4 msec
  2 192.168.34.4 1 msec *  1 msec
R1#
```

We will look into Administrative Distances in later in the chapter, but for now let's look at the actual mechanics behind how the packets move.

4.1.c Process Switching/Fast Switching/CEF

Process switching is the oldest and slowest method. When packets are sent, they trigger a process within the system called an interrupt (kind of like when someone catches your attention and you then need to listen to what they are saying). The interrupt handler identifies the protocol by using the EtherType in the packet and places the packet in a queue. When the packet is in the queue, it is scheduled for delivery. The IOS performs a context switch to the packet forwarding process. This reads the next entry in the input queue, looking at the destination address and sends the packet to the relevant output interface. The problem with this method is that it does incur very high CPU usage on the device.

Fast switching speeds things up (as the name suggests) by only process switching the first packet, subsequent packets are sent by using cached information. This cache contains the IP next hop, outgoing interface and outbound layer-2 header. If the destination address is not found then packet is moved down to the input process, which does a full destination address lookup and stores the result in the fast switching cache. This works much better than process switching, generally - it certainly does with smaller routing tables, but where there are 1000s of routes, as there are in many routers belonging to ISPs, the routers could crash due to all the packets being punted down to process switching. The command "*ip route-cache*" enables fast switching.

CEF is a Cisco proprietary technology; it stands for Cisco Express Forwarding. CEF uses another table, the FIB, or Forwarding Information Base. With CEF the RIB is copied into the FIB, there is no need to punt packets down to different processes, and the process is fast (again, hence the name). If the entry is not in the CEF table (another name for the FIB), then it simply does not exist.

4.2 Configure and verify utilizing the CLI to set basic Router configuration

We have already been through a large part of this section back in chapter two, but we will cover this again though so we can solidify the knowledge. There are also a couple of new bits.

4.2.a hostname

We set the hostname for our benefit more than anyone else's; it is certainly beneficial when we need to map out a network. Setting the hostname on a Cisco IOS router is no different to how we set it on our switches. We are using the same IOS software, and there are only a few differences between the software image used by a router and that used by a switch.

We will go through all of our routers, setting the hostnames. For each of the routers, right click on it and select start, connect to the console, then name them in the same way we did in chapter two. I have shown the full sequence of steps for the EIGRP routers, but am only showing the hostname command for the rest of the routers. I have not included the Frame-Relay routers now, as we will not need them until later on:

```
Router>en
Router#conf t
Enter configuration commands, one per line.  End with CNTL/Z.
Router(config)#hostname EIGRP1
EIGRP1(config)#

Router>en
Router#conf t
Enter configuration commands, one per line.  End with CNTL/Z.
Router(config)#hostname EIGRP2
EIGRP2(config)#

Router>en
Router#conf t
Enter configuration commands, one per line.  End with CNTL/Z.
Router(config)#hostname EIGRP3
EIGRP3(config)#

Router>en
Router#conf t
Enter configuration commands, one per line.  End with CNTL/Z.
Router(config)#hostname EIGRP4
EIGRP4(config)#
```

```
Router>en
Router#conf t
Enter configuration commands, one per line.  End with CNTL/Z.
Router(config)#hostname EIGRP5
EIGRP5(config)#

Router(config)#ho ISP

Router(config)#ho OSPF1

Router(config)#ho OSPF0

Router(config)#ho OSPF2

Router(config)#ho OSPF3

Router(config)#ho Gateway

Router(config)#ho Internet
```

Now that we can easily identify which router we are currently using, let's make sure that we can log into them.

4.2.b local user and password

For our routers we will create just the one administrative account. This account will be called "admin" and the password will be "cisco".

Because the configuration steps will be the same on each of the routers, it would make sense to write the commands in notepad, or a similar text editor, and then paste them into the routers. Open a text editor and type the following:

```
username admin password cisco
```

> Watch out for the editor doing auto-capitalization of the first word. Some text editors do, some don't.
>
> Cisco IOS is case-sensitive, and capitalized words will cause an error.

Now paste this into each of the routers:

```
EIGRP1(config)#username admin password cisco
EIGRP1(config)#
```

```
EIGRP2(config)#username admin password cisco
EIGRP2(config)#

EIGRP3(config)#username admin password cisco
EIGRP3(config)#

EIGRP4(config)#username admin password cisco
EIGRP4(config)#

EIGRP5(config)#username admin password cisco
EIGRP5(config)#

ISP(config)#username admin password cisco
ISP(config)#

OSPF1(config)#username admin password cisco
OSPF1(config)#

OSPF0(config)#username admin password cisco
OSPF0(config)#

OSPF2(config)#username admin password cisco
OSPF2(config)#

OSPF3(config)#username admin password cisco
OSPF3(config)#

Gateway(config)#username admin password cisco
Gateway(config)#

Internet(config)#username admin password cisco
Internet(config)#
```

4.2.c enable secret password

For all of the routers we will set an enable secret password of "cisco", so open notepad again and type in "enable secret cisco", then copy it and paste it into <u>all</u> of the routers. I am not going to show it for all of the routers, but here are a couple:

```
EIGRP1(config)#enable secret cisco
EIGRP1(config)#

OSPF1(config)#enable secret cisco
OSPF1(config)#
```

By now, I am sure you get the idea of what we are doing. Using notepad (or similar) is a great way of speeding up repetitive tasks. So much so that we can complete the next three topics in one hit.

4.2.d console & VTY logins
4.2.e exec-timeout
4.2.f service password encryption

Let's do these three in one go; it makes sense, as there is no variation in the commands. So, in your trusty notepad, type in the following:

```
line con 0
exec-timeout 0 0
line vty 0 4
exec-timeout 0 0
login local
service password-encryption
```

Now paste it into <u>all</u> of the routers. I have shown the commands being entered on EIGRP1.

```
EIGRP1(config)#line con 0
EIGRP1(config-line)#exec-timeout 0 0
EIGRP1(config-line)#line vty 0 4
EIGRP1(config-line)#exec-timeout 0 0
EIGRP1(config-line)#login local
EIGRP1(config-line)#service password-encryption
EIGRP1(config)#
```

Now that all of our routers are correctly named, have a user, and are set up as we need them to be, we can start to give them addresses and form the foundation of our wide area network.

4.2.g interface IP Address

Here is where we cannot use notepad anymore. Each router will need to be assigned one or more IP addresses. We will need an IP address configured on each connected interface and on any loopback interfaces we have, such as the one that will be on the Internet router at the top of our topology.

I will do a few of the configurations, the others you will need to do on your own. We will be using a table to work through.

Router	Int	IP address	Mask	No sh	Description	Complete
EIGRP1	S2/0	192.168.51.1	/24	☐	Link to EIGRP5	☐
EIGRP1	E0/1	192.168.1.2	/24	☐	Link to ISP	☐
EIGRP1	E1/2	192.168.21.1	/24	☐	Link to EIGRP2	☐
EIGRP2	E2/1	192.168.21.2	/24	☐	Link to EIGRP1	☐
EIGRP2	E2/3	192.168.32.2	/24	☐	Link to EIGRP3	☐
EIGRP3	E3/2	192.168.32.3	/24	☐	Link to EIGRP2	☐
EIGRP3	E0/1	192.168.43.3	/24	☐	Link to EIGRP4	☐
EIGRP4	E0/1	192.168.43.4	/24	☐	Link to EIGRP3	☐
EIGRP4	S1/1	192.168.54.4	/24	☐	Link to EIGRP5	☐
EIGRP5	S1/1	192.168.54.5	/24	☐	Link to EIGRP4	☐
EIGRP5	S1/0	192.168.51.5	/24	☐	Link to EIGRP1	☐
ISP	E0/0	192.168.20.1	/24	☐	Link to Gateway	☐
ISP	E0/1	192.168.1.1	/24	☐	Link to EIGRP1	☐
ISP	E1/1	172.16.1.1	/24	☐	Link to OSPF1	☐
ISP	E0/2	192.168.30.1	/24	☐	Link to Internet	☐
OSPF1	E1/1	172.16.1.2	/24	☐	Link to ISP	☐
OSPF1	E1/0	172.16.2.2	/24	☐	Link to OSPF0	☐
OSPF0	E0/1	172.16.2.1	/24	☐	Link to OSPF1	☐
OSPF0	E0/2	172.16.3.1	/24	☐	Link to OSPF2	☐
OSPF2	E2/0	172.16.3.2	/24	☐	Link to OSPF0	☐
OSPF2	E2/3	172.16.4.2	/24	☐	Link to OSPF3	☐
OSPF3	E3/2	172.16.4.3	/24	☐	Link to OSPF2	☐
Internet	E0/2	192.168.30.254	/24	☐	Link to ISP	☐
Gateway	E0/0	192.168.20.254	/24	☐	Link to ISP	☐
Gateway	E0/1	10.1.1.254	/24	☐	Link to SW1	☐
Gateway	E0/2	10.20.1.254	/24	☐	Link to SW2	☐

This table is also available as a PDF on the website in the download section, so that you can print it off and tick off the entries when you have completed each line.

Let's discuss the numbering for a moment. Because this is our topology, we can be a bit ordered about it. When you have someone else's network, then the numbering can be all over the place, it might make sense to them but not to others. At some stage you will have to explain your network to someone else, so try to make it as easy as you can when numbering devices.

Most of our network hinges around the ISP router. So that uses .1 for the last octet of all of its IP addresses. It's easy to remember. The Gateway and Internet routers use the last available IP in the range (.254) for their physical connections. Now we have two easy to remember IP numbering methods; using the first and last IP addresses in a range.

Where possible I have tried to make the interface and IP address used make sense. So from EIGRP3 to EIGRP2 we use e3/2 on EIGRP3 and e2/3 on EIGRP2. The IP address uses a similar scheme with the third octet using the highest router number and lowest router number. Therefore, the link between EIGRP3 and EIGRP2 uses the network 192.168.**32**.0/24. The final octet is the same as the router number, so for EIGRP2 we end up with an IP address of 192.168.32.2.

Moving over to the OSPF side of the network, we use a simpler method for the choice of interface, but for the IP address we are just incrementing the third octet. OSPF0 uses .1 for both of its IP addresses, we could not use .0, as that is a network address (therefore unusable for addressing on a device). OSPF2 and OSPF3 do use the method of addressing by name; OSPF2 uses .2 as its last octet, and OSPF3 uses .3 as its last octet.

By numbering them this way the most important devices (ISP, Gateway, Internet, OSPF0) all have an easy to remember IP address, by either using the first address in the range, or the last address in the range.

Below are some configurations for EIGRP1, ISP and OSPF1, as these have been referenced earlier in the book (in Chapter 1).

```
EIGRP1(config)#int s2/0
EIGRP1(config-if)#ip address 192.168.51.1 255.255.255.0
EIGRP1(config-if)#no shut
EIGRP1(config-if)#description Link to EIGRP5
EIGRP1(config-if)#exit
EIGRP1(config)#int e0/1
EIGRP1(config-if)#ip address 192.168.1.2 255.255.255.0
EIGRP1(config-if)#no shut
EIGRP1(config-if)#description Link to ISP
EIGRP1(config-if)#exit
EIGRP1(config)#int e1/2
EIGRP1(config-if)#ip address 192.168.21.1 255.255.255.0
EIGRP1(config-if)#no shut
EIGRP1(config-if)#description Link to EIGRP2
EIGRP1(config-if)#

ISP(config)#int e0/0
ISP(config-if)#ip address 192.168.20.1 255.255.255.0
ISP(config-if)#no shut
ISP(config-if)#description Link to Gateway
ISP(config-if)#int e0/1
ISP(config-if)#ip address 192.168.1.1 255.255.255.0
ISP(config-if)#no shut
ISP(config-if)#desc Link to EIGRP1
ISP(config-if)#int e1/1
ISP(config-if)#ip address 172.16.1.1 255.255.255.0
ISP(config-if)#no shut
```

```
ISP(config-if)#desc Link to OSPF1
ISP(config-if)#int e0/2
ISP(config-if)#ip add 192.168.30.1 255.255.255.0
ISP(config-if)#no shut
ISP(config-if)#desc Link to Internet
ISP(config-if)#

OSPF1(config)#int e1/1
OSPF1(config-if)#ip address 172.16.1.2 255.255.255.0
OSPF1(config-if)#no shut
OSPF1(config-if)#desc Link to ISP
OSPF1(config-if)#int e1/0
OSPF1(config-if)#ip add 172.16.2.2 255.255.255.0
OSPF1(config-if)#no shut
OSPF1(config-if)#desc Link to OSPF0
OSPF1(config-if)#
```

Now you can go through and set up the other routers!

4.2.g (i) loopback

Loopback interfaces are extremely useful, for a number of reasons. We can use them as the base IP for services. Because they do not belong to any one interface, they are always available, unless you purposefully shut them down. Many of the IGPs will use the addresses we assign to loopback interfaces as their router-id, for this exact reason. We will see this later on.

We can also set services up to listen and answer on their loopback interfaces, and they can be used to "fake" services, such as the test internet address of 8.8.8.8 we will assign to the Internet router.

To create a loopback interface we use the command "*interface loopback <number>*", assigning a number to it. We can have a large number of loopback interfaces, the Internet router will support 2,147,483,647 loopback addresses, as shown below. I have never seen a router running this many loopback interfaces though and cannot see a reason to do so, unless you want to replicate the entire internet routing table from the comfort of your own home, so let's just create one for the moment:

```
Internet(config-if)#exit
Internet(config)#interface loopback ?
  <0-2147483647>  Loopback interface number

Internet(config)#interface loopback 0
Internet(config-if)#ip address 8.8.8.8 255.255.255.255
Internet(config-if)#
```

Notice that I have used a subnet mask of /32 (255.255.255.255) for the loopback address. You can use other prefixes, such as a /8, /16 or /24, but this does have repercussions elsewhere. If you are creating an MPLS network, for example then you should use a /32 subnet mask for the loopback.

> MPLS uses a protocol called LDP (Label Distribution Protocol) to distribute the labels. It also requires an IGP, such as OSPF or IS-IS (Intermediate System to Intermediate System). Whilst using a /32 subnet is not a fixed requirement, the loopback interface's advertised subnet must be agreed between LDP and the IGP. If the Loopback address uses a /24 subnet, OSPF will actually advertise this as a /32, and there will be a failure between the control plane and data plane.
>
> If you want to read more about MPLS then pick up my other book: MPLS for Cisco Networks.

Many of the IGPs will use the first loopback interface's IP address as their router ID, so by creating a structured addressing scheme you can leverage control over this as well. It certainly makes life easier when seeing what adjacencies have formed with whom, as you will be able to visualize the network easier.

We will now create some more loopback addresses. We cannot address the routers as logically as we might like, but we can use 100.100.100.100 for the ISP router, and work (somewhat methodically) around our topology:

Router	Loopback 0 IP address
ISP	100.100.100.100/32
OSPF1	1.2.1.1/32
OSPF0	1.2.0.1/32
OSPF2	1.2.2.1/32
OSPF3	1.2.3.1/32
Gateway	50.50.50.50/32
EIGRP1	1.1.1.1/32
EIGRP2	2.2.2.2/32
EIGRP3	3.3.3.3/32
EIGRP4	4.4.4.4/32
EIGRP5	5.5.5.5/32
Internet	8.8.8.8/32
SW1	3.1.1.1/32
SW2	3.1.1.2/32
SW3	3.1.1.3/32
SW4	3.1.1.4/32

Now it's your turn to go ahead and set up the loopback interfaces with the IP addresses as shown in the table above. We have already created the loopback interface on the Internet router, and the process is no different for the other routers and switches.

As it currently stands, we now have a network where everything is fully addressed and are nearly at the stage where we can start to implement an IGP to actually give us the network-wide reachability. We should always be security-minded though, and nothing screams out "secure system!" like a good banner!

4.2.h banner

It is actually a requirement of becoming PCI (Payment Card Industry) certified, that devices must have banners displayed when someone logs into them, warning them that their activities are monitored and that unlawful access will lead to prosecution. Clearly, this will strike fear into any would-be intruder! Therefore, being security-minded as we are, we should configure banners as well.

There are a couple of places we can configure banners, if we use the context-sensitive help command "banner ?" we get a number of options:

```
EIGRP1(config)#banner ?
  LINE            c banner-text c, where 'c' is a delimiting character
  config-save     Set message for saving configuration
  exec            Set EXEC process creation banner
  incoming        Set incoming terminal line banner
  login           Set login banner
  motd            Set Message of the Day banner
  prompt-timeout  Set Message for login authentication timeout
  slip-ppp        Set Message for SLIP/PPP
EIGRP1(config)#banner
```

The key with configuring any banner is that you need to tell the operating system when the banner starts and when it ends. This is through the use of a "delimiting" character. It's a good idea to use something that you definitely won't need to use within the text of the banner. So, as per the output above, with a short enough banner you could start it with a "c" which would be the opening delimiter, and close it with a "c", if the banner does not contain any words that have a "c" in them. That is not exactly easy. The letter C occurs nine times in this paragraph, and that does not include the ones I have used to reference Cisco's instruction. It is therefore easier to use a more random character delimiter, such as ^, so you know that the chances of typing this within the body of the banner is very slim.

We will configure a banner on EIGRP1 with the following text:

```
This is EIGRP1. Stay out of my packets!
```

Using the delimiter of ^, the command looks like this:

```
EIGRP1(config-if)#banner ^ This is EIGRP1. Stay out of my packets! ^
EIGRP1(config)#
```

Now if we logout of the router, we can see our banner:

```
EIGRP1(config)#end
EIGRP1#logout

EIGRP1 con0 is now available

Press RETURN to get started.

 This is EIGRP1. Stay out of my packets!
EIGRP1>
```

I have removed a few of the blank lines, but see how literally the command is taken, including the space between the first ^ and the capital T of "This".

Banners can be very generic, allowing you to copy and paste the commands onto the routers. They can be one line, or multiple lines. So let's make a multiple line one, that would be more suitable. With multiple line banners we press enter after the first delimiter character:

```
EIGRP1>en
Password:
EIGRP1#conf t
EIGRP1(config)#banner ^
Enter TEXT message.  End with the character '^'.
This is a monitored system.
Unlawful access will be reported.
You may be prosecuted.
^
EIGRP1(config)#
```

Now when we log out we can see the following banner:

```
EIGRP1(config)#end
EIGRP1#logout

EIGRP1 con0 is now available

Press RETURN to get started.
```

```
This is a monitored system.
Unlawful access will be reported.
You may be prosecuted.

EIGRP1>
```

This looks a bit more professional! It also could be pasted onto a number of routers if you wanted a generic banner.

What if you wanted to use the same message on a number of routers, but needed to customize it? Well, thankfully we can do that as well, which we will do in our next banner message; the message of the day banner.

4.2.i motd

MOTD, or Message of the Day, was originally used to send a message to all users in a UNIX environment (easier than emailing everyone), and has stuck around. We can use this to display another banner message. In this one, we will use a bit of cleverness to personalize the message by using variables.

```
EIGRP1>en
Password:
EIGRP1#conf t
Enter configuration commands, one per line.  End with CNTL/Z.
EIGRP1(config)#banner motd ^
Enter TEXT message.  End with the character '^'.
Welcome to $(hostname).
You are attached to console $(line).
Please use this system responsibly.
^
EIGRP1(config)#
```

Now when we logout and back in we can see the following:

```
EIGRP1(config)#end
EIGRP1#logout

EIGRP1 con0 is now available

Press RETURN to get started.

Welcome to EIGRP1.
You are attached to console 0
Please use this system responsibly.

EIGRP1>
```

Our previous banner has been replaced with our MOTD one. The banner displays our hostname, by using the variable $(hostname), and the line we are connected (console 0). If we wanted to keep the original (generic) banner, and still show a customized banner, we can use the line command *"exec-banner"* to display the banner, and create a new banner using the *"banner exec"* command. This is set up below:

```
EIGRP1(config)#line con 0
EIGRP1(config-line)#exec-banner
EIGRP1(config-line)#exit
EIGRP1(config)#banner exec ^$(hostname) welcomes careful engineers!^
EIGRP1(config)#end
EIGRP1#logout

EIGRP1 con0 is now available

Press RETURN to get started.

Welcome to EIGRP1.
You are attached to console 0
Please use this system responsibly.
EIGRP1 welcomes careful engineers!
EIGRP1>
```

There is also the command *"banner incoming"*, which will show a banner upon telnet or SSH connection and *"banner login"*, which will show a banner between the username and password prompts.

We used the command *"exec-banner"* to control which banner we wanted to show, there is also *"motd-banner"*, which can achieve a similar result. We can even choose not to show the MOTD banner if we are connected to the console line, leaving us with just the exec banner:

```
EIGRP1(config)#line con 0
EIGRP1(config-line)#no motd-banner
EIGRP1(config-line)#end
EIGRP1#logout

EIGRP1 con0 is now available

Press RETURN to get started.

EIGRP1 welcomes careful engineers!
EIGRP1>
```

As you can see, we can be very selective as to where we show banners, what banners we show, and what we show in them.

We have done a lot of work this chapter so far, so we really should save our work.

4.2.j copy run start

Just as we used the command *"copy running-config startup-config"* on our switches, we can use the same command on our routers to achieve the same goal.

```
EIGRP1>en
Password:
EIGRP1#
EIGRP1#copy run start
Destination filename [startup-config]?
Building configuration...
[OK]
EIGRP1#
```

On all of your routers please type in the above commands, you can use the long format (*copy running-config startup-config*) or just use *"copy run start"*. Remember though that in the exam not all truncated commands may be available.

I hope that you found this section pretty easy. Most of it we covered in chapter two, but some of it was new to us. The next two sections should also be fairly relaxing as we go over some verification commands, to check out our interfaces, basic visibility and reachability.

4.3 Configure and verify operation status of a device interface

We have two types of interfaces in our topology; Ethernet and Serial. Whilst the configuration we have done so far has been fairly identical, in that both have an IP address and a subnet mask, these two interfaces actually operate very differently in real life.

4.3.a Serial

As we saw in chapter one, serial interfaces are either DCE or DTE. One sends the clock rate (DCE or Data Communication Equipment); the other receives the clock rate (DTE or Data Terminal Equipment). The cables themselves actually have DCE and DTE embossed on them, making life easier. Our clock rates do need to match. To see the clock rate we are either sending or receiving, we would use the command *"show controllers serial1/2"* (or whatever interface we needed to look at). This will tell us on which end of the cable we are.

We will start with some basic setup on the frame-relay routers. This will be the basic IP addressing, and the same set of commands for the creation of the admin user, exec-timeout and password encryption.

```
Router(config)#ho FR-Hub
FR-Hub(config)#username admin password cisco
FR-Hub(config)#enable secret cisco
FR-Hub(config)#line con 0
FR-Hub(config-line)#exec-timeout 0 0
FR-Hub(config-line)#line vty 0 4
FR-Hub(config-line)#exec-timeout 0 0
FR-Hub(config-line)#login local
FR-Hub(config-line)#service password-encryption
FR-Hub(config)#int s1/1
FR-Hub(config-if)#ip add 192.168.11.1 255.255.255.0
FR-Hub(config-if)#no shut
FR-Hub(config-if)#desc Link to FR-Spoke1
FR-Hub(config-if)#int s1/2
FR-Hub(config-if)#ip add 192.168.12.1 255.255.255.0
FR-Hub(config-if)#no shut
FR-Hub(config-if)#desc Link to FR-Spoke2
FR-Hub(config-if)#

Router(config)#ho FR-Spoke1
FR-Spoke1(config)#username admin password cisco
FR-Spoke1(config)#enable secret cisco
FR-Spoke1(config)#line con 0
FR-Spoke1(config-line)#exec-timeout 0 0
FR-Spoke1(config-line)#line vty 0 4
FR-Spoke1(config-line)#exec-timeout 0 0
FR-Spoke1(config-line)#login local
FR-Spoke1(config-line)#service password-encryption
FR-Spoke1(config)#int s1/1
FR-Spoke1(config-if)#ip add 192.168.11.2 255.255.255.0
FR-Spoke1(config-if)#no shut
FR-Spoke1(config-if)#desc Link to FR-Hub
FR-Spoke1(config-if)#

Router(config)#ho FR-Spoke2
FR-Spoke2(config)#username admin password cisco
FR-Spoke2(config)#enable secret cisco
FR-Spoke2(config)#line con 0
FR-Spoke2(config-line)#exec-timeout 0 0
FR-Spoke2(config-line)#line vty 0 4
FR-Spoke2(config-line)#exec-timeout 0 0
FR-Spoke2(config-line)#login local
FR-Spoke2(config-line)#service password-encryption
FR-Spoke2(config)#int s1/2
FR-Spoke2(config-if)#ip add 192.168.12.2 255.255.255.0
FR-Spoke2(config-if)#no shut
FR-Spoke2(config-if)#desc Link to FR-Hub
FR-Spoke2(config-if)#
```

Things do not work quite the same with a virtualized environment. Below we can see the output from FR-Hub and FR-Spoke1 (the output has been truncated a bit):

```
FR-Hub(config-if)#end
FR-Hub#show controller serial 1/1
M4T: show controller:
PAS unit 1, subunit 1, f/w version 1-45, rev ID 0xFFFF, version 1
idb = 0xF2596418, ds = 0xF2597750, ssb=0xF2597B08
Clock mux=0x0, ucmd_ctrl=0x1C, port_status=0x3B
Serial config=0x8, line config=0x200
maxdgram=1608, bufpool=78Kb, 120 particles
     DCD=up  DSR=up  DTR=up  RTS=up  CTS=up
line state: up
cable type : V.11 (X.21) DCE cable, received clockrate 2015232
running=1, port id=0x132E86B0
FR-Hub#

FR-Spoke1(config-if)#end
FR-Spoke1#show controllers serial 1/1
M4T: show controller:
PAS unit 1, subunit 1, f/w version 1-45, rev ID 0xFFFF, version 1
idb = 0xF2600C58, ds = 0xF2601F90, ssb=0xF2602348
Clock mux=0x0, ucmd_ctrl=0x1C, port_status=0x3B
Serial config=0x8, line config=0x200
maxdgram=1608, bufpool=78Kb, 120 particles
     DCD=up  DSR=up  DTR=up  RTS=up  CTS=up
line state: up
cable type : V.11 (X.21) DCE cable, received clockrate 2015232
running=1, port id=0x132FA6B0
FR-Spoke1#
```

As you can see, both cables are set as DCE (in bold text), nevertheless we still have connectivity:

```
FR-Hub#ping 192.168.11.2
Type escape sequence to abort.
Sending 5, 100-byte ICMP Echos to 192.168.11.2:
!!!!!
Success rate is 100 percent (5/5)
FR-Hub#
```

We can try to set the clock rate (to 56000 bps), but we do not see any change:

```
FR-Hub(config)#int s1/1
FR-Hub(config-if)#clock rate 56000
FR-Hub(config-if)#shut
FR-Hub(config-if)#
FR-Hub(config-if)#no shut
```

```
FR-Hub(config-if)#end
FR-Hub#show controller serial 1/1 | i cable
cable type : V.11 (X.21) DCE cable, received clockrate 56000
FR-Hub#ping 192.168.11.2
Type escape sequence to abort.
Sending 5, 100-byte ICMP Echos to 192.168.11.2:
!!!!!
Success rate is 100 percent (5/5)
FR-Hub#

FR-Spoke1#show controllers serial 1/1 | i cable
cable type : V.11 (X.21) DCE cable, received clockrate 2015232
FR-Spoke1#
```

The point is that in a proper environment with physical equipment, your clock rate needs to match at both ends.

What else can affect connectivity between serial interfaces? The encapsulation certainly can.

A mismatch in encapsulation can be easy to miss. The default encapsulation is HDLC. HDLC stands for High-Level Data Link Control, Cisco, of course, likes to use cHDLC (Cisco HDLC). A cHDLC frame looks like this:

Flag	Address	Control	Type code	Data	FCS		Flag

The address field will be either 0x0F for unicast, or 0x8F for broadcast. HDLC works through a set of requests and responses. The DCE sends commands and the DTE sends responses, and this is sent in the control field. The type code supports the EtherType code that we saw when we looked at the Ethernet frame. The flag fields at the beginning and end signify the start and end of the frame.

If we set the encapsulation of FR-Hub's serial interface to PPP (Point-to-Point Protocol), we then see that we lose the connection to FR-Spoke1:

```
FR-Hub(config)#int s1/1
FR-Hub(config-if)#
FR-Hub(config-if)#encapsulation ppp
FR-Hub(config-if)#
%LINEPROTO-5-UPDOWN: Line protocol on Interface Serial1/1, changed state
to down
FR-Hub(config-if)#
```

We will cover HDLC and PPP in greater depth in chapter eight, but for the moment, we will set FR-Spoke1 to use PPP encapsulation as well, and see our link come up again:

```
FR-Spoke1(config)#int s1/1
FR-Spoke1(config-if)#
FR-Spoke1(config-if)#encapsulation ppp
FR-Spoke1(config-if)#
%LINEPROTO-5-UPDOWN: Line protocol on Interface Serial1/1, changed state
to up
FR-Spoke1(config-if)#
```

We will cover PPP and serial interfaces in greater detail towards the end of the book, but this does illustrate the point that a mismatch in encapsulation can cause issues. Let's move forward and check our Ethernet connections.

4.3.b Ethernet

With Ethernet, we do not need to worry about encapsulation issues (there is no "*encapsulation*" command under an Ethernet interface). But, like any interface (and this includes serial interfaces) we should check that it is up, and the command "*show ip interface brief*" will tell us the current state:

```
ISP(config-if)#end
ISP#sh ip int bri
Interface      IP-Address     OK? Method Status                 Protocol
Ethernet0/0    192.168.20.1   YES manual up                     up
Ethernet0/1    192.168.1.1    YES manual up                     up
Ethernet0/2    192.168.30.1   YES manual up                     up
Ethernet0/3    unassigned     YES unset  administratively down down
Ethernet1/0    unassigned     YES unset  administratively down down
Ethernet1/1    172.16.1.1     YES manual up                     up
Ethernet1/2    unassigned     YES unset  administratively down down
Ethernet1/3    unassigned     YES unset  administratively down down
Loopback0      100.100.100.100 YES manual up                    up
ISP#
```

If our interfaces are up, then we know that we are at least physically cabled correctly and we can move our tests further up the stack, using tools such as ping and traceroute to confirm reachability.

4.4 Verify router configuration and network connectivity using

4.4.a ping

We can confirm that we have connectivity between the devices, using the ping command, as we saw back in chapter two. We will now confirm end-to-end connectivity using ping.

Starting on EIGRP1 make sure you can ping ISP, and that ISP can ping the Gateway and Internet routers, then move on to the OSPF routers, making sure that they can ping each other as well. The results should look like this:

```
EIGRP1#ping 192.168.1.1
Type escape sequence to abort.
Sending 5, 100-byte ICMP Echos to 192.168.1.1:
!!!!!
Success rate is 100 percent (5/5)
EIGRP1#

ISP#ping 192.168.20.1
Type escape sequence to abort.
Sending 5, 100-byte ICMP Echos to 192.168.20.1:
!!!!!
Success rate is 100 percent (5/5)
ISP#ping 192.168.30.1
Type escape sequence to abort.
Sending 5, 100-byte ICMP Echos to 192.168.30.1:
!!!!!
Success rate is 100 percent (5/5)
ISP#ping 172.16.1.2
Type escape sequence to abort.
Sending 5, 100-byte ICMP Echos to 172.16.1.2:
!!!!!
Success rate is 100 percent (5/5)
ISP#
```

I won't put the results for the other routers, but I am sure that you get the idea; ping is a great way to test basic reachability. We can also use extended ping to see how much we can send in a packet.

4.4.a (i) extended

Extended ping allows us to play with the various parts of the ping packet. To use an extended ping we can use the *"ping"* command on its own and then supply the information needed, such as destination, source and size. We can also press return to accept the default value, which is shown within square brackets:

```
ISP#ping
Protocol [ip]: ip
Target IP address: 172.16.1.2
Repeat count [5]: 5
Datagram size [100]: 1400
Timeout in seconds [2]: 2
Extended commands [n]: y
Source address or interface: 172.16.1.1
Type of service [0]: 0
Set DF bit in IP header? [no]: yes
Validate reply data? [no]: no
Data pattern [0xABCD]:
Loose, Strict, Record, Timestamp, Verbose[none]:
```

```
Sweep range of sizes [n]: n
Type escape sequence to abort.
Sending 5, 1400-byte ICMP Echos to 172.16.1.2:
Packet sent with a source address of 172.16.1.1
Packet sent with the DF bit set
!!!!!
Success rate is 100 percent (5/5)
ISP#
```

I have either used or accepted most of the defaults, apart from the DF-bit, which I have enabled, and the datagram size. The default packet size sent in a ping is 100 bytes, but above I am sending 1400 bytes, which is close to the maximum MTU size we spoke of earlier.

We can also supply these values with the ping command we have used before:

```
ISP#ping 172.16.1.2 size 1400 df-bit
Type escape sequence to abort.
Sending 5, 1400-byte ICMP Echos to 172.16.1.2:
Packet sent with the DF bit set
!!!!!
Success rate is 100 percent (5/5)
ISP#
```

Let's increase the size and see what happens:

```
ISP#ping 172.16.1.2 size 1499 df-bit
Type escape sequence to abort.
Sending 5, 1499-byte ICMP Echos to 172.16.1.2:
Packet sent with the DF bit set
!!!!!
Success rate is 100 percent (5/5)
ISP#
```

We are one byte beneath the default MTU size, let's push it up byte by byte, and see at what point it will fail:

```
ISP#ping 172.16.1.2 size 1500 df-bit
Type escape sequence to abort.
Sending 5, 1500-byte ICMP Echos to 172.16.1.2:
Packet sent with the DF bit set
!!!!!
Success rate is 100 percent (5/5)
ISP#
ISP#ping 172.16.1.2 size 1501 df-bit
Type escape sequence to abort.
Sending 5, 1501-byte ICMP Echos to 172.16.1.2:
Packet sent with the DF bit set
```

```
.....
Success rate is 0 percent (0/5)
ISP#
```

Therefore, the ping will fail at 1501 bytes with the df-bit set. The DF-bit means Do Not Fragment (do not send it in multiple packets), so we are trying to exceed the MTU of the interface. If we remove this bit, then we can pass a 1501-byte packet through:

```
ISP#ping 172.16.1.2 size 1501
Type escape sequence to abort.
Sending 5, 1501-byte ICMP Echos to 172.16.1.2:
!!!!!
Success rate is 100 percent (5/5)
ISP#
```

We can even pass a 2-megabyte packet through, if we can fragment it.

```
ISP#ping 172.16.1.2 size 2048
Type escape sequence to abort.
Sending 5, 2048-byte ICMP Echos to 172.16.1.2:
!!!!!
Success rate is 100 percent (5/5)
ISP#
```

What other options are available to us for verifying connectivity in Ethernet networks? None that are different to how we tested our switches earlier, but the syllabus says traceroute, so traceroute we shall.

4.4.b traceroute

Traceroute really won't show us much at the moment, but try it anyway:

```
ISP#traceroute 172.16.1.2
Type escape sequence to abort.
Tracing the route to 172.16.1.2
VRF info: (vrf in name/id, vrf out name/id)
  1 172.16.1.2 12 msec 16 msec *
ISP#
```

Wonderful! A great test! Yes, I am being sarcastic; it's actually quite slow and does not show us much. Whilst we cannot put more entries in it, we can speed it up:

```
ISP#traceroute 172.16.1.2 numeric
Type escape sequence to abort.
Tracing the route to 172.16.1.2
```

```
VRF info: (vrf in name/id, vrf out name/id)
  1 172.16.1.2 8 msec *  16 msec
ISP#
```

The *"numeric"* keyword has the effect of disabling DNS lookups, which is why it is much faster. We can instruct the router not to do DNS lookups from global configuration mode:

```
ISP(config)#no ip domain-lookup
ISP(config)#
```

This makes subsequent traceroutes much faster:

```
ISP(config)#end
ISP#traceroute 172.16.1.2
Type escape sequence to abort.
Tracing the route to 172.16.1.2
VRF info: (vrf in name/id, vrf out name/id)
  1 172.16.1.2 24 msec *  8 msec
ISP#
```

OK, I know that you can't gauge the speed by reading a page, but try it at home and you should see that it is much faster, and there is no need to use the *"numeric"* keyword. It also helps if we make a typing mistake. We can see this if we type *"endd"* on OSPF1, and the same on ISP:

```
OSPF1>endd
Translating "endd"...domain server (255.255.255.255)
 (255.255.255.255)
Translating "endd"...domain server (255.255.255.255)

Translating "endd"...domain server (255.255.255.255)

Translating "endd"...domain server (255.255.255.255)

% Bad IP address or host name
Translating "endd"...domain server (255.255.255.255)
% Unknown command or computer name, or unable to find computer address
OSPF1>
```

It takes a few minutes for OSPF1 to return to a usable state, whereas ISP returns much quicker with *"no ip domain-lookup"* configured:

```
ISP>endd
Translating "endd"

Translating "endd"
```

```
Translating "endd"

% Bad IP address or host name% Unknown command or computer name, or
unable to find computer address
ISP>
```

DNS querying is enabled by default, so by using command *"no ip domain-lookup"* we have disabled it.

Once we set up our IGPs we will, returning to the point in question, do proper traceroutes as a way of proving complete end-to-end connectivity. For the moment, we can only test connectivity to our neighbour router, but we can test the rest of the network layers using telnet and SSH, which we will run through quickly.

4.4.c telnet
4.4.d SSH

We covered telnet and SSH back in chapter two, so will run through them again quickly. We set up a local user (admin) and password (cisco) on all of our routers in section 4.2.b, and set the VTY line to use the local database to authenticate login attempts, now we can test this out:

```
ISP#telnet 172.16.1.2
Trying 172.16.1.2 ... Open

User Access Verification

Username: admin
Password:
OSPF1>exit

[Connection to 172.16.1.2 closed by foreign host]
ISP#
```

We can also set up SSH to test as well, which we will do this on the ISP router. Because the transport input is set to none (which is the default), we will enable just SSH:

```
ISP(config)#ip domain-name 802101.com
ISP(config)#ip ssh version 2
Please create RSA keys to enable SSH (and of at least 768 bits for SSH v2).
ISP(config)#
ISP(config)#crypto key generate rsa modulus 2048
The name for the keys will be: ISP.802101.com

% The key modulus size is 2048 bits
% Generating 2048 bit RSA keys, keys will be non-exportable...
[OK] (elapsed time was 10 seconds)
```

```
ISP(config)#
%SSH-5-ENABLED: SSH 2.0 has been enabled
ISP(config)#
ISP(config)#line vty 0 4
ISP(config-line)#transport input ssh
ISP(config-line)#end
```

We can test access from OSPF1:

```
OSPF1#ssh -l admin 172.16.1.1
Password:

ISP>exit

[Connection to 172.16.1.1 closed by foreign host]
OSPF1#
```

Lastly, in this section we will look at CDP.

4.4.e sh cdp neighbors

CDP, the Cisco Discovery Protocol, is great. It is very easy to forget what interface is connected to what device, and this is where CDP comes in handy. Often you may find that the logical topology of a network is quite different to the physical topology. CDP will be the saviour in such a case.

The most common CDP command will be *"show cdp neighbors"*, and we can see the output of this command on ISP:

```
ISP#sh cdp neighbors
Capability Codes: R - Router, T - Trans Bridge, B - Source Route Bridge
                  S - Switch, H - Host, I - IGMP, r - Repeater, P - Phone,
                  D - Remote, C - CVTA, M - Two-port Mac Relay

Device ID    Local Intrfce    Holdtme    Capability  Platform  Port ID
Internet     Eth 0/2          174              R B   Linux Uni Eth 0/2
OSPF1        Eth 1/1          146              R B   Linux Uni Eth 1/1
Gateway      Eth 0/0          155              R B   Linux Uni Eth 0/0
EIGRP1       Eth 0/1          166              R B   Linux Uni Eth 0/1

Total cdp entries displayed : 4
ISP#
```

From this we can see whom we are connected to in the first column (Device ID), and now aren't you glad we spent that time naming all of our devices! We can see which of our local interfaces we use to connect to that particular device, such as Ethernet 0/2 connect to the Internet router. We can also see the platform of the neighbour router and to which of their ports we are connected. From the output above, we can therefore see that OSPF1 is an IOU-based router and we connect to its Ethernet 1/1 interface through our Ethernet 1/1 interface. The capabilities field shows that these neighboring devices are Routers (R), and Source Route Bridges (B).

We can use CDP to dig a bit deeper into our neighboring routers, once we know who they are, using the (case-sensitive) command *"show cdp entry <neighbour hostname>"*:

```
ISP#sh cdp entry OSPF1
-------------------------
Device ID: OSPF1
Entry address(es):
  IP address: 172.16.1.2
  IPv6 address: 2001:DB8:A2::2  (global unicast)
  IPv6 address: FE80::A8BB:CCFF:FE00:B11  (link-local)
Platform: Linux Unix,  Capabilities: Router Source-Route-Bridge
Interface: Ethernet1/1,  Port ID (outgoing port): Ethernet1/1
Holdtime : 149 sec
Second Port Status: Unknown
Version :
Cisco IOS Software, Linux Software (I86BI_LINUX-ADVENTERPRISEK9-M),
Version 15.4(2)T, DEVELOPMENT TEST SOFTWARE
Technical Support: http://www.cisco.com/techsupport
Copyright (c) 1986-2014 by Cisco Systems, Inc.
Compiled Thu 27-Mar-14 01:08 by prod_rel_team
advertisement version: 2
Duplex: half
Management address(es):
  IP address: 172.16.1.2

ISP#
```

We do only get information pertinent to us; for example, we cannot see OSPF1's other IP address (the one connecting it to OSPF0). However, it is useful if you are troubleshooting an issue you think may be due to a firmware image and need to see what version of the IOS the other device is running. This gives us the same level of detail as the command *"show cdp neigh e1/2 detail"*. We can also look at CDP data on a per-interface basis, in order to check the CDP timers:

```
ISP#sh cdp interface e1/1
Ethernet1/1 is up, line protocol is up
  Encapsulation ARPA
  Sending CDP packets every 60 seconds
  Holdtime is 180 seconds
ISP#
```

We can also see the CDP traffic, broken down by version:

```
ISP#sh cdp traffic
CDP counters :
        Total packets output: 20520, Input: 16463
        Hdr syntax: 0, Chksum error: 0, Encaps failed: 0
        No memory: 0, Invalid packet: 0,
        CDP version 1 advertisements output: 0, Input: 0
        CDP version 2 advertisements output: 20520, Input: 16463
ISP#
```

As you can see above, there are two versions of CDP. Version 2 offers better device tracking and enhanced logging facilities within CDP. We can also get insight into VTP data, as shown on the CDP output from SW1:

```
SW1#sh cdp entry SW4.802101.local
-------------------------
Device ID: SW4.802101.local
Entry address(es):
  IP address: 10.1.1.4
Platform: Linux Unix,  Capabilities: Router Switch
Interface: Ethernet1/1,  Port ID (outgoing port): Ethernet1/1
Holdtime : 140 sec

Version :
Cisco IOS Software, Linux Software (I86BI_LINUX_L2-UPK9-M), Experimental
Version 15.0(20120621:060510) [dstivers-june20-2012-golden_spike 101]
Copyright (c) 1986-2012 by Cisco Systems, Inc.
Compiled Wed 20-Jun-12 23:58 by dstivers

advertisement version: 2
VTP Management Domain: '802101.com'
Duplex: half
Management address(es):
  IP address: 10.1.1.4

SW1#
```

Whilst CDP is turned on by default, and I can see no need to turn it off (unless you are supplying a transparent layer-2 network and wish to hide the underlying service provider infrastructure), it can be turned off using the command "*no cdp run*":

```
ISP(config)#no cdp run
ISP(config)#do sh cdp neigh
% CDP is not enabled
ISP(config)#
```

To turn it on again, use the command "*cdp run*". It will take a few moments for the entries to be populated. If you are in one of those curious situations where you do not want to use CDP on a particular interface, it can be disabled for that interface, rather than turning it off globally, by using the command "no cdp enable":

```
ISP(config)#cdp run
ISP(config)#int e1/1
ISP(config-if)#no cdp enable
ISP(config-if)#do sh cdp neigh
Capability Codes: R - Router, T - Trans Bridge, B - Source Route Bridge
                  S - Switch, H - Host, I - IGMP, r - Repeater, P - Phone,
                  D - Remote, C - CVTA, M - Two-port Mac Relay

Device ID    Local Intrfce    Holdtme    Capability  Platform  Port ID
Internet     Eth 0/2          178              R B   Linux Uni Eth 0/2
OSPF1        Eth 1/1          137              R B   Linux Uni Eth 1/1
Gateway      Eth 0/0          147              R B   Linux Uni Eth 0/0
EIGRP1       Eth 0/1          155              R B   Linux Uni Eth 0/1

Total cdp entries displayed : 4
ISP(config-if)#
```

This does not have the same immediate effect as turning it off globally using the command "no cdp run". Instead, the result can be more gradual. CDP uses a holdtimer, which is the third column. The holdtimer is 180 seconds, by default, which we saw in the output from "show cdp interface e1/1" a moment ago. The holdtimer is used to keep the CDP information fresh. Every minute we send CDP packets, which act as a keepalive. If we do not hear back from a CDP neighbour within the holdtime period, for which it has three chances, we flush it out, as we can see below (I have removed the capabilities section) with the entry for OSPF1:

```
ISP(config-if)#do sh cdp neigh | b Device
Device ID    Local Intrfce    Holdtme    Capability  Platform  Port ID
Internet     Eth 0/2          174              R B   Linux Uni Eth 0/2
OSPF1        Eth 1/1          75               R B   Linux Uni Eth 1/1
Gateway      Eth 0/0          140              R B   Linux Uni Eth 0/0
EIGRP1       Eth 0/1          147              R B   Linux Uni Eth 0/1

Total cdp entries displayed : 4
ISP(config-if)#
ISP(config-if)#do sh cdp neigh | b Device
Device ID    Local Intrfce    Holdtme    Capability  Platform  Port ID
Internet     Eth 0/2          168              R B   Linux Uni Eth 0/2
OSPF1        Eth 1/1          12               R B   Linux Uni Eth 1/1
Gateway      Eth 0/0          133              R B   Linux Uni Eth 0/0
EIGRP1       Eth 0/1          135              R B   Linux Uni Eth 0/1

Total cdp entries displayed : 4
ISP(config-if)#
ISP(config-if)#do sh cdp neigh | b Device
```

```
Device ID      Local Intrfce      Holdtme    Capability  Platform  Port ID
Internet       Eth 0/2            151              R B    Linux Uni Eth 0/2
OSPF1          Eth 1/1            0                R B    Linux Uni Eth 1/1
Gateway        Eth 0/0            171              R B    Linux Uni Eth 0/0
EIGRP1         Eth 0/1            172              R B    Linux Uni Eth 0/1

Total cdp entries displayed : 4
ISP(config-if)#
ISP(config-if)#do sh cdp neigh | b Device
Device ID      Local Intrfce      Holdtme    Capability  Platform  Port ID
Internet       Eth 0/2            146              R B    Linux Uni Eth 0/2
Gateway        Eth 0/0            166              R B    Linux Uni Eth 0/0
EIGRP1         Eth 0/1            167              R B    Linux Uni Eth 0/1

Total cdp entries displayed : 3
ISP(config-if)#
```

Once the timer expires, OSPF1 is flushed from our CDP table.

In this section we ran through some useful troubleshooting tools, allowing us to confirm our network is working. The traceroute, however, was a little lacklustre as we could only go as far as our neighboring router. In the next couple of sections, we are going to extend our network using routing protocols.

4.5 Configure and verify routing configuration for a static or default route given specific routing requirements

The first routing type we will create is a static route. A static route is one that is manually created, and will remain on the device unless it is manually removed. Static routes need a couple of values; the network (or host) we want to get to, the subnet mask and the next hop router.

The most common static route is probably a default route, to which we send all the traffic that does not match a more specific route. Here we will set up EIGRP1 and OSPF1 to have a default route pointing to the ISP router.

```
EIGRP1(config)#ip route 0.0.0.0 0.0.0.0 192.168.1.1
EIGRP1(config)#

OSPF1(config)#ip route 0.0.0.0 0.0.0.0 172.16.1.1
OSPF1(config)#
```

We have used the values of 0.0.0.0 for the network and 0.0.0.0 for the subnet mask. This means we are sending everything that does not match a more specific route to the ISP router. Once we have the route configured, we can check that it is there, by using the command "*show ip route*":

```
EIGRP1(config)#do sh ip route | b Gate
Gateway of last resort is 192.168.1.1 to network 0.0.0.0

S*     0.0.0.0/0 [1/0] via 192.168.1.1
       1.0.0.0/32 is subnetted, 1 subnets
C         1.1.1.1 is directly connected, Loopback0
       192.168.1.0/24 is variably subnetted, 2 subnets, 2 masks
C         192.168.1.0/24 is directly connected, Ethernet0/1
L         192.168.1.2/32 is directly connected, Ethernet0/1
       192.168.21.0/24 is variably subnetted, 2 subnets, 2 masks
C         192.168.21.0/24 is directly connected, Ethernet1/2
L         192.168.21.1/32 is directly connected, Ethernet1/2
       192.168.51.0/24 is variably subnetted, 2 subnets, 2 masks
C         192.168.51.0/24 is directly connected, Serial2/0
L         192.168.51.1/32 is directly connected, Serial2/0
EIGRP1(config)#
```

We can see a lot of connected (C) and local (L) routes. Local routes are the ones configured on the physical interfaces of our local router (192.168.1.2, 192.168.21.1 and 192.168.51.1). Notice how these are shown as a /32, but we also have the network above it, where it says, "variably subnetted". A local route is also known as a host route, and will always be shown as a /32 for an IPv4 route or a /128 for an IPv6 route.

We also have our static route (returning to the point in question). We can see this twice. It is our "Gateway of last resort", meaning if we don't have a better route, then send all traffic to 192.168.1.1. We also have it as our static route in the first line of our table (S* 0.0.0.0/0 [1/0] via 192.168.1.1).

If we are configuring a default route, as well as the "*ip route*" command, we can also use the command "*ip default-network*". Way back in section 2.3.c, we looked at the command "*ip default-gateway*" but did not discuss it any great depth. What would you expect the command to do? Give you a "gateway of last resort", right? Well, it does, but not all the time. It depends on what our device is actually doing. For the command "*ip default-gateway*" to work, we need to switch off IP routing, which is enabled by default on our switches. Returning to SW1 we can see that although we have the command configured (as we did in 2.3.c), we do not see it in our routing table:

```
SW1(config)#do sh ip route | b Gate
Gateway of last resort is not set

       3.0.0.0/32 is subnetted, 1 subnets
C         3.1.1.1 is directly connected, Loopback0
       10.0.0.0/8 is variably subnetted, 2 subnets, 2 masks
C         10.1.1.0/24 is directly connected, Vlan1
L         10.1.1.1/32 is directly connected, Vlan1
SW1(config)#
```

We have to turn off IP routing for the command to take effect:

```
SW1(config)#no ip routing
SW1(config)#
SW1(config)#do sh ip route
Default gateway is 10.1.1.254

Host                    Gateway            Last Use    Total Uses  Interface
ICMP redirect cache is empty
SW1(config)#
```

If we turn routing back on again, we see our routing table return:

```
SW1(config)#ip routing
SW1(config)#
SW1(config)#do sh ip route | b Gate
Gateway of last resort is not set

      3.0.0.0/32 is subnetted, 1 subnets
C        3.1.1.1 is directly connected, Loopback0
      10.0.0.0/8 is variably subnetted, 2 subnets, 2 masks
C        10.1.1.0/24 is directly connected, Vlan1
L        10.1.1.1/32 is directly connected, Vlan1
SW1(config)#
```

Now we can use the "*ip default-network*" command:

```
SW1(config)#ip default-network 10.1.1.0
SW1(config)#
SW1(config)#do sh ip route | b Gate
Gateway of last resort is not set

      3.0.0.0/32 is subnetted, 1 subnets
C        3.1.1.1 is directly connected, Loopback0
      10.0.0.0/8 is variably subnetted, 3 subnets, 3 masks
S        10.0.0.0/8 [1/0] via 10.1.1.0
C        10.1.1.0/24 is directly connected, Vlan1
L        10.1.1.1/32 is directly connected, Vlan1
SW1(config)#
```

This has injected a static route into our routing table, with the default subnet mask (/8) for that subnet. We cannot use this method with 0.0.0.0, though. We can try this, but our routing table does not change:

```
SW1(config)#ip default-network 0.0.0.0
SW1(config)#
SW1(config)#do sh ip route | b Gate
Gateway of last resort is not set
```

```
         3.0.0.0/32 is subnetted, 1 subnets
C           3.1.1.1 is directly connected, Loopback0
         10.0.0.0/8 is variably subnetted, 3 subnets, 3 masks
S           10.0.0.0/8 [1/0] via 10.1.1.0
C           10.1.1.0/24 is directly connected, Vlan1
L           10.1.1.1/32 is directly connected, Vlan1
SW1(config)#
```

Hopefully, you can start to see that whilst static routing is good, it is quite limited. Take the ISP router for example. If this were to have a default route, to where would it point? EIGRP1? OSPF1? The Internet or Gateway routers? All are good choices, but how would we route to the other networks? We can start to see the issues that might arise from a network that uses just static routes. Static routes are useful, but can become an administrative nightmare, as we will see in the next section.

4.6 Differentiate methods of routing and routing protocols

Static routes can only get us so far. They are great for a basic network, where you have an inside network (such as 10.1.1.0/24) and you can then use a static route pointing to the "outside", as we set up on EIGRP1 and OSPF1. However, if we have more networks behind us then we will need additional routes. Let's set up the OSPF side of the network using static routes and see how far we can get, and witness first-hand the administrative headache that this can become.

4.6.a Static vs. dynamic

We will be concentrating on the OSPF routers for the moment. The goal being that they can communicate with the ISP router and each other, including the loopback interfaces we configured earlier. We will start with the ISP router:

```
ISP(config)#ip route 172.16.2.0 255.255.255.0 172.16.1.2
ISP(config)#ip route 172.16.3.0 255.255.255.0 172.16.1.2
ISP(config)#ip route 172.16.4.0 255.255.255.0 172.16.1.2
ISP(config)#ip route 1.2.0.1 255.255.255.255 172.16.1.2
ISP(config)#ip route 1.2.1.1 255.255.255.255 172.16.1.2
ISP(config)#ip route 1.2.2.1 255.255.255.255 172.16.1.2
ISP(config)#ip route 1.2.3.1 255.255.255.255 172.16.1.2
ISP(config)#

OSPF1(config)#ip route 172.16.3.0 255.255.255.0 172.16.2.1
OSPF1(config)#ip route 172.16.4.0 255.255.255.0 172.16.2.1
OSPF1(config)#ip route 100.100.100.100 255.255.255.255 172.16.1.1
OSPF1(config)#ip route 1.2.0.1 255.255.255.255 172.16.2.1
OSPF1(config)#ip route 1.2.2.1 255.255.255.255 172.16.2.1
OSPF1(config)#ip route 1.2.3.1 255.255.255.255 172.16.2.1
OSPF1(config)#
```

```
OSPF0(config)#ip route 172.16.1.0 255.255.255.0 172.16.2.2
OSPF0(config)#ip route 172.16.4.0 255.255.255.0 172.16.3.2
OSPF0(config)#ip route 100.100.100.100 255.255.255.255 172.16.2.2
OSPF0(config)#ip route 1.2.1.1 255.255.255.255 172.16.2.2
OSPF0(config)#ip route 1.2.2.1 255.255.255.255 172.16.3.2
OSPF0(config)#ip route 1.2.3.1 255.255.255.255 172.16.3.2
OSPF0(config)#
```

Now I don't know about you, but this is already starting to become a hassle. Let's continue though.

```
OSPF2(config)#ip route 172.16.1.0 255.255.255.0 172.16.3.1
OSPF2(config)#ip route 172.16.2.0 255.255.255.0 172.16.3.1
OSPF2(config)#ip route 100.100.100.100 255.255.255.255 172.16.3.1
OSPF2(config)#ip route 1.2.0.1 255.255.255.255 172.16.3.1
OSPF2(config)#ip route 1.2.1.1 255.255.255.255 172.16.3.1
OSPF2(config)#ip route 1.2.3.1 255.255.255.255 172.16.4.3
OSPF2(config)#

OSPF3(config)#ip route 0.0.0.0 0.0.0.0 172.16.4.2
OSPF3(config)#
```

Because OSPF3 does not have any other connected networks we can use a default route and still have the desired end-to-end reachability (from OSPF3 to ISP):

```
OSPF3(config)#do ping 172.16.1.1
Type escape sequence to abort.
Sending 5, 100-byte ICMP Echos to 172.16.1.1:
!!!!!
Success rate is 100 percent (5/5)
OSPF3(config)#
OSPF3(config)#
OSPF3(config)#do trace 172.16.1.1 numeric
Type escape sequence to abort.
Tracing the route to 172.16.1.1
VRF info: (vrf in name/id, vrf out name/id)
  1 172.16.4.2 1 msec 0 msec 0 msec
  2 172.16.3.1 1 msec 0 msec 1 msec
  3 172.16.2.2 0 msec 1 msec 0 msec
  4 172.16.1.1 1 msec *  1 msec
OSPF3(config)#
```

Compared to earlier, we have a much more impressive traceroute now, and can even ping from the loopback of OSPF3 to the loopback of ISP:

```
OSPF3(config)#do ping 100.100.100.100 source 1.2.3.1
Type escape sequence to abort.
Sending 5, 100-byte ICMP Echos to 100.100.100.100:
```

```
Packet sent with a source address of 1.2.3.1
!!!!!
Success rate is 100 percent (5/5)
OSPF3(config)#
```

This configuration works. It is far from elegant, but it does work. It can also very easily go wrong, and a routing loop (where the packets bounced between two devices until they time-out) can easily be introduced into the network, as I did. Hopefully you won't see the following output, but try and guess which static route I got wrong:

```
ISP(config)#do trace 172.16.4.2 n
Type escape sequence to abort.
Tracing the route to 172.16.4.2
VRF info: (vrf in name/id, vrf out name/id)
  1 172.16.1.2 16 msec 8 msec 20 msec
  2 172.16.2.1 32 msec 28 msec 32 msec
  3 172.16.2.2 28 msec 20 msec 24 msec
  4 172.16.2.1 28 msec 32 msec 28 msec
  5 172.16.2.2 32 msec 28 msec 32 msec
  6 172.16.2.1 40 msec 40 msec 40 msec
  7 172.16.2.2 40 msec 40 msec 40 msec
  8 172.16.2.1 52 msec 52 msec 48 msec
  9 172.16.2.2 52 msec 52 msec 48 msec
 10 172.16.2.1 60 msec 60 msec 60 msec
 11 172.16.2.2 60 msec 60 msec 60 msec
 12 172.16.2.1 68 msec 72 msec 72 msec
 13 172.16.2.2 68 msec 72 msec 72 msec
 14 172.16.2.1 80 msec 80 msec 80 msec
 15 172.16.2.2 84 msec 80 msec 80 msec
 16 172.16.2.1 92 msec 88 msec 92 msec
 17 172.16.2.2 92 msec 88 msec 92 msec
 18 172.16.2.1 100 msec 104 msec 112 msec
 19 172.16.2.2 188 msec 172 msec 160 msec
 20 172.16.2.1 212 msec 184 msec 212 msec
 21 172.16.2.2 188 msec 212 msec 208 msec
 22 172.16.2.1 232 msec 232 msec 160 msec
 23 172.16.2.2 120 msec 120 msec 120 msec
 24 172.16.2.1 132 msec 128 msec 132 msec
 25 172.16.2.2 132 msec 132 msec 132 msec
 26 172.16.2.1 140 msec 140 msec 144 msec
 27 172.16.2.2 140 msec 152 msec 152 msec
 28 172.16.2.1 160 msec 160 msec 152 msec
 29 172.16.2.2 152 msec 152 msec 152 msec
 30 172.16.2.1 160 msec 164 msec 160 msec
ISP(config)#
```

If you get a traceroute that loops like the above one does, press Ctrl+Shift+6 to stop it.

Complex routing using static routes is not advised, because of this exact reason. It is prone to human error (layer eight) and hard to maintain, which is why dynamic routing protocols are so useful. Dynamic routing protocols allow us to "advertise" networks to our peers, and to propagate networks advertised to us by other peers. These peers do not always have to be directly connected, which is why I have said peers instead of neighbors. Routing protocols offer greater flexibility and simplicity and come in two variations; link-state and distance vector.

4.6.b Link state vs. distance vector

Distance vector protocols use distance in their decision-making. RIP (Routing Information Protocol) uses the distance between routers, known as hops, as its metric. RIP is not suited for large-scale deployments, as the maximum hop-count between devices cannot exceed fifteen. Our topology is far from large and the number of routers we have is right in the middle of RIPs limit. If we had twice the number of routers, we would not be able to run RIP from end-to-end.

RIP does not actually feature on the CCNA syllabus, possibly because it is not as widely used, possibly because Cisco wants to concentrate on OSPF and EIGRP. Nonetheless, we should still discuss it in order to learn of its limitations and why OSPF and EIGRP are preferred.

RIP was one of the earliest routing protocols and is still supported today. It is designed for smaller environments, hence the hop-count limit of 15. A route with a hop count of 16 is classed as an unreachable network. The key to understanding why RIP is no longer favoured is to remember that it is one of the oldest protocols, routing tables were much smaller back then and the volume of traffic was much lower. Because of the low volume of traffic, RIP could use more bandwidth, without impacting the network. RIP does send a lot of traffic for it to work. It sends updates every 30 seconds (by default), these updates include the entire routing table. RIP also supports triggered updates, which can reduce the amount of traffic RIP generates by only sending updates when a change occurs.

RIP comes in two versions (for IPv4, there is another for IPv6). RIP version 1 was "classless", so did not send the subnet mask in the routing update, meaning it was great if you wanted to route 10.0.0.0/8, 172.16.0.0/16, or 192.168.1.0/24, but not much good for anything more complex (10.1.1.0/24 for example), it also did not support any form of authentication.

Version 2 of RIP added support for CIDR, so we could use RIP for the 10.1.1.0/24 network. Version 2 also switched to a multicast delivery format, cutting down on unnecessary traffic and supports MD5 authentication.

RIP works in a request/response method. Once we enable RIP, the router sends a broadcast request message (for RIPv1) out of each interface that is RIP enabled. Neighbours running RIP will send back a response message, which includes their routing table. Once we receive the table, we need to make a decision:

- If we don't already have the route, then we add it to our routing table, including information about the router from which we received the route.
- If we already have the route, but the new one has a lower hop count (therefore a better route), then we install the new route in our routing table.
- If we already have the route, but the new one has a higher hop count (therefore a worse route), then we set the hop count to 16 (infinity).

RIP operates on a process of routing by rumor. We learn other routes because other routers tell us about them. We cannot validate them ourselves, we just have to assume that the information we have is correct. Whilst we don't explicitly need to know huge amounts about RIP (according to the syllabus), we really should configure it so we can see it in action.

We enable the RIP routing process using the command "*router rip*". We then add the networks we wish to advertise using the command "*network <network>*". Let's do this with EIGRP1, ISP and Gateway:

```
EIGRP1(config)#router rip
EIGRP1(config-router)#network 192.168.1.0
EIGRP1(config-router)#network 192.168.21.0
EIGRP1(config-router)#

ISP(config)#router rip
ISP(config-router)#network 192.168.1.0
ISP(config-router)#network 192.168.20.0
ISP(config-router)#

Gateway(config)#router rip
Gateway(config-router)#network 192.168.20.0
Gateway(config-router)#
```

We can see that Gateway now knows about the 192.168.1.0 and 192.168.21.0 routes (indicated with an "R"):

```
Gateway(config-router)#do sh ip route | b Gate
Gateway of last resort is not set

      10.0.0.0/8 is variably subnetted, 4 subnets, 2 masks
C        10.1.1.0/24 is directly connected, Ethernet0/1
L        10.1.1.254/32 is directly connected, Ethernet0/1
C        10.20.1.0/24 is directly connected, Ethernet0/2
```

```
L          10.20.1.254/32 is directly connected, Ethernet0/2
           50.0.0.0/32 is subnetted, 1 subnets
C          50.50.50.50 is directly connected, Loopback0
R       192.168.1.0/24 [120/1] via 192.168.20.1, 00:00:01, Ethernet0/0
        192.168.20.0/24 is variably subnetted, 2 subnets, 2 masks
C          192.168.20.0/24 is directly connected, Ethernet0/0
L          192.168.20.254/32 is directly connected, Ethernet0/0
R       192.168.21.0/24 [120/2] via 192.168.20.1, 00:00:01, Ethernet0/0
Gateway(config-router)#
```

We can get a much more succinct output, by adding the name of the protocol that we just want to see routes for:

```
Gateway(config-router)#do sh ip route rip | b Gate
Gateway of last resort is not set

R       192.168.1.0/24 [120/1] via 192.168.20.1, 00:00:28, Ethernet0/0
R       192.168.21.0/24 [120/2] via 192.168.20.1, 00:00:28, Ethernet0/0
Gateway(config-router)#
```

EIGRP1 knows about the networks advertised by Gateway, and here I have narrowed down the command to show just the RIP routes:

```
EIGRP1(config-router)#do sh ip route rip | b Gate
Gateway of last resort is 192.168.1.1 to network 0.0.0.0

R       192.168.20.0/24 [120/1] via 192.168.1.1, 00:00:07, Ethernet0/1
EIGRP1(config-router)#
```

There are a couple of commands that will give us greater insight into the routes we have (and this includes local, connected and static routes). We can use the "show ip route <network>" command:

```
EIGRP1(config-router)#do sh ip route 192.168.20.0
Routing entry for 192.168.20.0/24
  Known via "rip", distance 120, metric 1
  Redistributing via rip
  Last update from 192.168.1.1 on Ethernet0/1, 00:00:12 ago
  Routing Descriptor Blocks:
  * 192.168.1.1, from 192.168.1.1, 00:00:12 ago, via Ethernet0/1
      Route metric is 1, traffic share count is 1
EIGRP1(config-router)#
```

We can also use the command "show ip cef" to display the contents on the CEF table, which we spoke about in 4.1.c:

```
EIGRP1(config-router)#do sh ip cef 192.168.20.0
192.168.20.0/24
  nexthop 192.168.1.1 Ethernet0/1
EIGRP1(config-router)#
```

If we want to add an explicit entry into the routing table, we can daisy-chain the routes, as we will see next.

4.6.c next hop

The routing table and CEF table show us the next hop for our routes, this is the router we must go through to get to our destination. As mentioned above, the next hop can be anything we want, just so long as we have a route to that next hop.

Consider the following routing table:

```
EIGRP1(config-router)#do sh ip route | b Gate
Gateway of last resort is 192.168.1.1 to network 0.0.0.0

S*     0.0.0.0/0 [1/0] via 192.168.1.1
       1.0.0.0/32 is subnetted, 1 subnets
C         1.1.1.1 is directly connected, Loopback0
       192.168.1.0/24 is variably subnetted, 2 subnets, 2 masks
C         192.168.1.0/24 is directly connected, Ethernet0/1
L         192.168.1.2/32 is directly connected, Ethernet0/1
R      192.168.20.0/24 [120/1] via 192.168.1.1, 00:00:19, Ethernet0/1
       192.168.21.0/24 is variably subnetted, 2 subnets, 2 masks
C         192.168.21.0/24 is directly connected, Ethernet1/2
L         192.168.21.1/32 is directly connected, Ethernet1/2
       192.168.51.0/24 is variably subnetted, 2 subnets, 2 masks
C         192.168.51.0/24 is directly connected, Serial2/0
L         192.168.51.1/32 is directly connected, Serial2/0
EIGRP1(config-router)#
```

EIGRP1 does not know about the loopback address on the Gateway router (50.50.50.50). It has a default route via ISP, but ISP does not know about the loopback address either:

```
ISP(config)#do sh ip cef 50.50.50.50/32
%Prefix not found
ISP(config-router)#do sh ip cef 50.50.50.50
0.0.0.0/0
  no route
ISP(config-router)#
```

Therefore, any attempt by EIGRP1 to get to this address will fail:

```
EIGRP1(config-router)#do ping 50.50.50.50
Type escape sequence to abort.
Sending 5, 100-byte ICMP Echos to 50.50.50.50:
U.U.U
Success rate is 0 percent (0/5)
EIGRP1(config-router)#
```

Recall from chapter 2 that a U means destination unreachable and a dot means that there was a timeout while waiting for a reply.

EIGRP1 does however know about Gateway's 192.168.20.254 address, which it learnt via RIP, and it can reach it:

```
EIGRP1(config-router)#do ping 192.168.20.254
Type escape sequence to abort.
Sending 5, 100-byte ICMP Echos to 192.168.20.254:
!!!!!
Success rate is 100 percent (5/5)
EIGRP1(config-router)#
```

Therefore, we can use this address as the next hop address to get to 50.50.50.50:

```
EIGRP1(config)#ip route 50.50.50.50 255.255.255.255 192.168.20.254
EIGRP1(config)#
```

Does the traffic now completely jump over ISP?

```
EIGRP1(config)#do ping 50.50.50.50
Type escape sequence to abort.
Sending 5, 100-byte ICMP Echos to 50.50.50.50:
U.U.U
Success rate is 0 percent (0/5)
EIGRP1(config)#
```

No, it does not. If we look at the CEF table then we can see that it is headed in the right direction:

```
EIGRP1(config)#do sh ip cef 50.50.50.50
50.50.50.50/32
  nexthop 192.168.1.1 Ethernet0/1
EIGRP1(config)#
```

However, the traceroute shows that we stop at ISP:

```
EIGRP1(config)#do trace 50.50.50.50 numeric
Type escape sequence to abort.
Tracing the route to 50.50.50.50
```

```
VRF info: (vrf in name/id, vrf out name/id)
  1 192.168.1.1 2 msec 10 msec 10 msec
  2 192.168.1.1 !H  *  !H
EIGRP1(config)#
```

This is because ISP does not know about the 50.50.50.50 network, so for it to be able to route to that, we have to tell it where to go:

```
ISP(config-router)#ip route 50.50.50.50 255.255.255.255 192.168.20.254
ISP(config)#
```

As well as highlighting the benefits of using a routing protocol to ease the burden of static routes, now EIGRP1 can get to 50.50.50.50:

```
EIGRP1(config)#do trace 50.50.50.50 numeric
Type escape sequence to abort.
Tracing the route to 50.50.50.50
VRF info: (vrf in name/id, vrf out name/id)
  1 192.168.1.1 0 msec 1 msec 4 msec
  2 192.168.20.254 0 msec * 1 msec
EIGRP1(config)#do ping 50.50.50.50
Type escape sequence to abort.
Sending 5, 100-byte ICMP Echos to 50.50.50.50:
!!!!!
Success rate is 100 percent (5/5)
EIGRP1(config)#
```

Therefore, although we can set a next hop address that is not directly connected to us, we still need the routes that it relies on to have a full path to that destination. In order for us to understand how we are going to get somewhere, we need to understand the routing table a bit more.

4.6.d ip routing table

The routing table is our list of what is where. By the end of the book our routing tables will look very impressive, we will have lots of routes and will be able to get to anywhere in the network from any of our devices. This means that the routing table will be fairly large. Therefore, it makes sense that we know how to read this table early on. Let's start with EIGRP1's routing table:

```
EIGRP1(config)#do sh ip route | b Gate
Gateway of last resort is 192.168.1.1 to network 0.0.0.0

S*    0.0.0.0/0 [1/0] via 192.168.1.1
      1.0.0.0/32 is subnetted, 1 subnets
C        1.1.1.1 is directly connected, Loopback0
      50.0.0.0/32 is subnetted, 1 subnets
```

```
S          50.50.50.50 [1/0] via 192.168.20.254
           192.168.1.0/24 is variably subnetted, 2 subnets, 2 masks
C          192.168.1.0/24 is directly connected, Ethernet0/1
L          192.168.1.2/32 is directly connected, Ethernet0/1
R       192.168.20.0/24 [120/1] via 192.168.1.1, 00:00:21, Ethernet0/1
           192.168.21.0/24 is variably subnetted, 2 subnets, 2 masks
C          192.168.21.0/24 is directly connected, Ethernet1/2
L          192.168.21.1/32 is directly connected, Ethernet1/2
           192.168.51.0/24 is variably subnetted, 2 subnets, 2 masks
C          192.168.51.0/24 is directly connected, Serial2/0
L          192.168.51.1/32 is directly connected, Serial2/0
EIGRP1(config)#
```

Let's narrow it down to just the static routes and RIP routes. We can use the command *"show ip route static"* or *"show ip route rip"* but we cannot mix the two commands to get both, therefore we need to use the output modifier instead. This one is a bit tricky to get it nice and succinct. If we chose to include the S and the R, denoting static and RIP respectively, then we also include all the codes and any serial interfaces as well:

```
EIGRP1(config)#do sh ip route | include S|R
Codes: L - local, C - connected, S - static, R - RIP, M - mobile, B - BGP
       D - EIGRP, EX - EIGRP external, O - OSPF, IA - OSPF inter area
       N1 - OSPF NSSA external type 1, N2 - OSPF NSSA external type 2
       E1 - OSPF external type 1, E2 - OSPF external type 2
       i - IS-IS, su - IS-IS summary, L1 - IS-IS level-1, L2 - IS-IS level-2
       ia - IS-IS inter area, * - candidate default, U - per-user static route
       o - ODR, P - periodic downloaded static route, H - NHRP, l - LISP
S*     0.0.0.0/0 [1/0] via 192.168.1.1
S          50.50.50.50 [1/0] via 192.168.20.254
R       192.168.20.0/24 [120/1] via 192.168.1.1, 00:00:23, Ethernet0/1
C          192.168.51.0/24 is directly connected, Serial2/0
L          192.168.51.1/32 is directly connected, Serial2/0
EIGRP1(config)#
```

Instead, we can exclude the dashes (to get rid of the codes), the C and the L (denoting Connected and Local, respectively), and any line that includes the word "subnetted":

```
EIGRP1(config)#do sh ip route | e -|L|C|subnetted

Gateway of last resort is 192.168.1.1 to network 0.0.0.0

S*     0.0.0.0/0 [1/0] via 192.168.1.1
S          50.50.50.50 [1/0] via 192.168.20.254
R       192.168.20.0/24 [120/1] via 192.168.1.1, 00:00:24, Ethernet0/1

EIGRP1(config)#
```

At the top of our table, we have the static route for 0.0.0.0/0, meaning send all unmatched traffic to the ISP router. We then have another static entry, for 50.50.50.50 pointing to 192.168.20.254, and finally we have our RIP route for the 192.168.20.0/24 subnet, pointing to the ISP router.

Next to each of the destinations, we have a set of two numbers in square brackets. We have [1/0] for our static routes and [120/1] for our RIP route. The first number in the brackets is the administrative distance (AD) we spoke of earlier.

The AD is all about how much we believe a route to be true. We can't get any better than a connected route, as it is on us, either as a physical port (Ethernet or serial) or as a virtual loopback interface, so its AD is 0. Other routes get a different value:

Route type	AD
Connected	0
Static	1
eBGP	20
EIGRP (Internal)	90
IGRP	100
OSPF	110
IS-IS	115
RIP	120
EIGRP (External)	170
iBGP	200
EIGRP summary route	5

Static routes will have needed someone to enter them directly into the router, so they also get a very believe AD of 1. We then get to the dynamic protocols. The ones we will be most interested in are the three EIGRP ones, OSPF and RIP, but we will briefly talk about the others.

BGP is used on the Internet. It connects the Internet, which is a bunch of Autonomous Systems (AS), together. Each AS has a different number and each is responsible for its own set of prefixes, as well as propagating prefixes it has learned from other AS's. This is referred to as eBGP, the "e" meaning external, where the routes are passed to us from a different AS. There is a high level of trust put into BGP, therefore eBGP routes are given an AD of 20. BGP can also be run within a local area network (instead of OSPF, EIGRP or RIP), and is referred to as iBGP (internal). It works very well, but BGP has some rules and design constraints. One of these rules is that iBGP learned prefixes will not be propagated (sent on to neighboring routers) unless the router also knows about it through an IGP (Internal Gateway Protocol, such as OSPF, RIP or EIGRP). Therefore, we should already know about it through an IGP, which has a more believable AD, so iBGP gets an high AD of 200.

> There is a little more to the BGP rules than that. If you would like to learn more then grab a copy of my book: BGP for Cisco Networks.

Don't worry about IGRP; it's an old protocol that isn't supported nowadays and you would be very hard-pressed to find anywhere that still uses it. EIGRP, which we will discuss in much greater depth later on, replaced it.

Service providers use IS-IS (Intermediate-System to Intermediate-System), primarily. It is a link state protocol, like OSPF. It's not the easiest of protocols to understand within a few pages, and does not feature on the CCNA syllabus, so we won't go into details here.

The second number in the brackets is the metric. We use this to influence how we want our routing to behave.

Let's add another route for 50.50.50.50 on EIGRP1, this time pointing in completely the wrong direction (towards EIGRP2):

```
EIGRP1(config)#ip route 50.50.50.50 255.255.255.255 192.168.21.2
EIGRP1(config)#do sh ip route 50.50.50.50
Routing entry for 50.50.50.50/32
  Known via "static", distance 1, metric 0
  Routing Descriptor Blocks:
    192.168.21.2
      Route metric is 0, traffic share count is 1
  * 192.168.20.254
      Route metric is 0, traffic share count is 1
EIGRP1(config)#
```

We now have two routes for this destination. We can go in one way, or the other. One will work, the other will not. This may not be the best example, as we know that EIGRP2 does not have any knowledge of 50.50.50.50. However, if it did, then we would load-balance the traffic across the two routes, as shown by the traffic share count above. Now, what if one of those routes was intended purely as a backup route? By adding a metric we can influence our routing table, ensuring that the route through ISP is always favoured, below is the same command, but we are adding a metric of 250:

```
EIGRP1(config)#ip route 50.50.50.50 255.255.255.255 192.168.21.2 250
EIGRP1(config)#do sh ip route static | b Gate
Gateway of last resort is 192.168.1.1 to network 0.0.0.0

S*    0.0.0.0/0 [1/0] via 192.168.1.1
      50.0.0.0/32 is subnetted, 1 subnets
S        50.50.50.50 [1/0] via 192.168.20.254
EIGRP1(config)#
```

The route is gone! Let's see where it went.

4.6.e Passive Interfaces (how they work)

So where did our static route with the high metric go? We can find out by temporarily supressing RIP advertisements from ISP to EIGRP1, using the passive-interface command:

```
ISP(config)#router rip
ISP(config-router)#passive-interface e0/1
ISP(config-router)#
```

The command *"passive-interface <interface>"* in RIP routing prevents an interface from sending out advertisements, but not from receiving them. It works differently with OSPF, and will prevent OSPF neighborships forming, by blocking the sending of Hello packets.

So, what effect does this have on EIGRP1's routing table? Type in *"do sh ip route rip | b Gate"* and press enter, press the up arrow on the keyboard and press enter again to put the command back in again, do this a few times. Can you see the time increasing?

```
EIGRP1(config)#do sh ip route rip | b Gate
Gateway of last resort is 192.168.1.1 to network 0.0.0.0

R     192.168.20.0/24 [120/1] via 192.168.1.1, 00:01:49, Ethernet0/1
EIGRP1(config)#
EIGRP1(config)#do sh ip route rip | b Gate
Gateway of last resort is 192.168.1.1 to network 0.0.0.0

R     192.168.20.0/24 [120/1] via 192.168.1.1, 00:02:48, Ethernet0/1
EIGRP1(config)#do sh ip route rip | b Gate
Gateway of last resort is 192.168.1.1 to network 0.0.0.0

R     192.168.20.0/24 [120/1] via 192.168.1.1, 00:03:01, Ethernet0/1
EIGRP1(config)#do sh ip route rip | b Gate
Gateway of last resort is 192.168.1.1 to network 0.0.0.0

R     192.168.20.0/24 is possibly down, routing via 192.168.1.1, Eth0/1
EIGRP1(config)#
EIGRP1(config)#do sh ip route rip | b Gate
Gateway of last resort is 192.168.1.1 to network 0.0.0.0

EIGRP1(config)#
```

Because EIGRP1 is not receiving updates from ISP, we start to use different timers, apart from the standard 30-second update timer. By default, every 30 seconds RIP sends out an update, containing the full routing table. If we don't receive an update within 30 seconds, we wait a little longer, for the period of the Invalid timer, which by default is 180 seconds (3 minutes). The Invalid timer is the length of time we can have a route not be updated, or confirmed to still exist, before we declare it unreachable and set the hop count to 16. We then wait a bit longer (another 60 seconds by default) for the flush timer to expire, at which point the route is removed.

Once we get to around the 3-minute mark we can see that the router has now started to question the validity of the route, saying it is "possibly down". A little while longer the route is totally flushed out.

At about the 3-minute mark we can see the route details for 50.50.50.50 change. The route switches from pointing to ISP, and instead starts to point to OSPF2, with the distance (our metric) of 250 we configured earlier.

```
EIGRP1(config)#do sh ip route 50.50.50.50
Routing entry for 50.50.50.50/32
  Known via "static", distance 1, metric 0
  Routing Descriptor Blocks:
  * 192.168.20.254
      Route metric is 0, traffic share count is 1
EIGRP1(config)#do sh ip route 50.50.50.50
Routing entry for 50.50.50.50/32
  Known via "static", distance 250, metric 0
  Routing Descriptor Blocks:
  * 192.168.21.2
      Route metric is 0, traffic share count is 1
EIGRP1(config)#
```

This is (naturally) reflected in our routing table:

```
EIGRP1(config)#do sh ip route static | b Gate
Gateway of last resort is 192.168.1.1 to network 0.0.0.0

S*      0.0.0.0/0 [1/0] via 192.168.1.1
        50.0.0.0/32 is subnetted, 1 subnets
S          50.50.50.50 [250/0] via 192.168.21.2
EIGRP1(config)#
```

Let's finish by setting ISP back up to talk to EIGRP1. Although we disabled the sending of RIP updates through our Ethernet1/1 interface by using the passive-interface command, we can get around this, by switching to unicast. Let's look at the output of the command "*show ip protocols*" for a moment:

```
ISP(config-router)#do sh ip protocols
*** IP Routing is NSF aware ***

Routing Protocol is "application"
  Sending updates every 0 seconds
  Invalid after 0 seconds, hold down 0, flushed after 0
  Outgoing update filter list for all interfaces is not set
  Incoming update filter list for all interfaces is not set
```

```
Maximum path: 32
Routing for Networks:
Routing Information Sources:
  Gateway         Distance      Last Update
Distance: (default is 4)

Routing Protocol is "rip"
  Outgoing update filter list for all interfaces is not set
  Incoming update filter list for all interfaces is not set
  Sending updates every 30 seconds, next due in 23 seconds
  Invalid after 180 seconds, hold down 180, flushed after 240
  Redistributing: rip
  Default version control: send version 1, receive any version
    Interface              Send  Recv  Triggered RIP  Key-chain
    Ethernet0/0             1     1 2
  Automatic network summarization is in effect
  Maximum path: 4
  Routing for Networks:
    192.168.1.0
    192.168.20.0
  Passive Interface(s):
    Ethernet0/1
  Routing Information Sources:
    Gateway         Distance      Last Update
    192.168.1.2        120        00:00:14
  Distance: (default is 120)

ISP(config-router)#
```

This command tells us all about our timers, our neighbors, the versions we are using, our load balancing capabilities (maximum path), what networks we are routing, any passive interfaces and who we are receiving updates from. We cannot see any neighbors in the output above, which means that any communication we have is through broadcast (because we are sending using RIP version 1). We can set up EIGRP1 to be a unicast peer using the command *"neighbor <IP address>"*:

```
ISP(config-router)#neighbor 192.168.1.2
ISP(config-router)#
```

Now, we can use the *"show ip protocols"* command to see who our neighbor(s) are:

```
ISP(config-router)#do sh ip protocols | b rip
Routing Protocol is "rip"
  Outgoing update filter list for all interfaces is not set
  Incoming update filter list for all interfaces is not set
  Sending updates every 30 seconds, next due in 26 seconds
  Invalid after 180 seconds, hold down 180, flushed after 240
  Redistributing: rip
```

```
   Neighbor(s):
     192.168.1.2
   Default version control: send version 1, receive any version
     Interface              Send  Recv  Triggered RIP  Key-chain
     Ethernet0/0             1     1 2
   Automatic network summarization is in effect
   Maximum path: 4
   Routing for Networks:
     192.168.1.0
     192.168.20.0
   Passive Interface(s):
     Ethernet0/1
   Routing Information Sources:
     Gateway          Distance      Last Update
     192.168.1.2          120       00:00:26
   Distance: (default is 120)

 ISP(config-router)#
```

Given a few moments, we should see our RIP learned routes populate our routing tables, and EIGRP1's route to 50.50.50.50 reverts back to the original route (because the next-hop is again available):

```
 ISP(config-router)#do sh ip route rip | b Gate
 Gateway of last resort is not set

 R     192.168.21.0/24 [120/1] via 192.168.1.2, 00:00:06, Ethernet0/1
 ISP(config-router)#

 EIGRP1(config)#do sh ip route static | b Gate
 Gateway of last resort is 192.168.1.1 to network 0.0.0.0

 S*    0.0.0.0/0 [1/0] via 192.168.1.1
       50.0.0.0/32 is subnetted, 1 subnets
 S        50.50.50.50 [1/0] via 192.168.20.254
 EIGRP1(config)#
```

Our small-scale RIP deployment worked fine and hopefully you have seen how easy it is to deploy. However, RIP is not on the syllabus, so we should remove it and move on.

```
 EIGRP1(config)#no router rip
 EIGRP1(config)#

 ISP(config-router)#exit
 ISP(config)#no router rip
 ISP(config)#
```

```
Gateway(config-router)#exit
Gateway(config)#no router rip
Gateway(config)#
```

RIP is still a great way to start understanding how routing protocols operate, because it is a very simplistic protocol. There is still quite a bit of RIP that could be covered, but now it's time to start looking at OSPF.

4.7 Configure and verify OSPF

Networks grew quickly and soon RIP became unsuitable for modern networks. Hampered by the 15-hop limit, slow convergence times and the inability to support VLSM, the pressure was on to move to a new open standard for an Internal Gateway Protocol (IGP). This was around 1988, and in 1991 it became formalized. Now we have Open Shortest-Path First (OSPF), which is the de-facto standard for internal routing in local area networks, because it is an open standard it is supported on a very wide range of devices from different manufacturers.

OSPF is a link-state protocol, like IS-IS, both use Dijkstra's algorithm (RIP uses the Bellman-Ford algorithm) to determine the best path to a destination. Whereas IS-IS can carry IPv4 and IPv6 natively, OSPF had to be rewritten for IPv6, and now we have OSPFv2 for IPv4 and OSPFv3 for IPv6. The key difference between OSPF and IS-IS is that OSPF operates at layer-3, on top of IP, whereas IS-IS operates at layer-2. Both protocols use the concept of areas to segregate the network, but this is where we will leave IS-IS alone, and concentrate on OSPF.

The Dijkstra algorithm allows OSPF to find the best path through a network. It works on attributing a cost to a link. This cost is also the metric for OSPF. The cost is worked out as follows; reference interface bandwidth divided by interface bandwidth. The reference bandwidth will always be 100Mbps. Therefore, to work out the cost of a T1 line (1.544Mbps) we would divide 100,000,000 by 1,544,000, and get a cost of 64. The cost of a 10Mbps Ethernet interface would be 10 (100,000,000/10,000,000). A table of default OSPF costs is below:

Bandwidth	OSPF Cost
100 Gbps	1
40 Gbps	1
10 Gbps	1
1 Gbps	1
100 Mbps	1
10 Mbps	10
1.544 Mbps	64

In a multi-path network, the path with the lowest cumulative cost will be the one taken. This makes perfect sense, if we have a path with two 1Gbps links (a cost of two), it is clearly faster than a link with one 1Gbps link and a 10Mbps link (cost of 11). We can actually change the cost of a link, if we want to. This is useful if we have two links of equal speed and are paying a flat price for one, and paying by the megabyte for the other, for example.

The costs for a destination allow the router to form a path tree. The information built up by the routers, and any subsequent changes, is flooded to the other routers, through link-state updates (LSUs). OSPF's multicast behaviour works much better than RIP's broadcast behaviour, but still, flooding is hardly ideal. Areas can reduce the effect that this has; they create boundaries where link-state updates cannot cross. Nevertheless, is the creation of multiple areas actually beneficial to us?

4.7.a Benefit of single area

An area in OSPF is a grouping of hosts and networks. It is a way of carving a network up into logical, sensible units. Imagine a network that spans many offices across the globe. It would not make sense that these are all within the same network; it would be easier, but not sensible. Each area has its own link state database, which is good at keeping routing protocol traffic at manageable levels. If we ran just one area across a number of locations, the routing protocol traffic could impede user traffic. Instead, segregation into areas means that we can make better use of our bandwidth by summarizing routes between areas.

We seem to be digressing though, instead of singing about the benefits of a single area, the focus has been on the negative aspects. So, let's look at why you would use a single area.

Single areas make life so much easier. With OSPF, there is one "main" backbone area; area 0. All other areas should have connection to area 0, either physically, or virtually. A single area (area 0) makes this much easier.

Consider our topology. We have four dedicated OSPF routers and the ISP router, which will also take part in OSPF. The logical topology looks like this:

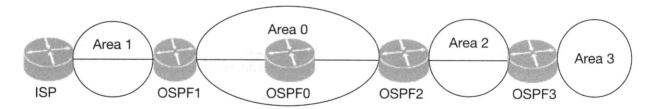

OSPF0 is our backbone router; it has all of its interfaces in Area 0. ISP and OSPF1 are in Area 1, and this area is connected to Area 0. OSPF2 is in Area 2, and OSPF1 and OSPF2 both have interfaces in Area 0. OSPF3 is in Area 2, and its Loopback interface will be in Area 3.

Let's start configuring these and see how this topology affects us.

4.7.b Configure OSPFv2

In the previous section, we used the command *"router rip"* to configure RIP, we can use the command *"router ospf"* to start configuring OSPF. We need to specify a process number, which is a way of running more than one instance of OSPF on a router. We will use process number one, so the command is *"router ospf 1"*:

```
OSPF0(config)#router ospf ?
  <1-65535>  Process ID

OSPF0(config)#router ospf 1
OSPF0(config-router)#
```

If we wanted to run more OSPF instances we could also configure *"router ospf 2"*, *"router ospf 3"* and so on. These process numbers are all locally significant. Next, we should specify a router-id. This acts as a way of OSPF knowing who supplied what route. By default, OSPF will choose a router-id on its own, first choosing the highest loopback interface as its router ID. If it does not find one, then it will choose the highest interface ID, and if it does not find one (if for any reason we have not configured an IP address yet), it will tell us to configure one manually.

It is wise, however, not to leave it up to chance, and manually enter one:

```
OSPF0(config-router)#router-id 1.2.0.1
OSPF0(config-router)#
```

Once we have done this, we can start to add in our networks, using the *"network"* command, as we did in RIP.

OSPF supports variable length subnet masks, making life easier. Here the network command requires a wildcard mask in order to match the subnet mask. The wildcard mask is like the reverse of the subnet mask.

If we wanted to match 172.16.2.0/24, instead of using the subnet mask of 255.255.255.0, we would use the wildcard mask of 0.0.0.255. If we wanted to match a /16 subnet mask of 255.255.0.0, the wildcard mask would be 0.0.255.255. An exact match to an IP address would use the wildcard mask 0.0.0.0.

We can use this to reduce the number of commands we need to enter. With OSPF0 we have three IP addresses, 172.16.2.1, 172.16.3.1 and 1.2.0.1 (as we want to include our loopback interface). We can choose to match just the IP address (172.16.2.1), just the subnet (172.16.2.0), or match more than one subnet (172.16.0.0). When we use the network command in OSPF we also need to supply the area as well.

If we wanted to match just the IP addresses configured on our interfaces, we would use the commands:

```
OSPF0(config-router)#network 172.16.2.1 0.0.0.0 area 0
OSPF0(config-router)#network 172.16.3.1 0.0.0.0 area 0
OSPF0(config-router)#network 1.2.0.1 0.0.0.0 area 0
```

If wanted to match the exact subnets, we could use the commands:

```
OSPF0(config-router)#network 172.16.2.0 0.0.0.255 area 0
OSPF0(config-router)#network 172.16.3.0 0.0.0.255 area 0
OSPF0(config-router)#network 1.2.0.1 0.0.0.0 area 0
```

The loopback uses all zeros for the wildcard mask as it has a /32 subnet mask (255.255.255.255), therefore the wildcard mask would be 0.0.0.0.

If we wanted to match on the first and second octets of the IP address, we could use the commands:

```
OSPF0(config-router)#network 172.16.0.0 0.0.255.255 area 0
```

This has left us with a lot of duplication in our configuration:

```
OSPF0(config-router)#do sh run | s ospf
router ospf 1
 router-id 1.2.0.1
 network 1.2.0.1 0.0.0.0 area 0
 network 172.16.2.1 0.0.0.0 area 0
 network 172.16.2.0 0.0.0.255 area 0
 network 172.16.3.1 0.0.0.0 area 0
 network 172.16.3.0 0.0.0.255 area 0
 network 172.16.0.0 0.0.255.255 area 0
OSPF0(config-router)#
```

Let's remove some of the duplicates:

```
OSPF0(config-router)#
OSPF0(config-router)#no network 172.16.2.0 0.0.0.255 area 0
OSPF0(config-router)#no network 172.16.3.0 0.0.0.255 area 0
OSPF0(config-router)#no network 172.16.0.0 0.0.255.255 area 0
OSPF0(config-router)#
```

We will test out the other methods on the other routers. For the moment, let's just confirm our settings. We can use the command "*show ip protocols*" to see some excellent information about OSPF:

```
OSPF0(config-router)#do sh ip protocols | b ospf
Routing Protocol is "ospf 1"
  Outgoing update filter list for all interfaces is not set
  Incoming update filter list for all interfaces is not set
  Router ID 1.2.0.1
  Number of areas in this router is 1. 1 normal 0 stub 0 nssa
  Maximum path: 4
  Routing for Networks:
    1.2.0.1 0.0.0.0 area 0
    172.16.2.1 0.0.0.0 area 0
    172.16.3.1 0.0.0.0 area 0
  Routing Information Sources:
    Gateway           Distance        Last Update
  Distance: (default is 110)

OSPF0(config-router)#
```

Above we can see our router-id and which networks we are routing. Let's press on and set up OSPF1:

```
OSPF1(config)#router ospf 1
OSPF1(config-router)#network 172.16.2.0 0.0.0.255 area 0
OSPF1(config-router)#
%OSPF-5-ADJCHG: Process 1, Nbr 1.2.0.1 on Ethernet1/0 from LOADING to
FULL, Loading Done
OSPF1(config-router)#
OSPF1(config-router)#network 172.16.1.0 0.0.0.255 area 1
OSPF1(config-router)#network 1.2.1.1 0.0.0.0 area 1
OSPF1(config-router)#
```

I was very specific with the subnet mask here. Because we have two interfaces, 172.16.2.0/24 and 172.16.1.0/24, and as they are in different areas, I cannot use the command "network 172.16.0.0 0.0.255.255 area 0" as this would put both interfaces in area 0.

Notice that I have not configured a router-id, but within a few moments of adding in the link connecting OSPF1 to OSPF0, we are told that process 1 has gone from "loading" to "full".

Let's use "sh ip protocols" on OSPF1:

```
OSPF1(config-router)#do sh ip protocols | b ospf
Routing Protocol is "ospf 1"
  Outgoing update filter list for all interfaces is not set
  Incoming update filter list for all interfaces is not set
  Router ID 1.2.1.1
  It is an area border router
  Number of areas in this router is 2. 2 normal 0 stub 0 nssa
  Maximum path: 4
  Routing for Networks:
```

```
       1.2.1.1 0.0.0.0 area 1
       172.16.1.0 0.0.0.255 area 1
       172.16.2.0 0.0.0.255 area 0
   Routing Information Sources:
     Gateway          Distance       Last Update
     1.2.0.1               110       00:00:26
   Distance: (default is 110)

OSPF1(config-router)#
```

Firstly, we can see that OSPF has chosen the router-id for us, selecting the IP address from loopback 0. We have two networks in area 1, and one in area 0. We are also receiving routes from 1.2.0.1. This means we should see them in our routing table:

```
OSPF1(config-router)#do sh ip route ospf | b Gate
Gateway of last resort is 172.16.1.1 to network 0.0.0.0

OSPF1(config-router)#
```

Where are our routes? Let's take a moment to think about this. We should see the some OSPF routes, right? Yes, we should, unless they are not being installed in the routing table due to us already having the routes but with a better administrative distance. Such is the case here, we never removed our static routes from earlier! Let's delete those now. The easiest way to do this is to type the command "*do show run |i route*":

```
OSPF1(config-router)#do sh run | i route
router ospf 1
ip route 0.0.0.0 0.0.0.0 172.16.1.1
ip route 1.2.0.1 255.255.255.255 172.16.2.1
ip route 1.2.2.1 255.255.255.255 172.16.2.1
ip route 1.2.3.1 255.255.255.255 172.16.2.1
ip route 100.100.100.100 255.255.255.255 172.16.1.1
ip route 172.16.3.0 255.255.255.0 172.16.2.1
ip route 172.16.4.0 255.255.255.0 172.16.2.1
ipv6 route ::/0 2001:DB8:A2::1
OSPF1(config-router)#
```

Select all of the lines that start with "ip route" and copy them into notepad. At the beginning of each line type in "no" followed by a space, so that it looks like this:

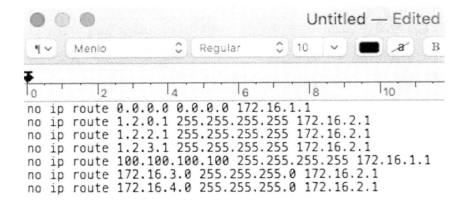

Now copy them from the text document and paste them back into the router:

```
OSPF1(config-router)#no ip route 0.0.0.0 0.0.0.0 172.16.1.1
OSPF1(config)#no ip route 1.2.0.1 255.255.255.255 172.16.2.1
OSPF1(config)#no ip route 1.2.2.1 255.255.255.255 172.16.2.1
OSPF1(config)#no ip route 1.2.3.1 255.255.255.255 172.16.2.1
OSPF1(config)#no ip route 100.100.100.100 255.255.255.255 172.16.1.1
OSPF1(config)#no ip route 172.16.3.0 255.255.255.0 172.16.2.1
OSPF1(config)#no ip route 172.16.4.0 255.255.255.0 172.16.2.1
OSPF1(config)#
```

With a clean slate, we can start to see the OSPF routes:

```
OSPF1(config)#do sh ip route ospf | b Gate
Gateway of last resort is not set

      1.0.0.0/32 is subnetted, 2 subnets
O        1.2.0.1 [110/11] via 172.16.2.1, 00:00:26, Ethernet1/0
      172.16.0.0/16 is variably subnetted, 5 subnets, 2 masks
O        172.16.3.0/24 [110/20] via 172.16.2.1, 00:00:26, Ethernet1/0
OSPF1(config)#
```

We should go and clean up the other routers now though, so we don't get confused later on:

```
ISP(config)#no ip route 1.2.0.1 255.255.255.255 172.16.1.2
ISP(config)#no ip route 1.2.1.1 255.255.255.255 172.16.1.2
ISP(config)#no ip route 1.2.2.1 255.255.255.255 172.16.1.2
ISP(config)#no ip route 1.2.3.1 255.255.255.255 172.16.1.2
ISP(config)#no ip route 50.50.50.50 255.255.255.255 192.168.20.254
ISP(config)#no ip route 172.16.2.0 255.255.255.0 172.16.1.2
ISP(config)#no ip route 172.16.3.0 255.255.255.0 172.16.1.2
ISP(config)#no ip route 172.16.4.0 255.255.255.0 172.16.1.2
ISP(config)#
```

```
OSPF0(config-router)#no ip route 1.2.1.1 255.255.255.255 172.16.2.2
OSPF0(config)#no ip route 1.2.2.1 255.255.255.255 172.16.3.2
OSPF0(config)#no ip route 1.2.3.1 255.255.255.255 172.16.3.2
OSPF0(config)#no ip route 100.100.100.100 255.255.255.255 172.16.2.2
OSPF0(config)#no ip route 172.16.1.0 255.255.255.0 172.16.2.2
OSPF0(config)#no ip route 172.16.4.0 255.255.255.0 172.16.3.2
OSPF0(config)#

OSPF2(config)#no ip route 1.2.0.1 255.255.255.255 172.16.3.1
OSPF2(config)#no ip route 1.2.1.1 255.255.255.255 172.16.3.1
OSPF2(config)#no ip route 1.2.3.1 255.255.255.255 172.16.4.3
OSPF2(config)#no ip route 100.100.100.100 255.255.255.255 172.16.3.1
OSPF2(config)#no ip route 172.16.1.0 255.255.255.0 172.16.3.1
OSPF2(config)#no ip route 172.16.2.0 255.255.255.0 172.16.3.1
OSPF2(config)#

OSPF3(config)#no ip route 0.0.0.0 0.0.0.0 172.16.4.2
OSPF3(config)#
```

Great! Now we can continue without getting any surprises. Let's have a look at OSPF0's routing table:

```
OSPF0(config)#do sh ip route ospf | b Gate
Gateway of last resort is not set

      1.0.0.0/32 is subnetted, 2 subnets
O IA    1.2.1.1 [110/11] via 172.16.2.2, 00:05:07, Ethernet0/1
      172.16.0.0/16 is variably subnetted, 5 subnets, 2 masks
O IA    172.16.1.0/24 [110/20] via 172.16.2.2, 00:04:42, Ethernet0/1
OSPF0(config)#
```

We can see the loopback interface and the interface connecting OSPF1 to ISP in our routing table. Notice that instead of "O" they are shown as "O IA". This means that they are Inter-Area routes, as in they are not from our area.

Let's set up ISP:

```
ISP(config)#router ospf 1
ISP(config-router)#router-id 100.100.100.100
ISP(config-router)#interface e1/1
ISP(config-if)#ip ospf 1 area 1
%OSPF-5-ADJCHG: Process 1, Nbr 1.2.1.1 on Ethernet1/1 from LOADING to
FULL, Loading Done
ISP(config-if)#int lo0
ISP(config-if)#ip ospf 1 area 1
ISP(config-if)#
```

With OSPF we can use the interface-level command *"ip ospf <process> area <area number>"*, instead of the network command. We will see this command a lot with OSPF for IPv6, as there is no network command with the new version. If we now go back to OSPF0, we can see the routes in the table:

```
OSPF0(config)#do sh ip route ospf | b Gate
Gateway of last resort is not set

      1.0.0.0/32 is subnetted, 2 subnets
O IA    1.2.1.1 [110/11] via 172.16.2.2, 00:07:05, Ethernet0/1
      100.0.0.0/32 is subnetted, 1 subnets
O IA     100.100.100.100 [110/21] via 172.16.2.2, 00:00:46, Ethernet0/1
      172.16.0.0/16 is variably subnetted, 5 subnets, 2 masks
O IA      172.16.1.0/24 [110/20] via 172.16.2.2, 00:06:40, Ethernet0/1
OSPF0(config)#
```

We also have reachability from OSPF0 to ISP:

```
OSPF0(config)#do ping 100.100.100.100
Type escape sequence to abort.
Sending 5, 100-byte ICMP Echos to 100.100.100.100:
!!!!!
Success rate is 100 percent (5/5)
OSPF0(config)#
```

Time for OSPF2:

```
OSPF2(config)#router ospf 1
OSPF2(config-router)#router-id 1.2.2.1
OSPF2(config-router)#network 172.16.3.2 0.0.0.0 area 0
OSPF2(config-router)#
%OSPF-5-ADJCHG: Process 1, Nbr 1.2.0.1 on Ethernet2/0 from LOADING to
FULL, Loading Done
OSPF2(config-router)#
OSPF2(config-router)#network 172.16.4.2 0.0.0.0 area 2
OSPF2(config-router)#network 1.2.2.1 0.0.0.0 area 2
OSPF2(config-router)#
```

Our adjacency to OSPF0 forms and the routes are added to OSPF0's routing table:

```
OSPF0(config)#do sh ip route ospf | b Gate
Gateway of last resort is not set

      1.0.0.0/32 is subnetted, 3 subnets
O IA    1.2.1.1 [110/11] via 172.16.2.2, 00:10:14, Ethernet0/1
O IA    1.2.2.1 [110/11] via 172.16.3.2, 00:00:53, Ethernet0/2
      100.0.0.0/32 is subnetted, 1 subnets
O IA     100.100.100.100 [110/21] via 172.16.2.2, 00:03:55, Ethernet0/1
```

```
             172.16.0.0/16 is variably subnetted, 6 subnets, 2 masks
O IA      172.16.1.0/24 [110/20] via 172.16.2.2, 00:09:49, Ethernet0/1
O IA      172.16.4.0/24 [110/20] via 172.16.3.2, 00:01:02, Ethernet0/2
OSPF0(config)#
```

OSPF2 can now see and reach ISP:

```
OSPF2(config-router)#do sh ip route ospf | b Gate
Gateway of last resort is not set

       1.0.0.0/32 is subnetted, 3 subnets
O         1.2.0.1 [110/11] via 172.16.3.1, 00:01:42, Ethernet2/0
O IA      1.2.1.1 [110/21] via 172.16.3.1, 00:01:42, Ethernet2/0
       100.0.0.0/32 is subnetted, 1 subnets
O IA      100.100.100.100 [110/31] via 172.16.3.1, 00:01:42, Ethernet2/0
       172.16.0.0/16 is variably subnetted, 6 subnets, 2 masks
O IA      172.16.1.0/24 [110/30] via 172.16.3.1, 00:01:42, Ethernet2/0
O         172.16.2.0/24 [110/20] via 172.16.3.1, 00:01:42, Ethernet2/0
OSPF2(config-router)#do ping 100.100.100.100
Type escape sequence to abort.
Sending 5, 100-byte ICMP Echos to 100.100.100.100:
!!!!!
Success rate is 100 percent (5/5)
OSPF2(config-router)#
```

Let's add OSPF3:

```
OSPF3(config)#router ospf 1
OSPF3(config-router)#router-id 1.2.3.1
OSPF3(config-router)#network 172.16.4.3 0.0.0.0 area 2
OSPF3(config-router)#
%OSPF-5-ADJCHG: Process 1, Nbr 1.2.2.1 on Ethernet3/2 from LOADING to
FULL, Loading Done
OSPF3(config-router)#network 1.2.3.1 0.0.0.0 area 3
OSPF3(config-router)#
```

Now let's check OSPF0:

```
OSPF0(config)#do sh ip route ospf | b Gate
Gateway of last resort is not set

       1.0.0.0/32 is subnetted, 3 subnets
O IA      1.2.1.1 [110/11] via 172.16.2.2, 00:12:36, Ethernet0/1
O IA      1.2.2.1 [110/11] via 172.16.3.2, 00:03:15, Ethernet0/2
       100.0.0.0/32 is subnetted, 1 subnets
O IA      100.100.100.100 [110/21] via 172.16.2.2, 00:06:17, Ethernet0/1
       172.16.0.0/16 is variably subnetted, 6 subnets, 2 masks
```

```
O IA      172.16.1.0/24 [110/20] via 172.16.2.2, 00:12:11, Ethernet0/1
O IA      172.16.4.0/24 [110/20] via 172.16.3.2, 00:03:24, Ethernet0/2
OSPF0(config)#
```

We can see that since adding OSPF3, nothing has changed in OSPF0's routing table. We still have the network 172.16.4.0/24, which connects OSPF2 to OSPF3, but we do not see OSPF3's loopback interface. This is the problem with not running a single area. We have what is known as a "discontiguous network". We will fix this problem in a short while, but before we do we need to discuss the mechanics of what we have just accomplished.

OSPF forms adjacencies between two routers, an adjacency is who can talk to whom and share routing information. In order to form an adjacency a number of factors need to match. The area ID must match, which is why both OSPF1 and OSPF2 need to have interfaces in area 0. The subnet mask of the interfaces must match. We could not, for example, form an adjacency between an interface with the IP address 172.16.1.1 255.255.255.0 and another with the subnet mask 172.16.1.2 255.255.240.0. OSPF has timers, just as RIP does, we will discuss the timers in a moment, but these need to match in order to form an adjacency. As we are running with the default timers, we have not needed to configure these. Our stub flags need to match. OSPF supports stub areas, which is another way of reducing OSPF traffic. We will look at these shortly as well.

The first indication of an adjacency forming was when we saw the message that we had moved from "loading" to "full". These are two of the states that a router will move through when forming an adjacency. The state changes are initiated by Hello packets, which are sent to the multicast address 224.0.0.5. It is best if we watch the process through the packet exchanges using Wireshark.

If you want to generate the capture yourself, right click on OSPF0, select "Capture", then select the e0/1 interface. Wireshark should start (but note that the line numbers will probably differ).

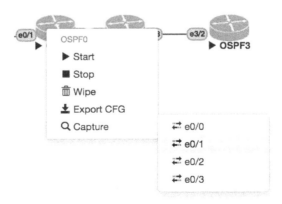

Once Wireshark has started, shut down e0/1 on OSPF0:

```
OSPF0(config)#int e0/1
OSPF0(config-if)#shut
OSPF0(config-if)#
%OSPF-5-ADJCHG: Process 1, Nbr 1.2.1.1 on Ethernet0/1 from FULL to DOWN,
Neighbor Down: Interface down or detached
OSPF0(config-if)#
%LINK-5-CHANGED: Interface Ethernet0/1, changed state to administratively
down
%LINEPROTO-5-UPDOWN: Line protocol on Interface Ethernet0/1, changed
state to down
OSPF0(config-if)#
```

Give it a few moments, and turn the interface back on again. Once you see the messages below, stop the Wireshark capture by clicking on the big red square:

```
OSPF0(config-if)#no shut
OSPF0(config-if)#
%LINK-3-UPDOWN: Interface Ethernet0/1, changed state to up
%LINEPROTO-5-UPDOWN: Line protocol on Interface Ethernet0/1, changed
state to up
OSPF0(config-if)#
%OSPF-5-ADJCHG: Process 1, Nbr 1.2.1.1 on Ethernet0/1 from LOADING to
FULL, Loading Done
OSPF0(config-if)#
```

We can then filter down the results to just display the OSPF packets by typing "ospf" in the filter bar at the top (the bar should turn green indicating the filter is correct):

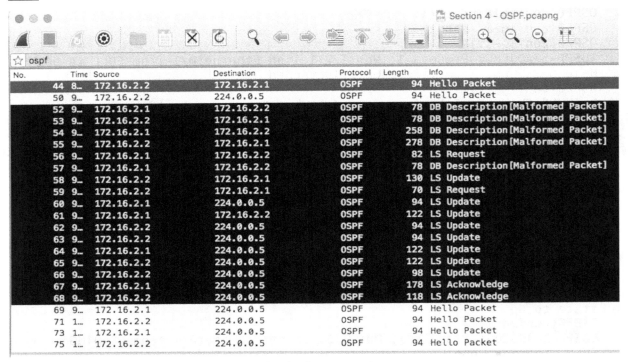

Wireshark capture: 4

We start in the OSPF Down state. In this state, we have not received any Hello packets, but we can still send them.

We start, at line 43 of the capture, by sending a multicast Hello packet to 224.0.0.5. This moves us to the Init stage. Our Hello packet contains our network mask, our Hello and Dead intervals, and we also (in the OSPF Header) include our router-id and the area. The data we send in the Hello packet must match the recipient; otherwise, we will not be able to form an adjacency.

```
▼ Open Shortest Path First
  ▼ OSPF Header
       Version: 2
       Message Type: Hello Packet (1)
       Packet Length: 44
       Source OSPF Router: 1.2.0.1 (1.2.0.1)
       Area ID: 0.0.0.0 (0.0.0.0) (Backbone)
       Checksum: 0xeb9b [correct]
       Auth Type: Null (0)
       Auth Data (none): 0000000000000000
  ▼ OSPF Hello Packet
       Network Mask: 255.255.255.0 (255.255.255.0)
       Hello Interval [sec]: 10
     ▶ Options: 0x12 ((L) LLS Data block, (E) External Routing)
       Router Priority: 1
       Router Dead Interval [sec]: 40
       Designated Router: 0.0.0.0 (0.0.0.0)
       Backup Designated Router: 0.0.0.0 (0.0.0.0)
  ▶ OSPF LLS Data Block
```

The packet we receive from OSPF1 (in line 44) contains its router-id, the same network mask and Hello and Dead intervals, and now it lists OSPF0 as the active neighbor:

```
▼ Open Shortest Path First
  ▼ OSPF Header
       Version: 2
       Message Type: Hello Packet (1)
       Packet Length: 48
       Source OSPF Router: 1.2.1.1 (1.2.1.1)
       Area ID: 0.0.0.0 (0.0.0.0) (Backbone)
       Checksum: 0x3b82 [correct]
       Auth Type: Null (0)
       Auth Data (none): 0000000000000000
  ▼ OSPF Hello Packet
       Network Mask: 255.255.255.0 (255.255.255.0)
       Hello Interval [sec]: 10
     ▶ Options: 0x12 ((L) LLS Data block, (E) External Routing)
       Router Priority: 1
       Router Dead Interval [sec]: 40
       Designated Router: 172.16.2.2 (172.16.2.2)
       Backup Designated Router: 0.0.0.0 (0.0.0.0)
       Active Neighbor: 1.2.0.1 (1.2.0.1)
  ▶ OSPF LLS Data Block
```

We have now entered the 2-way state. The 2-way state means that bi-directional communication has been established. We have exchanged hello packets and these hello packets include each other's router-id within the Active Neighbor field.

We then start to elect the Designated Router (DR) and Backup Designated Router (BDR). We will discuss these once we finish going through the different states.

Next, we move into the Exstart stage. Once the DR and BDR have been elected, the routers start to exchange link state information. They establish a Master/Slave relationship and choose an initial sequence number for adjacency formation. The router with the highest router ID will become the master and starts the Exchange stage.

In the Exchange stage the OSPF speaking routers exchange Database Descriptor (DBD) packets. These contain the link state advertisements (LSA) headers only and describe the contents of the entire link-state database. Each DBD packet has a sequence number, which can only be incremented by the master.

Line 52 shows the first DBD packet.

```
▼ Open Shortest Path First
  ► OSPF Header
  ▼ OSPF DB Description
      Interface MTU: 1500
    ► Options: 0x52 (O, (L) LLS Data block, (E) External Routing)
    ▼ DB Description: 0x07 ((I) Init, (M) More, (MS) Master)
        .... 0... = (R) OOBResync: Not set
        .... .1.. = (I) Init: Set
        .... ..1. = (M) More: Set
        .... ...1 = (MS) Master: Yes
      DD Sequence: 4071
  ► OSPF LLS Data Block
```

OSPF0 considers itself the master and has set the DD sequence to 4071. Line 53 shows OSPF1 thinking that it is the master, and set the DD sequence number to 4178:

```
▼ DB Description: 0x07 ((I) Init, (M) More, (MS) Master)
    .... 0... = (R) OOBResync: Not set
    .... .1.. = (I) Init: Set
    .... ..1. = (M) More: Set
    .... ...1 = (MS) Master: Yes
  DD Sequence: 4178
► OSPF LLS Data Block
```

Line 54 shows that the two routers have now agree on the master/slave relationship, OSPF0 agrees that it is not the master, and uses the same sequence number as set by OSPF1, at which stage we also start to see the LSA headers:

```
▼ OSPF DB Description
     Interface MTU: 1500
   ▶ Options: 0x52 (0, (L) LLS Data block, (E) External Routing)
   ▼ DB Description: 0x02 ((M) More)
         .... 0... = (R) OOBResync: Not set
         .... .0.. = (I) Init: Not set
         .... ..1. = (M) More: Set
         .... ...0 = (MS) Master: No
     DD Sequence: 4178
▶ LSA Header
▶ LSA Header
▶ LSA Header
▶ LSA Header
▶ LSA Header
▶ LSA Header
▶ LSA Header
▶ LSA Header
▶ LSA Header
▶ OSPF LLS Data Block
```

From this point, it is only OSPF1 that can increment the sequence number.

The LSA headers contain a mixture of Router LSAs, Network LSAs and Summary LSAs. We will discuss these in section 4.7.g.

We now are now in the Loading stage, where we start to see link-state request (line 56) and link-state update packets (line 58), which contain the entire LSA. The contents of the DBD packets received are compared to information in the routers' own link-state database to see if newer information is available.

The LS Request in line 56 is OSPF0's way of asking for new information; it sends what it thinks it knows about in order for OSPF1 to confirm that is correct. Through the requests and updates from lines 56 to 68, OSPF0 and OSPF1 exchange their databases and build up their view of the network.

Once the databases have been exchanged and acknowledged (lines 67 and 68) we reach the Full stage. Now the routers are fully adjacent with each other. Full is the state we want in the topology that we have.

The full process will be Down -> Init -> 2-way -> Exstart -> Exchange -> Loading -> Full.

If we had a different topology, such as five routers all connected to the same switch, we would see three remain at the 2-way stage. One router would be elected the DR and one would be elected the

BDR. The remaining three would show "2WAY/DROTHER" when we look at their neighbor table. To understand this, we need to look at what the DR and BDR are.

Designated Router and Backup Designated Router

OSPF is designed for scalability, speed and sensible bandwidth usage. It is not the loud and brash protocol that RIP is. In order to keep the number of LSAs sensible, one designated router and one backup designated router will be elected. It is with these routers that we form full adjacencies and exchange LSAs.

Stepping away from our main topology for a moment, we can see this in action. This is our logical topology:

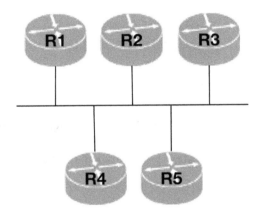

The physical topology is that all the routers connect to a single switch. Each router has a loopback interface; R1 has 1.1.1.1/32, R2 has 2.2.2.2/32 and so on. We are using the subnet mask 192.168.1.0/24, and each router uses their router number for the last octet (R1 is 192.168.1.1/24 and so on). OSPF has been enabled, and all interfaces have been advertised. R1's configuration is below:

```
R1(config)#int e0/0
R1(config-if)#ip add 192.168.1.1 255.255.255.0
R1(config-if)#no shut
R1(config-if)#int lo0
R1(config-if)#ip add 1.1.1.1 255.255.255.255
R1(config-if)#router ospf 1
R1(config-router)#router-id 1.1.1.1
R1(config-router)#network 0.0.0.0 0.0.0.0 area 0
R1(config-router)#
```

We can check our neighbors using the command "*show ip ospf neighbor*". We can see that R1 lists R2 as the BDR, and R3, R4 and R5 have established full adjacencies with them:

```
R1(config-router)#do sh ip ospf neighbor
Neighbor ID  Pri  State          Dead Time  Address       Interface
2.2.2.2        1  FULL/BDR       00:00:36   192.168.1.2   Ethernet0/0
3.3.3.3        1  FULL/DROTHER   00:00:33   192.168.1.3   Ethernet0/0
4.4.4.4        1  FULL/DROTHER   00:00:32   192.168.1.4   Ethernet0/0
5.5.5.5        1  FULL/DROTHER   00:00:38   192.168.1.5   Ethernet0/0
R1(config-router)#
```

R2 has full adjacencies to R1 (the DR) and to R3, R4 and R5.

```
R2(config-router)#do sh ip ospf neighbor
Neighbor ID  Pri  State          Dead Time  Address       Interface
1.1.1.1        1  FULL/DR        00:00:32   192.168.1.1   Ethernet0/0
3.3.3.3        1  FULL/DROTHER   00:00:32   192.168.1.3   Ethernet0/0
4.4.4.4        1  FULL/DROTHER   00:00:31   192.168.1.4   Ethernet0/0
5.5.5.5        1  FULL/DROTHER   00:00:37   192.168.1.5   Ethernet0/0
R2(config-router)#
```

R3 has a full adjacency to R1 and R2, and is in 2WAY/DROTHER to R4 and R5.

```
R3(config-router)#do sh ip ospf neighbor
Neighbor ID  Pri  State          Dead Time  Address       Interface
1.1.1.1        1  FULL/DR        00:00:30   192.168.1.1   Ethernet0/0
2.2.2.2        1  FULL/BDR       00:00:34   192.168.1.2   Ethernet0/0
4.4.4.4        1  2WAY/DROTHER   00:00:39   192.168.1.4   Ethernet0/0
5.5.5.5        1  2WAY/DROTHER   00:00:35   192.168.1.5   Ethernet0/0
R3(config-router)#
```

The same is true for R4:

```
R4(config-router)#do sh ip ospf neighbor
Neighbor ID  Pri  State          Dead Time  Address       Interface
1.1.1.1        1  FULL/DR        00:00:38   192.168.1.1   Ethernet0/0
2.2.2.2        1  FULL/BDR       00:00:32   192.168.1.2   Ethernet0/0
3.3.3.3        1  2WAY/DROTHER   00:00:38   192.168.1.3   Ethernet0/0
5.5.5.5        1  2WAY/DROTHER   00:00:34   192.168.1.5   Ethernet0/0
R4(config-router)#
```

Also for R5:

```
R5(config-router)#do sh ip ospf neighbor
Neighbor ID  Pri  State          Dead Time  Address       Interface
1.1.1.1        1  FULL/DR        00:00:36   192.168.1.1   Ethernet0/0
2.2.2.2        1  FULL/BDR       00:00:39   192.168.1.2   Ethernet0/0
3.3.3.3        1  2WAY/DROTHER   00:00:36   192.168.1.3   Ethernet0/0
4.4.4.4        1  2WAY/DROTHER   00:00:35   192.168.1.4   Ethernet0/0
R5(config-router)#
```

The DR and BDR election works by looking at the OSPF priority in the Hello packet. As you can see from the Wireshark captures from earlier, both OSPF0 and OSPF1 have the (default) priority of one. As the priority is a tie, the routers will then elect the roles based on the router ID (also referred to as the RID), with the highest RID winning. Do not confuse the highest number with the biggest number. Here one is a higher number than five, which is why R1 became the DR, and R2 became the BDR. Both 1.1.1.1 and 2.2.2.2 are higher numbers than 5.5.5.5. We can change who will be elected the DR by changing the priority value, using the command *"ip ospf priority <value>"*, under the connecting interface:

```
R5(config)#int e0/0
R5(config-if)#
R5(config-if)#ip ospf priority 200
R5(config-if)#
```

We then need to clear the OSPF process and let the election process take place again:

```
R1#clear ip ospf process
Reset ALL OSPF processes? [no]: yes
R1#

R2#clear ip ospf process
Reset ALL OSPF processes? [no]: yes
R2#
```

R1 and R2 will now drop and reform their adjacencies, after which R5 is now the Designated Router:

```
R2#sh ip ospf neigh

Neighbor ID  Pri  State          Dead Time  Address      Interface
1.1.1.1        1  2WAY/DROTHER   00:00:36   192.168.1.1  Ethernet0/0
3.3.3.3        1  2WAY/DROTHER   00:00:36   192.168.1.3  Ethernet0/0
4.4.4.4        1  FULL/BDR       00:00:38   192.168.1.4  Ethernet0/0
5.5.5.5      200  FULL/DR        00:00:37   192.168.1.5  Ethernet0/0

R2#

R1#sh ip ospf neigh

Neighbor ID  Pri  State          Dead Time  Address      Interface
2.2.2.2        1  2WAY/DROTHER   00:00:31   192.168.1.2  Ethernet0/0
3.3.3.3        1  2WAY/DROTHER   00:00:34   192.168.1.3  Ethernet0/0
4.4.4.4        1  FULL/BDR       00:00:36   192.168.1.4  Ethernet0/0
5.5.5.5      200  FULL/DR        00:00:30   192.168.1.5  Ethernet0/0

R1#
```

```
R5#sh ip ospf neigh

Neighbor ID  Pri  State         Dead Time  Address      Interface
1.1.1.1        1  FULL/DROTHER  00:00:37   192.168.1.1  Ethernet0/0
2.2.2.2        1  FULL/DROTHER  00:00:34   192.168.1.2  Ethernet0/0
3.3.3.3        1  FULL/DROTHER  00:00:39   192.168.1.3  Ethernet0/0
4.4.4.4        1  FULL/BDR      00:00:38   192.168.1.4  Ethernet0/0
R5#
```

We can even prevent a router from taking part in the election; by setting its priority to zero:

```
R3(config)#int e0/0
R3(config-if)#ip ospf priority 0
R3(config-if)#
```

Returning to our main topology, we have now set up OSPF for IPv4 (known as OSPFv2). Let's do the same for IPv6 (OSPFv3).

4.7.c Configure OSPFv3

Way back in chapter 3, we set up some of our routers to run IPv6. It was only a small deployment, and now we are going to extend this out, so that we have OSPFv2 and OSPFv3 running at the same time.

We won't be touching EIGRP1 now, we'll save that for much later, but we have IPv6 addresses set up on ISP and OSPF1.

Let's go and set up IPv6 addresses on the rest of our routers.

```
OSPF1(config-if)#int lo0
OSPF1(config-if)#ipv6 add 2001:db8:1:2:1:1::1/128
OSPF1(config)#int e1/0
OSPF1(config-if)#ipv6 add 2001:db8:a3::2/64
OSPF1(config-if)#

OSPF0(config-if)#int e0/1
OSPF0(config-if)#ipv6 add 2001:db8:a3::1/64
OSPF0(config-if)#int lo0
OSPF0(config-if)#ipv6 add 2001:db8:1:2:0:1::1/128
OSPF0(config-if)#int e0/2
OSPF0(config-if)#ipv6 add 2001:db8:a4::1/64
OSPF0(config-if)#

OSPF2(config-router)#int e2/0
OSPF2(config-if)#ipv6 add 2001:db8:a4::2/64
OSPF2(config-if)#int lo0
OSPF2(config-if)#ipv6 add 2001:db8:1:2:2:1::1/128
```

```
OSPF2(config-if)#int e2/3
OSPF2(config-if)#ipv6 add 2001:db8:a5::2/64
OSPF2(config-if)#

OSPF3(config-router)#int e1/3
OSPF3(config-if)#ipv6 add 2001:db8:a5::3/64
OSPF3(config-if)#int lo0
OSPF3(config-if)#ipv6 add 2001:db8:1:2:3:1::1/128
OSPF3(config-if)#
```

To make life easier, our OSPF network will all be in the same area. We start with the *"ipv6 router"* command:

```
ISP(config)#ipv6 router ospf 1
ISP(config-rtr)#
```

Then we specify our RID:

```
ISP(config-rtr)#router-id 100.100.100.100
```

We cannot use the *"network"* command here though. Instead, we need to head back into the interface configuration, where we specify which ospf process we want to add this network to, along with the area:

```
ISP(config-rtr)#exit
ISP(config)#int e1/1
ISP(config-if)#ipv6 ospf 1 area 0
ISP(config-if)#
```

We can do the same for our loopback interface, and here we see that if the interface is not already IPv6 enabled, we are told so:

```
ISP(config-if)#int lo0
ISP(config-if)#ipv6 ospf 1 area 0
% OSPFv3: IPV6 is not enabled on this interface
ISP(config-if)#ipv6 enable
ISP(config-if)#ipv6 ospf 1 area 0
ISP(config-if)#
```

Let's move on to OSPF1:

```
OSPF1(config-if)#int e1/1
OSPF1(config-if)#ipv6 ospf 1 area 0
OSPF1(config-if)#
%OSPFv3-5-ADJCHG: Process 1, Nbr 100.100.100.100 on Ethernet1/1 from
LOADING to FULL, Loading Done
```

```
OSPF1(config-if)#int lo0
OSPF1(config-if)#ipv6 enable
OSPF1(config-if)#ipv6 ospf 1 area 0
OSPF1(config-if)#
```

Notice that we have not configured the routing process on OSPF1, but the adjacency still forms. The process does get created for us, as we can see by comparing the output of "*sh run | i router*" (show me any line that begins with the word router) on ISP and OSPF1:

```
ISP(config-if)#do sh run | i router
router ospf 1
 router-id 100.100.100.100
ipv6 router ospf 1
 router-id 100.100.100.100
ISP(config-if)#

OSPF1(config-if)#do sh run | i router
router ospf 1
ipv6 router ospf 1
OSPF1(config-if)#
```

We should go in and manually set our RID though:

```
OSPF1(config-if)#ipv6 router ospf 1
OSPF1(config-rtr)#router-id 1.2.1.1
OSPF1(config-rtr)#
```

This is again one of those best-practice behaviours, which means no surprises later on.

Let's finish off the rest of the configurations (remembering that we need to enable IPv6 unicast routing):

```
OSPF1(config-rtr)#int e1/0
OSPF1(config-if)#ipv6 ospf 1 area 0
OSPF1(config-if)#

OSPF0(config-if)#ipv6 router ospf 1
% IPv6 routing not enabled
OSPF0(config)#ipv6 unicast-routing
OSPF0(config)#ipv6 router ospf 1
OSPF0(config-rtr)#router-id 1.2.0.1
OSPF0(config-rtr)#int e0/1
OSPF0(config-if)#ipv6 enable
OSPF0(config-if)#ipv6 ospf 1 area 0
OSPF0(config-if)#
%OSPFv3-5-ADJCHG: Process 1, Nbr 1.2.1.1 on Ethernet0/1 from LOADING to
FULL, Loading Done
```

```
OSPF0(config-if)#
OSPF0(config-if)#int lo0
OSPF0(config-if)#ipv6 enable
OSPF0(config-if)#ipv6 ospf 1 area 0
OSPF0(config-if)#int e0/2
OSPF0(config-if)#ipv6 enable
OSPF0(config-if)#ipv6 ospf 1 area 0
OSPF0(config-if)#

OSPF2(config-if)#ipv6 unicast-routing
OSPF2(config)#ipv6 router ospf 1
OSPF2(config-rtr)#router-id 1.2.2.1
OSPF2(config-rtr)#int e2/0
OSPF2(config-if)#ipv6 ospf 1 area 0
OSPF2(config-if)#
%OSPFv3-5-ADJCHG: Process 1, Nbr 1.2.0.1 on Ethernet2/0 from LOADING to
FULL, Loading Done
OSPF2(config-if)#
OSPF2(config-if)#int lo0
OSPF2(config-if)#ipv6 enable
OSPF2(config-if)#ipv6 ospf 1 area 0
OSPF2(config-if)#int e2/3
OSPF2(config-if)#ipv6 enable
OSPF2(config-if)#ipv6 ospf 1 area 0
OSPF2(config-if)#

OSPF3(config-if)#ipv6 unicast-routing
OSPF3(config)#ipv6 router ospf 1
OSPF3(config-rtr)#router-id 1.2.3.1
OSPF3(config-rtr)#int e3/2
OSPF3(config-if)#ipv6 enable
OSPF3(config-if)#ipv6 ospf 1 area 0
OSPF3(config-if)#
%OSPFv3-5-ADJCHG: Process 1, Nbr 1.2.2.1 on Ethernet3/2 from LOADING to
FULL, Loading Done
OSPF3(config-if)#int lo0
OSPF3(config-if)#ipv6 enable
OSPF3(config-if)#ipv6 ospf 1 area 0
OSPF3(config-if)#
```

Let's have a look at our routing tables and confirm end-to-end connectivity:

```
ISP(config-if)#do sh ipv6 route ospf
IPv6 Routing Table - default - 12 entries
Codes: C - Connected, L - Local, S - Static, U - Per-user Static route
       B - BGP, HA - Home Agent, MR - Mobile Router, R - RIP
       H - NHRP, I1 - ISIS L1, I2 - ISIS L2, IA - ISIS interarea
       IS - ISIS summary, D - EIGRP, EX - EIGRP external, NM - NEMO
       ND - ND Default, NDp - ND Prefix, DCE - Destination, NDr - Redirect
```

```
              O - OSPF Intra, OI - OSPF Inter, OE1 - OSPF ext 1, OE2 - OSPF ext 2
              ON1 - OSPF NSSA ext 1, ON2 - OSPF NSSA ext 2, la - LISP alt
              lr - LISP site-registrations, ld - LISP dyn-eid, a - Application
O    2001:DB8:1:2:0:1:0:1/128 [110/20]
         via FE80::A8BB:CCFF:FE00:B11, Ethernet1/1
O    2001:DB8:1:2:1:1:0:1/128 [110/10]
         via FE80::A8BB:CCFF:FE00:B11, Ethernet1/1
O    2001:DB8:1:2:2:1::/128 [110/30]
         via FE80::A8BB:CCFF:FE00:B11, Ethernet1/1
O    2001:DB8:1:2:3:1:0:1/128 [110/40]
         via FE80::A8BB:CCFF:FE00:B11, Ethernet1/1
O    2001:DB8:A3::/64 [110/20]
         via FE80::A8BB:CCFF:FE00:B11, Ethernet1/1
O    2001:DB8:A4::/64 [110/30]
         via FE80::A8BB:CCFF:FE00:B11, Ethernet1/1
O    2001:DB8:A5::/64 [110/40]
         via FE80::A8BB:CCFF:FE00:B11, Ethernet1/1
ISP(config-if)#
```

Now we can reach all the way from ISP to the loopback address of OSPF3:

```
ISP(config-if)#do ping ipv6 2001:DB8:1:2:3:1:0:1
Type escape sequence to abort.
Sending 5, 100-byte ICMP Echos to 2001:DB8:1:2:3:1:0:1:
!!!!!
Success rate is 100 percent (5/5)
ISP(config-if)#
```

This should also help with understanding the benefits of a single OSPF area. By running a single area, all of our routers have connectivity, unlike our OSPFv2 network, where there is no visibility to OSPF3's loopback interface.

Whilst what we have seen of OSPFv3 does not differ all that much from OSPFv2, there are some differences behind the scenes, mainly with the LSA types. We will cover these in 4.7.g. The key difference is that OSPFv3 can get you much further than OSPFv2 can, it can carry IPv6 and IPv4 traffic. It does this by using address families. Whilst this is outside of the CCNA scope, it is pretty neat.

OSPFv3 still uses the 32-bit router ID and following the same rules as OSPFv2, it will select one based on an available IPv4 address. If we do not have an IPv4 address then we would be asked to configure one manually:

```
%OSPFv3-4-NORTRID: OSPFv3 process 1 could not pick a router-id, please
configure manually
```

Why are router-id's so important? Let's find out.

4.7.d Router ID

The router ID, or RID, identifies us to our neighbors, therefore it needs to be unique. It can be anything we like, just so long as it is expressed in dotted-decimal notation (1.1.1.1, 2.2.2.2, 1.2.3.4 and so on).

So, what happens when we have a duplicate router ID?

```
OSPF3(config-if)#router ospf 1
OSPF3(config-router)#router-id 1.2.2.1
% OSPF: Reload or use "clear ip ospf process" command, for this to take
effect
OSPF3(config-router)#do clear ip ospf process
Reset ALL OSPF processes? [no]: yes
OSPF3(config-router)#
%OSPF-5-ADJCHG: Process 1, Nbr 1.2.2.1 on Ethernet3/2 from FULL to DOWN,
Neighbor Down: Interface down or detached
%OSPF-4-DUP_RTRID_NBR: OSPF detected duplicate router-id 1.2.2.1 from
172.16.4.2 on interface Ethernet3/2
OSPF3(config-router)#
OSPF3(config-router)#do sh ip ospf neighbor
OSPF3(config-router)#
```

We do not form adjacencies. Let's set it back again:

```
OSPF3(config-router)#router-id 1.2.3.1
OSPF3(config-router)#
%OSPF-5-ADJCHG: Process 1, Nbr 1.2.2.1 on Ethernet3/2 from LOADING to
FULL, Loading Done
OSPF3(config-router)#
```

Our adjacencies form.

As you can see, the RID must be unique for OSPF to form adjacencies with neighboring routers. However, in the event that you specifically want to prevent two OSPF routers for forming adjacencies, such as where we had five routers connected to one switch previously, then we could duplicate the router IDs.

Whilst having duplicate router IDs is a good way of making sure that a router does not form an adjacency with another (specific) router, if we wanted to make sure that it did not form any adjacencies at all over a particular interface, then we could use the passive interface command instead.

4.7.e Passive Interface

We used the passive interface command when we looked at RIP. There we saw that with the passive interface command configured we could still receive advertisements, but not send them. OSPF behaves very differently when this command is configured.

The command syntax is the same, it is still performed under the router configuration, but the effect is immediate:

```
OSPF3(config-router)#passive-interface e3/2
OSPF3(config-router)#
%OSPF-5-ADJCHG: Process 1, Nbr 1.2.2.1 on Ethernet3/2 from FULL to DOWN,
Neighbor Down: Interface down or detached
OSPF3(config-router)#
```

There are very valid usage scenarios for passive interfaces, such as where you are redistributing from one protocol into another.

Our topology does not necessitate the usage of passive interfaces, but it does need fixing to provide the same end-to-end reachability in the multi-area IPv4 network that we have in the single-area IPv6 one. So let's remove the passive interface and complete our OSPFv2 network:

```
OSPF3(config-router)#no passive-interface e3/2
OSPF3(config-router)#
%OSPF-5-ADJCHG: Process 1, Nbr 1.2.2.1 on Ethernet3/2 from LOADING to
FULL, Loading Done
OSPF3(config-router)#
```

4.7.f Discuss multi-area OSPF

We saw the benefits of a single area design when our OSPFv3 network ended up being far more complete than our multi-area OSPFv2 network. Our OSPFv3 design was simple and effective, however, from a design point of view, it was less than ideal.

In a large-scale deployment, it makes sense to implement a hierarchical design; by segregating the OSPF network into areas. This will reduce the amount of bandwidth used by the protocols, leaving more bandwidth for user traffic. The issue with this approach is that due to the design of the OSPF protocol, it specifies that all areas must have either a physical or a virtual connection to area 0. Therefore, a typical approach to designing OSPF networks looks a little like this:

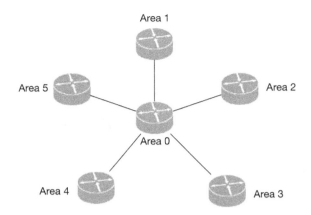

Each area has a physical connection to area 0 and everyone is happy. So, what about topologies that cannot, for one reason or another, have this configuration?

This is where we need to implement a virtual connection between the areas. This is called a virtual link. To create a virtual link you first identify which area is the transit area. In our case, area 2 is the transit area. We then specify the router IDs that will form the virtual link, which will be the RIDs for OSPF2 and OSPF3. The complete command would be *"area <transit area> virtual-link <RID of connecting router>"*, such as:

```
OSPF3(config-router)#area 2 virtual-link 1.2.2.1
```

OSPF2 will start to complain until we complete the other side of the virtual link:

```
%OSPF-4-ERRRCV: Received invalid packet: mismatched area ID, from
backbone area must be virtual-link but not found from 172.16.4.3,
Ethernet1/3
OSPF2(config-if)#router ospf 1
OSPF2(config-router)#area 2 virtual-link 1.2.3.1
OSPF2(config-router)#
%OSPF-5-ADJCHG: Process 1, Nbr 1.2.3.1 on OSPF_VL0 from LOADING to FULL,
Loading Done
OSPF2(config-router)#
```

Our virtual link acts the same way as our physical links, and will go through the same stages to form an adjacency:

```
OSPF3(config-router)#
%OSPF-5-ADJCHG: Process 1, Nbr 1.2.2.1 on OSPF_VL1 from LOADING to FULL,
Loading Done
OSPF3(config-router)#
```

We can now see ISP's loopback interface in OSPF3's routing table:

```
OSPF3(config-router)#do sh ip route ospf | b Gate
Gateway of last resort is not set

      1.0.0.0/8 is variably subnetted, 5 subnets, 2 masks
O        1.2.0.1/32 [110/21] via 172.16.4.2, 00:00:42, Ethernet3/2
O IA     1.2.1.1/32 [110/31] via 172.16.4.2, 00:00:42, Ethernet3/2
O        1.2.2.1/32 [110/11] via 172.16.4.2, 00:01:59, Ethernet3/2
      100.0.0.0/32 is subnetted, 1 subnets
O IA    100.100.100.100 [110/41] via 172.16.4.2, 00:00:42, Ethernet3/2
      172.16.0.0/16 is variably subnetted, 5 subnets, 2 masks
O IA    172.16.1.0/24 [110/40] via 172.16.4.2, 00:00:42, Ethernet3/2
O       172.16.2.0/24 [110/30] via 172.16.4.2, 00:00:42, Ethernet3/2
O       172.16.3.0/24 [110/20] via 172.16.4.2, 00:00:42, Ethernet3/2
OSPF3(config-router)#
```

We also have end-to-end reachability between the loopback interfaces:

```
ISP(config-if)#do ping 1.2.3.1 so lo0
Type escape sequence to abort.
Sending 5, 100-byte ICMP Echos to 1.2.3.1:
Packet sent with a source address of 100.100.100.100
!!!!!
Success rate is 100 percent (5/5)
ISP(config-if)#
```

Virtual links are useful when you have a network where area zero is divided by another area.

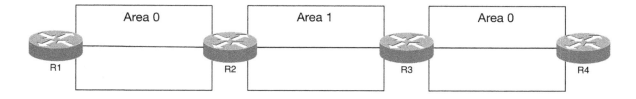

A virtual link here will extend area 0 across the transit area (area one).

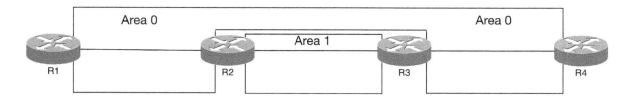

The areas we have configured so far are known as "standard" areas. OSPF0 is our backbone router, and OSPF1, OSPF2 and OSPF3 are Area Border routers (ABRs), as they border two areas. ISP will be (towards the end of the book) an Autonomous System Border Router (ASBR) as it will be performing redistribution between different domains (our OSPF and EIGRP networks).

The different area types determine what LSA types are passed from area to area, all with a view to simplifying routing tables and reducing OSPF traffic (LSAs). We will cover the LSA types in greater detail in the next section as this section is primarily to discuss the different area types, but there will be a lot of overlap between the two sections.

Within a standard area, we can have LSA types 1, 2, 3, 4 and 5.

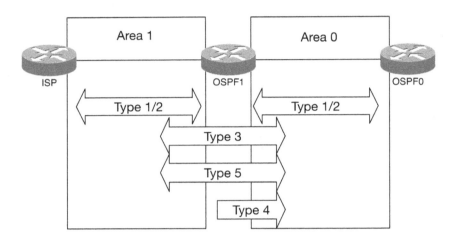

Using the contents of the routing table and the OSPF database (*show ip ospf database*) we can get a good view of how these different area types change our understanding of the network.

This is ISP's OSPF database and its routing table:

```
ISP(config-if)#do sh ip ospf database

        OSPF Router with ID (1.1.1.1) (Process ID 1)

        Router Link States (Area 1)

Link ID          ADV Router       Age      Seq#       Checksum Link count
1.2.1.1          1.2.1.1          1042     0x8000001C 0x00B8B5 2
100.100.100.100  100.100.100.100  912      0x8000001B 0x005B70 2

        Net Link States (Area 1)

Link ID     ADV Router    Age      Seq#       Checksum
172.16.1.2  1.2.1.1       19       0x80000034 0x00CA6E
```

```
                    Summary Net Link States (Area 1)

Link ID         ADV Router      Age         Seq#        Checksum
1.2.0.1         1.2.1.1         46          0x80000032  0x0040B7
1.2.2.1         1.2.1.1         46          0x80000032  0x008E5D
1.2.3.1         1.2.1.1         46          0x8000000A  0x0038D0
172.16.2.0      1.2.1.1         46          0x80000032  0x00C974
172.16.3.0      1.2.1.1         46          0x80000032  0x002310
172.16.4.0      1.2.1.1         46          0x80000009  0x00CE82
ISP(config-if)#
ISP(config-if)#do sh ip route ospf | b Gate
Gateway of last resort is not set

        1.0.0.0/32 is subnetted, 4 subnets
O IA    1.2.0.1 [110/21] via 172.16.1.2, 14:01:27, Ethernet1/1
O       1.2.1.1 [110/11] via 172.16.1.2, 14:13:41, Ethernet1/1
O IA    1.2.2.1 [110/31] via 172.16.1.2, 14:01:27, Ethernet1/1
O IA    1.2.3.1 [110/41] via 172.16.1.2, 00:02:48, Ethernet1/1
        172.16.0.0/16 is variably subnetted, 5 subnets, 2 masks
O IA    172.16.2.0/24 [110/20] via 172.16.1.2, 14:13:41, Ethernet1/1
O IA    172.16.3.0/24 [110/30] via 172.16.1.2, 14:01:27, Ethernet1/1
O IA    172.16.4.0/24 [110/40] via 172.16.1.2, 14:01:27, Ethernet1/1
ISP(config-if)#
```

This is ISP as a "standard" area. We can then have a stub area.

A stub area can contain LSA types 1, 2 and 3; it will also gain a default route. Type 5 LSAs will not be propagated, instead the ABR injects a default route in a type 3 LSA.

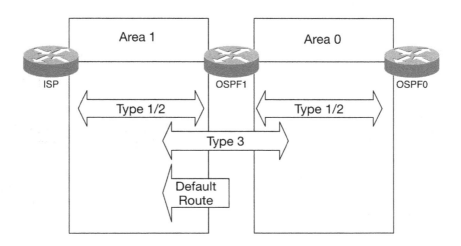

We create a stub area by using the command *"area <area number> stub"*. All routers belonging to this stub area must agree that it is a stub area, as you can see below the adjacency between OSPF1 and ISP does not re-establish until they are both configured as stub:

```
OSPF1(config-router)#area 1 stub
OSPF1(config-router)#
%OSPF-5-ADJCHG: Process 1, Nbr 100.100.100.100 on Ethernet1/1 from FULL
to DOWN, Neighbor Down: Adjacency forced to reset
OSPF1(config-router)#

ISP(config-if)#router ospf 1
ISP(config-router)#
%OSPF-5-ADJCHG: Process 1, Nbr 1.2.1.1 on Ethernet1/1 from FULL to DOWN,
Neighbor Down: Dead timer expired
ISP(config-router)#
ISP(config-router)#area 1 stub
ISP(config-router)#
%OSPF-5-ADJCHG: Process 1, Nbr 1.2.1.1 on Ethernet1/1 from LOADING to
FULL, Loading Done
ISP(config-router)#
```

The adjacency forms:

```
OSPF1(config-router)#
%OSPF-5-ADJCHG: Process 1, Nbr 100.100.100.100 on Ethernet1/1 from
LOADING to FULL, Loading Done
OSPF1(config-router)#
```

ISP's routing table shows us the effect of this command. Here is the table now that it is a stub area:

```
ISP(config-router)#do sh ip route ospf | b Gate
Gateway of last resort is 172.16.1.2 to network 0.0.0.0

O*IA  0.0.0.0/0 [110/11] via 172.16.1.2, 00:01:07, Ethernet1/1
         1.0.0.0/32 is subnetted, 4 subnets
O IA     1.2.0.1 [110/21] via 172.16.1.2, 00:01:07, Ethernet1/1
O        1.2.1.1 [110/11] via 172.16.1.2, 00:01:07, Ethernet1/1
O IA     1.2.2.1 [110/31] via 172.16.1.2, 00:01:07, Ethernet1/1
O IA     1.2.3.1 [110/41] via 172.16.1.2, 00:01:07, Ethernet1/1
         172.16.0.0/16 is variably subnetted, 5 subnets, 2 masks
O IA     172.16.2.0/24 [110/20] via 172.16.1.2, 00:01:07, Ethernet1/1
O IA     172.16.3.0/24 [110/30] via 172.16.1.2, 00:01:07, Ethernet1/1
O IA     172.16.4.0/24 [110/40] via 172.16.1.2, 00:01:07, Ethernet1/1
ISP(config-router)#
```

We now have a default route pointing towards OSPF1, which we can also see in our OSPF database:

```
ISP(config-router)#do sh ip ospf database

        OSPF Router with ID (100.100.100.100) (Process ID 1)

        Router Link States (Area 1)

Link ID          ADV Router       Age    Seq#       Checksum Link count
1.2.1.1          1.2.1.1          107    0x8000001E 0x00BCB2 2
100.100.100.100  100.100.100.100  106    0x8000001D 0x005F6D 2

        Net Link States (Area 1)

Link ID          ADV Router       Age    Seq#       Checksum
172.16.1.1       100.100.100.100  106    0x80000001 0x00F262

        Summary Net Link States (Area 1)

Link ID          ADV Router       Age    Seq#       Checksum
0.0.0.0          1.2.1.1          153    0x80000001 0x008BAD
1.2.0.1          1.2.1.1          153    0x8000001B 0x008C84
1.2.2.1          1.2.1.1          153    0x8000001B 0x00DA2A
1.2.3.1          1.2.1.1          153    0x80000002 0x0066AC
172.16.2.0       1.2.1.1          153    0x8000001C 0x001442
172.16.3.0       1.2.1.1          153    0x8000001B 0x006FDC
172.16.4.0       1.2.1.1          153    0x8000001B 0x00C878
ISP(config-router)#
```

Apart from the default router, there is not a huge difference between the standard and stub area.

The next type of area is a Totally Stubby area, which can contain LSA types 1 and 2 and a single type 3 LSA; a default route substituted for all external and inter-area routes.

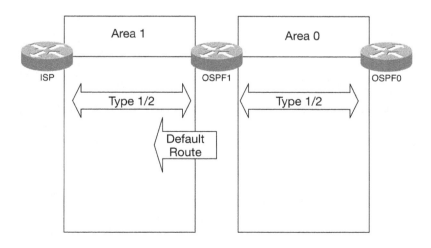

```
ISP(config-router)#area 1 stub no-summary
ISP(config-router)#

OSPF1(config-router)#area 1 stub no-summary
OSPF1(config-router)#
```

This gives us the biggest change:

```
ISP(config-router)#do sh ip ospf database

            OSPF Router with ID (100.100.100.100) (Process ID 1)

                Router Link States (Area 1)

Link ID            ADV Router        Age      Seq#        Checksum Link count
1.2.1.1            1.2.1.1           201      0x8000001E 0x00BCB2 2
100.100.100.100 100.100.100.100 200            0x8000001D 0x005F6D 2

                Net Link States (Area 1)

Link ID            ADV Router        Age      Seq#        Checksum
172.16.1.1         100.100.100.100 200        0x80000001 0x00F262

                Summary Net Link States (Area 1)

Link ID            ADV Router        Age      Seq#        Checksum
0.0.0.0            1.2.1.1           10       0x80000003 0x0087AF
ISP(config-router)#
ISP(config-router)#
ISP(config-router)#do sh ip route ospf | b Gate
Gateway of last resort is 172.16.1.2 to network 0.0.0.0

O*IA  0.0.0.0/0 [110/11] via 172.16.1.2, 00:00:25, Ethernet1/1
        1.0.0.0/32 is subnetted, 1 subnets
O          1.2.1.1 [110/11] via 172.16.1.2, 00:00:38, Ethernet1/1
ISP(config-router)#
```

The final type is the not-so-stubby area (nssa). NSSAs can be either standard stub, or totally stubby areas. The NSSA will send a type 7 LSA, which will be converted to a type 5 LSA by the ABR (OSPF1).

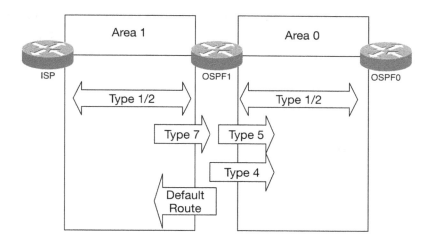

We need to remove any previous stub configuration before we can configure a not-so-stubby area.

```
OSPF1(config-router)#no area 1 stub no-summary
OSPF1(config-router)#do sh run | s router
router ospf 1
 area 1 stub
 network 1.2.1.1 0.0.0.0 area 1
 network 172.16.1.0 0.0.0.255 area 1
 network 172.16.2.0 0.0.0.255 area 0
ipv6 router ospf 1
 router-id 1.2.1.1
OSPF1(config-router)#no area 1 stub
OSPF1(config-router)#
%OSPF-5-ADJCHG: Process 1, Nbr 100.100.100.100 on Ethernet1/1 from FULL
to DOWN, Neighbor Down: Adjacency forced to reset
%OSPF-5-ADJCHG: Process 1, Nbr 100.100.100.100 on Ethernet1/1 from
LOADING to FULL, Loading Done
OSPF1(config-router)#

ISP(config-router)#no area 1 stub
ISP(config-router)#
%OSPF-5-ADJCHG: Process 1, Nbr 1.2.1.1 on Ethernet1/1 from FULL to DOWN,
Neighbor Down: Adjacency forced to reset
%OSPF-5-ADJCHG: Process 1, Nbr 1.2.1.1 on Ethernet1/1 from LOADING to
FULL, Loading Done
ISP(config-router)#do sh run | s router
router ospf 1
 router-id 100.100.100.100
 network 100.100.100.100 0.0.0.0 area 1
 network 172.16.0.0 0.0.255.255 area 1
ipv6 router ospf 1
ISP(config-router)#
```

Notice that for OSPF1 we needed to use two commands to remove the stub configuration, but only one on ISP. Removing the stub no-summary command first will still leave the first stub command, but removing the first stub command will remove the second command as well.

We set up NSSA areas using the following commands:

```
OSPF1(config-router)#
OSPF1(config-router)#area 1 nssa
OSPF1(config-router)#

ISP(config-router)#
ISP(config-router)#area 1 nssa
ISP(config-router)#
```

The adjacencies will drop and reform.

What effects has this change in area type had on our database?

```
ISP(config-router)#do sh ip ospf database

            OSPF Router with ID (100.100.100.100) (Process ID 1)

              Router Link States (Area 1)

Link ID           ADV Router        Age     Seq#       Checksum Link count
1.2.1.1           1.2.1.1           382     0x80000020 0x009AD0 2
100.100.100.100   100.100.100.100   377     0x8000001F 0x003D8B 2

              Net Link States (Area 1)

Link ID           ADV Router        Age     Seq#       Checksum
172.16.1.1        100.100.100.100   377     0x80000003 0x00D080

              Summary Net Link States (Area 1)

Link ID           ADV Router        Age     Seq#       Checksum
1.2.0.1           1.2.1.1           403     0x80000002 0x00A087
1.2.2.1           1.2.1.1           403     0x80000002 0x00EE2D
1.2.3.1           1.2.1.1           403     0x80000002 0x0048C8
172.16.2.0        1.2.1.1           403     0x80000002 0x002A44
172.16.3.0        1.2.1.1           403     0x80000002 0x0083DF
172.16.4.0        1.2.1.1           403     0x80000002 0x00DC7B

ISP(config-router)#
```

And the routing table?

```
ISP(config-router)#do sh ip route ospf | b Gate
Gateway of last resort is not set

      1.0.0.0/32 is subnetted, 4 subnets
O IA     1.2.0.1 [110/21] via 172.16.1.2, 00:06:36, Ethernet1/1
O        1.2.1.1 [110/11] via 172.16.1.2, 00:06:36, Ethernet1/1
O IA     1.2.2.1 [110/31] via 172.16.1.2, 00:06:36, Ethernet1/1
O IA     1.2.3.1 [110/41] via 172.16.1.2, 00:06:36, Ethernet1/1
      172.16.0.0/16 is variably subnetted, 5 subnets, 2 masks
O IA     172.16.2.0/24 [110/20] via 172.16.1.2, 00:06:36, Ethernet1/1
O IA     172.16.3.0/24 [110/30] via 172.16.1.2, 00:06:36, Ethernet1/1
O IA     172.16.4.0/24 [110/40] via 172.16.1.2, 00:06:36, Ethernet1/1
ISP(config-router)#
```

Back to where we were with a standard area, we do not get the default route injected by the ABR as we did with the stub area. We can instruct OSPF1 to do this though, by appending the option *"default-information-originate"* to the command:

```
OSPF1(config-router)#
OSPF1(config-router)#area 1 nssa default-information-originate
OSPF1(config-router)#
```

ISP now gets a default route, but it is displayed as an NSSA External type 2 route (remember that you can remove the *"| b Gate"* from the end of the command to see the codes and their meanings):

```
ISP(config-router)#do sh ip route ospf | b Gate
Gateway of last resort is 172.16.1.2 to network 0.0.0.0

O*N2  0.0.0.0/0 [110/1] via 172.16.1.2, 00:00:44, Ethernet1/1
      1.0.0.0/32 is subnetted, 4 subnets
O IA     1.2.0.1 [110/21] via 172.16.1.2, 00:06:05, Ethernet1/1
O        1.2.1.1 [110/11] via 172.16.1.2, 00:06:05, Ethernet1/1
O IA     1.2.2.1 [110/31] via 172.16.1.2, 00:06:05, Ethernet1/1
O IA     1.2.3.1 [110/41] via 172.16.1.2, 00:06:05, Ethernet1/1
      172.16.0.0/16 is variably subnetted, 5 subnets, 2 masks
O IA     172.16.2.0/24 [110/20] via 172.16.1.2, 00:06:05, Ethernet1/1
O IA     172.16.3.0/24 [110/30] via 172.16.1.2, 00:06:05, Ethernet1/1
O IA     172.16.4.0/24 [110/40] via 172.16.1.2, 00:06:05, Ethernet1/1
ISP(config-router)#
```

We can also use the command *"no-summary"* along with the nssa command to make the Not-so-stubby area function as a totally stubby area:

```
OSPF1(config-router)#area 1 nssa default-information-originate no-summary
OSPF1(config-router)#
```

The OSPF database shows us that the default route is injected via a type 7 LSA and the routing table shows it as an Inter-Area route:

```
ISP(config-router)#do sh ip ospf database

            OSPF Router with ID (100.100.100.100) (Process ID 1)

            Router Link States (Area 1)

Link ID         ADV Router      Age      Seq#       Checksum Link count
1.2.1.1         1.2.1.1         433      0x80000022 0x00421F 2
100.100.100.100 100.100.100.100 432      0x80000021 0x00DEE1 2

            Net Link States (Area 1)

Link ID         ADV Router      Age      Seq#       Checksum
172.16.1.1      100.100.100.100 427      0x80000005 0x0072D6

            Summary Net Link States (Area 1)

Link ID         ADV Router      Age      Seq#       Checksum
0.0.0.0         1.2.1.1         11       0x80000001 0x00131E

            Type-7 AS External Link States (Area 1)

Link ID         ADV Router      Age      Seq#       Checksum Tag
0.0.0.0         1.2.1.1         103      0x80000001 0x00E6C5 0
ISP(config-router)#do sh ip route ospf | b Gate
Gateway of last resort is 172.16.1.2 to network 0.0.0.0

O*IA  0.0.0.0/0 [110/11] via 172.16.1.2, 00:00:26, Ethernet1/1
         1.0.0.0/32 is subnetted, 1 subnets
O        1.2.1.1 [110/11] via 172.16.1.2, 00:07:20, Ethernet1/1
ISP(config-router)#
```

When we use the "no-summary" command when setting an area to be NSSA, we do not actually need the "default-information-originate" command as well, as the ABR will inject the default route, so we can use the below command, and neither the OSPF database or the routing table will be changed:

```
OSPF1(config-router)#no area 1 nssa default-information-originate no-
summary
OSPF1(config-router)#area 1 nssa no-summary
OSPF1(config-router)#do sh run | s router
router ospf 1
 area 1 nssa no-summary
 network 1.2.1.1 0.0.0.0 area 1
 network 172.16.1.0 0.0.0.255 area 1
 network 172.16.2.0 0.0.0.255 area 0
```

```
ipv6 router ospf 1
  router-id 1.2.1.1
OSPF1(config-router)#

ISP(config-router)#do sh ip route ospf | b Gate
Gateway of last resort is 172.16.1.2 to network 0.0.0.0

O*IA  0.0.0.0/0 [110/11] via 172.16.1.2, 00:01:08, Ethernet1/1
        1.0.0.0/32 is subnetted, 1 subnets
O          1.2.1.1 [110/11] via 172.16.1.2, 00:05:15, Ethernet1/1
ISP(config-router)#
```

We have seen that OSPF uses a large number of LSAs in order to create its view of the world. Let's now look at these in more detail.

4.7.g Understand LSA types and purpose

In this section we will be referring back to the output from *"sh ip ospf database"* for each of the LSAs. I will not include the full output, just the relevant portion.

The database shows a number of columns. We have the Link ID (link state ID to be exact). The link state ID (along with the LS type and advertising router) identifies the LSA within the Link State Database (LSDB). We then have the advertising router's RID (ADV Router) and then the age. The age is the time in seconds since the LSA was originated. The Seq# (which stands for LS Sequence Number) is used to detect old or duplicate LSAs. The checksum field is used for integrity checking and then we have the link count, which is the number of links in area 0.

Across all of the area types, we have two consistent LSA types; type 1 and type 2.

LSA type 1 is the Router LSA. This is announced by a router and lists the links to other routers and/or networks within the same area. This LSA also includes the associated metrics. Type 1 LSAs do not pass from one area to another; instead, they will stay within their own area (area 0 to area 0, area 1 to area 1, but never area 0 to area 1). We can see the type 1 LSA in the database:

```
              Router Link States (Area 0)

Link ID       ADV Router      Age          Seq#        Checksum Link count
1.2.0.1       1.2.0.1         345          0x80000039 0x009820 3
1.2.1.1       1.2.1.1         340          0x80000039 0x0088DA 1
1.2.2.1       1.2.2.1         129          0x80000039 0x000973 2
1.2.3.1       1.2.3.1         2     (DNA) 0x80000003 0x00E468 1
```

The Link ID is the RID of the originating router. We can see that OSPF0 has three links in area 0, OSPF1 has one link, OSPF2 has two links and OSPF3 has one link. The router LSA also indicates if the router is an ASBR or an ABR.

LSA type 2 is the Network LSA. This is advertised by the DR and only within the local area. The Network LSA contains a list of the routers on the segment. The Link ID is the interface address of the DR.

```
                Net Link States (Area 0)

Link ID        ADV Router      Age       Seq#        Checksum
172.16.2.2     1.2.1.1         87        0x80000038  0x00B67D
172.16.3.2     1.2.2.1         1896      0x80000037  0x00AF82
```

If we look at the output of "sh ip ospf neighbour" we can see the same information:

```
OSPF0#sh ip ospf neigh

Neighbor ID  Pri   State      Dead Time   Address      Interface
1.2.2.1        1   FULL/DR    00:00:31    172.16.3.2   Ethernet1/2
1.2.1.1        1   FULL/DR    00:00:38    172.16.2.2   Ethernet1/0
OSPF0#
```

Type 3 LSAs are Summary LSAs. An ABR, such as OSPF1 where it borders Area 1 and Area 0, will take the information it receives from one area and summarize it before sending it to the other area. The link ID is the destination network.

```
                Summary Net Link States (Area 0)

Link ID          ADV Router     Age         Seq#        Checksum
1.2.1.1          1.2.1.1        1693        0x8000001B  0x00FE19
1.2.2.1          1.2.2.1        421         0x8000001B  0x00EC29
1.2.2.1          1.2.3.1        73    (DNA) 0x80000001  0x007EA6
1.2.3.1          1.2.3.1        2     (DNA) 0x80000001  0x000F1F
100.100.100.100  1.2.1.1        580         0x80000001  0x00C7D3
172.16.1.0       1.2.1.1        580         0x8000001D  0x00FE55
172.16.4.0       1.2.2.1        421         0x8000001B  0x00DA77
172.16.4.0       1.2.3.1        73    (DNA) 0x80000001  0x000863
```

Notice that for ISP we just have the default route as the type 3 LSA:

```
                Summary Net Link States (Area 1)

Link ID        ADV Router      Age       Seq#        Checksum
0.0.0.0        1.2.1.1         779       0x80000006  0x000923
```

Type 4 LSAs are ASBR-Summary LSAs. We do not have any of these now but we will do later on. Type 4 LSAs are needed to provide the link between the information sent in a type 5 external LSA and the required next-hop information. The link ID is the RID of the described ASBR.

Type 5 LSAs are external LSAs, where we have other routing protocols being redistributed into OSPF. These are flooded without modification to all areas (apart from stub and NSSA). The link ID is the external network number.

Type 6 LSA was for Group Membership in Multicast OSPF (MOSPF). Multicast OSPF is not used anymore.

Type 7 LSAs are used instead of type 5 LSAs by not-so-stubby routers. These routers do not receive external LSAs from ABRs. Type 7 LSAs inform ABRs about external routes received from redistribution. The ABR translates this into a type 5 LSA and floods it to the rest of the network.

```
           Type-7 AS External Link States (Area 1)

  Link ID          ADV Router      Age      Seq#         Checksum Tag
  0.0.0.0          1.2.1.1         103      0x80000001 0x00E6C5 0
```

In OSPFv3 types 3 and 4 are named Inter-Area prefix LSA and Inter-Area Router LSA, and two more are added, Link LSA and Intra-Area Prefix LSA.

We can see the difference in the databases using the command "*show ipv6 ospf database*":

```
OSPF0#sh ipv6 ospf database

            OSPFv3 Router with ID (1.2.0.1) (Process ID 1)

            Router Link States (Area 0)

ADV Router          Age       Seq#         Fragment ID  Link count  Bits
  1.2.0.1           1623      0x8000001B   0            2           None
  1.2.1.1           1346      0x8000001B   0            2           None
  1.2.2.1           1293      0x8000001B   0            2           None
  1.2.3.1           890       0x8000001A   0            1           None
  100.100.100.100 1130        0x8000001B   0            1           None

            Net Link States (Area 0)

ADV Router          Age       Seq#         Link ID   Rtr count
  1.2.0.1           1623      0x8000001A   5         2
  1.2.1.1           1346      0x8000001A   7         2
  1.2.2.1           1293      0x8000001A   14        2
  100.100.100.100 1130        0x8000001A   8         2
```

```
                    Link (Type-8) Link States (Area 0)

ADV Router          Age         Seq#          Link ID    Interface
  1.2.0.1           1623        0x8000001A    5          Et0/2
  1.2.2.1           1293        0x8000001A    11         Et0/2
  1.2.0.1           1623        0x8000001A    4          Et0/1
  1.2.1.1           1591        0x8000001A    7          Et0/1

               Intra Area Prefix Link States (Area 0)

ADV Router          Age         Seq#          Link ID    Ref-lstype    Ref-LSID
  1.2.0.1           1623        0x8000001C    0          0x2001        0
  1.2.0.1           1623        0x8000001A    5120       0x2002        5
  1.2.1.1           1346        0x8000001C    0          0x2001        0
  1.2.1.1           1346        0x8000001A    7168       0x2002        7
  1.2.2.1           1293        0x8000001C    0          0x2001        0
  1.2.2.1           1293        0x8000001A    14336      0x2002        14
  1.2.3.1           890         0x8000001A    0          0x2001        0
  100.100.100.100 1130         0x8000001A    8192       0x2002        8
OSPF0#
```

OSPFv3 has the Inter-Area Prefix LSA, which is the IPv6 equivalent of the IPv4 type 3 summary LSA. They are originated by the ABR and specify the IPv6 prefixes that belong to other areas. We also have Inter-Area router LSAs, which are the equivalent of type 4 summary LSAs; they describe the route to the ASBR. The IPv6 version of the type 5 external LSA is the AS-External LSA. These are generated by an ASBR and describe the destinations outside of the local area.

In the output above, we can see the Link LSA. These are originated for each link attached to the router. They are never flooded beyond the link they are local to. Lastly, we have the Intra-Area Prefix LSA, which advertises IPv6 prefixes for the router, any attached stub network, and any attached transit segment.

We have completed our OSPF configuration on this side, but it is still very self-contained.

What we will do now is extend this to the Gateway router, adding it into area 1:

```
ISP(config-router)#network 192.168.20.1 0.0.0.255 area 1
ISP(config-router)#

Gateway(config)#router ospf 1
Gateway(config-router)#router-id 50.50.50.50
Gateway(config-router)#network 192.168.20.0 0.0.0.255 area 1
Gateway(config-router)#network 50.50.50.50 0.0.0.0 area 1
Gateway(config-router)#area 1 nssa
Gateway(config-router)#
```

```
%OSPF-5-ADJCHG: Process 1, Nbr 100.100.100.100 on Ethernet0/0 from
LOADING to FULL, Loading Done
Gateway(config-router)#
```

Now, hopefully, we should receive a default route from the ISP router:

```
Gateway(config-router)#do sh ip route ospf | b Gate
Gateway of last resort is 192.168.20.1 to network 0.0.0.0

O*IA  0.0.0.0/0 [110/21] via 192.168.20.1, 00:01:00, Ethernet0/0
      1.0.0.0/32 is subnetted, 1 subnets
O        1.2.1.1 [110/21] via 192.168.20.1, 00:01:00, Ethernet0/0
      100.0.0.0/32 is subnetted, 1 subnets
O        100.100.100.100 [110/11] via 192.168.20.1, 00:01:00, Ethernet0/0
      172.16.0.0/24 is subnetted, 1 subnets
O        172.16.1.0 [110/20] via 192.168.20.1, 00:01:00, Ethernet0/0
Gateway(config-router)#
```

Perfect! We even have reachability to OSPF3:

```
Gateway(config-router)#do ping 1.2.3.1
Type escape sequence to abort.
Sending 5, 100-byte ICMP Echos to 1.2.3.1:
!!!!!
Success rate is 100 percent (5/5)
Gateway(config-router)#
```

This puts us into a great position to complete our LAN setup, by getting our VLANs talking to each other, and to the outside world.

4.8 Configure and verify interVLAN routing (Router on a stick)

We have not touched our LAN in a while. It was getting off to a good start, and then we moved on and started configuring our WAN. Now we need to go back and get our LAN talking to our WAN and to get the VLANs talking to each other.

The first way we are going to do this is by implementing what is known as "router on a stick", often abbreviated to "ROAS". This is where our router will handle the passing of traffic from one VLAN to another (and to the outside world).

A basic diagram of the traffic flow looks like this:

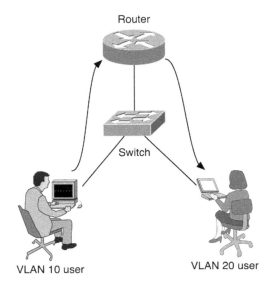

Router

Switch

VLAN 10 user

VLAN 20 user

When the user in VLAN 10 sends some data to the user in VLAN 20 the data flows to the switch, which then forwards it to the router using VLAN 10. The router in turn sends it back down to the switch in VLAN 20, where it is forwarded on to the user.

4.8.a sub interfaces

So far, we have reachability between SW1's VLAN 1 interface and the Gateway router:

```
Gateway(config-router)#do ping 10.1.1.1
Type escape sequence to abort.
Sending 5, 100-byte ICMP Echos to 10.1.1.1:
!!!!!
Success rate is 100 percent (5/5)
Gateway(config-router)#
```

This is great, but we have more VLANs than this. We also have an issue that (unlike switch interfaces) we cannot assign the router interface to a particular VLAN, nor can we make it into a trunk. We can, however, make more interfaces from the existing interface. These are called sub-interfaces.

To create a sub-interface we need to remove our existing IP address, create the sub interface and put the IP address on the sub interface instead. This will allow us to create a sub interface for each VLAN.

```
Gateway(config-router)#int e0/1
Gateway(config-if)#no ip address
Gateway(config-if)#int e0/1.1
Gateway(config-subif)#
```

We have created a new interface e0/1.1. We could use another number, but when you are creating a sub-interface it is customary to number it the same as the VLAN it is encapsulating for, it helps when looking at the configuration.

4.8.b upstream routing

The benefit of using sub-interfaces this is that, as well as allowing us to route from one VLAN to another, it will also allow us to pass traffic from our LAN to the networks beyond the Gateway router. This is referred to as "upstream routing". We can use any protocol that the Gateway router does, or just use static routing, which is what we will set up at the end of this section.

Whilst the sub-interfaces need to have an IP address configured on it for it to work, we cannot assign the address until we specify which VLAN we will be carrying, this is "encapsulation", which we have spoken about previously.

4.8.c encapsulation

We need to configure the VLAN information on the sub-interface before we can configure an IP address. We do this using the *"encapsulation"* command:

```
Gateway(config-subif)#ip address 10.1.1.254 255.255.255.0

% Configuring IP routing on a LAN subinterface is only allowed if that
subinterface is already configured as part of an IEEE 802.10, IEEE
802.1Q, or ISL vLAN.

Gateway(config-subif)#encapsulation dot1Q ?
  <1-4094>  IEEE 802.1Q VLAN ID required

Gateway(config-subif)#encapsulation dot1Q 1
Gateway(config-subif)#ip address 10.1.1.254 255.255.255.0
Gateway(config-subif)#
```

We will use 802.1Q here to match the encapsulation method used by our switches. At this stage, we should still be able to ping the VLAN 1 interface that is on SW1:

```
Gateway(config-subif)#do ping 10.1.1.1
Type escape sequence to abort.
Sending 5, 100-byte ICMP Echos to 10.1.1.1:
.!!!!
Success rate is 80 percent (4/5)
Gateway(config-subif)#
```

However, if we were to add more subinterfaces on the router for the other VLANs, these would not work, as the switch interface is only set up for VLAN 1. We need to change the connecting interface on the switch to be a trunk:

```
SW1(config)#int e0/0
SW1(config-if)#switchport trunk encapsulation dot
SW1(config-if)#switchport mode trunk
SW1(config-if)#
```

Our ping is successful (note that we might not get this result straight away, so wait a few seconds before trying):

```
Gateway(config-subif)#do ping 10.1.1.1
Type escape sequence to abort.
Sending 5, 100-byte ICMP Echos to 10.1.1.1:
!!!!!
Success rate is 100 percent (5/5)
Gateway(config-subif)#
```

This means that we can press on and set up VLAN 10, first by creating the SVI on the switch and then the sub-interface on the router:

```
SW1(config-if)#int vlan 10
SW1(config-if)#ip add 10.10.1.1 255.255.255.0
SW1(config-if)#no shut
SW1(config-if)#

Gateway(config)#int e0/1.10
Gateway(config-subif)#encapsulation dot1q 10
Gateway(config-subif)#ip add 10.10.1.254 255.255.255.0
Gateway(config-subif)#
Gateway(config-subif)#do ping 10.10.1.1
Type escape sequence to abort.
Sending 5, 100-byte ICMP Echos to 10.10.1.1:
.!!!!
Success rate is 80 percent (4/5)
Gateway(config-subif)#
```

The process is the same; create the VLAN interface on the switch, create the sub-interface on the router, set the encapsulation to the required VLAN and add the IP address.

Let's do the rest of the sub-interface on Gateway's e0/1 interface:

```
Gateway(config-subif)#int e0/1.30
Gateway(config-subif)#encap dot 30
Gateway(config-subif)#ip add 10.30.1.254 255.255.255.0
```

```
Gateway(config-subif)#exit
Gateway(config)#int e0/1.40
Gateway(config-subif)#encap dot 40
Gateway(config-subif)#ip add 10.40.1.254 255.255.255.0
Gateway(config-subif)#int e0/1.50
Gateway(config-subif)#encap dot 50
Gateway(config-subif)#ip add 10.50.1.254 255.255.255.0
Gateway(config-subif)#exit
Gateway(config)#
```

We will have VLAN 20 route (primarily) through SW2, so we will set the VLAN interface up on SW2, adding the sub-interface to e0/2 on the Gateway router (remembering to first remove the IP address from the interface):

```
Gateway(config)#int e0/2
Gateway(config-if)#no ip add
Gateway(config-if)#int e0/2.20
Gateway(config-subif)#encap dot 20
Gateway(config-subif)#ip add 10.20.1.254 255.255.255.0
Gateway(config-subif)#
```

We can use the command "*show ip int bri*" to check that all of our interfaces are there and that they are up. I have excluded the interfaces without IP address (unassigned) from the results purely for formatting reasons.

```
Gateway(config-subif)#do sh ip int bri | e unassigned
Interface          IP-Address      OK? Method Status          Protocol
Ethernet0/0        192.168.20.254  YES manual up              up
Ethernet0/1.1      10.1.1.254      YES manual up              up
Ethernet0/1.10     10.10.1.254     YES manual up              up
Ethernet0/1.30     10.30.1.254     YES manual up              up
Ethernet0/1.40     10.40.1.254     YES manual up              up
Ethernet0/1.50     10.50.1.254     YES manual up              up
Ethernet0/2.20     10.20.1.254     YES manual up              up
Loopback0          50.50.50.50     YES manual up              up
Gateway(config-subif)#
```

We can now test our connectivity from Dave's PC to the Gateway router, once we correct his IP address (we should already have the switch's port in the correct VLAN):

```
SW4#sh run int e0/0 | b interface
interface Ethernet0/0
 switchport access vlan 10
 switchport mode access
 duplex auto
end
SW4#
```

```
Dave-PC(config)#int e0/0
Dave-PC(config-if)#ip address 10.10.1.21 255.255.255.0
Dave-PC(config-if)#
Dave-PC(config-if)#do ping 10.10.1.1
Type escape sequence to abort.
Sending 5, 100-byte ICMP Echos to 10.10.1.1:
.!!!!
Success rate is 80 percent (4/5)
Dave-PC(config-if)#do ping 10.10.1.254
Type escape sequence to abort.
Sending 5, 100-byte ICMP Echos to 10.10.1.254:
.!!!!
Success rate is 80 percent (4/5)
Dave-PC(config-if)#
```

Now, from Dave-PC we can reach the SVI on the switch and the correct interface on the Gateway router. Let's set up Bob in his VLAN and give him an IP address so that we can test connectivity from Dave to Bob. SW3's e0/0 port should already be an access port for VLAN 30 and not shut down:

```
SW3(config)#do sh run int e0/0 | b interface
interface Ethernet0/0
 switchport access vlan 30
 switchport mode access
 duplex auto
end

SW3(config)#

Router(config)#ho Bob-PC
Bob-PC(config)#int e0/0
Bob-PC(config-if)#
Bob-PC(config-if)#ip add 10.30.1.21 255.255.255.0
Bob-PC(config-if)#no shut
Bob-PC(config-if)#
```

We should be able to get to the Gateway Router now:

```
Bob-PC(config-if)#do ping 10.30.1.254
Type escape sequence to abort.
Sending 5, 100-byte ICMP Echos to 10.30.1.254:
.!!!!
Success rate is 80 percent (4/5)
Bob-PC(config-if)#
```

Bob will not be able to reach Dave at this point. He only knows about the 10.30.1.0/24 network, similarly Dave only knows about the 10.10.1.0/24 network:

```
Bob-PC(config-if)#do sh ip route | b Gate
Gateway of last resort is not set

        10.0.0.0/8 is variably subnetted, 2 subnets, 2 masks
C          10.30.1.0/24 is directly connected, Ethernet0/0
L          10.30.1.21/32 is directly connected, Ethernet0/0
Bob-PC(config-if)#

Dave-PC(config-if)#do sh ip route | b Gate
Gateway of last resort is not set

        10.0.0.0/8 is variably subnetted, 2 subnets, 2 masks
C          10.10.1.0/24 is directly connected, Ethernet0/0
L          10.10.1.21/32 is directly connected, Ethernet0/0
Dave-PC(config-if)#
```

Let's give them a static route each, pointing to the Gateway router:

```
Bob-PC(config-if)#ip route 0.0.0.0 0.0.0.0 10.30.1.254
Bob-PC(config)#

Dave-PC(config-if)#ip route 0.0.0.0 0.0.0.0 10.10.1.254
Dave-PC(config)#
```

Now can they reach each other?

```
Dave-PC(config)#do ping 10.30.1.21
Type escape sequence to abort.
Sending 5, 100-byte ICMP Echos to 10.30.1.21:
!!!!!
Success rate is 100 percent (5/5)
Dave-PC(config)#

Bob-PC(config)#do ping 10.10.1.21
Type escape sequence to abort.
Sending 5, 100-byte ICMP Echos to 10.10.1.21:
!!!!!
Success rate is 100 percent (5/5)
Bob-PC(config)#
```

Yes, they can. If we do a traceroute, we can see that our router on a stick network is functioning as it should. The packets go up to the Gateway router in one VLAN and back down in the other VLAN. It works very well:

```
Bob-PC(config)#do trace 10.10.1.21 numeric
Type escape sequence to abort.
Tracing the route to 10.10.1.21
```

```
VRF info: (vrf in name/id, vrf out name/id)
  1 10.30.1.254 12 msec 16 msec 20 msec
  2 10.10.1.21 40 msec *  24 msec
Bob-PC(config)#
```

However, consider our network for a moment. In an ideal scenario we shouldn't even need to go near the router, all the traffic should be contained within the switches. Let's do that!

4.9 Configure SVI interfaces

The final step is to create the VLAN interfaces. These are known as "Switch Virtual Interfaces" or SVIs. Another name for them is VIF (Virtual Interface), which I have used before. The SVI connects the VLAN interfaces into a routed network. We already created one, for VLAN 10 on SW1, so let's configure the rest of our SVIs:

```
SW2(config)#int e0/0
SW2(config-if)#switchport trunk encapsulation dot1q
SW2(config-if)#switchport mode trunk
SW2(config-if)#int vlan 20
SW2(config-if)#ip address 10.20.1.1 255.255.255.0
SW2(config-if)#no shut
SW2(config-if)#

SW1(config-if)#int vlan 30
SW1(config-if)#ip add 10.30.1.1 255.255.255.0
SW1(config-if)#no shut
SW1(config-if)#int vlan 40
SW1(config-if)#ip address 10.40.1.1 255.255.255.0
SW1(config-if)#no shut
SW1(config-if)#int vlan 50
SW1(config-if)#ip add 10.50.1.1 255.255.255.0
SW1(config-if)#no shut
SW1(config-if)#
```

Above we have changed the e0/0 port on SW2, which connects it to the Gateway router, to a trunk port, then created four SVI interfaces. Our new SVIs should be able to reach the Gateway router's sub-interfaces:

```
SW2(config-if)#do ping 10.20.1.254
Type escape sequence to abort.
Sending 5, 100-byte ICMP Echos to 10.20.1.254:
!!!!!
Success rate is 100 percent (5/5)
SW2(config-if)#

SW1(config-if)#do ping 10.30.1.254
Type escape sequence to abort.
```

```
Sending 5, 100-byte ICMP Echos to 10.30.1.254:
.!!!!
Success rate is 80 percent (4/5)
SW1(config-if)#do ping 10.40.1.254
Type escape sequence to abort.
Sending 5, 100-byte ICMP Echos to 10.40.1.254:
.!!!!
Success rate is 80 percent (4/5)
SW1(config-if)#do ping 10.50.1.254
Type escape sequence to abort.
Sending 5, 100-byte ICMP Echos to 10.50.1.254:
.!!!!
Success rate is 80 percent (4/5)
SW1(config-if)#
```

SVIs bring the functions provided by the Router on a Stick based network, down into the switch. This means that inter-VLAN traffic is much faster, it no longer hits the switch, travels up to the router, and back down again to the destination. Instead, all of the inter-VLAN switching takes place within the switch itself. This will increase the routers performance, as it does not need to handle traffic that is not destined for the outside or external network, this is generally a preferred network design as well.

We can test this new configuration by changing the static route on Bob and Dave to point to the relevant SVI for their network:

```
Dave-PC(config)#ip route 0.0.0.0 0.0.0.0 10.10.1.1
Dave-PC(config)#

Bob-PC(config)#ip route 0.0.0.0 0.0.0.0 10.30.1.1
Bob-PC(config)#
```

Now, we should not need to touch the router:

```
Bob-PC(config)#do ping 10.10.1.21
Type escape sequence to abort.
Sending 5, 100-byte ICMP Echos to 10.10.1.21:
!!!!!
Success rate is 100 percent (5/5)
Bob-PC(config)#do trace 10.10.1.21 numeric
Type escape sequence to abort.
Tracing the route to 10.10.1.21
VRF info: (vrf in name/id, vrf out name/id)
  1 10.30.1.1 8 msec
    10.30.1.254 16 msec
    10.30.1.1 4 msec
  2 10.10.1.21 24 msec *  20 msec
Bob-PC(config)#
```

The ping works, but the traceroute looks odd. We are still going through the router, but also through the SVI on SW1. This is because we have two static routes:

```
Bob-PC(config)#do sh ip route | b Gate
Gateway of last resort is 10.30.1.254 to network 0.0.0.0

S*     0.0.0.0/0 [1/0] via 10.30.1.254
                 [1/0] via 10.30.1.1
       10.0.0.0/8 is variably subnetted, 2 subnets, 2 masks
C         10.30.1.0/24 is directly connected, Ethernet0/0
L         10.30.1.21/32 is directly connected, Ethernet0/0
Bob-PC(config)#do sh run | i ip route
ip route 0.0.0.0 0.0.0.0 10.30.1.254
ip route 0.0.0.0 0.0.0.0 10.30.1.1
Bob-PC(config)#
```

Let's remove the first one and do the same on Dave:

```
Bob-PC(config)#
Bob-PC(config)#no ip route 0.0.0.0 0.0.0.0 10.30.1.254
Bob-PC(config)#

Dave-PC(config)#
Dave-PC(config)#no ip route 0.0.0.0 0.0.0.0 10.10.1.254
Dave-PC(config)#
```

The traceroute now works as expected:

```
Bob-PC(config)#do trace 10.10.1.21 numeric
Type escape sequence to abort.
Tracing the route to 10.10.1.21
VRF info: (vrf in name/id, vrf out name/id)
  1 10.30.1.1 16 msec 4 msec 12 msec
  2 10.10.1.21 24 msec *  4 msec
Bob-PC(config)#
```

For completeness, we will now set up the Server and test that as well:

```
Router(config)#hostname Server
Server(config)#int e1/0
Server(config-if)#ip add 10.20.1.21 255.255.255.0
Server(config-if)#no shut
Server(config-if)#ip route 0.0.0.0 0.0.0.0 10.20.1.1
Server(config)#
```

Can we reach Bob or Dave?

```
Server(config)#do ping 10.10.1.21
Type escape sequence to abort.
Sending 5, 100-byte ICMP Echos to 10.10.1.21:
U.U.U
Success rate is 0 percent (0/5)
Server(config)#
```

No, we cannot. We can reach the SVI on SW2, but nothing else:

```
Server(config)#do ping 10.20.1.1
Type escape sequence to abort.
Sending 5, 100-byte ICMP Echos to 10.20.1.1:
!!!!!
Success rate is 100 percent (5/5)
Server(config)#
```

Think about the topology for the moment. Server will be able to reach the SVI on SW2, as the packets will be carried along VLAN 20, through SW1 to SW2, but it is unable to reach other VLANs. Where does the problem lie and how would you find it? More importantly, how can we fix the problem?

Traceroute would be the first step:

```
Server(config)#do trace 10.10.1.21 numeric
Type escape sequence to abort.
Tracing the route to 10.10.1.21
VRF info: (vrf in name/id, vrf out name/id)
  1 10.20.1.1 4 msec 12 msec 8 msec
  2 10.20.1.1 !H  *  !H
Server(config)#
```

The packets get to SW2, but stop there. It is therefore likely that SW2 has the issue. Let's check its routing table:

```
SW2(config-if)#do sh ip route | b Gate
Gateway of last resort is not set

      3.0.0.0/32 is subnetted, 1 subnets
C        3.1.1.2 is directly connected, Loopback0
      10.0.0.0/8 is variably subnetted, 4 subnets, 2 masks
C        10.1.1.0/24 is directly connected, Vlan1
L        10.1.1.2/32 is directly connected, Vlan1
C        10.20.1.0/24 is directly connected, Vlan20
L        10.20.1.1/32 is directly connected, Vlan20
SW2(config-if)#
```

SW2 has no knowledge of either network (at layer-3). So let's fix that:

```
SW2(config)#int vlan 10
SW2(config-if)#ip address 10.10.1.2 255.255.255.0
SW2(config-if)#no shut
SW2(config-if)#int vlan 30
SW2(config-if)#ip address 10.30.1.2 255.255.255.0
SW2(config-if)#no shut
SW2(config-if)#
SW2(config-if)#do sh ip route | b Gate
Gateway of last resort is not set

      3.0.0.0/32 is subnetted, 1 subnets
C        3.1.1.2 is directly connected, Loopback0
      10.0.0.0/8 is variably subnetted, 8 subnets, 2 masks
C        10.1.1.0/24 is directly connected, Vlan1
L        10.1.1.2/32 is directly connected, Vlan1
C        10.10.1.0/24 is directly connected, Vlan10
L        10.10.1.2/32 is directly connected, Vlan10
C        10.20.1.0/24 is directly connected, Vlan20
L        10.20.1.1/32 is directly connected, Vlan20
C        10.30.1.0/24 is directly connected, Vlan30
L        10.30.1.2/32 is directly connected, Vlan30
SW2(config-if)#
```

> If the VLAN interfaces do not come up straight away, do a shut and no shut on the interfaces:
>
> ```
> SW2(config-if)#interface Vlan30
> SW2(config-if)#shut
> %LINK-5-CHANGED: Interface Vlan30, changed state to
> administratively down
> SW2(config-if)#no shut
> %LINK-3-UPDOWN: Interface Vlan30, changed state to up
> %LINEPROTO-5-UPDOWN: Line protocol on Interface Vlan30, changed
> state to up
> SW2(config-if)#interface Vlan10
> SW2(config-if)#shut
> %LINK-5-CHANGED: Interface Vlan10, changed state to
> administratively down
> SW2(config-if)#no shut
> %LINK-3-UPDOWN: Interface Vlan10, changed state to up
> %LINEPROTO-5-UPDOWN: Line protocol on Interface Vlan10, changed
> state to up
> SW2(config-if)#
> ```

Naturally, we need to supply the same layer-3 connectivity for VLAN 20 between SW2 and SW1:

```
SW1(config-if)#int vlan 20
SW1(config-if)#ip add 10.20.1.2 255.255.255.0
SW1(config-if)#no shut
SW1(config-if)#
```

Now do we have connectivity?

```
Server(config)#do ping 10.10.1.21
Type escape sequence to abort.
Sending 5, 100-byte ICMP Echos to 10.10.1.21:
!!!!!
Success rate is 100 percent (5/5)
Server(config)#do ping 10.30.1.21
Type escape sequence to abort.
Sending 5, 100-byte ICMP Echos to 10.30.1.21:
.!!!!
Success rate is 80 percent (4/5)
Server(config)#
```

We do and we are still containing all our traffic within the switches, not passing it up to the router:

```
Server(config)#do trace 10.10.1.21 n
Type escape sequence to abort.
Tracing the route to 10.10.1.21
VRF info: (vrf in name/id, vrf out name/id)
  1 10.20.1.1 12 msec 8 msec 12 msec
  2 10.10.1.21 28 msec *  16 msec
Server(config)#
```

Really, we should create SVIs for VLAN 40 and VLAN 50, but as we are not actually going to use them, we don't need to. If you want to practice though, go ahead and create them.

Let's have a little break from routing. We have covered a lot of information so far in this chapter. We are not quite done yet as we still have EIGRP to complete, but we can rest a little while we discuss how to manage our IOS files, and licensing.

4.10 Manage Cisco IOS Files

This topic does not belong here. I have no idea why this is thrown into the middle of the routing technologies; it is totally out of place and should be in a section about maintenance or something. That said, it does give us a little break between OSPF and EIGRP and gives us a chance to see what actually happens when we boot our devices.

Before we dive in, we should get a quick over view of the memory types available to us. We have ROM, RAM, Flash and NVRAM.

- ROM stands for Read-Only memory. This holds the bootstrap program, amongst others.
- RAM or Random-Access Memory stores our routing tables and running config. The contents of RAM are lost during a reboot.
- Flash memory is erasable and is used to hold IOS images. Data here is retained upon reboot.
- NVRAM (Non-Volatile RAM) holds the startup-config. Data here is not lost on reboot.

When the router (or switch, but we will use the term router here) first boots up it runs a Power-On Self Test (POST). The POST checks the physical hardware, making sure that all the different parts of the router, such as the interfaces, are operational and present. The POST runs from the Read-only Memory (ROM).

After the POST is completed, we look for the IOS file. The location of which depends on our configuration-register value, which is usually 0x2102. We can find out what our configuration-register value is by looking at the results from the command *"show version"*:

```
Router#show version | i Configuration register
Configuration register is 0x2102
Router#
```

This is performed by the bootstrap code. The bootstrap is a program kept in the ROM, used to execute programs. The bootstrap will look for the line "boot system" in the startup-config file, we can have more than one of these commands and the router will try to load them in order, it the first one succeeds then the boot process continues, if not it will try the next file and so on. If the bootstrap cannot load any of the files, or if the command (or startup-config) is missing, then it will attempt to load an IOS images found on the Flash memory. If no IOS image is found on the flash, it will attempt to find one using TFTP, or one from ROM (which is referred to as mini-IOS).

We do not have this command available in our virtual environment, but it will be visible on a physical device. Once an IOS image is found it is loaded into the RAM.

The next step is to load the startup-config into RAM from the NVRAM. If none is found then the router will try to load one from TFTP and if it cannot find one there, it will enter the Setup mode, which is where we see prompts to enter "Initial Configuration Mode".

The full sequence is: POST -> Bootstrap -> IOS -> Config -> Run

The IOS file loaded in step 2 may not necessarily live in the NVRAM. Depending on the value of the configuration register it can live elsewhere, we control this via our boot preferences.

4.10.a Boot Preferences

The Configuration register is a 16-bit register that is divided into four sets of 4-bits. The default is 0x2102. This instructs the router to look in the flash memory for the IOS file. We can use this to instruct the router to load an IOS file from a TFTP server, and also use this to reset a lost password.

To reset a lost password we need to connect to the router using a rollover cable and a terminal program, such as PuTTY. The default serial port setting should be 9600 baud. The baud rate is the rate we can push data across a serial port, 9600 baud means we can transfer data at 9600 bits per second.

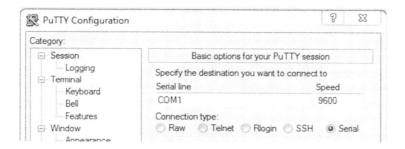

We also have to configure some other settings:

- No parity
- 8 data bits
- 1 stop bit
- No flow control

This is referred to as 8-N-1. The putty settings are shown next.

A data bit setting of eight suits most traffic, because each character matches one byte. 7-bits is used for ASCII and 5-bits were used for Baudot code, for the old Teletype printers, which is where most of this technology and terminology comes from. Stop bits are sent at the end of every character and allows the receiver to detect the end of a character and to resynchronize with the character stream. Parity is concerned with error detection. With parity set to none, we are letting the communication protocol handle the error checking, rather than the interface. Flow control is used to pause and resume traffic flow.

If your connecting device does not support 9600 baud (though most will), you can edit the configuration register to set a different baud rate using the below table. An incorrect baud rate will result in strange characters on the screen.

Confreg setting	Results
0x2102	Ignores break, boots into ROM if initial boot fails, 9600 baud rate
0x2122	Ignores break, boots into ROM if initial boot fails, 19200 baud rate
0x2124	Netboot, ignores break, boots into ROM if initial boot fails, 19200 baud rate
0x2142	Ignores break, boots into ROM if initial boot fails, 9600 baud rate, ignores contents of NVRAM

There are many more settings, but these are some of the more frequently used ones. We can also create (within limited parameters) our own.

Bit number	Hex	Boot field parameters / meaning
00-03	0x0000-0x000F	0x0000: Stays at bootstrap prompt 0x0001: Boots first image found in Flash 0x0002 – 0x000F: Look in the startup configuration for the system image name
06	0x0040	Ignore NVRAM contents
07	0x0080	Disable boot messages
08	0x0100	Break Disabled
10	0x0400	IP broadcast with all zeros
5, 11, 12	0x0020 0x0800 0x1000	Console line speed
13	0x2000	Boots default ROM software if network boot fails
14	0x4000	IP broadcasts do not have net numbers
15	0x8000	Enables diagnostic messages, ignores NVRAM contents

To work these out we need to go back to binary. 0x2142 when converted to binary equals 0000 0000 0010 0001 0100 0010. We can ignore the first two sets of zeros. The above table is a little confusing, so let's make a table to break it up a bit:

Bit number	15	14	13	12	11	10	9	8	7	6	5	4	3	2	1	0
Our value	0	0	1	0	0	0	0	1	0	1	0	0	0	0	1	0
Binary	0010				0001				0100				0010			
Converted	2				1				4				2			
Meaning	Boot to flash if netboot fails				Ignore console break				Ignore NVRAM				Boot field			

From the table above we have a bit in position 13, meaning we should boot using the default ROM. We have a bit in position 8, so we should ignore console break, we have a bit in position 6 so we should ignore the contents of NVRAM and we have a 2 in the boot field, meaning we should look at the startup configuration for the system image to load.

What do we do if we need to configure a different baud rate, such 57600 (such as the one used in a configuration register setting of 0x3122)?

Bit number	15	14	13	12	11	10	9	8	7	6	5	4	3	2	1	0
Our value	0	0	1	1	0	0	0	1	0	0	1	0	0	0	1	0
Binary	0011				0001				0010				0010			
Converted	3				1				2				2			
Meaning	Boot to flash if netboot fails				Ignore console break								Boot field			

Here we have a device connecting at 57600, the important bits here are positions 5, 11 and 12. We have a number of different possible baud rates and the configuration register uses these three fields, with 115200 being set to all ones and 9600 (the default) being set to all zeros:

Baud	Bit 5	Bit 11	Bit 12
115200	1	1	1
57600	1	0	1
38400	1	1	0
19200	1	0	0
9600	0	0	0
4800	0	1	0
2400	0	1	1
1200	0	0	1

Once we have connected to the COM port, we need to check and make a note of the existing settings, using the command "*show version*", as we saw above. Whilst we cannot do this on our virtual routers, we would use these steps to reset a password, which is useful if you purchase a second-hand router!

Once connected, turn the router off and back on again. As soon as you can (within 60 seconds) press the break key sequence on the keyboard, which is generally Ctrl+Break or you can click on Break under the Special commands menu in PuTTY:

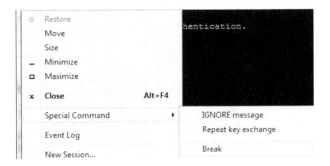

The prompt should now change to:

```
rommon 1 >
```

Now we need to enter the command *"confreg 0x2142"* and press enter so that we boot from flash. We have now bypassed the startup configuration file.

```
rommon 1 > confreg 0x2142
```

The prompt should now change to "rommon 2>". Type *"reset"*.

```
rommon 2 > reset
```

The router will reboot and enter the initial configuration set up mode. Type *"no"* to each of the setup prompts. Once you get to the prompt "Router>", type in *"enable"* and press return.

```
Router>en
```

The prompt should change to "Router#". Type in *"copy startup-config running-config"* and press enter to load the saved configuration, accepting the default filenames.

```
Router#copy startup-config running-config
```

Make sure that you do not copy the running-config over the startup-config though! The router prompt will change to the hostname configured in the startup-config:

```
R1#
```

Now type in *"conf t"* and press enter, then change the password using *"enable secret <password>"*:

```
R1#conf t
R1(config)#enable secret Password123
```

Make sure that the relevant interfaces are not shut down (*show ip interface brief*) and then reset the configuration register back to its original value (0x2102).

```
R1(config)#config-register 0x2101
R1(config)#
```

Lastly, type in "*end*" and then save the configuration using the command "*copy running-config startup-config*".

```
R1(config)#end
R1#copy running-config startup-config
```

Now you can reboot and have access to the router again.

The bootstrap and configuration register settings control how we load the IOS image, so let's look at the images themselves.

4.10.b Cisco IOS Images (15)

Why is there a fifteen in brackets? This is because how we license devices has changed dramatically. There used to be one IOS image per router model family, per version, per release and per feature set. Because different devices have different hardware, such as CPU, or the number of interfaces and interface card options, this meant that it could be very confusing. With the different versions there were also different feature sets; such as voice, data and security. This means that there were many images for different platforms and different abilities.

The basic feature set is IP Base. From there you could add on Security, Voice or data, or one or more of the options:

IP Base
IP Base + Security
IP Base + Data
IP Base + Voice
IP Base + Security + Data
IP Base + Security + Voice
IP Base + Security + Voice + Data

With IOS 15, came a big change in the way licensing is handled. We now have a universal image (per model family). The universal image contains all the feature sets (IP Base + Security + Voice + Data), you just buy the features you want and can upgrade an existing license when you need to.

Cisco offers CLM, the Cisco License Manager, to look after the licenses. CLM communicates with Cisco and resellers, allowing the licenses to be easily tracked and installed onto your devices.

We can also install new licenses manually. Each device has a unique identifying number (UDI), which contains the product ID (PID) and the serial number (SN). We can find these using the command "*show license udi*".

Upgrading requires a Product Authorization Key (PAK). We then connect this PAK to a particular device and this is done through Cisco's online portal. The steps to do this are to copy the PAK and UDI numbers onto the Cisco Product License Registration portal, if all is good (as in you have not used it before, it is going onto a real router and the PAK is valid), then Cisco emails you a license file.

The license file is then installed onto the device, using the command "*license install <source>*". Once confirmed and the device is reloaded, the license is applied.

4.10.c (i) Show license

We can look at the licenses on the system using the following commands:

```
show license
show license feature
show version
```

4.10.c (ii) Change license

Being the kind people Cisco are, we can also test out a license without buying it. This allows us to test the features for 60 days under a "right-to-use" license.

To do this we use the command "*license boot module*": such as

```
R1(config)#license boot module c3900 technology-package securityk9
```

Then we reload the device, and can carry on evaluating the new features for 60 days. For now, though it is time to return to routing protocols, and implement EIGRP.

4.11 Configure and verify EIGRP (single AS)

Enhanced Internal Gateway Routing Protocol (EIGRP) replaced the old Internal Gateway Routing Protocol (IGRP).

IGRP is a proprietary distance vector protocol developed by Cisco designed to replace RIP. It was designed to overcome the 15-hop limit and took into account many more metrics, such as bandwidth, delay, load, MTU and reliability. The hop count limit was increased to 255, but it retained the classless nature of RIP (by not advertising the subnet mask). The classless nature of IGRP was one of the reasons that EIGRP was created and why IGRP is now obsolete.

EIGRP built on IGRP, using the Diffusing Update Algorithm (DUAL) to improve routing and to provide loop-free networking. EIGRP remains (partially) a proprietary protocol. Parts of EIGRP are now an open standard, which is a good step towards EIGRP being supported by more vendors, though at present a multi-vendor environment (where you have a mix of Cisco, Juniper or other devices), in most likelihood, will run OSPF.

> Just because EIGRP was based on IGRP does not mean you should add IGRP to your resume. If you have thirty years networking experience you may have used IGRP. If you only have a few years experience then, unless you have discovered time travel, you shouldn't put it down when applying for jobs. It immediately looks like you are resume "stuffing" by adding any TLA (Three Letter Acronym) you can find.

EIGRP has a number of features, such as support for CIDR and VLSM, the ability to load-balance and strong authentication using MD5. From a traffic point of view, once the EIGRP peers have exchanged their full routing table during adjacency formation, they will then only send topology changes, rather than sending the entire table, which is beneficial for bandwidth usage across the network. Although EIGRP is still a distance vector protocol, it is often referred to as a hybrid because it only sends updates when a change occurs, borrowing this method from the link-state protocols (OSPF and IS-IS).

With EIGRP, we have additional tables. We have the standard routing table, also a neighbor table, and a topology table. The neighbor table is used to keep track of the directly connected EIGRP peers. The topology table stores the routes learned from EIGRP peers, along with the metrics for each route and the feasible successor and successors. These routes will be either passive or active. Passive routes are ones we have finished processing (the calculating of the best route), active ones are still being processed. The routes that are inserted into the routing table will be the ones that are not active, are a feasible successor or have an AD higher than an existing route.

Whereas OSPF can be hard to grasp because of the amount of LSAs and multi-area constraints, EIGRP is quite simple. The hardest part of EIGRP to understand is the concept of feasible successors. This is a very confusing subject, so don't expect to understand it right away, but as we go through, we will build up the EIGRP side of the topology, which will certainly help our understanding.

Let's start by doing a bit of a clean up on EIGRP1, by removing the static routes to 50.50.50.50:

```
EIGRP1(config)#no ip route 50.50.50.50 255.255.255.255 192.168.20.254
EIGRP1(config)#no ip route 50.50.50.50 255.255.255.255 192.168.21.2 250
EIGRP1(config)#
```

All routing protocol configurations on Cisco IOS start with the word *"router"* followed by the protocol. We saw that RIP did not need any additional commands (*"router rip"* was sufficient), whereas OSPF required us to include a process number (*"router ospf 1"*). EIGRP also needs additional information, in the form of the Autonomous System (AS) number, or the virtual instance name when using EIGRP named mode. We won't go into EIGRP named mode here, but there will be a downloadable guide and workbook on the website.

OSPF was configured using a process, we could have multiple OSPF processes on the router and these would be created using the commands *"router ospf 1"*, *"router ospf 2"* and so on. We would then join areas under this initial command. The process number in OSPF is only locally significant; we could have *"router ospf 1"* configured on one router, *"router ospf 2"* configured on another and they would still be able to form an adjacency (following the rules of forming an OSPF adjacency, that is). EIGRP Autonomous Systems are different, they do control to whom we can talk. Think of an Autonomous System (AS) as a group of interconnected devices. We are not bound by the same constraints with EIGRP as we are with OSPF. There is no "backbone" in EIGRP (unlike OSPF's Area 0), but we do have different constraints. Without additional configuration (redistribution), one EIGRP AS will not share data with another. Our concern is with a single AS though, so let's start getting that set up, we will be using EIGRP AS 1 throughout. We start with the command *"router eigrp"* and add either the AS number, which can be between 1 and 65535, or we can give it a name, for named mode (EIGRP Virtual-Instance Name):

```
EIGRP1(config)#
EIGRP1(config)#router eigrp ?
  <1-65535>  Autonomous System
  WORD       EIGRP Virtual-Instance Name

EIGRP1(config)#router eigrp 1
EIGRP1(config-router)#
```

We can support a very large number of numbered autonomous systems and increase this by using the named mode.

Like RIP and OSPF we form adjacencies by by using the "network" command to advertise a network, or an interface, again we need to use the wildcard mask method that we saw in OSPF:

```
EIGRP1(config-router)#network 192.168.21.0 ?
  A.B.C.D  EIGRP wild card bits
  <cr>

EIGRP1(config-router)#network 192.168.21.0 0.255.255.255
EIGRP1(config-router)#
```

What network am I advertising here?

A: 192.168.21.0 /24
B: 192.168.0.0 /16
C: 192.0.0.0 /8

The answer is C. We can see what networks we are advertising by checking the routing configuration.

```
EIGRP1(config-router)#do sh run | s router
router eigrp 1
 network 192.0.0.0 0.255.255.255
EIGRP1(config-router)#
```

What other command could I use to tell me what networks EIGRP is routing for?

"show ip protocols"

Therefore, by using the wildcard mask of 0.255.255.255 I am actually advertising the 192.0.0.0/8 network. Is it a mistake though?

We need to form adjacencies with EIGRP2 and EIGRP5, both of which are technically in the 192.0.0.0/8 subnet, as is ISP, which we will set up for EIGRP as well. So, really, it would work fine. However, what if you connected another interface that you did not want to advertise into EIGRP? Then you would have to rethink the situation. Therefore, it can be wise to be more concise with the configuration early on, saving on surprises later on. So, starting as we mean to carry on, let's change this:

```
EIGRP1(config-router)#no network 192.168.21.0 0.255.255.255
EIGRP1(config-router)#network 192.168.21.0 0.0.0.255
EIGRP1(config-router)#do sh run | s router
router eigrp 1
 network 192.168.21.0
EIGRP1(config-router)#
```

Let's get EIGRP2 added. We will advertise the 192.168.21.0/24 subnet, which joins the two routers together:

```
EIGRP2(config)#router eigrp 1
EIGRP2(config-router)#network 192.168.21.0 0.0.0.255
EIGRP2(config-router)#
%DUAL-5-NBRCHANGE: EIGRP-IPv4 1: Neighbor 192.168.21.1 (Ethernet2/1) is
up: new adjacency
EIGRP2(config-router)#
```

Our adjacency comes up very quickly, however we will not have any EIGRP routes in our routing table now. This is because the 192.168.21.0/24 network is also a connected network and the Administrative Distance of connected (0) is better than EIGRP's (90). However, we can start to look at the EIGRP topology:

```
EIGRP1(config-router)#do sh ip eigrp topology
EIGRP-IPv4 Topology Table for AS(1)/ID(1.1.1.1)
Codes: P - Passive, A - Active, U - Update, Q - Query, R - Reply,
       r - reply Status, s - sia Status

P 192.168.21.0/24, 1 successors, FD is 281600
        via Connected, Ethernet1/2

EIGRP1(config-router)#
```

Above we can see that we are in AS 1 and our router ID is 1.1.1.1 (the same as our loopback interface). We then have some codes, which we will discuss further in 4.11.b, and our topology entry:

```
P 192.168.21.0/24, 1 successors, FD is 281600
        via Connected, Ethernet1/2
```

The P means passive, then we have the network along with the number of successors and the FD, which stands for Feasible Distance.

4.11.a Feasible Distance/Feasible Successors/Administrative distance

Each EIGRP learned route will go through a feasibility condition check, after which the route will either be in a state of Passive or Active, which would be indicated with a P or an A as above. The Feasible Distance (FD) is the lowest distance to a destination since the last time the route went from active to passive. Our feasible distance for 192.168.21.0/24 is 281600.

We have one successor, which is actually the only successor as that is the only route we know about. A successor is the next-hop that is used to forward data traffic for a particular destination. A successor is chosen, usually, based on which has the least cost path to reach that destination.

A Feasible Successor is one that meets the feasibility condition and is therefore loop-free. It may not be the least cost path, but it can still be used. If for example, we use equal or unequal load sharing, or an existing successor became unreachable, a feasible successor would be used. Feasible Successors act as a backup route. Any route can be a backup route. We could have a network with two paths between Router A and Router B. The first path could be a direct link between the two routers, the second path could have twenty routers in between, if the first path fails then the second will be used, the differentiation though is what EIGRP considers as a viable backup path, and this is determined by the Feasibility condition.

4.11.b Feasibility condition

The Feasibility Condition (FC) verifies that a path is loop-free. Every path that meets the condition is therefore guaranteed to be loop-free, but not all loop-free paths may actually pass the feasibility condition. EIGRP uses the DUAL algorithm for path selection. Each path undergoes the Feasibility Condition check, after which the path will be Passive (providing the least cost path), or Active (none of the neighbors provided a least cost path).

The FC is met when a neighbors advertised cost (which is the Reported Distance, or RD) is less than feasible distance (FD) for that destination, meaning that the neighbor is closer to the destination than the local router has ever been since the destination entered the Passive state for the last time. Therefore, if our FD is 10 and a neighbour advertised a route to the same destination with an RD of 7, then this will pass the check and be installed as a feasible successor.

This will become easier to understand as our EIGRP network grows, but to understand the FD and RD we need to understand EIGRP metrics.

4.11.c Metric composition

When we added the network statement in EIGRP1 it started to send out EIGRP Hello messages to the multicast address 224.0.0.10. Here is one that was captured through Wireshark:

```
   2 1_  192.168.21.1        224.0.0.10         EIGRP      74 Hello
   3 1   aa:bb:cc:00:16:12   aa:bb:cc:00:16:12  LOOP       60 Reply
```

```
▶ Frame 2: 74 bytes on wire (592 bits), 74 bytes captured (592 bits) on interface 0
▶ Ethernet II, Src: aa:bb:cc:00:11:21 (aa:bb:cc:00:11:21), Dst: IPv4mcast_0a (01:00:5e:00:00:0a
▶ Internet Protocol Version 4, Src: 192.168.21.1 (192.168.21.1), Dst: 224.0.0.10 (224.0.0.10)
▽ Cisco EIGRP
     Version: 2
     Opcode: Hello (5)
     Checksum: 0xead1 [correct]
   ▶ Flags: 0x00000000
     Sequence: 0
     Acknowledge: 0
     Virtual Router ID: 0 (Address-Family)
     Autonomous System: 1
   ▽ Parameters
        Type: Parameters (0x0001)
        Length: 12
        K1: 1
        K2: 0
        K3: 1
        K4: 0
        K5: 0
        K6: 0
        Hold Time: 15
   ▽ Software Version: EIGRP=15.0, TLV=2.0
        Type: Software Version (0x0004)
        Length: 8
        EIGRP Release: 15.00
        EIGRP TLV version: 2.00
```

Wireshark capture: 5

We can see our Autonomous System number just before the parameters field, and then we have the parameters, which are used to calculate the EIGRP metric.

The actual metric calculation is:

256 * ((K1 * Bandwidth) + (K2 * Bandwidth) / (256 - Load) + K3 * Delay) * (K5 / (Reliability + K4)))

This looks pretty scary at first, but the trick is to take each bit in turn and break it down, as we will do. We can see the five K values in the above capture (it shows 6, as K6 is used in EIGRP Wide Metrics, but we just need to know about the first five). They are set at the defaults; where K1 and K3 are set to 1, and the others (K2, K4 and K5) are set to 0.

We do not have any EIGRP routes at the moment though, so we have nothing with which to test. To give ourselves something to play with, let's add in the loopback interfaces for EIGRP1 and EIGRP2:

```
EIGRP1(config-router)#network 1.1.1.1 0.0.0.0
EIGRP1(config-router)#

EIGRP2(config-router)#network 2.2.2.2 0.0.0.0
EIGRP2(config-router)#
```

Now we should see the 2.2.2.2 network:

```
EIGRP1(config-router)#do sh ip route eigrp | b Gate
Gateway of last resort is 192.168.1.1 to network 0.0.0.0

      2.0.0.0/32 is subnetted, 1 subnets
D        2.2.2.2 [90/409600] via 192.168.21.2, 00:00:22, Ethernet1/2
EIGRP1(config-router)#
```

We do.

The numbers in the square brackets are the Administrative Distance; 90; because it is an internal EIGRP route, and the metric, which is 409600.

We need a little more information than the above Hello packet shows us though in order to work out the calculation. We can get this information from a couple of sources, primarily from the EIGRP topology:

```
EIGRP1(config-router)#do sh ip eigrp topology 2.2.2.2/32
EIGRP-IPv4 Topology Entry for AS(1)/ID(1.1.1.1) for 2.2.2.2/32
  State is Passive, Query origin flag is 1, 1 Successor(s), FD is 409600
  Descriptor Blocks:
  192.168.21.2 (Ethernet1/2), from 192.168.21.2, Send flag is 0x0
      Composite metric is (409600/128256), route is Internal
      Vector metric:
        Minimum bandwidth is 10000 Kbit
        Total delay is 6000 microseconds
        Reliability is 255/255
        Load is 1/255
        Minimum MTU is 1500
        Hop count is 1
        Originating router is 2.2.2.2
EIGRP1(config-router)#
```

The metrics we need are the bandwidth, load, delay, reliability and the MTU. Bandwidth is the minimum bandwidth (measured in kilobits per second) along the path from the router to the destination. The load is a value from 1 to 255, where 255 indicates that the link is completely saturated. Delay is measured in 10's of a microsecond, or usec. Reliability is a value from 1 to 255, where 255 means the link is completely reliable. MTU is not actually used in the calculation. We do not use the hop count either.

Let's try to work out the metric with the numbers we now have.

Our K values (as we saw from the Wireshark capture) are:

K1 = 1
K2 = 0
K3 = 1
K4 = 0
K5 = 0

Our values are:

Bandwidth = 10000
Load = 1
Delay = 6000
Reliability = 255

Taking each part in turn, we can break it down. The original formula is:

256*((K1*Bandwidth) + (K2*Bandwidth)/(256-Load) + K3*Delay)*(K5/(Reliability + K4)))

Starting with the bandwidth, the bandwidth calculation actually uses a reference bandwidth (like OSPF does), of 10,000,000 (based on a 1Gb interface), which is then divided by the bandwidth we see above:

10,000,000 / 10,000 = 1000
K1 * bandwidth = 1 * 1000 = 1000

Our calculation now becomes:

256*(1000 + (K2*Bandwidth)/(256-Load) + K3*Delay)*(K5/(Reliability + K4)))

We can work out the next part of the formula:

K2 * bandwidth = 0 * 1000 = 0
256 - load = 256 - 1 = 255
0/255 = 0

Our ever-shortening calculation now becomes:

256*(1000 + 0 + K3*Delay)*(K5/(Reliability + K4)))

Delay is divided by 10 to convert it to the 10s of microseconds we need

6000/10 = 600
K3*delay = 1 * 600 = 600

Now the calculation is:

256*(1000 + 0 + 600)*(K5/(Reliability + K4)))

We can shorten this again:

256*(1600*(K5/(Reliability + K4)))

The last part of the formula is:

$$Reliability + K4 = 255 + 0 = 255$$
$$K5/255 = 0/255 = 0$$

Therefore, we end up with the following:

256*(1600*0)

Our calculation finally becomes:

$$256*1600 = 409600$$

We will look at the calculation again when we set up the rest of the routers and can compare a few more. However, hopefully you can already see that without any manipulation of the K values, the EIGRP metric will be 256*(bandwidth + delay).

Let's set up the rest of the routers now.

```
EIGRP2(config-router)#network 192.168.32.2 0.0.0.0
EIGRP2(config-router)#

EIGRP3(config)#router eigrp 1
EIGRP3(config-router)#
EIGRP3(config-router)#network 192.168.32.0 0.0.0.255
EIGRP3(config-router)#
%DUAL-5-NBRCHANGE: EIGRP-IPv4 1: Neighbor 192.168.32.2 (Ethernet3/2) is
up: new adjacency
EIGRP3(config-router)#network 192.168.43.0 0.0.0.255
EIGRP3(config-router)#network 3.3.3.3 0.0.0.0
EIGRP3(config-router)#
```

Notice the difference in the network statements for the 192.168.32.0/24 network between EIGRP2 and EIGRP3. This was deliberate to show that adjacencies will form, even though the network statement differs.

```
EIGRP4(config)#router eigrp 1
EIGRP4(config-router)#
EIGRP4(config-router)#network 192.168.43.0 0.0.0.255
%DUAL-5-NBRCHANGE: EIGRP-IPv4 1: Neighbor 192.168.43.3 (Ethernet0/1) is
up: new adjacency
EIGRP4(config-router)#network 192.168.54.0 0.0.0.255
EIGRP4(config-router)#network 4.4.4.4 0.0.0.0
EIGRP4(config-router)#

EIGRP5(config)#router eigrp 1
EIGRP5(config-router)#network 192.168.51.0 0.0.0.255
EIGRP5(config-router)#network 192.168.54.0 0.0.0.255
%DUAL-5-NBRCHANGE: EIGRP-IPv4 1: Neighbor 192.168.54.4 (Serial1/1) is up:
new adjacency
EIGRP5(config-router)#network 5.5.5.5 0.0.0.0
EIGRP5(config-router)#
```

We just need to add one last network statement to EIGRP1 to complete:

```
EIGRP1(config-router)#network 192.168.51.0 0.0.0.255
EIGRP1(config-router)#
%DUAL-5-NBRCHANGE: EIGRP-IPv4 1: Neighbor 192.168.51.5 (Serial2/0) is up:
new adjacency
EIGRP1(config-router)#
```

We now have a fully connected EIGRP network, as we can see from EIGRP1:

```
EIGRP1(config-router)#do sh ip route eigrp | b Gate
Gateway of last resort is 192.168.1.1 to network 0.0.0.0

      2.0.0.0/32 is subnetted, 1 subnets
D        2.2.2.2 [90/409600] via 192.168.21.2, 00:01:59, Ethernet1/2
      3.0.0.0/32 is subnetted, 1 subnets
D        3.3.3.3 [90/435200] via 192.168.21.2, 00:01:59, Ethernet1/2
      4.0.0.0/32 is subnetted, 1 subnets
D        4.4.4.4 [90/460800] via 192.168.21.2, 00:01:59, Ethernet1/2
      5.0.0.0/32 is subnetted, 1 subnets
D        5.5.5.5 [90/2297856] via 192.168.51.5, 00:01:59, Serial2/0
D     192.168.32.0/24 [90/307200] via 192.168.21.2, 00:01:59, Ethernet1/2
D     192.168.43.0/24 [90/332800] via 192.168.21.2, 00:01:59, Ethernet1/2
D     192.168.54.0/24 [90/2246656] via 192.168.21.2, 00:01:59, Eth1/2
EIGRP1(config-router)#
```

Let's do the metric calculation again, this time for the 192.168.54.0/24 network. This will be a little bit more interesting than the first one. The routing table shows the route with a metric of 2246656 going via EIGRP2, but this actually takes more hops (it is a less-direct route) than going through EIGRP5:

```
EIGRP1(config-router)#do sh ip eigrp topology 192.168.54.0
EIGRP-IPv4 Topology Entry for AS(1)/ID(1.1.1.1) for 192.168.54.0/24
  State is Passive, Query origin flag is 1, 1 Successor(s), FD is 2246656
  Descriptor Blocks:
  192.168.21.2 (Ethernet1/2), from 192.168.21.2, Send flag is 0x0
      Composite metric is (2246656/2221056), route is Internal
      Vector metric:
        Minimum bandwidth is 1544 Kbit
        Total delay is 23000 microseconds
        Reliability is 255/255
        Load is 1/255
        Minimum MTU is 1500
        Hop count is 3
        Originating router is 4.4.4.4
  192.168.51.5 (Serial2/0), from 192.168.51.5, Send flag is 0x0
      Composite metric is (2681856/2169856), route is Internal
      Vector metric:
        Minimum bandwidth is 1544 Kbit
        Total delay is 40000 microseconds
        Reliability is 255/255
        Load is 1/255
        Minimum MTU is 1500
        Hop count is 1
        Originating router is 5.5.5.5
EIGRP1(config-router)#
```

Right, lets work this out.

We have multiple values (as we have two routes), but because our K values are the default, we know we just need to use the simple calculation (256*(bandwidth + delay)):

The first route, through EIGRP2 has a metric of 2246656. The bandwidth is 1544, because this is the minimum bandwidth over-all, not just the minimum for the links in one path and the delay is 23000. We start by dividing the reference bandwidth by the minimum bandwidth value:

10,000,000 / 1544 = 6476

We then convert the delay from microseconds to tens of microseconds:

23000 / 10 = 2300

We add these two values together:

6476 + 2300 = 8776

Lastly, we multiply 256 by our value above:

$$256 * 8776 = 2246656$$

The route through EIGRP5 has the same minimum bandwidth, so we already know that this equals 6476 from the calculation above, but the delay is 40000.

$$40000 / 10 = 4000$$
$$6476 + 4000 = 10476$$
$$256 * 10476 = 2681856$$

Although the metric calculation looks scary at first, really it is not. We now have both the Feasible Distance (FD) values for our routes. The route installed into our routing table has a metric of 2246656 and we have a second route with a metric of 2681856:

```
EIGRP1(config-router)#do sh ip eigrp topology 192.168.54.0 | i Composite
        Composite metric is (2246656/2221056), route is Internal
        Composite metric is (2681856/2169856), route is Internal
EIGRP1(config-router)#
```

The second number in brackets is the reported distance (RD), which comes from the feasible distance of the other router (EIGRP2 or EIGRP5):

```
EIGRP2(config-router)#do sh ip eigrp topology 192.168.54.0 | i
from|Composite
    192.168.32.3 (Ethernet2/3), from 192.168.32.3, Send flag is 0x0
        Composite metric is (2221056/2195456), route is Internal
EIGRP2(config-router)#

EIGRP5(config-router)#do sh ip eigrp topology 192.168.54.0 | i
from|Composite
    0.0.0.0 (Serial1/1), from Connected, Send flag is 0x0
        Composite metric is (2169856/0), route is Internal
    192.168.51.1 (Serial1/0), from 192.168.51.1, Send flag is 0x0
        Composite metric is (2758656/2246656), route is Internal
EIGRP5(config-router)#
```

EIGRP2 will be our successor and it will be installed into our routing table, with a metric (FD) of 2246656:

```
EIGRP1(config-router)#do sh ip route 192.168.54.0
Routing entry for 192.168.54.0/24
  Known via "eigrp 1", distance 90, metric 2246656, type internal
  Redistributing via eigrp 1
  Last update from 192.168.21.2 on Ethernet1/2, 02:29:22 ago
```

```
       Routing Descriptor Blocks:
       * 192.168.21.2, from 192.168.21.2, 02:29:22 ago, via Ethernet1/2
           Route metric is 2246656, traffic share count is 1
           Total delay is 23000 microseconds, minimum bandwidth is 1544 Kbit
           Reliability 255/255, minimum MTU 1500 bytes
           Loading 1/255, Hops 3
     EIGRP1(config-router)#
```

The route through EIGRP5 will be our feasible successor. The route through EIGRP5 meets the feasibility requirement because its reported distance of 2169856 is lower than the successor routes FD of 2246656.

We can view the complete topology using the command "show ip eigrp topology all-links":

```
EIGRP1(config-router)#do sh ip eigrp topology all-links
EIGRP-IPv4 Topology Table for AS(1)/ID(1.1.1.1)
Codes: P - Passive, A - Active, U - Update, Q - Query, R - Reply,
       r - reply Status, s - sia Status

P 192.168.21.0/24, 1 successors, FD is 281600, serno 4
        via Connected, Ethernet1/2
P 4.4.4.4/32, 1 successors, FD is 460800, serno 11
        via 192.168.21.2 (460800/435200), Ethernet1/2
        via 192.168.51.5 (2809856/2297856), Serial2/0
P 192.168.54.0/24, 1 successors, FD is 2246656, serno 10
        via 192.168.21.2 (2246656/2221056), Ethernet1/2
        via 192.168.51.5 (2681856/2169856), Serial2/0
P 5.5.5.5/32, 1 successors, FD is 2297856, serno 14
        via 192.168.51.5 (2297856/128256), Serial2/0
P 192.168.51.0/24, 1 successors, FD is 2169856, serno 13
        via Connected, Serial2/0
P 192.168.32.0/24, 1 successors, FD is 307200, serno 7
        via 192.168.21.2 (307200/281600), Ethernet1/2
P 2.2.2.2/32, 1 successors, FD is 409600, serno 6
        via 192.168.21.2 (409600/128256), Ethernet1/2
P 3.3.3.3/32, 1 successors, FD is 435200, serno 9
        via 192.168.21.2 (435200/409600), Ethernet1/2
        via 192.168.51.5 (2835456/2323456), Serial2/0
P 192.168.43.0/24, 1 successors, FD is 332800, serno 8
        via 192.168.21.2 (332800/307200), Ethernet1/2
        via 192.168.51.5 (2707456/2195456), Serial2/0
P 1.1.1.1/32, 1 successors, FD is 128256, serno 5
        via Connected, Loopback0

EIGRP1(config-router)#
```

Above we can see that a number of routes have failed the Feasibility check. They will still be available as backup routes, but their RD is greater than our FD, these are called "non-successors".

Don't let this put you off EIGRP, this is the hardest part to grasp about it. The rest of EIGRP is very straightforward. One way of helping to work out whom a feasible successor might be is to put letters next to the values, like this:

<pre>
                      A   B
         via 192.168.21.2 (2246656/2221056), Ethernet1/2
         via 192.168.51.5 (2681856/2169856), Serial2/0
                      C   D
</pre>

If D is less than A, then the route is likely to be installed as a feasible successor. Use A, B, C, D; this doesn't work as well with using 1, 2, 3, 4, it's a purely psychological thing though as your brain knows that 4 is greater than 1. In this case, letters works better.

Let's go back to our Wireshark capture and look at EIGRP neighbor adjacency formation.

As soon as we enabled EIGRP on the e1/2 interface of EIGRP1, it started to send Hello packets to the multicast address 224.0.0.10 (line 16 overleaf). Once we enabled EIGRP2, it also started sending Hello packets, to the same multicast address. Like EIGRP1 these Hello packets include the AS number, the K values and it will also include the Hold time, which is used to detect when EIGRP peers have stopped sending Hellos. The default hold time is 15 seconds, and the Hello interval (the time between sending of Hellos) is five seconds, so if a peer stops sending Hellos for 15 seconds, we will consider these routes unavailable.

After the Hello packets we then start to send Update packets (line 17), these are sent via unicast instead of broadcast, using TCP port 88. These update packets contain the EIGRP routes known to the sender. Ours between EIGRP1 and EIGRP2 are empty, because they did not know about any routes at that stage. The adjacency is not yet completed; we are still in the "initialization process". We know this because the Initialization bit is set:

```
15 2..  192.168.21.1      192.168.21.2       EIGRP    60  Update
16 2..  192.168.21.2      224.0.0.10         EIGRP    84  Hello
17 2..  192.168.21.2      192.168.21.1       EIGRP    54  Update
18 2..  192.168.21.1      192.168.21.2       EIGRP    60  Hello (Ack)
```

```
► Frame 15: 60 bytes on wire (480 bits), 60 bytes captured (480 bits) on interface 0
► Ethernet II, Src: aa:bb:cc:00:11:21 (aa:bb:cc:00:11:21), Dst: aa:bb:cc:00:16:12 (aa:b
► Internet Protocol Version 4, Src: 192.168.21.1 (192.168.21.1), Dst: 192.168.21.2 (192
▼ Cisco EIGRP
    Version: 2
    Opcode: Update (1)
    Checksum: 0xfdfb [correct]
  ▼ Flags: 0x00000001, Init
        .... .... .... .... .... .... .... ...1 = Init: Set
        .... .... .... .... .... .... .... ..0. = Conditional Receive: Not set
        .... .... .... .... .... .... .... .0.. = Restart: Not set
        .... .... .... .... .... .... .... 0... = End Of Table: Not set
    Sequence: 1
    Acknowledge: 0
    Virtual Router ID: 0 (Address-Family)
    Autonomous System: 1
```

It is not until we send an Ack (line 18) that the adjacency has formed.

```
18 2..  192.168.21.1      192.168.21.2       EIGRP    60  Hello (Ack)
```

```
► Frame 18: 60 bytes on wire (480 bits), 60 bytes captured (480 bits) on interface 0
► Ethernet II, Src: aa:bb:cc:00:11:21 (aa:bb:cc:00:11:21), Dst: aa:bb:cc:00:16:12 (aa:
► Internet Protocol Version 4, Src: 192.168.21.1 (192.168.21.1), Dst: 192.168.21.2 (19
▼ Cisco EIGRP
    Version: 2
    Opcode: Hello (5)
    Checksum: 0xfdf8 [correct]
  ▼ Flags: 0x00000000
        .... .... .... .... .... .... .... ...0 = Init: Not set
        .... .... .... .... .... .... .... ..0. = Conditional Receive: Not set
        .... .... .... .... .... .... .... .0.. = Restart: Not set
        .... .... .... .... .... .... .... 0... = End Of Table: Not set
    Sequence: 0
    Acknowledge: 1
    Virtual Router ID: 0 (Address-Family)
    Autonomous System: 1
```

Since EIGRP1 and EIGRP2 formed their adjacency, our EIGRP network has gained a few more players. We now have more EIGRP routes, so let's send them over to ISP and see the traffic through Wireshark:

```
EIGRP1(config-router)#network 192.168.1.2 0.0.0.0
EIGRP1(config-router)#

ISP(config)#router eigrp 1
ISP(config-router)#network 192.168.1.1 0.0.0.0
ISP(config-router)#
```

```
%DUAL-5-NBRCHANGE: EIGRP-IPv4 1: Neighbor 192.168.1.2 (Ethernet0/1) is
up: new adjacency
ISP(config-router)#
```

From the capture, we can start to see some good traffic:

No.	Time	Source	Destination	Protocol	Length	Info
9	3...	192.168.1.2	224.0.0.10	EIGRP	74	Hello
11	3...	192.168.1.2	224.0.0.10	EIGRP	74	Hello
14	4...	192.168.1.2	224.0.0.10	EIGRP	74	Hello
17	4...	192.168.1.2	224.0.0.10	EIGRP	74	Hello
18	4...	192.168.1.2	224.0.0.10	EIGRP	74	Hello
21	5...	192.168.1.2	224.0.0.10	EIGRP	74	Hello
22	5...	192.168.1.1	224.0.0.10	EIGRP	74	Hello
23	5...	192.168.1.2	224.0.0.10	EIGRP	84	Hello
24	5...	192.168.1.2	192.168.1.1	EIGRP	60	Update
25	5...	192.168.1.1	224.0.0.10	EIGRP	84	Hello
26	5...	192.168.1.1	192.168.1.2	EIGRP	54	Update
27	5...	192.168.1.2	224.0.0.10	EIGRP	499	Update
28	5...	192.168.1.2	192.168.1.1	EIGRP	60	Hello (Ack)
29	5...	192.168.1.1	224.0.0.10	EIGRP	499	Update
30	5...	192.168.1.2	192.168.1.1	EIGRP	60	Hello (Ack)
31	5...	192.168.1.2	192.168.1.1	EIGRP	499	Update
32	5...	192.168.1.1	192.168.1.2	EIGRP	54	Hello (Ack)
34	6...	192.168.1.2	224.0.0.10	EIGRP	84	Hello
35	6...	192.168.1.1	224.0.0.10	EIGRP	84	Hello
37	6...	192.168.1.2	224.0.0.10	EIGRP	84	Hello

Wireshark capture: 6

The initial traffic is pretty much the same, but in packet 27, we can see that EIGRP1 has sent its EIGRP routes in a multicast Update packet. I have only shown one of the routes, but by default, they are all expanded fully, like the one for 1.1.1.1/32. We can see that the route type is internal and the Router ID (RID) of the router that originated the route, we also send the prefix length, which is the subnet mask.

```
        27 5_   192.168.1.2          224.0.0.10          EIGRP      499 Update
▶ Frame 27: 499 bytes on wire (3992 bits), 499 bytes captured (3992 bits) on inte
▶ Ethernet II, Src: aa:bb:cc:00:11:10 (aa:bb:cc:00:11:10), Dst: IPv4mcast_0a (01:
▶ Internet Protocol Version 4, Src: 192.168.1.2 (192.168.1.2), Dst: 224.0.0.10 (2
▼ Cisco EIGRP
       Version: 2
       Opcode: Update (1)
       Checksum: 0xc0bf [correct]
  ▶ Flags: 0x00000000
       Sequence: 19
       Acknowledge: 0
       Virtual Router ID: 0 (Address-Family)
       Autonomous System: 1
  ▶ Internal Route  =   192.168.21.0/24
  ▼ Internal Route  =   1.1.1.1/32
       Type: Internal Route (0x0602)
       Length: 45
       Topology: 0
       AFI: IPv4 (1)
       RouterID: 1.1.1.1 (1.1.1.1)
     ▶ Wide Metric
       NextHop: 0.0.0.0 (0.0.0.0)
       Prefix Length: 32
       Destination: 1.0.0.0 (1.0.0.0)
  ▶ Internal Route  =   2.2.2.2/32
  ▶ Internal Route  =   192.168.32.0/24
  ▶ Internal Route  =   192.168.43.0/24
  ▶ Internal Route  =   3.3.3.3/32
  ▶ Internal Route  =   192.168.54.0/24
  ▶ Internal Route  =   4.4.4.4/32
  ▶ Internal Route  =   192.168.51.0/24
  ▶ Internal Route  =   5.5.5.5/32
```

4.11.d Router ID

We saw with OSPF that having a unique router ID (RID) is important in ensuring proper adjacency formation. The RID in EIGRP is equally important, but for other reasons. We have not assigned any RIDs, but have let the router decide what to use. Like OSPF the RID is a 32-bit dotted decimal value, and the router will use the highest IP address assigned to a loopback interface, or if there are not any loopback addresses configured, the highest IP address assigned to any other interface.

Let's set the router IDs now.

```
EIGRP1(config-router)#eigrp router-id 1.1.1.1
EIGRP1(config-router)#
```

Notice that we need to use the command "*eigrp router-id*" and not just "*router-id*" as we did with OSPF, possibly because OSPF came first, and that the IOS would consider "*router-id*" to be an ambiguous command if we could use it under both of the protocols.

This does not have any effect as the RID we are using is the same as the one already set on the router. We will now set up EIGRP2 and EIGRP3, but they will use the same RID:

```
EIGRP2(config-router)#eigrp router-id 2.2.2.2
EIGRP2(config-router)#

EIGRP3(config-router)#eigrp router-id 2.2.2.2
EIGRP3(config-router)#
```

After a few moments, we should see the following messages:

```
EIGRP3(config-router)#
%DUAL-5-NBRCHANGE: EIGRP-IPv4 1: Neighbor 192.168.43.4 (Ethernet0/1) is
down: route configuration changed
%DUAL-5-NBRCHANGE: EIGRP-IPv4 1: Neighbor 192.168.32.2 (Ethernet3/2) is
down: route configuration changed
%DUAL-5-NBRCHANGE: EIGRP-IPv4 1: Neighbor 192.168.43.4 (Ethernet0/1) is
up: new adjacency
%DUAL-5-NBRCHANGE: EIGRP-IPv4 1: Neighbor 192.168.32.2 (Ethernet3/2) is
up: new adjacency
EIGRP3(config-router)#
```

Therefore, although EIGRP2 and EIGRP3 share the same RID, they can still form an adjacency. We can check their neighbor tables, and confirm this:

```
EIGRP3(config-router)#do sh ip eigrp neighbor
EIGRP-IPv4 Neighbors for AS(1)
H   Address          Interface      Hold Uptime    SRTT   RTO  Q   Seq
                                    (sec)          (ms)        Cnt Num
1   192.168.32.2     Et3/2          12   00:01:06  11     100  0   33
0   192.168.43.4     Et0/1          13   00:01:10  7      100  0   24
EIGRP3(config-router)#

EIGRP2(config-router)#do sh ip eigrp neighbor
EIGRP-IPv4 Neighbors for AS(1)
H   Address          Interface      Hold Uptime    SRTT   RTO  Q   Seq
                                    (sec)          (ms)        Cnt Num
1   192.168.32.3     Et2/3          12   00:01:45  14     100  0   26
0   192.168.21.1     Et2/1          12   2d00h     3      100  0   44
EIGRP2(config-router)#
```

We can tell that the adjacencies are healthy because of the Q Cnt (Queue Count) field in the output above. If the queue count is zero all is good, if it is one or more, then we have problems. So, does this mean that all EIGRP routers can have the same router ID? Well, no. Each should have a unique RID. A duplicate RID may not cause us any issues here now, but later on when we try to get from one side of the network to another it certainly will. Routers with duplicate RIDs will not accept external routes (those that come from redistribution) from the other. EIGRP external routes have a field in them called the "EIGRP router originator" containing the RID. If this is the same as the routers own RID then the router will not accept the route.

Let's set EIGRP3 to what is should be and carry on:

```
EIGRP3(config-router)#no eigrp router-id 2.2.2.2
EIGRP3(config-router)#
EIGRP3(config-router)#eigrp router-id 3.3.3.3
EIGRP3(config-router)#
%DUAL-5-NBRCHANGE: EIGRP-IPv4 1: Neighbor 192.168.32.2 (Ethernet3/2) is
down: route configuration changed
%DUAL-5-NBRCHANGE: EIGRP-IPv4 1: Neighbor 192.168.43.4 (Ethernet0/1) is
down: route configuration changed
%DUAL-5-NBRCHANGE: EIGRP-IPv4 1: Neighbor 192.168.43.4 (Ethernet0/1) is
up: new adjacency
%DUAL-5-NBRCHANGE: EIGRP-IPv4 1: Neighbor 192.168.32.2 (Ethernet3/2) is
up: new adjacency
EIGRP3(config-router)#

EIGRP4(config-router)#eigrp router-id 4.4.4.4
EIGRP4(config-router)#

EIGRP5(config-router)#eigrp router-id 5.5.5.5
EIGRP5(config-router)#

ISP(config-router)#eigrp router-id 100.100.100.100
ISP(config-router)#
```

Talking about route acceptance, let's have a look at auto-summarization.

4.11.e Auto summary

The default behaviour of EIGRP before IOS 15.0 was to perform auto-summarization each time it crossed a border between two major networks. This meant that the networks you advertised were not necessarily the ones that were advertised. Let's step away from our main topology for a moment and look at this in action.

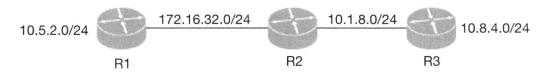

The basic configuration for the three routers is as follows:

```
R1(config)#int lo0
R1(config-if)#ip add 10.5.2.1 255.255.255.0
R1(config-if)#int e0/0
R1(config-if)#ip add 172.16.32.1 255.255.255.0
R1(config-if)#no shut
R1(config-if)#
R1(config-if)#router eigrp 1
R1(config-router)#eigrp router-id 1.1.1.1
R1(config-router)#network 172.16.32.0 0.0.0.255
R1(config-router)#network 10.5.2.0 0.0.0.255
R1(config-router)#

R2(config)#int e0/0
R2(config-if)#ip add 172.16.32.2 255.255.255.0
R2(config-if)#no shut
R2(config-if)#int e0/1
R2(config-if)#ip add 10.1.8.2 255.255.255.0
R2(config-if)#no shut
R2(config-if)#
R2(config-if)#router eigrp 1
R2(config-router)#eigrp router-id 2.2.2.2
R2(config-router)#network 172.16.32.0 0.0.0.255
R2(config-router)#network 10.1.8.0 0.0.0.255
R2(config-router)#

R3(config)#int e0/1
R3(config-if)#ip add 10.1.8.3 255.255.255.0
R3(config-if)#no shut
R3(config-if)#int lo0
R3(config-if)#ip add 10.8.4.3 255.255.255.0
R3(config-if)#
R3(config-if)#router eigrp 1
R3(config-router)#eigrp router-id 3.3.3.3
R3(config-router)#network 10.8.4.0 0.0.0.255
R3(config-router)#network 10.1.8.0 0.0.0.255
R3(config-router)#
```

We are running an earlier version of IOS (12.2), and are advertising the /24 networks. So, what routes does R1 and R3 see in their routing tables (with auto-summarization enabled)?:

```
R1(config-router)#do sh ip route eigrp | b Gate
Gateway of last resort is not set

      10.0.0.0/8 is variably subnetted, 3 subnets, 3 masks
D        10.0.0.0/8 is a summary, 00:00:29, Null0
      172.16.0.0/16 is variably subnetted, 3 subnets, 3 masks
D        172.16.0.0/16 is a summary, 00:00:46, Null0
R1(config-router)#
```

```
R3(config-router)#do sh ip route eigrp | b Gate
Gateway of last resort is not set

D     172.16.0.0/16 [90/307200] via 10.1.8.2, 00:01:02, Ethernet0/1
R3(config-router)#
```

We only receive the classful subnet. If we were unsure about whether we are summarizing or not (after all it is easy to get the wildcard masks wrong) we can use the command *"show ip protocols"*:

```
R1(config-router)#do sh ip protocols
*** IP Routing is NSF aware ***
Routing Protocol is "eigrp 1"
  Outgoing update filter list for all interfaces is not set
  Incoming update filter list for all interfaces is not set
  Default networks flagged in outgoing updates
  Default networks accepted from incoming updates
  Redistributing: eigrp 1
  EIGRP-IPv4 Protocol for AS(1)
    Metric weight K1=1, K2=0, K3=1, K4=0, K5=0
    NSF-aware route hold timer is 240
    Router-ID: 1.1.1.1
    Topology : 0 (base)
      Active Timer: 3 min
      Distance: internal 90 external 170
      Maximum path: 4
      Maximum hopcount 100
      Maximum metric variance 1

  Automatic Summarization: enabled
    172.16.0.0/16 for Lo0
      Summarizing 1 component with metric 281600
    10.0.0.0/8 for Et0/0
      Summarizing 1 component with metric 128256
  Maximum path: 4
  Routing for Networks:
    10.5.2.0/24
    172.16.32.0/24
  Routing Information Sources:
    Gateway         Distance      Last Update
    (this router)          5      00:01:51
    172.16.32.2           90      00:01:51
  Distance: internal 90 external 170

R1(config-router)#
```

Because of this summarization, we have an overlap on R3. R1'S 10.5.2.0/24 network, which is being advertised as 10.0.0.0/8, overlaps with R3's own loopback interface. Therefore it is not added to the routing table and is not reachable:

```
R3(config-router)#do ping 10.5.2.1
Type escape sequence to abort.
Sending 5, 100-byte ICMP Echos to 10.5.2.1:
.....
Success rate is 0 percent (0/5)
R3(config-router)#
```

The way around this is to turn off auto-summarization.:

```
R1(config-router)#no auto-summary
R1(config-router)#

R2(config-router)#no auto-summary
R2(config-router)#

R3(config-router)#no auto-summary
R3(config-router)#
```

After each router performs a resynchronization, our routing tables look much better and we have full reachability:

```
R1(config-router)#do sh ip route eigrp | b Gate
Gateway of last resort is not set

      10.0.0.0/8 is variably subnetted, 4 subnets, 2 masks
D        10.1.8.0/24 [90/307200] via 172.16.32.2, 00:00:48, Ethernet0/0
D        10.8.4.0/24 [90/435200] via 172.16.32.2, 00:00:48, Ethernet0/0
R1(config-router)#

R3(config-router)#do sh ip route eigrp | b Gate
Gateway of last resort is not set

      10.0.0.0/8 is variably subnetted, 5 subnets, 2 masks
D        10.5.2.0/24 [90/435200] via 10.1.8.2, 00:01:38, Ethernet0/1
      172.16.0.0/24 is subnetted, 1 subnets
D        172.16.32.0 [90/307200] via 10.1.8.2, 00:01:14, Ethernet0/1
R3(config-router)#
R3(config-router)#do ping 10.5.2.1
Type escape sequence to abort.
Sending 5, 100-byte ICMP Echos to 10.5.2.1:
!!!!!
Success rate is 100 percent (5/5)
R3(config-router)#
```

IOS 15 changed this behaviour, and now automatic summarization is disabled by default, making life much easier. That said, you might find yourself in a new environment where they are using an older IOS, maybe the flash memory and RAM does not support upgrading to a newer image, so you need to use the command "*no auto-summary*". You may be lucky and never touch an older IOS, but equally so, for the sake of one line, regardless of whether you need it or not, it can be a massive help and prevent unwanted surprises.

Let's configure this on our routers:

```
EIGRP1(config-router)#no auto-summary
EIGRP1(config-router)#

EIGRP2(config-router)#no auto-summary
EIGRP2(config-router)#

EIGRP3(config-router)#no auto-summary
EIGRP3(config-router)#

EIGRP4(config-router)#no auto-summary
EIGRP4(config-router)#

EIGRP5(config-router)#no auto-summary
EIGRP5(config-router)#

ISP(config-router)#no auto-summary
ISP(config-router)#
```

Again, this will have no effect on our routing tables, but setting this command should be second nature when configuring EIGRP and can eliminate surprises when using a mixture of IOS versions.

Don't think that this means you should never summarize your routes; in fact the opposite is true. Summarization allows us to reduce the size of our routing tables, which is always beneficial, but only when we are in control of it. With EIGRP we can use the interface-level command "*ip summary-address eigrp 1 192.168.0.0 255.255.0.0 80*" Here we would advertise a summary address of 192.168.0.0/16 in EIGRP AS 1, with an administrative distance of 80.

Now that we have a working EIGRP network, let's play around with it a bit and see how we can influence the way traffic flows around it.

4.11.f Path Selection

We already saw that through the metrics used by EIGRP to calculate the best path available, predominantly bandwidth and delay, that the "best path" may not necessarily be the shortest one. However, we still need to be able to exercise our influence over the choice of routing. For example, we have been made aware of some upcoming maintenance along a particular path (the link between EIGRP2 and EIGRP3), therefore want to send traffic from EIGRP1 to EIGRP4 via EIGRP5 instead. We can do this by manipulating the values used in the metrics.

First let's have a look at the numbers we can manipulate:

```
EIGRP1(config-router)#do sh int e1/2 | i DLY
  MTU 1500 bytes, BW 10000 Kbit/sec, DLY 1000 usec,
EIGRP1(config-router)#do sh int s2/0 | i DLY
  MTU 1500 bytes, BW 1544 Kbit/sec, DLY 20000 usec,
EIGRP1(config-router)#
```

Now let's have a look at the EIGRP viewpoint:

```
EIGRP1(config-router)#do sh ip eigrp topology 4.4.4.4/32
EIGRP-IPv4 Topology Entry for AS(1)/ID(1.1.1.1) for 4.4.4.4/32
  State is Passive, Query origin flag is 1, 1 Successor(s), FD is 460800
  Descriptor Blocks:
  192.168.21.2 (Ethernet1/2), from 192.168.21.2, Send flag is 0x0
      Composite metric is (460800/435200), route is Internal
      Vector metric:
        Minimum bandwidth is 10000 Kbit
        Total delay is 8000 microseconds
        Reliability is 255/255
        Load is 1/255
        Minimum MTU is 1500
        Hop count is 3
        Originating router is 4.4.4.4
  192.168.51.5 (Serial2/0), from 192.168.51.5, Send flag is 0x0
      Composite metric is (2809856/2297856), route is Internal
      Vector metric:
        Minimum bandwidth is 1544 Kbit
        Total delay is 45000 microseconds
        Reliability is 255/255
        Load is 1/255
        Minimum MTU is 1500
        Hop count is 2
        Originating router is 4.4.4.4
EIGRP1(config-router)#
```

There is a huge difference between the two lines. We need to reduce the metrics on the path through EIGRP5 so that they are lower than the path through EIGRP2. First let's try changing the delay:

```
EIGRP1(config-router)#int s2/0
EIGRP1(config-if)#
EIGRP1(config-if)#delay 100
EIGRP1(config-if)#
```

The command is accepted (notice that again there is a difference between the value we enter and the value shown (which is in tens of a second, or usec):

```
EIGRP1(config-if)#do sh int s2/0 | i DLY
  MTU 1500 bytes, BW 1544 Kbit/sec, DLY 1000 usec,
EIGRP1(config-if)#
```

Our delay now matches. Has this affected anything? Well, the metric has reduced a little (from 2809856 to 2323456), but we are still very far apart:

```
EIGRP1(config-if)#do sh ip eigrp topology 4.4.4.4/32 | i Composite
        Composite metric is (460800/435200), route is Internal
        Composite metric is (2323456/2297856), route is Internal
EIGRP1(config-if)#
```

Let's try changing the bandwidth on e1/2 (our link to EIGRP2).

```
EIGRP1(config-if)#int e1/2
EIGRP1(config-if)#bandwidth 10
EIGRP1(config-if)#do sh int e1/2 | i DLY
  MTU 1500 bytes, BW 10 Kbit/sec, DLY 1000 usec,
EIGRP1(config-if)#
```

Has this brought the desired change?

```
EIGRP1(config-if)#do sh ip eigrp topology 4.4.4.4/32 | i Composite
        Composite metric is (2323456/2297856), route is Internal
        Composite metric is (256204800/435200), route is Internal
EIGRP1(config-if)#
```

It has. We can see that the metric for the s2/0 interface is now on top. Our routing table has also been updated:

```
EIGRP1(config-if)#do sh ip route 4.4.4.4
Routing entry for 4.4.4.4/32
  Known via "eigrp 1", distance 90, metric 2323456, type internal
  Redistributing via eigrp 1
  Last update from 192.168.51.5 on Serial2/0, 00:01:44 ago
  Routing Descriptor Blocks:
  * 192.168.51.5, from 192.168.51.5, 00:01:44 ago, via Serial2/0
      Route metric is 2323456, traffic share count is 1
      Total delay is 26000 microseconds, minimum bandwidth is 1544 Kbit
      Reliability 255/255, minimum MTU 1500 bytes
      Loading 1/255, Hops 2
EIGRP1(config-if)#
```

We can even set the delay back to its original value and we still prefer the route through EIGRP5 to get to EIGRP4's loopback network.

```
EIGRP1(config-if)#int s2/0
EIGRP1(config-if)#
EIGRP1(config-if)#no delay 100
EIGRP1(config-if)#
EIGRP1(config-if)#do sh run int s2/0
Building configuration...

Current configuration : 118 bytes
!
interface Serial2/0
 description Link to EIGRP5
 ip address 192.168.51.1 255.255.255.0
 serial restart-delay 0
end

EIGRP1(config-if)#
EIGRP1(config-if)#do sh ip route 4.4.4.4
Routing entry for 4.4.4.4/32
  Known via "eigrp 1", distance 90, metric 2809856, type internal
  Redistributing via eigrp 1
  Last update from 192.168.51.5 on Serial2/0, 00:00:11 ago
  Routing Descriptor Blocks:
  * 192.168.51.5, from 192.168.51.5, 00:00:11 ago, via Serial2/0
      Route metric is 2809856, traffic share count is 1
      Total delay is 45000 microseconds, minimum bandwidth is 1544 Kbit
      Reliability 255/255, minimum MTU 1500 bytes
      Loading 1/255, Hops 2
EIGRP1(config-if)#
```

Lastly, just to make sure, we can do a traceroute confirming that we go through EIGRP5:

```
EIGRP1(config-if)#
EIGRP1(config-if)#do trace 4.4.4.4 numeric
Type escape sequence to abort.
Tracing the route to 4.4.4.4
VRF info: (vrf in name/id, vrf out name/id)
  1 192.168.51.5 9 msec 7 msec 8 msec
  2 192.168.54.4 6 msec *  9 msec
EIGRP1(config-if)#
```

As well as using these methods to influence how your traffic can flow in the event that you want to redirect it for a period of time, we can also use these methods to send our traffic over all the links available to us at the same time, which is known as load balancing.

4.11.g Load Balancing

Load balancing, as the name suggests, allows you to balance the traffic load over more than one connection. By default, if all the paths are equal, we can load balance across four paths. We can confirm this, using the show ip protocols command; looking at the "Maximum path" line:

```
EIGRP1(config-if)#do sh ip protocols | s EIGRP-IPv4
  EIGRP-IPv4 Protocol for AS(1)
    Metric weight K1=1, K2=0, K3=1, K4=0, K5=0
    NSF-aware route hold timer is 240
    Router-ID: 1.1.1.1
    Topology : 0 (base)
      Active Timer: 3 min
      Distance: internal 90 external 170
      Maximum path: 4
      Maximum hopcount 100
      Maximum metric variance 1

EIGRP1(config-if)#
```

We can actually use up to 32 paths to load balance in our IOS version, though some IOS versions only support up to 16 paths:

```
EIGRP1(config-if)#router eigrp 1
EIGRP1(config-router)#
EIGRP1(config-router)#maximum-paths ?
  <1-32>  Number of paths

EIGRP1(config-router)#maximum-paths 32
EIGRP1(config-router)#
EIGRP1(config-router)#do sh ip protocols | i Maximum path
  Maximum path: 32
      Maximum path: 32
  Maximum path: 32
EIGRP1(config-router)#
```

We don't have four paths in our topology, we only have two paths, and these are hardly equal. The good news is that we can still use both at the same time, we just have to do a little more playing around with the numbers.

4.11.g (i) Unequal

Whilst everyone prefers an even flow within the network, we can tweak the network to load balance across unequal links, which we will do with EIGRP1.

Let's start by setting EIGRP1's e1/2 interface back to normal:

```
EIGRP1(config-router)#int e1/2
EIGRP1(config-if)#bandwidth 10000
EIGRP1(config-if)#
EIGRP1(config-if)#do sh ip eigrp topology 4.4.4.4/32 | i Composite
        Composite metric is (460800/435200), route is Internal
        Composite metric is (2809856/2297856), route is Internal
EIGRP1(config-if)#
```

Before we start changing things, let's quickly remind ourselves of what our routing table looks like:

```
EIGRP1(config-router)#do sh ip route eigrp | b Gate
Gateway of last resort is 192.168.1.1 to network 0.0.0.0

      2.0.0.0/32 is subnetted, 1 subnets
D       2.2.2.2 [90/409600] via 192.168.21.2, 00:00:13, Ethernet1/2
      3.0.0.0/32 is subnetted, 1 subnets
D       3.3.3.3 [90/435200] via 192.168.21.2, 00:00:13, Ethernet1/2
      4.0.0.0/32 is subnetted, 1 subnets
D       4.4.4.4 [90/460800] via 192.168.21.2, 00:00:13, Ethernet1/2
      5.0.0.0/32 is subnetted, 1 subnets
D       5.5.5.5 [90/2297856] via 192.168.51.5, 00:00:13, Serial2/0
D     192.168.32.0/24 [90/307200] via 192.168.21.2, 00:00:13, Ethernet1/2
D     192.168.43.0/24 [90/332800] via 192.168.21.2, 00:00:13, Ethernet1/2
D     192.168.54.0/24 [90/2246656] via 192.168.21.2, 00:00:13, Ethernet1/2
EIGRP1(config-router)#
```

We don't need to manipulate the bandwidth or delay here. If we started down this road then we are actually destined to have a very under-performing network. Instead, we can use the metrics to our advantage.

Our largest metric is 2809856, our smallest is 460800. How many times does 460800 go into 2809856? Just over six times (2809856 divided by 460800 leaves us with 6.09 and change).

We can use the command *"variance"*, followed by a value between 1 and 128 to allow for unequal paths. It is an EIGRP command, so we need to pop back into router configuration mode to use it:

```
EIGRP1(config-if)#router eigrp 1
EIGRP1(config-router)#variance ?
  <1-128>  Metric variance multiplier

EIGRP1(config-router)#variance 7
EIGRP1(config-router)#
```

We can only use whole numbers. The command "*variance 6*" would not be enough as the difference is 6.09, so we have to round up to 7. Now will we see more routes to 4.4.4.4/32?

```
EIGRP1(config-router)#variance 7
EIGRP1(config-router)#do sh ip route eigrp | b Gate
Gateway of last resort is 192.168.1.1 to network 0.0.0.0

      2.0.0.0/32 is subnetted, 1 subnets
D        2.2.2.2 [90/409600] via 192.168.21.2, 00:00:02, Ethernet1/2
      3.0.0.0/32 is subnetted, 1 subnets
D        3.3.3.3 [90/435200] via 192.168.21.2, 00:00:02, Ethernet1/2
      4.0.0.0/32 is subnetted, 1 subnets
D        4.4.4.4 [90/460800] via 192.168.21.2, 00:00:02, Ethernet1/2
      5.0.0.0/32 is subnetted, 1 subnets
D        5.5.5.5 [90/2297856] via 192.168.51.5, 00:00:02, Serial2/0
D     192.168.32.0/24 [90/307200] via 192.168.21.2, 00:00:02, Ethernet1/2
D     192.168.43.0/24 [90/332800] via 192.168.21.2, 00:00:02, Ethernet1/2
D     192.168.54.0/24 [90/2681856] via 192.168.51.5, 00:00:02, Serial2/0
                      [90/2246656] via 192.168.21.2, 00:00:02, Ethernet1/2
EIGRP1(config-router)#
```

No, we do not. We have gained one for 192.168.54.0/24, but not for anything else. Why is this? We now need to go back and look at the feasibility condition. :

```
EIGRP1(config-router)#do sh ip eigrp topology all-links
EIGRP-IPv4 Topology Table for AS(1)/ID(1.1.1.1)
Codes: P - Passive, A - Active, U - Update, Q - Query, R - Reply,
       r - reply Status, s - sia Status

P 192.168.21.0/24, 1 successors, FD is 281600, serno 90
        via Connected, Ethernet1/2
P 4.4.4.4/32, 1 successors, FD is 460800, serno 84
        via 192.168.21.2 (460800/435200), Ethernet1/2
        via 192.168.51.5 (2809856/2297856), Serial2/0
P 192.168.54.0/24, 2 successors, FD is 2246656, serno 95
        via 192.168.51.5 (2681856/2169856), Serial2/0
        via 192.168.21.2 (2246656/2221056), Ethernet1/2
P 5.5.5.5/32, 1 successors, FD is 1811456, serno 65
        via 192.168.51.5 (2297856/128256), Serial2/0
P 192.168.1.0/24, 1 successors, FD is 281600, serno 15
        via Connected, Ethernet0/1
P 192.168.51.0/24, 1 successors, FD is 2169856, serno 70
        via Connected, Serial2/0
P 192.168.32.0/24, 1 successors, FD is 307200, serno 86
        via 192.168.21.2 (307200/281600), Ethernet1/2
P 2.2.2.2/32, 1 successors, FD is 409600, serno 87
        via 192.168.21.2 (409600/128256), Ethernet1/2
P 3.3.3.3/32, 1 successors, FD is 435200, serno 88
```

```
            via 192.168.21.2 (435200/409600), Ethernet1/2
            via 192.168.51.5 (2835456/2323456), Serial2/0
 P 192.168.43.0/24, 1 successors, FD is 332800, serno 89
            via 192.168.21.2 (332800/307200), Ethernet1/2
            via 192.168.51.5 (2707456/2195456), Serial2/0
 P 1.1.1.1/32, 1 successors, FD is 128256, serno 5
            via Connected, Loopback0

EIGRP1(config-router)#
```

Remember that for EIGRP to consider route as a backup route it must pass the feasibility check, and as such, the advertising routers RD (reported distance) must be lower than our FD. We only have one route that satisfies this condition, which is 192.168.54.0/24, explaining why we now have another route for this network. The other routes all fail the FC, which is why even with a high variance of 7 (or even going all the way up to 128) they still will not be considered for unequal load balancing. A quicker way (and more succinct) would be to just include the word successors:

```
EIGRP1(config-router)#do sh ip eigrp topology all-links | i successors
 P 192.168.21.0/24, 1 successors, FD is 281600, serno 90
 P 4.4.4.4/32, 1 successors, FD is 460800, serno 84
 P 192.168.54.0/24, 2 successors, FD is 2246656, serno 95
 P 5.5.5.5/32, 1 successors, FD is 1811456, serno 65
 P 192.168.1.0/24, 1 successors, FD is 281600, serno 15
 P 192.168.51.0/24, 1 successors, FD is 2169856, serno 70
 P 192.168.32.0/24, 1 successors, FD is 307200, serno 86
 P 2.2.2.2/32, 1 successors, FD is 409600, serno 87
 P 3.3.3.3/32, 1 successors, FD is 435200, serno 88
 P 192.168.43.0/24, 1 successors, FD is 332800, serno 89
 P 1.1.1.1/32, 1 successors, FD is 128256, serno 5
EIGRP1(config-router)#
```

None of the other routes (those via EIGRP5) have met the feasibility condition, therefore they are not considered as a backup route by EIGRP. They can still be used in the event that EIGRP1's E1/2 interface goes down, but from an EIGRP calculation they will not be considered, regardless of how high we set the variance.

It would be unfair to leave EIGRP without looking at the IPv6 version, so we will cover that now.

EIGRP for IPv6 (EIGRPv6)

Whilst EIGRPv6 is not explicitly stated on the syllabus, it makes sense that we cover it, after-all we did do OSPFv3. We will run this on top of our existing EIGRP IPv4 network.

We start by enabling IPv6 on our five EIGRP routers:

```
EIGRP1(config-router)#ipv6 unicast-routing
EIGRP1(config)#

EIGRP2(config-router)#ipv6 unicast-routing
EIGRP2(config)#

EIGRP3(config-router)#ipv6 unicast-routing
EIGRP3(config)#

EIGRP4(config-router)#ipv6 unicast-routing
EIGRP4(config)#

EIGRP5(config-router)#ipv6 unicast-routing
EIGRP5(config)#
```

Next, we create the EIGRPv6 routing process:

```
EIGRP1(config)#ipv6 router eigrp 1
EIGRP1(config-rtr)#

EIGRP2(config)#ipv6 router eigrp 1
EIGRP2(config-rtr)#

EIGRP3(config)#ipv6 router eigrp 1
EIGRP3(config-rtr)#

EIGRP4(config)#ipv6 router eigrp 1
EIGRP4(config-rtr)#

EIGRP5(config)#ipv6 router eigrp 1
EIGRP5(config-rtr)#
```

We will be using a manual router ID configuration, borrowing it from the loopback interface:

```
EIGRP1(config-rtr)#eigrp router-id 1.1.1.1
EIGRP1(config-rtr)#

EIGRP2(config-rtr)#eigrp router-id 2.2.2.2
EIGRP2(config-rtr)#

EIGRP3(config-rtr)#eigrp router-id 3.3.3.3
EIGRP3(config-rtr)#

EIGRP4(config-rtr)#eigrp router-id 4.4.4.4
EIGRP4(config-rtr)#

EIGRP5(config-rtr)#eigrp router-id 5.5.5.5
EIGRP5(config-rtr)#
```

Next, we add the respective interfaces to EIGRPv6. Like OSPF we are not using a *"network"* command, rather we advertise whatever is configured on the interface, remember also that we need to enable the interface for IPv6. We will start to see the adjacencies form:

```
EIGRP1(config-rtr)#int e1/2
EIGRP1(config-if)#ipv6 eigrp 1
EIGRP1(config-if)#ipv6 enable
EIGRP1(config-if)#int s2/0
EIGRP1(config-if)#ipv6 eigrp 1
EIGRP1(config-if)#ipv6 enable
EIGRP1(config-if)#int lo0
EIGRP1(config-if)#ipv6 eigrp 1
EIGRP1(config-if)#ipv6 enable
EIGRP1(config-if)#

EIGRP2(config-if)#int e2/1
EIGRP2(config-if)#ipv6 eigrp 1
EIGRP2(config-if)#ipv6 enable
%DUAL-5-NBRCHANGE: EIGRP-IPv6 1: Neighbor FE80::A8BB:CCFF:FE00:1121
(Ethernet2/1) is up: new adjacency
EIGRP2(config-if)#int e2/3
EIGRP2(config-if)#ipv6 eigrp 1
EIGRP2(config-if)#ipv6 enable
EIGRP2(config-if)#int lo0
EIGRP2(config-if)#ipv6 eigrp 1
EIGRP2(config-if)#ipv6 enable
EIGRP2(config-if)#

EIGRP3(config-rtr)#int e3/2
EIGRP3(config-if)#ipv6 eigrp 1
EIGRP3(config-if)#ipv6 enable
%DUAL-5-NBRCHANGE: EIGRP-IPv6 1: Neighbor FE80::A8BB:CCFF:FE00:1632
(Ethernet3/2) is up: new adjacency
EIGRP3(config-if)#int e0/1
EIGRP3(config-if)#ipv6 eigrp 1
EIGRP3(config-if)#ipv6 enable
%DUAL-5-NBRCHANGE: EIGRP-IPv6 1: Neighbor FE80::A8BB:CCFF:FE00:1510
(Ethernet0/1) is up: new adjacency
EIGRP3(config-if)#int lo0
EIGRP3(config-if)#ipv6 eigrp 1
EIGRP3(config-if)#ipv6 enable
EIGRP3(config-if)#

EIGRP4(config-rtr)#int e0/1
EIGRP4(config-if)#ipv6 eigrp 1
EIGRP4(config-if)#ipv6 enable
%DUAL-5-NBRCHANGE: EIGRP-IPv6 1: Neighbor FE80::A8BB:CCFF:FE00:1310
(Ethernet0/1) is up: new adjacency
```

```
EIGRP4(config-if)#int s1/1
EIGRP4(config-if)#ipv6 eigrp 1
EIGRP4(config-if)#ipv6 enable
%DUAL-5-NBRCHANGE: EIGRP-IPv6 1: Neighbor FE80::4FF:FE00:14 (Serial1/1)
is up: new adjacency
EIGRP4(config-if)#int lo0
EIGRP4(config-if)#ipv6 eigrp 1
EIGRP4(config-if)#ipv6 enable
EIGRP4(config-if)#

EIGRP5(config)#int s1/0
EIGRP5(config-if)#ipv6 eigrp 1
EIGRP5(config-if)#ipv6 enable
%DUAL-5-NBRCHANGE: EIGRP-IPv6 1: Neighbor FE80::A8BB:CCFF:FE00:1100
(Serial1/0) is up: new adjacency
EIGRP5(config-if)#int s1/1
EIGRP5(config-if)#ipv6 eigrp 1
EIGRP5(config-if)#ipv6 enable
%DUAL-5-NBRCHANGE: EIGRP-IPv6 1: Neighbor FE80::A8BB:CCFF:FE00:1500
(Serial1/1) is up: new adjacency
EIGRP5(config-if)#int lo0
EIGRP5(config-if)#ipv6 eigrp 1
EIGRP5(config-if)#ipv6 enable
EIGRP5(config-if)#
```

We can check our EIGRPv3 adjacencies using the command *"show ipv6 eigrp neighbors"*:

```
EIGRP1(config-if)#do sh ipv6 eigrp neigh
EIGRP-IPv6 Neighbors for AS(1)
H   Address             Interface    Hold Uptime    SRTT   RTO   Q   Seq
                                     (sec)          (ms)         Cnt Num
1   Link-local address: Se2/0        12 00:00:53    654    3924  0   1
    FE80::4FF:FE00:14
0   Link-local address: Et1/2        14 00:04:17    1986   5000  0   1
    FE80::A8BB:CCFF:FE00:1612
EIGRP1(config-if)#

EIGRP3(config-if)#do sh ipv6 eigrp neigh
EIGRP-IPv6 Neighbors for AS(1)
H   Address             Interface    Hold Uptime    SRTT   RTO   Q   Seq
                                     (sec)          (ms)         Cnt Num
1   Link-local address: Et0/1        14 00:02:49    1992   5000  0   1
    FE80::A8BB:CCFF:FE00:1510
0   Link-local address: Et3/2        10 00:04:07    1998   5000  0   2
    FE80::A8BB:CCFF:FE00:1632
EIGRP3(config-if)#
```

```
EIGRP4(config-if)#do sh ipv6 eigrp neigh
EIGRP-IPv6 Neighbors for AS(1)
H   Address              Interface    Hold Uptime    SRTT   RTO   Q   Seq
                                      (sec)          (ms)        Cnt Num
1   Link-local address:  Se1/1         12 00:02:01   516   3096   0   2
    FE80::4FF:FE00:14
0   Link-local address:  Et0/1         10 00:03:02     1   3000   0   2
    FE80::A8BB:CCFF:FE00:1310
EIGRP4(config-if)#
```

So far, this is good, but we do not have any IPv6 addresses configured! Let's add some. We will be using 2001 followed by dbX, where X is incremented from 8 upwards, followed by 88 (EIGRP's protocol number), then the IP address. Each will use a /64 subnet, apart from the loopback interfaces, which will all use 2001:db20, followed by the address and these will be /128 addresses. Because IPv6 is so flexible with how we can address our interfaces, we can do little thing to help us, like using the protocol number in the address to indicate which protocol should be advertising the address:

```
EIGRP1(config-if)#int e1/2
EIGRP1(config-if)#ipv6 add 2001:db8:88:192:168:21::1/46
EIGRP1(config-if)#int s2/0
EIGRP1(config-if)#ipv6 add 2001:db9:88:192:168:51::1/64
EIGRP1(config-if)#int lo0
EIGRP1(config-if)#ipv6 add 2001:db20:1:1:1::1/128
EIGRP1(config-if)#

EIGRP2(config-if)#int e2/1
EIGRP2(config-if)#ipv6 add 2001:db8:88:192:168:21::2/64
EIGRP2(config-if)#int e2/3
EIGRP2(config-if)#ipv6 add 2001:db10:88:192:168:32::2/64
EIGRP2(config-if)#int lo0
EIGRP2(config-if)#ipv6 add 2001:db20:2:2:2::2/128
EIGRP2(config-if)#

EIGRP3(config-if)#int e0/1
EIGRP3(config-if)#ipv6 add 2001:db11:88:192:168:43::3/64
EIGRP3(config-if)#int e3/2
EIGRP3(config-if)#ipv6 add 2001:db10:88:192:168:32::3/64
EIGRP3(config-if)#int lo0
EIGRP3(config-if)#ipv6 add 2001:db20:3:3:3::3/128
EIGRP3(config-if)#

EIGRP4(config-if)#int e0/1
EIGRP4(config-if)#ipv6 add 2001:db11:88:192:168:43::4/64
EIGRP4(config-if)#int s1/1
EIGRP4(config-if)#ipv6 add 2001:db12:88:192:168:54::4/64
EIGRP4(config-if)#int lo0
EIGRP4(config-if)#ipv6 add 2001:db20:4:4:4::4/128
EIGRP4(config-if)#
```

```
EIGRP5(config-if)#int s1/0
EIGRP5(config-if)#ipv6 add 2001:db9:88:192:168:51::5/64
EIGRP5(config-if)#int s1/1
EIGRP5(config-if)#ipv6 add 2001:db12:88:192:168:54::5/64
EIGRP5(config-if)#int lo0
EIGRP5(config-if)#ipv6 add 2001:db20:5:5:5::5/128
EIGRP5(config-if)#
```

We can now check EIGRP1 to make sure that it has a route to EIGRP5's loopback interface:

```
EIGRP1(config-if)#do sh ipv6 route eigrp
IPv6 Routing Table - default - 15 entries
Codes: C - Connected, L - Local, S - Static, U - Per-user Static route
       B - BGP, HA - Home Agent, MR - Mobile Router, R - RIP
       H - NHRP, I1 - ISIS L1, I2 - ISIS L2, IA - ISIS interarea
       IS - ISIS summary, D - EIGRP, EX - EIGRP external, NM - NEMO
       ND - ND Default, NDp - ND Prefix, DCE - Destination, NDr - Redirect
       O - OSPF Intra, OI - OSPF Inter, OE1 - OSPF ext 1, OE2 - OSPF ext 2
       ON1 - OSPF NSSA ext 1, ON2 - OSPF NSSA ext 2, la - LISP alt
       lr - LISP site-registrations, ld - LISP dyn-eid, a - Application
D   2001:DB10:88:192::/64 [90/307200]
     via FE80::A8BB:CCFF:FE00:1612, Ethernet1/2
D   2001:DB11:88:192::/64 [90/332800]
     via FE80::A8BB:CCFF:FE00:1612, Ethernet1/2
D   2001:DB12:88:192::/64 [90/2246656]
     via FE80::A8BB:CCFF:FE00:1612, Ethernet1/2
D   2001:DB20:2:2:2::2/128 [90/409600]
     via FE80::A8BB:CCFF:FE00:1612, Ethernet1/2
D   2001:DB20:3:3:3::3/128 [90/435200]
     via FE80::A8BB:CCFF:FE00:1612, Ethernet1/2
D   2001:DB20:4:4:4::4/128 [90/460800]
     via FE80::A8BB:CCFF:FE00:1612, Ethernet1/2
D   2001:DB20:5:5:5::5/128 [90/2297856]
     via FE80::4FF:FE00:14, Serial2/0
EIGRP1(config-if)#
```

The route is there, now let's check end-to-end connectivity:

```
EIGRP1(config-if)#do ping ipv6 2001:DB20:5:5:5::5 so lo0
Type escape sequence to abort.
Sending 5, 100-byte ICMP Echos to 2001:DB20:5:5:5::5:
Packet sent with a source address of 2001:DB20:1:1:1::1
!!!!!
Success rate is 100 percent (5/5)
EIGRP1(config-if)#
```

Perfect! As you can see there is no big mystery to IPv6, either for OSPF or EIGRP. The hardest part is figuring out the addressing scheme, making sure that there is no overlap in addresses. Refer back to the IPv6 routing table on EIGRP1, look at how the addresses are shown, I have shown them again below for ease of reading:

```
EIGRP1(config-if)#do sh ipv6 route | i 88
C   2001:DB8:88:192::/64 [0/0]
L   2001:DB8:88:192:168:21:0:1/128 [0/0]
C   2001:DB9:88:192::/64 [0/0]
L   2001:DB9:88:192:168:51:0:1/128 [0/0]
D   2001:DB10:88:192::/64 [90/307200]
D   2001:DB11:88:192::/64 [90/332800]
D   2001:DB12:88:192::/64 [90/2246656]
EIGRP1(config-if)#
```

We have five prefixes. Each with a /64 subnet. The way I have had to differentiate the networks is within the first half of the address (the first 64-bits), using DB8, DB9, DB10 and so on. If I wanted to be extremely strict with the IP address, so that each were to be unique at the same place as the IPv4 address I would need to change them to something like 2001:db8:88:88:192:168:54:0/112. For this address the start of the range would be 2001:db8:88:88:192:168:54:0, and the end of the range would be 2001:db8:88:88:192:168:54:ffff. This would give us 65536 host addresses!

We will leave routing protocols for a while and look at some services now.

5. IP Services

IP services accounts for 10% of the exam topics. In this section we will deploy a DHCP server, start to secure our network through access-lists, "hide" our internal LAN from the WAN and provide a way for them to all be at the same local time. We will also look at making our LAN more resilient using First Hop Reachability protocols (FHRP) and we'll look at how we can better monitor our environment through syslog and SNMP.

Cisco routers can provide a number of services, such as time synchronization (through NTP), DNS services, which although is not covered on the syllabus we will discuss in the Beyond CCNA chapter and IP addressing (DHCP), which we will discuss now.

5.1 Configure and verify DHCP (IOS Router)

DHCP, or the Dynamic Host Configuration Protocol, is used to supply a client machine with an IP address and additionally default gateway, domain name, NTP server addresses and a lot of other information. It works in a client-server model based on the original BOOTP or Bootstrap Protocol. We will set up the Server to be, well, the server, and Dave and Bob to be the clients. We will need to do a little reconfiguration of one of our PCs to look at the basic operation, but this will also help solidify the idea of what broadcasts can and cannot do.

DHCP uses UDP, as it is a connectionless protocol, utilising UDP port 67 on the server and port 68 on the client. We can serve IP addresses from a pool, or make sure that a client always receives the same IP address, known as a reservation. DHCP has four phases. The easiest way to remember these is with the acronym DORA.

The first stage is the DHCP Discovery. The client broadcasts a DHCPDISCOVER message to the destination address 255.255.255.255 (on UDP port 67). If it has had an IP address assigned before, it will also request the previous address. If this previous address has not been assigned to another computer then the client will receive it again. If the server cannot give the client the requested address, the client will send a new request.

The next stage is the DHCP Offer. The receipt of a DHCPDISCOVER message by the server causes the server to reserve an IP address from the available pool. It then offers this IP address in a DHCPOFFER message back to the client. This message contains the MAC address of the client, the IP address being offered, along with the subnet mask, lease duration and the DHCP servers own IP address.

Once the client receives the DHCPOFFER message, it responds with a DHCPREQUEST message, requesting the address being offered. This is then broadcast to the server.

Because we are using broadcast messages we may see the scenario where we have more than one DHCP server, so the client may get more than one offer. The client will only accept one of these. The server identification option in the request is then used to inform the other DHCP servers which offer the client is going to accept and they withdraw their own offers. The IP address they are offering is returned to their own pool.

> It is common practice to have two DHCP servers; following the 80/20 rule. One server will hand out 80% of the address pool and another will be configured to hand out the remaining 20%. In the event that one DHCP server is unavailable the other can take over.

Once the server receives the DHCPREQUEST it will acknowledge this though a DHCPACK message back to the client. The process looks like this:

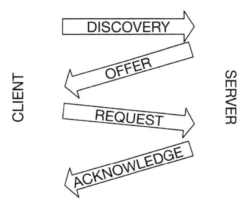

Let's start setting up our server to hand out IP addresses for Bob and Dave. Although they are in different subnets this will not be a problem, we can still hand out addresses for more than one subnet. Our server will be able to offer addresses for VLAN 10, VLAN 20 and VLAN 30 (we only need 10 and 30 though).

We start by defining a pool name. We then add the network range we want to hand out addresses for, and can add options such as the domain name and default router. Before we do that we need to exclude some addresses, we will get to why we are doing this a little later. We can do this in two ways, individually, as I do for the VLAN 10 addresses, or by specifying the start of the range and the end of the range, as I do for the VLAN 20 and 30 addresses:

```
Server(config)#ip dhcp excluded-address 10.10.1.1
Server(config)#ip dhcp excluded-address 10.10.1.2
Server(config)#ip dhcp excluded-address 10.20.1.1 10.20.1.2
Server(config)#ip dhcp excluded-address 10.30.1.1 10.30.1.2
Server(config)#ip dhcp excluded-address 10.20.1.21
```

```
Server(config)#ip dhcp excluded-address 10.10.1.254
Server(config)#ip dhcp excluded-address 10.20.1.254
Server(config)#ip dhcp excluded-address 10.30.1.254
Server(config)#
```

We will now create three DHCP pools:

```
Server(config)#ip dhcp pool VLAN-10
Server(dhcp-config)#network 10.10.1.0 /24
Server(dhcp-config)#domain-name 802101.com
Server(dhcp-config)#default-router 10.10.1.1
Server(dhcp-config)#exit
Server(config)#ip dhcp pool VLAN-20
Server(dhcp-config)#network 10.20.1.0 /24
Server(dhcp-config)#domain-name 802101.com
Server(dhcp-config)#default-router 10.20.1.1
Server(dhcp-config)#exit
Server(config)#ip dhcp pool VLAN-30
Server(dhcp-config)#network 10.30.1.0 /24
Server(dhcp-config)#domain-name 802101.com
Server(dhcp-config)#default-router 10.30.1.1
Server(dhcp-config)#
```

All set, we now just need someone to start requesting an IP address!

5.1.a Configuring router interfaces to use DHCP

We will now set up Bob's PC to be a DHCP client, as well as removing the static route, as we should get this through DHCP.

```
Bob-PC(config)#no ip route 0.0.0.0 0.0.0.0 10.30.1.1
Bob-PC(config)#int e0/0
Bob-PC(config-if)#ip address dhcp
Bob-PC(config-if)#
```

 There is a problem with how our network is defined and how DHCP operates. Can you see what it is?

A: We have not specified the DHCP server on Bob's PC
B: Bob is in a different VLAN therefore DHCP will not work
C: The switch Bob is connected to has not been enabled for DHCP

B is the correct answer. C is also partially correct. A is totally incorrect.

Bob is in a different VLAN, so broadcast traffic is isolated to that particular VLAN (as it should be). To be able to see how DHCP operates we will move Bob into the same VLAN as the server, but just for the moment. This will allow is to capture the DHCP traffic so that we can look at the contents. After that, we will put Bob back in the correct VLAN and look at why answer C is partially correct.

At this point, I have started to capture the traffic on Bob's E0/0 interface.

```
SW3(config)#int e0/0
SW3(config-if)#switchport access vlan 20
SW3(config-if)#
```

We may need to shut and no shut the interface on Bob's PC:

```
Bob-PC(config-if)#shut
Bob-PC(config-if)#
%LINK-5-CHANGED: Interface Ethernet0/0, changed state to administratively
down
%LINEPROTO-5-UPDOWN: Line protocol on Interface Ethernet0/0, changed
state to down
Bob-PC(config-if)#
Bob-PC(config-if)#no shut
Bob-PC(config-if)#
%LINK-3-UPDOWN: Interface Ethernet0/0, changed state to up
%LINEPROTO-5-UPDOWN: Line protocol on Interface Ethernet0/0, changed
state to up
Bob-PC(config-if)#
%DHCP-6-ADDRESS_ASSIGN: Interface Ethernet0/0 assigned DHCP address
10.20.1.3, mask 255.255.255.0, hostname Bob-PC
Bob-PC(config-if)#
```

We now have an IP address of 10.20.1.3 and a default route:

```
Bob-PC(config-if)#do sh ip route | b Gate
Gateway of last resort is 10.20.1.1 to network 0.0.0.0

S*    0.0.0.0/0 [254/0] via 10.20.1.1
      10.0.0.0/8 is variably subnetted, 2 subnets, 2 masks
C        10.20.1.0/24 is directly connected, Ethernet0/0
L        10.20.1.3/32 is directly connected, Ethernet0/0
Bob-PC(config-if)#
```

Let's have a look at the Wireshark capture. We can look at just the DHCP traffic by using a filter of "bootp":

```
 bootp
No.      Time          Source           Destination        Protocol Length Info
   2 0.944636      0.0.0.0          255.255.255.255    DHCP     337 DHCP Discover - Transaction ID 0x1b77
   7 4.953345      0.0.0.0          255.255.255.255    DHCP     337 DHCP Discover - Transaction ID 0x1b77
  45 56.160943     0.0.0.0          255.255.255.255    DHCP     337 DHCP Discover - Transaction ID 0xbc9
  50 58.180536     10.20.1.21       255.255.255.255    DHCP     342 DHCP Offer    - Transaction ID 0xbc9
  51 58.180729     0.0.0.0          255.255.255.255    DHCP     349 DHCP Request  - Transaction ID 0xbc9
  52 58.181797     10.20.1.21       255.255.255.255    DHCP     342 DHCP ACK      - Transaction ID 0xbc9
```

Wireshark capture: 7

We can see two initial DHCPDISCOVER messages followed by a third, which is the start of our client/server communication. The discovery message contains our MAC address, and our hostname, but not much else:

```
▼ Bootstrap Protocol (Discover)
      Message type: Boot Request (1)
      Hardware type: Ethernet (0x01)
      Hardware address length: 6
      Hops: 0
      Transaction ID: 0x00000bc9
      Seconds elapsed: 0
   ▶ Bootp flags: 0x8000, Broadcast flag (Broadcast)
      Client IP address: 0.0.0.0
      Your (client) IP address: 0.0.0.0
      Next server IP address: 0.0.0.0
      Relay agent IP address: 0.0.0.0
      Client MAC address: aa:bb:cc:00:0e:00 (aa:bb:cc:00:0e:00)
      Client hardware address padding: 00000000000000000000
      Server host name not given
      Boot file name not given
      Magic cookie: DHCP
   ▶ Option: (53) DHCP Message Type (Discover)
   ▶ Option: (57) Maximum DHCP Message Size
   ▶ Option: (61) Client identifier
   ▼ Option: (12) Host Name
         Length: 6
         Host Name: Bob-PC ◀
   ▶ Option: (55) Parameter Request List
   ▼ Option: (255) End
         Option End: 255
```

The DHCPOFFER contains the IP address we are being offered (in the "Your (client) IP address" field), and by which server, in the DHCP Server Identifier field. We can also see how long we can lease the IP address for, and at which point during the lease time we can request to keep using the address we have (in the IP Address Lease Time and Renewal Time Value fields respectively). We then have the subnet mask to go along with the IP address we are being offered, the domain name and lastly our default router.

```
▼ Bootstrap Protocol (Offer)
      Message type: Boot Reply (2)
      Hardware type: Ethernet (0x01)
      Hardware address length: 6
      Hops: 0
      Transaction ID: 0x00000bc9
      Seconds elapsed: 0
   ▶ Bootp flags: 0x8000, Broadcast flag (Broadcast)
      Client IP address: 0.0.0.0
      Your (client) IP address: 10.20.1.3   ◀━━━━━
      Next server IP address: 0.0.0.0
      Relay agent IP address: 0.0.0.0
      Client MAC address: aa:bb:cc:00:0e:00 (aa:bb:cc:00:0e:00)
      Client hardware address padding: 00000000000000000000
      Server host name not given
      Boot file name not given
      Magic cookie: DHCP
   ▶ Option: (53) DHCP Message Type (Offer)
   ▼ Option: (54) DHCP Server Identifier
      Length: 4
      DHCP Server Identifier: 10.20.1.21   ◀━━━━━
   ▼ Option: (51) IP Address Lease Time
      Length: 4
      IP Address Lease Time: (86400s) 1 day   ◀━━━━━
   ▼ Option: (58) Renewal Time Value
      Length: 4
      Renewal Time Value: (43200s) 12 hours   ◀━━━━━
   ▶ Option: (59) Rebinding Time Value
   ▼ Option: (1) Subnet Mask
      Length: 4
      Subnet Mask: 255.255.255.0   ◀━━━━━
   ▼ Option: (15) Domain Name
      Length: 10
      Domain Name: 802101.com   ◀━━━━━
   ▼ Option: (3) Router
      Length: 4
      Router: 10.20.1.1   ◀━━━━━
   ▶ Option: (255) End
      Padding: 0000000000000000
```

We then sent a DHCPREQUEST back, still using the broadcast address because at this stage we have not yet assigned the offered address to an interface. In this request we state which IP address we are willing to accept (Requested IP address) and from which server (DHCP Server Identifier):

```
▼ Bootstrap Protocol (Request)
     Message type: Boot Request (1)
     Hardware type: Ethernet (0x01)
     Hardware address length: 6
     Hops: 0
     Transaction ID: 0x00000bc9
     Seconds elapsed: 0
   ▶ Bootp flags: 0x8000, Broadcast flag (Broadcast)
     Client IP address: 0.0.0.0
     Your (client) IP address: 0.0.0.0
     Next server IP address: 0.0.0.0
     Relay agent IP address: 0.0.0.0
     Client MAC address: aa:bb:cc:00:0e:00 (aa:bb:cc:00:0e:00)
     Client hardware address padding: 00000000000000000000
     Server host name not given
     Boot file name not given
     Magic cookie: DHCP
   ▶ Option: (53) DHCP Message Type (Request)
   ▶ Option: (57) Maximum DHCP Message Size
   ▶ Option: (61) Client identifier
   ▼ Option: (54) DHCP Server Identifier
       Length: 4
       DHCP Server Identifier: 10.20.1.21  ◀━━━━━━━━
   ▼ Option: (50) Requested IP Address
       Length: 4
       Requested IP Address: 10.20.1.3  ◀━━━━━━━━
   ▶ Option: (12) Host Name
   ▶ Option: (55) Parameter Request List
   ▼ Option: (255) End
       Option End: 255
```

The final step is for the server to acknowledge the request. The packet data is nearly identical to the offer, so I have shown a smaller section of the packet:

```
▼ Bootstrap Protocol (ACK)
     Message type: Boot Reply (2)
     Hardware type: Ethernet (0x01)
     Hardware address length: 6
     Hops: 0
     Transaction ID: 0x00000bc9
     Seconds elapsed: 0
   ▶ Bootp flags: 0x8000, Broadcast flag (Broadcast)
     Client IP address: 0.0.0.0
     Your (client) IP address: 10.20.1.3
     Next server IP address: 0.0.0.0
     Relay agent IP address: 0.0.0.0
     Client MAC address: aa:bb:cc:00:0e:00 (aa:bb:cc:00:0e:00)
     Client hardware address padding: 00000000000000000000
     Server host name not given
     Boot file name not given
     Magic cookie: DHCP
   ▶ Option: (53) DHCP Message Type (ACK)
```

Returning to the question earlier, Answer C is partially correct because although the switch Bob is connected to does not need to hand out addresses itself, it does need to know where to forward requests to if the client and server are in different subnets. This is known as DHCP relaying. The DHCP relay agent receives the DHCPDISCOVER message and then sends it via unicast to the DHCP server. The contents of the messages now change a bit, with the relay agents IP address populating the GIADDR (Gateway IP address) field. The server looks at this to determine which subnet the message originated from, allocating an IP address based on that. the standard messages are exchanged, but the server talks to the relay agent instead.

Let's start by moving Bob back to his correct VLAN:

```
SW3(config)#int e0/0
SW3(config-if)#switchport access vlan 30
SW3(config-if)#
```

We set up a relay agent under the VLAN interface by using the command *"ip helper-address <ip address of DHCP Server>"*:

```
SW1(config)#int vlan 30
SW1(config-if)#ip helper-address 10.20.1.21
SW1(config-if)#
```

We should shut and no shut the interface to start the DHCP Discover process again:

```
Bob-PC(config)#int e0/0
Bob-PC(config-if)#shut
Bob-PC(config-if)#
%LINK-5-CHANGED: Interface Ethernet0/0, changed state to administratively
down
%LINEPROTO-5-UPDOWN: Line protocol on Interface Ethernet0/0, changed
state to down
Bob-PC(config-if)#
Bob-PC(config-if)#no shut
Bob-PC(config-if)#
%LINK-3-UPDOWN: Interface Ethernet0/0, changed state to up
%LINEPROTO-5-UPDOWN: Line protocol on Interface Ethernet0/0, changed
state to up
Bob-PC(config-if)#
%DHCP-6-ADDRESS_ASSIGN: Interface Ethernet0/0 assigned DHCP address
10.30.1.3, mask 255.255.255.0, hostname Bob-PC

Bob-PC(config-if)#
```

Although we still get an IP address on Bob-PC, which is using broadcast, all the communication between the Server and the virtual IP address for VLAN 30 on SW1 is unicast:

34	4...	10.30.1.1	10.20.1.21	DHCP	337	DHCP Discover
38	4...	10.20.1.21	10.30.1.1	DHCP	342	DHCP Offer
40	4...	10.30.1.1	10.20.1.21	DHCP	337	DHCP Discover
41	4...	10.20.1.21	10.30.1.1	DHCP	342	DHCP Offer
42	4...	10.30.1.1	10.20.1.21	DHCP	349	DHCP Request
43	4...	10.20.1.21	10.30.1.1	DHCP	342	DHCP ACK

Wireshark capture: 8

Throughout the communication the Client MAC address (Bob-PC) remains the same, but we now make use of the Relay Agent IP address field, which is set to 10.30.1.1; the VIP for VLAN 30, as we can see in the Offer message below:

```
▼ Bootstrap Protocol (Offer)
    Message type: Boot Reply (2)
    Hardware type: Ethernet (0x01)
    Hardware address length: 6
    Hops: 0
    Transaction ID: 0x00000bc8
    Seconds elapsed: 0
  ▶ Bootp flags: 0x8000, Broadcast flag (Broadcast)
    Client IP address: 0.0.0.0
    Your (client) IP address: 10.30.1.3
    Next server IP address: 0.0.0.0
    Relay agent IP address: 10.30.1.1
    Client MAC address: aa:bb:cc:00:0e:00 (aa:bb:cc:00:0e:00)
```

Let's set up Dave as well now, starting with the VLAN interface (note the inclusion of SW2):

```
SW1(config-if)#int vlan 10
SW1(config-if)#ip helper-address 10.20.1.21
SW1(config-if)#

SW2(config)#int vlan 10
SW2(config-if)#ip helper-address 10.20.1.21
SW2(config-if)#
```

Dave needs to have the static route removed; the interface changed to use DHCP and the interface shutdown and brought up again:

```
Dave-PC(config)#no ip route 0.0.0.0 0.0.0.0 10.10.1.1
Dave-PC(config)#int e0/0
Dave-PC(config-if)#ip address dhcp
Dave-PC(config-if)#shut
Dave-PC(config-if)#
```

```
%LINK-5-CHANGED: Interface Ethernet0/0, changed state to administratively
down
%LINEPROTO-5-UPDOWN: Line protocol on Interface Ethernet0/0, changed
state to down
Dave-PC(config-if)#
Dave-PC(config-if)#no shut
Dave-PC(config-if)#
%LINK-3-UPDOWN: Interface Ethernet0/0, changed state to up
%LINEPROTO-5-UPDOWN: Line protocol on Interface Ethernet0/0, changed
state to up
Dave-PC(config-if)#
%DHCP-6-ADDRESS_ASSIGN: Interface Ethernet0/0 assigned DHCP address
10.10.1.3, mask 255.255.255.0, hostname Dave-PC

Dave-PC(config-if)#do sh ip route 0.0.0.0
Routing entry for 0.0.0.0/0, supernet
  Known via "static", distance 254, metric 0, candidate default path
  Routing Descriptor Blocks:
  * 10.10.1.1
      Route metric is 0, traffic share count is 1
Dave-PC(config-if)#
```

Now we have the capability to hand out IP addresses across all the different departments in our LAN. DHCP can do so much more than this though, as we have seen by configuring a domain name and a default router. These were shown in the options fields of the packets we captured. There are many options available to us, and we can even create our own.

5.1.b DHCP options (Basic overview and functionality)

Options are octet strings. The first is the option code, the second is the number of octets to follow and the rest of them are code dependent. A DHCPOFFER message will be 0x35,0x01,0x02. 0x35 mean it is a DHCP Message Type (53), 0x01 means we have one octet coming next and 0x02 means a value of "Offer". We have already configured a couple of these, they were standard ones, as defined under RFC2132.

Options allow us to configure the network from one single place. When an IP phone boots up we can tell it (through DHCP) where to download firmware, or we can use it to install an operating system through PXE (Preboot Execution Environment).

We can create our own options from the private use range (224 – 254), such as:

```
Server(dhcp-config)#option 230 ascii 802101.com Rocks!!
Server(dhcp-config)#
```

We will add on a few more options shortly, but we need to return to something we implemented earlier, but did not discuss.

5.1.c Excluded addresses

When we first set up Server to hand out IP addresses we excluded a number of IP addresses, using the command "*ip dhcp excluded-address <ip address>*". Why did we do this?

DHCP hands out addresses (new addresses that is) sequentially. That means that the DHCP server would start at the first available addresses and work its way through the range until the range is exhausted. It would not be able to discern whether another device already had the same IP address, and we would end up with devices with duplicate addresses.

Duplicate addresses have a number of repercussions on the network. At best you and another workstation will get messages about having duplicate addresses, at worst other devices on the network now see you as a default gateway, are sending you all their traffic, and finding that they are not getting anywhere.

For this reason we have excluded a number of addresses from being used as client addresses. These are the IP addresses of the VLAN interfaces, the Server's own IP address and the IP addresses of the router's sub-interfaces. When creating exclusions it's best to try and make the excluded addresses easy to remember, say from the beginning or end of the range. For this reason when planning your IP addressing place the devices that need to be easily remembered and need to have fixed IP addresses either towards the beginning or the end of the subnet (or both).

5.1.d Lease time

We saw from the Wireshark captures that there was a "lease time" when we received an offer:

```
▼ Option: (51) IP Address Lease Time
    Length: 4
    IP Address Lease Time: (86400s) 1 day
▼ Option: (58) Renewal Time Value
    Length: 4
    Renewal Time Value: (43200s) 12 hours
▼ Option: (59) Rebinding Time Value
    Length: 4
    Rebinding Time Value: (75600s) 21 hours
```

We have a lease time of one day. This is known as being "bound" to an IP address. Once we are initially bound to an IP address a timer starts. This timer is the T1 timer, which is the renewal time, or DHCP option 58. The renewal time is (by default) 50% of the lease time. After the T1 timer has expired we request to keep our IP address by sending a unicast DHCPREQUEST, to the original DHCP server, hoping to get a DHCPACK, we will send three requests in order to give the DHCP server a fair chance at responding. If we do not get a response then we start to take notice of the rebinding timer (known as the T2 timer, or DHCP option 59), which is 87.5% of the lease time. At 50% of the remaining time till the T2 expires we will send another DHCPREQUEST (well, three) and if, again, we do not get a response then once the T2 expires we will send one more attempt via unicast and two via broadcast. If we still do not receive a response we will start sending DHCPDISCOVER packets, hoping that another DHCP server will respond.

5.2 Describe the types, features, and applications of ACLs

ACLs, or Access Control Lists, are a way of permitting or denying traffic based on if they match or do not match a set of criteria, this is referred to as "filtering". Think of them as a list of people allowed into a party that is written on a sheet and checked by the doorman. It can be permissive, allowing everyone, or restrictive, allowing a subset of people and denying everyone else. The important thing to remember with ACLs is that no matter what the access list contains it must be put into force, i.e. the doorman. It would be no good to have an access list, if there was no one to check it.

When we write access lists, as we will do shortly, they must be assigned to an interface, this puts the ACL into effect, acting as the doorman.

With ACLs placement is key. So, plan them carefully. Picture a straight road. We have the destination (a shop) and the source (your home). We want to get from home to the shop, but will be blocked by an ACL (i.e. a sign saying that the road to the shop is blocked). Where would we place the ACL? If we place the ACL at the destination then the traffic has already traversed the network only to be blocked at the end. This means we are letting traffic bounce around the network needlessly. Returning to the analogy, we have just driven many miles to find the shop is shut. It has wasted your time and resources. In this scenario, the ACL should be placed as close to the source as possible.

Now, what if the road was different, with multiple side roads joining on to it. There are probably more people that want to get to the shop, so do we put in more ACLs? Keeping with the road analogy, more signs informing everyone that the shop is shut will mean more people to stand at the signs and increases the chances of missing a point on the road. In this scenario the ACL would be placed closer to the destination, minimising the chances of mistake (human error), and ensuring that we capture all the sources. Granted this does mean that we will have more traffic bouncing around only to be turned away, but this is the trade-off we have as a network engineer between ensuring we minimise our chances for error and the number of ACLs we need to write, whilst maximising the effectiveness of our network and its security.

Let's start by looking at some of the ACLs we can use and then we will implement a couple within our LAN and WAN. The different ACLs also dictate where they should be placed; also, we can only have one access-list per direction on an interface (inbound or outbound). There are two formats of ACLs; numbered or named. Within this, we can have standard or extended filtering.

ACLs are always processed from the top-down. If we find a match then no more action is taken. There is also an implicit deny at the end of every ACL.

Let's start to put this in a little context, with some rules for being let into a restaurant.

1.   Permit anyone wearing trousers.
2.   Permit anyone wearing a skirt.
3.   Permit anyone wearing a shirt.
4.   Permit anyone wearing a red tie.
5.   Permit anyone wearing shoes.

Now if I tried to get into the restaurant wearing a jumper, shorts and trainers, would I be allowed in? No. The default deny rule at the end would make sure I did not get in. The default deny rule is "implicit". This means that it does not show up in the configuration. So, what happens if I went to a nearby shop and bought a red tie? Then the fourth line would allow me in. I might look odd, but I would satisfy one of the permissive statements.

What if the ACL was written differently?

1.   Deny anyone wearing sandals with socks
2.   Permit anyone else

The good news here is that people who wear socks and sandals would be denied. I would be allowed, but the implicit default deny rule would not match anyone else, as we have already permitted everything else.

One last one:

1.   Permit anyone
2.   Deny anyone wearing socks with sandals
3.   Deny anyone wearing a Nickleback t-shirt

Who gets in now? Everyone. Because we go from top-down, anyone would be allowed in because of the first rule. We would not get to the second or third rule, or to the default deny rule.

Proper ordering of ACLs is critical, whilst we should always have a permit statement; any deny statement should go at the top. Now let's have a look at some actual ACLs.

5.2.a standard (editing and sequence numbers)

Standard ACLs work based on the source network or host. They should be placed as close to the destination as possible. With a standard ACL, we can permit or deny traffic based on the source address. Standard access lists are number between 1 and 99, and from 1300 to 1999 (if we are using the extended range).

For the next section we are going to look at ACLs using two routers; R1 and R2, we will then put some of this into practice with our main topology.

An example of a standard access list would be:

```
R1(config)#ip access-list 1 permit 10.10.1.0 0.0.0.255
```

This would permit any host from 10.10.1.1 to 10.10.1.254 because of the wildcard mask of 0.0.0.255 (remembering that 0 will be the subnet address and 255 will be the broadcast address). A host with an IP address of 10.20.1.3 would be denied due to the implicit deny rule.

In our second example, we could permit one host (10.10.1.2) using the command:

```
R1(config)#access-list 1 permit 10.10.1.2
```

Any other host would be denied. Alternatively, if we wanted to deny a single host and permit everyone else, we would use:

```
R1(config)#access-list 1 deny 10.10.1.2
R1(config)#access-list 1 permit 0.0.0.0 255.255.255.255
```

Again, this should be placed as close to the destination as possible and the way to do this would be:

```
R1(config)#int e0/0
R1(config-if)#ip access-group 1 in
R1(config-if)#
```

This would deny the host 10.10.1.2 from accessing the e0/0 interface of R1, so it would block Telnet, SSH and even block access to the routing protocols between the two hosts. If we wanted to deny Telnet and allow SSH we would need to use an extended access list.

Returning to the second example, we have a basic access-list of "*access-list 1 permit 10.10.1.2 0.0.0.0*", this is set as an access-group inbound on our e0/0 interface, and this is the way we put the ACL into effect (the doorman). This is a good example as we have the implicit deny statement. Therefore it does not show up in the configuration, or in our ACL rules. We can check our access-lists using the command "*show access-lists*":

```
R1#show access-lists
Standard IP access list 1
    10 permit 10.10.1.2
R1#
```

The access-lists we have will be separated into the standard access-lists and extended access-lists. Our single line ACL has a sequence number (10). This is to enable us to edit our access-list, but the editing abilities are limited. Let's add another line to our ACL:

```
R1(config)#access-list 1 permit 2.2.2.2 0.0.0.0
R1(config)#
```

Now our ACL looks like this:

```
R1(config)#do sh access-lists
Standard IP access list 1
    20 permit 2.2.2.2
    10 permit 10.10.1.2
R1(config)#
```

We have the new entry at sequence number 20. Can we remove number 10?

```
R1(config)#no access-list 1 ?
  <cr>
R1(config)#no access-list 1
```

No, we can only remove the entire access-list. We cannot (in a standard access-list) add an entry between 10 and 20 either:

```
R1(config)#access-list 1 ?
  deny    Specify packets to reject
  permit  Specify packets to forward
  remark  Access list entry comment
R1(config)#access-list 1 permit ?
  Hostname or A.B.C.D  Address to match
  any                  Any source host
  host                 A single host address
R1(config)#access-list 1 permit 3.3.3.3 ?
  /nn or A.B.C.D  Wildcard bits
  log             Log matches against this entry
  <cr>
R1(config)#access-list 1 permit 3.3.3.3 0.0.0.0 ?
  log  Log matches against this entry
  <cr>
R1(config)#access-list 1 permit 3.3.3.3 0.0.0.0
```

If we wanted to edit our access-list (this way), we would need to delete it and recreate it from scratch.

```
R1(config)#no access-list 1
R1(config)#do sh run | i access-list
R1(config)#access-list 1 permit 2.2.2.2
R1(config)#do sh access-lists
Standard IP access list 1
    10 permit 2.2.2.2
R1(config)#
```

The effect of this ACL is that we can telnet from R2 (10.10.1.2) to R1 (10.10.1.1), but only by using its loopback 0 interface (2.2.2.2) as our source:

```
R2(config)#do telnet 10.10.1.1
Trying 10.10.1.1 ...
% Destination unreachable; gateway or host down

R2(config)#do telnet 10.10.1.1 /source-interface lo0
Trying 10.10.1.1 ... Open

Password required, but none set

[Connection to 10.10.1.1 closed by foreign host]
R2(config)#
```

All other traffic from R2 would be blocked, unless sourced from the loopback interface, which is less than ideal. It would be better if we could be more specific, and specify a protocol in our ACL. We can do this using an extended ACL.

5.2.b extended

Extended ACLs should be placed as close to the source as possible. With an extended ACL, we can check the "5-tuple", which is the source address/port, destination address/port and the protocol. Extended ACLs are numbered from 100 to 199 and from 2000 to 2699 in the extended range.

An example of an extended ACL would be:

```
R1(config)#access-list 101 permit tcp 10.10.1.0 0.0.0.255 1.1.1.1 0.0.0.0
eq telnet
```

This would be applied in the same way as the standard ACL:

```
R1(config)#int e0/0
R1(config-if)#ip access-group 101 out
```

This would permit Telnet traffic from the 10.10.1.0/24 network to the loopback interface of R1 (1.1.1.1), but deny it from the loopback address of R2. We need to ensure that this is applied though:

```
R1(config)#int e0/0
R1(config-if)#no ip access-group 1 in
R1(config-if)#ip access-group 101 in
R1(config-if)#

R2#telnet 1.1.1.1
Trying 1.1.1.1 ... Open


Password required, but none set

[Connection to 1.1.1.1 closed by foreign host]
R2#telnet 1.1.1.1 /source-interface lo0
Trying 1.1.1.1 ...
% Destination unreachable; gateway or host down
R2#
```

We currently have one line in our extended ACL, which looks like this:

```
R1#sh access-lists
Extended IP access list 101
    10 permit tcp 10.10.1.0 0.0.0.255 host 1.1.1.1 eq telnet (10 matches)
R1#
```

We can add to our ACL:

```
R1(config)#access-list 101 permit tcp 2.2.2.2 0.0.0.0 host 1.1.1.1 eq
telnet
R1(config)#
```

However, we cannot remove a singular entry through this method (as we saw with the standard access list), despite the numbering (10, 20 and so on):

```
R1(config)#do sh access-lists
Extended IP access list 101
    10 permit tcp 10.10.1.0 0.0.0.255 host 1.1.1.1 eq telnet (10 matches)
    20 permit tcp host 2.2.2.2 host 1.1.1.1 eq telnet
R1(config)#no access-list 101 ?
  <cr>

R1(config)#no access-list 101
```

Instead, and as we will see again shortly, we need to get into the ACL in a different way:

```
R1(config)#ip access-list extended 101
R1(config-ext-nacl)#no 20
R1(config-ext-nacl)#do sh access-lists
Extended IP access list 101
    10 permit tcp 10.10.1.0 0.0.0.255 host 1.1.1.1 eq telnet
R1(config-ext-nacl)#
```

If we make a mistake we do not need to remove the entire ACL and start again from scratch. Whilst the command "*access-list*" versus "*ip access-list*" looks quite different, really we end up in the same place, for the most part, and you can see this by comparing the numbers for both methods:

```
R1(config)#access-list ?
  <1-99>              IP standard access list
  <100-199>           IP extended access list
  <1100-1199>         Extended 48-bit MAC address access list
  <1300-1999>         IP standard access list (expanded range)
  <200-299>           Protocol type-code access list
  <2000-2699>         IP extended access list (expanded range)
  <2700-2799>         MPLS access list
  <300-399>           DECnet access list
  <700-799>           48-bit MAC address access list
  compiled            Enable IP access-list compilation
  dynamic-extended    Extend the dynamic ACL absolute timer
  rate-limit          Simple rate-limit specific access list

R1(config)#ip access-list ?
  extended     Extended Access List
  helper       Access List acts on helper-address
  log-update   Control access list log updates
  logging      Control access list logging
  resequence   Resequence Access List
  standard     Standard Access List

R1(config)#ip access-list standard ?
  <1-99>        Standard IP access-list number
  <1300-1999>   Standard IP access-list number (expanded range)
  WORD          Access-list name

R1(config)#ip access-list extended ?
  <100-199>     Extended IP access-list number
  <2000-2699>   Extended IP access-list number (expanded range)
  WORD          Access-list name

R1(config)#ip access-list extended
```

The major difference is that with the command "*ip access-list*" we can give them names.

5.2.c named

Named ACLs allow us to have more control and to be more descriptive. Rather than *"access-list 1"* we can have *"access-list DenyR2"*. With named ACLs we can have standard ACLs, just matching the source, or extended, allowing us to match on source and destination address and ports and protocol (the 5–tuple). We can also add and remove entries based on their sequence number.

```
R1(config)#ip access-list standard MyStandardACL
R1(config-std-nacl)#permit 10.1.1.2 0.0.0.0
R1(config-std-nacl)#do sh access-list
Standard IP access list MyStandardACL
    10 permit 10.1.1.2
R1(config-std-nacl)#exit
R1(config)#
```

Now we can add an entry at sequence number 15, and remove the entry at sequence number 10:

```
R1(config)#ip access-list standard MyStandardACL
R1(config-std-nacl)#15 permit 2.2.2.2 0.0.0.0
R1(config-std-nacl)#no 10
R1(config-std-nacl)#do sh access-list
Standard IP access list MyStandardACL
    15 permit 2.2.2.2
R1(config-std-nacl)#
```

The access-list is applied to an interface using the name instead of the number:

```
R1(config)#int e0/0
R1(config-if)#no ip access-group 101 in
R1(config-if)#
R1(config-if)#ip access-group ?
  <1-199>     IP access list (standard or extended)
  <1300-2699> IP expanded access list (standard or extended)
  WORD        Access-list name

R1(config-if)#ip access-group MyStandardACL in
R1(config-if)#
```

This works as it should, but this time permits telnet from R2's loopback only:

```
R2#telnet 10.10.1.1
Trying 10.10.1.1 ...
% Destination unreachable; gateway or host down

R2#telnet 10.10.1.1 /source-interface lo0
Trying 10.10.1.1 ... Open
```

```
Password required, but none set

[Connection to 10.10.1.1 closed by foreign host]
R2#
```

Creating an extended named ACL is no different:

```
R1(config)#no ip access-list standard MyStandardACL
R1(config)#do sh access-list
R1(config)#
R1(config)#ip access-list extended MyExtendedACL
R1(config-ext-nacl)#5 permit tcp 2.2.2.2 0.0.0.0 1.1.1.1 0.0.0.0 eq
telnet
R1(config-ext-nacl)#do sh access-list
Extended IP access list MyExtendedACL
    5 permit tcp host 2.2.2.2 host 1.1.1.1 eq telnet
R1(config-ext-nacl)#int e0/0
R1(config-if)#no ip access-group MyStandardACL in
R1(config-if)#ip access-group MyExtendedACL in
R1(config-if)#
```

If we test it, it works as it should:

```
R2#telnet 1.1.1.1
Trying 1.1.1.1 ...
% Destination unreachable; gateway or host down

R2#telnet 1.1.1.1 /source-interface lo0
Trying 1.1.1.1 ... Open

Password required, but none set

[Connection to 1.1.1.1 closed by foreign host]
R2#
```

5.2.d numbered

When we looked at standard and extended access lists we just used the command *"access-list"* followed by the number. When we created our named access-list, we had to use the command *"ip access-list"* followed by the option of standard or extended. Either way is fine, but if you choose the first method, as we have, then it may then be harder to remember how to create a named ACL. So practice both methods.

The second method (*ip access-list*) allows us to find what we need a little more quickly and allows us to create named ACLs. Here we can see the number ranges for both standard and extended, along with the option to create a named ACL for both:

```
R1(config)#ip access-list standard ?
  <1-99>       Standard IP access-list number
  <1300-1999>  Standard IP access-list number (expanded range)
  WORD         Access-list name

R1(config)#ip access-list extended ?
  <100-199>    Extended IP access-list number
  <2000-2699>  Extended IP access-list number (expanded range)
  WORD         Access-list name

R1(config)#ip access-list extended
```

5.2.e Log option

Because of the implicit deny rule at the end of every ACL it can be easy to miss traffic that has been dropped. By using the "*log*" option at the end of the ACL entries, we can start to see the hits (the number of times we have a match to an ACL entry), which are then logged. This allows us to view them in the syslog. Adding logging to an ACL entry is as simple as adding the word "*log*" at the end of it:

```
R1(config)#ip access-list extended MyExtendedACL
R1(config-ext-nacl)#permit tcp host 2.2.2.2 host 1.1.1.1 eq telnet log
R1(config-ext-nacl)#
```

If we test this:

```
R2#telnet 1.1.1.1 /source-interface lo0
Trying 1.1.1.1 ... Open

Password required, but none set

[Connection to 1.1.1.1 closed by foreign host]
R2#
```

We can see an entry logged on R1's console:

```
R1#
%SEC-6-IPACCESSLOGP: list MyExtendedACL permitted tcp 2.2.2.2(16434) ->
1.1.1.1(23), 1 packet
R1#
```

The real benefit is that in the event that we need to troubleshoot an ACL, we can make the implicit deny rule an *explicit* deny rule and log the hits against it:

```
R1(config)#ip access-list extended MyExtendedACL
R1(config-ext-nacl)#deny ip any any log
R1(config-ext-nacl)#
```

If we try again:

```
R2#telnet 1.1.1.1
Trying 1.1.1.1 ...
% Destination unreachable; gateway or host down

R2#
```

We get a syslog message on the console showing that the connection is denied:

```
R1#
%SEC-6-IPACCESSLOGP: list MyExtendedACL denied tcp 10.10.1.2(61631) ->
1.1.1.1(23), 1 packet
R1#
```

This then allows us to identify the issue and correct our ACL, if we did want to permit the traffic.

Let's put all of this into some context with our own network.

5.3 Configure and verify ACLs in a network environment

ACLs increase security, this is not their only role as they can also be used to control routing updates, but we will look at them from a security aspect. Therefore, with this in mind, we will start to make our network more secure. One of our primary concerns will be the ISP router. ISPs tend to get a little upset if you try and get into their routers, so we will prevent everyone apart from the Gateway router from accessing the ISP's loopback interface by either telnet or SSH. First of all, let's confirm that it is working, using the username admin and password of "cisco":

```
ISP(config-if)#line vty 0 4
ISP(config-line)#transport input telnet ssh
ISP(config-line)#exit

Gateway#ssh -l admin 100.100.100.100
Password:
ISP>
ISP>exit

[Connection to 100.100.100.100 closed by foreign host]
```

```
Gateway#
Gateway#telnet 100.100.100.100
Trying 100.100.100.100 ... Open

User Access Verification

Username: admin
Password:
ISP>exit

[Connection to 100.100.100.100 closed by foreign host]
Gateway#
```

How would we go about securing this with an ACL? The easiest way to do this would be to permit the Gateway router and to let the default deny rule take care of everything else. We will need to use an extended rule as we want to restrict access down at the protocol level, and because we may need to open up this restriction later on, we will use a named ACL.

5.3.a named

We start with a descriptive name.

```
ISP(config)#ip access-list extended PermitSSH-Telnet
```

Now, do we want IP or TCP? If we use IP that will either permit or prevent all communication, as we cannot specify a port:

```
ISP(config-ext-nacl)#permit ip host 192.168.20.254 100.100.100.100
0.0.0.0 ?
  dscp        Match packets with given dscp value
  fragments   Check non-initial fragments
  log         Log matches against this entry
  log-input   Log matches against this entry, including input interface
  option      Match packets with given IP Options value
  precedence  Match packets with given precedence value
  reflect     Create reflexive access list entry
  time-range  Specify a time-range
  tos         Match packets with given TOS value
  ttl         Match packets with given TTL value
  <cr>

ISP(config-ext-nacl)#
```

If we change to TCP, we can than use the eq (or equals) operator and specify our desired protocols. Some protocols, however, must be specified by their protocol number, rather than the name:

```
ISP(config-ext-nacl)#permit tcp host 192.168.20.254 100.100.100.100
0.0.0.0 eq 22
ISP(config-ext-nacl)#permit tcp host 192.168.20.254 100.100.100.100
0.0.0.0 eq telnet
ISP(config-ext-nacl)#
```

We can also add a note to the ACL, in the form of a remark, so that anyone else looking at the configuration can see its purpose:

```
ISP(config-ext-nacl)#remark Permit SSH & Telnet from Gateway
```

We then need to assign it. But where do we assign it? Let's try the E0/0 interface, as that is the one nearest to the Gateway router:

```
ISP(config-ext-nacl)#int e0/0
ISP(config-if)#ip access-group PermitSSH-Telnet in
ISP(config-if)#
```

Now try testing SSH and Telnet from the Gateway router.

Does it work? Possibly it does, possibly it does not. It depends how long you wait. Give it a few moments and we should see:

```
ISP(config-if)#
%OSPF-5-ADJCHG: Process 1, Nbr 50.50.50.50 on Ethernet0/0 from FULL to
DOWN, Neighbor Down: Dead timer expired
ISP(config-if)#
```

Because we have only allowed in SSH and Telnet traffic we have also blocked OSPF communication. Let's remove it from the interface and put it on the VTY line instead:

```
ISP(config-line)#int e0/0
ISP(config-if)#no ip access-group PermitSSH-Telnet in
ISP(config-if)#
%OSPF-5-ADJCHG: Process 1, Nbr 50.50.50.50 on Ethernet0/0 from LOADING to
FULL, Loading Done
ISP(config-if)#
```

Instead of the *access-group* command we used earlier, we need to use *access-class* for VTY lines:

```
ISP(config-if)#line vty 0 4
ISP(config-line)#access-class ?
  <1-199>       IP access list
  <1300-2699>   IP expanded access list
  WORD          Access-list name
```

```
ISP(config-line)#access-class PermitSSH-Telnet ?
  in   Filter incoming connections
  out  Filter outgoing connections

ISP(config-line)#access-class PermitSSH-Telnet in
ISP(config-line)#
```

Does it work now?

```
Gateway#telnet 100.100.100.100
Trying 100.100.100.100 ...
% Connection refused by remote host

Gateway#ssh -l admin 100.100.100.100
% Connection refused by remote host

Gateway#
```

No, it does not, and we will find out why in a moment when we add logging to our named ACL.

5.3.b numbered

Let's do a quick numbered access-list before we dig back into our ACL problem. We will set up the Gateway router to deny any traffic from OSPF3's loopback address (1.2.3.1). It has access at the moment:

```
OSPF3#ping 192.168.20.254 so lo0
Type escape sequence to abort.
Sending 5, 100-byte ICMP Echos to 192.168.20.254:
Packet sent with a source address of 1.2.3.1
!!!!!
Success rate is 100 percent (5/5)
OSPF3#
```

Let's stop that:

```
Gateway(config)#access-list 1 deny 1.2.3.1
Gateway(config)#access-list 1 permit any
Gateway(config)#int e0/0
Gateway(config-if)#ip access-group 1 in
Gateway(config-if)#
```

Notice that we have had to enter a permit statement otherwise all other traffic would be dropped.

Now if we test we can see that OSPF3 can get to the Gateway router from its e3/2 interface, but not from its loopback interface:

```
OSPF3#ping 192.168.20.254
Type escape sequence to abort.
Sending 5, 100-byte ICMP Echos to 192.168.20.254:
!!!!!
Success rate is 100 percent (5/5)
OSPF3#ping 192.168.20.254 so lo0
Type escape sequence to abort.
Sending 5, 100-byte ICMP Echos to 192.168.20.254:
Packet sent with a source address of 1.2.3.1
U.U.U
Success rate is 0 percent (0/5)
OSPF3#
```

This is working as we would expect. Now let's go and fix our problem, by setting up some logging.

5.3.c Log option

The idea was that only the Gateway router would be able to access the ISP router through its VTY lines. It did not go according to plan. Why not? Let's start by revisiting our access-list:

```
ISP(config-line)#do sh access-list
Extended IP access list PermitSSH-Telnet
    10 permit tcp host 192.168.20.254 host 100.100.100.100 eq 22 (43 matches)
    20 permit tcp host 192.168.20.254 host 100.100.100.100 eq telnet (36 matches)
ISP(config-line)#
```

Although we intend to access the VTY lines through the loopback address, I have actually made a very incorrect assumption. Let's think about this logically. If I were to telnet to a router by its physical interface address, I would end up where? At the VTY line. If I were to telnet to the same router by its loopback address, where would I end up? On its VTY line again. So actually, the VTY lines are not bound to an individual IP address. Enabling logging on an explicit deny rule will confirm this:

```
ISP(config-line)#ip access-list extended PermitSSH-Telnet
ISP(config-ext-nacl)#deny tcp any any log
ISP(config-ext-nacl)#do sh access-list
Extended IP access list PermitSSH-Telnet
    10 permit tcp host 192.168.20.254 host 100.100.100.100 eq 22 (43 matches)
    20 permit tcp host 192.168.20.254 host 100.100.100.100 eq telnet (36 matches)
    30 deny tcp any any log
ISP(config-ext-nacl)#
```

If we try again from the Gateway router, we can see the logged messages:

```
Gateway#ssh -l admin 100.100.100.100
% Connection refused by remote host

Gateway#telnet 100.100.100.100
Trying 100.100.100.100 ...
% Connection refused by remote host

Gateway#

ISP(config-ext-nacl)#
%SEC-6-IPACCESSLOGP: list PermitSSH-Telnet denied tcp
192.168.20.254(45420) -> 0.0.0.0(22), 1 packet
%SEC-6-IPACCESSLOGP: list PermitSSH-Telnet denied tcp
192.168.20.254(58057) -> 0.0.0.0(23), 1 packet
ISP(config-ext-nacl)#
```

Above we can see that the VTY lines are listening on all interfaces (0.0.0.0). So let's correct our ACL, first by removing the entries, then by adding new ones:

```
ISP(config-ext-nacl)#no 10
ISP(config-ext-nacl)#no 20
ISP(config-ext-nacl)#do sh access-list
Extended IP access list PermitSSH-Telnet
    30 deny tcp any any log (2 matches)
ISP(config-ext-nacl)#
ISP(config-ext-nacl)#
ISP(config-ext-nacl)#10 permit tcp host 192.168.20.254 any eq 22
ISP(config-ext-nacl)#20 permit tcp host 192.168.20.254 any eq telnet
ISP(config-ext-nacl)#do sh access-list
Extended IP access list PermitSSH-Telnet
    10 permit tcp host 192.168.20.254 any eq 22
    20 permit tcp host 192.168.20.254 any eq telnet
    30 deny tcp any any log (2 matches)
ISP(config-ext-nacl)#
```

Now we find that EIGRP1 cannot access ISP via its VTY lines (as we would hope):

```
EIGRP1#ssh -l admin 100.100.100.100
% Connection refused by remote host

EIGRP1#telnet 100.100.100.100
Trying 100.100.100.100 ...
% Connection refused by remote host

EIGRP1#
```

These are still logged by ISP because of the deny rule:

```
ISP(config-ext-nacl)#
%SEC-6-IPACCESSLOGP: list PermitSSH-Telnet denied tcp 192.168.1.2(43670)
-> 0.0.0.0(22), 1 packet
ISP(config-ext-nacl)#
%SEC-6-IPACCESSLOGP: list PermitSSH-Telnet denied tcp 192.168.1.2(57165)
-> 0.0.0.0(23), 1 packet
ISP(config-ext-nacl)#
```

However, Gateway can (again, as we would hope):

```
Gateway#telnet 100.100.100.100
Trying 100.100.100.100 ... Open

User Access Verification

Username: admin
Password:
ISP>exit

[Connection to 100.100.100.100 closed by foreign host]
Gateway#
Gateway#ssh -l admin 100.100.100.100
Password:
ISP>
ISP>exit

[Connection to 100.100.100.100 closed by foreign host]
Gateway#
```

My original plan for this section was to have Server being the only device able to access ISP. Unfortunately ISP does not have any knowledge about the 10.0.0.0/8 networks sitting behind Gateway, therefore will drop the traffic. We don't want it to either, for very good reasons, namely that we would (in real-life) be using a public IP address between the ISP and Gateway, and not a private address. However, we still want Server and the rest of our LAN to be able to access ISP (and the rest of our network). Let's move on and find out why and how.

5.4 Identify the basic operation of NAT

Although I am just using private IP ranges throughout our topology we need to pretend for a moment that we do have a mixture of true LAN and WAN. Our WAN would use public IP addresses and our LAN would use private IP addresses. Private addresses are not routable on the Internet, only public ones are. So how does a device such as a computer in a LAN with a private IP address get access to the Internet? It does this through Network Address Translation (NAT), where private addresses become public ones and vice versa.

5.4.a purpose

The basic idea of NAT is to switch two IP addresses around, hiding the true source or destination, or both. We can achieve NAT in a number of ways; we can dynamically assign addresses from a pool, give certain devices their own specific NAT address, or hide everyone behind a single address. We will look at these now.

5.4.b pool

With pool translation, we need to have a pool of public addresses, enough to support each user that will be accessing the Internet at the same time. We do not need a perfect 1-to-1 match, unless everyone will be on the Internet at the same time. NATs time out, so addresses will be re-used. There is no guarantee that a device will get the same address each time as the address allocation is dynamic; we specify a range of inside addresses and a range of public addresses to map to.

5.4.c static
5.4.d 1to1

I really do not know why these two are separated in the syllabus when they are the same. With 1to1 (also known as Static NAT) there is a constant mapping between a particular private address and a particular public address. This type of NAT allows us to keep public facing servers using the same public address at all times. This does increase the administrative overhead if we have a number of servers, but it also gives us, and anyone wanting to access our services, a fixed point of contact.

5.4.e overloading

The above solutions all rely on one factor; having a large number of public IP addresses. It is becoming increasingly harder to get public IPv4 addresses now, so it will soon become nearly impossible to get enough addresses to do pool translation, or set static translations for a large number of servers.

Overloading can help in such a case. We have one private IP address and this is used for NAT, each client then is translated to this address, but each has a separate port. We are "overloading" the single address. This way we can perform NAT for thousands of hosts. This is also (more commonly) referred to as Port Address Translation (PAT), which follows the same principles as multiplexing which we discussed earlier.

5.4.f source addressing

If Cisco's layout of the syllabus wasn't confusing enough, their terminology just seems to add to this confusion sometimes. Cisco define some terms for NAT, which are either Inside or Outside and then global or local. Think of Inside as "our network" and outside as "their network":

Inside Local – An IP address (usually from the RFC1918 private IP addresses range) assigned to a host inside the network.

Inside Global – Usually a public IP address assigned by an ISP, representing one or more Inside Local address to the outside world.

Outside Global – Usually a public IP address assigned by an ISP, this is the public address of the outside network.

Outside Local – the IP address is an outside host as it appears to *their* inside network.

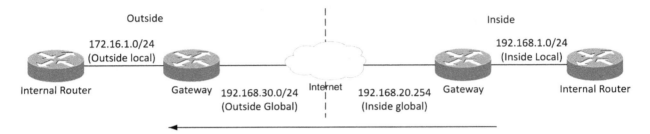

5.4.g one way NAT

With the pool and the PAT methods the translations is initiated from the inside-out. We need someone on the inside to make the traffic that results in the NAT being set up. The NAT cannot be initiated from the outside-in, after all, the outside source has no knowledge of the inside host, therefore can only address it to the public address. The device performing NAT will not know which device inside the network is the intended recipient. For this reason, Pool and PAT (overloading) are referred to as one-way NATs.

Enough talking now, let's set up some network address translation.

5.5 Configure and verify NAT for given network requirements

Let's start by defining some requirements.

- Requirement #1: Server will have a static NAT address of 192.168.20.21
- Requirement #2: Bob and Dave will receive "external" addresses from a pool (192.168.20.10 – 192.168.20.20)
- Requirement #3: The VLAN IP addresses on the switches will use NAT overloading (PAT).

By the end of this, we should see some excellent connectivity from our LAN to our WAN.

We will start with the Server.

NAT commands start with the words *"ip nat"* and as we are setting up a translation for our network, we will need the command *"inside"*:

```
Gateway(config)#ip nat inside ?
  destination  Destination address translation
  source       Source address translation

Gateway(config)#ip nat inside
```

Next, we need to specify our source:

```
Gateway(config)#ip nat inside source ?
  list       Specify access list describing local addresses
  route-map  Specify route-map
  static     Specify static local->global mapping

Gateway(config)#ip nat inside source
```

Here we can now specify an access-list, a route-map, which we have not covered, or we can use the *"static"* command:

```
Gateway(config)#ip nat inside source static ?
  A.B.C.D  Inside local IP address
  esp      IPSec-ESP (Tunnel mode) support
  network  Subnet translation
  tcp      Transmission Control Protocol
  udp      User Datagram Protocol

Gateway(config)#ip nat inside source static
```

We set the source to be that of Server's IP address:

```
Gateway(config)#ip nat inside source static 10.20.1.21 ?
  A.B.C.D    Source global IP address
  interface  Specify interface for global address

Gateway(config)#ip nat inside source static 10.20.1.21 ?
```

Lastly, we specify the address we want to translate it to:

```
Gateway(config)#ip nat inside source static 10.20.1.21 192.168.20.21
Gateway(config)#
```

Now we need to enable our interfaces and place them in their respective roles, inside or outside. We will have multiple inside interfaces (the connections to SW1 and SW2) and one outside interface (the connection to ISP). This is done under the interface, using the command *"ip nat <inside|outside>"*:

```
Gateway(config)#int e0/0
Gateway(config-if)#ip nat outside
Gateway(config-if)#interface Ethernet0/2.20
Gateway(config-subif)#ip nat inside
Gateway(config-subif)#
```

Do not be surprised if it takes a few moments for the *"ip nat outside"* command to return you to the prompt.

We need to give SW2 a default route (otherwise the traffic from Server will not get past SW2):

```
SW2(config-if)#ip route 0.0.0.0 0.0.0.0 10.20.1.254
SW2(config)#
```

In addition, to prove we have a two-way NAT (not just a one-way NAT), we can enable telnet on Server:

```
Server(config)#line vty 0 4
Server(config-line)#transport input telnet
Server(config-line)#end
```

Let's test! First, we will try to ping ISP on its public interface, and then on its loopback interface:

```
Server#ping 192.168.20.1
Type escape sequence to abort.
Sending 5, 100-byte ICMP Echos to 192.168.20.1:
.!!!!
Success rate is 80 percent (4/5)
Server#ping 100.100.100.100
Type escape sequence to abort.
Sending 5, 100-byte ICMP Echos to 100.100.100.100:
!!!!!
Success rate is 100 percent (5/5)
Server#
```

Now let's try and telnet from ISP, which will prove that the communication is two-way:

```
ISP(config-ext-nacl)#do telnet 192.168.20.21
Trying 192.168.20.21 ... Open


Password required, but none set

[Connection to 192.168.20.21 closed by foreign host]
ISP(config-ext-nacl)#
```

We can confirm that the NAT is working by looking at the NAT translations (*show ip nat translations*):

```
Gateway(config-subif)#do sh ip nat translations
Pro Inside global     Inside local  Outside local   Outside global
tcp 192.168.20.21:23  10.20.1.21:23 192.168.20.1:96    192.168.20.1:39096
icmp 192.168.20.21:36 10.20.1.21:36 100.100.100.100:36 100.100.100.100:36
--- 192.168.20.21     10.20.1.21    ---                ---
Gateway(config-subif)#
```

We can tell from the translations table that this is static NAT because whilst the protocol entries (tcp and icmp above) will timeout when there is no traffic, we will still see the static NAT entry, as shown below, once we wait a few minutes for the translation to time out:

```
Gateway(config-subif)#do sh ip nat translations
Pro Inside global     Inside local   Outside local   Outside global
--- 192.168.20.21     10.20.1.21     ---             ---
Gateway(config-subif)#
```

So far, so good, let's move on to the second requirement; Bob and Dave will receive addresses from a pool of addresses (192.168.20.10 – 192.168.20.20). We start with the same command as before; "*ip nat inside source*", but now we specify an access list, which will be the hosts, or range of IPs we want to translate, followed by the word "*pool*" and then the name of the nat pool:

```
Gateway(config-subif)#exit
Gateway(config)#ip nat inside source list DaveAndBob pool TenToTwenty
Gateway(config)#
```

We create a standard access list, we could just use a numbered ACL, but it's a good idea to give yourself scope to add and remove entries without having to delete the entire ACL:

```
Gateway(config)#ip access-list standard DaveAndBob
Gateway(config-std-nacl)#permit 10.10.1.3
Gateway(config-std-nacl)#permit 10.30.1.3
Gateway(config-std-nacl)#
```

Then we create the NAT pool, calling it TenToTwenty, specifying the starting address (192.168.20.10) and the end address (192.168.20.20), along with the netmask.

```
Gateway(config-std-nacl)#exit
Gateway(config)#
Gateway(config)#ip nat pool TenToTwenty 192.168.20.10 192.168.20.20
netmask 255.255.255.0
```

We can also specify a prefix-length instead of the netmask, but we cannot change a pool that is in use:

```
Gateway(config)#ip nat pool TenToTwenty 192.168.20.10 192.168.20.20
prefix-length 24
%Pool TenToTwenty in use, cannot redefine
Gateway(config)#
```

We need to set the sub interface for VLAN 1 to be the inside for our NAT. We did similar on Gateway's E0/2.20 interface. This is because SW2 has that as the default gateway, and SW1 has 10.1.1.254 as the default gateway, which is Gateway's e0/1.1 interface:

```
Gateway(config)#int e0/1.1
Gateway(config-subif)#ip nat inside
Gateway(config-subif)#exit

SW1(config)#ip route 0.0.0.0 0.0.0.0 10.1.1.254
SW1(config)#
```

Lastly, we can test:

```
Bob-PC#ping 100.100.100.100
Type escape sequence to abort.
Sending 5, 100-byte ICMP Echos to 100.100.100.100:
.!!!!
Success rate is 80 percent (4/5)
Bob-PC#

Dave-PC#ping 100.100.100.100
Type escape sequence to abort.
Sending 5, 100-byte ICMP Echos to 100.100.100.100:
.!!!!
Success rate is 80 percent (4/5)
Dave-PC#
```

If we return to Gateway, we can see the translations that have been created:

```
Gateway(config)#do sh ip nat trans
Pro Inside global      Inside local    Outside local       Outside global
icmp 192.168.20.11:12  10.10.1.3:12    100.100.100.100:12 100.100.100.100:12
--- 192.168.20.11      10.10.1.3       ---                 ---
--- 192.168.20.21      10.20.1.21      ---                 ---
icmp 192.168.20.10:10  10.30.1.3:10    100.100.100.100:10 100.100.100.100:10
--- 192.168.20.10      10.30.1.3       ---                 ---
Gateway(config)#
```

> One word can make all the difference. It can also be hard to spot. Can you spot why the pool translation didn't work with the following configuration:
>
> ```
> ip nat pool TenToTwenty 192.168.20.10 192.168.20.20 netmask
> 255.255.255.0
> ip nat source list DaveAndBob pool TenToTwenty
> ip nat inside source static 10.20.1.21 192.168.20.21
> ```
>
> The second line is missing the word "*inside*" and should be:
>
> ```
> ip nat inside source list DaveAndBob pool TenToTwenty
> ```
>
> The first command is accepted as it belongs to a different method of NAT, called NAT Virtual Interface (NVI). Whilst the two can be confusing, NVI dispenses with the inside/outside local/global terms, in fact there is no inside or outside at all. NAT is enabled on an interface using the command "*ip nat enable*".

Our final configuration will be to set up NAT overload, or PAT, as per our third and final requirement.

We start with the same command: "*ip nat inside source*", we set the source to be a list (called VLAN-IPs) and we set the interface we want to use for overloading, remembering to add the very important word "*overload*", otherwise only one entry from the access-list would be translated. The full command ends up as:

```
Gateway(config)#ip nat inside source list VLAN-IPs interface Ethernet0/0
overload
Gateway(config)#
```

Now we need to create the access list:

```
Gateway(config)#ip access-list standard VLAN-IPs
Gateway(config-std-nacl)#permit 10.10.1.1
Gateway(config-std-nacl)#permit 10.20.1.1
Gateway(config-std-nacl)#permit 10.30.1.1
Gateway(config-std-nacl)#permit 10.40.1.1
Gateway(config-std-nacl)#permit 10.50.1.1
Gateway(config-std-nacl)#
```

Now let's test by pinging 100.100.100.100 from VLAN 10, 30, 40 and 50 on SW1 and from VLAN 20 on SW2:

```
SW1#ping 100.100.100.100 source vlan 10
Type escape sequence to abort.
Sending 5, 100-byte ICMP Echos to 100.100.100.100:
Packet sent with a source address of 10.10.1.1
```

```
!!!!!
Success rate is 100 percent (5/5)
SW1#
SW1#ping 100.100.100.100 source vlan 30
Type escape sequence to abort.
Sending 5, 100-byte ICMP Echos to 100.100.100.100:
Packet sent with a source address of 10.30.1.1
!!!!!
Success rate is 100 percent (5/5)
SW1#
SW1#ping 100.100.100.100 source vlan 40
Type escape sequence to abort.
Sending 5, 100-byte ICMP Echos to 100.100.100.100:
Packet sent with a source address of 10.40.1.1
!!!!!
Success rate is 100 percent (5/5)
SW1#
SW1#ping 100.100.100.100 source vlan 50
Type escape sequence to abort.
Sending 5, 100-byte ICMP Echos to 100.100.100.100:
Packet sent with a source address of 10.50.1.1
!!!!!
Success rate is 100 percent (5/5)
SW1#

SW2#ping 100.100.100.100 so vlan 20
Type escape sequence to abort.
Sending 5, 100-byte ICMP Echos to 100.100.100.100:
Packet sent with a source address of 10.20.1.1
!!!!!
Success rate is 100 percent (5/5)
SW2#
```

Completely successful! We can see the translations in the translation table as well:

```
Gateway(config-std-nacl)#do sh ip nat transl
Pro Inside global      Inside local Outside local    Outside global
icmp 192.168.20.254:14 10.10.1.1:14 100.100.100.100:14 100.100.100.100:14
--- 192.168.20.11      10.10.1.3    ---                ---
icmp 192.168.20.254:1  10.20.1.1:1  100.100.100.100:1  100.100.100.100:1
icmp 192.168.20.254:2  10.20.1.1:2  100.100.100.100:2  100.100.100.100:2
--- 192.168.20.21      10.20.1.21   ---                ---
icmp 192.168.20.254:15 10.30.1.1:15 100.100.100.100:15 100.100.100.100:15
--- 192.168.20.10      10.30.1.3    ---                ---
icmp 192.168.20.254:16 10.40.1.1:16 100.100.100.100:16 100.100.100.100:16
icmp 192.168.20.254:17 10.50.1.1:17 100.100.100.100:17 100.100.100.100:17
Gateway(config-std-nacl)#
```

Now we have three different implementations of NAT all working together. You know what also helps us work together? Having synchronized clocks.

5.6 Configure and verify NTP as a client

NTP is easy to set up, but extremely important. NTP is the Network Time Protocol; its function is to allow devices to all have the same time, gained from one authoritative source. Why is this important? Most devices have an internal clock. We can set the clock manually on each device and, assuming nothing goes wrong with the battery, the devices will keep to the same time. Then we have different time zones, GMT, UTC, PST and so on, so we need to, on a per-device basic, ensure that these are all correct. This all means administrative overhead on your part, having to manually configure these settings. NTP solves this issue. Having a constant time source is also important for auditing and security. It is a mandatory requirement of some processes, such as PCI compliance. This is so that in the event of an issue, when you are looking through the logs trying to correlate issues on more than one device, you can accurately pinpoint when the problem occurred. In addition, if you use a centralized authentication system, such as Microsoft's Active Directory, the device's clock must be within 5 minutes of the Active Directory's clock.

NTP is an old technology, having been in place since the early 1980's. It runs as a client-server model, and uses UDP as its transport mechanism, on port 123. The current version of NTP is NTPv4. NTP uses hierarchical layers, known as stratums. Stratum 0 is the highest layer, and here are the likes of atomic, GPS or radio clocks. These are reference clocks. Stratum 1 clocks are synchronized to stratum 0 clocks to a few microseconds, they can peer with other stratum 1 clocks, and are known as primary time-servers. Stratum 2 clocks synchronize to stratum 1 clocks and peer to other stratum 2 clocks. Then we have stratum 3 clocks that synchronize to stratum 2, and peer to other stratum 3 servers, and we continue this method right down to stratum 15. Stratum 16 means that we are not synchronized with an upper layer clock, so it will use its own internal clock as the time source.

An NTP client will poll a server in order to synchronize its clock. It is best practice to have more than one NTP server, so the client can poll each of them.

Our goal is to configure and verify NTP as a client. In order to do this we need an NTP source though. Setting a router up as an NTP server is a simple one-line command:

```
Server(config)#ntp master 1
Server(config)#
```

Here we instruct the server that it is now an authoritative time source, at stratum 1. If we had another NTP server at the same stratum, we could peer with that, using the command "*ntp peer <peer IP address>*".

To configure a device as an NTP client we point it to the NTP server:

```
Bob-PC(config)#ntp server 10.20.1.21
Bob-PC(config)#
```

How do we know we are getting the time from NTP? There are a couple of ways. We can look at the clock in detail, using the command "*show clock detail*":

```
Bob-PC(config)#do sh clock detail
21:13:33.928 UTC Wed Nov 4 2015
Time source is NTP
Bob-PC(config)#
```

You can see that it says our time source is NTP. We can also look at the NTP associations, and see that we are synchronizing to the right server (denoted by the *), and that the server is a stratum 1 source (the "st" column).

```
Bob-PC(config)#do show ntp associations

   address      ref clock   st   when  poll reach  delay  offset   disp
*~10.20.1.21  .LOCL.       1     41    64     1   2.000   0.000 189.44
 * sys.peer, # selected, + candidate, - outlyer, x falseticker, ~
configured
Bob-PC(config)#
```

We can also look at the status, using "*show ntp status*":

```
Bob-PC(config)#do sh ntp status
Clock is synchronized, stratum 2, reference is 10.20.1.21
nominal freq is 250.0000 Hz, actual freq is 250.0000 Hz, precision is 2**10
ntp uptime is 41300 (1/100 of seconds), resolution is 4000
reference time is D9E4F4F6.B9999B98 (21:19:50.725 UTC Wed Nov 4 2015)
clock offset is 0.5000 msec, root delay is 1.00 msec
root dispersion is 7.45 msec, peer dispersion is 3.56 msec
loopfilter state is 'CTRL' (Normal Controlled Loop), drift is 0.000000007 s/s
system poll interval is 64, last update was 7 sec ago.
Bob-PC(config)#
```

We can see that we are synchronized and that we are a stratum 2 source now. We could extend this out and have all of our LAN devices synchronizing to the server, which will certainly keep the people in compliance and security happy. For the moment though, we will press on and implement some high availability.

5.7 Recognize High availability (FHRP)

Although we only need to "recognize" high availability, it is more fun to implement. Therefore, that is what we will do now. We will implement high availability (HA), using First Hop Redundancy Protocols

(FHRP). The caveat is, though, we will only have limited success in our environment. There are three technologies we will discuss, VRRP, HSRP and GLBP. VRRP and HSRP are pretty similar as we will see, and the way they operate is the reason why we will only have limited success. Both work by creating a virtual MAC address and this does not play well with our virtualized environment. It is only as of October 2015 that Cisco's VIRL added support for VRRP and HSRP to its IOSv line, and even then it comes under the heading of "Features likely to work for IOSv", i.e. they have had some success, but when people say it doesn't work, they can reply with "well, we only said likely". If you can get to test this out (on IOSv, or real switches, then do). Regardless, let's give it a go.

To make life a little easier, we will switch Dave and Bob back to static addresses:

```
Bob-PC(config)#int e0/0
Bob-PC(config-if)#ip add 10.30.1.21 255.255.255.0
Bob-PC(config-if)#ip route 0.0.0.0 0.0.0.0 10.30.1.1
Bob-PC(config)#

Dave-PC(config)#int e0/0
Dave-PC(config-if)#ip add 10.10.1.21 255.255.255.0
Dave-PC(config-if)#ip route 0.0.0.0 0.0.0.0 10.10.1.1
Dave-PC(config)#
```

Let's start with VRRP.

5.7.a VRRP

VRRP is the industry standard; its full name is Virtual Router Redundancy Protocol. It shares many concepts with HSRP, but the two are not compatible. As the name suggests, we have a "virtual router", this will be the one using the 10.30.1.1 address currently used by VLAN 30. SW1 and SW2 will act as the master and backup for this virtual router. The virtual router that is created gets a MAC address of 00-00-5e-00-01-XX, where XX is the Virtual Router Identifier, or VRID. In order to assign the 10.30.1.1 address to the virtual router, we need to reconfigure our switches, and we will be using .2 and .3 as their IP addresses:

```
SW2(config)#int vlan 30
SW2(config-if)#ip add 10.30.1.3 255.255.255.0
SW2(config-if)#end

SW1(config-if)#int vlan 30
SW1(config-if)#ip add 10.30.1.2 255.255.255.0
SW1(config-if)#end
```

We start to create our virtual router under the VLAN interface by creating a VRRP group. We can have 255 groups in total. The group number can be anything you like, but for ease of reading, we will number the same as the VLAN. We assign an IP address to this group, but note that we do not need to include a subnet mask, as the switch will use the subnet mask from the main IP address.

```
SW1(config-if)#vrrp ?
  <1-255>  Group number

SW1(config-if)#vrrp 30 ?
  authentication  Authentication string
  description     Group specific description
  ip              Enable Virtual Router Redundancy Protocol (VRRP) for IP
  preempt         Enable preemption of lower priority Master
  priority        Priority of this VRRP group
  timers          Set the VRRP timers
  track           Event Tracking

SW1(config-if)#vrrp 30 ip 10.30.1.1
SW1(config-if)#
```

Once we have enabled this command we will see VRRP working:

```
SW1(config-if)#
%VRRP-6-STATECHANGE: Vl30 Grp 30 state Init -> Backup
%VRRP-6-STATECHANGE: Vl30 Grp 30 state Backup -> Init
SW1(config-if)#
%VRRP-6-STATECHANGE: Vl30 Grp 30 state Init -> Backup
%VRRP-6-STATECHANGE: Vl30 Grp 30 state Backup -> Master
SW1(config-if)#
```

In order to set up the master and backup roles we need to assign a priority. The default priority is 100, but as we want to be in control we will assign our own priority of 110, which means it is more preferred (as the master role) than 100. If we leave both routers at the default priority the one with the highest IP address will become the master (the same is true for HSRP).

```
SW1(config-if)#vrrp 30 priority 110
SW1(config-if)#
```

In a moment we will set up SW2, but at this point SW1 is already sending VRRP multicast traffic on VLAN 30 (using the multicast address 224.0.0.18 and IP protocol number 112). SW2 will act as the backup for the virtual router in the event that anything should happen to SW1. If SW1 goes down, SW2 will take over. If SW1 comes back, it will take over the master role again (which is known as "preemption"). This all sounds great, but what if SW1 has an underlying issue and starts to reboot again? Ideally, we want to know that our switches are stable before we hand control back over. For this reason we should put in a delay, known a "preempt delay". We will set this at a minimum of 60 seconds:

```
SW1(config-if)#vrrp 30 preempt ?
  delay  Wait before preempting
  <cr>

SW1(config-if)#vrrp 30 preempt delay ?
  minimum  Delay at least this long

SW1(config-if)#vrrp 30 preempt delay minimum 60
SW1(config-if)#
```

Now let's set up SW2:

```
SW2(config-if)#vrrp 30 ip 10.30.1.1
%VRRP-6-STATECHANGE: Vl30 Grp 30 state Init -> Backup
%VRRP-6-STATECHANGE: Vl30 Grp 30 state Backup -> Init
%VRRP-6-STATECHANGE: Vl30 Grp 30 state Init -> Backup
SW2(config-if)#vrrp 30 priority 90
```

I have set the priority to 90, this way I can easily see from the configuration who should be the master and who should be the backup. We can see state changes above and we go to our intended role of Backup.

If we wanted to see more details about our VRRP groups, we can use "show vrrp brief":

```
SW1(config-if)#do sh vrrp brief
Interface     Grp Pri Time  Own Pre State    Master addr    Group addr
Vl30          30  110 3570      Y   Master   10.30.1.2      10.30.1.1
SW1(config-if)#
```

We can look further into the group by looking at the VLAN interface for VRRP:

```
SW1(config-if)#do sh vrrp interface vlan 30
Vlan30 - Group 30
  State is Master
  Virtual IP address is 10.30.1.1
  Virtual MAC address is 0000.5e00.011e
  Advertisement interval is 1.000 sec
  Preemption enabled, delay min 60 secs
  Priority is 110
  Master Router is 10.30.1.2 (local), priority is 110
  Master Advertisement interval is 1.000 sec
  Master Down interval is 3.570 sec

SW1(config-if)#
```

Here we can see the state (master), the Virtual IP address and the Virtual MAC address, which means our VRID is 1e. 1e in hex gives us 0001 1110. If we work this out, we can find the binary value of 1e (refer to Appendix C for a table of Hex to binary conversion):

128	64	32	16	8	4	2	1
0	0	0	1	1	1	1	0

When we add these up, we get to a familiar number: 30 (16+8+4+2 = 30). Therefore, the VRID will use the group number, converted into binary.

If we had more VRRP groups set up, we can look at all of them using the command "*show vrrp all*". If we look at SW2, we can see that it has the state of "backup", and that the master router is SW1:

```
SW2(config-if)#do sh vrrp interface vl30
Vlan30 — Group 30
  State is Backup
  Virtual IP address is 10.30.1.1
  Virtual MAC address is 0000.5e00.011e
  Advertisement interval is 1.000 sec
  Preemption enabled
  Priority is 90
  Master Router is 10.30.1.2, priority is 110
  Master Advertisement interval is 1.000 sec
  Master Down interval is 3.648 sec (expires in 3.188 sec)

SW2(config-if)#
```

Because of the inherent issues with virtualized router and switches at the layer-2 level, we will have some issues. in that Bob can see (via ARP) the VRRP MAC address for 10.30.1.1, but he will not be able to reach it:

```
Bob-PC#sh arp
Protocol  Address          Age (min)  Hardware Addr   Type   Interface
Internet  10.30.1.1               0   0000.5e00.011e  ARPA   Ethernet0/0
Internet  10.30.1.21              -   aabb.cc00.0e00  ARPA   Ethernet0/0
Bob-PC#ping 10.30.1.1
Type escape sequence to abort.
Sending 5, 100-byte ICMP Echos to 10.30.1.1:
.....
Success rate is 0 percent (0/5)
Bob-PC#
```

Sadly, he won't be able to get to it, but again this is an issue with trying to virtualize advanced layer-2 functions.

5.7.b HSRP

HSRP, the Hot Router Standby Protocol, is very similar to VRRP. We switch the word *"vrrp"* for *"standby"* and the commands are the same. Again, we need to start by reconfiguring our existing VLAN IP addresses before we get started:

```
SW2(config-if)#int vlan 10
SW2(config-if)#
SW2(config-if)#ip add 10.10.1.3 255.255.255.0
SW2(config-if)#

SW1(config-if)#int vlan 10
SW1(config-if)#
SW1(config-if)#ip add 10.10.1.2 255.255.255.0
SW1(config-if)#
```

Like VRRP, we need to start by specifying the group number and by default we can have 255 groups:

```
SW1(config-if)#standby ?
  <0-255>         group number
  arp             HSRP interface ARP subcommands
  authentication  Authentication
  delay           HSRP initialisation delay
  follow          Name of HSRP group to follow
  ip              Enable HSRP IPv4 and set the virtual IP address
  ipv6            Enable HSRP IPv6
  mac-address     Virtual MAC address
  mac-refresh     Refresh MAC cache on switch by periodically sending
packet from virtual mac address
  name            Redundancy name string
  preempt         Overthrow lower priority Active routers
  priority        Priority level
  redirect        Configure sending of ICMP Redirect messages with an
HSRP virtual IP address as the gateway IP address
  timers          Hello and hold timers
  track           Priority tracking
  use-bia         HSRP uses interface's burned in address
  version         HSRP version

SW1(config-if)#standby
```

If 255 groups are not enough for your environment, we can increase this to 4095 groups. All we need to do is change our version from version 1 to version 2 (but we'll put it back to version 1):

```
SW1(config-if)#standby version ?
  <1-2>  Version number
```

```
SW1(config-if)#standby version 2
SW1(config-if)#standby ?
  <0-4095>         group number
  arp              HSRP interface ARP subcommands
  authentication   Authentication
  delay            HSRP initialisation delay
  follow           Name of HSRP group to follow
  ip               Enable HSRP IPv4 and set the virtual IP address
  ipv6             Enable HSRP IPv6
  mac-address      Virtual MAC address
  mac-refresh      Refresh MAC cache on switch by periodically sending packet from
virtual mac address
  name             Redundancy name string
  preempt          Overthrow lower priority Active routers
  priority         Priority level
  redirect         Configure sending of ICMP Redirect messages with an HSRP
virtual IP address as the gateway IP address
  timers           Hello and hold timers
  track            Priority tracking
  use-bia          HSRP uses interface's burned in address
  version          HSRP version

SW1(config-if)#standby version 1
```

We will use HSRP group 10, to match our VLAN and, like we did with VRRP, assign an IP address:

```
SW1(config-if)#standby 10 ip 10.10.1.1
```

We then assign a priority

```
SW1(config-if)#standby 10 priority 110
%HSRP-5-STATECHANGE: Vlan10 Grp 10 state Standby -> Active
SW1(config-if)#
```

Immediately we move into the Active state. We have started to send HSRP multicast traffic to 224.0.0.2 on UDP port 1985. HSRP version 2 uses the multicast address 224.0.0.102 and the same port number of 1985. We also set the pre-emption delay to 60 seconds:

```
SW1(config-if)#standby 10 preempt delay minimum 60
```

We set up SW2, but put the priority at 90 :

```
SW2(config)#int vlan 10
SW2(config-if)#standby 10 ip 10.10.1.1
SW2(config-if)#standby 10 priority 90
%HSRP-5-STATECHANGE: Vlan10 Grp 10 state Speak -> Standby
SW2(config-if)#
```

SW2 goes into the standby state. We can use the command *"show standby"* to list the details for all of our HSRP groups, or to look at an individual one; we can use *"show standby vlan <vlan id>"*:

```
SW1(config-if)#
SW1(config-if)#do sh standby
Vlan10 - Group 10
  State is Active
    2 state changes, last state change 00:42:56
  Virtual IP address is 10.10.1.1
  Active virtual MAC address is 0000.0c07.ac0a
    Local virtual MAC address is 0000.0c07.ac0a (v1 default)
  Hello time 3 sec, hold time 10 sec
    Next hello sent in 0.256 secs
  Preemption enabled, delay min 60 secs
  Active router is local
  Standby router is 10.10.1.3, priority 90 (expires in 9.472 sec)
  Priority 110 (configured 110)
  Group name is "hsrp-Vl10-10" (default)
SW1(config-if)#

SW2(config-if)#
SW2(config-if)#do sh standby vlan 10
Vlan10 - Group 10
  State is Standby
    13 state changes, last state change 00:04:35
  Virtual IP address is 10.10.1.1
  Active virtual MAC address is 0000.0c07.ac0a
    Local virtual MAC address is 0000.0c07.ac0a (v1 default)
  Hello time 3 sec, hold time 10 sec
    Next hello sent in 1.040 secs
  Preemption disabled
  Active router is 10.10.1.2, priority 110 (expires in 8.208 sec)
  Standby router is local
  Priority 90 (configured 90)
  Group name is "hsrp-Vl10-10" (default)
SW2(config-if)#
```

Like VRRP, we have a Virtual MAC address. For HSRP version 1 it is 00:00:0c:07:ac:XX, and for version 2 it is 00:00:0c:9f:fX:XX. Both will use the HSRP group for the X's. Our Virtual MAC address ends with 0a, which equals 10:

128	64	32	16	8	4	2	1
0	0	0	0	1	0	1	0

We can see the Virtual MAC address from Dave's PC, but again due to issues with virtualizing layer-2 we won't have much luck actually using it.

```
Dave-PC(config-if)#do sh arp
Protocol  Address         Age (min)  Hardware Addr   Type   Interface
Internet  10.10.1.21          -      aabb.cc00.0500  ARPA   Ethernet0/0
Dave-PC(config-if)#do ping 10.10.1.1
Type escape sequence to abort.
Sending 5, 100-byte ICMP Echos to 10.10.1.1:
.....
Success rate is 0 percent (0/5)
Dave-PC(config-if)#do sh arp
Protocol  Address         Age (min)  Hardware Addr   Type   Interface
Internet  10.10.1.1           0      0000.0c07.ac0a  ARPA   Ethernet0/0
Internet  10.10.1.21          -      aabb.cc00.0500  ARPA   Ethernet0/0
Dave-PC(config-if)#
```

Before we move on to GLBP, which should be a little more reliable in our virtual environment, let's take a moment to talk about the group numbering. Group numbers must be the same between all members of the same group and this is pretty obvious. Now, imagine you have two separate sites. Both have the same set of VLANs (VLAN 10, 20, 30 and so on), but they have different IP addressing schemes. Site 1 uses 1.1.X.0/24, where X is the VLAN and site 2 uses 1.2.X.0/24. It makes sense to work from a standard process, if you number your HSRP (or VRRP) groups after the VLAN they are for, then you have a standard template and anyone can understand what is going on, which is a good thing. Now let's throw a spanner in the works. What if these two sites are connected by a layer-2 connection? Then we will start to see some issues. I call it HSRP-crosstalk. One site, with its completely separate set of IP addresses will actually take control, based on the priority; either configured or because of the highest IP address. So you will get into a scenario where the virtual IP address for an HSRP group in site 2 actually uses the IP address for the same HSRP group in site 1, effectively breaking your network at layers-2 and 3. So, if you have multiple sites, are using a first-hop redundancy protocol such as HSRP or VRRP, and have or may have a layer-2 connection between the sites, do bear this in mind and work out a sensible, but protected, group numbering system early on.

There is nothing worse when doing maintenance in one site and taking down another by mistake! Anyway, enough of the scary stories, let's look at GLBP.

5.7.c GLBP

GLBP (Gateway Load Balancing Protocol) is also Cisco proprietary, the commands to set up GLBP are pretty identical to both VRRP and HSRP, but the difference between GLBP and the others is in the title, it performs load balancing. We can have two or more routers in a GLBP group and they will answer the traffic requests in turn, so with three routers the traffic serving would be R1, R2, R3 and then back to R1, R2 and so on. This is the default round-robin approach to load balancing – each router taking an equal share of the traffic. We can play with the weights of each of the routers, making one more preferred and therefore taking more of the traffic, but round-robin works well in most scenarios.

GLBP elects an Active Virtual Gateway (AVG) for each group, another router will be placed in the Standby state, and if we have more, these will be placed in the listen state. The AVG gives each member of the group, including itself, a virtual MAC address, and now we have Active Virtual Forwarders (AVFs).

We start by changing the IP address on SW2 (from 10.20.1.2 to 10.20.1.3). We do not need to change the IP address on SW1:

```
SW2(config)#int vlan 20
SW2(config-if)#ip add 10.20.1.3 255.255.255.0
SW2(config-if)#
```

Now we can set up GLBP, starting with the group number (matching our VLAN) and the IP address.

```
SW1(config-if)#int vlan 20
SW1(config-if)#glbp 20 ip 10.20.1.1
SW1(config-if)#
%GLBP-6-STATECHANGE: Vlan20 Grp 20 state Speak -> Active
SW1(config-if)
```

We then set the priority:

```
SW1(config-if)#glbp 20 priority 110
SW1(config-if)#
%GLBP-6-FWDSTATECHANGE: Vlan20 Grp 20 Fwd 1 state Listen -> Active
SW1(config-if)#
```

And the delay:

```
SW1(config-if)#glbp 20 preempt delay minimum 60
SW1(config-if)#
```

By now SW1 is happily sending GLBP multicast traffic to 224.0.0.102, using UDP port 3222. Note that this is the same address as HSRP version 2, but the port number is different, which, again, is multiplexing at work. SW2 is set up similarly:

```
SW2(config-if)#glbp 20 ip 10.20.1.1
SW2(config-if)#glbp 20 priority 90
SW2(config-if)#
```

SW2 changes its state to Active:

```
SW2(config-if)#
%GLBP-6-FWDSTATECHANGE: Vlan20 Grp 20 Fwd 2 state Listen -> Active
SW2(config-if)#
```

We can check our GBLP groups using the command *"show glbp"*:

```
SW1(config-if)#
SW1(config-if)#do sh glbp
Vlan20 - Group 20
  State is Active
    1 state change, last state change 00:01:27
  Virtual IP address is 10.20.1.1
  Hello time 3 sec, hold time 10 sec
    Next hello sent in 0.960 secs
  Redirect time 600 sec, forwarder timeout 14400 sec
  Preemption enabled, min delay 60 sec
  Active is local
  Standby is 10.20.1.3, priority 90 (expires in 9.152 sec)
  Priority 110 (configured)
  Weighting 100 (default 100), thresholds: lower 1, upper 100
  Load balancing: round-robin
  Group members:
    aabb.cc80.0100 (10.20.1.2) local
    aabb.cc80.0200 (10.20.1.3)
  There are 2 forwarders (1 active)
  Forwarder 1
    State is Active
      1 state change, last state change 00:01:16
    MAC address is 0007.b400.1401 (default)
    Owner ID is aabb.cc80.0100
    Redirection enabled
    Preemption enabled, min delay 30 sec
    Active is local, weighting 100
  Forwarder 2
    State is Listen
    MAC address is 0007.b400.1402 (learnt)
    Owner ID is aabb.cc80.0200
    Redirection enabled, 599.168 sec remaining (maximum 600 sec)
    Time to live: 14399.168 sec (maximum 14400 sec)
    Preemption enabled, min delay 30 sec
    Active is 10.20.1.3 (primary), weighting 100 (expires in 10.240 sec)
SW1(config-if)#
```

We can see that SW1 is active, it knows that the standby router is SW2 (10.20.1.3) and that SW2's priority is 90. SW1's priority is 110, and we are using round-robin load balancing. We have two group members, identified by their MAC addresses. SW1 is currently forwarding and SW2 is listening. We also have the virtual MAC addresses; 0007.b400.1401 for SW1 and 0007.b400.1402 for SW2. The MAC address does use the group number, just like HSRP and VRRP. 14 in hex can be converted to binary (0001 0100) which when added up equals 20:

128	64	32	16	8	4	2	1
0	0	0	1	0	1	0	0

If we look at the ARP cache on Server, we can see that it has picked up the Virtual MAC address for the GLBP group, however we do not have reachability:

```
Server#sh arp
Protocol  Address      Age (min)  Hardware Addr   Type   Interface
Internet  10.20.1.1          43   0007.b400.1402  ARPA   Ethernet1/0
Internet  10.20.1.2          22   aabb.cc80.0100  ARPA   Ethernet1/0
Internet  10.20.1.3          22   aabb.cc80.0200  ARPA   Ethernet1/0
Internet  10.20.1.21          -   aabb.cc00.0601  ARPA   Ethernet1/0
Internet  10.20.1.254        43   aabb.cc00.0820  ARPA   Ethernet1/0
Server#ping 10.20.1.1
Type escape sequence to abort.
Sending 5, 100-byte ICMP Echos to 10.20.1.1, timeout is 2 seconds:
.....
Success rate is 0 percent (0/5)
Server#
```

Remember though, that the failures here would not be seen on physical equipment, or as and when Cisco supplies a virtual image that fully supports these technologies at a layer-2 level. This is solely a problem with running a virtualized lab that depends on more advanced layer-2 functionality. These technologies run very well on physical equipment. With this in mind, let's revert our configurations and finish this section.

Removing the HSRP and VRRP configuration is very simple; we just use the command "*no <protocol> <group number>*":

```
SW1(config-if)#int vlan 10
SW1(config-if)#no standby 10
SW1(config-if)#
%HSRP-5-STATECHANGE: Vlan10 Grp 10 state Active -> Disabled
SW1(config-if)#do sh run int vlan 10 | b interface
interface Vlan10
 ip address 10.10.1.2 255.255.255.0
 ip helper-address 10.20.1.21
end

SW1(config-if)#

SW2(config-if)#int vlan 10
SW2(config-if)#no standby 10
SW2(config-if)#
%HSRP-5-STATECHANGE: Vlan10 Grp 10 state Active -> Disabled
SW2(config-if)#
```

We then set SW1 up with the original IP address:

```
SW1(config-if)#ip add 10.10.1.1 255.255.255.0
SW1(config-if)#
%HSRP-5-STATECHANGE: Vlan10 Grp 10 state Active -> Disabled
SW1(config-if)#do sh run int vlan 10 | b interface
interface Vlan10
  ip address 10.10.1.1 255.255.255.0
  ip helper-address 10.20.1.21
end
SW1(config-if)#
```

We remove VRRP in the same way:

```
SW2(config-if)#int vlan 30
SW2(config-if)#no vrrp 30
SW2(config-if)#do sh run int vlan 30 | b interface
interface Vlan30
  ip address 10.30.1.3 255.255.255.0
end
SW2(config-if)#

SW1(config-if)#int vlan 30
SW1(config-if)#no vrrp 30
SW1(config-if)#ip add 10.30.1.1 255.255.255.0
SW1(config-if)#do sh run int vlan 30 | b interface
interface Vlan30
  ip address 10.30.1.1 255.255.255.0
  ip helper-address 10.20.1.21
end
SW1(config-if)#
```

Removing GLBP takes little more work, as we have to remove all of the commands:

```
SW1(config-if)#int vlan 20
SW1(config-if)#no glbp 20
% Incomplete command.

SW1(config-if)#no glbp 20 ?
  authentication   Authentication method
  client-cache     Client cache
  forwarder        Forwarder configuration
  ip               Enable group and set virtual IP address
  ipv6             Enable group for IPv6 and set the virtual IPv6 address
  load-balancing   Load balancing method
  name             Redundancy name
  preempt          Overthrow lower priority designated routers
```

```
      priority        Priority level
      timers          Adjust GLBP timers
      weighting       Gateway weighting and tracking

SW1(config-if)#no glbp 20 ip 10.20.1.1
SW1(config-if)#do sh run int vlan 20 | b interface
interface Vlan20
 ip address 10.20.1.2 255.255.255.0
 glbp 20 priority 110
 glbp 20 preempt delay minimum 60
end
SW1(config-if)#no glbp 20 priority 110
SW1(config-if)#no glbp 20 preempt delay minimum 60
SW1(config-if)#do sh run int vlan 20 | b interface
interface Vlan20
 ip address 10.20.1.2 255.255.255.0
end
SW1(config-if)#
```

Let's do the same for SW2:

```
SW2(config-if)#int vlan 20
SW2(config-if)#no glbp 20 ip 10.20.1.1
%GLBP-6-FWDSTATECHANGE: Vlan20 Grp 20 Fwd 1 state Active -> Init
%GLBP-6-FWDSTATECHANGE: Vlan20 Grp 20 Fwd 2 state Active -> Init
%GLBP-6-STATECHANGE: Vlan20 Grp 20 state Active -> Disabled
SW2(config-if)#no glbp 20 pri 90
SW2(config-if)#do sh run int vlan 20 | b interface
interface Vlan20
 ip address 10.20.1.3 255.255.255.0
end

SW2(config-if)#ip add 10.20.1.1 255.255.255.0
SW2(config-if)#
```

Let's check our IP addresses now (excluding any interfaces without an assigned IP address):

```
SW1(config-if)#do sh ip int bri | e unas
Interface      IP-Address      OK? Method Status       Protocol
Loopback0      3.1.1.1         YES NVRAM  up           up
Vlan1          10.1.1.1        YES NVRAM  up           up
Vlan10         10.10.1.1       YES NVRAM  up           up
Vlan20         10.20.1.2       YES NVRAM  up           up
Vlan30         10.30.1.1       YES NVRAM  up           up
Vlan40         10.40.1.1       YES NVRAM  up           up
Vlan50         10.50.1.1       YES NVRAM  up           up
SW1(config-if)#
```

```
SW2(config-if)#do sh ip int bri | e unas
Interface       IP-Address      OK? Method Status         Protocol
Loopback0       3.1.1.2         YES manual up             up
Vlan1           10.1.1.2        YES manual up             up
Vlan10          10.10.1.3       YES manual up             up
Vlan20          10.20.1.1       YES manual up             up
Vlan30          10.30.1.3       YES manual up             up
SW2(config-if)#
```

We will end this chapter with a look at how we can monitor our network through syslog and SNMP.

5.8 Configure and verify syslog

Earlier we made sure that our devices were using the same time settings (well, one of them at least). This was important for a number of reasons, primarily for authentication (a devices clock need to be within 5 minutes of an Active Directory controllers clock for authentication) and for when we need to produce a timeline of events if we have a security incident. The second part of this is to make sure that we are correctly logging events. This is done through a system called "syslog".

Syslog gathers messages about system events, such as someone logging into a device, access rule hits and interface state transitions (like an interface being switched off, or a cable being unplugged). These can then be sent to a syslog server, actually, they should be sent, and all your device logs should be in one place. There are a number of such servers available, such as the open source (free) Syslog-ng, Kiwi Syslog server by SolarWinds, or paid for servers such as LogRythym or AlienVault. These allow the logs to be aggregated and stored. Routers and switches only have a finite amount of storage, so moving the syslog from the devices on to a centralised management platform is key to proper network security and auditing.

Syslog can be configured to collect information at different levels. These levels range from 0 to 7, with 0 just telling us about emergencies and 7 giving us absolutely everything. Finding a happy medium between these two is vital, but you may need to switch between levels depending on the scenario and requirements of other divisions. The different levels are shown in the following table:

Level	Severity	Description
0	Emergency	System is unusable
1	Alert	Immediate action needed
2	Critical	Critical conditions
3	Error	Errors
4	Warning	Warnings
5	Notice	Normal but significant conditions
6	Informational	Informational
7	Debug	Everything

If you type *"show logging"* on Server you will see a lot of information. Too much to paste in here, but there are some key things we should look at:

```
Server#show logging
Syslog logging: enabled (0 messages dropped, 3 messages rate-limited, 0
flushes, 0 overruns, xml disabled, filtering disabled)

No Active Message Discriminator.



No Inactive Message Discriminator.


    Console logging: level debugging, 55 messages logged, xml disabled,
                    filtering disabled
    Monitor logging: level debugging, 0 messages logged, xml disabled,
                    filtering disabled
    Buffer logging:  level debugging, 55 messages logged, xml disabled,
                    filtering disabled
    Exception Logging: size (4096 bytes)
    Count and timestamp logging messages: disabled
    Persistent logging: disabled

No active filter modules.

    Trap logging: level informational, 58 message lines logged
        Logging Source-Interface:        VRF Name:

Log Buffer (4096 bytes):
```

Here we can see that logging is enabled. Our default level is "debugging". We have 55 console messages, which are also stored in the buffer (though this is dependent on the IOS version), and our buffer is 4096 bytes, which is not very large; hence the need to stored them elsewhere.

The level we are logging at means we capture a lot of information, much more than we need to. If this is the case then we can change the logging level using the command *"logging <destination> <level>"*:

```
Server(config)#logging console warnings
Server(config)#
```

Now if we look at the *"show logging"* command, we can see that our logging level has changed:

```
Server(config)#do show logging | i logging
Syslog logging: enabled (0 messages dropped, 3 messages rate-limited, 0
flushes, 0 overruns, xml disabled, filtering disabled)
    Console logging: level warnings, 55 messages logged, xml disabled,
```

```
    Monitor logging: level debugging, 0 messages logged, xml disabled,
    Buffer logging:  level debugging, 55 messages logged, xml disabled,
    Count and timestamp logging messages: disabled
    Persistent logging: disabled
    Trap logging: level informational, 58 message lines logged
Server(config)#
```

We can also use the numerical equivalent to specify our desired logging level:

```
Server(config)#logging buffered 4
Server(config)#do show logging | i logging
Syslog logging: enabled (0 messages dropped, 3 messages rate-limited, 0
flushes, 0 overruns, xml disabled, filtering disabled)
    Console logging: level warnings, 55 messages logged, xml disabled,
    Monitor logging: level debugging, 0 messages logged, xml disabled,
    Buffer logging:  level warnings, 55 messages logged, xml disabled,
    Count and timestamp logging messages: disabled
    Persistent logging: disabled
    Trap logging: level informational, 58 message lines logged
Server(config)#
```

By setting our level to 4 (Warning) we also capture levels 0, 1, 2 and 3 as well. If we set our logging level to 6 (Informational) we would capture levels 0 – 5 as well.

If we wanted to (and we should) send our logs to a different destination (a syslog server for instance) we can use the following:

```
Server(config)#logging host 1.2.3.4
Server(config)#
```

Now we can see that our logs will be sent to the host with the IP address 1.2.3.4:

```
Server(config)#do sh logging
<truncated>
    Trap logging: level informational, 61 message lines logged
        Logging to 1.2.3.4  (udp port 514, audit disabled,
            link up),
            1 message lines logged,
            0 message lines rate-limited,
            0 message lines dropped-by-MD,
            xml disabled, sequence number disabled
            filtering disabled
        Logging Source-Interface:       VRF Name:

Log Buffer (4096 bytes):
Server(config)#
```

Consistency is important. If we have a device with more than one interface then we should make sure that the syslog server knows exactly where the logs it receives are coming from, otherwise we lose the ability to correlate logs from a source correctly, such as if we have a router that can get to the syslog server via one of two IGP-learned routes and one of these routes goes down. In this scenario, the alternate route through a different interface will be used, and we would lose the ability to correlate the logs sourced from the old address with those sourced from the new address. To mitigate this we can tell the router to send its logs from a loopback interface (assuming that the loopback interface is also being advertised):

```
Server(config)#logging source-interface loopback 0
Server(config)#
```

We do not have a loopback interface on Server, so we will source our logs from the e0/0 interface:

```
Server(config)#logging source-interface ethernet 0/0
Server(config)#
```

We can then check this by looking at the logging configuration:

```
Server(config)#do sh logging | b Source
        Logging Source-Interface:       VRF Name:
        Ethernet0/0

Log Buffer (4096 bytes):
Server(config)#
```

Let's put some of our logs to good use.

5.8.a Utilize syslog output

Our network has been running for quite a while now, we have made many changes and implemented lots of new things. This means we should have some pretty decent logs to look at. Let's look at a few from ISP. I have truncated the output and removed the dates and times, interface up/down notifications and the lines saying "Configured from console" to make it easier to read:

```
ISP#sh logging
<truncated>

Log Buffer (4096 bytes):
RA on Ethernet1/1 has been previously configured on another interface
%IPV6_ND-6-ADDRESS: 2001:DB8::/64 can not generate auto-configured
address on Ethernet0/1, 2001:DB8::A8BB:CCFF:FE00:C10 already configured
using a different method
%SSH-5-ENABLED: SSH 2.0 has been enabled
```

```
%OSPF-5-ADJCHG: Process 1, Nbr 1.2.1.1 on Ethernet1/1 from LOADING to
FULL, Loading Done
%OSPFv3-5-ADJCHG: Process 1, Nbr 1.2.1.1 on Ethernet1/1 from LOADING to
FULL, Loading Done
%DUAL-5-NBRCHANGE: EIGRP-IPv4 1: Neighbor 192.168.1.2 (Ethernet0/1) is
up: new adjacency
%SEC-6-IPACCESSLOGP: list PermitSSH-Telnet denied tcp
192.168.20.254(45420) -> 0.0.0.0(23), 1 packet
%OSPF-5-ADJCHG: Process 1, Nbr 50.50.50.50 on Ethernet0/0 from LOADING to
FULL, Loading Done
ISP#
```

Barring the removal of the timestamps, we still have some good information. We can break these down into its respective components.

First, we have the facility that generated the log:

```
%IPV6_ND
%SSH
%OSPF
%OSPFv3
%DUAL
%SEC
```

Then we have the severity level:

```
-6-
-5-
```

Then a mnemonic, which is a short description explaining the event:

```
ADDRESS
ENABLED
ADJCHG
NBRCHANGE
IPACCESSLOGP
```

And the description of the event:

```
: SSH 2.0 has been enabled
: Process 1, Nbr 1.2.1.1 on Ethernet1/1 from LOADING to FULL, Loading
Done
: EIGRP-IPv4 1: Neighbor 192.168.1.2 (Ethernet0/1) is up: new adjacency
: list PermitSSH-Telnet denied tcp 192.168.1.2(64743) -> 0.0.0.0(22), 1
packet
```

With this information we can finely tune what level we log at, making sure we gather the information we need.

5.9 Describe SNMP v2 and v3

SNMP (Simple Network Management Protocol) is something every engineer should understand. "What is SNMP used for?" is one of my basic questions whenever I am interviewing someone looking to fill a networking role. I wouldn't be looking for the in-depth ins-and-outs, but would expect a basic understanding.

SNMP works at the application layer, we have SNMP managers and agents. SNMP uses databases called MIBs, Management Information Bases, to organize pretty much everything about a device and to tell a manager where to look for data.

Because network devices are all pretty similar, in that they have interfaces, CPUs, memory, fans and power, we can have fairly generalized MIBs, and then more device specific MIBs, which look after the variations in devices, such as VPN capabilities or reporting on the amount of free space on a hard disk.

An SNMP manager is used to pull out data (referred to as GET) and also to write data or perform actions such as shutting down an interface (SET). These abilities depend on whether we have read-only (RO) or read-write (RW) access. SNMP uses communities, which is a fancy name for a password. The community (password) we use dictates what we can do. We can also send data directly from an agent in the event that we see a particular event (such as an interface going down). This is known as a trap. The SNMP manager can then react based on the information it either pulls out of the agent, or is sent by the agent. Ideally, we should have some traps configured. SNMP managers usually poll a device (use GET messages to pull out data) every so often. Too many requests can cause the agent (router) to suffer (CPU usage, spending more time answering SNMP requests than routing traffic), too few requests means we can miss vital information. We can help the balance by sending traps (notifications) when an event occurs, because you want to be alerted if an interface goes down straight away, rather than waiting ten minutes for the manager to pull in the status information for the interface. The manager then can perform actions, such as updating a status page (go from green to amber or red), or send an email alert. With SNMPv3 came Inform messages, which perform an acknowledgement to trap messages.

There are a number of free and paid-for SNMP managers (also known as Network Management Stations, or NMS), such as Nagios, Cisco Prime and Zabbix. We can also use a basic Linux machine and install snmpget on it to query devices.

In order to be able to query a device we need to set up SNMP. We will set up two communities; one will be read-only, the other will be read-write. Because allowing read-write access does open up security issues, both will then have their access limited down to our NMS, which will be the mythical 1.2.3.4 that we are also sending Server's syslogs to.

We will start by setting our contact information and our location:

```
ISP(config)#snmp-server contact Me@Once
ISP(config)#snmp-server location The Internet
ISP(config)#
```

This is not essential, but is useful. We then set our read-only (RO) community, which is called MyROCommunity:

```
ISP(config)#snmp-server community MyROCommunity ro
ISP(config)#
```

Setting a read-write (RW) community is just as simple:

```
ISP(config)#snmp-server community MyRWCommunity rw
ISP(config)#
```

This is a fine setup, but lacks security. Because of this, we can attach an access list to the community settings to limit down our exposure. We will create a standard access list, called PermitNMS, for this. First let's check our existing ACLs to make sure we don't (accidentally) edit an existing one:

```
ISP(config)#do sh access-lists
Extended IP access list PermitSSH-Telnet
    10 permit tcp host 192.168.20.254 any eq 22 (2 matches)
    20 permit tcp host 192.168.20.254 any eq telnet (2 matches)
    50 deny tcp any any log (4 matches)
ISP(config)#
```

That's fine, now let's create the access list.

```
ISP(config)#ip access-list standard PermitNMS
ISP(config-std-nacl)#permit 1.2.3.4
ISP(config-std-nacl)#exit
ISP(config)#
```

If we look at the options for our community configuration, we can see that we can add the new ACL using its name, but also note that we do not get an option to use the extended ACLs (100-199 or 2000-2699):

```
ISP(config)#snmp-server community MyROCommunity ro ?
  <1-99>       Std IP accesslist allowing access with this community string
  <1300-1999>  Expanded IP accesslist allowing access with this community
               string
  WORD         Access-list name
  ipv6         Specify IPv6 Named Access-List
  <cr>
```

```
ISP(config)#snmp-server community MyROCommunity ro PermitNMS
ISP(config)#snmp-server community MyRWCommunity rw PermitNMS
```

Lastly, we should make sure that in doing this we have overwritten our existing commands with the new ones:

```
ISP(config)#do sh run | i community
snmp-server community MyROCommunity RO PermitNMS
snmp-server community MyRWCommunity RW PermitNMS
ISP(config)#
```

We have implemented SNMP version 2c here (as well as v1 by default); 2c is the preferred version of SNMPv2. While we have implemented a basic form of security, SNMPv2c is still inherently insecure. SNMPv3 is now the standard version of SNMP. It adds much more security by way of integrity, authentication and encryption. Integrity means that a packet has not been tampered with (intercepted) along the route, authentication means we know who the packet came from, and encryption means that the packet cannot be read if it is intercepted. We do not have to use all of these features, as SNMPv3 offers three different security modes:

Mode	Command	Authentication method	Encryption
noAuthNoPriv	noauth	Username	None
authNoPriv	auth	MD5 or SHA	None
authPriv	priv	MD5 or SHA	3DES, DES-56 or AES

We can set up SNMPv3 using the following:

```
ISP(config)#snmp-server group MySNMPv3Group v3 priv
ISP(config)#snmp-server user MySNMPUser MySNMPv3Group v3
ISP(config)#
Configuring snmpv3 USM user, persisting snmpEngineBoots. Please Wait...

ISP(config)#
```

SNMPv3 needs users and groups. Above we have the most basic commands we can use to create both. We have not assigned any authentication to it, nor do we have any encryption:

```
ISP(config)#do sh snmp user

User name: MySNMPUser
Engine ID: 800000090300AABBCC000C00
storage-type: nonvolatile          active
Authentication Protocol: None
Privacy Protocol: None
Group-name: MySNMPGroup
ISP(config)#
```

We can change the configuration to use a password:

```
ISP(config)#snmp-server user MySNMPUser MySNMPGroup v3 auth sha MyPassword
```

Now we have a SHA encrypted authentication password:

```
ISP(config)#do sh snmp user

User name: MySNMPUser
Engine ID: 800000090300AABBCC000C00
storage-type: nonvolatile        active
Authentication Protocol: SHA
Privacy Protocol: None
Group-name: MySNMPGroup

ISP(config)#
```

If we want to add privacy we can, but now the command gets pretty long, and the beginning of the command is replaced with a dollar sign:

```
ISP(config)#$ user MySNMPUser MySNMPGroup v3 auth sha MyPassword priv ?
   3des  Use 168 bit 3DES algorithm for encryption
   aes   Use AES algorithm for encryption
   des   Use 56 bit DES algorithm for encryption

ISP(config)#$ user MySNMPUser MySNMPGroup v3 auth sha MyPassword priv
3des ?
   WORD  privacy password for user

ISP(config)#
```

This makes it a little harder to read, so what we can do here is increase the width of our console to accommodate more characters:

```
ISP(config)#line con 0
ISP(config-line)#width 255
ISP(config-line)#exit
ISP(config)#
```

Now you'll find that the command is fully readable and not truncated:

```
ISP(config)#snmp-server user MySNMPUser MySNMPGroup v3 auth sha
MyPassword priv 3des MyPrivPassword
ISP(config)#
```

Now, with this extremely long command, we have a fully secured SNMPv3 user:

```
ISP(config)#do sh snmp user

User name: MySNMPUser
Engine ID: 800000090300AABBCC000C00
storage-type: nonvolatile        active
Authentication Protocol: SHA
Privacy Protocol: 3DES
Group-name: MySNMPGroup

ISP(config)#
```

So that's how we setup SNMP on a router, but how do we actually use it? The easiest way to get started with SNMP is to install snmpwalk on a Linux machine, you get the added bonus of learning a little bit of Linux and that is never a bad thing (though you can install snmpwalk on Windows as well, just head over to http://www.net-snmp.org/).

Once snmpwalk is installed you can then run a command such as:

```
snmpwalk -v 2c -c MyROCommunity 100.100.100.100 1.3.6.1.2.1.1.5.0
```

This will use SNMP v2c with the community string "MyROCommunity". We are querying a device with the IP address of 100.100.100.100, and we are looking for the OID 1.3.6.1.2.1.1.5.

To use SNMPv3 we would use the command

```
snmpwalk -v 3 -l authPriv -u MySNMPUser -a SHA -A MyPassword -x 3DES -X
MyPrivPassword 100.100.100.100 1.3.6.1.2.1.1.5.0
```

OID stands for Object Identifier. These OIDs live within the MIBs we mentioned at the start. The OID referenced above comes from the SNMPv2-MIB and is the OID for the object sysName. Because objects may have more than one entry (such as multiple interfaces), they are assigned a number, starting from zero. So when we want to query the hostname (1.3.6.1.2.1.1.5) we also need to specify the index (0). Thankfully there is a much easier way to do this, and that is by using the named value in the MIB, such as sysName.0:

```
snmpwalk -v 2c -c MyROCommunity 100.100.100.100 sysName.0
```

The actual usage of which would look like this:

```
[root@box ~]# snmpwalk -v 2c -c MyRoCommunity 100.100.100.100
1.3.6.1.2.1.1.5.0
SNMPv2-MIB::sysName.0 = STRING: SW1.802101.com
[root@box ~]#
```

The sysName OID lives underneath a much bigger OID, called "system". We can query this either by using:

```
snmpwalk -v 2c -c MyROCommunity 100.100.100.100 1.3.6.1.2.1.1
```

Or:

```
snmpwalk -v 2c -c MyROCommunity 100.100.100.100 system
```

This will return a much larger set of results:

```
[root@box ~]# snmpwalk -v 2c -c MyROCommunity 100.100.100.100 system
SNMPv2-MIB::sysDescr.0 = STRING: Cisco IOS Software, C3750E Software
(C3750E-UNIVERSALK9-M), Version 12.2(55)SE3, RELEASE SOFTWARE (fc1)

Technical Support: http://www.cisco.com/techsupport

Copyright (c) 1986-2011 by Cisco Systems, Inc.

Compiled Thu 05-May-11 15:40 by prod_rel_team
SNMPv2-MIB::sysObjectID.0 = OID: SNMPv2-SMI::enterprises.9.1.516
DISMAN-EVENT-MIB::sysUpTimeInstance = Timeticks: (4140334814) 479 days,
4:55:48.14
SNMPv2-MIB::sysContact.0 = STRING: stu@802101.com
SNMPv2-MIB::sysName.0 = STRING: SW1.802101.com
SNMPv2-MIB::sysLocation.0 = STRING: Bedfordshire
SNMPv2-MIB::sysServices.0 = INTEGER: 6
<truncated>
```

We are going to leave SNMP now, but do spend some time getting to know it, it is one of the tools that will help you going forward. It's like one of those cool tools Batman has in his utility belt; you should have it in yours too.

Next up; Security!

6. Network Device Security

This chapter accounts for 10% of the CCNA exam weighting. We have actually covered a large section of this already, so the first section (6.1) will act as a nice bit of revision. The second section (6.2) will be a bit new and then in section 6.3 and 6.4 we'll do a few more access control lists.

6.1 Configure and verify network device security features

We looked at device security quite early on, first in section 2.3 and then again in section 4.2. Cisco like this topic so much they have it three times on the syllabus, so it must be important.

6.1.a Device password security

Every device should have a password on each of its management entry points. We can connect to a router through the physical console port, or through the VTY lines. These should have a password and we should also require a password when switching between levels (such as going to privileged exec mode). The easiest way to set this up is through the *"enable"* command.

6.1.b Enable secret vs. enable

The enable command sets a password for moving from user exec mode to privileged exec mode. We can have the standard enable password command, or the enable secret command:

```
ISP(config)#enable ?
  algorithm-type  Algorithm to use for hashing the plaintext 'enable' secret
  password        Assign the privileged level password (MAX of 25 characters)
  secret          Assign the privileged level secret (MAX of 25 characters)
ISP(config)#enable
```

The first command is used as follows:

```
ISP(config)#enable password Secret123
```

This will be stored in clear-text though, but with service password-encryption enabled, we can see that the password is encrypted:

```
ISP(config)#do sh run | s password
service password-encryption
enable password 7 15210E0F162F3F757A6075
username admin password 7 121A0C041104
ISP(config)#
```

The second option is used like this, but note that some versions of the IOS will not let us use the same password as the enable password:

```
ISP(config)#enable secret Cisco123
ISP(config)#do sh run | s enable
enable secret 5 $1$O5cr$4CLF2q5QTFbJQ3tpJsKJl0
enable password 7 04680E051D24581F5B4A
 ipv6 enable
ISP(config)#
```

The enable secret password uses MD5 hashing to hide it. The difference between the two is that type 7 passwords can be decrypted using a few lines of JavaScript (or any other programming language):

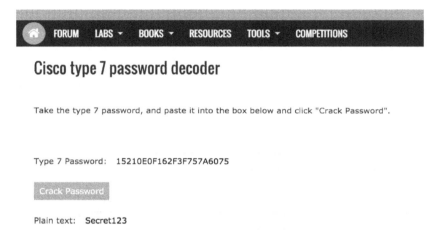

Type 5 passwords are much harder to crack. So, wherever possible always use enable secret.

6.1.c Transport

Transport refers to the protocols we allow in and out of our VTY and AUX lines, and what we allow out from our console port.

```
ISP(config)#line vty 0 4
ISP(config-line)#transport ?
  input      Define which protocols to use when connecting to the
terminal server
  output     Define which protocols to use for outgoing connections
  preferred  Specify the preferred protocol to use

ISP(config-line)#transport
```

We can disable entry to the VTY lines completely using the command *"no transport input"*:

```
ISP(config-line)#no transport input
```

However, this would be a little silly as you then lose remote management. Instead to make the VTY lines secure, we should disable telnet and enable SSH.

6.1.c.1 disable telnet
6.1.c.2 SSH

Disabling telnet on a VTY line and enabling SSH is performed through one command:

```
ISP(config-line)#transport input ssh
```

By explicitly enabling SSH, we are disabling Telnet. We can check the VTY lines and see that they are set to only use SSH:

```
ISP(config-line)#do sh run | s vty
line vty 0 4
 access-class PermitSSH-Telnet in
 exec-timeout 0 0
 login local
 transport input ssh
ISP(config-line)#
```

Apart from being secure by nature when compared to Telnet, there are many more commands that can be configured to increase our SSH security. We can set a timeout, so that if anyone walks away from his or her open connection, it will close after 90 seconds:

```
ISP(config)#ip ssh time-out 90
```

We can make sure we don't let people have too many goes at guessing passwords (known as brute-force attacks). Three goes and they have to try to connect again:

```
ISP(config)#ip ssh authentication-retries 3
```

We can make sure that we don't let too many people on at the same time. Here we set the amount of times SSH sessions can be started (at the same time) to two:

```
ISP(config)#ip ssh maxstartups 2
```

Lastly, we can log SSH activity:

```
ISP(config)#ip ssh logging events
```

An alternative approach to the above command would be:

```
ISP(config)#login on-failure log
ISP(config)#login on-success log
ISP(config)#
```

That's SSH covered, so how else can we secure our VTY lines?

6.1.d VTYs

As we saw from our look at ACLs earlier, the VTY lines listen to all our interfaces, physical and virtual. Meaning for every IP address we have, we have one more avenue of attack. Therefore, we should protect the VTY lines as much as possible. We can instruct them to log user off after a period of inactivity. We turned this off earlier on our console lines (because it is a little annoying to have to log back in again), but we are more security conscious now and so we are going to turn it on for our VTY lines, setting the timeout period to five minutes:

```
ISP(config)#line vty 0 4
ISP(config-line)#exec-timeout ?
  <0-35791>  Timeout in minutes

ISP(config-line)#exec-timeout 5 ?
  <0-2147483>  Timeout in seconds
  <cr>

ISP(config-line)#exec-timeout 5 0
ISP(config-line)#exit
```

We can (and should) also limit down what hosts and networks can access our VTY lines, by using an ACL and the access-class command. So, now we have secured our remote access we should be fine, right? Not so much. We have bigger concerns.

6.1.e physical security

As much as we can secure ourselves against remote attacks, we need to make sure that our physical security is equally strong. Social engineering (getting passwords or physical access to equipment) is a massive threat to companies and end-users alike.

It can be easy to gain physical access to an office, so make sure that your equipment is locked away in a dedicated server room (or comms rooms depending on which terminology you prefer) and that there is sufficient security to ensure only those who should have access actually have access. Review the need for people to have access every six months and make sure that if you use a combination lock that the code is changed regularly. When staff leave, or ID badges are lost, make sure this is reported immediately and access is revoked.

If someone does manage to get access to your devices, we should make it as hard as possible for them to see what passwords we are using.

6.1.f service password

Passwords have a tendency to be written down on post-it notes, kept in text documents and so on, which is less than ideal. The Cisco IOS is no different and will store passwords in clear text:

```
Dave-PC#sh run | i password
no service password-encryption
Dave-PC#conf t
Dave-PC(config)#username Dave password Dave123
Dave-PC(config)#enable password cisco
Dave-PC(config)#
```

Our passwords are stored in clear text:

```
Dave-PC(config)#do sh run | i password
no service password-encryption
enable password cisco
username Dave password 0 Dave123
Dave-PC(config)#
```

We can encrypt these though, using the command *"service password-encryption"*:

```
Dave-PC(config)#service password-encryption
Dave-PC(config)#do sh run | i password
service password-encryption
enable password 7 121A0C041104
username Dave password 7 1433131D09557878
Dave-PC(config)#
```

Whilst this is still not as secure as using enable secret passwords, it is better than clear text. It will cause the sneaky intruder literally seconds of frustration (whilst they Google "Cisco type-7 decoder"). Let's make their job harder by setting a secret password:

```
Dave-PC(config)#username Dave secret Dave123
ERROR: Can not have both a user password and a user secret.
Please choose one or the other.
Dave-PC(config)#no username Dave password Dave123
```

```
This operation will remove all username related configurations with same
name.Do you want to continue? [confirm]
Dave-PC(config)#username Dave secret Dave123
Dave-PC(config)#do sh run | i password
service password-encryption
enable password 7 121A0C041104
Dave-PC(config)#do sh run | i usern
username Dave secret 5 $1$1uDf$t1JWaI3jReS.dUCMls/E3/
Dave-PC(config)#no enable password
Dave-PC(config)#enable secret cisco
Dave-PC(config)#do sh run | i password
service password-encryption
Dave-PC(config)#do sh run | i secret
enable secret 5 $1$Cne5$cD8flqP1.ye6wd5X1dI2b1
username Dave secret 5 $1$POP$NghcjR8KC2paQeqIUN9t71
Dave-PC(config)#
```

Ideally though, the attacker would not even be able to see type 5 passwords. From the above configuration we can deduce that there is a user called Dave. It is therefore likely that Dave has accounts on other devices (that may not be as secure). Dave also provides us with a target for social engineering. For this reason we should remove the reliance on local accounts and instead have our devices use a centralized (external) authentication system.

6.1.g Describe external authentication methods

External authentication can take a number of forms, these are RADIUS, TACACS+ and Kerberos (used by Microsoft's Active Directory). Authentication is only one part of the equation though; usually we would discuss this as part of AAA, which stands for Authentication, Authorization and Accounting. We can authenticate (login), we are authorized (we can run commands) and these actions are logged (accounted). We do not have to implement all parts of AAA and this does come down to requirements (by the Company), or cost. There are free implementations of RADIUS (FreeRadius) and TACACS+ (TacPlus or TACACS.net for Windows).

The basic premise behind all of them is that we move the authentication of users away from the router and onto a third-party system. It makes managing multiple routers much easier, and reduces the security risk. We always still need one local account, to be used in the event that we cannot communicate with the AAA server, but this is deemed an acceptable risk.

Radius (Remote Authentication Dial-In User Service), when running under Microsoft's Internet Authentication Service (IAS), can also read from Active Directory and allows the separation of users and user groups to functions (i.e. we can let them log in at a specific level), by passing different strings, known as AV pairs, back to the router.

For us, though, we only need a basic understanding of what external authentication allows us to achieve. There is another topic we need to look at in more depth; port security.

6.2 Configure and verify Switch Port Security

We saw back in chapter 2 that attaching an older switch to the network could overwrite our VLAN configuration, we could protect this using VTP passwords, but this still does not prevent someone adding a switch to a network and guessing passwords. We need to be able to react quicker to such an intrusion and we can do this by implementing port security on our switches.

Port security offers a way to limit which devices (based on their MAC address), or how many devices, connect into our network on a particular port. We use it to keep track of MAC addresses, and react if the number of MAC addresses on an interface changes. We can react to changes beyond our allowed configuration (known as a "violation") in a number of ways; we can shutdown the port, restrict it or protect it, and we'll cover these different actions in a moment.

We are back to Bob now. Bob is very important; he has his own VLAN and is very security conscious. We still are not sure what Bob does exactly, but he's been around for years and no one wants to be the one to question him. Bob has become a bit worried about people connecting into his VLAN and has asked us to implement port-security.

The basic command we need to start with is "*switchport port-security*"; this enables the function under the interface:

```
SW3(config)#int e0/0
SW3(config-if)#switchport port-security
SW3(config-if)#
```

On its own this achieves very little, but we do need this command, if we enter the commands we are going to look at next, without adding this command, they will have no effect. The next step is for the switch to always know who Bob is.

6.2.a Sticky MAC

When we implement port-security, we start to build up a database. We can limit the amount of entries in this database from anywhere between 1 and 4097 entries. Therefore, what happens if we say that five people are allowed to connect to a port (they could be connected via a switch attached to the port)? The first five will be OK. Bob can run a number of devices, and if anyone else tries to connect, they will not be able to. This is fine and achieves the desired goal. But, what if someone were to reboot the switch and attach to the port before Bob can get his devices attached?

Thankfully, we can make MAC addresses "sticky", and the switch will remember them after a reboot. Therefore, we can attach the devices we want to have attached and instruct the switch to remember them, or we can enter our own chosen MAC addresses into the database:

```
SW3(config-if)#switchport port-security mac-address ?
  H.H.H    48 bit mac address
  sticky   Configure dynamic secure addresses as sticky

SW3(config-if)#switchport port-security mac-address sticky
SW3(config-if)#
```

The learned addresses should then be converted into an entry under the interface. We can check what MAC address Bob's PC has by looking for the "bia" (Burned In Address):

```
Bob-PC#sh int e0/0 | i bia
  Hardware is AmdP2, address is aabb.cc00.0e00 (bia aabb.cc00.0e00)
Bob-PC#
```

Now if we look at the port configuration on the switch, we can see this:

```
SW3(config-if)#do sh run int e0/0
Building configuration...

Current configuration : 224 bytes
!
interface Ethernet0/0
 switchport access vlan 30
 switchport mode access
 switchport port-security
 switchport port-security mac-address sticky
 switchport port-security mac-address sticky aabb.cc00.0e00
 duplex auto
end

SW3(config-if)#
```

Bob is now safe in the event that the switch is rebooted.

6.2.b MAC address limitation

Bob has asked us to prove that this is a secure measure; he is concerned that people can still connect to his port and gain access to the network.

To show him this is the case, we can look at the port security settings using the command "*show port-security*":

```
SW3(config-if)#do sh port-security
Secure Port MaxSecureAddr CurrentAddr SecurityViolation Security Action
                 (Count)       (Count)       (Count)
--------------------------------------------------------------------------
     Et0/0            1             1                0         Shutdown
--------------------------------------------------------------------------
Total Addresses in System (excluding one mac per port)    : 0
Max Addresses limit in System (excluding one mac per port) : 4096

SW3(config-if)#switchport port-security ?
  aging         Port-security aging commands
  mac-address   Secure mac address
  maximum       Max secure addresses
  violation     Security violation mode
  <cr>

SW3(config-if)#
```

Here we can see that we only allow one address on interface E0/0 (MaxSecureAddr) and currently we are at the limit (CurrentAddr). We have not exceeded the limit (SecurityViolation), but if we do then the default action is to shutdown the port (Security Action).

Bob asks us if we can prove this. We can, by changing his MAC address:

```
Bob-PC(config)#int e0/0
Bob-PC(config-if)#mac-address aabb.cc00.0e01
Bob-PC(config-if)#shut
Bob-PC(config-if)#
Bob-PC(config-if)#no shut
Bob-PC(config-if)#
```

Pretty quickly, we can see the port being shut down:

```
SW3(config-if)#
%PM-4-ERR_DISABLE: psecure-violation error detected on Et0/0, putting
Et0/0 in err-disable state
SW3(config-if)#
%PORT_SECURITY-2-PSECURE_VIOLATION: Security violation occurred, caused
by MAC address aabb.cc00.0e01 on port Ethernet0/0.
%LINEPROTO-5-UPDOWN: Line protocol on Interface Ethernet0/0, changed
state to down
SW3(config-if)#
%LINK-3-UPDOWN: Interface Ethernet0/0, changed state to down
SW3(config-if)#
```

This works as desired. Bob, however, needs a couple of devices to be able to connect, so asks you to increase the Maximum Secure Addresses count:

```
SW3(config-if)#switchport port-security maximum 3
SW3(config-if)#do sh port-security
Secure Port MaxSecureAddr CurrentAddr SecurityViolation  Security Action
              (Count)      (Count)      (Count)
----------------------------------------------------------------------
    Et0/0          3            1             1             Shutdown
----------------------------------------------------------------------
Total Addresses in System (excluding one mac per port)    : 0
Max Addresses limit in System (excluding one mac per port) : 4096

SW3(config-if)#
```

The port is still shut down though. We need to manually shut and no shut the port to get it back up:

```
SW3(config-if)#shut
%LINK-5-CHANGED: Interface Ethernet0/0, changed state to administratively
down
SW3(config-if)#no shut
SW3(config-if)#
%LINK-3-UPDOWN: Interface Ethernet0/0, changed state to up
%LINEPROTO-5-UPDOWN: Line protocol on Interface Ethernet0/0, changed
state to up
SW3(config-if)#
```

If we return to the interface configuration, we can see that the new MAC address has been added to the configuration:

```
SW3(config-if)#do sh run int e0/0
Building configuration...

Current configuration : 320 bytes
!
interface Ethernet0/0
 switchport access vlan 30
 switchport mode access
 switchport port-security
 switchport port-security maximum 3
 switchport port-security mac-address sticky
 switchport port-security mac-address sticky aabb.cc00.0e00
 switchport port-security mac-address sticky aabb.cc00.0e01
 duplex auto
end

SW3(config-if)#
```

We currently have two addresses in the database:

```
SW3(config-if)#do sh port-security
Secure Port MaxSecureAddr CurrentAddr SecurityViolation  Security Action
              (Count)       (Count)       (Count)
--------------------------------------------------------------------------
     Et0/0         3             2             1          Shutdown
--------------------------------------------------------------------------
Total Addresses in System (excluding one mac per port)    : 1
Max Addresses limit in System (excluding one mac per port) : 4096

SW3(config-if)#
```

These have both been learned dynamically, but we can also add static addresses.

6.2.c static/dynamic

Bob needs one more device added to the system, he does not have it with him so it cannot be learnt dynamically, but he does (somewhat oddly) know the MAC address.

We saw this as an option just a moment ago, and now we will add one:

```
SW3(config-if)#switchport port-security mac-address ?
  H.H.H   48 bit mac address
  sticky  Configure dynamic secure addresses as sticky

SW3(config-if)#switchport port-security mac-address aabb.cc00.0e02
SW3(config-if)#
```

We can see this as a command under the interface (like the two dynamically learned ones):

```
SW3(config-if)#do sh run int e0/0 | b interface
interface Ethernet0/0
 switchport access vlan 30
 switchport mode access
 switchport port-security
 switchport port-security maximum 3
 switchport port-security mac-address sticky
 switchport port-security mac-address sticky aabb.cc00.0e00
 switchport port-security mac-address sticky aabb.cc00.0e01
 switchport port-security mac-address aabb.cc00.0e02
 duplex auto
end

SW3(config-if)#
```

We are also now at our limit:

```
SW3(config-if)#do sh port-security
Secure Port MaxSecureAddr CurrentAddr SecurityViolation  Security Action
               (Count)       (Count)       (Count)
--------------------------------------------------------------------------
     Et0/0           3             3               1            Shutdown
--------------------------------------------------------------------------
Total Addresses in System (excluding one mac per port)    : 2
Max Addresses limit in System (excluding one mac per port) : 4096

SW3(config-if)#
```

We can now change Bob's MAC address to the new static entry and see that we do not trigger a violation:

```
Bob-PC(config-if)#mac-address aabb.cc00.0e02
```

If we change it once more, we trigger a violation:

```
Bob-PC(config-if)#mac-address aabb.cc00.0e03

SW3(config-if)#
%PM-4-ERR_DISABLE: psecure-violation error detected on Et0/0, putting
Et0/0 in err-disable state
%PORT_SECURITY-2-PSECURE_VIOLATION: Security violation occurred, caused
by MAC address aabb.cc00.0e03 on port Ethernet0/0.
%LINEPROTO-5-UPDOWN: Line protocol on Interface Ethernet0/0, changed
state to down
%LINK-3-UPDOWN: Interface Ethernet0/0, changed state to down
SW3(config-if)#
```

Let's have a look at the different violation options we have.

6.2.d violation modes

Above we can see that the default security violation action is to shutdown the port. It is one of three options:

```
SW3(config-if)#switchport port-security violation ?
  protect    Security violation protect mode
  restrict   Security violation restrict mode
  shutdown   Security violation shutdown mode

SW3(config-if)#switchport port-security violation
```

During this shutdown, the port is placed in an "err-disabled" state.

6.2.d (i) err disable
6.2.d (ii) shutdown

The default action of shutdown places our port in an err-disabled state:

```
%PM-4-ERR_DISABLE: psecure-violation error detected on Et0/0, putting
Et0/0 in err-disable state
```

Err-disable means we have to manually shut down the port and then un-shut it to bring it back up again.

We can though instruct the switch to recover, once the violation is fixed. This should be discussed further down, according to the syllabus, but it makes sense to talk about it now. We do this through errdisable recovery and we can use this feature to recover from a number of actions that would cause a switchport to be disabled (for formatting reasons I have removed the words "Enable timer to" from the descriptions, apart from the first one):

```
SW3(config-if)#errdisable recovery cause ?
  all                   Enable timer to recover from all causes
  arp-inspection        recover from arp inspection error disable state
  bpduguard             recover from BPDU Guard error disable state
  channel-misconfig     recover from channel misconfig disable state
  dhcp-rate-limit       recover from dhcp-rate-limit error disable state
  dtp-flap              recover from dtp-flap error disable state
  gbic-invalid          recover from invalid GBIC error disable state
  l2ptguard             recover from l2protocol-tunnel error state
  link-flap             recover from link-flap error disable state
  link-monitor-failure  recover from link monitoring failure
  loopback              recover from loopback disable state
  mac-limit             recover from mac limit disable state
  oam-remote-failure    recover from remote failure detected by OAM
  pagp-flap             recover from pagp-flap error disable state
  psecure-violation     recover from psecure violation disable state
  security-violation    recover from 802.1x violation disable state
  storm-control         recover from storm-control error disable state
  udld                  recover from udld error disable state
  unicast-flood         recover from unicast flood disable state
  vmps                  recover from vmps shutdown error disable state

SW3(config-if)#errdisable recovery cause
```

If we wanted to set our switches to recover from a port-security violation, we would use the command:

```
SW3(config-if)#errdisable recovery cause psecure-violation
SW3(config)#
```

We can test this by putting Bob back to his original MAC address and clearing the errdisable state

```
Bob-PC(config)#int e0/0
Bob-PC(config-if)#
Bob-PC(config-if)#mac-address aabb.cc00.0e00
Bob-PC(config-if)#

SW3(config-if)#int e0/0
SW3(config-if)#
SW3(config-if)#shut
SW3(config-if)#
%LINK-5-CHANGED: Interface Ethernet0/0, changed state to administratively
down
SW3(config-if)#no shut
SW3(config-if)#
%LINK-3-UPDOWN: Interface Ethernet0/0, changed state to up
%LINEPROTO-5-UPDOWN: Line protocol on Interface Ethernet0/0, changed
state to up
SW3(config-if)#
```

Now we can generate a violation, watch the port being placed in the errdisabled state, and then change it back again:

```
Bob-PC(config-if)#mac-address aabb.cc00.0e03
Bob-PC(config-if)#

SW3(config-if)#
%PM-4-ERR_DISABLE: psecure-violation error detected on Et0/0, putting
Et0/0 in err-disable state
SW3(config-if)#
%PORT_SECURITY-2-PSECURE_VIOLATION: Security violation occurred, caused
by MAC address aabb.cc00.0e03 on port Ethernet0/0.
%LINEPROTO-5-UPDOWN: Line protocol on Interface Ethernet0/0, changed
state to down
SW3(config-if)#
%LINK-3-UPDOWN: Interface Ethernet0/0, changed state to down
SW3(config-if)#

Bob-PC(config-if)#mac-address aabb.cc00.0e00
Bob-PC(config-if)#
```

Recovery is not instantaneous. There is a timer of 300 seconds, though this can be changed using the command *"errdisable recovery interval"* (I have truncated some of the output):

```
SW3(config-if)#do sh errdisable recovery
Recovery Status                        Timer Status
---------------                        ------------
udld                                   Disabled
bpduguard                              Disabled
security-violation                     Disabled
<truncated>

Timer interval: 300 seconds

Interfaces that will be enabled at the next timeout:

Interface          Errdisable reason          Time left(sec)
---------          -----------------          --------------
Et0/0              psecure-violation          205

SW3(config-if)#
```

Once the timer expires, in the "Time left(sec)" column, the port is brought back up again:

```
SW3(config)#
%PM-4-ERR_RECOVER: Attempting to recover from psecure-violation err-
disable state on Et0/0
SW3(config)#
%LINK-3-UPDOWN: Interface Ethernet0/0, changed state to up
%LINEPROTO-5-UPDOWN: Line protocol on Interface Ethernet0/0, changed
state to up
SW3(config)#
```

The shutdown option is definitely the best of the available options, it offers more flexibility, and when joined with errdisable recovery, reduces administrative work on your part.

6.2.d(iii) protect restrict

The other two modes are protect and restrict. With both of these modes, the interface will stay in the connected state and both will discard the frames from the offending device.

The difference between the two is when it comes to how the violations are logged. Protect will not increase the violations counter, but restrict will.

Wherever possible, use the shutdown method.

This covers ports we know devices are connected to, but what about the other ports that are, as yet, unused?

6.2.e Shutdown unused ports

Yep, it's as simple as that. If a port is not being used, then shut it down. This is only part of the equation though, as we will see in a moment, but it makes sense. If a port is shut down then people connecting to it will not be able to get anywhere.

6.2.f err disable recovery

We discussed this just now in conjunction with err-disable.

6.2.g Assign unused ports in unused VLANs

As well as shutting down the ports that are not being used, they should be placed in a separate VLAN. Pick a VLAN with a nice, easy to remember number, such as 999, 666, 1024 or something like that and put the ports into that.

You can make life easier on yourself by starting every switch basic configuration like this. Once you have named your switch and added it to the network as a VTP client (with your unused VLAN being sent by VTP), then use the range command to assign all the ports apart from the one that connects the switch to the rest of the network) to the unused VLAN. The commands would look similar to:

```
SwitchA(config)#interface range gi0/1 - 47
SwitchA(config-if-range)#switchport mode access
SwitchA(config-if-range)#switchport access vlan 999
SwitchA(config-if-range)#shutdown
```

This would leave port gi0/48 as your trunk to the rest of the network, the access ports would then be shut down and in a separate VLAN. You would then have to manually move them into the correct VLAN and unshut them when you add a device to that switch.

6.2.h Putting Native VLAN to other than VLAN 1

There is a security exploit known as VLAN hopping. This uses VLAN tagging, by having two tags. When we configure an access port, we specify an access vlan (*switchport access vlan X*). If a port is in the native VLAN then the switch does not apply a VLAN tag. Therefore, an attacker can add another VLAN tag to the packet, in order to get around any filtering on the switches. Imagine we have a secure server in VLAN 30. Only devices in VLAN 30 can access this server. The attacker creates a packet with two VLAN headers. One is for the legitimate traffic, VLAN 1 to VLAN 1 (the default native VLAN), but the other VLAN header is for VLAN 30. The switch will remove the first VLAN header (VLAN 1) and passes the packet, the second switch would then see the VLAN 30 header and pass the packet. The secure server will receive the packet, as it is perceived to have come from another host in the secure VLAN.

Network hacking aside, there is a basic reason to make sure that native VLANs always match. If we have a switch whose native VLAN is VLAN 1, and another whose native VLAN is VLAN 2, then both will send untagged frames. Therefore switch 2 will pass frames belonging to VLAN 1 from the first switch into VLAN 2, and Switch 2 will send native VLAN 2 frames to Switch 1, which will end up in VLAN 1 on the first switch.

As well as making sure that the native VLAN matches, we should also use a separate VLAN as the native VLAN. We can set this up by adding VLAN 999 to SW4 (our VTP server):

```
SW4(config)#vlan 999
SW4(config-vlan)#name DungeonVLAN
SW4(config-vlan)#exit
% Applying VLAN changes may take few minutes.  Please wait...

SW4(config)#
```

Making sure that it is picked up by SW3 and SW2:

```
SW3(config-if)#do sh vlan | i 9
999  DungeonVLAN                          active
999  enet  100999    1500  -     -     -     -    -         0         0
SW3(config-if)#

SW2#sh vlan | i 9
999  DungeonVLAN                          active
999  enet  100999    1500  -     -     -     -    -         0         0
SW2#
```

Then we can place the trunk between SW3 and SW2 into this VLAN.

```
SW3(config-if)#int e1/1
SW3(config-if)#switchport trunk native vlan 999
SW3(config-if)#

SW2(config-if)#int e1/1
SW2(config-if)#switchport trunk native vlan 999
SW2(config-if)#
```

For the last part of this chapter, we will revisit access control lists.

6.3 Configure and verify ACLs to filter network traffic

We have a server that, at the moment, just looks after DHCP. We'll add DNS in a later chapter, but for the moment let's give it something else to serve up; Web pages.

Enabling the (very basic) web server that comes with the router is just a case of using the command
"*ip http server*":

```
Server(config)#ip http server
Server(config)#
```

We can now telnet from Dave and Bob onto the IP address of Server, specifying port 80 as the port we
want to connect to (HTTP, instead of the default telnet port of 23):

```
Dave-PC#telnet 10.20.1.21 80
Trying 10.20.1.21, 80 ... Open
get
HTTP/1.1 400 Bad Request
Date: Mon, 09 Nov 2015 13:41:37 GMT
Server: cisco-IOS
Accept-Ranges: none

400 Bad Request
[Connection to 10.20.1.21 closed by foreign host]
Dave-PC#

Bob-PC#telnet 10.20.1.21 80
Trying 10.20.1.21, 80 ... Open
get
HTTP/1.1 400 Bad Request
Date: Mon, 09 Nov 2015 13:42:03 GMT
Server: cisco-IOS
Accept-Ranges: none

400 Bad Request
[Connection to 10.20.1.21 closed by foreign host]
Bob-PC#
```

We need to type "*get*", which I have bolded in the above examples. This is not a perfect example, but
we can see an HTTP response, date and server. It's not much, but it does give us something to play
with.

For our ACL we just want Bob to have access. First of all, think about what we want to close down and
from where, and what we need to leave open.

It will be an inbound filter on Server's e0/0 interface, but do we want a standard ACL, or an extended
one? If we have a standard one we can only match on the source, but we have a few services and this
would block the other users from the services that they legitimately need. Therefore, we need an
extended ACL. We will call this "DenyWeb":

```
Server(config)#ip access-list extended DenyWeb
Server(config-ext-nacl)#
```

How would we write the statements? We could start with permitting Bob:

```
Server(config-ext-nacl)#permit tcp 10.20.1.0 0.0.0.255 host 10.20.1.21 eq
www
```

This would give Bob access and the default deny would block everyone else from the web server, but this would also block other traffic. Therefore, we can add another clause to deny all other web traffic:

```
Server(config-ext-nacl)#deny tcp any host 10.20.1.21 eq www
```

We still have the default deny rule at the end though, so let's be more permissive:

```
Server(config-ext-nacl)#permit tcp any any
Server(config-ext-nacl)#
```

We then apply it to the interface:

```
Server(config-ext-nacl)#int e1/0
Server(config-if)#ip access-group DenyWeb in
Server(config-if)#
```

Now, can Bob still access the web site?

```
Bob-PC#telnet 10.20.1.21 80
Trying 10.20.1.21, 80 ... Open
get
HTTP/1.1 400 Bad Request
Date: Mon, 09 Nov 2015 14:00:58 GMT
Server: cisco-IOS
Accept-Ranges: none

400 Bad Request
[Connection to 10.20.1.21 closed by foreign host]
Bob-PC#
```

Yes. Can Dave?

```
Dave-PC#telnet 10.20.1.21 80
Trying 10.20.1.21, 80 ...
% Connection timed out; remote host not responding

Dave-PC#
```

No, he cannot. Can he telnet to Server? According to our ACL, that should still be fine. Let's just set Server up to accept Telnet:

```
Server(config)#line vty 0 4
Server(config-line)#transport input telnet
Server(config-line)#password cisco
Server(config-line)#
```

Now we can test:

```
Dave-PC#telnet 10.20.1.21
Trying 10.20.1.21 ... Open


User Access Verification

Password:
Server>exit

[Connection to 10.20.1.21 closed by foreign host]
Dave-PC#
```

This good, it means our ACL is working correctly. Now let's stop Dave telnetting to Server.

6.4 Configure and verify ACLs to limit telnet and SSH access to the router

We will now create a final ACL to prevent Dave from telnetting to Server. It is pretty similar to the one we did above, the only major difference is that we cannot use the "*ip access-group*" command, instead we need to use "*ip access-class*".

Let's create the ACL. We can deny just Dave, but what if his IP address changes? He could be using DHCP, so this is a very real possibility. We could deny the network he is on, but then we lose the ability to get to Server from VLAN 10 on SW1. Ideally, we need to exclude 10.10.1.1 – 10.10.1.3 from this ACL (and 10.10.1.254).

For this we can create an object group, into which we can enter a range of IP addresses:

```
Server(config)#object-group network SwitchesOK
Server(config-network-group)#?
Network object group configuration commands:
  A.B.C.D       Network address of the group members
  any           Any host
  description   Network object group description
  exit          Exit from IP policy-group configuration mode
```

```
    group-object  Nested object group
    host          Host address of the object-group member
    no            Negate or set default values of a command
    range         Match only packets in the range of IP address

  Server(config-network-group)#range ?
    A.B.C.D  IP address1

  Server(config-network-group)#range 10.10.1.4 ?
    A.B.C.D  IP address2

  Server(config-network-group)#range 10.10.1.4 10.10.1.253
  Server(config-network-group)#exit
  Server(config)#
```

Above, I have excluded the VLAN interfaces and Gateway sub-interface addresses. Now we have an object we can call in our ACL:

```
  Server(config)#ip access-list extended DenyDave
  Server(config-ext-nacl)#deny tcp object-group SwitchesOK any eq telnet
  Server(config-ext-nacl)#permit tcp any any eq telnet
  Server(config-ext-nacl)#line vty 0 4
  Server(config-line)#access-class DenyDave in
  Server(config-line)#
```

Bob still has access:

```
  Bob-PC#telnet 10.20.1.21
  Trying 10.20.1.21 ... Open

  User Access Verification

  Password:
  Server>exit

  [Connection to 10.20.1.21 closed by foreign host]
  Bob-PC#
```

Dave does not:

```
  Dave-PC#telnet 10.20.1.21
  Trying 10.20.1.21 ...
  % Connection refused by remote host

  Dave-PC#
```

Excellent stuff! Now we are ready to move on to the next chapter, which is troubleshooting.

7. Troubleshooting

This should be the next chapter, really. When we get to section 7.12 we are supposed to be able to troubleshoot and resolve WAN issues, but we have not even looked at them yet. So, skip ahead to chapters 8 and 9, and come back afterwards.

Back? Great!

We have an important section here, accounting for 20% of the exam weighting.

Troubleshooting can be a mixture of frustration, fun and learning. We have a problem, we need to fix it and, hopefully, we can learn something along the way. With this in mind, we are going to play a little game. Have you every heard of a game called "Capture the Flag"? The idea is that you have to get from point A to point B, grab a flag, and return to point A with it. That is what we are going to do now. Save all the existing configurations, and then stop all of the routers. Now load up the troubleshooting lab in UNetLab, and start all the devices.

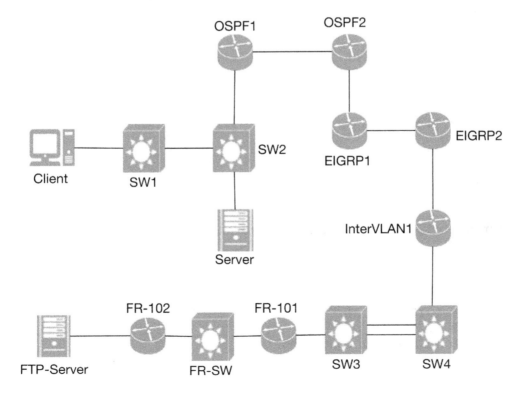

You have been called in to fix the network in the Brooklyn office. Due to a mistake by someone else, the network there has had all of the configurations replaced with backups from varying dates. This means that it is broken! It's up to you to fix it.

You have received this email:

> Hi
>
> Someone replaced all the device configurations with old backups; the entire network is messed up. There is a server that has all the payroll information on it, and we need that ASAP.
>
> We need you to get over to Brooklyn and fix it. There is a terminal there you can work from, which should get you onto the network.
>
> There will be a nice bonus in it for you if you can fix it!
>
> Thanks
>
> Bob.

Therefore, you head over to Brooklyn, get to the office and sit at the desk. The people there inform you that there are a number of routers and switches. There are some servers and client machines in different VLANs, as well as running OSPF and EIGRP, there is redistribution between OSPF and EIGRP, but this has been unaffected by the problem. All the usernames and passwords to the devices are "cisco". There is an FTP server at the end of the network; on this server is the file with all the payroll information on it (our "flag"). We need to get this file (we can't create files on it though, so we will need to connect to it via Telnet and pretend instead).

There are a couple of rules to this chapter:

- Do not try to fix a device, until you can see it through CDP from the previous device (the only exception is when moving from FR-101 to FR-102).
- You cannot remove any commands, but you can fix the ones already there.

The end goal is that we can perform the following:

```
Client#trace FTP-Server numeric
Type escape sequence to abort.
Tracing the route to 10.103.1.1
VRF info: (vrf in name/id, vrf out name/id)
  1 10.10.10.1 0 msec 0 msec 1 msec
  2 1.1.1.2 0 msec 1 msec 0 msec
```

```
   3 100.89.1.89 0 msec 1 msec 0 msec
   4 89.89.1.2 0 msec 1 msec 1 msec
   5 89.88.2.1 1 msec 1 msec 0 msec
   6 88.88.21.1 1 msec 0 msec 0 msec
   7 10.100.1.101 2 msec 2 msec 1 msec
   8 10.102.1.102 18 msec 20 msec 19 msec
   9 10.103.1.1 27 msec *  28 msec
Client#
Client#telnet FTP-Server
Trying FTP-Server (10.103.1.1)... Open


User Access Verification

Password:
FTP-Server>exit

[Connection to FTP-Server closed by foreign host]
Client#
```

Let's get started.

> Note: If you perform this more than once, you may need to delete the vlan.dat file on SW2 and reload the device first:
>
> ```
> SW2#dir
> Directory of unix:/
>
> 5122417  -rw-        0  Jan 1 2016 16:31:20 +00:00  wrapper.txt
> 5122499  -rw-      736  Jan 1 2016 13:48:29 +00:00  vlan.dat-00012
> 5122418  -rw-      812  Jan 1 2016 16:31:20 +00:00  NETMAP
> 5122485  -rw-  1048576  Jan 1 2016 13:37:45 +00:00  nvram_00012
> 5122416  -rw-        0  Jan 1 2016 11:55:14 +00:00  .configured
> 5122415  -rw-     1391  Jan 1 2016 11:55:14 +00:00  startup-config
>
> 2147479552 bytes total (2147479552 bytes free)
> SW2#del vlan.dat-00012
> Delete filename [vlan.dat-00012]?
> Delete unix:/vlan.dat-00012? [confirm]
> SW2#reload
> Proceed with reload? [confirm]
>
> %SYS-5-RELOAD: Reload requested by console. Reload Reason: Reload
> command.
> ```

7.1 Troubleshoot and correct common problems associated with IP addressing and host configurations

From Client we need to get to SW1. We can see it through CDP, which helps us eliminate any physical connectivity problems (like a port being shut down):

```
Client#sh cdp neigh | b Device
Device ID     Local Intrfce    Holdtme    Capability  Platform  Port ID
SW1           Eth 0/0          160                R S I  Linux Uni Eth 0/1

Total cdp entries displayed : 1
Client#
```

We can also use CDP to tell us some IP information:

```
Client#sh cdp entry SW1
-------------------------
Device ID: SW1
Entry address(es):
  IP address: 1.1.1.1
Platform: Linux Unix,  Capabilities: Router Switch IGMP
Interface: Ethernet0/0,  Port ID (outgoing port): Ethernet0/1
Holdtime : 137 sec
Second Port Status: Unknown

Version :
Cisco IOS Software, Solaris Software (I86BI_LINUXL2-ADVENTERPRISEK9-M),
Experimental Version 15.1(20130726:213425) [dstivers-july26-2013-
team_track 104]
Copyright (c) 1986-2013 by Cisco Systems, Inc.
Compiled Fri 26-Jul-13 15:56 by dstivers

advertisement version: 2
VTP Management Domain: '802101.local'
Native VLAN: 10
Duplex: half
Management address(es):
  IP address: 1.1.1.1

Client#
```

We know that SW1 has at least one IP address (1.1.1.1), and that the native VLAN is VLAN 10. It is also running VTP.

Can we see 1.1.1.1 in our routing table?

```
Client#sh ip route | b Gate
Gateway of last resort is not set

      10.0.0.0/8 is variably subnetted, 2 subnets, 2 masks
C        10.10.100.0/24 is directly connected, Ethernet0/0
L        10.10.100.10/32 is directly connected, Ethernet0/0
Client#
```

No, we cannot. We also do not have a default route. Do we have any special configuration on Ethernet0/0?

```
Client#sh run int e0/0 | b interface
interface Ethernet0/0
 ip address 10.10.100.10 255.255.255.0
end

Client#
```

This looks pretty standard. Because we have a static IP address assigned to interface Ethernet0/0, this rules out a DHCP problem and increases the likelihood that this is a problem with IP addressing.

If we look at the output from "show ip protocols", we can see that we do not have any routing protocols configured:

```
Client#sh ip protocols
*** IP Routing is NSF aware ***

Routing Protocol is "application"
  Sending updates every 0 seconds
  Invalid after 0 seconds, hold down 0, flushed after 0
  Outgoing update filter list for all interfaces is not set
  Incoming update filter list for all interfaces is not set
  Maximum path: 32
  Routing for Networks:
  Routing Information Sources:
    Gateway         Distance      Last Update
  Distance: (default is 4)

Client#
```

There is no OSFP, EIGRP or RIP configuration. We can confirm this a second way:

```
Client#sh run | i router
Client#
```

This increases the chances that we are using static routing to reach SW1 and beyond. Although we cannot see a static route in our routing table, this does not mean that we do not have one configured. A route will only be added to the routing table if it is a viable and working route. So let's see if we have one:

```
Client#sh run | i ip route
ip route 0.0.0.0 0.0.0.0 10.10.10.1
Client#
```

We have a static route, and it is very close to our own IP address:

```
Client#sh run int e0/0 | i address
 ip address 10.10.100.10 255.255.255.0
Client#
```

So, we have a mismatch in IP addresses, but who is the guilty party? Well, on the basis that we cannot yet reach SW1, let's assume the issue is with us, locally. We'll change our IP address to 10.10.10.10 and see what happens:

```
Client#conf t
Client(config)#int e0/0
Client(config-if)#ip add 10.10.10.10 255.255.255.0
Client(config-if)#end
Client#
```

Now let's check our routing table. If changing our IP address has resolved the issue, we should see the static default route, and be able to reach it:

```
Client#sh ip route | b Gate
Gateway of last resort is 10.10.10.1 to network 0.0.0.0

S*     0.0.0.0/0 [1/0] via 10.10.10.1
       10.0.0.0/8 is variably subnetted, 2 subnets, 2 masks
C         10.10.10.0/24 is directly connected, Ethernet0/0
L         10.10.10.10/32 is directly connected, Ethernet0/0
Client#ping 10.10.10.1
Type escape sequence to abort.
Sending 5, 100-byte ICMP Echos to 10.10.10.1:
!!!!!
Success rate is 100 percent (5/5)
Client#
```

Because we can now reach SW1, we can move on.

7.2 Troubleshoot and resolve VLAN problems

Let's start by seeing if we can see SW2 from SW1:

```
SW1#sh cdp neigh | b Device
Device ID      Local Intrfce    Holdtme   Capability Platform  Port ID
SW2            Eth 0/0          133             R S I Linux Uni Eth 0/0
Client         Eth 0/1          177             R B   Linux Uni Eth 0/0
SW1#
```

We can. Can we find any IP information about SW2?

```
SW1#sh cdp entry SW2 | i address
Entry address(es):
  IP address: 1.1.1.2
Management address(es):
  IP address: 1.1.1.2
SW1#sh arp
Protocol  Address          Age (min)  Hardware Addr   Type    Interface
Internet  1.1.1.1              -       aabb.cc80.0e00  ARPA    Vlan1
Internet  1.1.1.2             184      aabb.cc80.0c00  ARPA    Vlan1
Internet  10.10.10.1           -       aabb.cc80.0e00  ARPA    Vlan10
Internet  10.10.10.10         13       aabb.cc00.0100  ARPA    Vlan10
SW1#
```

We know that we already have an IP address of 1.1.1.1 on SW1. Now we also know that SW2 has an IP address of 1.1.1.2 (in VLAN 1). We can also see that our 1.1.1.1 address is in the same VLAN. Let's try pinging SW2:

```
SW1#ping 1.1.1.2
Type escape sequence to abort.
Sending 5, 100-byte ICMP Echos to 1.1.1.2:
!!!!!
Success rate is 100 percent (5/5)
SW1#
```

We have visibility and reachability to SW2, so we can start to compare the two:

```
SW1#sh vlan bri | e unsup
VLAN Name                 Status    Ports
---- -------------------- --------- --------------------------------
1    default              active    Et0/0, Et0/2, Et0/3
10   Client-VLAN          active    Et0/1
89   OSPF-VLAN            active

SW1#
```

```
SW2#sh vlan bri | e unsup
```

VLAN	Name	Status	Ports
1	default	active	Et0/0, Et0/3

```
SW2#
```

We have no VLANs (apart from VLAN 1) on SW2. Let's dig a bit deeper. We have a server connected to SW2 on its e0/1 port, but this port is not assigned to a VLAN in our list. So, what vlan is it assigned to?

```
SW2#sh run int e0/1 | i vlan
 switchport access vlan 20
SW2#
```

VLAN 20 it would seem. Why do we not know about VLAN 20 then and why is it missing from our VLAN list? We can learn about VLANs by either having them manually created on the switch, or through VTP. From looking at SW1 using CDP on Client, we know that SW1 is running VTP, so there is a good chance that SW2 is as well:

```
SW2#sh vtp status | i Mode
VTP Pruning Mode            : Disabled
VTP Operating Mode          : Server
SW2#
```

We are running VTP, and we are in server mode. Let's check SW1:

```
SW1#sh vtp status | i Mode
VTP Pruning Mode            : Disabled
VTP Operating Mode          : Server
SW1#
```

Both are running in Server mode, which is the default. Let's look a little mode closely:

```
SW1#sh vtp status | i Domain
VTP Domain Name             : 802101.local
SW1#

SW2#sh vtp status | i Domain
VTP Domain Name             :
SW2#
```

SW1 looks more like a VTP server as it has a domain name configured, but we could have both as a server, and manually create the required VLANs. Let's go ahead and set up SW2 to be a VTP client:

```
SW2(config)#vtp mode client
Setting device to VTP Client mode for VLANS.
SW2(config)#vtp domain 802101.local
Changing VTP domain name from NULL to 802101.local
SW2(config)#
```

As SW1 is now the VTP server, we need to configure VLAN 20 on there:

```
SW1#conf t
SW1(config)#vlan 20
SW1(config-vlan)#name Server-VLAN
SW1(config-vlan)#exit
SW1(config)#
```

However, this still does not account for why all the VLANs are missing from SW2, so there is something else wrong.

7.2.a Identify that VLANs are configured

VLAN 20 is definitely there on SW1:

```
SW1(config)#do sh vlan bri | e unsup

VLAN Name                 Status    Ports
---- -------------------- --------- ------------------------------
1    default              active    Et0/0, Et0/2, Et0/3
10   Client-VLAN          active    Et0/1
20   Server-VLAN          active
89   OSPF-VLAN            active

SW1(config)#
```

So, what could account for it being missing on SW2?

7.2.b Verify port membership correct

We have already confirmed that the Server is in the correct VLAN. Therefore, an incorrect port membership would not account for VLAN 20 (or the others) being missing from SW2. Extending this out, what are some useful troubleshooting steps to confirm correct port membership? Well, we can look at all the port configurations and compare this against the list of VLANs we have:

```
SW2#sh run | i access vlan
 switchport access vlan 20
 switchport access vlan 89
SW2#
```

A switch in VTP client mode can have ports configured in access mode for a particular VLAN, but this will not create the VLANs on it, only the VTP server can do this. We can tell from this that we need to have at least two VLANs (20 and 89) to support our port membership configuration. However, how do we confirm that the port is configured correctly? This will require a little deduction; confirming IP addressing on the end device and where default routes point (i.e. to the VLAN interface), but mainly knowledge of who should be where.

7.2.c Correct IP address configured

We can confirm the client IP addresses (making sure they are in the same subnet as their default gateway) by looking at the VLAN interfaces and by comparing the subnet masks configured on the interfaces.

```
SW2#sh ip int bri | e unas
Interface        IP-Address      OK? Method Status    Protocol
Vlan1            1.1.1.2         YES NVRAM  up        up
Vlan20           20.20.20.1      YES NVRAM  up        up
Vlan89           100.89.1.1      YES NVRAM  up        up

SW2#sh run int vlan 20 | b interface
interface Vlan20
 ip address 20.20.20.1 255.255.255.0
end

SW2#
```

This, however, would not account for why SW2 does not have VLAN 20 in its database.

We have already established that we have connectivity between SW1 and SW2. We know that SW1 should be the VTP server, and SW2 the client. We added the missing VLAN to SW1, but it has not been added to SW2. The next logical place to look would be the trunk between the two switches.

7.3 Troubleshoot and resolve trunking problems on Cisco switches

Let's have a look at our trunks. There is not a huge amount to look at when troubleshooting trunks, we need to confirm they are set up as trunks, the encapsulation is correct, and that the interfaces are up.

7.3.a Verify correct trunk states

We can verify our trunk status using the command "*show interface trunk*":

```
SW2#show int trunk
SW2#

SW1(config)#end
SW1#
SW1#show int trunk
SW1#
```

Nothing is returned. This means we do not have any trunks, which also means that the interfaces must have defaulted, or moved to access ports instead of trunk ports. We can confirm this by looking at the VLAN assignments:

```
SW1#sh vlan | i Et0/0
1    default                    active    Et0/0, Et0/2, Et0/3
SW1#

SW2#sh vlan | i Et0/0
1    default                    active    Et0/0, Et0/3
SW2#
```

Now we need to look at the interface configuration:

```
SW1#sh run int e0/0 | b interface
interface Ethernet0/0
 switchport trunk encapsulation isl
 duplex auto
end

SW1#

SW2#sh run int e0/0 | b interface
interface Ethernet0/0
 switchport trunk encapsulation dot1q
 switchport trunk allowed vlan 1,10,89
 duplex auto
end

SW2#
```

Now we can see a difference in the encapsulation.

7.3.b Verify correct encapsulation configured

We have one switch using ISL encapsulation, the other using dot1q. We cannot form a trunk with these settings, so we need to change one. Dot1q is the standard, so let's use that:

```
SW1#conf t
SW1(config)#int e0/0
SW1(config-if)#switchport trunk encapsulation dot1q
SW1(config-if)#do sh int trunk

Port          Mode            Encapsulation  Status     Native vlan
Et0/0         desirable       802.1q         trunking   1

Port          Vlans allowed on trunk
Et0/0         1-4094

Port          Vlans allowed and active in management domain
Et0/0         1,10,20,89

Port          Vlans in spanning tree forwarding state and not pruned
Et0/0         1,10,20,89
SW1(config-if)#
```

That looks better. Let's check it from SW2:

```
SW2#show interface trunk

Port          Mode            Encapsulation  Status     Native vlan
Et0/0         desirable       802.1q         trunking   1

Port          Vlans allowed on trunk
Et0/0         1,10,89

Port          Vlans allowed and active in management domain
Et0/0         1,10,89

Port          Vlans in spanning tree forwarding state and not pruned
Et0/0         1,10,89
SW2#
```

We now have a properly formed trunk, but are still missing VLAN 20. Notice the difference between SW1 and SW2. SW1 has VLANs 1, 10, 20 and 89 allowed and active in the management domain. SW2 just has 1, 10 and 89.

7.3.c Correct VLANs allowed

VLAN 20 is not "allowed". This is confirmed by the interface configuration we looked at before (when we were confirming the encapsulation), so we should have picked up on it rather quickly:

```
SW2#sh run int e0/0 | i allowed
 switchport trunk allowed vlan 1,10,89
SW2#
```

We are only allowing the three VLANs. Let's add VLAN 20. We do this using the command *"switchport trunk allowed vlan add <vlan number>"*:

```
SW2(config)#int e0/0
SW2(config-if)#switchport trunk allowed vlan add 20
SW2(config-if)#
SW2(config-if)#do sh vlan bri | e unsup

VLAN Name                     Status    Ports
---- -------------------- --------- --------------------------------
1    default               active    Et0/3
10   Client-VLAN           active
20   Server-VLAN           active    Et0/1
89   OSPF-VLAN             active    Et0/2

SW2(config-if)#
```

Now we have all the VLANs we can move on.

7.4 Troubleshoot and resolve ACL issues

We have a server, but what can we do with it? Well, as we cannot see it in SW2's list of CDP neighbors, not a lot:

```
SW2(config-if)#do sh cdp neigh | b Device
Device ID    Local Intrfce    Holdtme    Capability Platform  Port ID
SW1          Eth 0/0          138              R S I Linux Uni Eth 0/0
OSPF1        Eth 0/2          137              R B   Linux Uni Eth 0/2
SW2(config-if)#
```

Why not? Let's start with the basics:

```
SW2(config-if)#do sh ip int bri | i Ethernet0/1
Ethernet0/1      unassigned      YES unset  administratively down down
SW2(config-if)#
```

The interface is down. Let's bring it up and move forward:

```
SW2(config-if)#int e0/1
SW2(config-if)#
SW2(config-if)#no shut
SW2(config-if)#
%LINK-3-UPDOWN: Interface Ethernet0/1, changed state to up
%LINEPROTO-5-UPDOWN: Line protocol on Interface Ethernet0/1, changed
state to up
SW2(config-if)#
```

```
SW2(config-if)#do sh cdp neigh | b Device
Device ID      Local Intrfce     Holdtme    Capability Platform  Port ID
Server         Eth 0/1           162              R B  Linux Uni Eth 0/0
SW1            Eth 0/0           121            R S I  Linux Uni Eth 0/0
OSPF1          Eth 0/2           177              R B  Linux Uni Eth 0/2
SW2(config-if)#
```

This is one of the first troubleshooting steps you should take. Always start from the most basic of causes. Is it plugged in? Is it turned on? Is the network cable connected? Then you can start working your way up the layers.

Now we can move on to the Server. The server is a web server, providing a secure Intranet (an internal website). Access is reserved for users on the client PC, and from interface e0/2.200 on InterVLAN1.

We can see the access-list using the command *"show access-lists"*:

```
Server#sh access-lists
Extended IP access list SecureHTTP
    10 permit tcp host 10.10.10.10 any eq www
    20 permit tcp host 10.200.1.200 any eq www
    30 deny ip any any log
Server#
```

Let's try telnetting to it from the Client; first, we need to find the IP address of the Server:

```
Server#sh ip int bri | e unas
Interface      IP-Address      OK? Method Status       Protocol
Ethernet0/0    20.20.20.20     YES NVRAM  up           up

Server#
```

Now we can telnet to it on port 80 and use the *"get"* command:

```
Client#telnet 20.20.20.20 80
Trying 20.20.20.20, 80 ... Open
get
HTTP/1.1 400 Bad Request
Date: Tue, 24 Nov 2015 10:39:15 GMT
Server: cisco-IOS
Accept-Ranges: none

400 Bad Request
[Connection to 20.20.20.20 closed by foreign host]
Client#
```

We can also telnet from SW2, which actually should be denied:

```
SW2(config-if)#do telnet 20.20.20.20 80
Trying 20.20.20.20, 80 ... Open
get
HTTP/1.1 400 Bad Request
Date: Tue, 24 Nov 2015 11:58:31 GMT
Server: cisco-IOS
Accept-Ranges: none

400 Bad Request
[Connection to 20.20.20.20 closed by foreign host]
SW2(config-if)#
```

Again, we need to type in the "*get*" command to see the rest of the output. Now lets look at the access-list again.

7.4.a Verify statistics

```
Server#sh access-lists
Extended IP access list SecureHTTP
    10 permit tcp host 10.10.10.10 any eq www
    20 permit tcp host 10.200.1.200 any eq www
    30 deny ip any any log
Server#
```

We do not see any hits on the ACL. The access-list syntax looks fine; we are permitting access from the Client (10.10.10.10) to the Server (any) if the connection is through http (www), and from 10.200.1.200. Let's continue troubleshooting.

7.4.b Verify permitted networks

It is very easy to incorrectly configure an access-list, mainly because of the use of wildcard masks, and the same is true for setting up our routing protocols, such as EIGRP. We can end up being far more permissive or restrictive than we want to be. We get so used to writing network addresses, such as 10.10.10.0 255.255.255.0, that when we come to write ACLs, we forget to switch to wildcards.

Here are two ACL configurations:

```
Server(config)#ip access-list extended TestACL
Server(config-ext-nacl)#permit tcp 10.10.10.0 255.255.255.0 any eq www
Server(config-ext-nacl)#exit
Server(config)#ip access-list extended TestACL-2
Server(config-ext-nacl)#permit tcp 10.10.10.0 0.0.0.255 any eq www
Server(config-ext-nacl)#exit
```

One is incorrect (TestACL), the other is correct (TestACL-2). What does the result give us?

```
Server(config)#do sh access-list TestACL
Extended IP access list TestACL
    10 permit tcp 0.0.0.0 255.255.255.0 any eq www
Server(config)#
```

TestACL looks pretty messed up. Whereas TestACL-2 looks ideal:

```
Server(config)#do sh access-list TestACL-2
Extended IP access list TestACL-2
    10 permit tcp 10.10.10.0 0.0.0.255 any eq www
Server(config)#
```

This is where the context sensitive help comes in handy. Do not be afraid to use it. Every engineer does, and that is why it's there. The help tells us what is expected:

```
Server(config-ext-nacl)#permit tcp 10.10.10.0 ?
  A.B.C.D  Source wildcard bits

Server(config-ext-nacl)#
```

It is far better to use the help than to mess up an ACL. Let's remove the new ones:

```
Server(config)#no ip access-list extended TestACL
Server(config)#no ip access-list extended TestACL-2
Server(config)#
```

Anyway, we know that the ACL is OK; we have allowed all the correct hosts. So, what else do we need to check?

7.4.c Verify direction

We can have one access list per interface, per protocol (IPv4/IPv6) and per direction. The same is true for our virtual interfaces. We use the command "*ip access-group <ACL>*" on a physical interface, and "*access-group <ACL>*" on our virtual lines.

For obvious reasons the direction of an ACL is vitally important. Depending on the contents of our access-list we could permit unwanted traffic or block critical communication to other networks or services.

How do we find where an ACL has been applied? Well, for that we need to look at the interface or line configurations:

```
Server(config)#do sh run int e0/0 | b interface
interface Ethernet0/0
 ip address 20.20.20.20 255.255.255.0
 ip access-group SecureHTTP out
end

Server(config)#do sh run | s line vty 0 4
line vty 0 4
 access-class SecureHTTP out
 login
 transport input telnet
Server(config)#
```

We could also just search for the ACL name, though this does not tell us where to look, just that it is there. This is useful for confirming that there have not been any spelling mistakes though:

```
Server(config)#do sh run | i SecureHTTP
 ip access-group SecureHTTP out
ip access-list extended SecureHTTP
 access-class SecureHTTP out
Server(config)#
```

Both the Ethernet interface and the VTY lines have the access-list applied, but in the wrong direction (out rather than in). Do we need both the interface and the VTY line to have the ACL applied? Let's find out:

```
Server(config)#int e0/0
Server(config-if)#no ip access-group SecureHTTP out
Server(config-if)#ip access-group SecureHTTP in
Server(config-if)#
```

With this change, we can still access the HTTP server on Server from the Client machine, and our ACL statistics start to increase:

```
Client#telnet 20.20.20.20 80
Trying 20.20.20.20, 80 ... Open
get
HTTP/1.1 400 Bad Request
Date: Tue, 24 Nov 2015 12:22:24 GMT
Server: cisco-IOS
Accept-Ranges: none

400 Bad Request

[Connection to 20.20.20.20 closed by foreign host]
Client#
```

```
Server(config-if)#do sh access-lists
Extended IP access list SecureHTTP
    10 permit tcp host 10.10.10.10 any eq www (10 matches)
    20 permit tcp host 10.200.1.200 any eq www
    30 deny ip any any log (14 matches)
Server(config-if)#
```

Can we still access it from SW2?

```
SW2(config-if)#do telnet 20.20.20.20 80
Trying 20.20.20.20, 80 ...
% Destination unreachable; gateway or host down

SW2(config-if)#
```

No, we cannot, which is exactly the desired behaviour. This should have also resulted in a log entry for the denied traffic:

```
%SEC-6-IPACCESSLOGRP: list SecureHTTP denied ospf 20.20.20.1 ->
224.0.0.5, 1 packet
Server(config-if)#
%SEC-6-IPACCESSLOGP: list SecureHTTP denied tcp 20.20.20.1(51468) ->
20.20.20.20(80), 1 packet
Server(config-if)#
%SEC-6-IPACCESSLOGRP: list SecureHTTP denied ospf 20.20.20.1 ->
224.0.0.5, 32 packets
Server(config-if)#
```

The denied OSPF traffic is due to SW2 advertising OSPF out of all of its interfaces, so let's stop that behaviour (without breaking OSPF). Whilst this is not essential, the reason for doing this goes back to what we were talking about with logging, that usually the logs will be passed on to some form of log aggregation and storage system, unnecessary logs will fill up the space. Therefore we'll make the security guys happy, and our life easier by creating an ACL to filter out this traffic:

```
SW2(config-if)#ip access-list extended BlockOSPF->Server
SW2(config-ext-nacl)#
```

Give it a nice helpful name, remember that someone else will look at your configurations from time to time, so do make your ACL names easy to understand. Now, what are our options?

```
SW2(config-ext-nacl)#deny ?
  <0-255>  An IP protocol number
  ahp      Authentication Header Protocol
  eigrp    Cisco's EIGRP routing protocol
  esp      Encapsulation Security Payload
  gre      Cisco's GRE tunneling
```

```
icmp      Internet Control Message Protocol
igmp      Internet Gateway Message Protocol
ip        Any Internet Protocol
ipinip    IP in IP tunneling
nos       KA9Q NOS compatible IP over IP tunneling
ospf      OSPF routing protocol
pcp       Payload Compression Protocol
pim       Protocol Independent Multicast
tcp       Transmission Control Protocol
udp       User Datagram Protocol

SW2(config-ext-nacl)#deny
```

OSPF looks like a good choice:

```
SW2(config-ext-nacl)#deny ospf ?
  A.B.C.D  Source address
  any      Any source host
  host     A single source host

SW2(config-ext-nacl)#deny ospf
```

Let's make it easy and do "any/any":

```
SW2(config-ext-nacl)#deny ospf any any
SW2(config-ext-nacl)#
```

Are we done? This ACL will definitely block OSPF traffic. So let's try it. However, where do we put it?

7.4.c (i) Interface

Let's try putting the ACL on the interface connecting to the Server:

```
SW2(config-ext-nacl)#int e0/1
SW2(config-if)#ip access-group BlockOSPF->Server out
                                                   ^
% Invalid input detected at '^' marker.

SW2(config-if)#ip access-group BlockOSPF->Server ?
  in  inbound packets

SW2(config-if)#ip access-group BlockOSPF->Server
```

Hmmm, ok, not there, but why?

Switches act a little differently to routers. We have an access-port, which is a layer-2 interface; therefore, we can only apply inbound ACLs.

Look at the log entry from the server, notice that it states the source of the OSPF messages as coming from the VLAN IP address (20.20.20.1), lets put it on the VLAN interface instead:

```
SW2(config-if)#int vlan 20
SW2(config-if)#ip access-group BlockOSPF->Server out
SW2(config-if)#
```

The switch is happy with the command and we should not see any OSPF messages on the logs of the server. Let's test that we still have the right level of access:

```
SW2(config-if)#do telnet 20.20.20.20 80
Trying 20.20.20.20, 80 ...
% Destination unreachable; gateway or host down

SW2(config-if)#
```

SW2 is still blocked.

```
Client#telnet 20.20.20.20 80
Trying 20.20.20.20, 80 ...
% Destination unreachable; gateway or host down

Client#
```

So is Client. Looks like we forgot the most vital part of creating ACLs; they must have at least one permit clause, or else everything will be blocked by the implicit deny rule at the end. So let's fix it:

```
SW2(config-if)#ip access-list extended BlockOSPF->Server
SW2(config-ext-nacl)#permit ip any any
SW2(config-ext-nacl)#do sh access-lists
Extended IP access list BlockOSPF->Server
    10 deny ospf any any
    20 permit ip any any
SW2(config-ext-nacl)#
```

Now let's test:

```
SW2(config-ext-nacl)#do telnet 20.20.20.20 80
Trying 20.20.20.20, 80 ...
% Destination unreachable; gateway or host down

SW2(config-ext-nacl)#end
```

Good, now can we telnet from Client?

```
Client#telnet 20.20.20.20 80
Trying 20.20.20.20, 80 ... Open
get
HTTP/1.1 400 Bad Request
Date: Tue, 24 Nov 2015 12:50:30 GMT
Server: cisco-IOS
Accept-Ranges: none

400 Bad Request
[Connection to 20.20.20.20 closed by foreign host]
Client#
```

Lastly, if we return to Server's console we can see that the denied traffic is logged, but we are not seeing any OSPF messages, confirming that our ACL is working as expected.

```
Server(config-if)#
%SEC-6-IPACCESSLOGP: list SecureHTTP denied tcp 20.20.20.1(65455) ->
20.20.20.20(80), 1 packet
Server(config-if)#
%SEC-6-IPACCESSLOGP: list SecureHTTP denied tcp 20.20.20.1(55538) ->
20.20.20.20(80), 1 packet
Server(config-if)#
```

So far, so good. Let's move on to some layer-1 issues we could encounter.

7.5 Troubleshoot and resolve Layer 1 problems

Most layer-1 problems are caused either by a cable not being plugged in, or faulty cables. Problems caused through collisions are rare now in wired networks, but we are still expected to understand what these issues could be.

When packets collide, they can combine, resulting in broken or corrupt packets. Collisions can only occur at the physical layer when you have multiple devices connected to a hub.

Collisions can produce the following errors:

7.5.a Framing

Framing errors are where we have an illegal format, and the packets are received with an invalid frame checksum (FCS). Bad cabling, a faulty network interface card or a duplex mismatch can cause this.

7.5.b CRC

CRC errors (Cyclic Redundancy Check) can be caused by late collisions (packets colliding after the first 64-bytes have been sent), using incorrect cabling (Cat 3 instead of Cat 5 for instance), or duplex mismatches.

7.5.c Runts

Runts are frames that did not meet minimum frame size of 64-bytes; again, this can be caused by late collisions.

7.5.d Giants

This is the opposite of runts; these are frames that exceed the maximum frame size (1518 bytes).

7.5.e Dropped packets

Packets can be dropped if there are too many in the buffer. We can increase the buffers using the command *"buffers <interface>"* followed by one of the available options:

```
OSPF1(config)#buffers ethernet 0/0 ?
  initial    Temporary buffers allocated at system reload
  max-free   Maximum number of free buffers
  min-free   Minimum number of free buffers
  permanent  Number of permanent buffers

OSPF1(config)#buffers ethernet 0/0
OSPF1(config)#
```

We can see our current buffer using the command *"show buffers"*, and look at the buffer drops using the *"show interface"* command, below you can see interface VLAN 20 in SW1 has had 20 drops:

```
SW2#sh int vlan 20 | i drop
  Input queue: 0/75/0/0 (size/max/drops/flushes); Total output drops: 20
SW2#
```

7.5.f Late collisions

Late collisions occur after the 64th byte of the frame has been transmitted, these indicate a duplex mismatch. Recall from chapter to when we discussed the different ways in which a switch can pass traffic, using store or cut-through switching, this relates to that concept.

7.5.g Input/output errors

Input errors are the total of runts, giants, no buffer, CRC, frame, overrun and ignored counters. Output errors are the number of packets that a port tried to transmit but which had a problem.

When trying to fix the errors it is useful to clear the counters, so we can easily see whether the errors have been resolved, or whether the counters continue to increase, indicating that the problem still exists.

The counters can be cleared using the command *"clear counters <interface>"*. We need to confirm the action by pressing return on the keyboard:

```
SW2#clear counters vlan 20
Clear "show interface" counters on this interface [confirm]
SW2#
%CLEAR-5-COUNTERS: Clear counter on interface Vlan20 by console
SW2#sh int vlan 20
Vlan20 is up, line protocol is up
  Hardware is EtherSVI, address is aabb.cc80.0c00 (bia aabb.cc80.0c00)
  Internet address is 10.20.1.2/24
  MTU 1500 bytes, BW 1000000 Kbit, DLY 10 usec,
     reliability 255/255, txload 1/255, rxload 1/255
  Encapsulation ARPA, loopback not set
  Keepalive not supported
  ARP type: ARPA, ARP Timeout 04:00:00
  Last input 00:08:07, output never, output hang never
  Last clearing of "show interface" counters 00:00:09
  Input queue: 0/75/0/0 (size/max/drops/flushes); Total output drops: 0
  Queueing strategy: fifo
  Output queue: 0/40 (size/max)
  5 minute input rate 0 bits/sec, 0 packets/sec
  5 minute output rate 0 bits/sec, 0 packets/sec
     0 packets input, 0 bytes, 0 no buffer
     Received 0 broadcasts (0 IP multicasts)
     0 runts, 0 giants, 0 throttles
     0 input errors, 0 CRC, 0 frame, 0 overrun, 0 ignored
     0 packets output, 0 bytes, 0 underruns
     0 output errors, 0 interface resets
     0 output buffer failures, 0 output buffers swapped out
SW2#
```

As you can see above the counter were cleared nine seconds ago (*Last clearing of "show interface counters*).

7.6 Identify and correct common network problems

This is one of those annoyingly vague topics, but the most common network problems are usually due to misconfiguration, such as incorrect IP addressing, or cabling.

Start with the basics, make sure that the right cables are plugged in, in the right ports and the cables are of the correct type (try also replacing the cable as they can break). If they are all OK then try pinging the localhost IP address (*ping 127.0.0.1*), if this is successful it will eliminate any problems from being with the underlying software stack.

If we can ping 127.0.0.1 then try pinging another host on the same network, then the default gateway (making sure that we actually have a default gateway configured). Use traceroute to look at the path the data is using, and remember to check that the subnet masks are correct.

If you do find any misconfigurations only make one change at a time, go through the tests again. If you go through making many changes without testing then it is easy to miss which change actually resolved the problem.

7.7 Troubleshoot and resolve spanning tree operation issues

We are sticking with SW1 and SW2 for the moment. Everything looks good. We have pretty good connectivity; Client can reach Server and both are in different VLANs, which would indicate that our trunking is correct and our port to VLAN assignment is working. Let's go through STP though just to make sure that all is working, as it should, concentrating on VLANs 10 and 20.

7.7.a Verify root switch

```
SW2#sh spanning-tree vlan 10

VLAN0010
  Spanning tree enabled protocol ieee
  Root ID    Priority    32778
             Address     aabb.cc00.0c00
             This bridge is the root
             Hello Time   2 sec  Max Age 20 sec  Forward Delay 15 sec

  Bridge ID  Priority    32778  (priority 32768 sys-id-ext 10)
             Address     aabb.cc00.0c00
             Hello Time   2 sec  Max Age 20 sec  Forward Delay 15 sec
             Aging Time  300 sec

Interface    Role Sts Cost      Prio.Nbr Type
------------ ---- --- --------- -------- --------------------------------
Et0/0        Desg FWD 100       128.1    Shr
```

```
SW2#sh spanning-tree vlan 20 | i ID|root
  Root ID    Priority    32788
             This bridge is the root
  Bridge ID  Priority    32788  (priority 32768 sys-id-ext 20)
SW2#
```

SW2 is the root for VLANs 10 and 20. SW2 is the root as its MAC address is lower than that of SW1. We can see SW1's MAC address by looking at the bridge details:

```
SW1#sh span vlan 10 | s Bridge
  Bridge ID  Priority    32778  (priority 32768 sys-id-ext 10)
             Address     aabb.cc00.0e00
             Hello Time  2 sec  Max Age 20 sec  Forward Delay 15 sec
             Aging Time  300 sec

SW1#
```

The last part of SW2's MAC address is 0c00 and SW1's is 0e00. Therefore, SW2 becomes the root switch.

7.7.b Verify priority

Both switches take the default priority of 32768 and add on the VLAN number; VLAN 10's priority becomes 32778 and VLAN 20's priority becomes 32788. This is because of the extended system-id feature that is enabled:

```
SW2#sh run | i spanning
spanning-tree mode pvst
spanning-tree extend system-id
SW2#
```

This command also shows us that there has been no additional configuration made to spanning-tree which might influence the priorities.

7.7.c Verify mode is correct

We can see, from the above output, that SW2 is running PVST (technically PVST+), let's run the same command on SW1:

```
SW1#sh run | i spanning
spanning-tree mode rapid-pvst
spanning-tree extend system-id
SW1#
```

SW1 is running Rapid-PVST. Rapid-PVST is backwardly compatible with PVST, which is why everything is working fine. However, we do lose the timesaving benefits of Rapid-PVST with SW2, as it is running the slower PVST+.

```
SW2(config)#spanning-tree mode rapid-pvst
SW2(config)#do sh run | i spanning
spanning-tree mode rapid-pvst
spanning-tree extend system-id
SW2(config)#
```

We can confirm the mode change using the command "*show spanning-tree summary*":

```
SW2(config)#do sh spanning-tree summary
Switch is in rapid-pvst mode
Root bridge for: VLAN0001, VLAN0010, VLAN0020, VLAN0089
Extended system ID           is enabled
Portfast Default             is disabled
PortFast BPDU Guard Default  is disabled
Portfast BPDU Filter Default is disabled
Loopguard Default            is disabled
EtherChannel misconfig guard is enabled
Configured Pathcost method used is short
UplinkFast                   is disabled
BackboneFast                 is disabled
```

Name	Blocking	Listening	Learning	Forwarding	STP Active
VLAN0001	0	0	0	2	2
VLAN0010	0	0	0	1	1
VLAN0020	0	0	0	2	2
VLAN0089	0	0	0	2	2
4 vlans	0	0	0	7	7

```
SW2(config)#
```

The above command also shows us some port information. We can see the same on SW1:

```
SW1#sh spanning summary | b Name
```

Name	Blocking	Listening	Learning	Forwarding	STP Active
VLAN0001	0	0	0	3	3
VLAN0010	0	0	0	2	2
VLAN0020	0	0	0	1	1
VLAN0089	0	0	0	1	1
4 vlans	0	0	0	7	7

```
SW1#
```

If you look at the numbers above, we seem to have far more going on than the simple connectivity we have would suggest. Take SW1 as the example. SW1 is connected to Client and to SW2. That is it. However, it has three ports forwarding in VLAN 1. Why is this?

7.7.d Verify port states

If we look at the spanning tree statistics for VLAN 1, we can see why:

```
SW1#sh spanning-tree vlan 1

VLAN0001
  Spanning tree enabled protocol rstp
  Root ID    Priority    32769
             Address     aabb.cc00.0c00
             Cost        100
             Port        1 (Ethernet0/0)
             Hello Time   2 sec  Max Age 20 sec  Forward Delay 15 sec

  Bridge ID  Priority    32769  (priority 32768 sys-id-ext 1)
             Address     aabb.cc00.0e00
             Hello Time   2 sec  Max Age 20 sec  Forward Delay 15 sec
             Aging Time  300 sec

Interface        Role Sts Cost      Prio.Nbr Type
---------------- ---- --- --------- -------- --------------------------------
Et0/0            Root FWD 100       128.1    Shr
Et0/2            Desg FWD 100       128.3    Shr
Et0/3            Desg FWD 100       128.4    Shr


SW1#
```

SW1 still has two ports in VLAN 1; E0/2 and E0/3. We can confirm this by looking at the VLAN database:

```
SW1#sh vlan | i active
1    default                          active    Et0/2, Et0/3
10   Client-VLAN                      active    Et0/1
20   Server-VLAN                      active
89   OSPF-VLAN                        active
SW1#
```

Remember that any port that is not a trunk port and that is not specifically assigned to a VLAN will be placed in VLAN 1. These ports are not shut down, so they will be in a forwarding state. The same is true for SW2:

```
SW2#sh vlan | i active
1    default                            active   Et0/3
10   Client-VLAN                        active
20   Server-VLAN                        active   Et0/1
89   OSPF-VLAN                          active   Et0/2
SW2#
```

E0/3 has not been assigned to a VLAN, so it is automatically placed in VLAN 1, it is also not shut down, so it will be forwarding:

```
SW2#sh spanning-tree vlan 1 | b Interface
Interface       Role Sts Cost      Prio.Nbr Type
--------------- ---- --- --------- -------- --------------------------
Et0/0           Desg FWD 100       128.1    Shr
Et0/3           Desg FWD 100       128.4    Shr

SW2#
```

VLAN 89 has one interface assigned to it; it is also carried along the trunk (port e0/0):

```
SW2#sh spanning-tree vlan 89 | b Interface
Interface       Role Sts Cost      Prio.Nbr Type
--------------- ---- --- --------- -------- --------------------------
Et0/0           Desg FWD 100       128.1    Shr
Et0/2           Desg FWD 100       128.3    Shr

SW2#
```

Moving on, from Client we should be able to reach OSPF1:

```
Client#ping 89.89.1.1
Type escape sequence to abort.
Sending 5, 100-byte ICMP Echos to 89.89.1.1:
!!!!!
Success rate is 100 percent (5/5)
Client#
```

We can, and as we confirmed that SW2 has OSPF1 in its CDP table back in section 7.4, we can see what OSPF1 has in store for us.

7.8 Troubleshoot and resolve routing issues

OSPF1 should make it easy for us to start troubleshooting, as the error messages will be on the console:

```
OSPF1#
%OSPF-4-ERRRCV: Received invalid packet: mismatched area ID from backbone
area from 89.89.1.2, Ethernet0/0
OSPF1#
```

Clearly, this would direct us immediately to looking at the OSPF configuration, but sometimes we do not get the helpful messages.

7.8.a Verify routing is enabled (sh ip protocols)

With the Cisco IOS, one line can make all the difference, and it may not be an obvious one. Consider the following:

```
OSPF1#
OSPF1#sh ip protocols | b ospf
Routing Protocol is "ospf 1"
  Outgoing update filter list for all interfaces is not set
  Incoming update filter list for all interfaces is not set
  Router ID 11.11.11.11
  It is an area border router
  Number of areas in this router is 2. 2 normal 0 stub 0 nssa
  Maximum path: 4
  Routing for Networks:
    11.11.11.11 0.0.0.0 area 0
    89.89.1.0 0.0.0.255 area 1
    100.89.1.0 0.0.0.255 area 0
  Routing Information Sources:
    Gateway         Distance      Last Update
    1.1.1.1              110      5d20h
    22.22.22.22          110      5d21h
    1.1.1.2              110      5d21h
  Distance: (default is 110)

OSPF1#
```

Everything looks fine here. We can tell that OSPF is enabled and all looks good. Now, let's see what happens if we try this:

```
OSPF1#conf t
OSPF1(config)#
OSPF1(config)#no ip routing
OSPF1(config)#
```

What does *"show ip protocols"* tell us now?

```
OSPF1(config)#do sh ip protocols
*** IP Routing is NSF aware ***

OSPF1(config)#
```

Not much, but neither does it explicitly state that routing has been disabled. Let's turn it back on again:

```
OSPF1(config)#ip routing
OSPF1(config)#
```

Now what does it tell us?

```
OSPF1(config)#do sh ip protocols
*** IP Routing is NSF aware ***

OSPF1(config)#
```

Still nothing. We have also lost our OSPF configuration:

```
OSPF1(config)#do sh run | s router ospf
OSPF1(config)#
```

So from this we can see that the command "*show ip protocols*" looks the same whether we have a brand new router (with routing enabled), or whether routing has been explicitly disabled. So how do we catch this one? We could use "*show run | i routing*":

```
OSPF1(config)#no ip routing
OSPF1(config)#
OSPF1(config)#do sh run | i routing
no ip routing
OSPF1(config)#
```

Alternatively, we can try to access the routing configuration mode:

```
OSPF1(config)#router ospf 1

IP routing not enabled
OSPF1(config)#
```

Either way, we need to go and look for it.

Let's enable routing and set up OSPF again. We'll take the same information as the successful "*sh ip protocols*" output at the start of this section:

```
OSPF1(config)#ip routing
OSPF1(config)#router ospf 1
OSPF1(config-router)#router-id 11.11.11.11
OSPF1(config-router)#network 11.11.11.11 0.0.0.0 area 0
OSPF1(config-router)#network 89.89.1.0 0.0.0.255 area 1
OSPF1(config-router)#network 100.89.1.0 0.0.0.255 area 0
OSPF1(config-router)#
%OSPF-4-ERRRCV: Received invalid packet: mismatched area ID from backbone
area from 89.89.1.2, Ethernet0/0
OSPF1(config-router)#
%OSPF-5-ADJCHG: Process 1, Nbr 1.1.1.2 on Ethernet0/2 from LOADING to
FULL, Loading Done
OSPF1(config-router)#
%OSPF-4-ERRRCV: Received invalid packet: mismatched area ID from backbone
area from 89.89.1.2, Ethernet0/0
OSPF1(config-router)#
```

Already we should have seen the errors start to come in and it should be pretty obvious why. Don't fix it just yet though; we have a couple of bits to look at before we do that.

7.8.b Verify routing table is correct

How do we know our routing table is correct? Let's have a look:

```
OSPF1(config-router)#do sh ip route | b Gate
Gateway of last resort is not set

      1.0.0.0/24 is subnetted, 1 subnets
O        1.1.1.0 [110/11] via 100.89.1.1, 00:04:16, Ethernet0/2
      10.0.0.0/24 is subnetted, 1 subnets
O        10.10.10.0 [110/12] via 100.89.1.1, 00:04:16, Ethernet0/2
      11.0.0.0/32 is subnetted, 1 subnets
C        11.11.11.11 is directly connected, Loopback0
      20.0.0.0/24 is subnetted, 1 subnets
O        20.20.20.0 [110/11] via 100.89.1.1, 00:04:16, Ethernet0/2
      89.0.0.0/8 is variably subnetted, 2 subnets, 2 masks
C        89.89.1.0/24 is directly connected, Ethernet0/0
L        89.89.1.1/32 is directly connected, Ethernet0/0
      100.0.0.0/8 is variably subnetted, 2 subnets, 2 masks
C        100.89.1.0/24 is directly connected, Ethernet0/2
L        100.89.1.89/32 is directly connected, Ethernet0/2
OSPF1(config-router)#
```

We don't have much in there to look at. This would be our first clue that we are missing entries, just by looking at the size. Nevertheless, how do we know what entries are missing? Well, looking at other devices, knowing what they are advertising to us, can only really do this. It is clear from the output above that we lack routing entries for the rest of the network, but what if an adjacent router were advertising a default route to us? Of if we had a default route statically set? Then it makes it harder to see what is missing.

Never be afraid to resort to a pen and paper, map out the flow of routing entries, look for summarized routes (where instead of 10.0.1.0/24, 10.0.2.0/24, 10.0.3.0/24 we have 10.0.0.0/16 in the routing table). This brings us nicely to path selection.

7.8.c Verify correct path selection

Routers will always prefer the longest match in the routing table, by default; 10.1.1.1/32, will be preferred over 10.1.1.0/24, which will be preferred over 10.1.0.0/16, which will be preferred over 10.0.0.0/8. Use traceroute to make sure that the traffic flow is going in the right direction and that the traffic is not looping anywhere in the network.

7.9 Troubleshoot and resolve OSPF problems

Let's go and make OSPF1 happy again.

7.9.a Verify neighbor adjacencies

The message on OSPF1 makes it very clear what the problem is, we have an area mismatch. Hopefully you didn't go ahead and fix it already!

Let's assume that for a moment we do not know what area we should use. We can find out what the other side is sending us if we are lucky enough to have access, but this is not always guaranteed. Debugging using the command "*debug ip ospf <process number> hello*" does sometimes help. If you are lucky, this will show what area was received, but as you can see, we are not so lucky here:

```
OSPF1#debug ip ospf 1 hello
OSPF hello debugging is on for process 1
OSPF1#
OSPF-1 HELLO Et0/0: Send hello to 224.0.0.5 area 1 from 89.89.1.1
OSPF1#
%OSPF-4-ERRRCV: Received invalid packet: mismatched area ID from backbone
area from 89.89.1.2, Ethernet0/0
OSPF1#
OSPF-1 HELLO Et0/2: Send hello to 224.0.0.5 area 0 from 100.89.1.89
OSPF-1 HELLO Et0/2: Rcv hello from 1.1.1.2 area 0 100.89.1.1
OSPF1#
OSPF-1 HELLO Et0/0: Send hello to 224.0.0.5 area 1 from 89.89.1.1
OSPF1#
%OSPF-4-ERRRCV: Received invalid packet: mismatched area ID from backbone
area from 89.89.1.2, Ethernet0/0
```

```
OSPF1#
OSPF-1 HELLO Et0/2: Send hello to 224.0.0.5 area 0 from 100.89.1.89
OSPF-1 HELLO Et0/2: Rcv hello from 1.1.1.2 area 0 100.89.1.1
OSPF1#un all
All possible debugging has been turned off
OSPF1#
```

We are sending OSPF hellos from the e0/0 interface:

```
OSPF1#
OSPF-1 HELLO Et0/0: Send hello to 224.0.0.5 area 1 from 89.89.1.1
OSPF1#
```

However, we cannot see any received messages coming from OSPF2. The good news is that we can see OSPF2 from CDP though, and (most importantly) we have reachability:

```
OSPF1#sh cdp neigh | b Device
Device ID      Local Intrfce    Holdtme    Capability  Platform  Port ID
SW2            Eth 0/2          149              R S I  Linux Uni Eth 0/2
OSPF2          Eth 0/0          155              R B    Linux Uni Eth 0/0

Total cdp entries displayed : 2
OSPF1#
OSPF1#ping 89.89.1.2
Type escape sequence to abort.
Sending 5, 100-byte ICMP Echos to 89.89.1.2:
.!!!!
Success rate is 80 percent (4/5)
OSPF1#
```

Therefore, we can connect to it and have a look. Once we are on OSPF2, we can use the same debug command (ok, running "*show run | s router ospf*" would be easier, I know):

```
OSPF2#debug ip ospf hello
OSPF2#
OSPF hello debugging is on
OSPF2#
OSPF2#
OSPF-1 HELLO Et0/0: Send hello to 224.0.0.5 area 0 from 89.89.1.2
OSPF2#
```

We can now see that we are sending a hello from area 0 on OSPF2 (Send hello to 224.0.0.5 area 0 from 89.89.1.2), but from area 1 on OSPF1 (Send hello to 224.0.0.5 area 1 from 89.89.1.1). Now we know what area they should be in, we can change OSPF1:

```
OSPF1#sh run | s router o
router ospf 1
 router-id 11.11.11.11
 network 11.11.11.11 0.0.0.0 area 0
 network 89.89.1.0 0.0.0.255 area 1
 network 100.89.1.0 0.0.0.255 area 0
OSPF1#conf t
Enter configuration commands, one per line.  End with CNTL/Z.
OSPF1(config)#router ospf 1
OSPF1(config-router)#no network 89.89.1.0 0.0.0.255 area 1
OSPF1(config-router)#network 89.89.1.0 0.0.0.255 area 0
OSPF1(config-router)#
%OSPF-5-ADJCHG: Process 1, Nbr 22.22.22.22 on Ethernet0/0 from LOADING to
FULL, Loading Done
OSPF1(config-router)#
```

Once the areas are corrected, we can see some useful output from the debug:

```
OSPF2#
OSPF-1 HELLO Et0/0: Send hello to 224.0.0.5 area 0 from 89.89.1.2
OSPF-1 HELLO Et0/0: Rcv hello from 11.11.11.11 area 0 89.89.1.1
OSPF2#
```

But why did we change OSPF1 to area 0, and not OSPF2 to area 1? Remember that with OSPF, every OSPF-speaking router needs a connection to area 0 (the backbone), therefore (and as we saw from chapter 4) it is easier to have all your interfaces in area 0. However, having the E0/0 interfaces of OSPF1 and OSPF2 in area 1 would have worked equally as well, as OSPF1 is in Area 0 (via its loopback and E0/2 interfaces). When in doubt try area 0.

So, what else could have tripped us up with OSPF? Let's have a look.

7.9.b Verify hello and dead timers

The hello and dead must match. We can find what these are set to by looking at the OSPF interface:

```
OSPF1#sh ip ospf interface Ethernet 0/0
Ethernet0/0 is up, line protocol is up
  Internet Address 89.89.1.1/24, Area 0, Attached via Network Statement
  Process ID 1, Router ID 11.11.11.11, Network Type BROADCAST, Cost: 10
  Topology-MTID    Cost    Disabled    Shutdown    Topology Name
        0           10       no          no           Base
  Transmit Delay is 1 sec, State BDR, Priority 1
  Designated Router (ID) 22.22.22.22, Interface address 89.89.1.2
  Backup Designated router (ID) 11.11.11.11, Interface address 89.89.1.1
  Timer intervals configured, Hello 10, Dead 40, Wait 40, Retransmit 5
    oob-resync timeout 40
    Hello due in 00:00:08
```

```
      Supports Link-local Signaling (LLS)
      Cisco NSF helper support enabled
      IETF NSF helper support enabled
      Index 3/2, flood queue length 0
      Next 0x0(0)/0x0(0)
      Last flood scan length is 1, maximum is 1
      Last flood scan time is 0 msec, maximum is 0 msec
      Neighbor Count is 1, Adjacent neighbor count is 1
        Adjacent with neighbor 22.22.22.22  (Designated Router)
      Suppress hello for 0 neighbor(s)
OSPF1#

OSPF2#sh ip ospf interface ethernet 0/0 | i Timer
    Timer intervals configured, Hello 10, Dead 40, Wait 40, Retransmit 5
OSPF2#
```

If our timers do not match, we will not form an adjacency.

7.9.c Verify OSPF area

We can confirm what areas we are configured for in a couple of ways. We can use the output from
"show ip protocols", or we can look at OSPF:

```
OSPF1#sh ip ospf interface brief
Interface    PID    Area      IP Address/Mask     Cost    State Nbrs F/C
Lo0          1      0         11.11.11.11/32      1       LOOP  0/0
Et0/0        1      0         89.89.1.1/24        10      BDR   1/1
Et0/2        1      0         100.89.1.89/24      10      BDR   1/1
OSPF1#

OSPF2#sh ip ospf interface brief
Interface    PID    Area      IP Address/Mask     Cost    State Nbrs F/C
Lo0          1      0         22.22.22.22/32      1       LOOP  0/0
Et0/0        1      0         89.89.1.2/24        10      DR    1/1
OSPF2#
```

As we saw earlier, a mismatch in areas will cause the routers not to form an adjacency.

7.9.d Verify interface MTU

A mismatch in the MTU will cause adjacencies not to form. The MTU mismatch will be detected when
the two routers come to exchange the Database Description (DBD) packets during adjacency
formation. We can see this happen:

```
OSPF1(config)#int e0/0
OSPF1(config-if)#ip mtu ?
  <68-1500>  MTU (bytes)
```

```
OSPF1(config-if)#ip mtu 1000
OSPF1(config-if)#
```

Now we will shut down the interface, set up some debugging, and look for that all-critical line (please note that I have truncated the debug output, just to make it easier to read and see what we are looking for):

```
1.  OSPF1(config-if)#shut
2.  OSPF1(config-if)#
3.  <adjacency gets torn down, interface shuts down fully>
4.  OSPF1(config-if)#
5.  OSPF1(config-if)#do debug condition interface e0/0
6.  Condition 1 set
7.  OSPF1(config-if)#do debug ip packet detail
8.  IP packet debugging is on (detailed)
9.  OSPF1(config-if)#do debug ip ospf adj
10. OSPF adjacency debugging is on
11. OSPF1(config-if)#
12. OSPF1(config-if)#no shut
13. OSPF1(config-if)#
14. %LINK-3-UPDOWN: Interface Ethernet0/0, changed state to up
15. OSPF1(config-if)#
16. OSPF-1 ADJ    Et0/0: Rcv DBD from 22.22.22.22 seq 0x5F7 opt 0x52
    flag 0x7 len 32  mtu 1500 state EXSTART
17. OSPF-1 ADJ    Et0/0: Nbr 22.22.22.22 has larger interface MTU
18. OSPF1(config-if)#
19. OSPF-1 ADJ    Et0/0: Neighbor change event
20. OSPF-1 ADJ    Et0/0: DR/BDR election
21. OSPF-1 ADJ    Et0/0: Elect BDR 11.11.11.11
22. OSPF-1 ADJ    Et0/0: Elect DR 22.22.22.22
23. OSPF-1 ADJ    Et0/0: DR: 22.22.22.22 (Id)   BDR: 11.11.11.11 (Id)
24. OSPF-1 ADJ    Et0/0: Send DBD to 22.22.22.22 seq 0x88D opt 0x52 flag
    0x7 len 32
25. OSPF-1 ADJ    Et0/0: Retransmitting DBD to 22.22.22.22 [2]
26. OSPF-1 ADJ    Et0/0: Rcv DBD from 22.22.22.22 seq 0x5F7 opt 0x52
    flag 0x7 len 32  mtu 1500 state EXSTART
27. OSPF-1 ADJ    Et0/0: Nbr 22.22.22.22 has larger interface MTU
28. OSPF1(config-if)#
29. OSPF1(config-if)#do un all
30. All possible debugging has been turned off
31. OSPF1(config-if)#
```

We start by shutting down the interface (line 1), I have removed the interface and adjacency down notifications to save space. We set up a debug condition in line 5 (we only want to look at the traffic on our E0/0 interface), we then set up debugging for ip packet (detailed) on line 7 and OSPF adjacencies on line 9.

The interface is brought up again on line 12 and we start to see the OSPF traffic. I have removed some of the traffic, but we can see that we start to exchange the DBD (line 16) and this is when the MTU discovery occurs. We are informed that the MTU is different in line 17.

The process then starts again, until OSPF decides that it has tried too many times and gives us this message:

```
OSPF1(config-if)#
%OSPF-5-ADJCHG: Process 1, Nbr 22.22.22.22 on Ethernet0/0 from EXSTART to
DOWN, Neighbor Down: Too many retransmissions
OSPF1(config-if)#
```

Without the debugging, we would have to start looking at the configuration to find why the OSPF adjacency did not form.

Let's fix it so that we can move on. How shall we fix it? The easy way; by removing the MTU command, or interesting way? Let's do the interesting way:

```
OSPF1(config-if)#ip ospf mtu-ignore
OSPF1(config-if)#
```

Now let's shut and no shut the interface:

```
OSPF1(config-if)#shut
OSPF1(config-if)#
%LINEPROTO-5-UPDOWN: Line protocol on Interface Ethernet0/0, changed
state to down
OSPF1(config-if)#no shut
OSPF1(config-if)#
```

Remember that the checks that OSPF1 does to ensure that the MTU matches are also performed by OSPF2, so we should do the exact same commands on OSPF2 as well:

```
OSPF2(config)#int e0/0
OSPF2(config-if)#ip ospf mtu-ignore
OSPF2(config-if)#shut
OSPF2(config-if)#
%OSPF-5-ADJCHG: Process 1, Nbr 11.11.11.11 on Ethernet0/0 from DOWN to
DOWN, Neighbor Down: Interface down or detached
OSPF2(config-if)#
OSPF2(config-if)#no shut
OSPF2(config-if)#
%OSPF-5-ADJCHG: Process 1, Nbr 11.11.11.11 on Ethernet0/0 from LOADING to
FULL, Loading Done
OSPF2(config-if)#end
```

OSPF1 should also show the adjacency form:

```
OSPF1(config-if)#
%OSPF-5-ADJCHG: Process 1, Nbr 22.22.22.22 on Ethernet0/0 from LOADING to
FULL, Loading Done
OSPF1(config-if)#end
```

You might get the adjacency form with just one of the routers having the *"ip ospf mtu-ignore"* command on it, but it is a good idea to have the command on both sides of the link.

7.9.e Verify network types

We can verify our network types by looking at the interface through OSPF:

```
OSPF1#sh ip ospf int e0/0
Ethernet0/0 is up, line protocol is up
  Internet Address 89.89.1.1/24, Area 0, Attached via Network Statement
  Process ID 1, Router ID 11.11.11.11, Network Type BROADCAST, Cost: 10
  Topology-MTID    Cost   Disabled   Shutdown    Topology Name
        0           10       no         no          Base
  Transmit Delay is 1 sec, State DR, Priority 1
  Designated Router (ID) 11.11.11.11, Interface address 89.89.1.1
  Backup Designated router (ID) 22.22.22.22, Interface address 89.89.1.2
  Timer intervals configured, Hello 10, Dead 40, Wait 40, Retransmit 5
    oob-resync timeout 40
    Hello due in 00:00:02
  Supports Link-local Signaling (LLS)
  Cisco NSF helper support enabled
  IETF NSF helper support enabled
  Index 3/2, flood queue length 0
  Next 0x0(0)/0x0(0)
  Last flood scan length is 1, maximum is 1
  Last flood scan time is 0 msec, maximum is 0 msec
  Neighbor Count is 1, Adjacent neighbor count is 1
    Adjacent with neighbor 22.22.22.22  (Backup Designated Router)
  Suppress hello for 0 neighbor(s)
OSPF1#
```

Interface e0/0 has a network type of BROADCAST, whilst the loopback interface has a network type of LOOPBACK:

```
OSPF1#sh ip ospf int loopback0
Loopback0 is up, line protocol is up
  Internet Address 11.11.11.11/32, Area 0, Attached via Network Statement
  Process ID 1, Router ID 11.11.11.11, Network Type LOOPBACK, Cost: 1
  Topology-MTID    Cost   Disabled   Shutdown    Topology Name
        0            1        no         no          Base
  Loopback interface is treated as a stub Host
OSPF1#
```

The network type will influence with whom we can form an adjacency. We can form adjacencies with:

- Broadcast to Broadcast
- Non-broadcast to non-broadcast
- Point-to-point to point-to-point
- Broadcast to non-broadcast (need to adjust the hello and dead timers)
- Point-to-point and point-to-multipoint (hello and dead timers will need to be adjusted)

A table of the differences is below.

	Default for interface type	Default hello timer (seconds)	Default dead timer (seconds)	Requires DR/BDR
Broadcast	Ethernet	10	40	Yes
Non-Broadcast	Frame Relay	30	120	Yes
Point-to-Point		10	40	No
Point-to-Multipoint		30	120	No
Point-to-Multipoint non-broadcast		30	120	No
loopback	Loopback			No

The non-broadcast network types will require the manually configuration of neighbors. We can change the network type using the interface level command *"ip ospf network <network type>"*:

```
OSPF1(config)#int e0/0
OSPF1(config-if)#
OSPF1(config-if)#ip ospf network ?
  broadcast              Specify OSPF broadcast multi-access network
  non-broadcast          Specify OSPF NBMA network
  point-to-multipoint    Specify OSPF point-to-multipoint network
  point-to-point         Specify OSPF point-to-point network

OSPF1(config-if)#ip ospf network
```

Let's change the network type to be non-broadcast and then manually configure our neighbors:

```
OSPF1(config-if)#ip ospf network non-broadcast
OSPF1(config-if)#
%OSPF-5-ADJCHG: Process 1, Nbr 22.22.22.22 on Ethernet0/0 from FULL to
DOWN, Neighbor Down: Interface down or detached
OSPF1(config-if)#
OSPF1(config-if)#router ospf 1
OSPF1(config-router)#
OSPF1(config-router)#neighbor 89.89.1.2
OSPF1(config-router)#
```

Naturally, we need to do the same on OSPF2 (a non-broadcast interface cannot form an adjacency with a broadcast interface):

```
OSPF2(config)#router ospf 1
OSPF2(config-router)#neighbor 89.89.1.1
% OSPF: Configured Nbr 89.89.1.1 is incompatible with OSPF network type
on Ethernet0/0
OSPF2(config-router)#
OSPF2(config-router)#
%OSPF-4-CFG_NBR_INVALID_NET_TYPE: Can not use configured neighbor
89.89.1.1 on Ethernet0/0. Neighbor command only allowed on NBMA and P2MP
networks
OSPF2(config-router)#int e0/0
OSPF2(config-if)#ip ospf network non-broadcast
OSPF2(config-if)#router ospf 1
OSPF2(config-router)#neighbor 89.89.1.1
OSPF2(config-router)#priority 2
OSPF2(config-router)#
%OSPF-5-ADJCHG: Process 1, Nbr 11.11.11.11 on Ethernet0/0 from LOADING to
FULL, Loading Done
OSPF2(config-router)#
```

We must set the priority, otherwise the routers will not elect a DR/BDR. Eventually, OSPF1 also shows the adjacency form (though it may take quite a few moments):

```
OSPF1(config-router)#
%OSPF-5-ADJCHG: Process 1, Nbr 22.22.22.22 on Ethernet0/0 from LOADING to
FULL, Loading Done
OSPF1(config-router)#
```

7.9.f Verify neighbor states

We can use the command "*sh ip ospf neighbor*" to see what state we are in with our neighbor:

```
OSPF1(config-router)#
OSPF1(config-router)#do sh ip ospf neigh

Neighbor ID     Pri    State             Dead Time    Address       Interface
N/A             0      ATTEMPT/DROTHER   00:01:55     89.89.1.2     Ethernet0/0
1.1.1.2         1      FULL/DR           00:00:38     100.89.1.1    Ethernet0/2
OSPF1(config-router)#
OSPF1(config-router)#do sh ip ospf neigh

Neighbor ID     Pri    State             Dead Time    Address       Interface
22.22.22.22     1      2WAY/DROTHER      00:01:37     89.89.1.2     Ethernet0/0
1.1.1.2         1      FULL/DR           00:00:32     100.89.1.1    Ethernet0/2
OSPF1(config-router)#
```

```
OSPF1(config-router)#do sh ip ospf neigh
Neighbor ID   Pri   State         Dead Time   Address      Interface
22.22.22.22    1    EXSTART/BDR   00:01:52    89.89.1.2    Ethernet0/0
1.1.1.2        1    FULL/DR       00:00:37    100.89.1.1   Ethernet0/2
OSPF1(config-router)#
OSPF1(config-router)#do sh ip ospf neigh

Neighbor ID   Pri   State         Dead Time   Address      Interface
22.22.22.22    1    FULL/DR       00:01:45    89.89.1.2    Ethernet0/0
1.1.1.2        1    FULL/DR       00:00:39    100.89.1.1   Ethernet0/2
OSPF1(config-router)#
```

We can also use this command to dig deeper into our neighbor:

```
OSPF1(config-router)#do sh ip ospf neigh 22.22.22.22
 Neighbor 22.22.22.22, interface address 89.89.1.2
    In the area 0 via interface Ethernet0/0
    Neighbor priority is 1 (configured 0), State is FULL, 22 state
changes
    DR is 89.89.1.2 BDR is 89.89.1.1
    Poll interval 120
    Options is 0x12 in Hello (E-bit, L-bit)
    Options is 0x52 in DBD (E-bit, L-bit, O-bit)
    LLS Options is 0x1 (LR)
    Dead timer due in 00:01:37
    Neighbor is up for 00:02:17
    Index 2/2, retransmission queue length 0, number of retransmission 0
    First 0x0(0)/0x0(0) Next 0x0(0)/0x0(0)
    Last retransmission scan length is 0, maximum is 0
    Last retransmission scan time is 0 msec, maximum is 0 msec
OSPF1(config-router)#
```

This includes the current state (FULL), but notice that the priorities do not show the priority configured on OSPF2 (2). For that we need to look at the topology table.

7.9.g Review OSPF topology table

The last step is to check our OSPF topology table.

```
OSPF1(config-router)#do sh ip ospf topology

            OSPF Router with ID (11.11.11.11) (Process ID 1)


                 Base Topology (MTID 0)

 Topology priority is 64
```

```
        Router is not originating router-LSAs with maximum metric
        Number of areas transit capable is 0
        Initial SPF schedule delay 5000 msecs
        Minimum hold time between two consecutive SPFs 10000 msecs
        Maximum wait time between two consecutive SPFs 10000 msecs
            Area BACKBONE(0)
                SPF algorithm last executed 00:15:19.283 ago
                SPF algorithm executed 23 times
                Area ranges are
    OSPF1(config-router)#
```

And for OSPF2:

```
    OSPF2(config-router)#do sh ip ospf topology

                OSPF Router with ID (22.22.22.22) (Process ID 1)


                    Base Topology (MTID 0)

        Topology priority is 2
        Redistributing External Routes from,
            eigrp 1, includes subnets in redistribution
        Router is not originating router-LSAs with maximum metric
        Number of areas transit capable is 0
        Initial SPF schedule delay 5000 msecs
        Minimum hold time between two consecutive SPFs 10000 msecs
        Maximum wait time between two consecutive SPFs 10000 msecs
            Area BACKBONE(0)
                SPF algorithm last executed 00:15:45.284 ago
                SPF algorithm executed 16 times
                Area ranges are
    OSPF2(config-router)#
```

We can see that OSPF2 is redistributing EIGRP (or will do, once we fix the EIGRP adjacency), and we can see the different priorities, including our priority of 2 that we configured on OSPF2. Now let's go and fix EIGRP so we get it redistributing those routes.

7.10 Troubleshoot and resolve EIGRP problems

Troubleshooting EIGRP is not very different from OSPF; it's all about process.

7.10.a Verify neighbor adjacencies

OSPF2 has been complaining for some time now:

```
OSPF2(config-router)#
%DUAL-5-NBRCHANGE: EIGRP-IPv4 1: Neighbor 89.88.1.1 (Ethernet0/1) is
down: K-value mismatch
OSPF2(config-router)#
%DUAL-5-NBRCHANGE: EIGRP-IPv4 1: Neighbor 89.88.2.1 (Ethernet0/2) is
down: K-value mismatch
OSPF2(config-router)#
```

Recall from chapter 4 that the K values are our metric weights. So we have an issues with the metrics we are sending over to our peers. It's time to use *"show ip protocols"* to see what metrics we are using:

```
OSPF2(config-router)#end
OSPF2#
OSPF2#sh ip protocols | s eigrp
Routing Protocol is "eigrp 1"
  Outgoing update filter list for all interfaces is not set
  Incoming update filter list for all interfaces is not set
  Default networks flagged in outgoing updates
  Default networks accepted from incoming updates
  Redistributing: ospf 1
  EIGRP-IPv4 Protocol for AS(1)
    Metric weight K1=1, K2=1, K3=1, K4=1, K5=0
    NSF-aware route hold timer is 240
    Router-ID: 22.22.22.22
    Topology : 0 (base)
      Active Timer: 3 min
      Distance: internal 90 external 170
      Maximum path: 4
      Maximum hopcount 100
      Maximum metric variance 1
    eigrp 1, includes subnets in redistribution
OSPF2#
```

How do we tackle this one? We can start by looking at our own configuration:

```
OSPF2#sh run | s router eigrp
router eigrp 1
 metric weights 0 1 1 1 1 0
 network 89.88.1.2 0.0.0.0
 network 89.88.2.2 0.0.0.0
 redistribute ospf 1 match internal external 1 external 2 metric 10000 0
255 1 1500
 eigrp router-id 22.22.22.22
OSPF2#
```

We can see that the metric weights have been manually configured. We know that they have been manually configured as they show up in the configuration, whereas default settings do not show up in the configuration.

So we could remove the command, which should set it have to the defaults, but how do we know that the other two routers are using the defaults? We don't, not from here anyway.

We can use some debugging, and in this case, this will be the most informative:

```
OSPF2#debug eigrp packets hello detail
    (HELLO Detail)
EIGRP Packet debugging is on
OSPF2#
*Nov 26 19:16:30.190: EIGRP: Sending HELLO on Et0/2 - paklen 30
*Nov 26 19:16:30.190:    AS 1, Flags 0x0:(NULL), Seq 0/0 interfaceQ 0/0
iidbQ un/rely 0/0
*Nov 26 19:16:30.190:    {type = 1, length = 12}
*Nov 26 19:16:30.190:    {vector = {
*Nov 26 19:16:30.190:            {01010101 0000000F}
*Nov 26 19:16:30.190:    }
*Nov 26 19:16:30.190:    {type = 4, length = 8}
*Nov 26 19:16:30.190:    {vector = {
*Nov 26 19:16:30.190:            {0F000200}
*Nov 26 19:16:30.190:    }
*Nov 26 19:16:30.190:    {type = F5, length = 10}
*Nov 26 19:16:30.190:    {vector = {
*Nov 26 19:16:30.190:            {00000002 0000}
*Nov 26 19:16:30.190:    }
*Nov 26 19:16:32.796: EIGRP: Received HELLO on Et0/1 - paklen 30 nbr
89.88.1.1
*Nov 26 19:16:32.796:    AS 1, Flags 0x0:(NULL), Seq 0/0 interfaceQ 0/0
*Nov 26 19:16:32.796:    {type = 1, length = 12}
*Nov 26 19:16:32.796:    {vector = {
*Nov 26 19:16:32.796:            {01000100 0000000F}
*Nov 26 19:16:32.796:    }
*Nov 26 19:16:32.796:    {type = 4, length = 8}
*Nov 26 19:16:32.796:    {vector = {
*Nov 26 19:16:32.796:            {0F000200}
*Nov 26 19:16:32.796:    }
*Nov 26 19:16:32.796:    {type = F5, length = 10}
*Nov 26 19:16:32.796:    {vector = {
*Nov 26 19:16:32.796:            {00000002 0000}
*Nov 26 19:16:32.796:    }
*Nov 26 19:16:32.796:            K-value mismatch
OSPF2#un all
All possible debugging has been turned off
OSPF2#
```

Notice that we are sending our parameters, which are the "type 1" vectors, and these differ to the ones we are receiving; we send 01010101 and are receiving 01000100. Let's do a Wireshark capture to help us visualize this:

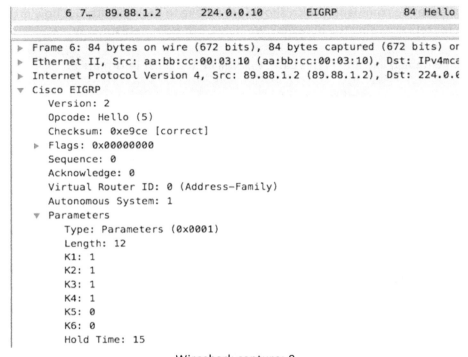

Wireshark capture: 9

OSPF2 is using K1, K2, K3 and K4. So does this match up with the debug output, and if so, can we work out what the other side is using?

	K1	K2	K3	K4	K5, K6 & Hold
OSPF2	01	01	01	01	0000000F
EIGRP1	01	00	01	00	0000000F

This looks very plausible, as the defaults are K1 and K3 only. Wireshark can confirm this though:

```
     10  1.  89.88.1.1      224.0.0.10      EIGRP       84 Hello
```

```
▶ Frame 10: 84 bytes on wire (672 bits), 84 bytes captured (672 bits) c
▶ Ethernet II, Src: aa:bb:cc:00:04:10 (aa:bb:cc:00:04:10), Dst: IPv4mca
▶ Internet Protocol Version 4, Src: 89.88.1.1 (89.88.1.1), Dst: 224.0.0
▼ Cisco EIGRP
     Version: 2
     Opcode: Hello (5)
     Checksum: 0xe9d0 [correct]
   ▶ Flags: 0x00000000
     Sequence: 0
     Acknowledge: 0
     Virtual Router ID: 0 (Address-Family)
     Autonomous System: 1
   ▼ Parameters
       Type: Parameters (0x0001)
       Length: 12
       K1: 1
       K2: 0
       K3: 1
       K4: 0
       K5: 0
       K6: 0
       Hold Time: 15
```

Looks good. We have confirmed that EIGRP1 (and EIGRP2 if you want to work it out) are using the default K values, so let's use them on OSPF2 as well:

```
OSPF2(config)#router eigrp 1
OSPF2(config-router)#no metric weights 0 1 1 1 1 0
OSPF2(config-router)#
%DUAL-5-NBRCHANGE: EIGRP-IPv4 1: Neighbor 89.88.2.1 (Ethernet0/2) is up:
new adjacency
OSPF2(config-router)#
%DUAL-5-NBRCHANGE: EIGRP-IPv4 1: Neighbor 89.88.1.1 (Ethernet0/1) is up:
new adjacency
OSPF2(config-router)#
```

We now have adjacencies to both the EIGRP routers in Autonomous System 1.

7.10.b Verify AS number

Because we can be joined to more than one AS, we need to see which peers are in which AS. This is important as routes learned from one AS will not be advertised into another AS, unless we configure redistribution between the two AS's. Therefore, if we are trying to track down why one router does not see a particular route in a more complex EIGRP topology, we may need to look at if and how one AS is being redistributed into another.

We can see what neighbors are active in which AS using the command *"show ip eigrp neighbors"*

```
OSPF2(config-router)#end
OSPF2#
OSPF2#sh ip eigrp neigh
EIGRP-IPv4 Neighbors for AS(1)
H   Address      Interface   Hold Uptime    SRTT   RTO  Q   Seq
                             (sec)          (ms)        Cnt Num
1   89.88.1.1    Et0/1        11 00:02:49      7   100  0   174
0   89.88.2.1    Et0/2        14 00:02:50      4   100  0   161
OSPF2#
```

7.10.c Verify load balancing

By default, EIGRP will load-balance across multiple paths (four of them). We can use *"show ip protocols"* to look at the entry for "maximum paths". We can see the effect of this in our routing table:

```
OSPF2#sh ip route eigrp | b Gate
Gateway of last resort is not set

      1.0.0.0/24 is subnetted, 1 subnets
D        1.1.1.0 [90/332800] via 89.88.2.1, 00:27:14, Eth0/2
                 [90/332800] via 89.88.1.1, 00:27:14, Eth0/1
      10.0.0.0/24 is subnetted, 3 subnets
D        10.100.1.0 [90/332800] via 89.88.2.1, 00:27:14, Eth0/2
                    [90/332800] via 89.88.1.1, 00:27:14, Eth0/1
D        10.200.1.0 [90/332800] via 89.88.2.1, 00:27:14, Eth0/2
                    [90/332800] via 89.88.1.1, 00:27:14, Eth0/1
      88.0.0.0/8 is variably subnetted, 5 subnets, 2 masks
D        88.88.11.0/24 [90/307200] via 89.88.1.1, 00:27:14, Ethernet0/1
D        88.88.12.0/24 [90/307200] via 89.88.2.1, 00:27:14, Ethernet0/2
D        88.88.21.0/24 [90/307200] via 89.88.2.1, 00:27:14, Ethernet0/2
D        88.88.88.1/32 [90/409600] via 89.88.1.1, 00:27:14, Ethernet0/1
D        88.88.88.2/32 [90/409600] via 89.88.2.1, 00:27:14, Ethernet0/2
OSPF2#
```

The entries that are bolded are the ones we can load balance across. We can see how this works if we do a traceroute to one of the addresses (an address on InterVLAN1):

```
OSPF2#trace 1.1.1.1 numeric
Type escape sequence to abort.
Tracing the route to 1.1.1.1
VRF info: (vrf in name/id, vrf out name/id)
  1 89.88.1.1 1 msec
    89.88.2.1 5 msec
```

```
     89.88.1.1 0 msec
  2 88.88.21.1 1 msec
     88.88.11.1 4 msec *
OSPF2#
```

We need to look for issues such as interface bandwidth mismatches across the paths, anything that can affect the metric, if we change the bandwidth on EIGRP2; we lose the ability to load-balance across both paths:

```
EIGRP2(config)#int e0/1
EIGRP2(config-if)#bandwidth 1000
EIGRP2(config-if)#

OSPF2#sh ip route 1.0.0.0
Routing entry for 1.0.0.0/24, 1 known subnets
  Redistributing via eigrp 1
D        1.1.1.0 [90/332800] via 89.88.1.1, 00:00:52, Ethernet0/1
OSPF2#
```

We can set it back and load balance again:

```
EIGRP2(config-if)#no band 1000
EIGRP2(config-if)#

OSPF2#sh ip route 1.0.0.0
Routing entry for 1.0.0.0/24, 1 known subnets
  Redistributing via eigrp 1
D        1.1.1.0 [90/332800] via 89.88.2.1, 00:00:10, Ethernet0/2
                 [90/332800] via 89.88.1.1, 00:00:10, Ethernet0/1
OSPF2#
```

Remember that by default we can load balance, so if we cannot, then something must have been changed and should show up in the configuration, most likely under the interface configuration or under the routing protocol configuration.

7.10.d Split horizon

The last section in EIGRP troubleshooting to cover is split horizon. Split horizon is a rule (of sorts) that says we should not advertise a route we learn about over the interface we learned it on. This would be like someone telling you a joke, and once they have finished, you try telling them the exact same joke. They already know about it and will probably ignore your efforts in telling them.

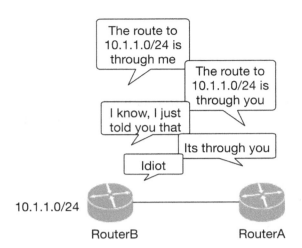

This makes sense, if RouterB advertises the 10.1.1.0/24 network to RouterA, why would RouterA need to tell RouterB about a route he is already advertising? Split horizon prevents this behaviour.

However, sometimes split horizon can cause us issues, example cases are with DMVPN (Dynamic Multipoint VPN), where we do need to turn off split horizon, the same is true where we have a number of EIGRP-speaking routers connected to a LAN segment. In the following diagram, RouterA and RouterB are set as static neighbors. RouterB does not have adjacencies to RouterC or RouterD:

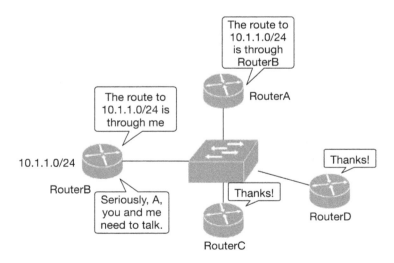

We can switch off split horizon using the interface-level command "*no ip split-horizon*":

```
EIGRP2(config-if)#no ip split-horizon
EIGRP2(config-if)#
```

We can turn it back on again using the command "*ip split-horizon*":

```
EIGRP2(config-if)#ip split-horizon
EIGRP2(config-if)#
```

Our network is starting to recover now. SW1's routing table is looking much better:

```
SW1#sh ip route | b Gate
Gateway of last resort is not set

      1.0.0.0/8 is variably subnetted, 2 subnets, 2 masks
C        1.1.1.0/24 is directly connected, Vlan1
L        1.1.1.1/32 is directly connected, Vlan1
      10.0.0.0/8 is variably subnetted, 4 subnets, 2 masks
C        10.10.10.0/24 is directly connected, Vlan10
L        10.10.10.1/32 is directly connected, Vlan10
O E2     10.100.1.0/24 [110/20] via 1.1.1.2, 01:16:15, Vlan1
O E2     10.200.1.0/24 [110/20] via 1.1.1.2, 01:16:15, Vlan1
      11.0.0.0/32 is subnetted, 1 subnets
O        11.11.11.11 [110/3] via 1.1.1.2, 05:13:18, Vlan1
      20.0.0.0/24 is subnetted, 1 subnets
O        20.20.20.0 [110/2] via 1.1.1.2, 6d04h, Vlan1
      22.0.0.0/32 is subnetted, 1 subnets
O        22.22.22.22 [110/13] via 1.1.1.2, 02:24:03, Vlan1
      88.0.0.0/8 is variably subnetted, 5 subnets, 2 masks
O E2     88.88.11.0/24 [110/20] via 1.1.1.2, 01:16:15, Vlan1
O E2     88.88.12.0/24 [110/20] via 1.1.1.2, 01:16:15, Vlan1
O E2     88.88.21.0/24 [110/20] via 1.1.1.2, 01:16:15, Vlan1
O E2     88.88.88.1/32 [110/20] via 1.1.1.2, 01:16:15, Vlan1
O E2     88.88.88.2/32 [110/20] via 1.1.1.2, 01:16:15, Vlan1
      89.0.0.0/24 is subnetted, 3 subnets
O E2     89.88.1.0 [110/20] via 1.1.1.2, 02:24:03, Vlan1
O E2     89.88.2.0 [110/20] via 1.1.1.2, 02:24:03, Vlan1
O        89.89.1.0 [110/12] via 1.1.1.2, 02:24:03, Vlan1
      100.0.0.0/24 is subnetted, 1 subnets
O        100.89.1.0 [110/2] via 1.1.1.2, 05:24:53, Vlan1
SW1#
```

We can even reach from Client to InterVLAN1:

```
Client#ping 10.200.1.200
Type escape sequence to abort.
Sending 5, 100-byte ICMP Echos to 10.200.1.200:
!!!!!
Success rate is 100 percent (5/5)
Client#
```

Let's press on!

7.11 Troubleshoot and resolve interVLAN routing problems

On the console of InterVLAN1, nothing seems wrong. We can see both the EIGRP routers and SW4:

```
InterVLAN1#sh cdp neigh | b Device
Device ID      Local Intrfce   Holdtme    Capability  Platform  Port ID
SW4            Eth 0/2.1       155              R S I  Linux Uni Eth 0/0
EIGRP1         Eth 0/0         134              R B    Linux Uni Eth 0/2
EIGRP2         Eth 0/1         143              R B    Linux Uni Eth 0/1

Total cdp entries displayed : 3
InterVLAN1#
```

We have a number of interfaces and can see that we also have sub-interfaces, all are up/up:

```
InterVLAN1#sh ip int bri | e Serial|down
Interface            IP-Address      OK? Method Status    Protocol
Ethernet0/0          88.88.11.1      YES NVRAM  up        up
Ethernet0/1          88.88.21.1      YES NVRAM  up        up
Ethernet0/2          unassigned      YES NVRAM  up        up
Ethernet0/2.1        1.1.1.11        YES manual up        up
Ethernet0/2.100      10.100.1.200    YES NVRAM  up        up
Ethernet0/2.200      10.200.1.200    YES NVRAM  up        up

InterVLAN1#
```

We can also telnet to the secure server:

```
InterVLAN1#telnet 20.20.20.20 80 /source-interface e0/2.200
Trying 20.20.20.20, 80 ... Open
get
HTTP/1.1 400 Bad Request
Date: Tue, 05 Jan 2016 17:51:10 GMT
Server: cisco-IOS
Accept-Ranges: none

400 Bad Request
[Connection to 20.20.20.20 closed by foreign host]
InterVLAN1#
```

So let's look at the other side of the network.

7.11.a Verify connectivity

If all is working well, we should be able to ping the VLAN 1 interfaces on SW3 and SW4, as well as the VLAN 100 and VLAN 200 interfaces:

```
InterVLAN1#ping 1.1.1.3
Type escape sequence to abort.
Sending 5, 100-byte ICMP Echos to 1.1.1.3:
.....
Success rate is 0 percent (0/5)
InterVLAN1#ping 1.1.1.4
Type escape sequence to abort.
Sending 5, 100-byte ICMP Echos to 1.1.1.4:
!!!!!
Success rate is 100 percent (5/5)
InterVLAN1#ping 10.100.1.1
Type escape sequence to abort.
Sending 5, 100-byte ICMP Echos to 10.100.1.1:
.....
Success rate is 0 percent (0/5)
InterVLAN1#ping 10.200.1.1
Type escape sequence to abort.
Sending 5, 100-byte ICMP Echos to 10.200.1.1:
.!!!!
Success rate is 100 percent (4/5)
InterVLAN1#
```

We have mixed results, we can reach SW4, but not SW3.

7.11.b Verify encapsulation

Let's start by looking at our interfaces on the InterVLAN1 router:

```
InterVLAN1#sh run int e0/2.100 | b interface
interface Ethernet0/2.100
 encapsulation dot1Q 10
 ip address 10.100.1.200 255.255.255.0
end

InterVLAN1#sh run int e0/2.200 | b interface
interface Ethernet0/2.200
 encapsulation dot1Q 200
 ip address 10.200.1.200 255.255.255.0
end

InterVLAN1#
```

We need to use sub-interfaces so that we can assign a dot1q tag to it. Can you see what is wrong in the output above? Well, without more information, nothing is actually wrong. We have a sub-interface, E0/2.100, with an IP address of 10.100.1.200 and the interface is set up for dot1q encapsulation, for VLAN 10. The idea of numbering the sub-interface to be the same as the dot1q

VLAN it encapsulates is just an idea, it is just done to aid us, but is not mandatory, so a sub-interface of e0/2.100 can happily pass traffic for VLAN 10 (or VLAN 4, 5, 28 or whatever).

Unfortunately, this is one of those times we do need to connect to the other device in order to find out what our dot1q VLAN should actually be, and to show that we are taking a leap of faith in assuming that it is the VLAN encapsulation that is incorrect.

Let's jump onto SW4 to confirm or deny this:

```
SW4#sh ip int bri | e unas
Interface         IP-Address      OK? Method Status       Protocol
Loopback0         44.44.44.44     YES NVRAM  up           up
Vlan1             1.1.1.4         YES NVRAM  up           up
Vlan200           10.200.1.1      YES NVRAM  up           up

SW4#
SW4#sh vlan brief | e unsup

VLAN Name                             Status    Ports
---- -------------------------------- --------- --------------
1    default                          active    Et0/3
100  FR-VLAN                          active
200  Secure-VLAN                      active
SW4#sh int trunk | i Et0/0
Et0/0         on             802.1q         trunking      1
Et0/0         1-4094
Et0/0         1,100,200
Et0/0         1,100,200
SW4#
```

The outputs above would all indicate that it is indeed a configuration mistake on InterVLAN1 and the dot1q encapsulation should be for VLAN 100, not VLAN 10. We do not have a VLAN 100 interface on SW4, so we still may have some surprises to come, but let's fix InterVLAN1 and see what happens:

```
InterVLAN1(config)#int e0/2.100
InterVLAN1(config-subif)#encapsulation dot1Q 100
InterVLAN1(config-subif)#
```

Can we get to the VLAN interface now?

```
InterVLAN1(config-subif)#do ping 10.100.1.1
Type escape sequence to abort.
Sending 5, 100-byte ICMP Echos to 10.100.1.1:
.....
Success rate is 0 percent (0/5)
InterVLAN1(config-subif)#
```

Not yet.

OK, so where do we start looking?

7.11.c Verify subnet

First, let's make sure we are sticking to the rules of this challenge, can we see SW3 from SW4 using CDP?

```
SW4#sh cdp neigh | b Device
Device ID       Local Intrfce   Holdtme   Capability  Platform  Port ID
SW3             Eth 0/2         136             R S I  Linux Uni Eth 0/2
SW3             Eth 0/1         136             R S I  Linux Uni Eth 0/1
InterVLAN1      Eth 0/0         132             R B    Linux Uni Eth 0/2.1

SW4#
```

We can, so let's move on to SW3 and make sure that we are trying to talk to the correct device:

```
SW3#sh ip int bri | e unas
Interface           IP-Address        OK? Method Status    Protocol
Loopback0           33.33.33.33       YES NVRAM  up        up
Vlan1               1.1.1.3           YES NVRAM  up        up
Vlan100             10.100.1.1        YES NVRAM  up        up

SW3#
```

So now we know we are trying to reach SW3 from InterVLAN1, are we on the same subnet?

```
InterVLAN1(config-subif)#
InterVLAN1(config-subif)#do sh run int e0/2.100 | i address
 ip address 10.100.1.200 255.255.255.0
InterVLAN1(config-subif)#

SW3#sh run int vlan 100 | i address
 ip address 10.100.1.1 255.255.255.0
SW3#
```

Both are in the same subnet.

7.11.d Verify native VLAN

The native VLAN is used for untagged traffic, anything that is not explicitly tagged will use VLAN 1. We can see from SW4 that the native VLAN is VLAN 1:

```
SW4#sh int e0/0 trunk | i Status|trunking
Port       Mode            Encapsulation  Status       Native vlan
Et0/0      on              802.1q         trunking     1
SW4#
```

Is the traffic from InterVLAN1 tagged, or untagged?

If we start Wireshark, and then try to ping 10.100.1.1 from InterVLAN1 we can find out. We will not be able to see any ICMP packets, but we can look at the ARP request (the ARP request will need to be replied to, in order to build up the MAC address table):

```
    86 2…  aa:bb:cc:00:…  Broadcast      ARP      64 Who has 10.100.1.1? Tell 10.100.1.200
▶ Frame 86: 64 bytes on wire (512 bits), 64 bytes captured (512 bits) on interface 0
▶ Ethernet II, Src: aa:bb:cc:00:06:20 (aa:bb:cc:00:06:20), Dst: Broadcast (ff:ff:ff:ff:ff:ff)
▼ 802.1Q Virtual LAN, PRI: 0, CFI: 0, ID: 100
      000. .... .... .... = Priority: Best Effort (default) (0)
      ...0 .... .... .... = CFI: Canonical (0)
      .... 0000 0110 0100 = ID: 100
      Type: ARP (0x0806)
      Padding: 00000000000000000000000000000000
      Trailer: 00000000
▶ Address Resolution Protocol (request)
```

Wireshark capture: 10

Our traffic is tagged, so it should reach the correct VLAN (100, as shown next to "ID"). Now we know that the traffic from InterVLAN1 is leaving the router in the correct VLAN, and will be received by SW4 (as SW4 is trunking for that VLAN on the port connecting it to InterVLAN1). The VLAN interface is up on SW3, so it looks like the traffic is not getting from SW4 to SW3.

This looks like a trunking issue.

7.11.e Port mode trunk status

Let's look at the trunks between SW4 and SW3:

```
SW4#show int trunk | i Status|trunking
Port       Mode            Encapsulation  Status       Native vlan
Et0/0      on              802.1q         trunking     1
Et0/1      on              isl            trunking     1
Et0/2      on              isl            trunking     1

SW4#
```

We have ISL encapsulation running on the links between SW4 and SW3 (e0/1 and e0/2). How is SW3 set up?

```
SW3#sh int trunk | i Status|trunking
Port         Mode              Encapsulation  Status      Native vlan
Et0/1        on                802.1q         trunking    1
Et0/2        on                802.1q         trunking    1
SW3#
```

We have 802.1q on SW3. These two are not compatible. Trunking is not like STP (where Rapid-PVST can live happily with PVST), our trunks must match.

Another way we could see the issue would be by looking at the logs on the router, where we might see something like this:

```
SW4(config)#do sh log
<truncated>
%SPANTREE-2-RECV_1Q_NON_1QTRUNK: Received 802.1Q BPDU on non 802.1Q trunk
Ethernet0/1 VLAN1.
%SPANTREE-7-BLOCK_PORT_TYPE: Blocking Ethernet0/1 on VLAN0001.
Inconsistent port type.
%SPANTREE-2-RECV_1Q_NON_1QTRUNK: Received 802.1Q BPDU on non 802.1Q trunk
Ethernet0/1 VLAN200.
%SPANTREE-7-BLOCK_PORT_TYPE: Blocking Ethernet0/1 on VLAN0200.
Inconsistent port type.
%SPANTREE-2-RECV_1Q_NON_1QTRUNK: Received 802.1Q BPDU on non 802.1Q trunk
Ethernet0/1 VLAN100.
%SPANTREE-7-BLOCK_PORT_TYPE: Blocking Ethernet0/1 on VLAN0100.
Inconsistent port type.
```

In the event that we did not have access to the other router, these logs would be extremely helpful. They tell us what the other side is sending; "Received 802.1Q BPDU", it also tells us that we are not using an 802.1Q trunk; "on non 802.1Q trunk Ethernet0/1". It would then allow us to change our encapsulation method to match the other router, hoping that the trunk will work and our traffic will pass along it:

```
SW4(config)#int e0/1
SW4(config-if)#switchport trunk encapsulation dot1q
SW4(config-if)#
```

After a few moments, we should see EIGRP adjacencies appear:

```
SW3#
%DUAL-5-NBRCHANGE: EIGRP-IPv4 1: Neighbor 1.1.1.1 (Vlan1) is up: new
adjacency
%DUAL-5-NBRCHANGE: EIGRP-IPv4 1: Neighbor 10.100.1.200 (Vlan100) is up:
new adjacency
SW3#
```

We should also have a successful ping result:

```
InterVLAN1#ping 10.100.1.1
Type escape sequence to abort.
Sending 5, 100-byte ICMP Echos to 10.100.1.1:
..!!!
Success rate is 60 percent (3/5)
InterVLAN1#
```

> If the ping fails, and you see the EIGRP adjacencies dropping and being re-established, try shutting down port e0/2 on SW3 and SW4.

All being well, we should be able to get to here from Client as well:

```
Client#ping 10.100.1.1
Type escape sequence to abort.
Sending 5, 100-byte ICMP Echos to 10.100.1.1:
!!!!!
Success rate is 100 percent (5/5)
Client#
```

We are nearly at our destination! We just need to fix our WAN.

7.12 Troubleshoot and resolve WAN implementation issues

We only have a couple more steps to go through before we can capture the flag, and this is to fix the "WAN" (which is a couple of Frame Relay routers and a Frame Relay switch that connect us to the FTP-Server). We can already see that we are connected to FR-101 from SW3, which means we are (according to the rules) able to connect to FR-101:

```
SW3#sh cdp neigh | b Device
Device ID       Local Intrfce    Holdtme   Capability  Platform  Port ID
FR-101          Eth 0/0          142             R B   Linux Uni Eth 0/0
SW4             Eth 0/2          179           R S I   Linux Uni Eth 0/2
SW4             Eth 0/1          179           R S I   Linux Uni Eth 0/1
SW3#
```

We can also reach it (we can find the IP address using the command *"show cdp entry FR-101"*):

```
SW3#ping 10.100.1.101
Type escape sequence to abort.
Sending 5, 100-byte ICMP Echos to 10.100.1.101:
!!!!!
Success rate is 100 percent (5/5)
SW3#
```

Let's jump on to FR-101 and see what is happening there.

```
FR-101#sh cdp neigh | b Device
Device ID        Local Intrfce     Holdtme   Capability Platform  Port ID
SW3              Eth 0/0           148            R S I  Linux Uni Eth 0/0

Total cdp entries displayed : 1
FR-101#
```

From FR-101, we can only see SW3. Is the interface shutdown, or do we have a different issue?

```
FR-101#sh ip int bri s1/0
Interface           IP-Address      OK? Method Status      Protocol
Serial1/0           10.101.1.101    YES NVRAM  up          down
FR-101#
```

The interface is not shut down; the Status is "up", but the line protocol is "down". This usually indicates an issue with encapsulation. The next step would be to look at the interface configuration:

```
FR-101#sh run int s1/0
Building configuration...

Current configuration : 103 bytes
!
interface Serial1/0
 ip address 10.101.1.101 255.255.255.0
 serial restart-delay 0
end

FR-101#
```

Not much to help us there. So, what do we know about serial interfaces?

7.12.a Serial interfaces

Despite the sometimes confusing array of interface cards and cables that are available for serial communication, serial interfaces are pretty simple things to configure. We have two things we need; the interface to be up (by using the "*no shutdown*" command) and for the line protocol to be up. The line protocol must match, and can be HDLC (which is the default), PPP, Frame Relay, or a number of other options:

```
FR-101(config)#int s1/0
FR-101(config-if)#encapsulation ?
  atm-dxi           ATM-DXI encapsulation
  bstun             Block Serial tunneling (BSTUN)
```

```
frame-relay       Frame Relay networks
hdlc              Serial HDLC synchronous
lapb              LAPB (X.25 Level 2)
ppp               Point-to-Point protocol
sdlc              SDLC
sdlc-primary      SDLC (primary)
sdlc-secondary    SDLC (secondary)
smds              Switched Megabit Data Service (SMDS)
stun              Serial tunneling (STUN)
x25               X.25

FR-101(config-if)#encapsulation
```

Let's try setting the encapsulation to Frame Relay and see what happens.

7.12.b Frame Relay

```
FR-101(config-if)#encapsulation frame-relay
FR-101(config-if)#
%LINEPROTO-5-UPDOWN: Line protocol on Interface Serial1/0, changed state
to up
FR-101(config-if)#
```

Our line protocol comes up, meaning we have a match to the interface setting on the other side of the cable. After a few moments, we should see an EIGRP adjacency form:

```
FR-101(config-if)#
%DUAL-5-NBRCHANGE: EIGRP-IPv4 1: Neighbor 10.102.1.102 (Serial1/0) is up:
new adjacency
FR-101(config-if)#
```

We do not have a CDP entry though:

```
FR-101(config-if)#do sh cdp neigh | b Device
Device ID    Local Intrfce   Holdtme   Capability Platform  Port ID
SW3          Eth 0/0         139              R S I Linux Uni Eth 0/0

Total cdp entries displayed : 1
FR-101(config-if)#
```

We can fix this, but let's talk about why first.

We are running a slightly different Frame Relay configuration here (compared to our main topology); we are using a dedicated Frame Relay switch (FR-SW). CDP is disabled (by default) on Frame Relay interfaces. CDP operates at layer-2, so FR-SW will ignore these particular packets, in that the FR-SW will be "invisible" but it will pass them. When we have a successful PVC, such as the one we now have between FR-101 and FR-102, we can enable CDP and they should be able to see each other through CDP:

```
FR-101(config-if)#int s1/0
FR-101(config-if)#cdp enable
FR-101(config-if)#

FR-102(config)#int s1/0
FR-102(config-if)#cdp enable
FR-102(config-if)#
```

After we give it a moment or two, we should see the new CDP entry:

```
FR-101(config-if)#do sh cdp neigh | b Device
Device ID       Local Intrfce   Holdtme   Capability  Platform  Port ID
FR-102          Ser 1/0         138             R B   Linux Uni Ser 1/0
SW3             Eth 0/0         138           R S I   Linux Uni Eth 0/0

Total cdp entries displayed : 2
FR-101(config-if)#
```

When we use a Frame Relay switch, as we are doing here, the switch will not originate packets itself. It will just switch them. Therefore, even if we enable CDP on the serial interfaces on the switch, it will stay "invisible" to the Frame Relay routers. Let's take a moment to look at the configuration of the switch:

```
FR-SW#sh run int s1/1 |b interface
interface Serial1/1
 ip address 10.101.1.1 255.255.255.0
 encapsulation frame-relay
 serial restart-delay 0
 clock rate 56000
 frame-relay intf-type dce
 frame-relay route 101 interface Serial1/2 102
end
FR-SW#sh run int s1/2 | b interface
interface Serial1/2
 ip address 10.102.1.1 255.255.255.0
 encapsulation frame-relay
 serial restart-delay 0
 clock rate 56000
 frame-relay intf-type dce
 frame-relay route 102 interface Serial1/1 101
end
FR-SW#
```

Both interfaces are set to use Frame Relay encapsulation, both are acting as the DCE, as they have the clock rate command set, as well as the interface type. Then we have a *"frame-relay route"* command. The route command does just that, it routes the different DLCIs between each other, handling all the switching of the tags. The command syntax is *"frame-relay route <inbound DLCI> interface <outbound interface> <outbound DLCI>"*. So for the command configured under S1/1 it means "this interface is DLCI 101, make a PVC to interface (Serial 1/2) which will be using a DLCI of 102".

We can confirm that the routes are working in a couple of ways, the most useful will be the command *"show frame-relay route"*:

```
FR-SW#sh frame-relay route
Input Intf     Input Dlci     Output Intf     Output Dlci     Status
Serial1/1      101            Serial1/2       102             active
Serial1/2      102            Serial1/1       101             active
FR-SW#
```

Other useful commands will be *"show frame-relay pvc"* and *"show frame-relay lmi"*. One last step to go!

7.12.c PPP

Our last step is to get from FR-102 to the FTP-Server. We cannot, however, see it in CDP:

```
FR-102#sh cdp neigh | b Device
Device ID      Local Intrfce   Holdtme   Capability Platform  Port ID
FR-101         Ser 1/0         125            R B   Linux Uni Ser 1/0
Total cdp entries displayed : 1
FR-102#
```

Our line protocol is down as well:

```
FR-102#sh ip int bri | e unas
Interface         IP-Address       OK? Method Status      Protocol
Serial1/0         10.102.1.102     YES NVRAM  up          up
Serial1/1         10.103.1.102     YES NVRAM  up          down
Loopback0         102.102.102.102  YES NVRAM  up          up
FR-102#
```

As it is a line protocol issue we should know where to start looking; at the encapsulation on the interface. The default encapsulation is HDLC, as we can see below:

```
FR-102#sh int s1/1 | i Encapsulation
  Encapsulation HDLC, crc 16, loopback not set
FR-102#
```

So let's try PPP instead (the topic heading kind of gives this away!):

```
FR-102(config)#int s1/1
FR-102(config-if)#encapsulation ppp
FR-102(config-if)#
%LINEPROTO-5-UPDOWN: Line protocol on Interface Serial1/1, changed state
to up
FR-102(config-if)#end
```

The line comes up, and we have a CDP entry for the FTP-Server:

```
FR-102#sh cdp neigh | b Device
Device ID      Local Intrfce   Holdtme   Capability Platform  Port ID
FR-101         Ser 1/0         168              R B  Linux Uni Ser 1/0
FTP-Server     Ser 1/1         150              R B  Linux Uni Ser 1/0

Total cdp entries displayed : 2
FR-102#
```

Now we can head over to the FTP server and check that out:

```
FTP-Server#
%LINEPROTO-5-UPDOWN: Line protocol on Interface Serial1/0, changed state
to up
FTP-Server#sh ip route | b Gate
Gateway of last resort is 10.103.1.102 to network 0.0.0.0

S*    0.0.0.0/0 [1/0] via 10.103.1.102
      10.0.0.0/8 is variably subnetted, 3 subnets, 2 masks
C        10.103.1.0/24 is directly connected, Serial1/0
L        10.103.1.1/32 is directly connected, Serial1/0
C        10.103.1.102/32 is directly connected, Serial1/0
FTP-Server#
```

We have a default route through FR-102, which, if we look at the interface configuration, is being supplied through the IP Control Protocol (using the command "*ppp ipcp route default*"):

```
FTP-Server#sh run int s1/0 | b interface
interface Serial1/0
 ip address 10.103.1.1 255.255.255.0
 encapsulation ppp
 ppp ipcp route default
 serial restart-delay 0
end

FTP-Server#
```

Now, if all went well and we have fixed all the issues, we should be able to reach the FTP-Server from the client:

```
Client#ping 10.103.1.1
Type escape sequence to abort.
Sending 5, 100-byte ICMP Echos to 10.103.1.1:
!!!!!
Success rate is 100 percent (5/5)
Client#
Client#trace 10.103.1.1 numeric
Type escape sequence to abort.
Tracing the route to 10.103.1.1
VRF info: (vrf in name/id, vrf out name/id)
  1 10.10.10.1 5 msec 4 msec 5 msec
  2 1.1.1.2 0 msec 4 msec 4 msec
  3 100.89.1.89 5 msec 1 msec 4 msec
  4 89.89.1.2 1 msec 1 msec 1 msec
  5 89.88.2.1 1 msec 1 msec 1 msec
  6 88.88.21.1 1 msec 1 msec 1 msec
  7 10.100.1.101 2 msec 1 msec 2 msec
  8 10.102.1.102 18 msec 19 msec 19 msec
  9 10.103.1.1 26 msec *  29 msec
Client#
```

Can we telnet (using the password of "cisco")?

```
Client#telnet 10.103.1.1
Trying 10.103.1.1 ... Open


User Access Verification

Password:
FTP-Server>!!! hurrah !!!
FTP-Server>exit

[Connection to 10.103.1.1 closed by foreign host]
Client#
```

Whilst there is no actual file for us to grab, we have been able to get from one side of the network to the other. Which is pretty much mission accomplished, but we still have a couple of things to discuss before we finish this chapter.

7.13 Monitor NetFlow statistics

We need to monitor NetFlow statistics, which is something we have not discussed yet. NetFlow is all about collecting data about your network traffic. It can look at the source, the destination, protocols and so on. A "flow" is made of number of factors:

- Ingress interface
- Source IP address
- Destination IP address
- IP protocol
- Source port
- Destination port
- Type of Service

These, when all put together, classify as a flow. Flows are then exported to a collector, which looks after the collecting of flows, storing them and pre-processing them. Flows are then examined using an analysis application.

We do not have an analysis engine, but this will not stop us from having a look at NetFlow and the kind of data we can get from it.

We enable NetFlow on a per-interface level, using the command "*ip flow ingress*" for traffic coming into the interface, or "*ip flow egress*" if we want to see what traffic leaves the interface. We can use both commands to see what comes in and what goes out of an interface, but here we are just going to look at what is coming in:

```
FTP-Server(config)#int s1/0
FTP-Server(config-if)#
FTP-Server(config-if)#ip flow ingress
FTP-Server(config-if)#
```

We have enabled NetFlow now. The most common version of NetFlow is version 5, but version 9 offers support for IPv6, MPLS and BGP nexthop. We can make sure we are running version 9 using the global command "*ip flow-export version 9*":

```
FTP-Server(config-if)#exit
FTP-Server(config)#
FTP-Server(config)#ip flow-export version 9
FTP-Server(config)#
```

Now we can make some traffic and see what NetFlow gives us:

```
Client#ping 10.103.1.1
Type escape sequence to abort.
Sending 5, 100-byte ICMP Echos to 10.103.1.1:
!!!!!
Success rate is 100 percent (5/5)
Client#telnet 10.103.1.1
Trying 10.103.1.1 ... Open

User Access Verification

Password:
FTP-Server>exit

[Connection to 10.103.1.1 closed by foreign host]
Client#
```

To look at the NetFlow data we have collected we can use the command *"show ip cache flow"*:

```
FTP-Server(config)#do sh ip cache flow
IP packet size distribution (137 total packets):
   1-32   64   96  128  160  192  224  256  288  320  352  384  416  448  480
   .000 .963 .000 .036 .000 .000 .000 .000 .000 .000 .000 .000 .000 .000 .000

    512  544  576 1024 1536 2048 2560 3072 3584 4096 4608
   .000 .000 .000 .000 .000 .000 .000 .000 .000 .000 .000

IP Flow Switching Cache, 278544 bytes
  1 active, 4095 inactive, 3 added
  499 ager polls, 0 flow alloc failures
  Active flows timeout in 30 minutes
  Inactive flows timeout in 15 seconds
IP Sub Flow Cache, 34056 bytes
  0 active, 1024 inactive, 0 added, 0 added to flow
  0 alloc failures, 0 force free
  1 chunk, 1 chunk added
  last clearing of statistics never
Protocol         Total   Flows  Packets Bytes Packets Active(Sec) Idle(Sec)
--------         Flows   /Sec   /Flow   /Pkt  /Sec    /Flow       /Flow
TCP-Telnet           1   0.0       28    41   0.0        3.5         1.2
ICMP                 1   0.0        5   100   0.0        0.1        15.7
Total:               2   0.0       16    50   0.0        1.8         8.5

SrcIf      SrcIPaddress   DstIf       DstIPaddress     Pr SrcP DstP  Pkts

SrcIf      SrcIPaddress   DstIf       DstIPaddress     Pr SrcP DstP  Pkts
Se1/0      10.103.1.102   Null        224.0.0.10       58 0000 0000   104
FTP-Server(config)#
```

We can see that NetFlow has captured both the ICMP ping and the TCP Telnet sessions. Usually we would want to export this data, to make it available for a dedicated application that can report on the data collected, whilst we do not have one to use, the command would be:

```
FTP-Server(config)#ip flow-export destination MyFlowApp
```

Where MyFlowApp is a DNS hostname, or we can use the IP address:

```
FTP-Server(config)#ip flow-export destination 10.10.10.10
```

One last thing to look at and then we have completed this chapter!

7.14 TS EtherChannel problems

We are not making the best use of our network, it's all working, but we could still make it perform a little better. We have an EtherChannel between SW3 and SW4, now it is time to troubleshoot (TS) it. However, when we looked at the trunking issues, we only fixed one interface:

```
SW3#sh int trunk | i trunking
Et0/1        on              802.1q          trunking     1
Et0/2        on              802.1q          trunking     1
SW3#

SW4#sh int trunk | i trunking
Et0/0        on              802.1q          trunking     1
Et0/1        on              802.1q          trunking     1
Et0/2        on              isl             trunking     1
SW4#
```

Let's fix SW4:

```
SW4(config)#int e0/2
SW4(config-if)#swi trunk encap dot
SW4(config-if)#
```

> Note: You may need to perform these steps, and then turn the interface on as the last step.

Now if we look at our trunks, we can see that the portchannel (Po1) is working as a trunk.

```
SW4(config-if)#do sh int trunk | i trunking
Et0/0        on              802.1q          trunking     1
Et0/1        on              802.1q          trunking     1
Po1          on              802.1q          trunking     1
SW4(config-if)#
```

```
SW3#sh int trunk | i trunking
Et0/1       on              802.1q         trunking      1
Po1         on              802.1q         trunking      1
SW3#
```

Let's make sure our EtherChannel is healthy:

```
SW3#sh etherchannel summary
Flags:  D - down         P - bundled in port-channel
        I - stand-alone  s - suspended
        H - Hot-standby (LACP only)
        R - Layer3       S - Layer2
        U - in use       f - failed to allocate aggregator

        M - not in use, minimum links not met
        u - unsuitable for bundling
        w - waiting to be aggregated
        d - default port


Number of channel-groups in use: 1
Number of aggregators:           1

Group  Port-channel  Protocol    Ports
------+-------------+-----------+-----------------------------------
1      Po1(SU)       PAgP        Et0/1(I)    Et0/2(P)

SW3#

SW4(config-if)#do sh etherchannel summary | b Group
Group  Port-channel  Protocol    Ports
------+-------------+-----------+-----------------------------------
1      Po1(SU)       PAgP        Et0/2(P)

SW4(config-if)#
```

PAgP is working, but the ports do not match. SW3 has ports e0/1 and e0/2, whereas SW4 only has e0/2. Let's look at the port configurations:

```
SW3#sh run int e0/1
interface Ethernet0/1
 switchport trunk encapsulation dot1q
 switchport mode trunk
 duplex auto
 channel-group 1 mode desirable
end

SW3#
```

```
SW3#sh run int e0/2
interface Ethernet0/2
 switchport trunk encapsulation dot1q
 switchport mode trunk
 duplex auto
 channel-group 1 mode desirable
end
SW3#

SW4(config-if)#do sh run int e0/1
interface Ethernet0/1
 switchport trunk encapsulation dot1q
 switchport mode trunk
 duplex auto
end
SW4(config-if)#
SW4(config-if)#do sh run int e0/2
interface Ethernet0/2
 switchport trunk encapsulation dot1q
 switchport mode trunk
 duplex auto
 channel-group 1 mode desirable
end
SW4(config-if)#
```

Notice anything missing? That's right, E0/1 on SW4 has not been added to the group. Let's fix it:

```
SW4(config-if)#int e0/1
SW4(config-if)#
SW4(config-if)#channel-group 1 mode desirable
SW4(config-if)#
```

Now let's check them again:

```
SW3#sh etherchannel summary | b Number
Number of channel-groups in use: 1
Number of aggregators:          1

Group  Port-channel  Protocol    Ports
------+-------------+-----------+-----------------------------------
1      Po1(SU)       PAgP        Et0/1(P)   Et0/2(P)
SW3#
```

We should get an equally good result from SW4:

```
SW4(config-if)#do sh etherchannel summary | b Number
Number of channel-groups in use: 1
Number of aggregators:           1

Group  Port-channel  Protocol    Ports
------+-------------+-----------+-------------------------------
1       Po1(SU)        PAgP        Et0/1(P)    Et0/2(P)
SW4(config-if)#
```

Excellent! We have now fixed the entire Brooklyn network and everyone is very pleased.

8. WAN Technologies

A WAN is a network that extends over a large distance. We can connect WANs in a number of ways, from slow and cheap, to fast and expensive. We will discuss these technologies here, then set up some of them. Most of the technologies are commonly referred to as "leased lines"; the customer leases them from the provider. These lines can be Ethernet based (metro Ethernet), use serial connections (PPP and HDLC), use existing copper telephone cabling or even cellular or satellite communications.

8.1 Identify different WAN Technologies

8.1.a Metro Ethernet

Ethernet is cheap and fairly resilient; therefore, it makes sense that this is used to connect the consumer to the ISP. However, Ethernet has distance limitations (as we saw at the start of the book), though these are being pushed further. Ethernet is also much faster than the T and E standards of North American and Europe (discussed below).

8.1.b VSAT

VSAT (Very Small Aperture Terminal) is a two-way satellite based solution using a dish antenna smaller than 3 meters. VSAT uses satellite communication for narrowband (such as credit card transactions) or broadband communication. This is generally a very expensive solution, but does offer the bonus of enabling connectivity to remote locations.

8.1.c Cellular 3g/4g

Cellular services, also known as mobile Internet, are experiencing a swift rise in speeds and reduction in costs. This makes it a very good solution for backup Internet lines. Many routers now ship with modules allowing you to insert a SIM card (Subscriber Identity Module), or 3g/4g USB dongle. In the event that your main line experiences a failure, access to the Internet is still possible through the cellular service. Access will be comparably slower than with dedicated lines. 3g (third generation), 4g (fourth generation) and LTE (Long-Term Evolution, which is part of 4g) all rely on the service providers wireless network connecting to the wider Internet.

8.1.d MPLS

MPLS (Multiprotocol Label Switching) is fun, sounds very geeky I know, but it is a very cool technology. It can be used to join customers together within an ISP's network and it is private (these are referred to as MPLS VPNs). The ISP looks after the customer's traffic, even allowing the customer to use OSPF at one end and EIGRP at the other and performing redistribution for the customer (for example, but they can also use static routing, BGP, IS-IS, or even RIP). The ISP can even have different customers using the same address spaces without worrying about traffic from one customer leaking into another. This is achieved through the insertion of an MPLS "shim" between layer-2 and layer-3, containing labels that identify customers, by their Route Distinguisher (RD).

MPLS is highly flexible; it is only really concerned about IP traffic and offers easy management on the consumer's part, leaving the hard work to the ISP.

8.1.e T1/E1

T1 and E1 are standards for carrying digital telecommunications. T1 is the North American version and E1 is European. Both use two pairs of copper cables, achieving full duplex communication.

T1 lines have a 1.544Mbps data rate, and can have 24 channels, with 64Kbps per channel. E1 can have 32 channels and achieves a data rate of 2048Kbps. Both provide the basis for more services, such as Frame Relay and ISDN.

There are improvements to these standards, offering more speeds:

North America		Europe	
Name	Speed (Mbit/s)	Name	Speed (Mbit/s)
T1 (DS1)	1.544	E1	2.048
T2 (DS2)	6.312	E2	8.448
T3 (DS3)	44.736	E3	34.368
DS4	274.176	E4	139.264
DS5	400.352	E5	565.148

8.1.f ISDN

We will discuss analog modems here as well as ISDN (Integrated Services Digital Network), as the two go hand-in-hand.

Analog modems work by dialling a telephone number that belongs to an ISP. This is then converted into a digital signal by a modem (Modulator-Demodulator). The digital computer signal is modulated into an analog signal on the customer's "local loop" (their telephone cable), travels along the telephone cable and is then demodulated back into a digital signal by the ISP's modem.

Whilst dial-up services are not as popular as DSL or Cable now, due to the slower speeds of dial-up (56Kbps), they are still used.

ISDN is similar to dial-up, still requiring you to make a call to the ISP, but it is a digital signal, and is faster, offering two 64 Kbps calls at the same time resulting in 128Kbps of Internet. Instead of using an analog modem an ISDN BRI modem is used. BRI stands for Basic Rate Interface, whilst the ISP uses PRI (Primary Rate Interface), which offers 23 64Kbps channels from one T1 line.

8.1.g DSL

DSL, Digital Subscriber Line, is replacing analog (dialup) and ISDN services at a very fast rate. DSL offers excellent speeds (certainly compared to dialup and ISDN), an "always-on" service, and the competition between the different telecommunications companies, collectively referred to as "Telcos", is driving down prices.

The real boost in DSL is the fact that it can run on existing twisted pair telephone cabling, carrying both analog voice (baseband) and digital data traffic (wide-band). The traffic on the wire, exiting the customer, is sent at different frequencies, maintaining the separation of voice and data.

The carrying of the different streams within the customers premises is performed through the use of a small box, officially called a low-pass DSL filter, but commonly called a splitter, that separates the single cable coming into the building into a line for the telephone and a line for the DSL modem.

Once the Telco receives the streams they are passed into a DSL Access Multiplexer (DSLAM), where digital data is passed to routers and on to the Internet, whilst voice traffic is passed onto the voice-specific hardware.

There are a number of variations of DSL technologies, the most common is ADSL, or Asymmetric DSL, which offers speeds up to 24Mbit/s download and 3.5Mbit/s upload. These speeds are far greater than analog or ISDN, but do suffer with degradation of signal the further away from the exchange you are. Most ADSL implementations have a maximum distance of 5.5Km from the exchange to the customer.

8.1.h Frame Relay

Frame Relay is becoming out-dated. Cisco seem to have a love/hate relationship with it though and is slowly reducing its importance in exams. When I started studying for my CCIE, which at the time was version 4, Frame Relay was the part I was dreading, predominantly because I could never envisage a time when I would actually use it. Then they released v5 of the CCIE and removed Frame Relay completely. I was pleased. Nevertheless, it still exists in the current version of the CCNA. I do think that it will be removed in later versions and this reflects the current market for Frame Relay; Ethernet is cheaper, both for the provider and for the consumer. We have an entire section about Frame Relay coming up soon, so let's move on.

8.1.i Cable

Cable technology is similar to DSL. Both use existing cable to supply more than one service (cable supplies television as well). Both are asymmetric (download speeds are much better than upload speeds) and both have the signals split in the customers' premises and at the provider's premises, in order to separate the different streams. Cable is also an "always-on" service.

8.1.j VPN

MPLS is expensive (but cool), dial-up can be expensive and slow, and Metro Ethernet can be expensive. So, what do you do when you want to connect two or more offices together? You can use VPNs and take advantage of your existing ISP connections.

A VPN is a Virtual Private Network and joins two site together; all it needs is a route from one side to another. VPNs can take a number of forms, from a single user connecting to an office, or an IPSec VPN connecting two offices (and all the users in the offices) together, which provides secure end-to-end communication.

VPNs are secure (hence being called "Private networks"). They offer confidentiality (are encrypted), authentication and integrity (temper detection). Collectively this is known as the CIA triangle.

Because VPNs can use any underlying transport mechanism, they offer reduced cost (as opposed a dedicated MPLS network), security, and are very scalable.

If you want to learn more about VPNs then have a look at VPNs and NAT for Cisco Networks book.

Let's move on and do some configuration.

8.2 Configure and verify a basic WAN serial connection

Serial connections are full duplex and symmetric, meaning the consumer has the same speed download and upload. They do require a data link protocol, such as HDLC or PPP in order to carry the higher layer protocols. They use a WAN Interface Card (WIC) to connect the providers DCE serial cable to the router (which then becomes the DTE), as we spoke about in chapter one.

We are going to start configuring our Frame-Relay side of the network now. We will start with HDLC; move on to PPP and then to Frame Relay.

We will start with a brief recap of serial interfaces, as we have not touched them since section 4.3.a when we set up the basic IP addressing.

As you will recall, the basic configuration of a serial interface is no different to an Ethernet interface. The difference would be if we were working with physical equipment. Here the clocking (DTE/DCE) becomes important. We would set our FR-Hub to supply the clocking information to the spoke routers (it would be our DCE, or Data Communications Equipment):

```
FR-Hub(config)#int s1/2
FR-Hub(config-if)#clock rate ?
  With the exception of the following standard values not subject to
rounding,

        1200 2400 4800 9600 14400 19200 28800 38400
        56000 64000 128000 2015232

  accepted clockrates will be bestfitted (rounded) to the nearest value
  supportable by the hardware.

  <246-8064000>    DCE clock rate (bits per second)

FR-Hub(config-if)#clock rate 56000
FR-Hub(config-if)#int s1/1
FR-Hub(config-if)#clock rate 56000
FR-Hub(config-if)#
```

We do not need to set this command on the spokes, as they will pick this up from the hub. We can also use the command *"show controllers serial 1/1"*, which will also tell us the clocking information:

```
FR-Hub(config-if)#do show controllers serial 1/1
<truncated>
maxdgram=1608, bufpool=78Kb, 120 particles
    DCD=up  DSR=up  DTR=up  RTS=up  CTS=up
line state: up
cable type : V.11 (X.21) DCE cable, received clockrate 56000
<truncated>
FR-Hub(config-if)#
```

Like Ethernet interfaces, we can check the operational status of our interface using the command *"show interface s<slot>/<interface>"*:

```
FR-Spoke1(config)#int s1/1
FR-Spoke1(config-if)#do sh int s1/1
Serial1/1 is up, line protocol is up
  Hardware is M4T
  Description: Link to FR-Hub
```

```
        Internet address is 192.168.11.2/24
        MTU 1500 bytes, BW 1544 Kbit/sec, DLY 20000 usec,
            reliability 255/255, txload 1/255, rxload 1/255
        Encapsulation HDLC, crc 16, loopback not set
        Keepalive set (10 sec)
        Restart-Delay is 0 secs
        Last input 00:00:01, output 00:00:00, output hang never
        Last clearing of "show interface" counters never
        <truncated>
            2 carrier transitions     DCD=up  DSR=up  DTR=up  RTS=up  CTS=up

   FR-Spoke1(config-if)#
```

The encapsulation is set to HDLC. HDLC (High-Level Data Link Control) is a synchronous data link layer protocol. HDLC is an ISO standard and can be used for point-to-point and point-to-multipoint topologies. HDLC also forms the basis for PPP. HDLC is the default encapsulation and the encapsulation should always match on each side. If one side is set to *"encapsulation ppp"*, we can change it back to HDLC either using the command *"encapsulation hdlc"* or even *"no encapsulation ppp"*.

HDLC encapsulates the higher-level protocols between a flag field and an FCS (Frame Check Sequence) field. Despite this being a solely point-to-point technology (in that the destination can only be the other end of the link), there is an address field. This goes back to the olden-days when providers offered multi-drop circuits, where there was more than one possible destination, so an address similar to MAC addresses was used. The actual HDLC packet looks like this:

Header				Trailer	
Flag	Address	Control	Type	Data	FCS

The flag is used for synchronization, using a certain bit pattern so that the receiving router knows that a new frame is arriving. The type indicates the type of the layer-3 packet encapsulated within the frame (either IPv4 or IPv6). The FCS (similar to Ethernet frames) is used for error detection. The important thing to note, here, is that we are talking about the Cisco version of HDLC; routers need to know what is inside the packet (IPv4 or IPv6), so Cisco included the Type field to accommodate this.

In our network, once FR-Hub receives data from the rest of the network, which is intended for one of the spokes, it will de-encapsulate the IP packet from the Ethernet frame, discarding the Ethernet header and trailer. The IP packet will then be encapsulated into a new HDLC frame (with an HDLC header and trailer) and encoded into the electrical signal to be passed along the serial cable at layer-1.

The spoke will receive the HDLC frame, check the FCS, and then de-encapsulate the IP packet from the HDLC frame, discarding the HDLC header and trailer. The IP packet is then re-encapsulated into an Ethernet frame and passed along to the intended host (if we had hosts on the spokes), using their MAC address.

Returning to the output from FR-Spoke1, we also have a keepalive (10 seconds). This is important when we make changes and need to shut and no shut an interface. Although we will be notified on the local router, we should wait until the other router also notifies us that its interface is down, before we bring the interface back up again.

Serial interfaces are a little more unforgiving than Ethernet interfaces, but this actually allows us a greater level of troubleshooting assistance. To see what I mean, let's shut down FR-Spoke1's serial interface:

```
FR-Spoke1(config-if)#shut
FR-Spoke1(config-if)#
%LINK-5-CHANGED: Interface Serial1/1, changed state to administratively
down
%LINEPROTO-5-UPDOWN: Line protocol on Interface Serial1/1, changed state
to down
FR-Spoke1(config-if)#
```

After a few moments (as long as it takes the 10 second keepalive to detect the other side being down), FR-Hub's own Serial1/1 interface changes its state to down:

```
FR-Hub(config-if)#do sh ip int bri | i Serial
Serial1/0          unassigned      YES manual administratively down down
Serial1/1          192.168.11.1    YES manual up                   up
Serial1/2          192.168.12.1    YES manual up                   up
Serial1/3          unassigned      YES NVRAM  administratively down down
FR-Hub(config-if)#
%LINEPROTO-5-UPDOWN: Line protocol on Interface Serial1/1, changed state
to down
FR-Hub(config-if)#do sh ip int bri | i Serial
Serial1/0          unassigned      YES manual administratively down down
Serial1/1          192.168.11.1    YES manual up                   down
Serial1/2          192.168.12.1    YES manual up                   up
Serial1/3          unassigned      YES NVRAM  administratively down down
FR-Hub(config-if)#
```

If we look at the interface, we can see that the line protocol is down:

```
FR-Hub(config-if)#do sh int s1/1 | i protocol
Serial1/1 is up, line protocol is down
     0 unknown protocol drops
FR-Hub(config-if)#
```

This allows us to see that either the other side is down, or we have a mismatch in encapsulation. Serial interfaces do actually make troubleshooting quite easy for us; we just need to look at the interface status and the protocol status. If both are down, it's a layer-1 problem. If it is Up/Down

(Interface is up, protocol is down) it's a layer-2 problem, and if both are up and we still have issues; it's a layer-3 or above problem.

With Serial interfaces, we have a number of options for encapsulation:

```
FR-Spoke1(config-if)#encapsulation ?
  atm-dxi         ATM-DXI encapsulation
  bstun           Block Serial tunneling (BSTUN)
  frame-relay     Frame Relay networks
  hdlc            Serial HDLC synchronous
  lapb            LAPB (X.25 Level 2)
  ppp             Point-to-Point protocol
  sdlc            SDLC
  sdlc-primary    SDLC (primary)
  sdlc-secondary  SDLC (secondary)
  smds            Switched Megabit Data Service (SMDS)
  stun            Serial tunneling (STUN)
  x25             X.25

FR-Spoke1(config-if)#encapsulation
```

The encapsulation types we will use most are PPP and Frame Relay. If we have a mismatch in the encapsulation we would see the same "line protocol is down" message. We will see this when we set up PPP.

8.3 Configure and verify a PPP connection between Cisco routers

PPP (Point-to-Point Protocol) offers a lot more than HDLC does, but is still very similar to HDLC. It is still a data-link protocol, is used by ISPs for dial-up access and forms the basis for PPPoE and PPPoA in DSL services (PPP over Ethernet and PPP over ATM respectively). PPP supports authentication using PAP or CHAP, compression, PPP multilink (a bit like the etherchannels we set up earlier) and error detection and error recovery. All in all, it is very useful!

The PPP frame is also identical to the HDLC frame:

Header				Trailer	
Flag	Address	Control	Type	Data	FCS

Possibly the most importantly aspect of PPP is the inclusion of *Control Protocols* (CP). These control protocols allow easier integration and support of higher-layer protocols.

We have a Link Control Protocol (LCP); this looks after our layer-2. LCP handles loops in the link through the "magic number" and will disable an interface if it detects a loop. This allows the router to use an alternate route. We have Link-Quality Monitoring (LQM), which performs error detection and will disable an interface if error percentage thresholds are exceeded. LCP also handles Multilink PPP, and authentication, through PAP or CHAP.

The Network Control Protocols (NCP) handles the layer-3 protocols (IPv4 and IPv6). IPCP controls IPv4, IPV6CP controls IPv6 and CDPCP handles the Cisco Discovery Protocol (CDP).

In order to set up PPP, we need to set the encapsulation type to PPP. Both sides need to use the same encapsulation type. We cannot have HDLC on one side and PPP on the other; they are incompatible. We'll bring back up the serial interface on FR-Spoke1, watch the line come back up on the hub, then change the encapsulation:

```
FR-Spoke1(config-if)#no shut
FR-Spoke1(config-if)#
%LINK-3-UPDOWN: Interface Serial1/1, changed state to up
%LINEPROTO-5-UPDOWN: Line protocol on Interface Serial1/1, changed state
to up
FR-Spoke1(config-if)#

FR-Hub(config-if)#
%LINEPROTO-5-UPDOWN: Line protocol on Interface Serial1/1, changed state
to up
FR-Hub(config-if)#do sh int s1/1 | i protocol
Serial1/1 is up, line protocol is up
     0 unknown protocol drops
FR-Hub(config-if)#
```

Now let's change the encapsulation:

```
FR-Spoke1(config-if)#encapsulation ppp
FR-Spoke1(config-if)#
```

We then see the line change its state to down on both routers:

```
FR-Spoke1(config-if)#
%LINEPROTO-5-UPDOWN: Line protocol on Interface Serial1/1, changed state
to down
FR-Spoke1(config-if)#

FR-Hub(config-if)#
%LINEPROTO-5-UPDOWN: Line protocol on Interface Serial1/1, changed state
to down
FR-Hub(config-if)#do sh int s1/1 | i protocol
Serial1/1 is up, line protocol is down
     20 unknown protocol drops
FR-Hub(config-if)#
```

If we change FR-Hub's interface to use PPP encapsulation, the line comes back up again:

```
FR-Hub(config-if)#int s1/1
FR-Hub(config-if)#encapsulation ppp
FR-Hub(config-if)#
%LINEPROTO-5-UPDOWN: Line protocol on Interface Serial1/1, changed state
to up
FR-Hub(config-if)#
```

The cool thing about PPP encapsulation is that we don't even need to be on the same subnet for communication to work:

```
FR-Spoke1(config-if)#ip address 192.168.111.2 255.255.255.0
FR-Spoke1(config-if)#do sh ip route | b Gate
Gateway of last resort is not set

     192.168.11.0/32 is subnetted, 1 subnets
C        192.168.11.1 is directly connected, Serial1/1
     192.168.111.0/24 is variably subnetted, 2 subnets, 2 masks
C        192.168.111.0/24 is directly connected, Serial1/1
L        192.168.111.2/32 is directly connected, Serial1/1
FR-Spoke1(config-if)#do ping 192.168.11.1
Type escape sequence to abort.
Sending 5, 100-byte ICMP Echos to 192.168.11.1:
!!!!!
Success rate is 100 percent (5/5)
FR-Spoke1(config-if)#
```

Through PPP we can even install a default route, using the command "ppp ipcp route default". This uses the IPCP NCP. Here we can see the routing table before and after we use the command (once we have shut the interface down and brought it back up again):

```
FR-Spoke1(config-if)#do sh ip route | b Gate
Gateway of last resort is not set

     192.168.11.0/32 is subnetted, 1 subnets
C        192.168.11.1 is directly connected, Serial1/1
     192.168.111.0/24 is variably subnetted, 2 subnets, 2 masks
C        192.168.111.0/24 is directly connected, Serial1/1
L        192.168.111.2/32 is directly connected, Serial1/1
FR-Spoke1(config-if)#ppp ipcp route default
FR-Spoke1(config-if)#shut
FR-Spoke1(config-if)#
%LINEPROTO-5-UPDOWN: Line protocol on Interface Serial1/1, changed state
to down
%LINK-5-CHANGED: Interface Serial1/1, changed state to administratively
down
```

```
FR-Spoke1(config-if)#
FR-Spoke1(config-if)#no shut
FR-Spoke1(config-if)#
%LINK-3-UPDOWN: Interface Serial1/1, changed state to up
FR-Spoke1(config-if)#
%LINEPROTO-5-UPDOWN: Line protocol on Interface Serial1/1, changed state
to up
FR-Spoke1(config-if)#do sh ip route | b Gate
Gateway of last resort is 192.168.11.1 to network 0.0.0.0

S*    0.0.0.0/0 [1/0] via 192.168.11.1
      192.168.11.0/32 is subnetted, 1 subnets
C        192.168.11.1 is directly connected, Serial1/1
      192.168.111.0/24 is variably subnetted, 2 subnets, 2 masks
C        192.168.111.0/24 is directly connected, Serial1/1
L        192.168.111.2/32 is directly connected, Serial1/1
FR-Spoke1(config-if)#
```

Let's set up the other spoke:

```
FR-Hub(config-if)#int s1/2
FR-Hub(config-if)#encapsulation ppp
FR-Hub(config-if)#

FR-Spoke2(config-if)#encapsulation ppp
FR-Spoke2(config-if)#
%LINEPROTO-5-UPDOWN: Line protocol on Interface Serial1/2, changed state
to down
%LINEPROTO-5-UPDOWN: Line protocol on Interface Serial1/2, changed state
to up
FR-Spoke2(config-if)#
```

We will also give it a default route, note that we need to shut the interface and bring it back up again for the default route to be installed in our routing table:

```
FR-Spoke2(config-if)#ppp ipcp route default
FR-Spoke2(config-if)#do sh ip route | b Gate
Gateway of last resort is not set

      192.168.12.0/24 is variably subnetted, 3 subnets, 2 masks
C        192.168.12.0/24 is directly connected, Serial1/2
C        192.168.12.1/32 is directly connected, Serial1/2
L        192.168.12.2/32 is directly connected, Serial1/2
FR-Spoke2(config-if)#shut
FR-Spoke2(config-if)#
%LINEPROTO-5-UPDOWN: Line protocol on Interface Serial1/2, changed state
to down
```

```
%LINK-5-CHANGED: Interface Serial1/2, changed state to administratively
down
FR-Spoke2(config-if)#no shut
FR-Spoke2(config-if)#
%LINK-3-UPDOWN: Interface Serial1/2, changed state to up
FR-Spoke2(config-if)#
%LINEPROTO-5-UPDOWN: Line protocol on Interface Serial1/2, changed state
to up
FR-Spoke2(config-if)#
FR-Spoke2(config-if)#do sh ip route | b Gate
Gateway of last resort is 192.168.12.1 to network 0.0.0.0

S*     0.0.0.0/0 [1/0] via 192.168.12.1
       192.168.12.0/24 is variably subnetted, 3 subnets, 2 masks
C          192.168.12.0/24 is directly connected, Serial1/2
C          192.168.12.1/32 is directly connected, Serial1/2
L          192.168.12.2/32 is directly connected, Serial1/2
FR-Spoke2(config-if)#
```

Hopefully, we should be able to get from FR-Spoke1 to FR-Spoke2:

```
FR-Spoke2(config-if)#do ping 192.168.111.2
Type escape sequence to abort.
Sending 5, 100-byte ICMP Echos to 192.168.111.2:
!!!!!
Success rate is 100 percent (5/5)
FR-Spoke2(config-if)#
```

Looks good!

Let's add some authentication now. The options we have are CHAP or PAP. PAP stands for Password Authentication Protocol, and CHAP stands for Challenge Handshake Authentication Protocol.

With PAP, the client sends a username and password. Although the password can be encrypted, PAP is vulnerable to eavesdropping on the connection.

CHAP is more secure. The server sends a challenge string to the client with its hostname. The client will then look to see if it has an entry in its user database for that hostname and, if it does, then combines that with the challenge it receives and sends it back, encrypted with a one-way hash. The server then performs the same process and if they agree, the connection is made. CHAP will also repeat this process periodically during the lifetime of the connection.

For this reason we will use CHAP. By default, we will send our hostnames in the CHAP traffic, so we need to create corresponding usernames (and passwords) on the routers:

```
FR-Hub(config-if)#exit
FR-Hub(config)#
FR-Hub(config)#username FR-Spoke1 password cisco
FR-Hub(config)#username FR-Spoke2 password cisco
FR-Hub(config)#

FR-Spoke1(config-if)#exit
FR-Spoke1(config)#
FR-Spoke1(config)#username FR-Hub password cisco
FR-Spoke1(config)#
```

We need to enable the interface for PPP authentication, specifying the authentication mechanism:

```
FR-Hub(config)#int s1/1
FR-Hub(config-if)#
FR-Hub(config-if)#ppp authentication chap
FR-Hub(config-if)#
%LINEPROTO-5-UPDOWN: Line protocol on Interface Serial1/1, changed state
to down
%LINEPROTO-5-UPDOWN: Line protocol on Interface Serial1/1, changed state
to up
FR-Hub(config-if)#

FR-Spoke1(config)#int s1/1
FR-Spoke1(config-if)#
FR-Spoke1(config-if)#ppp authentication chap
FR-Spoke1(config-if)#
%LINEPROTO-5-UPDOWN: Line protocol on Interface Serial1/1, changed state
to down
How %LINEPROTO-5-UPDOWN: Line protocol on Interface Serial1/1, changed
state to up
FR-Spoke1(config-if)#
```

How can we check that our authentication commands are working? The line protocol is up on both routers, which is a good sign, however this does not mean we are actually using authentication. We could have missed a vital command. The same is true for reachability, we may have it, but again we could have forgotten to turn something on:

```
FR-Spoke1(config-if)#do ping 192.168.12.2
Type escape sequence to abort.
Sending 5, 100-byte ICMP Echos to 192.168.12.2:
!!!!!
Success rate is 100 percent (5/5)
FR-Spoke1(config-if)#
```

We can look at our PPP status, using the command "*show ppp all*". This will list all the active sessions, and will tell us if they are using authentication:

```
FR-Hub(config-if)#do sh ppp all
Interface/ID OPEN+ Nego* Fail-      Stage   Peer Address  Peer Name
------------ ---------------------- ------  ------------- -----------
Se1/1        LCP+ CHAP+ IPCP+ CDP>  LocalT  192.168.111.2 FR-Spoke1
Se1/2        LCP+ IPCP+ CDPCP+      LocalT  192.168.12.2
FR-Hub(config-if)#
```

We can see that the PPP link on Serial 1/1 (to FR-Spoke1) is using CHAP authentication. Because we have an entry for it, we know all is good. The "*show ppp all*" command also shows us the LCP and NCP functions that are being used. We can see that IPCP, CDPCP and CHAP are all being used between FR-Hub and FR-Spoke1.

Let's try and break it by having a password mismatch and see what effect this has:

```
FR-Spoke1(config-if)#exit
FR-Spoke1(config)#username FR-Hub password cisco1
FR-Spoke1(config)#int s1/1
FR-Spoke1(config-if)#shut
FR-Spoke1(config-if)#
%LINEPROTO-5-UPDOWN: Line protocol on Interface Serial1/1, changed state
to down
%LINK-5-CHANGED: Interface Serial1/1, changed state to administratively
down
FR-Spoke1(config-if)#
```

As usual, we should wait for the timer to expire:

```
FR-Hub(config-if)#
%LINEPROTO-5-UPDOWN: Line protocol on Interface Serial1/1, changed state
to down
FR-Hub(config-if)#end
```

Then we can bring the interface back up again:

```
FR-Spoke1(config-if)#no shut
FR-Spoke1(config-if)#
%LINK-3-UPDOWN: Interface Serial1/1, changed state to up
FR-Spoke1(config-if)#do sh int s1/1 | i proto
Serial1/1 is up, line protocol is down
     12 unknown protocol drops
FR-Spoke1(config-if)#
```

The line protocol does not transition to the up state; this is because CHAP is part of LCP. Because CHAP authentication fails, LCP does not complete. If we fix the issue by correcting the password, the line protocol comes up:

```
FR-Spoke1(config-if)#username FR-Hub password cisco
FR-Spoke1(config)#
%LINEPROTO-5-UPDOWN: Line protocol on Interface Serial1/1, changed state
to up
FR-Spoke1(config)#
FR-Spoke1(config)#do sh int s1/1 | i proto
Serial1/1 is up, line protocol is up
     12 unknown protocol drops
FR-Spoke1(config)#
```

We can also look (in much greater depth) at the PPP status of the interface using the command *"show ppp interface s1/1"*. There is a lot of information within this output, so I have truncated it to show the useful information:

```
FR-Hub#sh ppp interface s1/1
PPP Serial Context Info
-------------------
Interface       : Se1/1

PPP Session Info
----------------
Interface       : Se1/1
Phase           : UP
Peer Name       : FR-Spoke1
Peer Address    : 192.168.111.2
Control Protocols: LCP[Open] CHAP+ IPCP[Open] CDPCP[Open]

Se1/1 LCP: [Open]
Our Negotiated Options
Se1/1 LCP:     AuthProto CHAP (0x0305C22305)
Peer's Negotiated Options
Se1/1 LCP:     AuthProto CHAP (0x0305C22305)

Se1/1 IPCP: [Open]
Our Negotiated Options
Se1/1 IPCP:     Address 192.168.11.1 (0x0306C0A80B01)
Peer's Negotiated Options
Se1/1 IPCP:     Address 192.168.111.2 (0x0306C0A86F02)

FR-Hub#
```

Above we have proof that the authentication is working (AuthProto CHAP) and that our routers are communicating correctly (they are in the "UP" phase). We are going to use debugging here. Because of the amount of PPP traffic, we need to limit the debugging down to just the essential traffic. Here we can set a debugging condition, to match just our serial 1/1 traffic, and then enable debugging of ppp negotiation:

```
FR-Hub#debug condition interface s1/1
Condition 1 set
FR-Hub# debug ppp negotiation
PPP protocol negotiation debugging is on
FR-Hub#
```

Then we can shut down the interface on FR-Spoke1, wait for the timer to tell us that the line protocol is down on FR-Hub, and enable the interface again. We will see FR-Hub start to gather some information. There is a lot of information, so we will break it down and take it in chunks.

We start from a PPP phase of "DOWN", by moving from a state of "Initial" to "Starting":

```
FR-Hub#
Se1/1 PPP: Phase is DOWN
Se1/1 PPP: Using default call direction
Se1/1 PPP: Treating connection as a dedicated line
```

PPP supports different directions. We can configure the router to treat the connection as outgoing (callout), incoming (callin), or dedicated, which is the default.

```
Se1/1 PPP: Session handle[DB00006B] Session id[103]
Se1/1 LCP: Event[OPEN] State[Initial to Starting]
Se1/1 LCP: O CONFREQ [Starting] id 1 len 15
Se1/1 LCP:    AuthProto CHAP (0x0305C22305)
Se1/1 LCP:    MagicNumber 0xBD702C13 (0x0506BD702C13)
Se1/1 LCP: Event[UP] State[Starting to REQsent]
Se1/1 LCP: I CONFREQ [REQsent] id 1 len 15
Se1/1 LCP:    AuthProto CHAP (0x0305C22305)
Se1/1 LCP:    MagicNumber 0xBD702DA6 (0x0506BD702DA6)
Se1/1 LCP: O CONFACK [REQsent] id 1 len 15
Se1/1 LCP:    AuthProto CHAP (0x0305C22305)
Se1/1 LCP:    MagicNumber 0xBD702DA6 (0x0506BD702DA6)
Se1/1 LCP: Event[Receive ConfReq+] State[REQsent to ACKsent]
Se1/1 LCP: I CONFACK [ACKsent] id 1 len 15
Se1/1 LCP:    AuthProto CHAP (0x0305C22305)
Se1/1 LCP:    MagicNumber 0xBD702C13 (0x0506BD702C13)
Se1/1 LCP: Event[Receive ConfAck] State[ACKsent to Open]
Se1/1 PPP: Phase is AUTHENTICATING, by both
```

We start performing loop detection; this is the MagicNumber LCP feature. The O's and I's referrer to Outgoing and Incoming, and this is our request/acknowledge dialog between the two routers. Once this is completed, we move to the Authenticating phase.

```
Se1/1 CHAP: O CHALLENGE id 1 len 27 from "FR-Hub"
Se1/1 LCP: State is Open
Se1/1 CHAP: I CHALLENGE id 1 len 30 from "FR-Spoke1"
Se1/1 CHAP: I RESPONSE id 1 len 30 from "FR-Spoke1"
```

```
Se1/1 PPP: Phase is FORWARDING, Attempting Forward
Se1/1 PPP: Phase is AUTHENTICATING, Unauthenticated User
Se1/1 CHAP: Using hostname from configured hostname
Se1/1 CHAP: Using password from AAA
Se1/1 CHAP: O RESPONSE id 1 len 27 from "FR-Hub"
Se1/1 IPCP: Authorizing CP
Se1/1 IPCP: CP stalled on event[Authorize CP]
Se1/1 IPCP: CP unstall
Se1/1 PPP: Phase is FORWARDING, Attempting Forward
Se1/1 PPP: Phase is AUTHENTICATING, Authenticated User
Se1/1 CHAP: O SUCCESS id 1 len 4
Se1/1 CHAP: I SUCCESS id 1 len 4
%LINEPROTO-5-UPDOWN: Line protocol on Interface Serial1/1, changed state
to up
Se1/1 PPP: Outbound cdp packet dropped, line protocol not up
Se1/1 PPP: Phase is UP
```

The O's and I's again indicate whether the packet was sent by us (O) or received by us (I). We exchange our hostnames and check the received hostname against our local database (Using the password from AAA). This occurs through a set of challenge/response messages. We are then authenticated and LCP completes, allowing the line protocol to change its state to up.

```
Se1/1 IPCP: Protocol configured, start CP. state[Initial]
Se1/1 IPCP: Event[OPEN] State[Initial to Starting]
Se1/1 IPCP: O CONFREQ [Starting] id 1 len 10
Se1/1 IPCP:     Address 192.168.11.1 (0x0306C0A80B01)
Se1/1 IPCP: Event[UP] State[Starting to REQsent]
Se1/1 CDPCP: Protocol configured, start CP. state[Initial]
Se1/1 CDPCP: Event[OPEN] State[Initial to Starting]
Se1/1 CDPCP: Authorizing CP
Se1/1 CDPCP: CP stalled on event[Authorize CP]
Se1/1 IPCP: I CONFREQ [REQsent] id 1 len 10
Se1/1 IPCP:     Address 192.168.111.2 (0x0306C0A86F02)
Se1/1 IPCP AUTHOR: Start.  Her address 192.168.111.2, we want 0.0.0.0
Se1/1 IPCP AUTHOR: Reject 192.168.111.2, using 0.0.0.0
Se1/1 IPCP AUTHOR: Done.  Her address 192.168.111.2, we want 0.0.0.0
Se1/1 IPCP: O CONFACK [REQsent] id 1 len 10
Se1/1 IPCP:     Address 192.168.111.2 (0x0306C0A86F02)
Se1/1 IPCP: Event[Receive ConfReq+] State[REQsent to ACKsent]
Se1/1 IPCP: I CONFACK [ACKsent] id 1 len 10
Se1/1 IPCP:     Address 192.168.11.1 (0x0306C0A80B01)
Se1/1 IPCP: Event[Receive ConfAck] State[ACKsent to Open]
Se1/1 CDPCP: I CONFREQ [Starting] id 1 len 4
Se1/1 CDPCP: Store stalled packet [0xF32EBAA0]
Se1/1 CDPCP: CP unstall
Se1/1 CDPCP: O CONFREQ [Starting] id 1 len 4
Se1/1 CDPCP: Event[UP] State[Starting to REQsent]
Se1/1 CDPCP: Continue processing stalled packet:
```

```
Se1/1 CDPCP: I CONFREQ [REQsent] id 1 len 4
Se1/1 CDPCP: O CONFACK [REQsent] id 1 len 4
Se1/1 CDPCP: Event[Receive ConfReq+] State[REQsent to ACKsent]
Se1/1 CDPCP: I CONFACK [ACKsent] id 1 len 4
Se1/1 CDPCP: Event[Receive ConfAck] State[ACKsent to Open]
Se1/1 IPCP: State is Open
Se1/1 CDPCP: State is Open
Se1/1 Added to neighbor route AVL tree: topoid 0, address 192.168.111.2
FR-Hub#
Se1/1 IPCP: Install route to 192.168.111.2
FR-Hub#
```

We then move to the Network Control Protocols. We can see the exchange of IP addresses (192.168.11.1 out and 192.168.111.2 in). The received route is then installed in our routing table. Let's turn off debugging now:

```
FR-Hub#undebug all
All possible debugging has been turned off
FR-Hub#
```

We could just use "*no debug ppp negotiation*" instead as this would achieve the same goal, and we may be in a scenario where we have multiple debugs happening and only want to stop one of them. We should also remove the debugging condition, as later on we may want to debug something else and may find ourselves without any debug output (as it is constrained to the wrong interface):

```
FR-Hub#no debug condition interface s1/1
This condition is the last interface condition set.
Removing all conditions may cause a flood of debugging
messages to result, unless specific debugging flags
are first removed.

Proceed with removal? [yes/no]: yes
Condition 1 has been removed
FR-Hub#
```

We can confirm that CDP is working:

```
FR-Hub#sh cdp neigh | b Device
Device ID    Local Intrfce   Holdtme   Capability   Platform   Port ID
FR-Spoke2    Ser 1/2         165              R B   Linux Uni  Ser 1/2
FR-Spoke1    Ser 1/1         157              R B   Linux Uni  Ser 1/1

Total cdp entries displayed : 2
FR-Hub#
```

We can also confirm the route is installed in our routing table:

```
FR-Hub#sh ip route 192.168.111.2
Routing entry for 192.168.111.2/32
  Known via "connected", distance 0, metric 0 (connected, via interface)
  Routing Descriptor Blocks:
  * directly connected, via Serial1/1
      Route metric is 0, traffic share count is 1
FR-Hub#
```

PPP is very flexible and works extremely well. However, there is an inherent problem with PPP and larger networks. Because it is a point-to-point technology once we start adding sites and extend our connectivity, we start to run into scalability issues. A network with five sites would require ten different PPP connections; six sites would require fifteen connections:

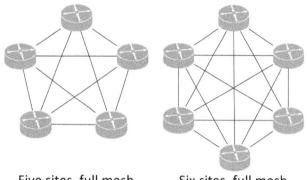

Five sites, full mesh   Six sites, full mesh

This proves to be a costly solution. An alternative would be a partial mesh, only directly connecting those sites that need to be connected and route traffic through a centralized "hub". The dotted lines represent the traffic that must route through the central router at the top:

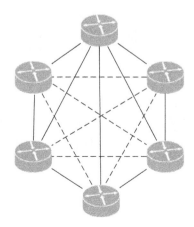

This puts greater load on a particular site as it then has to re-route traffic for different sites, so while PPP works well between two routers, it does lack scalability. Frame Relay offers a better solution in this scenario.

8.4 Configure and verify Frame Relay on Cisco routers

Frame Relay is a big topic for the CCNA, so expect a few questions on it in the exam. Frame Relay can solve the above issue by allowing sites to connect to each other through a single connection. These connections form "virtual circuits" through the Service Provider's infrastructure:

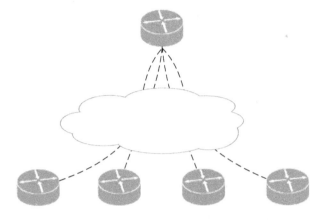

We can therefore keep our costs down as there is no need to invest in separate WAN connections for each peer, and we leave much of the work to the Service Provider. Each of our routers would be a DTE (Data Terminal Equipment), and the Service Provider would be the DCE, supplying the clocking information required. The logical path between the endpoints is referred to as a Virtual Circuit (VC). If the Service Provider predefines the circuit, it is referred to as a "Permanent Virtual Circuit" (PVC). We also have Switched Virtual Circuits (SVCs), which are more akin to dial-up and are only used when needed. VCs have a Committed Information Rate (CIR), which is the guaranteed minimum bandwidth that a line will receive from the provider and this is one of the real benefits of Frame Relay; you know exactly what you are getting in terms of speed.

In the following diagram, the box represents the points at which the provider connects to the customer (commonly referred to as the "demarcation point"). The square devices are the Frame Relay routers.

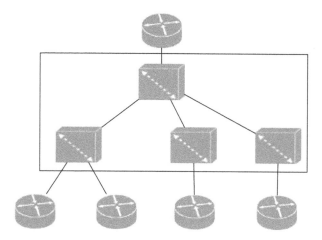

Because Frame Relay is a layer-2 technology, we cannot depend on IP addresses to send our traffic to the correct destination. Instead, we use Data Link Connection Identifiers (DLCIs). DLCIs identify the VC. A DLCI is a 10-bit decimal value and is locally significant. This means that whilst the DLCI values do not have to be unique across the network, they must be unique on the local router:

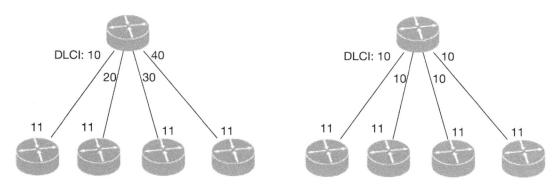

Correct DLCI numbering   Incorrect DLCI numbering

Within the providers network, the DLCI values are swapped. In the next image, the top router knows that the PVC has a local DLCI of 10; the bottom router knows that the local DLCI is 20. Both send frames with the local DLCI in the header. The Service Provider then changes the DLCI value in the header, so that while it leaves the top router with a value of 10, it arrives at the bottom router with a value of 20.

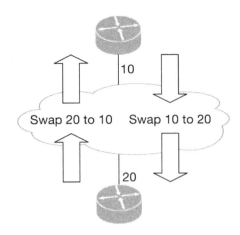

Let's start configuring Frame Relay. Because we do not have a Frame Relay switch between the hub and the spokes, we will be using the same DLCIs for each side of the connection. FR-Hub and FR-Spoke1 will use 101 and FR-Hub and FR-Spoke2 will use 102.

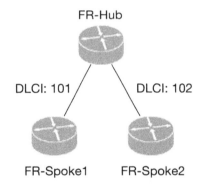

We need to start by disabling keepalives on the interface. If we do not do this then the line protocol will stay down.

```
FR-Hub(config)#int s1/2
FR-Hub(config-if)#no keepalive
FR-Hub(config-if)#
```

We start with the encapsulation:

```
FR-Hub(config-if)#encapsulation frame-relay ?
  MFR   Multilink Frame Relay bundle interface
  ietf  Use RFC1490/RFC2427 encapsulation
  <cr>

FR-Hub(config-if)#encapsulation frame-relay
```

We actually have three encapsulation types, MFR, IETF and Cisco. As we saw with HDLC and PPP, the encapsulation needs to match at both ends. Cisco encapsulation is the default, but if we are using non-Cisco equipment, we should use the IETF standard. We will use Cisco encapsulation:

```
FR-Hub(config-if)#encapsulation frame-relay
FR-Hub(config-if)#
```

We configure the local DLCI value using the command *"frame-relay interface-dlci <dlci number>"*:

```
FR-Hub(config-if)#frame-relay interface-dlci 102
FR-Hub(config-fr-dlci)#exit
FR-Hub(config-if)#
```

FR-Spoke2 is set up in the same way:

```
FR-Spoke2(config)#int s1/2
FR-Spoke2(config-if)#
%LINEPROTO-5-UPDOWN: Line protocol on Interface Serial1/2, changed state
to down
FR-Spoke2(config-if)#encapsulation frame-relay
%LINEPROTO-5-UPDOWN: Line protocol on Interface Serial1/2, changed state
to up
FR-Spoke2(config-if)#
FR-Spoke2(config-if)#frame-relay interface-dlci 102
FR-Spoke2(config-fr-dlci)#exit
FR-Spoke2(config-if)#no keepalive
FR-Spoke2(config-if)#
```

We can test using a ping from the hub to the spoke:

```
FR-Hub(config-if)#do ping 192.168.12.2
Type escape sequence to abort.
Sending 5, 100-byte ICMP Echos to 192.168.12.2:
!!!!!
Success rate is 100 percent (5/5)
FR-Hub(config-if)#
```

We can also look at the interface details:

```
FR-Hub(config-if)#do sh int s1/2
Serial1/2 is up, line protocol is up
  Hardware is M4T
  Description: Link to FR-Spoke2
  Internet address is 192.168.12.1/24
  MTU 1500 bytes, BW 1544 Kbit/sec, DLY 20000 usec,
     reliability 255/255, txload 1/255, rxload 1/255
```

```
  Encapsulation FRAME-RELAY, crc 16, loopback not set
  Keepalive not set
  Restart-Delay is 0 secs
  LMI DLCI 1023  LMI type is CISCO  frame relay DTE
  FR SVC disabled, LAPF state down
 <truncated>

 FR-Hub(config-if)#
```

Notice that we did not set an LMI type, but we still have one. We can set the LMI type using the following command:

```
 FR-Hub(config-if)#frame-relay lmi-type ?
   cisco
   ansi
   q933a

 FR-Hub(config-if)#frame-relay lmi-type
```

We again have three options. Cisco, ANSI, and ITU (q933a). The LMI type is used to manage physical access. By default, we will perform auto-sensing, which, as you may guess, defaults to the Cisco LMI type. LMI is actually disabled between the hub and Spoke2 though, we can tell this because the PVC status shows as "static" (instead of active):

```
 FR-Spoke2(config-if)#do sh frame-relay pvc 102

 PVC Statistics for interface Serial1/2 (Frame Relay DTE)

 DLCI = 102, DLCI USAGE = LOCAL, PVC STATUS = STATIC, INTERFACE =
 Serial1/2

   input pkts 16          output pkts 12          in bytes 1244
   out bytes 1108         dropped pkts 0          in pkts dropped 0
   out pkts dropped 0              out bytes dropped 0
   in FECN pkts 0         in BECN pkts 0          out FECN pkts 0
   out BECN pkts 0        in DE pkts 0            out DE pkts 0
   out bcast pkts 2       out bcast bytes 68
   5 minute input rate 0 bits/sec, 0 packets/sec
   5 minute output rate 0 bits/sec, 0 packets/sec
   pvc create time 00:23:05, last time pvc status changed 00:23:05
 FR-Spoke2(config-if)#
```

In addition, if we use the command *"show frame-relay lmi"*, we get no results:

```
 FR-Hub(config-if)#do sh frame-relay lmi
 FR-Hub(config-if)#
```

We will now set up FR-Spoke1. This time we will be using LMI, as well as sub-interfaces. Because we are using sub-interfaces, we need to remove the IP addresses from the physical interface, and set the encapsulation to frame-relay.

```
FR-Hub(config-if)#int s1/1
FR-Hub(config-if)#no ip address
FR-Hub(config-if)#encapsulation frame-relay
FR-Hub(config-if)#
FR-Hub(config-if)#clock rate 64000
FR-Hub(config-if)#frame-relay intf-type dce
FR-Hub(config-if)#
FR-Hub(config-if)#int s1/1.101 point-to-point
FR-Hub(config-subif)#ip address 192.168.11.1 255.255.255.0
FR-Hub(config-subif)#
%LINEPROTO-5-UPDOWN: Line protocol on Interface Serial1/1, changed state
to down
FR-Hub(config-subif)#frame-relay interface-dlci 101
FR-Hub(config-fr-dlci)#
FR-Hub(config-fr-dlci)#exit
FR-Hub(config-subif)#exit
FR-Hub(config)#
```

FR-Hub is set as the DCE, with a clock rate of 64000. We then create the sub-interface, specifying that it is a point-to-point interface, and moving the IP address to the sub-interface. We also specify the interface-dlci as well. FR-Spoke1 is very similar, but does not need the interface type command, or the clock rate to be set.

```
FR-Spoke1(config-if)#int s1/1
FR-Spoke1(config-if)#no ip address
FR-Spoke1(config-if)#encapsulation frame-relay
FR-Spoke1(config-if)#
FR-Spoke1(config)#int s1/1.101 point-to-point
FR-Spoke1(config-subif)#ip address 192.168.11.2 255.255.255.0
FR-Spoke1(config-subif)#frame-relay interface-dlci 101
FR-Spoke1(config-fr-dlci)#
```

Our most basic test will be a ping from FR-Spoke1 to FR-Hub:

```
FR-Spoke1(config-fr-dlci)#do ping 192.168.11.1
Type escape sequence to abort.
Sending 5, 100-byte ICMP Echos to 192.168.11.1:
!!!!!
Success rate is 100 percent (5/5)
FR-Spoke1(config-fr-dlci)#
```

This works fine. We can also see the LMI status:

```
FR-Hub(config)#do show frame-relay lmi
LMI Statistics for interface Serial1/1 (Frame Relay DCE) LMI TYPE = CISCO
  Invalid Unnumbered info 0          Invalid Prot Disc 0
  Invalid dummy Call Ref 0           Invalid Msg Type 0
  Invalid Status Message 0           Invalid Lock Shift 0
  Invalid Information ID 0           Invalid Report IE Len 0
  Invalid Report Request 0           Invalid Keep IE Len 0
  Num Status Enq. Rcvd 10            Num Status msgs Sent 10
  Num Update Status Sent 0           Num St Enq. Timeouts 6
FR-Hub(config)#
```

We can now compare the PVC status to the link between FR-Hub and the spokes, confirming that without LMI, the PVC status is "static" and with LMI it is "active":

```
FR-Hub(config)#do sh frame-relay pvc | i DLCI
DLCI=101, DLCI USAGE=LOCAL, PVC STATUS=ACTIVE, INTERFACE=Serial1/1.101
DLCI=102, DLCI USAGE=LOCAL, PVC STATUS=STATIC, INTERFACE=Serial1/2
FR-Hub(config)#
```

LMI (Local Management Interface) performs a couple of functions, such as keepalive notifications, inverse ARP and is used to signal whether the PVC is active or inactive. It is actually an enhancement to Frame Relay. The choice in LMI does have ramifications; Cisco's LMI allows DLCI numbering between 16 and 1007, and has its own LMI DLCI of 1023. ANSI and ITU allow numbering between 16 and 976, they have a DLCI of 0. Therefore, if you plan to use a specific DLCI numbering method, the choice of LMI type may affect this. LMI messages are sent every 10 seconds, as a standard "hello", if three hello messages are missed the interface will be shut down.

We have one side using LMI and the other, which does not. What do we lose by not using LMI? Our routing table looks fine (sparse, but fine), but we lose CDP information:

```
FR-Hub(config)#sh ip route | b Gate
Gateway of last resort is not set

      192.168.11.0/24 is variably subnetted, 2 subnets, 2 masks
C        192.168.11.0/24 is directly connected, Serial1/1.101
L        192.168.11.1/32 is directly connected, Serial1/1.101
      192.168.12.0/24 is variably subnetted, 2 subnets, 2 masks
C        192.168.12.0/24 is directly connected, Serial1/2
L        192.168.12.1/32 is directly connected, Serial1/2
FR-Hub(config)#do sh cdp neigh | b Device
Device ID   Local Intrfce   Holdtme  Capability  Platform  Port ID
FR-Spoke1   Ser 1/1.101     126          R B     Linux Uni Ser 1/1.101

Total cdp entries displayed : 1
FR-Hub(config)#
```

Frame Relay is a big topic and we are not done with it yet. We are going to save some of the important Frame Relay topics for the troubleshooting section though, as it is easier to explain them there.

Let's finish this chapter by setting up our connection between FR-Hub and EIGRP4.

8.5 Implement and troubleshoot PPPoE

The last step we need to do in order to complete our network, is get FR-Hub and EIGRP4 talking to each other. To do this we will use PPPoE, PPP over Ethernet. A benefit of this is that it will allow us the ability to capture some of the CHAP traffic, which we could not do on our serial interfaces.

PPPoE is primarily used in DSL technologies; it has all the benefits of PPP, such as authentication, with the added bonus of the speeds offered by Ethernet. PPPoE is an emulated form of PPP, primarily used across a shared medium (multiple clients calling one server through one interface).

EIGRP4 will act as our PPPoE server and FH-Hub will act as the client. We will start by setting up the server. Because FR-Hub will authenticate to us, we need to create a username and password for FR-Hub:

```
EIGRP4(config)#username FR-Hub password cisco
```

EIGRP4 also needs an IP address on its interface:

```
EIGRP4(config)#int e0/0
EIGRP4(config-if)#ip add 192.168.100.1 255.255.255.252
EIGRP4(config-if)#no shut
EIGRP4(config-if)#
```

We need to enable this interface for PPPoE, and we can step through the commands using the context sensitive help:

```
EIGRP4(config-if)#pppoe ?
  enable  Enable pppoe

EIGRP4(config-if)#pppoe enable ?
  group  attach a BBA group
  <cr>

EIGRP4(config-if)#pppoe enable group ?
  WORD    BBA Group name
  global  Attach global PPPoE group

EIGRP4(config-if)#pppoe enable group global
EIGRP4(config-if)#
```

```
%LINEPROTO-5-UPDOWN: Line protocol on Interface Virtual-Access1, changed
state to up
EIGRP4(config-if)#
%LINK-3-UPDOWN: Interface Virtual-Access1, changed state to up
EIGRP4(config-if)#
```

We now have a global PPPoE group and a new interface, Virtual-Access1. This new interface does not have an IP address, but it is in an up/up state:

```
EIGRP4(config-if)#do sh ip int bri | i Virtual
Virtual-Access1           unassigned      YES unset  up          up
EIGRP4(config-if)#
```

We then need to create an interface virtual template:

```
EIGRP4(config-if)#interface Virtual-Template1
EIGRP4(config-if)#mtu 1492
EIGRP4(config-if)#ip unnumbered ethernet0/0
EIGRP4(config-if)#ppp authentication pap chap
EIGRP4(config-if)#peer default ip address pool FR-Hub-Pool
EIGRP4(config-if)#
```

The virtual template contains our settings. We set the MTU of the interface to 1492 to account for the overhead created by the encapsulation (an 8-byte header). We instruct the template to "borrow" the IP address from our Ethernet0/0 interface. We could bind it to a loopback address, offering more stability (loopback interfaces never go down unless we forcefully make them). We also enable the authentication options of PAP and CHAP (as this will allow us to look at the differences). EIGRP4 will also use a basic form of DHCP to assign an address to FR-Hub, selecting an address from a range that we need to configure:

```
EIGRP4(config-if)#ip local pool FR-Hub-Pool 10.20.30.40 10.20.30.50
EIGRP4(config)#
```

Above we create a pool of ten addresses, from 10.20.30.40 to 10.20.30.50. As PPPoE is predominantly used in a shared medium environment, we may have more than one client dialing in to us. So how do we connect the template to our virtual-access interface? To do this we create another group, a BBA group. BBA stands for Broadband Aggregation.

```
EIGRP4(config)#bba-group pppoe global
EIGRP4(config-bba-group)#
EIGRP4(config-bba-group)#virtual-template 1
```

Now, if we look at our interfaces (excluding those that are in a status of "administratively down"), we can see our virtual template, which uses the same address as our Ethernet0/0 interface:

```
EIGRP4(config-bba-group)#do sh ip int bri | e administratively
Interface          IP-Address      OK? Method Status        Protocol
Ethernet0/0        192.168.100.1   YES manual up            up
Ethernet0/1        192.168.43.4    YES NVRAM  up            up
Serial1/0          unassigned      YES NVRAM  up            down
Serial1/1          192.168.54.4    YES NVRAM  up            down
Loopback4          4.4.4.4         YES NVRAM  up            up
Virtual-Access1    unassigned      YES unset  up            up
Virtual-Access2    unassigned      YES unset  down          down
Virtual-Template1  192.168.100.1   YES unset  down          down

EIGRP4(config-bba-group)#
```

Let's move onto FR-Hub.

```
FR-Hub(config)#int e0/0
FR-Hub(config-if)#no ip address
FR-Hub(config-if)#pppoe enable
FR-Hub(config-if)#
%LINEPROTO-5-UPDOWN: Line protocol on Interface Virtual-Access1, changed
state to up
FR-Hub(config-if)#
%LINK-3-UPDOWN: Interface Virtual-Access1, changed state to up
FR-Hub(config-if)#pppoe-client dial-pool-number 1
FR-Hub(config-if)#exit
FR-Hub(config)#interface Dialer1
FR-Hub(config-if)#ip address negotiated
FR-Hub(config-if)#encapsulation ppp
FR-Hub(config-if)#dialer pool 1
FR-Hub(config-if)#dialer-group 1
FR-Hub(config-if)#ppp authentication pap chap callin
FR-Hub(config-if)#ppp pap sent-username FR-Hub password cisco
FR-Hub(config-if)#ppp chap password cisco
FR-Hub(config-if)#
```

Above we start by removing the IP address from the interface, and setting it to be a PPPoE client. We create a dialer interface, telling it to use the IP address we receive from EIGRP4 and set up authentication (PAP and CHAP).

The last step is to enable the interface (I have removed the interfaces we are not interested in from the "sh ip int brief" command):

```
FR-Hub(config-if)#int e0/0
FR-Hub(config-if)#no shut
FR-Hub(config-if)#
%LINK-3-UPDOWN: Interface Ethernet0/0, changed state to up
```

```
%LINEPROTO-5-UPDOWN: Line protocol on Interface Ethernet0/0, changed
state to up
FR-Hub(config-if)#
FR-Hub(config-if)#do sh ip int bri
Interface            IP-Address       OK? Method Status      Protocol
Ethernet0/0          unassigned       YES NVRAM  up          up
Serial1/1            unassigned       YES manual up          up
Serial1/1.101        192.168.11.1     YES manual up          up
Serial1/2            192.168.12.1     YES manual up          up
Dialer1              unassigned       YES manual up          up
Virtual-Access1      unassigned       YES unset  up          up
FR-Hub(config-if)#
%DIALER-6-BIND: Interface Vi2 bound to profile Di1
%LINK-3-UPDOWN: Interface Virtual-Access2, changed state to up
FR-Hub(config-if)#
%LINEPROTO-5-UPDOWN: Line protocol on Interface Virtual-Access2, changed
state to up
FR-Hub(config-if)#
FR-Hub(config-if)#do sh ip int bri
Interface            IP-Address       OK? Method Status      Protocol
Ethernet0/0          unassigned       YES NVRAM  up          up
Serial1/1            unassigned       YES manual up          up
Serial1/1.101        192.168.11.1     YES manual up          up
Serial1/2            192.168.12.1     YES manual up          up
Dialer1              10.20.30.40      YES IPCP   up          up
Virtual-Access1      unassigned       YES unset  up          up
Virtual-Access2      unassigned       YES unset  up          up
FR-Hub(config-if)#
```

We can confirm basic connectivity using a ping:

```
FR-Hub(config-if)#do ping 192.168.100.1
Type escape sequence to abort.
Sending 5, 100-byte ICMP Echos to 192.168.100.1:
!!!!!
Success rate is 100 percent (5/5)
FR-Hub(config-if)#
```

We can also check our routing table:

```
FR-Hub(config-if)#do sh ip route | b Gateway
Gateway of last resort is not set

      10.0.0.0/32 is subnetted, 1 subnets
C        10.20.30.40 is directly connected, Dialer1
      192.168.11.0/24 is variably subnetted, 2 subnets, 2 masks
C        192.168.11.0/24 is directly connected, Serial1/1.101
L        192.168.11.1/32 is directly connected, Serial1/1.101
```

```
          192.168.12.0/24 is variably subnetted, 2 subnets, 2 masks
C             192.168.12.0/24 is directly connected, Serial1/2
L             192.168.12.1/32 is directly connected, Serial1/2
          192.168.100.0/32 is subnetted, 1 subnets
C             192.168.100.1 is directly connected, Dialer1
FR-Hub(config-if)#
```

At the moment, we cannot get very far, so let's add a default route. Because this is effectively PPP, we have the same control protocols, including IPCP, so we can utilize this to give us a default route:

```
FR-Hub(config-if)#int dialer1
FR-Hub(config-if)#ppp ipcp route default
FR-Hub(config-if)#shut
FR-Hub(config-if)#
%DIALER-6-UNBIND: Interface Vi2 unbound from profile Di1
Di1 DDR: dialer shutdown complete
%LINEPROTO-5-UPDOWN: Line protocol on Interface Virtual-Access2, changed
state to down
FR-Hub(config-if)#
%LINK-3-UPDOWN: Interface Virtual-Access2, changed state to down
FR-Hub(config-if)#
FR-Hub(config-if)#no shut
FR-Hub(config-if)#
%LINK-3-UPDOWN: Interface Dialer1, changed state to up
%DIALER-6-BIND: Interface Vi2 bound to profile Di1
%LINK-3-UPDOWN: Interface Virtual-Access2, changed state to up
FR-Hub(config-if)#
%LINEPROTO-5-UPDOWN: Line protocol on Interface Virtual-Access2, changed
state to up
FR-Hub(config-if)#
```

Now we have a default route pointing to EIGRP4 (but get a new address of 10.20.30.42):

```
FR-Hub(config-if)#do sh ip route | b Gate
Gateway of last resort is 192.168.100.1 to network 0.0.0.0

S*     0.0.0.0/0 [1/0] via 192.168.100.1
       10.0.0.0/32 is subnetted, 1 subnets
C          10.20.30.42 is directly connected, Dialer1
       192.168.11.0/24 is variably subnetted, 2 subnets, 2 masks
C          192.168.11.0/24 is directly connected, Serial1/1.101
L          192.168.11.1/32 is directly connected, Serial1/1.101
       192.168.12.0/24 is variably subnetted, 2 subnets, 2 masks
C          192.168.12.0/24 is directly connected, Serial1/2
L          192.168.12.1/32 is directly connected, Serial1/2
       192.168.100.0/32 is subnetted, 1 subnets
C          192.168.100.1 is directly connected, Dialer1
FR-Hub(config-if)#
```

This allows us to ping 4.4.4.4 (EIGRP4's loopback interface):

```
FR-Hub(config-if)#do ping 4.4.4.4
Type escape sequence to abort.
Sending 5, 100-byte ICMP Echos to 4.4.4.4:
!!!!!
Success rate is 100 percent (5/5)
FR-Hub(config-if)#
```

Let's shut down the interface again, and capture some of the traffic in Wireshark:

```
FR-Hub(config-if)#shut
FR-Hub(config-if)#
%DIALER-6-UNBIND: Interface Vi2 unbound from profile Di1
Di1 DDR: dialer shutdown complete
%LINEPROTO-5-UPDOWN: Line protocol on Interface Virtual-Access2, changed
state to down
FR-Hub(config-if)#
%LINK-3-UPDOWN: Interface Virtual-Access2, changed state to down
FR-Hub(config-if)#
%LINK-5-CHANGED: Interface Dialer1, changed state to administratively
down
FR-Hub(config-if)#
FR-Hub(config-if)#no shut
FR-Hub(config-if)#
%LINK-3-UPDOWN: Interface Dialer1, changed state to up
FR-Hub(config-if)#
%DIALER-6-BIND: Interface Vi2 bound to profile Di1
%LINK-3-UPDOWN: Interface Virtual-Access2, changed state to up
FR-Hub(config-if)#
%LINEPROTO-5-UPDOWN: Line protocol on Interface Virtual-Access2, changed
state to up
FR-Hub(config-if)#do ping 4.4.4.4
Type escape sequence to abort.
Sending 5, 100-byte ICMP Echos to 4.4.4.4:
!!!!!
Success rate is 100 percent (5/5)
FR-Hub(config-if)#
```

The captured conversation shows that we start with the PPPoE Discovery phase. This phase has four parts to the conversation. These parts are the Initiation (PADI), the Offer (PADO), the Request (PADR) and the Session confirmation (PADS). The PAD part stands for "PPPoE Active Discovery". I like to try to remember the acronym "I Offer Random Stuff" to remember the phases. There is another phase, once we disconnect, and that is PADT (termination).

This is the relevant part of the Wireshark capture:

```
11 3_   aa:bb:cc:00:0_  Broadcast        PPPoED     60 Active Discovery Initiation (PADI)
12 3_   aa:bb:cc:00:1_  aa:bb:cc:00:0f_  PPPoED     66 Active Discovery Offer (PADO) AC-Name='EIGRP4'
13 4_   aa:bb:cc:00:0_  aa:bb:cc:00:15_  PPPoED     66 Active Discovery Request (PADR) AC-Name='EIGRP4'
14 4_   aa:bb:cc:00:1_  aa:bb:cc:00:0f_  PPPoED     66 Active Discovery Session-confirmation (PADS) AC-Name='EIGRP4'
```

Wireshark capture: 11

The initiation goes from the client to the server. This uses an Ethernet broadcast, and it contains the MAC address of FR-Hub:

```
▶ Frame 11: 60 bytes on wire (480 bits), 60 bytes captured (480 bits) on interface 0
▶ Ethernet II, Src: aa:bb:cc:00:0f:00 (aa:bb:cc:00:0f:00), Dst: Broadcast (ff:ff:ff:ff:ff:ff)
▼ PPP-over-Ethernet Discovery
    0001 .... = Version: 1
    .... 0001 = Type: 1
    Code: Active Discovery Initiation (PADI) (0x09)
    Session ID: 0x0000
    Payload Length: 16
  ▼ PPPoE Tags
      Host-Uniq: 6100000100001265
```

The server then responds with an offer. The offer contains its own MAC address and its hostname:

```
▶ Frame 12: 66 bytes on wire (528 bits), 66 bytes captured
▶ Ethernet II, Src: aa:bb:cc:00:15:00 (aa:bb:cc:00:15:00),
▼ PPP-over-Ethernet Discovery
    0001 .... = Version: 1
    .... 0001 = Type: 1
    Code: Active Discovery Offer (PADO) (0x07)
    Session ID: 0x0000
    Payload Length: 46
  ▼ PPPoE Tags
      Host-Uniq: 6100000100001265
      AC-Name: EIGRP4
      AC-Cookie: abf0fd7b74149eaa6dcb5c184886ab5d
```

FR-Hub then sends back a request, accepting the offer:

```
▶ Frame 13: 66 bytes on wire (528 bits), 66 bytes captured
▶ Ethernet II, Src: aa:bb:cc:00:0f:00 (aa:bb:cc:00:0f:00),
▼ PPP-over-Ethernet Discovery
    0001 .... = Version: 1
    .... 0001 = Type: 1
    Code: Active Discovery Request (PADR) (0x19)
    Session ID: 0x0000
    Payload Length: 46
  ▼ PPPoE Tags
      Host-Uniq: 6100000100001265
      AC-Name: EIGRP4
      AC-Cookie: abf0fd7b74149eaa6dcb5c184886ab5d
```

The final stage is for EIGRP4 to send a session confirmation:

```
▶ Frame 14: 66 bytes on wire (528 bits), 66 bytes captured (52
▶ Ethernet II, Src: aa:bb:cc:00:15:00 (aa:bb:cc:00:15:00), Dst
▼ PPP-over-Ethernet Discovery
      0001 .... = Version: 1
      .... 0001 = Type: 1
      Code: Active Discovery Session-confirmation (PADS) (0x65)
      Session ID: 0x0003
      Payload Length: 46
   ▼ PPPoE Tags
        Host-Uniq: 61000001000001265
        AC-Name: EIGRP4
        AC-Cookie: abf0fd7b74149eaa6dcb5c184886ab5d
```

Now that the PPPoE session is created, we hand over to the PPP control protocols:

PPP LCP	60 Configuration Request
PPP LCP	60 Configuration Request
PPP LCP	60 Configuration Ack
PPP LCP	60 Configuration Nak
PPP LCP	60 Configuration Request
PPP LCP	60 Configuration Ack
PPP PAP	60 Authenticate-Request (Peer-ID='FR-Hub', Password='cisco')
PPP PAP	60 Authenticate-Ack (Message='')
PPP IPCP	60 Configuration Request
PPP IPCP	60 Configuration Request
PPP CDPCP	60 Configuration Request
PPP IPCP	60 Configuration Ack
PPP IPCP	60 Configuration Nak
PPP LCP	60 Protocol Reject
PPP IPCP	60 Configuration Request
PPP IPCP	60 Configuration Ack

There are many messages here, so we will not go through all of them in depth. In the capture, they are numbered from 16 to 31, and we will be using these numbers as our reference. FR-Hub starts by sending a request (16); this includes the magic number (used for looped link detection). Packet 17 then has a request from EIGRP4 to FR-Hub, containing the magic number, the MTU of 1492, and the request for FR-Hub to start sending PAP authentication details. Packets 18, 19, 20 and 21 then acknowledge this (albeit with a little toing and froing about the MTU).

In packet 22, we start to send our PAP authentication details. Notice that the password is sent in clear text, which is hardly a secure method. Packet 23 is EIGRP4's acknowledgement of successful PAP authentication.

Packet 24 is where we start to exchange our routing data. EIGRP4 sends its IP address, FR-Hub then requests an IP address (because the interface is set to "*ip address negotiated*"), it then is offered an IP address in packet 28, which it accepts in packet 30.

Now shut down interface dialer1 on FR-Hub, and we'll change the authentication to CHAP:

```
FR-Hub(config-if)#shut
%LINK-3-UPDOWN: Interface Virtual-Access2, changed state to down
%LINK-5-CHANGED: Interface Dialer1, changed state to administratively
down
FR-Hub(config-if)#
FR-Hub(config-if)#do sh run | i pap
 ppp authentication pap chap callin
 ppp pap sent-username FR-Hub password 7 060506324F41
FR-Hub(config-if)#no ppp pap sent-username FR-Hub password 7 060506324F41
FR-Hub(config-if)#ppp authentication chap callin
FR-Hub(config-if)#no shut
FR-Hub(config-if)#
%LINEPROTO-5-UPDOWN: Line protocol on Interface Virtual-Access2, changed
state to up
FR-Hub(config-if)#
<truncated>
FR-Hub(config-if)#do ping 4.4.4.4
Type escape sequence to abort.
Sending 5, 100-byte ICMP Echos to 4.4.4.4:
!!!!!
Success rate is 100 percent (5/5)
FR-Hub(config-if)#
```

The new Wireshark capture looks like this:

```
PPP CHAP      60 Challenge (NAME='EIGRP4', VALUE=0x5c78eb5ad5381410bdcad45b56cf6847)
PPP CHAP      60 Response (NAME='FR-Hub', VALUE=0xec9b98df8c6bc9c46c762cd5e4c11d82)
PPP CHAP      60 Success (MESSAGE='')
```

Wireshark capture: 12

We exchange usernames and the hash, but we cannot see a clear-text password. We then get a success message from EIGRP4. CHAP is obviously much more preferable than the easily hacked PPP.

The last step we need to do, in order to complete our network, is to extend our EIGRP routing across the Frame Relay routers.

```
FR-Hub(config-if)#router eigrp 1
FR-Hub(config-router)#network 192.168.11.0
FR-Hub(config-router)#network 192.168.12.0
FR-Hub(config-router)#
```

```
FR-Spoke1(config)#router eigrp 1
FR-Spoke1(config-router)#network 192.168.11.0
FR-Spoke1(config-router)#
%DUAL-5-NBRCHANGE: EIGRP-IPv4 1: Neighbor 192.168.11.1 (Serial1/1.101) is
up: new adjacency
FR-Spoke1(config-router)#

FR-Spoke2(config)#router eigrp 1
FR-Spoke2(config-router)#network 192.168.12.0
FR-Spoke2(config-router)#
%DUAL-5-NBRCHANGE: EIGRP-IPv4 1: Neighbor 192.168.12.1 (Serial1/2) is up:
new adjacency
FR-Spoke2(config-router)#
```

How do we deal with the adjacency between FR-Hub and EIGRP4? There is no guarantee that FR-Hub will always get the same IP address, also we are issued a /32 address, so cannot wildcard a subnet.

```
FR-Hub(config-router)#do sh int dialer1 | i address
  Internet address is 10.20.30.42/32
FR-Hub(config-router)#
```

Well, in this scenario we just have to hope that our address does not change too often:

```
EIGRP4(config-bba-group)#router eigrp 1
EIGRP4(config-router)#network 192.168.100.0
EIGRP4(config-router)#

FR-Hub(config-router)#do sh ip int bri | i Dialer1
Dialer1           10.20.30.42     YES IPCP    up              up
FR-Hub(config-router)#
FR-Hub(config-router)#network 10.20.30.42 0.0.0.0
FR-Hub(config-router)#
%DUAL-5-NBRCHANGE: EIGRP-IPv4 1: Neighbor 192.168.100.1 (Dialer1) is up:
new adjacency
FR-Hub(config-router)#
```

We should now have a few more routes on the spoke(s):

```
FR-Spoke1(config-router)#do sh ip route eigrp | b Gate
Gateway of last resort is not set

     1.0.0.0/32 is subnetted, 1 subnets
D       1.1.1.1 [90/46942976] via 192.168.11.1, 00:00:16, Ser1/1.101
     2.0.0.0/32 is subnetted, 1 subnets
D       2.2.2.2 [90/46917376] via 192.168.11.1, 00:00:16, Ser1/1.101
     3.0.0.0/32 is subnetted, 1 subnets
D       3.3.3.3 [90/46891776] via 192.168.11.1, 00:00:16, Ser1/1.101
```

```
        4.0.0.0/32 is subnetted, 1 subnets
D          4.4.4.4 [90/46866176] via 192.168.11.1, 00:00:16, Ser1/1.101
        5.0.0.0/32 is subnetted, 1 subnets
D          5.5.5.5 [90/47378176] via 192.168.11.1, 00:00:16, Ser1/1.101
        10.0.0.0/32 is subnetted, 1 subnets
D          10.20.30.42 [90/46738176] via 192.168.11.1, 00:00:16, Ser1/1.101
D        192.168.1.0/24 [90/46840576] via 192.168.11.1, 00:00:16, Ser1/1.101
D        192.168.12.0/24 [90/2681856] via 192.168.11.1, 00:01:59, Ser1/1.101
D        192.168.21.0/24 [90/46814976] via 192.168.11.1, 00:00:16, Ser1/1.101
D        192.168.32.0/24 [90/46789376] via 192.168.11.1, 00:00:16, Ser1/1.101
D        192.168.43.0/24 [90/46763776] via 192.168.11.1, 00:00:16, Ser1/1.101
D        192.168.51.0/24 [90/47326976] via 192.168.11.1, 00:00:16, Ser1/1.101
D        192.168.54.0/24 [90/47250176] via 192.168.11.1, 00:00:16, Ser1/1.101
        192.168.100.0/30 is subnetted, 1 subnets
D          192.168.100.0 [90/46763776] via 192.168.11.1, 00:00:16, Ser1/1.101
FR-Spoke1(config-router)# FR-Spoke1(config-router)#do ping 1.1.1.1
Type escape sequence to abort.
Sending 5, 100-byte ICMP Echos to 1.1.1.1:
!!!!!
Success rate is 100 percent (5/5)
FR-Spoke1(config-router)#
```

This is one of those times that IPv6 would really be of benefit here (at least if we could borrow the configuration aspect of IPv6), we could enable EIGRP at an interface level on the client (FR-Hub), and then if our IP address did change, we could still form an adjacency without needing to reconfigure EIGRP over and over again. We could achieve the same end goal, if we were running OSPF, by using the interface-level command "*ip ospf <process> area <area number>*".

Barring the troubleshooting section, we have now been through the entire CCNA syllabus. However, the network is not complete. We do not have full end-to-end reachability. We need to be able to get from the Frame Relay network, through the EIGRP network to the OSPF network. At the moment these are to completely separate networks. To join them up, we need to look at redistribution. We will do this in the next chapter, as well as adding a nicety to the network, in the form of DNS.

9. Beyond the CCNA: Redistribution

One thing that does not feature in the CCNA syllabus is redistribution, but it does feature heavily in the CCNP exams. This will be our final hands-on chapter, we are going to do a lot of tidying up and, by the end of the chapter, we will have complete end-to-end visibility and reachability.

We want to be able to reach the loopback interface on OSPF3 (1.2.3.1) from anywhere in the network. At the moment we have a couple of ACLs, so let's make life easier and remove them:

```
Gateway(config)#int e0/0
Gateway(config-if)#no ip access-group 1 in
Gateway(config-if)#

Server(config)#int e1/0
Server(config-if)#
Server(config-if)#no ip access-group DenyWeb in
Server(config-if)#
Server(config-if)#end
Server#ping 1.2.3.1
Type escape sequence to abort.
Sending 5, 100-byte ICMP Echos to 1.2.3.1:
!!!!!
Success rate is 100 percent (5/5)
Server#
```

We can check that NAT is working by looking at the NAT translation table:

```
Gateway(config-if)#do sh ip nat trans
Pro Inside global      Inside local      Outside local    Outside global
--- 192.168.20.11      10.10.1.3         ---              ---
icmp 192.168.20.21:24  10.20.1.21:24     1.2.3.1:24       1.2.3.1:24
--- 192.168.20.21      10.20.1.21        ---              ---
--- 192.168.20.10      10.30.1.3         ---              ---
Gateway(config-if)#
```

EIGRP4, however, cannot reach the same interface:

```
EIGRP4(config-router)#do ping 1.2.3.1
Type escape sequence to abort.
Sending 5, 100-byte ICMP Echos to 1.2.3.1:
.....
Success rate is 0 percent (0/5)
EIGRP4(config-router)#
```

This is because EIGRP4 cannot see it in its routing table:

```
EIGRP4(config-router)#do sh ip route 1.2.3.1
% Subnet not in table
EIGRP4(config-router)#
```

Similarly, OSPF3 cannot see EIGRP4 (192.168.43.4 or 192.168.54.4):

```
OSPF3#sh ip route | b Gate
Gateway of last resort is not set

        1.0.0.0/8 is variably subnetted, 5 subnets, 2 masks
O          1.2.0.1/32 [110/21] via 172.16.4.2, 00:26:31, Ethernet3/2
O IA       1.2.1.1/32 [110/31] via 172.16.4.2, 00:26:31, Ethernet3/2
O          1.2.2.1/32 [110/11] via 172.16.4.2, 00:26:51, Ethernet3/2
C          1.2.3.0/24 is directly connected, Loopback0
L          1.2.3.1/32 is directly connected, Loopback0
        50.0.0.0/32 is subnetted, 1 subnets
O IA       50.50.50.50 [110/51] via 172.16.4.2, 00:26:21, Ethernet3/2
        100.0.0.0/32 is subnetted, 1 subnets
O IA       100.100.100.100 [110/41] via 172.16.4.2, 00:26:31, Ethernet3/2
        172.16.0.0/16 is variably subnetted, 5 subnets, 2 masks
O IA       172.16.1.0/24 [110/40] via 172.16.4.2, 00:26:31, Ethernet3/2
O          172.16.2.0/24 [110/30] via 172.16.4.2, 00:26:31, Ethernet3/2
O          172.16.3.0/24 [110/20] via 172.16.4.2, 00:26:31, Ethernet3/2
C          172.16.4.0/24 is directly connected, Ethernet3/2
L          172.16.4.3/32 is directly connected, Ethernet3/2
O IA 192.168.20.0/24 [110/50] via 172.16.4.2, 00:26:31, Ethernet3/2
OSPF3#
```

The two domains (OSPF and EIGRP) are completely separate. This is why we need to implement redistribution. To do this we need to find where the two protocols meet, which is on the ISP router. From there, we need to redistribute the protocols into each other. The basic command for this is *"redistribute <from protocol> <process or AS number>"*. Some protocols require some additional information, as we will see.

EIGRP requires us to add in the metrics, which relate to our K values:

```
ISP(config)#router eigrp 1
ISP(config-router)#
ISP(config-router)#redistribute ospf 1 ?
  match      Redistribution of OSPF routes
  metric     Metric for redistributed routes
  route-map  Route map reference
  <cr>

ISP(config-router)#redistribute ospf 1 metric ?
  <1-4294967295>  Bandwidth metric in Kbits per second

ISP(config-router)#redistribute ospf 1 metric 10000 ?
```

```
     <0-4294967295>  EIGRP delay metric, in 10 microsecond units

  ISP(config-router)#redistribute ospf 1 metric 10000 10 ?
    <0-255>  EIGRP reliability metric where 255 is 100% reliable

  ISP(config-router)#redistribute ospf 1 metric 10000 10 255 ?
    <1-255>  EIGRP Effective bandwidth metric (Loading) where 255 is 100%
  loaded

  ISP(config-router)#redistribute ospf 1 metric 10000 10 255 1 ?
    <1-65535>  EIGRP MTU of the path

  ISP(config-router)#redistribute ospf 1 metric 10000 10 255 1 1500 ?
    match       Redistribution of OSPF routes
    route-map   Route map reference
    <cr>

  ISP(config-router)#redistribute ospf 1 metric 10000 10 255 1 1500
```

Above we have specified the bandwidth, delay, reliability, load and MTU. At the moment have only redistributed OSPF into EIGRP; the EIGRP speaking routers will be able to see the OSPF routes, but the OSPF speaking routers will not have any route back to the EIGRP routers, so we need to do mutual redistribution, and get the EIGRP routes into OSPF.

Redistributing EIGRP into OSPF is much easier. We specify the AS number, and specify that we want to include the subnets:

```
  ISP(config-router)#router ospf 1
  ISP(config-router)#
  ISP(config-router)#redistribute eigrp ?
    <1-65535>  AS number

  ISP(config-router)#redistribute eigrp 1 ?
    metric        Metric for redistributed routes
    metric-type   OSPF/IS-IS exterior metric type for redistributed routes
    nssa-only     Limit redistributed routes to NSSA areas
    route-map     Route map reference
    subnets       Consider subnets for redistribution into OSPF
    tag           Set tag for routes redistributed into OSPF
    <cr>

  ISP(config-router)#redistribute eigrp 1 subnets
  ISP(config-router)#
```

Now if we look at EIGRP4, we can see a much larger number of routes (as we would expect). These new routes appear as EIGRP External routers (D EX):

```
EIGRP4(config)#do sh ip route eigrp | b Gate
Gateway of last resort is not set

         1.0.0.0/32 is subnetted, 2 subnets
D           1.1.1.1 [90/460800] via 192.168.43.3, 10:37:59, Ethernet0/1
D EX        1.2.1.1 [170/360960] via 192.168.43.3, 00:01:14, Ethernet0/1
         2.0.0.0/32 is subnetted, 1 subnets
D           2.2.2.2 [90/435200] via 192.168.43.3, 10:25:24, Ethernet0/1
         3.0.0.0/32 is subnetted, 1 subnets
D           3.3.3.3 [90/409600] via 192.168.43.3, 10:37:59, Ethernet0/1
         5.0.0.0/32 is subnetted, 1 subnets
D           5.5.5.5 [90/2297856] via 192.168.54.5, 10:32:19, Serial1/1
         50.0.0.0/32 is subnetted, 1 subnets
D EX       50.50.50.50 [170/360960] via 192.168.43.3, 00:01:14, Ethernet0/1
         100.0.0.0/32 is subnetted, 1 subnets
D EX       100.100.100.100 [170/360960] via 192.168.43.3, 00:01:14, Eth0/1
         172.16.0.0/24 is subnetted, 1 subnets
D EX       172.16.1.0 [170/360960] via 192.168.43.3, 00:01:14, Ethernet0/1
D        192.168.1.0/24 [90/358400] via 192.168.43.3, 10:37:59, Ethernet0/1
D        192.168.11.0/24
              [90/4729856] via 10.20.30.42, 00:16:28, Virtual-Access1.1
D        192.168.12.0/24
              [90/4729856] via 10.20.30.42, 00:16:28, Virtual-Access1.1
D EX    192.168.20.0/24 [170/360960] via 192.168.43.3, 00:01:14, Eth0/1
D        192.168.21.0/24 [90/332800] via 192.168.43.3, 10:25:24, Ethernet0/1
D        192.168.32.0/24 [90/307200] via 192.168.43.3, 10:37:59, Ethernet0/1
D        192.168.51.0/24 [90/2246656] via 192.168.43.3, 10:32:19, Eth0/1
EIGRP4(config)#
```

OSPF3 also has more routes, appearing as OSPF External 2 (O E2):

```
OSPF3#sh ip route | b Gate
Gateway of last resort is not set

         1.0.0.0/32 is subnetted, 5 subnets
O E2     1.1.1.1 [110/20] via 172.16.4.2, 00:02:21, Ethernet3/2
O        1.2.0.1 [110/21] via 172.16.4.2, 1d01h, Ethernet3/2
O IA     1.2.1.1 [110/31] via 172.16.4.2, 1d01h, Ethernet3/2
O        1.2.2.1 [110/11] via 172.16.4.2, 1d01h, Ethernet3/2
C        1.2.3.1 is directly connected, Loopback0
         2.0.0.0/32 is subnetted, 1 subnets
O E2     2.2.2.2 [110/20] via 172.16.4.2, 00:02:21, Ethernet3/2
         3.0.0.0/32 is subnetted, 1 subnets
O E2     3.3.3.3 [110/20] via 172.16.4.2, 00:02:21, Ethernet3/2
         4.0.0.0/32 is subnetted, 1 subnets
O E2     4.4.4.4 [110/20] via 172.16.4.2, 00:02:21, Ethernet3/2
         5.0.0.0/32 is subnetted, 1 subnets
O E2     5.5.5.5 [110/20] via 172.16.4.2, 00:02:21, Ethernet3/2
         50.0.0.0/32 is subnetted, 1 subnets
```

```
O IA      50.50.50.50 [110/51] via 172.16.4.2, 08:49:49, Ethernet3/2
          100.0.0.0/32 is subnetted, 1 subnets
O IA      100.100.100.100 [110/41] via 172.16.4.2, 1d01h, Ethernet3/2
          172.16.0.0/16 is variably subnetted, 5 subnets, 2 masks
O IA      172.16.1.0/24 [110/40] via 172.16.4.2, 1d01h, Ethernet3/2
O         172.16.2.0/24 [110/30] via 172.16.4.2, 1d01h, Ethernet3/2
O         172.16.3.0/24 [110/20] via 172.16.4.2, 1d01h, Ethernet3/2
C         172.16.4.0/24 is directly connected, Ethernet3/2
L         172.16.4.3/32 is directly connected, Ethernet3/2
O E2 192.168.1.0/24 [110/20] via 172.16.4.2, 00:02:21, Ethernet3/2
O E2 192.168.11.0/24 [110/20] via 172.16.4.2, 00:02:21, Ethernet3/2
O E2 192.168.12.0/24 [110/20] via 172.16.4.2, 00:02:21, Ethernet3/2
O IA 192.168.20.0/24 [110/50] via 172.16.4.2, 08:49:49, Ethernet3/2
O E2 192.168.21.0/24 [110/20] via 172.16.4.2, 00:02:21, Ethernet3/2
O E2 192.168.32.0/24 [110/20] via 172.16.4.2, 00:02:21, Ethernet3/2
O E2 192.168.43.0/24 [110/20] via 172.16.4.2, 00:02:21, Ethernet3/2
O E2 192.168.51.0/24 [110/20] via 172.16.4.2, 00:02:21, Ethernet3/2
O E2 192.168.54.0/24 [110/20] via 172.16.4.2, 00:02:21, Ethernet3/2
          192.168.100.0/30 is subnetted, 1 subnets
O E2      192.168.100.0 [110/20] via 172.16.4.2, 00:02:21, Ethernet3/2
OSPF3#
```

We still cannot reach 1.2.3.1 though (it is not in our routing table and we do not have a default route):

```
EIGRP4(config)#do ping 1.2.3.1
Type escape sequence to abort.
Sending 5, 100-byte ICMP Echos to 1.2.3.1:
.....
Success rate is 0 percent (0/5)
EIGRP4(config)#
```

EIGRP1 does have a default route, but cannot access 1.2.3.1 either:

```
EIGRP1#sh ip route 1.2.3.1
% Subnet not in table
EIGRP1#sh ip route 0.0.0.0
Routing entry for 0.0.0.0/0, supernet
  Known via "static", distance 1, metric 0, candidate default path
  Routing Descriptor Blocks:
  * 192.168.1.1
      Route metric is 0, traffic share count is 1
EIGRP1#ping 1.2.3.1
Type escape sequence to abort.
Sending 5, 100-byte ICMP Echos to 1.2.3.1:
U.U.U
Success rate is 0 percent (0/5)
EIGRP1#
```

Why is this? This is because ISP does not have an explicit route to it, nor does it have a default route:

```
ISP(config-router)#do sh ip route 1.2.3.0
% Subnet not in table
ISP(config-router)#
ISP(config-router)#do sh ip route 0.0.0.0
% Network not in table
ISP(config-router)#
```

The reason for this is that ISP is still set as a Not-So Stubby area:

```
ISP(config-router)#do sh run | s router o
router ospf 1
 router-id 100.100.100.100
 area 1 nssa
 redistribute eigrp 1 subnets
 network 100.100.100.100 0.0.0.0 area 1
 network 172.16.0.0 0.0.255.255 area 1
 network 192.168.20.0 0.0.0.255 area 1
ipv6 router ospf 1
ISP(config-router)#
```

We could either add a default route on ISP to OSPF1, but then we would need to also add it to EIGRP1, EIGRP2 and so on, losing any benefit we get from running a routing protocol. Instead, let's remove the stub area

```
ISP(config-router)#router ospf 1
ISP(config-router)#no area 1 nssa
ISP(config-router)#
%OSPF-5-ADJCHG: Process 1, Nbr 50.50.50.50 on Ethernet0/0 from FULL to
DOWN, Neighbor Down: Adjacency forced to reset
%OSPF-5-ADJCHG: Process 1, Nbr 1.2.1.1 on Ethernet1/1 from FULL to DOWN,
Neighbor Down: Adjacency forced to reset
ISP(config-router)#

OSPF1(config)#router ospf 1
OSPF1(config-router)#
%OSPF-5-ADJCHG: Process 1, Nbr 100.100.100.100 on Ethernet1/1 from FULL
to DOWN, Neighbor Down: Dead timer expired
OSPF1(config-router)#
OSPF1(config-router)#no area 1 nssa default-information-originate no-
summary
OSPF1(config-router)#no area 1 nssa
OSPF1(config-router)#

Gateway(config-if)#router ospf 1
Gateway(config-router)#no area 1 nssa
Gateway(config-router)#
```

```
%OSPFv3-5-ADJCHG: Process 1, Nbr 100.100.100.100 on Ethernet1/1 from
LOADING to FULL, Loading Done
OSPF1(config-if)#
```

The OSPF adjacencies should reform, giving ISP a fuller routing table:

```
ISP(config-router)#do sh ip route 1.2.3.1
Routing entry for 1.2.3.1/32
  Known via "ospf 1", distance 110, metric 41, type inter area
  Redistributing via eigrp 1
  Advertised by eigrp 1 metric 10000 10 255 1 1500
  Last update from 172.16.1.2 on Ethernet1/1, 00:00:47 ago
  Routing Descriptor Blocks:
  * 172.16.1.2, from 1.2.1.1, 00:00:47 ago, via Ethernet1/1
      Route metric is 41, traffic share count is 1
ISP(config-router)#
```

Because of the redistribution, EIGRP4 should now see the routes:

```
EIGRP4(config)#do sh ip route 1.2.3.1
Routing entry for 1.2.3.1/32
  Known via "eigrp 1", distance 170, metric 360960, type external
  Redistributing via eigrp 1
  Last update from 192.168.43.3 on Ethernet0/1, 00:01:58 ago
  Routing Descriptor Blocks:
  * 192.168.43.3, from 192.168.43.3, 00:01:58 ago, via Ethernet0/1
      Route metric is 360960, traffic share count is 1
      Total delay is 4100 microseconds, minimum bandwidth is 10000 Kbit
      Reliability 255/255, minimum MTU 1500 bytes
      Loading 1/255, Hops 4
EIGRP4(config)#
```

We should also have reachability, as well as visibility:

```
EIGRP4(config)#do ping 1.2.3.1 source loopback 0
Type escape sequence to abort.
Sending 5, 100-byte ICMP Echos to 1.2.3.1:
Packet sent with a source address of 4.4.4.4
!!!!!
Success rate is 100 percent (5/5)
EIGRP4(config)#
```

As we are making sure that we have complete end-to-end reachability, we should make sure that the FR-Spoke routers can also reach the rest of the network. When we left them in chapter 8 the spokes had very limited reachability. We will give them a static route, pointing to the FR-Hub router:

```
FR-Spoke1(config)#ip route 0.0.0.0 0.0.0.0 192.168.11.1
FR-Spoke1(config)#
```

```
FR-Spoke2(config)#ip route 0.0.0.0 0.0.0.0 192.168.12.1
FR-Spoke2(config)#
```

We also need to make sure that FR-Hub has an EIGRP adjacency to EIGRP4.

```
EIGRP4(config)#do sh ip eigrp neighbors
EIGRP-IPv4 Neighbors for AS(1)
H   Address          Interface    Hold Uptime    SRTT   RTO  Q   Seq
                                  (sec)          (ms)        Cnt Num
2   10.20.30.42      Vi1.1        14  23:43:28      5    100  0   24
0   192.168.43.3     Et0/1        11  1d10h         5    100  0   53
1   192.168.54.5     Se1/1        11  1d10h        10    100  0   59
EIGRP4(config)#
```

We do, but remember that FR-Hub is using PPPoE, therefore the address *may* change, so do compare FR-Hub's assigned IP address with the network being advertised by EIGRP using the "*show ip protocols*" command.

We should now be able to test end-to-end connectivity, from Server to OSPF3's loopback interface:

```
Server#ping 192.168.12.2
Type escape sequence to abort.
Sending 5, 100-byte ICMP Echos to 192.168.12.2:
!!!!!
Success rate is 100 percent (5/5)
Server#
Server#ping 1.2.3.1
Type escape sequence to abort.
Sending 5, 100-byte ICMP Echos to 1.2.3.1:
!!!!!
Success rate is 100 percent (5/5)
Server#
```

Then from FR-Spoke2 to OSPF2's loopback, and to Server (which also confirms that NAT is working):

```
FR-Spoke2(config)#do ping 1.2.3.1
Type escape sequence to abort.
Sending 5, 100-byte ICMP Echos to 1.2.3.1:
!!!!!
Success rate is 100 percent (5/5)
FR-Spoke2(config)#
FR-Spoke2(config)#do ping 192.168.20.21
Type escape sequence to abort.
Sending 5, 100-byte ICMP Echos to 192.168.20.21:
!!!!!
Success rate is 100 percent (5/5)
FR-Spoke2(config)#
```

The last test is from OSPF3 into Server, again this confirms that NAT is working:

```
OSPF3#ping 192.168.20.21
Type escape sequence to abort.
Sending 5, 100-byte ICMP Echos to 192.168.20.21:
!!!!!
Success rate is 100 percent (5/5)
OSPF3#
```

Things are looking good now, we have proved connectivity from both ends of the network into the LAN (ensuring that our NAT works incoming when we ping 192.168.20.21), and from one side of the network to the other.

We have not touched the Internet router so far, and in the spirit of providing a fully working network, we should bring this in as well. We will add it to EIGRP, making it accessible to the entire network:

```
Internet(config)#router eigrp 1
Internet(config-router)#
Internet(config-router)#eigrp router-id 8.8.8.8
Internet(config-router)#network 8.8.8.8 0.0.0.0
Internet(config-router)#network 192.168.30.254 0.0.0.0
Internet(config-router)#

ISP(config-router)#router eigrp 1
ISP(config-router)#
ISP(config-router)#network 192.168.30.1 0.0.0.0
ISP(config-router)#
%DUAL-5-NBRCHANGE: EIGRP-IPv4 1: Neighbor 192.168.30.254 (Ethernet0/2) is
up: new adjacency
ISP(config-router)#
```

We can now test this from Server, FR-Spoke2 and OSPF3:

```
Server#ping 8.8.8.8
Type escape sequence to abort.
Sending 5, 100-byte ICMP Echos to 8.8.8.8:
!!!!!
Success rate is 100 percent (5/5)
Server#

FR-Spoke2(config)#do ping 8.8.8.8
Type escape sequence to abort.
Sending 5, 100-byte ICMP Echos to 8.8.8.8:
!!!!!
Success rate is 100 percent (5/5)
FR-Spoke2(config)#
```

```
OSPF3#ping 8.8.8.8
Type escape sequence to abort.
Sending 5, 100-byte ICMP Echos to 8.8.8.8:
!!!!!
Success rate is 100 percent (5/5)
OSPF3#
```

These are all successful, however, tests from Bob are not successful:

```
Bob-PC#ping 8.8.8.8
Type escape sequence to abort.
Sending 5, 100-byte ICMP Echos to 8.8.8.8:
.....
Success rate is 0 percent (0/5)
Bob-PC#
```

Remember that our LAN is now hidden behind NAT on the Gateway router. We saw that we could get to Server's NAT IP address of 192.168.20.21, but we cannot get from Bob to 8.8.8.8. Let's have a look at our NAT rules:

```
Gateway(config-router)#do sh run | i nat
 ip nat outside
 encapsulation dot1Q 1 native
 ip nat inside
 ip nat inside
ip nat pool TenToTwenty 192.168.20.10 192.168.20.20 netmask 255.255.255.0
ip nat inside source list DaveAndBob pool TenToTwenty
ip nat inside source list VLAN-IPs interface Ethernet0/0 overload
ip nat inside source static 10.20.1.21 192.168.20.21
Gateway(config-router)#
```

Now we need to look at the DaveAndBob access list:

```
Gateway(config-router)#do sh access-list DaveAndBob
Standard IP access list DaveAndBob
    10 permit 10.10.1.3 (1 match)
    20 permit 10.30.1.3 (1 match)
Gateway(config-router)#
```

Does this match up to their current IP addresses?

```
Bob-PC#sh ip int bri | e unas
Interface          IP-Address      OK? Method Status    Protocol
Ethernet0/0        10.30.1.21      YES manual up        up

Bob-PC#
```

```
Dave-PC#sh ip int bri | e unas
Interface        IP-Address     OK? Method Status    Protocol
Ethernet0/0      10.10.1.21     YES manual up        up

Dave-PC#
```

It does not. When we switched both of them back to static IP addresses we did not update the ACL.
We should do that.

For this to be successful we have to make a change to our NAT configuration. Using our existing ACL
we will remove the existing host entries and add the subnets for VLAN 10 and VLAN 30:

```
Gateway(config-router)#exit
Gateway(config)#ip access-list standard DaveAndBob
Gateway(config-std-nacl)#
Gateway(config-std-nacl)#no 10
Gateway(config-std-nacl)#no 20
Gateway(config-std-nacl)#
Gateway(config-std-nacl)#do sh access-list DaveAndBob
Standard IP access list DaveAndBob
Gateway(config-std-nacl)#
Gateway(config-std-nacl)#10 permit 10.10.1.0 0.0.0.255
Gateway(config-std-nacl)#20 permit 10.30.1.0 0.0.0.255
Gateway(config-std-nacl)#do sh access-list DaveAndBob
Standard IP access list DaveAndBob
    10 permit 10.10.1.0, wildcard bits 0.0.0.255
    20 permit 10.30.1.0, wildcard bits 0.0.0.255
Gateway(config-std-nacl)#
```

Once this is done, we should have successful pings from both Bob and Dave:

```
Bob-PC#ping 8.8.8.8
Type escape sequence to abort.
Sending 5, 100-byte ICMP Echos to 8.8.8.8:
!!!!!
Success rate is 100 percent (5/5)
Bob-PC#

Dave-PC#ping 8.8.8.8
Type escape sequence to abort.
Sending 5, 100-byte ICMP Echos to 8.8.8.8:
!!!!!
Success rate is 100 percent (5/5)
Dave-PC#
```

Wouldn't it be nice though if we could use hostnames instead? We can, by setting up our Server to be
a DNS server. We first create a host object (www.google.com) pointing to 8.8.8.8:

```
Server(config)#ip host www.google.com 8.8.8.8
Server(config)#
```

Next, we configure Server to be a DNS server and enable domain name lookups:

```
Server(config)#ip dns server
Server(config)#ip domain-lookup
Server(config)#
```

On Bob and Dave, we point them to use Server as a name-server:

```
Bob-PC(config)#ip name-server 10.20.1.21
Bob-PC(config)#

Dave-PC(config)#ip name-server 10.20.1.21
Dave-PC(config)#
```

Now we should be able to ping 8.8.8.8 by name:

```
Server(config)#do ping www.google.com
Type escape sequence to abort.
Sending 5, 100-byte ICMP Echos to 8.8.8.8:
!!!!!
Success rate is 100 percent (5/5)
Server(config)#

Bob-PC(config)#do ping www.google.com
Translating "www.google.com"...domain server (10.20.1.21) [OK]

Type escape sequence to abort.
Sending 5, 100-byte ICMP Echos to 8.8.8.8:
!!!!!
Success rate is 100 percent (5/5)
Bob-PC(config)#

Dave-PC#ping www.google.com
Translating "www.google.com"...domain server (10.20.1.21) [OK]

Type escape sequence to abort.
Sending 5, 100-byte ICMP Echos to 8.8.8.8:
!!!!!
Success rate is 100 percent (5/5)
Dave-PC#
```

Notice that both the PCs are now using Server (10.20.1.21) to resolve the hostname to the IP address.

We now have a fully functioning LAN and WAN, with complete end-to-end reachability. We are using two different IPv4 IGPs and have some IPv6 functionality. Our LAN is secure; hidden from the WAN through Network Address Translation, we have used spanning tree and VTP incorporating DHCP and DNS. You have used Wireshark and IOS debugging to find and fix issues, but more importantly, hopefully had some fun along the way.

Now we can go (back) on to some troubleshooting in Section 7.

10. Exam time

Exams can be stressful, there is no denying this, and so what can you do to make it easier for yourself?

Arrive early.

Rushing late into the exam is not going to help; you need to arrive early. Give yourself time to sign in and get prepared. Most places will let you start the exam early if you get there a little before your scheduled start time.

Avoid food and drink that gives you a sugar rush.

Taking caffeinated drinks and sugary snacks sounds like a good idea to give you a boost, but there will be a drop in sugar levels after about an hour or so. If you are allowed to take food and drink in (and some testing centers differ on this), stick to water and fruit, this will allow you to stay hydrated, and the fruit will be absorbed slowly, avoiding the peaks and troughs associated with high-sugar foods.

Take your time, but not too much!

There are between 50 and 60 questions. You have 90 minutes, and the passmark is around 80%.

This means you need to spend about 1.5 minutes per questions, and need to get approximately 48 questions correct (the emphasis is on approximately). If a question is proving difficult, do not spend 10 minutes trying to work it out, move on after two minutes. If you spend 10 minutes on a question, you could potentially miss getting five other questions correct for the sake of getting one question correct.

Good luck!

(and let me know how you get on!)

Appendix A: CIDR Notation

Subnet mask	CIDR prefix	Total IPs	Usable IPs
255.255.255.255	/32	1	1
255.255.255.254	/31	2	0
255.255.255.252	/30	4	2
255.255.255.248	/29	8	6
255.255.255.240	/28	16	14
255.255.255.224	/27	32	30
225.255.255.192	/26	64	62
255.255.255.128	/25	128	126
255.255.255.0	/24	256	254
255.255.254.0	/23	512	510
255.255.252.0	/22	1,024	1,022
255.255.248.0	/21	2,048	2,046
255.255.240.0	/20	4,096	4,094
255.255.224.0	/19	8,192	8,190
255.255.192.0	/18	16,384	16.382
255.255.128.0	/17	32,768	32,766
255.255.0.0	/16	65,536	65,534
255.254.0.0	/15	131,072	131,070
255.252.0.0	/14	262,144	262,142
255.248.0.0	/13	524,288	524,286
255.240.0.0	/12	1,048,567	1,048,574
255.224.0.0	/11	2,097,152	2,097,150
255.192.0.0	/10	4,194,304	4,194,302
255.128.0.0	/9	8,388,608	8,388,606
255.0.0.0	/8	16,777,216	16,777,214
254.0.0.0	/7	33,554,432	33,554,430
252.0.0.0	/6	67,108,864	67,108,862
248.0.0.0	/5	134,217,728	134,217,726
240.0.0.0	/4	268,435,456	268,435,454
224.0.0.0	/3	536,870,912	536,870,910
192.0.0.0	/2	1,073,741,824	1,073,741,822
128.0.0.0	/1	2,147,483,648	2,147,483,646
0.0.0.0	/0	4,294,967,296	4,294,967,294

Appendix B: Powers of 2

2^0	1
2^1	2
2^2	4
2^3	8
2^4	16
2^5	32
2^6	64
2^7	128
2^8	256
2^9	512
2^{10}	1,024
2^{11}	2,048
2^{12}	4,096
2^{13}	8,192
2^{14}	16,384
2^{15}	32,768
2^{16}	65,536
2^{17}	131,072
2^{18}	262,144
2^{19}	524,288
2^{20}	1,048,576
2^{21}	2,097,152
2^{22}	4,194,304
2^{23}	8,388,608
2^{24}	16,777,216
2^{25}	33,554,432
2^{26}	67,108,864
2^{27}	134,217,728
2^{28}	268,435,456
2^{29}	536,870,912
2^{30}	1,073,741,824
2^{31}	2,147,483,648
2^{32}	4,294,967,296

Appendix C: Binary to Hex conversion

Binary Value	Hex Value
0000	0
0001	1
0010	2
0011	3
0100	4
0101	5
0110	6
0111	7
1000	8
1001	9
1010	A
1011	B
1100	C
1101	D
1110	E
1111	F

Appendix D: Wireshark Captures

This page lists the Wireshark capture filenames, as they are listed in the book. You can download the captures from the download section of the website:

Wireshark capture	Filename
1	Section 1 - initial-ping-and-arp.pcapng
2	Section 1 - interface-down-telnet.pcapng
3	Section 1 - telnet.pcapng
4	Section 4 - OSPF.pcapng
5	Section 4 - EIGRP.pcapng
6	Section 4 - EIGRP-1-ISP.pcapng
7	Section 5 - DHCP-1.pcapng
8	Section 5 - DHCP-2.pcapng
9	Section 7 - EIGRP adjacencies.pcapng
10	Section 7 - InterVLAN.pcapng
11	Section 8 - PPPoE.pcapng
12	Section 8 - PPPoE-w.CHAP.pcapng

www.ingramcontent.com/pod-product-compliance
Lightning Source LLC
Chambersburg PA
CBHW060920060326
40690CB00041B/2777